TEACHER'S EDITION

HRW READING

READING TODAY AND TOMOR

SPOTLIGHTS

LEVEL 6

Level	Grade	Title
K	Readiness	Rainbows
1	Readiness	Sundrops
2	PP1	Surprises
3	PP2	Treasures
4	PP3	Kingdoms
5	P	Snapshots
6	1	Spotlights
7	2	Patterns
8	2	Pathways
9	3	Souvenirs
10	3	Signposts
11	4	Banners
12	5	Festivals
13	6	Passages
14	7	Seascapes
15	8	Voyages

Isabel Beck, Senior Author

Bonnie Armbruster   Taffy Raphael

Margaret McKeown   Lenore Ringler

Donna Ogle

HOLT, RINEHART AND WINSTON, INC.

Austin   New York   Chicago   San Diego   Toronto   Montreal

ACKNOWLEDGMENTS

For permission to reprint copyrighted material, grateful acknowledgment is made to the following sources:

Grosset & Dunlap, Inc.: "Choosing a Kitten" written anonymously.

Instructor Publications, Inc.: "A Pumpkin Seed" by Alice Crowell Hoffman and "A House for One" by Laura Arlon from *Poetry Place Anthology.* Copyright © 1983 by The Instructor Publications, Inc.

A *Teacher's Edition* is not automatically included with each shipment of a classroom set of textbooks; however, a *Teacher's Edition* will be forwarded when requested by a teacher, an administrator, or a representative of Holt, Rinehart and Winston, Inc.

Requests for permission to make copies of any part of the work should be mailed to:

Permissions
Holt, Rinehart and Winston, Inc.
1627 Woodland Avenue
Austin, Texas 78741

Printed in the United States of America
ISBN 0-15-718051-4
89012 125 7654321

PROGRAM COMPONENTS

	K	1	2	3	4	5	6	7	8	9	10	11	12	13	14	15
LEVEL	K	1	2	3	4	5	6	7	8	9	10	11	12	13	14	15
GRADE	R	R	PP1	PP2	PP3	P	1	2	2	3	3	4	5	6	7	8
INSTRUCTIONAL MATERIALS																
Write-In Pupil's Edition		●														
Pupil's Edition			●	●	●	●	●	●	●	●	●	●	●	●	●	●
Teacher's Edition	●	●	●	●	●	●	●	●	●	●	●	●	●	●	●	●
Kindergarten Kit*	●															
PRACTICE MATERIALS																
Workbook**			●	●	●	●	●	●	●	●	●	●	●	●	●	●
Practice Masters/Reteach Masters**	●	●	●	●	●	●	●	●	●	●	●	●	●	●	●	●
SUPPORT MATERIALS																
Teacher's Idea Book	●	●	●	●	●	●	●	●	●	●	●	●	●	●	●	●
Teacher's Resource Organizer		●	●	●	●	●	●	●	●	●	●	●	●	●	●	●
Resource Box		●	●	●	●	●	●									
Instructional Charts			●	●	●	●	●	●	●	●	●	●	●	●	●	●
Pocket Chart	●	●	●	●	●	●	●									
Word Builder and Word Builder Cards		●	●	●	●											
Big Books for Shared Reading	●	●	●	●	●	●	●	●	●	●						
TESTING AND MANAGEMENT MATERIALS																
Primary Placement Test**		●	●	●	●	●	●	●	●	●						
Intermediate Placement Test**												●	●	●	●	●
End-of-Unit Tests** (Forms A and B)						●	●	●	●	●	●	●	●	●	●	●
End-of-Book Test																
Skills Mastery Test**		●	●	●	●	●	●	●	●	●	●	●	●	●	●	●
Assessment of Reading Comprehension**						●	●	●	●	●	●	●	●	●	●	●
Individual Record Folders		●	●	●	●	●	●	●	●	●	●	●	●	●	●	●
Class II Management System**		●	●	●	●	●	●	●	●	●	●	●	●	●	●	●
MICROCOMPUTER COMPONENTS																
Writer's Notebook II** (Word-Processing)										●	●	●	●	●	●	●
Story Branches** (Skills Practice)										●	●	●	●	●	●	●
ADDITIONAL MATERIALS																
Stories on Tape** (Audio Cassettes)	●	●	●	●	●	●	●	●	●	●	●	●	●	●	●	●
HRW Literature Libraries**		●	●	●	●	●	●	●	●	●	●	●	●	●	●	●
Writing Folder		●	●	●	●	●	●	●	●	●	●	●	●	●	●	●

* A complete multi-component kit for reading and oral language development.
  For a complete description, please see page xlii.

** Accompanied by a *Teacher's Edition* or *User's Guide*.

TABLE OF CONTENTS

THE AUTHORS

DR. ISABEL L. BECK, SENIOR AUTHOR

Dr. Isabel L. Beck, senior author, is Professor of Education and Senior Scientist in the Learning Research and Development Center at the University of Pittsburgh, where she teaches graduate courses and conducts and directs research. Dr. Beck is a former elementary teacher and reading supervisor. She has authored over fifty journal articles and book chapters and is a member of the Commission on Reading of the National Academy of Education that developed *Becoming a Nation of Readers.* Dr. Beck is currently a member of the editorial boards of *Reading Research Quarterly, Cognition and Instruction,* and *Reading Psychology,* and is a member of the Board of Scientific Advisors of the Center for the Study of Reading. She has served as a consultant and advisor to such organizations as the National Assessment of Educational Programs, the U.S. Department of Education, and National Educational Television, and she has been a member of many committees of the International Reading Association, the American Educational Research Association, and the National Reading Conference. Dr. Beck received her Ph.D. from the University of Pittsburgh.

DR. LENORE H. RINGLER

Dr. Lenore H. Ringler, Professor of Educational Psychology at New York University, teaches courses in reading, language, and developmental psychology. She is a former classroom teacher and reading specialist, past president of the National Reading Conference, and a member of the Commission on Reading of the National Academy of Education that developed *Becoming a Nation of Readers.* Dr. Ringler serves as a consultant to a number of school districts and has participated in over thirty national educational conferences. Her numerous publications include *A Language—Thinking Approach to Reading* (1984, Harcourt Brace Jovanovich, Inc.). Dr. Ringler received her Ph.D. from New York University.

DR. DONNA M. OGLE

Dr. Donna M. Ogle is chairperson of the Reading Department and Faculty at National College of Education in Evanston, Illinois, where she teaches graduate courses and conducts research. Dr. Ogle is a former reading and Chapter I teacher, and has also taught English and Social Studies. She was the Director of Study Skills at Oklahoma Baptist University and an instructor at the University of Virginia. Dr. Ogle currently serves as associate editor of the *Journal of Reading Behavior,* as a member of the Program Committee of IRA, and as chair of NCTE's Research Assembly. She is a member of the Illinois Reading Council Hall of Fame and author of numerous journal articles and book chapters, including "K-W-L: A Teaching Model that Develops Active Reading of Expository Text"(*The Reading Teacher,* February, 1986.) Dr. Ogle received her Ed.D. from Oklahoma State University.

DR. TAFFY E. RAPHAEL

Dr. Taffy E. Raphael, Associate Professor of Education at Michigan State University, teaches reading and writing methods courses and conducts doctoral-level seminars in the psychology and pedagogy of reading and the metacognitive processes in reading and writing. She is a former elementary classroom teacher. Reports of Dr. Raphael's research have appeared in such journals as *Reading Research Quarterly, American Educational Research Journal, Reading Teacher, Journal of Reading, Journal of Reading Behavior,* and the *Michigan Reading Journal.* She has also written numerous book chapters and serves as guest editor of several educational journals. Dr. Raphael is a consultant to international schools in Indonesia and Taiwan and lecturer at universities in Thailand and China. She received her Ph.D. from the University of Illinois and was the recipient of the IRA's Elva Knight Award for research in reading in 1984.

DR. MARGARET G. McKEOWN

Dr. Margaret G. McKeown is a Research Associate at the University of Pittsburgh, where she is responsible for research on vocabulary development and social studies instruction and for development of vocabulary computer software. She is a former elementary teacher and recipient of the IRA's Outstanding Dissertation Award in 1985. Dr. McKeown is a member of the editorial boards for the *Reading Research Quarterly* and the *Journal of Reading Behavior* and serves as Chair of the Vocabulary Special Interest Group of the American Educational Research Association. She received her Ph.D. in Language Communication from the University of Pittsburgh.

DR. BONNIE B. ARMBRUSTER

Dr. Bonnie B. Armbruster is Associate Professor of Elementary and Early Childhood Education and a Senior Scientist at the Center for the Study of Reading at the University of Illinois. She teaches courses in reading and edu-

cational psychology and conducts research on reading in the content areas. In 1984 she was the recipient of the IRA's Elva Knight Award for research in reading. She has authored over thirty journal articles and book chapters, most of which focus on learning from reading in the content areas and on evaluating/selecting "considerate" textbooks. Dr. Armbruster received her Ph.D. from the University of Illinois.

PROGRAM CONSULTANTS

David Adams
Director of Curriculum and
   Elementary Education
Shoreline School District
Seattle, WA

Arnold Adoff
Distinguished Visiting Professor
Queens College, CUNY
New York, NY

June Allred
Assistant Coordinator
Teacher Education Center
University of Maryland
Columbia, MD

LaDonna Buffington
Education Specialist for Preschool Program
Capital Area Intermediate Unit
Millersburg, PA

George Canney
Professor of Reading
University of Idaho
Moscow, ID

Sandra Forester
Director of ESL Programs
Knox County Schools
Knoxville, TN

Fannie Gibson
Instructional Coordinator
Chicago City Schools
Chicago, IL

Phillip Gonzales
Educational Consultant
Torrance, CA

Pauline Hodges-McLain
Coordinator of Language Arts
Jefferson County Schools
Golden, CO

Shirley Jackson
Director of Education
Young Astronauts' Council
Washington, DC

James Worthington
Dean, School of Education
Seattle Pacific University
Seattle, WA

CRITICAL READERS

Adelia Ball
Milton Elementary School
Milton, WV

Brenda Blakenship
William Southern Elementary
Independence, MO

Dr. Helen Brown
Director of Elementary Programs
Metropolitan Public Schools
Nashville, TN

George Bryk
Spry School
Chicago, IL

Pamela A. Burbank
La Quinta Intermediate
La Quinta, CA

Janet Crossland
Ott School
Independence, MO

Sharon Davidson
Luff Elementary
Independence, MO

Jane Decker
Columbus Academy
Westerville, OH

Susy Desilet
Sycamore Hills School
Independence, MO

Sherrill Donahoe
R.C. Longan Elementary School
Richmond, VA

Rita Fox
Kenwood Elementary School
Minneapolis, MN

June Gilch
Ossipee Central School
Center Ossipee, NH

Barbara Ginsberg
Spry School
Chicago, IL

Dr. Deanna Gordon
Director of Elementary Education
Roanoke County Schools
Salem, VA

Peggy Gordon
Maple Street Elementary School
Carrollton, GA

Dr. John Grant
St. Louis City School District
St. Louis, MO

Martha Hall
Victoria Elementary School
San Bernardino, CA

Darlene Hardcastle
F.J. White Learning Center
Woodlake, CA

Nancy Harper
Anderson Contemporary School
Minneapolis, MN

Joann Harwell
Alabama Street Elementary School
Carrollton, GA

Patricia Jones
Carpenter School
Wolfeboro, NH

Doris Kennon
Chalmers School
Chicago, IL

Linda Kiser
College Street Elementary School
Carrollton, GA

Linda Knowles
Chattanooga City Schools
Chattanooga, TN

Susan Krieger
Forest Edge Elementary
Reston, VA

Marilou Linman
F.J. White Learning Center
Woodlake, CA

Joan Lynch
Westside Catholic Regional School
Manchester, NH

Susan Merrell
Tuftonboro Central School
Center Tuftonboro, NH

Geraldine S. McGlohon
Benview Elementary School
Rocky Mount, NC

Victoria McIver
St. Mary's Schools
Houlton, ME

Linda Moran
Wilder Contemporary School
Minneapolis, MN

Willye Nance
Forest Edge Elementary
Reston, VA

Marylce Nessen
Driffill School
Oxnard, CA

Gail Olson
Columbus Academy
Colombus, OH

Norma Osborn
Assistant Superintendent
Independence Schools
Independence, MO

Cynthia Parker
Irwin Avenue Open School
Charlotte, NC

Nancy T. Parker
Lynn Road Elementary School
Raleigh, NC

Beverly Rieschl
Sheridan Elementary School
Minneapolis, MN

Gracie Sanchez
F.J. White Learning Center
Woodlake, CA

Donna Sawyer
Deputy Superintendent
Diocese of Portland
Portland, ME

Carrie Seaton
Fulton School
Minneapolis, MN

Louise Swift
Howland School
Chicago, IL

Bridget Thomas
St. Acquinas Elementary School
Derry, NH

Vicki Thompson
Maple Park Middle School
Kansas City, MO

Judy Tyson
Santa Fe Trails Elementary
Independence, MO

Patsy Upchurch
College Street Elementary School
Carrollton, GA

Carol Viens
Effengham School
Center Ossipee, NH

Marilynn Walker
Waite Park Intermediate School
Minneapolis, MN

Roberta Wermelskirchen
Eastgate Middle School
Kansas City, MO

Kris Wilson
Leonard Lawrence Elementary
Bellevue, NE

DR. ISABEL BECK
TALKS ABOUT HRW READING

The development of *HRW READING: Reading Today and Tomorrow* was guided by a number of fundamental understandings about the nature of reading and the kinds of conditions that help children learn to read.

THE FOCUS OF INSTRUCTION

> **We begin with comprehension because there is no reading without it.**

We begin with comprehension because there is no reading without it. The view of comprehension that serves as a backdrop to many instructional features in *HRW READING* is that it is an active, constructive process. Comprehension is constructive because readers create meaning from a text — they do not ferret meaning out of printed pages. Readers create meaning by using information in the text together with knowledge they already possess. The constructive nature of comprehension emphasizes the importance of the knowledge a reader brings to a text. Of course, the role of prior knowledge is not a new discovery, but recent research persuades us that it has far deeper implications for comprehension than was previously assumed.

The importance of prior knowledge is acknowledged throughout *HRW READING,* in various parts of the lessons, and in both direct and subtle ways. The most direct way is by the inclusion of carefully developed suggestions and strategies to help teachers find out what students already know and what they need to know in order to comprehend an upcoming selection. The orientation in this part of the lesson is that background knowledge brought to a text provides a framework that helps students understand and remember new information.

LITERATURE

Quality literature is one of the finest sources for adding to one's knowledge. By definition, quality literature deals with fundamental human ideas and feelings and does so through exemplary uses of language. The higher the quality of what is read, the higher the quality of what can be experienced and learned. Hence, in *HRW READING,* the selections that students read have been chosen

> **Quality literature is one of the finest sources for adding to one's knowledge.**

from a core of recognized quality literature, both contemporary and traditional. The authors represented in the program range from the classic—Twain, Thurber, O'Henry, London—to the most current, award-winning names—Konigsberg, Cleary, O'Dell, Van Allsburg. In every case, however, a particular selection was chosen because it contained elements of character, plot or theme that would strike a responsive chord in children. The power of good literature to motivate students to read is a fundamental principal of *HRW READING.*

The literature in *HRW READING* is organized around meaningful themes and topics (Levels 5–15). Each thematic unit includes a balance of genrés—such as stories, plays, poetry, and nonfiction—representative of different times and cultures. In addition, the non-

> **One of the most wonderful ways children's knowledge of the world will grow and develop is by having good stories read aloud to them.**

fiction strand also includes an emphasis on content-area reading, utilizing informational articles and actual textbook excerpts.

The thematic organization and the balance of genrés serve several important functions. First, the strong content connections between and among selections make it possible for what has been learned in one selection to provide background for another. Second, the variety of types of literature impresses upon students the need to adjust reading strategies for different purposes and materials. Third, this organization helps students develop new interests and explore the possibilities of different literary forms.

One of the most wonderful ways children's knowledge of the world will grow and develop is by having good stories read aloud to them. Certainly, reading programs must share in the responsibility for arranging and encouraging situations in which students are read to *throughout* the grades. *HRW READING* has done so. Students of all ages profit from hearing a good reader share the joys, sorrows, ideas, and adventures that talented storytellers have set down for the younger members of our culture, as well as for adults. Whether stories are read *by* children or read *to* children, reading instruction must be focused, from the very beginning, to help children become aware that reading is a **meaning-centered process.** Anyone who has interacted with beginning readers recognizes the great gap between what they can understand aurally and what they can read. Their word recognition at the early levels is quite limited, of course, and as a result, the few printed sentences in beginning reading materials do not usually contain all the elements needed to tell a good story or to convey a coherent message.

In order to give beginning readers stories that are coherent and meaningful, but which they can read and understand, *HRW READING* has created a new approach to its preprimer stories. Perhaps of greatest importance is the fact that the preprimers were written by talented, professional children's authors, Marjorie and Mitchell Sharmat. After all, one of the essential ingredients for the development of a good story is a good storyteller.

Then, the stories are arranged in a format in which the teacher and the children *share* in constructing the stories. That is, the narratives are presented as stories to be partly told by the teacher and partly read by the children. This new orientation to the earliest reading materials allows the kind of meaningful encounters with written language that can help children understand, from the very beginning, that reading is a process not simply of recognizing words, but of gaining ideas.

DECODING

Fluent decoding serves comprehension and is, therefore, an essential component of reading. *HRW READING* acknowledges the pattern of research findings that has accumulated for many decades and which shows significant benefits from direct phonics instruction. In terms of instructional strategies, *HRW READING* uses the strongest features from both explicit and implicit phonics approaches, and does so in direct, uncomplicated, uncluttered ways.

The goal of phonics instruction in *HRW READING* is not to teach "rules," but rather to lay bare the principle that there *are* systematic relationships between letters and sounds. Therefore, we teach only the most important and regular sound/letter relationships, and we teach them only as there are immediate opportunities for using what has been learned in reading words in sentences and stories. The order in which sound/letter correspondences are introduced is one that makes available the largest possible number of interesting words for stories. Direct instruction in *blending* sounds to produce words is included, and the introduction of sound/ letter correspondences is completed by the end of grade two.

For phonics to become a tool in the service of comprehension, students need to be so familiar with the phonic elements that they pay little, if any, conscious attention to decoding words. This kind of decoding fluency is achieved when a very close relationship exists between phonics instruction and words children encounter in what they read. Therefore, in *HRW READING* the majority of words in each selection are completely decodable. That is, all of the sound/symbol correspondences have been taught. In addition, some irregular high frequency words (such as *the, said, is, what* and *have)* and some vivid, interesting words not yet decodable on the basis of sound/ symbol correspondences are also introduced. Without such words, authors are severely limited in the development of interesting, coherent stories that children will be motivated to read.

The major features of phonics instruction in *HRW READING* are the ones recommended in *Becoming a Nation of Readers*—phonics instruction is done early, approached systematically, and kept simple. It uses the strongest features of both explicit and implicit approaches, and it is immediately applied in the vocabulary of meaningful reading selections, written by talented professional children's authors.

COMPREHENSION AND CRITICAL THINKING

Good questions promote comprehension and critical thinking. When children read a story or hear a story read to them, they share an experience that offers valuable opportunities for discussion and extension of ideas and concepts. Traditionally, questions are the first vehicles for initiating discussions. Research about questions emphasizes that they are most likely to enhance comprehension when they are logically organized to follow events, encourage predictions about what will happen next, highlight important ideas, and establish connections between related concepts. To design logical sequences of questions *HRW*

> **Decoding fluency is achieved when a very close relationship exists between phonics instruction and the words children encounter in what they read.**

> **Good questions promote comprehension and critical thinking.**

READING uses the concept of a **story map**—a unified representation of a story—based on a logical organization of events and ideas of central importance and the interrelationships of those events and ideas.

Another aspect of questioning involves critical-thinking questions. The importance of consistently moving discussions of what children read toward higher-order thinking cannot be underestimated. Hence, in *HRW READING* **critical-thinking** questions are consistently included and, depending on the selection, may develop several story interpretations, probe the use of various literary conventions, speculate about certain symbolic references, or promote a multitude of other thoughtful and interpretative aspects of critical thinking.

It is also important to emphasize what an enormously useful source literature is for working with **problem solving.** By definition, stories have problems, and often there are characters in stories who are models of both good and poor attempts at problem solving. In *HRW READING,* attention has been given to taking instructional advantage of such powerful problem-solving models.

INTEGRATION OF LISTENING, SPEAKING, READING AND WRITING

Reading materials should present the integrated whole of language including listening, speaking, writing, and reading. Using what students have read as a catalyst for thinking, talking, and writing about ideas, issues, and problems suggested in a selection makes contact with the obvious connection between reading and the other language arts. The issue here is that reading needs to be viewed under the higher-order context of language. Reading, writing, listening, and speaking are not entities in themselves; they are elements of language. Certainly, attention to fostering language must be a priority within each subject area, throughout each day, over all the years of schooling. And certainly a reading program must assume a large share of the responsibility for fostering language.

A major concept underlying the development of *HRW READING* is that language grows in a language-rich environment. Therefore, throughout the program, in both direct and informal ways, attention is given to the development of all language arts—reading, writing, speaking, and listening—as well as to their integration. One of the places in which this is consistently done is in the Using Language activities that follow the reading

selections, using those selections as springboards for a variety of language activities. Often these activities encourage student writing and involve appropriate writing process stages. But the activities are not limited to writing. Many of the Using Language activities focus on the development of oral language.

Different learning styles were given careful consideration throughout the development of *HRW READING.* As a result, the program includes "big books," audio cassette recordings of text selections, picture cards, and manipulative materials. Lesson plans suggest art and music activities, choral reading, dramatization, readers theatre, role-playing, and a variety of other activities that engage all aspects of learning and promote language growth.

Although many of the language activities in *HRW READING* may be done independently, a great many of them have been designed to encourage and accommodate students working together. Such activities are arranged so that sometimes students serve as resources for each other as they complete a group project. In this regard, *HRW READING* acknowledges the recent research findings about cooperative learning that indicate important positive outcomes from students working together in small learning groups.

> **Reading materials should present the integrated whole of language including listening, speaking, writing, and reading.**

VOCABULARY

Vocabulary knowledge is strongly related to reading comprehension and a large, rich vocabulary is, in addition, a hallmark of the educated person. Reading programs need to assume a large share of the responsibility for fostering students' vocabulary growth. By taking advantage of the rich vocabulary found in good literature, reading programs are in an excellent position to do that.

In *HRW READING,* instruction in words from selections is provided in several ways. One is by directly teaching some important vocabulary before students read a selection; another is by looking back into a selection after reading to examine some of the eloquent, interesting, and creative ways professional writers use words.

HRW READING recognizes that all words are not "created equal" in terms of their importance to comprehension of a selection, their usefulness in other language situations, and the ease with which

Vocabulary knowledge is strongly related to reading comprehension.

they can be taught. Therefore, careful consideration was given to determining which words from each selection should be targeted for direct instruction. Depending on the particular set of words that will be worked with from any selection, one of three instructional approaches—definitional, contextual, or conceptual—is used. However, underlying each of these approaches are instructional strategies that require students to think about the words rather than merely to memorize definitions. Many lessons include provisions for the teacher to model the process of thinking about the way a word was used in context in order to figure out its meaning. Moreover, underlying *HRW READING*'s vocabulary strand are the higher-order goals of helping children develop an interest in words, master strategies for determining word meanings, and experience a growing curiosity—indeed, a delight—about words.

DIRECT INSTRUCTION IN COMPREHENSION STRATEGIES

Skilled readers are strategic readers, and students profit greatly from direct instruction in the strategies that good readers use. Recent research has brought to the attention of the field new insights about the role of **metacognition** in reading. Two elements—awareness of one's own

Skilled readers are strategic readers, and students profit greatly from direct instruction in the strategies that good readers use.

comprehension processes and strategies to "fix things up" when comprehension is not proceeding smoothly—are the components of metacognition. While good readers are not necessarily conscious of using specific strategies, it is certain that good readers do have a reservoir of strategies that they can call upon in the course of reading. Therefore, throughout *HRW READING,* a variety of strategies are made available to student in both direct and indirect ways.

Direct instruction emphasizes teacher modeling of a variety of important reading behaviors. For instance, in Level 1, as the teacher reads to the children, the *Teacher's Edition* provides suggestions that the teacher make some "asides" that model such strategies as updating earlier text information

("It sounds as if Arthur is in the city now. Let's see what happens."), that draw inferences ("I don't think Arthur's mother really thinks he went to the moon."), etc.

Specific strategies model for students the active thinking involved in reading. For example, in the case of nonfiction, including content-area selections, students are taught to begin by thinking about what they may know about a topic and then to consider what else they may want to learn. Students are also taught where to find the information needed to answer questions.

Another way students' awareness of their own comprehension processes is fostered is through a feature in the students' books entitled Be an Active Reader. In these skills lessons, fiction and nonfiction selections, as well as content-area textbook selections, are accompanied by sidenotes that help students think about what they are reading. Be an Active Reader lessons teach students to ask questions, to make predictions, and to pay attention to what the author is saying.

■   ■   ■

To a large extent, the major goal for *HRW READING* is to realize the potential for enhancing reading instruction that recent research has provided. However, although research suggests features that have some educational advantage, research does not specify how those findings can be woven into the educational environment. To do this, research findings must be developed into instructional ideas, and those ideas crafted into the teaching and learning materials. In many instances, what was needed was to enhance a component that has traditionally existed in basal reading programs; in other instances, some new features had to be developed. In all instances, the authors and publisher of *HRW READING: Reading Today and Tomorrow* were guided by a firm belief that it is motivated, knowledgeable teachers who teach children to read. Our goal has been to develop a program that will support and enhance the efforts of such teachers in developing lifelong readers— readers who *can* read, and *do* read, and who are effective users of language.

Isabel L. Beck

HRW READING

Share the experience

Perhaps few of us remember exactly *how* we learned to read, but what we almost certainly do remember is the delight we found in our first experiences with literature — the sheer pleasure of the patterned sound structures of poetry, the excitement of sharing adventures with memorable characters, our fascination with wondrous tales from other worlds and times. *HRW READING* capitalizes on this motivational aspect of reading by including in every level a rich blend of the finest literature and quality nonfiction selections. In every book, students will find the joy and involvement that makes them want to read on and on — today and tomorrow.

Quality literature motivates students to read—today and tomorrow.

Comprehension instruction moves students into, through, and beyond each reading selection.

Comprehension instruction is more than questions after reading. Direct instruction in essential vocabulary, a focus on prior knowledge, and questions that help students set purposes for reading allow students to move into reading with success. Focused, worthwhile questioning guides students through each selection, and a variety of listening, speaking, and writing activities after reading provide opportunities for students to understand fully the meaning of what they have read and to relate it to their own lives.

Direct instruction in comprehension and thinking strategies helps students become skilled, independent readers.

Skilled readers are strategic readers who know how to change the way they read in response to different purposes for reading. They recognize when they fail to comprehend, and they have strategies for resolving problems with comprehension. *HRW READING* directly teaches strategies for understanding not only stories but also content-area materials.

"Readers must be able to decode words quickly and accurately so that this process can coordinate fluidly with the process of constructing meaning from text." (*Becoming a Nation of Readers*, p. 11) In *HRW READING*, systematic, carefully crafted phonics instruction in meaningful contexts is the foundation of a decoding strategy that leads to fast, accurate word identification and gives students an essential tool in the service of comprehension.

Systematic instruction in decoding skills gives students early independence in reading.

The integration of listening, speaking, reading and writing helps students make sense of what they learn.

The development of reading ability and the desire to read is closely related to all aspects of language and of thought. In *HRW READING*, both the students' books and the *Teachers' Editions* provide activities that reinforce the unity of language and advance students' proficiencies in all the language arts.

QUALITY LITERATURE
FROM THE VERY BEGINNING!

One of the challenges of beginning reading instruction has been to provide worthwhile stories written in natural language that children can actually read. *HRW READING* meets that challenge.

The three Preprimers were written by Marjorie and Mitchell Sharmat, talented authors of award-winning children's books. Each book tells a continuing story whose plot and characters delight young readers.

The Hopping Toad

"Will I find the king's dragon?"
Kip asked the magic egg.

"Why not?" said the egg.

"The king's guards did not find it,"
said Kip.
"They did not get to the sun.
They went down in a heap."

32

FROM LEVEL 4

Umbrellas

"Nan has a hat," said Mitzie.

"Maxwell has a hat," said Stan.

24

FROM LEVEL 2

Samson Finds a Note

"I'm looking for the treasure,"
sang Pam.

"I'm looking for the treasure, too,"
sang Todd.

"I'm looking for Samson," said Rosa.
"Have you seen him?"

18

FROM LEVEL 3

Each story in the three Preprimers is a **shared reading experience** in which the teacher reads part of the story from the *Teacher's Edition,* and the children read the parts printed in their books.

FROM LEVEL 2

Umbrellas

"Nan *has* a *hat*," said Mitzie.

"Maxwell has a hat," said Stan.

24

"I am sad," said Mitzie.

"I am sad," said Stan.
"*We* need hats."

25

Before reading page 24

READ Nan, Maxwell, Stan, and Mitzie had seen the dark clouds cover the sun. They had packed up their things and started for home. But they were too late. It started to rain.

SAY What do you think the friends will do now? Read page 24 to find out.

After reading page 24

1. What did Stan and Mitzie notice about Nan and Maxwell? (They had on hats.) Literal
2. What good would a hat do? (A hat might help keep the rain off.) Inferential

Before reading page 25

READ Mitzie and Stan had no hats. They could see that the hats would help Nan and Maxwell stay dry. Even if Maxwell's hat wasn't a real hat, it was better than no hat at all.

SAY How do you think Mitzie and Stan will feel about not having hats? Read page 25 to find out.

After reading page 25

1. How did Mitzie and Stan feel? (They felt sad.) Literal
2. What did Stan and Mitzie decide they needed? (hats) Literal

Students and teachers **share** the experience of reading. The stories are rich in meaning and complete in story structure, leading students to understand—from the beginning—that reading is a process of constructing meaning, not simply of recognizing words.

SURPRISES

adapted from stories
by Steven Kroll

"The Biggest Pumpkin Ever"

"Thumbelina"

"Toot! Toot!"

"Happy Mother"

"Gifts to M

Clayton and Desmond are two mice
who are in for some surprises.
Read to find out what happens.

The Biggest Pumpkin Ever

One day, two mice fell in love
with the same pumpkin.

Clayton, the village mouse, saw
it on the vine in his mother's garden.

It was still little and green, but
Clayton was sure he could make it
grow very big.

Maybe it could get so big
that it could win the ribbon
at the pumpkin contest.

116

The contents of the Primer (Level 5) and
the first Reader (Level 6) were the responsibility of talented, well-known children's
authors: Joan Lexau, Bernice Myers,
Florence and Roxanne Heide, Lilian Moore,
Joanna Cole, and Steven Kroll. Each unit
in these books includes stories and informational articles written by one of these
authors, and adaptations of selections were
done by the authors themselves.

Contemporary stories, poems, plays, nonfiction
selections, and traditional favorites fill the pages
of the Primer and first Reader.

The shoemaker and his wife find
new friends.
How do the friends help?

The Elves and the Shoemaker

Long ago, there lived a man
who made shoes.

He made them from the best leather
he could find.

The man worked days and days
to make each shoe.

He did not make a lot of money.

Who will think of a way
to help Theodore?

That's What Friends Are For

ACT 2

Reader: *Along comes Theodore's
friend Crab.*

Crab: Why are you sitting
in the road?

97

Animal friends can help each other.
Read to find out how.

Animal Friends

Animals can help each other.
Honey birds and honey badgers help
each other.

The honey bird and the honey badger
like the same thing.
They like the taste of honey.
They help each other get honey.

QUALITY LITERATURE
AT EVERY GRADE, IN EVERY LEVEL!

At every level of **HRW READING** the selections have been chosen from a core of recognized, quality literature, both contemporary and traditional. Fiction and nonfiction, poems, plays, and content-area selections capture students' individual interests and motivate them to read far beyond their classroom texts.

Every book is filled with the work of **award-winning authors** and with literary selections that have received the most prestigious awards given for children's literature.

Frog tells of a time when he wanted spring to come. How did he know when it did?

The Corner
by Arnold Lobel

132

FROM LEVEL 7

Children "meet" authors on the pages of their readers through biographies, personal notes, and introductions to selections.

A NOTE FROM
THE POET

When I was a child, I often read my grandma's big book of English nursery rhymes. "The House That Jack Built" was one of my favorites.

Nearly a lifetime later, I discovered "The Nandi House That Jack Built" in the book *The Nandi: Their Language and Folklore* by Claude Hollis. The only similarity I could see between that and the English poem, was that in it, also, one thing led to another.

It took me ten years and a couple of hours to write my version. The ten years were spent in reading the source story now and then—each time deciding it was impossible. For I wanted to do it to the tune of the English *House That Jack Built*.

But one evening I really studied the story. Then I went to bed and wrestled with the tale. By four o'clock, the first stanza had come together in my mind. The next day the whole poem rolled out of my typewriter within two hours. I count it as the best inspirational experience that I have ever had.

Verna Aardema

FROM LEVEL 10

216

A dark cloud hangs over the Kapiti Plain, but no rain falls. How does Ki-Pat make the rain come?

Bringing the Rain to Kapiti Plain
by Verna Aardema

This is the great
Kapiti Plain,
All fresh and green
from the African rains—
A sea of grass for the
ground birds to nest in;
And patches of shade for
wild creatures to rest in;
With acacia trees for
browse on,
rdsmen
ows on.

217

So the grass grew green,
and the cattle fat!
And Ki-pat got a wife
and a little Ki-pat—
Who tends the cows now,
and shoots down the rain,
When black clouds shadow
Kapiti Plain.

The original source of every selection and awards it has won are identified in the student's book right after the selection.

This is the art and entire text of the book *Bringing the Rain to Kapiti Plain* by Verna Aardema. Ms. Aardema has won several awards, including two listings for the American Library Association's Notable Children's Books.

Discussing the Selection
1. What did Ki-Pat do to make the rain fall?
2. Why were the cows on the plain hungry and dry?
3. What happened when the eagle dropped a feather?
4. Why is Kapiti Plain now safe from a drought?
5. What are some other ways that drought affects people? How could it affect you?

FROM LEVEL 10

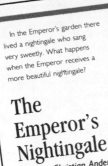

In the Emperor's garden there lived a nightingale who sang very sweetly. What happens when the Emperor receives a more beautiful nightingale?

The Emperor's Nightingale

by Hans Christian Andersen
adapted by Adele Thane

CAST OF CHARACTERS

Narrator

Tu Chin, the Emperor's sister

Emperor of China

Chan Tung, the Emperor's Lord-in-Waiting

Yu Lang, the kitchen maid

Nightingale

Toy Nightingale

294

FROM LEVEL 10

Literature selections span every genre and include both **classic** and **contemporary** choices.

Beyond the Arctic Circle, it is often difficult to find food to eat. In this story, an Eskimo girl is lost and hungry in northern Alaska. Read to find out how a pack of wolves can help her.

Julie of the Wolves

by Jean Craighead George

Miyax pushed back the hood of her sealskin parka and looked at the Arctic sun. It was a yellow disk in a limegreen sky, the colors of six o'clock in the evening and the time when the wolves awoke. Quietly she put down her cooking pot and crept to the top of a dome-shaped frost heave, one of the many earth buckles that rise and fall in the crackling cold of the Arctic winter. Lying on her stomach, she looked across a vast lawn of grass and moss and focused her attention on the wolves she had come upon two sleeps ago. They were wagging their tails as they awoke and saw each other.

Her hands trembled and her heartbeat quickened, for she was frightened, not so much of the wolves, who were shy and many harpoon shots away, but because of her desperate predicament. Miyax was lost. She had been lost without food for many sleeps on the North Slope of Alaska. The barren slope stretches for three hundred miles from the Brooks Range to the Arctic Ocean, and for more than eight hundred miles from the Chukchi to the Beaufort Sea. No roads

551

FROM LEVEL 14

Nonfiction and **content-area** selections provide opportunities for students to "fine tune" their reading skills to match different materials and purposes.

I, T Vocabulary: word meaning (mastery words)

DIRECT INSTRUCTION Write the following words on the chalkboard:

| IC | **abruptly channel identify urged** |

Have the words read aloud and review with students their meanings.

GUIDED PRACTICE Tell students that now that they have read "Snowshoe Trek to Otter River," they are going to talk about how the vocabulary words were used in the selection. Point to each of the words on the chalkboard as you ask the following questions:

1. **Abruptly**—When Daniel was following the tracks of the snowshoe hare, he noticed that they stopped *abruptly*. How can footprints stop abruptly? (They can stop suddenly because they might be covered up by fresh snow.) **Did Daniel start out abruptly on his trip to Otter River?** (No, his trip was carefully planned; it was not sudden or unexpected.)
2. **Channel**—Why did Daniel have to chop a *channel* through the ice in the river? (He had to make a passageway so he could get to the shore.) **How wide do you think Daniel's channel was?** (It was probably very narrow, just wide enough for him to squeeze through.)
3. **Identify**—What were some of the things in the wilderness that Daniel was able to *identify*? (He was able to recognize different flowers and trees, as well as the tracks made by different animals.) **How was Daniel able to identify the beaver house in the pond?** (He saw a large hump in the snow near a beaver dam.)
4. **Urged**—When Daniel got lost, something inside him *urged* him to get up and run. How did Daniel feel when this happened? (He felt as if something was forcing him to run.) **What would Mr. Bateau have urged him to do?** (Mr. Bateau probably would have urged him to calm down and think carefully, which is what Daniel did.)

※ **RETEACH** For those students who need additional instruction, see "Reteaching Lesson Skills," page T37, under "Reteaching and Extending."

COMPREHENSION/THINKING

I, T Story structure: mood

DIRECT INSTRUCTION Remind students that writers frequently use description and characterization to create a particular mood. The mood of a story is the feeling that it gives the reader. Direct students to listen as you read an excerpt from the book *Frozen Fire.* Tell them to try to describe the mood that the writer is attempting to create.

> Matthew had to fight against the force of the wind to make his way—a dozen steps between the bus and the house. He could scarcely see the door, for he was almost blinded by the lashing blizzard.
> "Dad, are you here?" called Matthew, once he got inside.
> There was no answer. The gray house trembled in the freezing gloom. With shaking fingers Matthew flipped the light switch. Nothing happened. He tried another. Nothing. For this house, at least, the power had failed. He got one of the fat white emergency candles from the cupboard and lighted it and with the same match lit the propane stove.
> Keep calm, he told himself. If you think this is bad for you, think what it must be like for Dad and Charlie out there somewhere in this storm.

Ask students to describe the mood, or feeling, of this passage. (scared, nervous, alarmed) Have them tell how the writer created the mood. (The writer used both a description of the setting and a description of the character's thoughts to create the mood.) Reread the passage and ask students to identify some words and phrases that created the particular mood of the passage. (*lashing blizzard, trembled, freezing gloom, emergency candles, keep calm*)

Like finding the right music teacher, finding the right instrument to play can be difficult for a young musician. As you read about Louis Armstrong as a boy, you'll learn how he discovered the horn as his musical instrument.

Louis Armstrong: Strike Up the Band!

by James Lincoln Collier

Louis Armstrong was born in New Orleans, Louisiana, in 1898. He grew up in a very poor family with little to eat, few clothes, and no toys. But one thing Louis did have around him all the time was music, and he loved music. At an early age, he formed a quartet with three other boys. They sang in the streets to earn a little money for food.

It was a very unhappy time in Louis's life when a judge decided that Louis should be sent to the Waifs' Home. Captain Joseph Jones had started the Waifs' Home to care for homeless boys. Louis's father had left the family when Louis was very young, and Louis's mother spent most of her time working.

This excerpt from a biography of Louis Armstrong describes how young Louis's stay at the Waifs' Home was an important step on his road to becoming one of the world's great jazz musicians.

266

FROM LEVEL 14

Reading aloud to students is encouraged at every level. Listening to good literature promotes oral language development, enlarges vocabularies, and develops a common background of content.

QUALITY LITERATURE
ORGANIZED TO PROMOTE COMPREHENSION

The **thematic organization** of selections in Levels 5–15 provides strong content connections between and among selections and encourages independent reading in pursuit of individual interests.

FROM LEVEL 11

A **unit opener** generates interest in the unit theme, accesses students' prior knowledge, provides an overview of the unit's selections, and helps students set initial purposes for reading.

UNIT 1

FRIENDS AND FAMILIES

Friends and family—we all have them and enjoy them. Sometimes our best friends are members of our own family.

Friends and family members are people we often take for granted. Think about what you already know about friendship. What makes a good friend? How can a member of your family be a friend? Also think about what it means to be a member of a family. What kinds of things are expected of each member of your family?

In this unit, you'll read about different kinds of friendships and family relationships. The unit is divided into three parts. The first part, "Special Friends," has selections about some unusual friendships between animals and between people. "Brothers and Sisters" is the title of the second group of selections. You'll see how brothers and sisters get along in different situations. The selections in the last part, "Families," add to our understanding of how members of a family can work together to help each other.

Here are some of the words you'll find in this unit:

patient	respect	protect
impatient	faithful	obey

Think about what these words tell you about friends and families...

FROM LEVEL 11

FAMILIES

Life on the prairie was often dangerous for pioneer families. Wild animals and bad weather were two of the dangers they had to face. But such dangers often brought families closer together.

In this last part of Unit 1, you'll be reading about two pioneer families. You'll also discover some things about the wolf, one of the animals pioneers feared most.

- "Wolves on Silver Lake" by Laura Ingalls Wilder
- "How to Own a Word" (Skills Lesson)
- "Make Room for the Wolf" by George Laycock
- "A House, A Home" (Poem) by Lorraine M. Halli

BONUS
- "Sarah, Plain and Tall" by Patricia MacLachlan

Pioneer families faced special kinds of problems. Read this story to find out how a dangerous event leads to the discovery of the perfect place for Laura's family to build their home.

Wolves on Silver Lake
by Laura Ingalls Wilder

For three years during the 1800's Laura Ingalls and her family lived in Minnesota. Pa didn't like living in a place that was old and worn out. He wanted to move west, where the land was unsettled and the hunting was good. Pa's chance came when someone offered him a job as a storekeeper, bookkeeper, and timekeeper for the railroad camps in the Dakota Territory. The family traveled west and lived in a shanty by the shores of Silver Lake. Winter approached and the railroad work was completed, but the Ingalls remained. They moved into the empty surveyors' house. This was to be their home until Pa could find a suitable place for a homestead.

101

In Levels 11–15, each unit is divided into three parts, each part focusing on a different aspect of the central unit theme.

FROM LEVEL 11

In the story "Wolves on Silver Lake," Laura and Carrie met a lone wolf. But most wolves live and hunt together in groups called packs. As you read, think about how members of a wolf pack help each other.

Make Room for the Wolf
by George Laycock

Our fear of wolves goes back hundreds of years. As small children, we hear about "the big bad wolf" and the three little pigs. Or we read the story of "Little Red Riding Hood" and we see pictures of wolves with big fangs. Children in Europe and Russia hear stories of wolves chasing people in the dark of night. These are all scary stories, but they are unfair to the wolf because most of them are not true.

Here is what is true of the wolf. These largest members of the wild dog family are powerful animals. A large, male gray wolf may weigh one hundred pounds, sometimes more, and stands three feet high at the shoulders. The female will weigh about fifteen pounds less.

116

Selections are closely related, providing opportunities for students to explore relationships among selections, to synthesize related ideas and concepts, and to think critically about the meaning of what they are reading.

Bonus Selections in each unit (Levels 11–15) and at the end of each book in Levels 5–10 are award-winning stories that provide independent reading experiences with unusually high-quality literature.

This is the story of a pioneer family that has someone special come to visit them. As you read, predict whether this new friend will stay and become a member of the family.

Sarah, Plain and Tall

by Patricia MacLachlan

Anna and Caleb lived with their papa on a farm on the prairie. Young Caleb didn't remember his mama because she died a day after he was born. His older sister Anna helped him to build memories of her. She told Caleb of the times when Papa and Mama used to sing.

One day, Papa put an ad in the newspaper for a wife. Soon he received an answer from a woman named Sarah, who lived in Maine. Sarah wrote that she would be coming to visit the family.

Sarah was a plain, tall woman. She arrived in the springtime, bringing sea shells for the children and a cat named Seal. But Anna and Caleb knew from the beginning that Sarah was lonely on the vast prairie. She missed the sea.

Anna and Caleb waited to see whether Sarah would decide to stay with them and their father. Anna tells the story.

126   127

FROM LEVEL 11

A **Unit Closer** provides questions that summarize the unit and help students think critically about the unit's selections and unifying theme.

FRIENDS AND FAMILIES

The selections in this unit have explored different kinds of friendships and family relationships. You have learned about some unusual animal friends, such as a fox and a mole and a zebra and an ostrich. You have read of special bonds between people, such as between Tía Rosa and Carmela and between twins. You have read about both human and wolf families and discovered ways a family takes care of its members.

Think about how some of the friendships in this unit began: a lonely mole, children born as twins, a family needing a wife and mother.

Some sentences from the selections follow. What do they tell us friendship is? What do they tell us about the importance of families?

• . . . the fox suddenly discovered who and what the mole was. He

was someone to be trusted, to be company, to be loved.

• Annie's voice trembled. "You can make me a costume, can't you, Henry?"

• Brother on the beach. Sister on the sand. Rolling in the water. Strolling hand in hand.

• Other wolves of the pack also may bring food for the mother and her young.

• Papa kept his promise to Sarah. When work was done, he took her out into the fields. Papa riding Jack, who was sly, and Sarah riding Old Bess. Sarah was quick to learn.

Now that you have read the selections in this unit, think about what you have learned about friendship and families.

1. In "Maybe, a Mole" and "A Gift for Tía Rosa," the special friends gave each other things that they didn't get from their own families. What were some of these things? Why were they important?

2. We're not used to seeing animals being friends the way we as humans are friends. But the two nonfiction selections, "Strange Partners" and "Make Room for the Wolf," show that animals can be friends in many of the ways we understand. Find at least four examples of animals being friends

4. You've read several selections about brothers and sisters who are not the same age and one selection about twins who are the same age. How is being a twin different from being an older or younger brother or sister?

5. How were Judy and Peter in the story "Jumanji" like the brother and sister in the poem "Today We Are Brother and Sister"?

6. In "Sarah, Plain and Tall," Sarah argued with her future husband. She wanted to learn how to ride

FROM LEVEL 11

A **Bibliography** at the end of each unit encourages reading beyond the text. It includes the titles of all the books represented in the unit, plus additional annotated entries that relate to the unit theme or to the content of selections. Bibliographies for **independent reading** and for **reading aloud** to students are included in the *Teacher's Editions* for Levels 1–15.

Bibliography

Books in This Unit

Today We Are Brother and Sister by Arnold Adoff. Lothrop, Lee & Shepard, 1981.

Maybe, a Mole by Julia Cunningham. Pantheon, 1974.

Strange Partners by Anabel Dean. Lerner, 1976.

Sarah, Plain and Tall by Patricia MacLachlan. Harper & Row, 1985.

Blue Moose by Manus Pinkwater. Dodd, Mead, 1975.

Being a Twin, Having a Twin by Maxine Rosenberg. Lothrop, Lee & Shepard, 1985.

Help! There's a Cat Washing in Here! by Alison Smith. E. P. Dutton, 1981.

A Gift for Tía Rosa by Karen T. Taha. Dillon Press, 1986.

Jumanji by Chris Van Allsburg. Houghton Mifflin, 1981.

By the Shores of Silver Lake by Laura Ingalls Wilder. Harper & Row, 1953.

Additional Books to Read

Floramel and Esteban by Emilie Buchwald. Harcourt Brace Jovanovich, 1982. Set on a Caribbean island, this is a funny story about the special friendship between a cow and a cattle egret.

The Secret Grove by Barbara Cohen. Union of American Hebrew Congregations, 1985. Two boys, one Israeli and one Jordanian, form a special friendship in this interesting story. Although their countries are at war, they spend one afternoon together and make a secret peace.

A Matter of Pride by Emily Crofford. Carolrhoda, 1981. Meg is at first ashamed of her mother's fear. Then she learns what courage is really all about. Read this absorbing family story to find out what happens to change her mind.

How My Parents Learned to Eat by Ina Friedman. Houghton Mifflin, 1984. A young girl tells the story of how her American father and Japanese mother met.

Blackberries in the Dark by Mavis Jukes. Alfred A. Knopf, 1985. A boy's grandmother helps him get over his grandfather's death. Find out how in this book.

The Wolves by Jana McConoughey. Crestwood House, 1983. Learn more about these interesting animals and what is being done to save them. This book has many color photographs.

Oh Honestly, Angela! by Nancy K. Robinson. Scholastic, 1985. This is a funny novel about two sisters and a brother and how they convince their parents to adopt a child.

Cornrows by Camille Yarbrough. Coward, 1979. A girl and her younger brother listen to their mother and grandmother tell stories of cornrowed hair and the history of their people.

146   147

FROM LEVEL 11

COMPREHENSION
BEFORE READING

"Useful approaches to building background knowledge...focus on the concepts...central to understanding the upcoming selection, concepts that children either do not possess or may not think of without prompting." *(Becoming a Nation of Readers,* p. 50)

Prereading activities in **HRW READING** develop an understanding of key vocabulary and concepts, activate and expand upon prior knowledge, and help students set purposes for reading.

Vocabulary instruction and practice help students see the relationships among words and understand the concepts these words represent.

The development of a single **Comprehension/Thinking Focus** skill through each step of the lesson plan helps students understand the *what, how*, and *why* of reading, and provides opportunities to apply this knowledge in a variety of reading situations.

FROM LEVEL 5

I, T Vocabulary: word meaning

DIRECT INSTRUCTION Tell pupils that they are going to talk about some words they will read in the next story. Print the following words and sentences on the chalkboard, omitting the underlining.

IC 18

cold	hatches	move	new	other

1. A robin sits on her new nest.
2. She cannot move far from the nest.
3. She must not let the eggs get cold.
4. One egg hatches.
5. Then the other eggs hatch.

brushes	clean	grub	hill
lays	rushes	stacked	

Read the first sentence and point to the word *new*. Ask pupils to tell what is new. (th... teers to point to and read th... pupils read the sentence with...

Read Sentence 2 aloud. Point... it. Ask what the robin cannot... from the nest.) Have pupils re... and then ask them to find and...

Read Sentence 3 and point to t... robin keeps the eggs from g... them.) Then call on pupils to... read it.

Read Sentence 4 and point to t... happens to an egg when it... open, and a baby bird come... sentence with you. Then hav... word *hatches*.

Read Sentence 5 and point to... if the robin has more than on... eggs.) Have pupils read the se... ask them to find and read the...

The words in the second set a... known phonic elements. You... read the words, using what th... sounds.

Point to and read the word *gru...* an ant first hatches, it is called... read *stacked* and explain that s... describe things that are piled... eggs are stacked on top of an a...

GUIDED PRACTICE Print the following sentences on the chalkboard, omitting the underlining.

IC 19

1. A robin lays eggs in a nest.
2. A fish lays eggs in a cold pond.
3. Ant eggs are stacked in a hill.
4. An ant egg hatches into a grub.
5. Grubs have no feet.
6. They cannot move.
7. One ant rushes to feed the grub.
8. Other ants clean the new grub.
9. A girl brushes away the ants.

Provide opportunities for pupils to practice reading the

T76 *Snapshots,* Level 5

---

1 PREPARING FOR THE SELECTION

DECODING/VOCABULARY

I, T Vocabulary: word meaning (mastery words)

DIRECT INSTRUCTION Tell students that they are going to learn some words that they will read in the next selection. Write the following words and sentences on the chalkboard:

IC 16

warriors	invaded	defense	ruins
	evidence		

1. The warriors came rushing to attack, armed with spears and swords.
2. The army surrounded the town at night and invaded the next day, smashing through the gates and climbing the walls.
3. The guards, using the few weapons they had to try to stop the attackers, provided little defense for their town.
4. The soldiers destroyed everything in their path, leaving the town in ruins.
5. Scientists found the remains of looms and pots of dye for yarn, evidence that the town had been a center of fabric making.

Provide an opportunity for students to pronounce each word and tell what they might know about it. Then help students use the context clues in each sentence to develop a definition for the underlined word. Model, or ask a student to model how to do this using the first sentence.

The first part of the sentence says that the warriors rushed to attack. You know from this that warriors are people who fight. The second part of the sentence says that the warriors had spears and swords. So the warriors had come prepared to fight with weapons and were experienced soldiers. Let's put that information into a definition.

State a definition for *warriors* and write the definition on the chalkboard. An example follows.

warriors "experienced, armed soldiers"

Use the same procedure for each vocabulary word. Help students use the context clues in each sentence to develop definitions. Use the following definitions as guides:

invaded "entered by force in order to take over"
defense "protection from danger"
ruins "the remains of something that has been destroyed"
evidence "material that proves something to be true or false"

GUIDED PRACTICE Tell students that you are going to ask them some questions and that each question will use two of the new words. If students have difficulty answering the questions, have them read the meaning of each word on the chalkboard, and then discuss with them the relationship between the words.

1. **What kind of *evidence* shows that a town was *invaded?*** (A town that was invaded would look destroyed.)
2. **Why would *warriors* invade other countries?** (Warriors are experienced soldiers who might want to capture other lands for themselves or their ruler.)
3. **How could the *defense* against invaders of one's village end in *ruins?*** (If a person could not defend the village, it would probably be destroyed.)

T430 *Banners,* Level 11

FROM LEVEL 11

FROM LEVEL 13

I Vocabulary: word meaning (non-mastery words)

DIRECT INSTRUCTION Tell students that you are going to talk about more words they will read in the next selection. Write the following words and definitions on the chalkboard. Read the words aloud:

IC 43

soothing	morosely	preserve
stifling	patriarch	diverted

1. "elderly respected man who is the ruler of a group of people"
2. "gloomily; sullenly"
3. "calming; comforting"
4. "turned aside"
5. "a place where wild animals are protected"
6. "smothering; hot and enclosed and difficult to breathe freely"

Tell students that you will read them a story that uses these words. Read the following story:

Debby squirmed uncomfortably in the back seat of the car. The summer day was hot, making the car feel *stifling*. She stared *morosely* at the back of her older brother's head as he steered towards a parking spot. Why was he acting like such a *patriarch*, ordering everyone around, just because Mom and Dad were out of town? He had insisted on visiting the wildlife *preserve*, even though Debby didn't want to go. When they finally climbed out of the car, however, the *soothing*, cool fresh air calmed some of Debby's anger. When her attention was *diverted* from her own misery to a pair of young raccoons up a tree, she looked happy to be where she was.

Reread each sentence containing a vocabulary word. Help students use the context clues in the story to choose a definition for each word from the list on the chalkboard. (*soothing,* 3.; *morosely,* 2.; *preserve,* 5.; *stifling,* 6.; *patriarch,* 1.; *diverted,* 4.)

GUIDED PRACTICE Read each definition aloud. Have students match the definitions to the vocabulary words and use the words in sentences.

COMPREHENSION/THINKING

Focus
M Literal: cause and effect (signal words)

DIRECT INSTRUCTION Write *cause and effect* on the chalkboard, explaining that this relationship tells what happened and why it happened. What happened is the *effect;* why it happened is the *cause.*

Tell students that sometimes a cause-and-effect relationship is signaled by words such as *because, since, therefore,* and *so.* Read aloud the sentence "The bird flew north because it was springtime," and ask students to name the effect (The bird flew north.) and the cause. (It was springtime.) Point out the use of the word *because* to signal the cause-and-effect relationship. Have students use other cause-and-effect clue words in the sentence to see that they all signal this relationship. (For example, "Since it was springtime, the bird flew north.")

GUIDED PRACTICE Read aloud the following sentences. Have students name the effect and the cause, and the signal word in each.

1. **Since I hadn't seen Jacob in two years, I was amazed to see that he had grown so tall.** (I was amazed to see that he [Jacob] had grown so tall; I hadn't seen Jacob in two years; *Since*)
2. **Because Peggy had been sick, she missed the class party.** (She [Peggy] missed the class party; Peggy had been sick; *Because*)
3. **Michael was eager to get a letter from his grandmother, so he checked the mailbox each day.** (He [Michael] checked the mailbox each day; Michael was eager to get a letter from his grandmother; *so*)
4. **Suzy's softball game was rained out; therefore, she returned home.** (She [Suzy] returned home; Suzy's softball game was rained out; *therefore*)

T190 *Passages,* Level 13

Prereading discussion in **HRW READING** focuses on students' prior knowledge and their expectations of what they will find in the text. Bringing students' *own* experience to the *reading* experience raises interest and sets the stage for comprehension.

Using Prior Knowledge encourages discussion that helps teachers discover what students already know and what they need to know for comprehending the selection.

Setting a Purpose for Reading guides students to make predictions about selection information and story outcomes and to set purposes for reading. Establishing a purpose for reading helps students construct the meaning of a selection and provides a model for them to use in their independent reading.

2 READING FOR COMPREHENSION

Background for the Teacher

SUMMARY A young girl tells about her family's trip west to make a new home. Traveling was very tiring, and when the family stopped for the night, there was always work to do. When they arrive at their new land, neighbors come and help them build a shanty to live in.

INFORMATION This story is an adaptation based on *The Early Family Home* from The Early Settler Life Series by Bobbie Kalman.

Using Prior Knowledge

Explain that pupils are going to read a story told by a young girl moving west in the early 1800's. Have pupils describe what moving to a new home might be like. Then discuss what moving in the early 1800's might involve. List pupil ideas in a cluster diagram similar to the one below.

[cluster diagram: Moving in the 1800's — leaving belongings, leaving friends, a long trip, difficult travel, covered wagon]

Then ask pupils to use the words in the diagram to summarize what moving in the 1800's was probably like.

Setting a Purpose for Reading

Instruct pupils to open their books to page 50. Read the title "A Settler Story." Point to the headnote at the top of page 50 and explain that this note will help them think about the story they are going to read. Ask a volunteer to read the headnote aloud. Have pupils predict how the family will work together to make a new home.

Reading Silently

Some pupils may be able to read this story independently. Direct them to read the whole story to find out more about the settler family's trip west. For those pupils who need more guidance, suggestions for directed reading follow. As pupils read and answer questions, periodically ask, "How did you know that?" or "Where did you find the answer?"

T116   *Patterns, Level 7*

FROM LEVEL 7

A **headnote** introducing each selection in the student's book (Levels 5–15) provides additional help in establishing background and setting a purpose for reading.

A girl tells about when she and her family went west to make a new home. Read to find out how they work together to make a new life.

A Settler Story

by Bobbie Kalman

My family and I left our home for the West in the summer of 1817. There were my mother and father, my Uncle Pete, and my four brothers and sisters, Marcus, Tom, Ann, and Emily.

We had already been traveling for three weeks, over bumpy dirt roads, in a wagon pulled by a team of oxen. It was almost dark when we came to a place where we could spend the night.

50

FROM LEVEL 7

The citizens plan to let only the most beautiful horses into their city. What will happen to change their minds?

Fritz and the Beautiful Horses

by Jan Brett

254

FROM LEVEL 8

COMPREHENSION
DURING AND AFTER READING

As students read each selection, the emphasis is on understanding and appreciating the content of the selection. Well-crafted questions, both during and after reading, probe for important information and ideas, and encourage critical thinking.

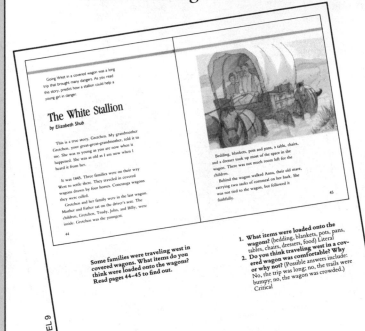

Successful readers make **predictions** about what will happen. As they read, they evaluate and revise those predictions. Directed-reading questions that accompany each reading selection (Levels 2–15) encourage this behavior and help students make connections between what they read and what they already know.

Discussing the Selection questions focus attention on ideas of central importance to the selection and promote critical thinking. The questions appear in the student's book, Levels 6–15, and in the *Teacher's Editions* at all levels.

Reader 1: And so Thumbelina and the prince were happy ever after.

Discussing the Selection
1. How did Bird surprise Thumbelina?
2. Why didn't she want to marry Mole?
3. Why did Bird want her to fly away with him?
4. When did you know Thumb would fly away with Bird?
5. How do you think Thumb friends felt after she left?

Whether or not Nibby "remembers" me I do not know, but he seems to understand that I am not to be feared, and he does not run away when I am near. He is two years old now and since cottontail rabbits often live five years in captivity, Nibby will probably live just as long in our protected garden.

This selection is taken from the book *Animals Come to My House* by Esther Kellner.

Discussing the Selection
1. What did Esther Kellner do to care for Nibby? Give some examples.
2. What may happen if you carelessly handle a baby rabbit?
3. Ms. Kellner states, "When we take in wild animals to care for, we are not looking for pets." What should be the aim of anyone who cares for wild animals?
4. In "The Pet Parade," many of Farley's pets, such as the gophers and owls, were wild animals. How would taking care of pets like these be different from taking care of more usual pets like cats, dogs, hamsters, and gerbils? How would it be the same?

328

Follow-up activities move students beyond each reading selection to help them relate what they have read to their own lives and to integrate reading with the other language arts.

Listening, speaking, reading, and writing activities that expand selection themes and relate reading to various content areas help students see reading as an important, useful, and enjoyable part of their daily lives.

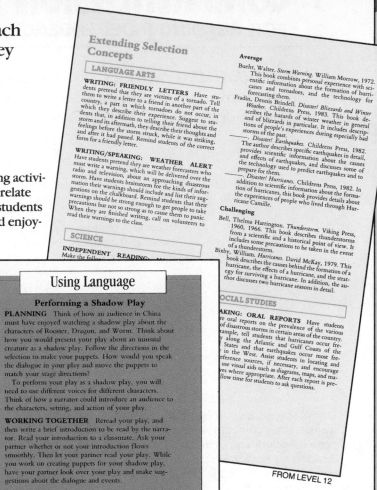

FROM LEVEL 12

Using Language activities that appear in the *Pupil's Edition* Levels 7–15, and in the *Teacher's Edition* at all levels, offer a wide variety of ways for students to respond to each selection. Both oral and written activities focus on *meaning*—not on the subskills of reading.

FROM LEVEL 12

"Independent reading is probably a major source of reading fluency...children should spend more time in independent reading." *(Becoming a Nation of Readers,* pp.78, 119) **Bibliographies** in the students' books, Levels 7–15, and in the *Teacher's Editions* at all levels, give high priority to independent reading by guiding students to outstanding literature that is both appropriate and interesting.

Unit Closer discussions engage students in higher level thinking processes as they are called upon to apply, analyze, synthesize, and evaluate information from the unit's selections.

COMPREHENSION STRATEGIES
FOR READING INDEPENDENCE

HRW READING provides direct instruction in the active comprehension strategies that good readers use.

In Level 1, reading a story aloud to students includes **modeling** the way good readers think as they read.

One of several approaches to vocabulary instruction, a context-to-definition approach, includes modeling the process of developing a definition by thinking about how a word was used in context.

SAY Do you think Henry will be able to get the ant now? (Allow time for response.)

Henry took the food he was cooking off the stove. Then he shut off the flame and pulled the stove away from the wall. He saw the ant!

The ant saw Henry and ran into a small crack in the wall. Henry went and got a hammer.

SAY Henry really wants to get that ant!

Henry pounded a big hole in the wall where the crack was. But he couldn't find the ant. So he kept on pounding.

The hole got bigger and bigger. At last, Henry saw the ant sitting on a pipe inside the wall.

Henry aimed the hammer at the ant—and missed. The blow of the hammer broke the pipe.

SAY Uh-oh. Now what will happen? Look at the second picture.

Water came shooting out of the pipe. Henry couldn't stop it.

Henry grabbed a towel. He tied it around the pipe, and the water stopped shooting out.

But Henry hadn't stopped the water soon enough. It had sprayed all over the kitchen. Everything was soaking wet, except for Clara's supper, thank goodness.

Henry began mopping the puddles of water. All at once he slipped and banged against the kitchen table. Everything came crashing down. Henry was covered with pots and pans and food.

The supper was ruined. There was nothing He could do now but to call Clara and tell her not to co...

While Henry was talking on the telephone, the to... came loose from the pipe. The water came shooting... and flooded the whole house. Henry was carried ri... out the front door by the flood.

SAY Poor Henry! The ant ruined everything.

There was no going back. Poor Henry's house wa... washed away by the flood. He saved what he could a... moved into a new house.

SAY Henry made a real mess chasing that ant!

When Henry was settled in his new house, he again asked Clara over for supper. Just as he went to the door to let Clara in, he saw an ant.

SAY Oh no! Not again! What do you think Henry will do? Let's find out.

He looked the other way!

ASK Why do you think he looked the other way? (because he didn't want to chase the ant) Of all the things that Henry did, what was the really awful mistake?

Pupils may suggest breaking the pipe or hammering a hole in the wall. Help them understand that Henry's biggest mistake was chasing the ant i... ...ace.

● **Listening:** story comprehension
● **Directions:** Look at the pictures as the teacher reads the story "Henry's Awful Mistake."
● **To the Parent:** Ask your child to tell the story of "Henry's Awful Mistake."

19

FROM LEVEL 1

---

1 PREPARING FOR THE SELECTION

DECODING/VOCABULARY

I, T Vocabulary: word meaning (mastery words)

DIRECT INSTRUCTION Tell students that they are going to learn some words that they will read in the next selection. Write the following words and sentences on the chalkboard:

IC 40

> **perilous solemnly**
> **muttered squirmed**
>
> 1. Mary was frightened during her _perilous_ drive down the icy mountain road.
> 2. After reading about the dangers of swimming alone, Rivke _solemnly_ promised never to swim alone again.
> 3. Mother _muttered_ to herself because we had all forgotten to hang up our coats.
> 4. After picking up his drumstick, Adam _squirmed_ with embarrassment when he saw that everyone else was using a knife and fork to eat the chicken.

Provide an opportunity for students to pronounce each word and tell what they might know about the word. Then help students use the context clues in each sentence to develop a definition for the underlined word. Model how to do this, using the first sentence. An example follows.

> **The first part of the sentence says that Mary was frightened during the drive. The second part of the sentence says that she was driving down an icy mountain road.** _Perilous_ **must mean "dangerous" because Mary is frightened, and because going down an icy mountain road is dangerous.**

State a definition for _perilous_ and write the definition on the chalkboard. An example follows.

perilous   "full of danger"

T182 _Festivals_, Level 12

FROM LEVEL 12

xxvi

Use the same procedure for each vocabulary word. Help students use the context clues in each sentence to develop definitions. Use the following definitions as guides:

solemnly   "in a serious and formal way"
muttered   "spoke in a low, unclear voice, usually to complain about something"

COMPREHENSION/THINKING

Focus
I, T Nonfiction structure: comparison and contrast

DIRECT INSTRUCTION Remind students that when authors write about more than one topic, they often compare and contrast the characteristics of each topic.

Write the following paragraph on the chalkboard from an information selection about two types of flowers that are in the same family. Read the paragraph aloud and have students listen to find out how the author organizes and presents the information.

IC 38

> The two flowers, black-eyed Susan and purple-headed sneezeweed, are both in the daisy family. Both have yellow petals. The center of the black-eyed Susan is chocolate brown, but the center of the purple-headed sneezeweed is a deep purple color. Both flowers bloom from June to October. The black-eyed Susan blooms in Canada, but the purple-headed sneezeweed blooms in Michigan, New York, and the New England states. They both grow from one to three feet tall, but the black-eyed Susan has one flower on its long stem, while the purple-headed sneezeweed may have four.

Ask students to tell how the author presented the information about the black-eyed Susan and the purple-headed sneezeweed. (The author compared and contrasted the two types of flowers.) Remind students that once they have figured out how the author organizes the information, they can develop some type of chart to help them better understand the information.

GUIDED PRACTICE The following charts are examples that may be used to organize the information. You may wish to copy the following charts on the chalkboard, omitting the information in the boxes.

How Black-eyed Susans and
Purple-headed Sneezeweed Are Alike

1. Both belong to the daisy family.
2. Both have yellow petals.
3. Both bloom in June to October.
4. Both grow one to three feet tall.

How Black-eyed Susans and
Purple-headed Sneezeweed Are Different

Black-eyed Susans	Purple-headed Sneezeweed
1. has a chocolate brown center	1. has a deep purple center
2. blooms in Canada	2. blooms in Michigan, New York, and New England states
3. has one flower on the stem	3. has four flowers on the stem

Reread the paragraph to students about the two flowers. Ask them to listen for things that are alike and things that are different about the two flowers. Then have volunteers complete the charts with information from the paragraph.

WB 23 INDEPENDENT PRACTICE _Workbook_ page 23 may be used for more practice with comparison and contrast.

PM 17 ADDITIONAL PRACTICE _Practice Masters_ page 17 may be used as an optional practice with comparison and contrast. (See page T148 for reduced pages with answers.)

RETEACH For those students who need additional instruction, see "Reteaching Lesson Skills," page T146 under "Reteaching and Extending."

Direct Instruction and **Guided Practice** as well as *Workbook* practice activities, help students develop strategies for understanding the structure of different kinds of text.

FROM LEVEL 11

Skills Lessons in the *Pupil's Edition* provide instruction in many aspects of comprehension and critical thinking.

Be an Active Reader lessons use marginal notes to "talk" with students about the structure of fiction and nonfiction selections. These notes provide students with a model for monitoring their own comprehension.

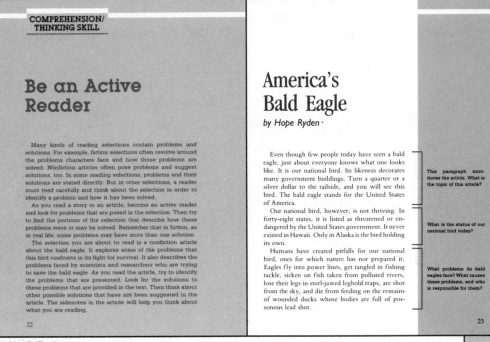

COMPREHENSION/
THINKING SKILL

Be an Active Reader

Many kinds of reading selections contain problems and solutions. For example, fiction selections often revolve around the problems characters face and how those problems are solved. Nonfiction articles often pose problems and suggest solutions, too. In some reading selections, problems and their solutions are stated directly. But in other selections, a reader must read carefully and think about the selection in order to identify a problem and how it has been solved.

As you read a story or an article, become an active reader and look for problems that are posed in the selection. Then try to find the portions of the selection that describe how these problems were or may be solved. Remember that in fiction, as in real life, some problems may have more than one solution.

The selection you are about to read is a nonfiction article about the bald eagle. It explores some of the problems that this bird confronts in its fight for survival. It also describes the problems faced by scientists and researchers who are trying to save the bald eagle. As you read the article, try to identify the problems that are presented. Look for the solutions to these problems that are provided in the text. Then think about other possible solutions that have not been suggested in the article. The sidenotes in the article will help you think about what you are reading.

22

America's Bald Eagle

by Hope Ryden

Even though few people today have seen a bald eagle, just about everyone knows what one looks like. It is our national bird. Its likeness decorates many government buildings. Turn a quarter or a silver dollar to the tailside, and you will see this bird. The bald eagle stands for the United States of America.

Our national bird, however, is not thriving. In forty-eight states, it is listed as threatened or endangered by the United States government. It never existed in Hawaii. Only in Alaska is the bird holding its own.

Humans have created pitfalls for our national bird, ones for which nature has not prepared it. Eagles fly into power lines, get tangled in fishing tackle, sicken on fish taken from polluted rivers, lose their legs in steel-jawed leghold traps, are shot from the sky, and die from feeding on the remains of wounded ducks whose bodies are full of poisonous lead shot.

This paragraph introduces the article. What is the topic of this article?

What is the status of our national bird today?

What problems do bald eagles face? What causes these problems, and who is responsible for them?

23

FROM LEVEL 15

How to Own a Word lessons help students organize ideas about words and reinforce the connection between reading and word meaning.

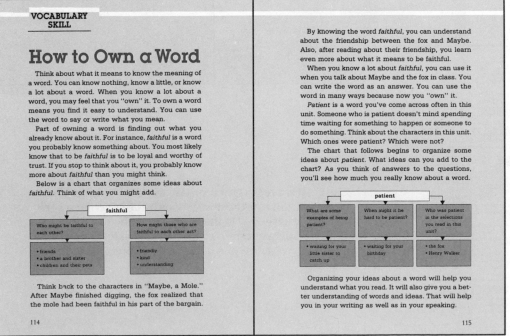

VOCABULARY
SKILL

How to Own a Word

Think about what it means to know the meaning of a word. You can know nothing, know a little, or know a lot about a word. When you know a lot about a word, you may feel that you "own" it. To own a word means you find it easy to understand. You can use the word to say or write what you mean.

Part of owning a word is finding out what you already know about it. For instance, *faithful* is a word you probably know something about. You most likely know that to be *faithful* is to be loyal and worthy of trust. If you stop to think about it, you probably know more about *faithful* than you might think.

Below is a chart that organizes some ideas about *faithful*. Think of what you might add.

faithful

Who might be faithful to each other?
• friends
• a brother and sister
• children and their pets

How might those who are faithful to each other act?
• friendly
• kind
• understanding

Think back to the characters in "Maybe, a Mole." After Maybe finished digging, the fox realized that the mole had been faithful in his part of the bargain.

114

By knowing the word *faithful*, you can understand about the friendship between the fox and Maybe. Also, after reading about their friendship, you learn even more about what it means to be faithful.

When you know a lot about *faithful*, you can use it when you talk about Maybe and the fox in class. You can write the word as an answer. You can use the word in many ways because now you "own" it.

Patient is a word you've come across often in this unit. Someone who is patient doesn't mind spending time waiting for something to happen or someone to do something. Think about the characters in this unit. Which ones were patient? Which were not?

The chart that follows begins to organize some ideas about *patient*. What ideas can you add to the chart? As you think of answers to the questions, you'll see how much you really know about a word.

patient

What are some examples of being patient?
• waiting for your little sister to catch up

When might it be hard to be patient?
• waiting for your birthday

Who was patient in the selections you read in this unit?
• the fox
• Henry Walker

Organizing your ideas about a word will help you understand what you read. It will also give you a better understanding of words and ideas. That will help you in your writing as well as in your speaking.

115

FROM LEVEL 11

COMPREHENSION STRATEGIES
FOR STUDYING AND LEARNING

Content-area reading is emphasized in lessons that instruct students in strategies for extracting and organizing critical information from texts.

Be an Active Reader

Paul Bunyan, Mark Twain, and many other American heroes came from the American Midwest. The selection you are about to read is the first chapter of a social studies unit about the Midwest. The title of the chapter is "People and Places." What do you already know about the Midwest?

Before you read, scan the article to find the objectives of the chapter, the headings and subheadings, the words in boldface, and the review questions. The notes at the bottom of the page will help you.

The article you are going to read tells how the Midwest was settled from the 1670's to the 1920's. To help you understand the sequence of events, make a chart including some of these dates mentioned in the selection.

Dates	Places settled	Settlers	Why settlers came
1673			
1775			
1869			
1890–1920			

Copy the chart onto another sheet of paper. What do you think you will find out about who settled in the Midwest and why they came?

234

CHAPTER 8

People and Places

Some Important People

As a young woman in Mattoon (ma-**toon**), Illinois, Patricia Harris wanted to become a lawyer. After her studies, she decided to teach law to others. She also worked hard for equal rights for black people. In 1977, she became the first black woman to hold an important job in the national government. In this job, Harris was able to help the people in cities who needed better housing and jobs.

Amelia Earhart (ar-**hahrt**) came from Atchison, Kansas. In the 1920's, she wanted to learn to fly a plane. In those days, there were few women pilots. But Earhart worked hard and became a very good pilot. In 1932, she was the first woman to fly a plane across the Atlantic Ocean alone.

Harry Houdini (hoo-**dee**-nee) was from Appleton, Wisconsin. As a boy, he joined a circus and learned to do magic tricks. But he wanted to entertain people with very exciting tricks. So he became an escape artist. One of his escapes was from a large box that had been nailed shut. Houdini was one of the greatest magicians of his time.

Patricia Harris

Amelia Earhart

Harry Houdini

Section Review

Write your answers on a sheet of paper.
1. What contributions did the French make to the early settlement of the Midwest?
2. Why did settlers come to the Midwest?
3. Did the railroad help all people of the Midwest? Explain.

Some **Be an Active Reader** lessons in the *Pupil's Editions* (Levels 11–15) teach specific strategies for understanding the organization of textbook content and help students learn to use the study aids included in textbook selections.

Thinking About What You've Read

What did you learn about the people and places of the Midwest? Why did settlers come to live there?

After you have completed your chart, it will probably look something like the one below.

Dates	Places settled	Settlers	Why settlers came
1673	Mississippi River	French from Canada	fur trade
1775	Northwest Territory	early Americans from the original colonies	better farming
1869	Great Plains	Americans (homesteaders)	land for farming provided by the government
1890–1920	Cities in the Midwest	from Sweden, Norway, Denmark, Eastern Europe, Italy, Greece	better jobs

Using this information, explain how the Midwest was settled. How has completing this chart added to your knowledge of the Midwest?

Active readers know how to use study aids in textbooks. They also learn to organize ideas so that new information can be added to what they already know.

243

Note: Reading aloud is an important daily activity throughout all grade levels. It is a way to share books with your students and expose them to all types of literature. As students are working in Unit 1, plan to read aloud *The Wind in the Willows*. Read a portion of the book each day. Encourage students to relate characters and events in this book to selections they read in the "Friends and Families" unit. Ask them to keep in mind the unit theme and how it relates to *The Wind in The Willows*. Ask them to think about what the book and its characters have to say about friendship.

WB **INDEPENDENT PRACTICE** *Workbook* page 5 may be used for more practice with identifying character traits.

PM **ADDITIONAL PRACTICE** *Practice Masters* page 3 may be used as an optional practice with identifying character traits. (See page T35 for reduced pages with answers.)

❋ **RETEACH** For those students who need additional instruction, see "Reteaching Lesson Skills," page T33, under "Reteaching and Extending."

STUDY SKILLS

M Study aids: question-answer relationships

DIRECT INSTRUCTION Have students turn to page 12 in their books. Indicate the questions and explain that questions such as these will be at the end of every selection in the book. Ask students to tell how they go about finding the answers to questions. Through discussion, help students understand that there are two basic sources for answering questions: information in the book and information in their heads. Write the following chart on the chalkboard:

IC 4

```
    Where Can I Find That Answer?

  ( In the Book )        ( In My Head )

  Right    Think       Author    On Your
  There   and Search   and You     Own
```

Call attention to the heading "In the Book" and explain that sometimes the question is answered right there in a sentence on the page and sometimes you have to search through the story for the answer. The answer might be found in different places in the story. Ask the following questions:

1. **How was Maybe different from the other moles?** (He could see.)
2. **Where did you find the answer?** (in the book; page 5, line 13: "I can see.")
3. **Was the answer right there in one sentence or was it given in different sentences throughout the story?** (in one sentence)
4. **How did the fox's feelings about Maybe change after the hunt for the treasure?** (At first, the fox was trying to use the mole in order to get the gold, but after he saw how hard Maybe had worked, he discovered that the mole was a true friend, someone to be trusted.)
5. **Did you find all the information in the same sentence?** (no) **Where did you find the information?** (Page 7, "And that's where . . . uneven bargain."; pages 9–10: "Looking at the . . . to be loved.)
6. **What did you have to do in order to answer this question?** (put the different pieces of information together)

The **QAR** strategy (Question-Answer-Relationships) helps students learn to answer questions by discovering *where* to find the answers: "in the book" or "in their heads." Understanding question-answer relationships heightens students' awareness of reading as a thinking, interactive process.

HRW READING makes extensive use of the **K-W-L model** as students read expository selections. This classroom-tested strategy models the active thinking needed when reading expository text and is particularly useful in reading content-area materials. The letters *K, W,* and *L* stand for the activities that help students recall what they KNOW, determine what they WANT to know prior to reading, and identify what they want to LEARN as they read.

The **K-W-L** strategy is fully developed in the **Using Prior Knowledge** part of the lesson plan.

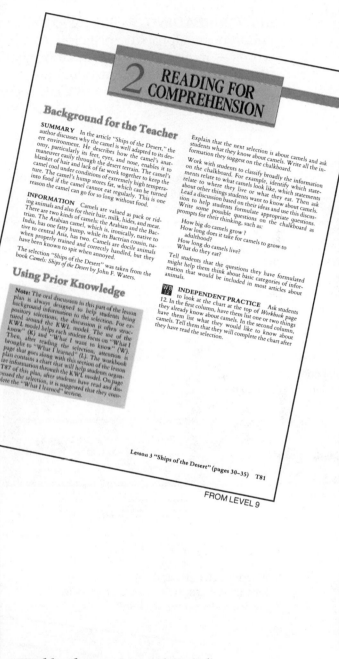

2 READING FOR COMPREHENSION

Background for the Teacher

SUMMARY In the article "Ships of the Desert," the author discusses why the camel is well adapted to its desert environment. He describes how the camel's anatomy, particularly its feet, eyes, and nose, enables it to maneuver easily through the desert terrain. The camel's blanket of hair and lack of fat work together to keep the camel cool under conditions of extremely high temperature. The camel's hump stores fat, which can be turned into food if the camel cannot eat regularly. This is one reason the camel can go for so long without food.

INFORMATION Camels are valued as pack or riding animals and also for their hair, milk, hides, and meat. There are two kinds of camels: the Arabian and the Bactrian. The Arabian camel, which is, ironically, native to India, has one fatty hump, while its Bactrian cousin, native to central Asia, has two. Camels are docile animals when properly trained and correctly handled, but they have been known to spit when annoyed.

The selection "Ships of the Desert" was taken from the book *Camels: Ships of the Desert* by John F. Waters.

Using Prior Knowledge

Note: The oral discussion in this part of the lesson plan is always designed to help students bring background information to the selection. For expository selections, the discussion is often structured around the KWL model. The use of the KWL model helps each student focus on "What I know" (K) and "What I want to know" (W). Then, after reading the selection, attention is brought to "What I learned" (L). The workbook page that goes along with this section of the lesson plan contains a chart that will help students organize information through the KWL model. On page T87 of this plan, after students have read and discussed the selection, it is suggested that they complete the "What I learned" section.

Explain that the next selection is about camels and ask students what they know about camels. Write all the information they suggest on the chalkboard.

Work with students to classify broadly the information on the chalkboard. For example, identify which statements relate to what camels look like, which statements relate to where they live or what they eat. Then ask about other things students want to know about camels. Lead a discussion based on their ideas and use this discussion to help students formulate appropriate questions. Write some possible questions on the chalkboard as prompts for their thinking, such as:

How big do camels grow?
How long does it take for camels to grow to adulthood?
How long do camels live?
What do they eat?

Tell students that the questions they have formulated might help them think about basic categories of information that would be included in most articles about animals.

WB 12 INDEPENDENT PRACTICE Ask students to look at the chart at the top of *Workbook* page 12. In the first column, have them list one or two things they already know about camels. In the second column, have them list what they would like to know about camels. Tell them that they will complete the chart after they have read the selection.

Comprehension/Thinking
Use with "Ships of the Desert," Lesson 3

Name

A. Use what you already know about camels to complete the first two columns of the chart. Then use story information to complete the last column of the chart.

Camels		
What I know:	What I want to know:	What I learned:

B. Use complete sentences to answer the questions below.

1. Why are camels called "ships of the desert"?

   Camels carry people and goods across deserts.

2. Why are camels the perfect animals for desert travel?

   Camels have feet that make it easy for them to walk in the sand. They can keep

   cool in the hot desert. They can travel for a long time without needing water.

12 *Souvenirs*
Level 9

• Selection comprehension: "Ships of the Desert"
• To the Parent: Have your child tell you about "Ships of the Desert."

A **Workbook** page gives students individual opportunities to create charts that will serve as a guide to reading using the K-W-L strategy.

DECODING INSTRUCTION
THAT PROMOTES COMPREHENSION

"One of the cornerstones of skilled reading is fast, accurate word identification." (*Becoming a Nation of Readers*, p. 36)

In **HRW READING**, well-designed, systematic phonics instruction teaches children the alphabetic principle of our language so that they can identify words — in and out of the basal program — very quickly. Phonics instruction begins in Level 1. Introduction of sound/symbol correspondences is completed in Level 8 (Grade 2). Review and maintenance is provided in Grade 3.

Phonics instruction is often drawn from **whole text**, and sound/symbol relationships are explored in whole, meaningful words.

Instruction moves beyond individual sounds to include direct instruction in **blending** sounds to form words. *Pocket Charts* and individual *Word Builders* and *Word Builder Cards* encourage active, every-pupil-response in teacher-directed lessons.

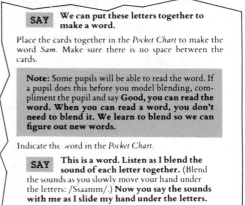

SAY We can put these letters together to make a word.

Place the cards together in the *Pocket Chart* to make the word *Sam*. Make sure there is no space between the cards.

Note: Some pupils will be able to read the word. If a pupil does this before you model blending, compliment the pupil and say **Good, you can read the word. When you can read a word, you don't need to blend it. We learn to blend so we can figure out new words.**

Indicate the word in the *Pocket Chart*.

SAY This is a word. Listen as I blend the sound of each letter together. (Blend the sounds as you slowly move your hand under the letters: /Ssaamm/.) **Now you say the sounds with me as I slide my hand under the letters.**

Move your hand more quickly this time. Call on a volunteer to identify the word. (*Sam*)

Unit 3 "The Sun" (pages 27–36)   T123

FROM LEVEL 1

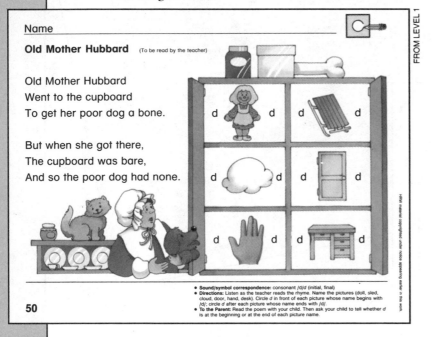

Name _____

Old Mother Hubbard (To be read by the teacher)

Old Mother Hubbard
Went to the cupboard
To get her poor dog a bone.

But when she got there,
The cupboard was bare,
And so the poor dog had none.

FROM LEVEL 1

- **Sound/symbol correspondence:** consonant /d/d (initial, final)
- **Directions:** Listen as the teacher reads the rhyme. Name the pictures (doll, sled, cloud, door, hand, desk). Circle *d* in front of each picture whose name begins with /d/; circle *d* after each picture whose name ends with /d/.
- **To the Parent:** Read the poem with your child. Then ask your child to tell whether *d* is at the beginning or at the end of each picture name.

50

Word structure and the use of **context clues** are important elements in the total decoding strategy.

Instruction utilizes all learning modalities as students listen to the sounds in words, visually associate sounds with letters, and reinforce this association through a variety of kinesthetic responses.

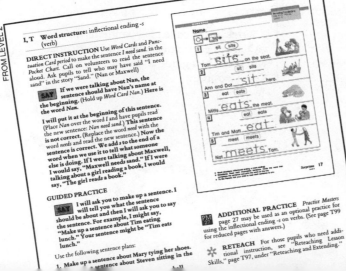

FROM LEVEL 2

I, T   Word structure: inflectional ending *-s* (verb)

DIRECT INSTRUCTION Use *Word Cards* and *Punctuation Card* period to make the sentence *I need sand.* in the *Pocket Chart*. Call on volunteers to read the sentence aloud. Ask pupils to tell who may have said "I need sand" in the story "Sand." (Nan or Maxwell)

SAY If we were talking about Nan, the sentence should have Nan's name at the beginning. (Hold up *Word Card Nan*.) Here is the word *Nan*.

I will put it at the beginning of this sentence. (Place *Nan* over the word *I* and have pupils read the new sentence: *Nan need sand.*) **This sentence is not correct.** (Replace the word *need* with the word *needs* and read the new sentence.) Now the sentence is correct. **We add *s* to the end of a word when we use it to tell what someone else is doing.** If I were talking about Maxwell, I would say, "Maxwell needs sand." If I were talking about a girl reading a book, I would say, "The girl reads a book."

GUIDED PRACTICE

SAY I will ask you to make up a sentence. I will tell you what the sentence should be about and then I will ask you to say the sentence. For example, I might say, "Make up a sentence about Tim eating lunch." Your sentence might be "Tim eats lunch."

Use the following sentence plans:
1. Make up a sentence about Mary tying her shoes.

ADDITIONAL PRACTICE *Practice Masters* page 27 may be used as an optional practice for using the inflectional ending *-s* on verbs. (See page T99 for reduced pages with answers.)

✳ **RETEACH** For those pupils who need additional instruction, see "Reteaching Lesson Skills," page T97, under "Reteaching and Extending."

Workbook pages, the *Practice/Reteach Masters*, and the Level 1 student's text provide abundant opportunities for reinforcing sound/letter knowledge in written activities.

XXX

THE BEST PRACTICE IS IN READING WHOLE TEXT.

"A high proportion of the words in the earliest selections children read should conform to the phonics they have already been taught." (*Becoming a Nation of Readers*, p. 47)

In **HRW READING** sound/symbol correspondences are introduced only as rapidly as they can be illustrated in meaningful reading selections. Thus, every sound/symbol correspondence that children learn is immediately illustrated in selection vocabulary. Most of the words in every story are completely decodable on the basis of sound/letter knowledge.

FROM LEVEL 2

HOW, THEN, CAN **HRW READING** HAVE SUCH DELIGHTFUL STORIES, EVEN IN THE PREPRIMERS?

- First, the sequence for introducing phonic elements is one that makes many good story words quickly accessible. (For example, long *e* is introduced early.)
- Second, some irregular, high frequency words are included, as well as some useful words with sound/letter correspondences not yet taught.
- Third, the entire texts were written by gifted authors of children's literature.
- And finally, shared reading in the preprimers makes possible strong, predictable story structure.

The King's Dragon

One day, the king was sad.
He said, "Where is my pet dragon?
I like to see it hop and skip.
It makes me happy.
Where is my pet dragon?"

FROM LEVEL 4

14

"The issue is no longer whether children should be taught phonics ... just how it should be done." (*Becoming a Nation of Readers*, p. 37)

INTEGRATED LANGUAGE
INSTRUCTION IN MEANINGFUL CONTEXTS

Activities that integrate listening, speaking, reading, and writing, and encourage cooperative learning fill the pages of *HRW READING.*

Using Language activities (Levels 7–15) following each fiction and nonfiction selection provide carefully planned opportunities for students to discover how readers, writers, speakers, and listeners use language to communicate effectively with one another.

Many **Using Language** activities are composition-based and guide students through the steps of the writing process. These lessons use the reading selections as springboards for a wide variety of writing experiences that focus on **meaning**—not on the subskills of reading.

Some **Using Language** activities can be done independently, while others involve students working together in cooperative learning situations.

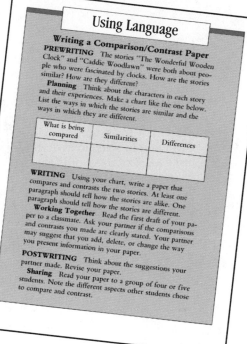

Using Language
Writing a Comparison/Contrast Paper

PREWRITING The stories "The Wonderful Wooden Clock" and "Caddie Woodlawn" were both about people who were fascinated by clocks. How are the stories similar? How are they different?

Planning Think about the characters in each story and their experiences. Make a chart like the one below. List the ways in which the stories are similar and the ways in which they are different.

What is being compared	Similarities	Differences

WRITING Using your chart, write a paper that compares and contrasts the two stories. At least one paragraph should tell how the stories are alike. One paragraph should tell how the stories are different.

Working Together Read the first draft of your paper to a classmate. Ask your partner if the comparisons and contrasts you made are clearly stated. Your partner may suggest that you add, delete, or change the way you present information in your paper.

POSTWRITING Think about the suggestions your partner made. Revise your paper.

Sharing Read your paper to a group of four or five students. Note the different aspects other students chose to compare and contrast.

FROM LEVEL 12

Other **Using Language** activities encourage the development of oral language as students role play, do choral reading, read aloud, perform readers theater, tell stories, or create dialogue—activities that promote both proficiency and creativity.

Using Language
Giving a Talk

PLANNING In "What's in a Name?" you read about all the different ways names have developed over the years. Do you know anything about the origin of your last name, or surname? Perhaps you know the meaning of your first name or why you were given your name. Think about giving a talk to your classmates about how you got your first or last name. If you don't know the story behind your names, how could you find out?

WORKING TOGETHER Working with a group of three or four classmates, think about possible sources for researching the origins of your first and last names. Ideas might include asking your parents or looking in name books in the library. Also, discuss with your group what information should be presented in a talk about your name. You might want to jot down some questions such as:

First Name
- Was I named for someone?
- What does my name mean?
- Is my name taken from another language?

Last Name
- What nationality is my name?
- Does my name mean something in another language?
- Does my name refer to a locality, an occupation, a relationship, or something else?

Answer these questions to make notes for your talk. Practice giving your talk to your group.

SHARING When you've practiced giving your talk in your small group, share it with the entire class.

181

FROM LEVEL 15

In Levels 2 through 6, **Using Language** activities are a regular part of the lesson plan in the *Teacher's Edition.*

Discussing the Selection

PURPOSE Remind pupils that at the beginning of the story they wanted to know what kind of parade would take place. Have pupils tell what they found out about the parade. (The friends took turns leading each other around the block. They did what the leader did.)

STORY MAPPING Ask pupils to think about the way each character led the parade. Then ask the questions that follow.

1. **What problem did the friends have at the beginning of the story?** (They wanted to find something to do.) Literal
2. **What did Mitzie suggest that the four friends should do?** (have a parade) Literal
3. **How did Mitzie start the parade?** (She had Nan, Maxwell, and Stan hop with her.) Literal
4. **What did each of the other friends do when they led the parade?** (Stan sang, Maxwell tap-danced, and Nan had them spin.) Literal
5. **Why did the parade stop?** (Spinning made them all dizzy.) Inferential

CRITICAL THINKING

1. **What might you do if you were the leader in a game of "Follow the Leader?"** (Possible answers include: skip, jump, clap hands.)
2. **Have you ever said, "I'm bored. There's nothing to do"? What are some things you could do when you think there's nothing to do?** (Possible answers include: read a book, have a parade, draw a picture; ask a friend to play.)

Using Language

ORAL READING/SPEAKING: EXPRESSION Remind pupils that the animal characters in their story talk the way people do. Ask pupils to say "I'm bored," in the way they might say it if they really were bored. Then have pupils turn to page 56 in their books. Ask volunteers to read the words Maxwell said in a bored way. Point out that Mitzie was excited about her idea. Have pupils read the words Mitzie said in the way she would have said them.

Page 57: Ask volunteers to read the words Stan said in the way he might have said them.

Page 58: Ask how Nan might have felt when she spoke about the parade. (Possible answers include: excited, happy.) Have pupils read the words Nan said.

Page 59: Have pupils read what Maxwell said to the others.

Page 60: Remind pupils that the friends are having a very good time with their parade. Ask pupils to read the words Nan said.

Page 61: Explain that Mitzie is getting tired of spinning. Have pupils read the words Mitzie says in a tired way.

Pages 62–63: Have pupils choral-read the word *stop* in the way Mitzie would have said it.

SPEAKING: ROLE PLAYING Tell pupils that they can act out the parade that Mitzie, Nan, Maxwell, and Stan had. Have a small group of pupils form a line to make a parade. Have the first person in line say, "Do what I do. Hop." Then let the "parade" hop. Send the leader to the end of the line and have the new leader say, "Do what I do. Sing." Continue having the "parade" perform each action as the characters did in "The Parade." You might invite pupils to lead other activities for the parade to follow.

FROM LEVEL 2

Throughout *HRW READING,* listening, speaking and writing are integrated with reading instruction. In lesson after lesson, *HRW READING* provides opportunities for students to interact with the teacher and with each other to apply and expand their skills in all the language arts.

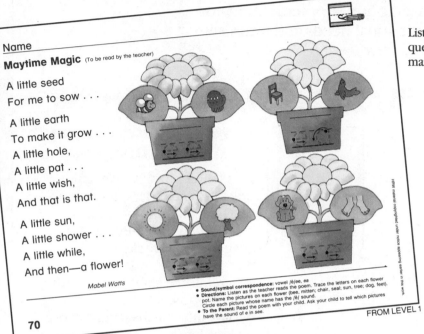

Name _____

Maytime Magic (To be read by the teacher)

A little seed
For me to sow . . .

A little earth
To make it grow . . .

A little hole,
A little pat . . .

A little wish,
And that is that.

A little sun,
A little shower . . .

A little while,
And then—a flower!

Mabel Watts

• **Sound/symbol correspondence:** vowel /ē/ee, ea
• **Directions:** Listen as the teacher reads the poem. Trace the letters on each flower pot. Name the pictures on each flower (bee, mitten, chair, seal; sun, tree; dog, feet). Circle each picture whose name has the /ē/ sound.
• **To the Parent:** Read the poem with your child. Ask your child to tell which pictures have the sound of e in see.

70   FROM LEVEL 1

Listening to brief narratives and poetry is frequently an integrated part of instruction in many aspects of reading.

Children's early composition abilities are developed through the writing of language-experience stories in response to stories they have heard or read.

FROM LEVEL 1

3 Developing the Skills

I Writing: language-experience stories

Remind pupils of the poem about a child's pretend trip into space. Display chart paper and tell pupils that they can work together to make up a story about a pretend trip into space. Explain that you will write the story on the chart paper for them. Tell pupils to think about who will travel in space in their story. Have them suggest names for their space travelers and tell where they might like to go. If necessary, help organize the story by asking questions such as the following:

    How should our story start?
    What will (character's name) use to travel?
    What might happen when (character) gets to (place)?
    Will there be any space creatures there?
    What will we call the creatures?
    What might the creatures do?
    What will (character) do?
    What might happen when (character) comes home?

As pupils dictate to you, write on the chart the words

✳ Practicing and Extending

The activities that follow provide practice and extension of skills developed in this lesson. Not every pupil needs to complete these activities. Choose only the activities that are needed to provide for the individual differences in your classroom.

Extending Selection Concepts

LITERATURE

LISTENING: FICTION Choose a book about an imaginary trip into space to read aloud. Discuss with pupils what happens to the characters in space.

Keats, Ezra Jack. *Regards to the Man in the Moon.* Four Winds Press, 1981. Louie learns that his imagination can take him anywhere, even into space.

Yolen, Jane. *Commander Toad in Space.* Coward-McCann, 1980. A band of space explorers board the ship Star Warts for a funny adventure.

Reading good literature to students is encouraged in every level, and students are urged to experiment with language in their responses.

The **Extending Selection Concepts** section of each lesson plan offers a great variety of listening, speaking, reading, and writing activities that promote growth in language while relating reading to the content areas.

Out in Space (To be read by the teacher)

When Mom and Dad turn out the lights
and I'm tucked in my room,
I pretend my bed's a rocket ship
And out in space I zoom.

I always wave to the man in the moon.
He'd like for me to stay,
But I pretend my friends on Mars
Want me to come and play.

Linda Cave

• **Listening:** poetry
• **Directions:** Listen as the teacher reads the poem.
• **To the Parent:** Read and discuss the poem with your child

17

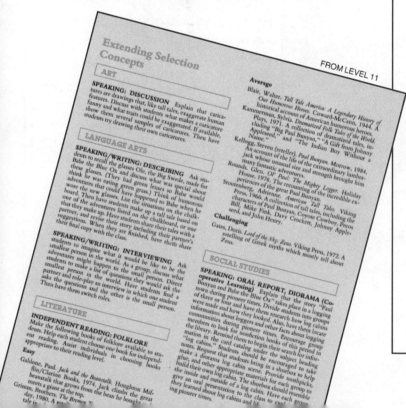

Extending Selection Concepts

ART

SPEAKING: DISCUSSION Explain that caricatures are drawings that, like tall tales, exaggerate human features. Discuss with students what makes a caricature funny and what traits could be exaggerated. If available, show them several samples of caricatures. Then have students try drawing their own caricatures.

LANGUAGE ARTS

SPEAKING/WRITING: DESCRIBING Ask students to recall the glasses Ole, the Big Swede, made for Babe the Blue Ox and discuss what was special about these glasses. (They had green lenses so Babe would think he was eating green grass.) Think of other adventures that could have happened to Babe when he wore the new glasses. List the situation on the chalkboard. Then have students make up a tall tale based on one of the adventures listed on the chalkboard, or one that they make up. Have students share their tales with a partner, and revise their story including their partner's suggestions. When they are finished, have them share their final copy with the class.

SPEAKING/WRITING: INTERVIEWING Ask students to imagine what it would be like to be the smallest person in the world. As a group, discuss what adventures might happen to the small person. Direct students to make a list of questions they would ask the smallest person in the world. Have students find a partner and role-play an interview in which one student asks the questions and the other is the small person. Then have them switch roles.

LITERATURE

INDEPENDENT READING: FOLKLORE Make the following books of folklore available to students. Help each student choose one book for independent reading. Assist individuals in choosing books appropriate to their reading level.

Easy

Galdone, Paul. *Jack and the Beanstalk.* Houghton Mifflin/Clarion Books, 1974. Jack climbs the great beanstalk that grows from the bean he bought.

Grimm, Brothers. *The Bremen T__* day, 1980. A s__ tale in __

Average

Blair, Walter. *Tall Tale America: A Legendary History of Our Humorous Heroes.* Coward-McCann, 1944. A historical account of American humorous heroes.

Kammerman, Sylvia. *Dramatized Folk Tales of the World.* Plays, 1971. A collection of dramatized tales, including "Big Paul Bunyan," "A Gift from Johnny Appleseed," and "The Indian Boy Without a Name."

Kellogg, Steven (reteller). *Paul Bunyan.* Morrow, 1984. An account of the life of the extraordinary lumberjack whose unusual size and strength brought him many fantastic adventures.

Rounds, Glen. *Ol' Paul: The Mighty Logger.* Holiday House, 1976. The recounting of the incredible experiences of the great Paul Bunyan.

Stoutenberg, Adrien. *American Tall Tales.* Viking Press, 1966. A collection of tall tales, including the characters of Paul Bunyan, Coyote Cowboy, Pecos Bill, Mike Fink, Davy Crockett, Johnny Appleseed, and John Henry.

Challenging

Gates, Doris. *Lord of the Sky: Zeus.* Viking Press, 1972. A retelling of Greek myths which mostly tell about Zeus.

SOCIAL STUDIES

SPEAKING: ORAL REPORT, DIORAMA (Cooperative Learning) Explain that the story "Paul Bunyan and Babe the Blue Ox" takes place in a logging town during pioneer times. Divide students into groups of three or four and have them research how log cabins were made and have them look. Also, have them locate information about loggers and other facts about logging communities during pioneer times. Encourage group members to look for nonfiction books of this period in the library. Remind them to begin their search for information in the card catalog under the subject heading "log cabins." Students should be encouraged to take notes. Request that students bring in a shoebox to take make a diorama log cabin in a shoebox to help glue, and other appropriate materials for their project. Provide toothpicks, build their own log cabin. The shoebox should resemble the inside and outside of a log cabin. Have each group give an oral presentation to the class to resemble how they learned about log cabins and __ ing pioneer times.

2 Using the page

R Listening: poetry

Help pupils find page 17 in their books. Ask pupils to listen as you read the poem to find out where the child is going. Run your hand under the words as you read the poem aloud.

ASK When does the child pretend to fly on a rocket? (when she goes to bed) Why is the man-in-the-moon winking? (He wants the child to stay.) Why won't the child stay with the man-in-the-moon? (She wants to play with her friends on Mars.)

Reread the poem, leaving off the last word of each stanza and ask pupils to supply the rhyming word. (zoom, play) Then read the poem a third time and ask pupils to join you.

SAY I will read each line of the poem. You tell me what word or words in the line have the /m/ sound. (line 1: *Mom;* line 2: *I'm, my, room;* line 3: *my;* line 4: *zoom;* line 5: *man, moon;* line 6: *me;* line 7: *my, Mars;* line 8: *me, come*)

FROM LEVEL 1

xxxiii

THE LESSON PLAN

Lesson plans in *HRW READING: Reading Today and Tomorrow* offer the resources, the options, and the flexibility teachers need for teaching reading in the way most effective in their classrooms. Each lesson plan includes provisions for varying and supplementing core instruction to meet a wide range of individual needs and interests.

STEP ONE

Preparing for the Selection

offers direct instruction, guided practice, and independent practice in—
- decoding skills
- vocabulary
- a comprehension/thinking Focus Skill

—all applied in the lesson's reading selection.

STEP TWO

Reading for Comprehension

offers—
- background information
- discussion for activating prior knowledge and setting purposes
- directed reading (shared reading in Levels 2–4) for use as needed in helping students understand the selection
- activities for Using Language, Applying the Focus Skill, Expanding Vocabulary (Levels 9–15), and Evaluating Comprehension.

STEP THREE

Developing Reading and Thinking Skills

offers direct instruction, guided practice, and independent practice in decoding/vocabulary, comprehension/thinking, language, and study skills—
- to introduce skills
- to reinforce skills taught earlier in the same level
- to maintain skills taught in previous levels
- to provide additional practice and application of the lesson's Focus Skill and new vocabulary.

RETEACHING AND EXTENDING

offers additional opportunities for meeting individual needs through—
- activities for reteaching and practicing lesson skills
- activities that relate reading to the other language arts and content areas
- suggestions for related independent reading.

SAMPLE LESSON PLAN

An **overview** of each lesson* helps teachers plan effective instruction.

(A) Objectives for each lesson are identified and grouped in four skills categories.

LESSON 1   "Go Away, Dog"
pages 2–9 (T12–T31)

(A) Skill Strands

(B) DECODING/VOCABULARY

I, T	**Sound/symbol correspondence:** consonant /l/ *l, ll* (initial, medial, final)
R	**Accumulated elements:** phonograms *-ell, -ill*
M	**Vocabulary:** antonyms
I	**Vocabulary:** word building
I, T	**Vocabulary:** word meaning

(C) COMPREHENSION/THINKING

Focus

I, T	**Inferential:** drawing conclusions

LANGUAGE

I	**Conventions of language:** commas in direct address

STUDY SKILLS

M	**Study aids:** summarizing

(D) Lesson Vocabulary

Decodable words: *aren't, beat, bring, feel, leap, legs, let, let's, lick, lost, lot, stick, still, tell*

Special words: *away, don't, girl, home*

(E) Materials

Snapshots, Level 5: pages 2–9
Workbook: pages 1–6
Practice Masters: pages 1–5
Instructional Charts: pages 1–3
Resource Box: Letter Cards a, c, d, e, i, k, l (2), L, o, p,
   Word Cards away, bell, dog, don't, fill, girl,
   Go, home, lamp, leap, lost, lot, still, tell
   Picture Card lion
   Punctuation Cards comma, period
Pocket Chart
Teacher's Idea Book
Reteach Masters: pages 1–2

(F) Language Applications

USING LANGUAGE

Oral reading: expression
Speaking: role playing

EXTENDING SELECTION CONCEPTS

Independent reading: vocabulary words
Writing: stories (Cooperative Learning)
Listening: poetry
Listening: fiction

(G) Special Populations

See *Teacher's Idea Book* for additional suggestions to help pupils with limited English proficiency.

Key to Symbols
I   Introduced in this lesson
R   Reinforced from an earlier lesson in this level
M   Maintained from previous levels
T   Tested in this level

(H) Idea Center

WORD BANKS

Have pupils bring a shoe box or tissue box to class. Gather construction paper, markers, paste, scissors, and other materials for pupils to decorate the boxes. See the *Teacher's Idea Book* for word cards that may be duplicated and cut apart. Or you can make your own word cards. (See page T12 for a list of words introduced in this story.) Each pupil will store the word cards in the completed word banks.

BIBLIOGRAPHY

Set up a reading corner or a reading table where books will be available throughout the year. Encourage pupils to use the books and to take care of them. For this first story, include various books about children and their dogs. A suggested bibliography follows. Annotations and suggestions for reading aloud appear in the lesson plan.

The first book is the original text that was adapted by the author for the selection "Go Away, Dog." Nodset, Joan. *Go Away, Dog.* Harper & Row, 1963.

Bridwell, Norman. *Clifford's Pals.* Scholastic, 1985.
Gackenbach, Dick. *Dog for a Day.* Clarion, 1987.
Griffith, Helen V. *Alex and the Cat.* Greenwillow, 1982.
Oxenbury, Helen. *Our Dog.* Dial Press, 1984.
Schwartz, Amy. *Oma and Bobo.* Bradbury Press, 1987.

(I) Planning Chart

		Instruction	Written Practice	Extending
Step 1 Preparing for the Selection	I, T	**Sound/symbol correspondence:** consonant /l/ *l, ll* (initial, medial, final)	*Workbook* page 1 *Practice Masters* pages 1–2 *Reteach Masters* page 1	
	I	**Vocabulary:** word building		**Independent reading:** vocabulary words
	I, T	**Vocabulary:** word meaning	*Workbook* page 2 *Practice Masters* page 3 *Reteach Masters* page 2	
	I, T	**Inferential:** drawing conclusions		
Step 2 Reading for Comprehension		**Oral reading:** expression **Speaking:** role playing **Inferential:** drawing conclusions **Story comprehension**	*Workbook* page 3	**Writing:** stories (Cooperative Learning)
Step 3 Developing Reading and Thinking Skills	R	**Accumulated elements:** phonograms *-ell, -ill*	*Workbook* page 4	**Listening:** poetry
	M	**Vocabulary:** antonyms	*Workbook* page 5 *Practice Masters* page 4	
	I, T	**Inferential:** drawing conclusions	*Workbook* page 6 *Practice Masters* page 5	
	M	**Study aids:** summarizing		**Listening:** fiction
	I	**Conventions of language:** commas in direct address		

(B) Symbols identify whether an objective is **introduced (I)** in this lesson, **reinforced (R)** from an earlier lesson in this level, or **maintained (M)** from a previous level. **T** indicates that an objective is **tested** in this level.

(C) The lesson's **Comprehension/Thinking Focus skill** is identified.

(D) Lesson Vocabulary lists all new words in the lesson's reading selection. **Decodable words** are those children should be able to decode easily, since all sound/symbol correspondences have been taught. **Special words** include irregular, high-frequency function words, as well as story-useful words with sound/symbol correspondences not yet taught.

(E) A **Materials** list includes the selection in the *Pupil's Edition,* related *Workbook* pages, and other program components available for use with the lesson.

*The content of this sample lesson is representative of lessons in Levels 5–8 of *HRW READING: Reading Today and Tomorrow.*

(F) Language Applications lists the major suggestions in each lesson for listening, speaking, writing, and independent reading activities, including listening and responding to books teachers read to students.

(G) Special Populations refers teachers to the *Teacher's Idea Book,* which includes suggested strategies for helping students with limited English proficiency.

(H) The **Idea Center** recommends alternatives for the program's components, lists any materials called for in the lesson that may not be readily available in the classroom, suggests games and other materials to reinforce learning, and includes a **Bibliography** of books for students to explore on their own and for teachers to read to students.

(I) A **Planning Chart** provides a summary of objectives and corresponding written practice materials. Also included are extension activities described in the **Reteaching and Extending** section of the lesson.

XXXV

Step 1 Preparing for the Selection

Step 1 provides instruction in skills and vocabulary to be applied in the lesson's reading selection.

---

1 PREPARING FOR THE SELECTION

DECODING/VOCABULARY

I, T   Sound/symbol correspondence: consonant /l/ (initial)

Note: Learning to read requires understanding the alphabetic principle. This principle is that a written symbol—a letter or letters—is associated with a unit of speech—a sound. Direct teaching of sound/symbol correspondence makes gaining understanding of the alphabetic principle easier. Associating a sound with a letter (or letters) helps pupils quickly gain independent decoding strategies.

DIRECT INSTRUCTION   Ask pupils to solve the following riddle:

READ
I can roar like anything.
In the jungle, I am king.
What am I? (a lion)

If necessary, display *Picture Card lion*. When pupils guess the answer, place *Letter Card l* in the *Pocket Chart*.

SAY   The word *lion* begins with the letter *l*. Letter *l* stands for the beginning sound in *lion*. Say *lion* with me: *lion*. Now say *lemon* with me: *lemon*. Do *lion* and *lemon* begin with the same sound? (yes) *Lion* and *lemon* both begin with the letter *l*. Listen as I say some words. If the word I say begins with /l/, raise your hand.

Use the following words: *leaf, lime, goat, laugh, list, lunch, bucket, listen.*

Place *Letter Card L* in the *Pocket Chart.*

SAY   Here is capital *L*. Capital *L* stands for the /l/ sound at the beginning of names such as *Lucy* and *Larry*. Both small *l* and capital *L* stand for the /l/ sound.

GUIDED PRACTICE   Ask pupils to listen to each sentence that you read and to finish it with a word that begins with /l/ as in lion. Use the following sentences. The answers are provided in parentheses for your convenience.

1. If something is not big, then it is _____. (little)
2. A yellow, sour fruit is a _____. (lemon)
3. When something is funny, you _____. (laugh)
4. At noon we eat _____. (lunch)
5. A baby sheep is called a _____. (lamb)
6. A place to get books is a _____. (library)

WB 1   INDEPENDENT PRACTICE   *Workbook* page 1 may be used to practice identifying sound/symbol correspondence /l/l.

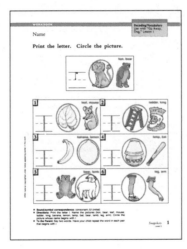

PM 1   ADDITIONAL PRACTICE   *Practice Masters* page 1 may be used as an optional practice for identifying sound/symbol correspondence /l/l. (See page T30 for reduced pages with answers.)

✳ RETEACH   For those pupils who need additional instruction, see "Reteaching Lesson Skills," page T28, under "Reteaching and Extending."

I, T   Sound/symbol correspondence: consonant /l/l, ll (medial, final)

DIRECT INSTRUCTION   Place *Letter Card l* in the *Pocket Chart.*

SAY   The letter *l* stands for the sound at the *beginning* of words such as *lion* and *lemon*. Now I'm going to say a word that *ends* with the /l/ sound. Listen for the /l/ sound at the end: *bell*. Say *bell: bell*. Now say *call: call*. Do *bell* and *call* end with the same sound? (yes)

Place *Word Card bell* in the *Pocket Chart.*

SAY   This is the word *bell*. Where do you hear the /l/ sound in *bell*? (∂: the end) What two letters stand for the /l' sound at the end of *bell*? (ll) When the /l/ sound is at the end of a word, it is often spelled with *ll.*

Sometimes the /l/ sound is in the middle of a word, such as in the word *yellow*. Let's say *yellow* together: *yellow*. The /l/ sound is in the middle of the word *yellow*. Two *l*'s together stand for the /l/ sound in *yellow*. Where do you hear the /l/ sound in *hello*? (in the middle) Where do you hear the /l/ sound in *follow*? (in the middle)

GUIDED PRACTICE   Call on a pupil to read the word as you hold up each of the following *Word Cards: bell, lamp, fill, lost, lot, still, leap.* Then display the *Word Cards* and have pupils select and read a word.

PM 2   ADDITIONAL PRACTICE   *Practice Masters* page 2 may be used as an optional practice for identifying sound/symbol correspondence /l/l, ll. (See page T30 for reduced pages with answers.)

✳ RETEACH   For those pupils who need additional instruction, see "Reteaching Lesson Skills," page T28, under "Reteaching and Extending."

I   Vocabulary: word building

Note: The word building activity that is provided in this section of the lesson plan contributes strongly to the development of pupil's blending skills. The consistent use of the word building activity supports the development of independent decoding.

DIRECT INSTRUCTION   Place *Letter Cards* in the *Pocket Chart* to make the word *lost* and have the word read. Remove letter *s* and ask pupils to read the new word. (lot) Ask pupils how *lot* can be changed to *dot*. (by changing *l* to *d*) Then change *lot* to *dot* and have the new word read.

GUIDED PRACTICE   Place *Letter Cards* in the *Pocket Chart* to make the word *doll* and have it read. Display *Letter Cards a, c, e, i, k, p, s,* and *t*. Ask a pupil to replace letters *ll* in *doll* with letters *c, k* and have the new word read. (dock) Continue by giving the following directions:

1. Replace the *d* with *l*. What word did you make? (lock)
2. Replace the *o* with *i*. What word did you make? (lick)
3. Replace the *ck* with *d*. What word did you make? (lid)
4. Replace letter *i* with letter *a*. What word did you make? (lad) A lad is a boy.
5. Replace letter *l* with letter *s*. What word did you make? (sad)
6. Replace letter *d* with letter *p*. What word did you make? (sap) Sap is what is used to make maple syrup.
7. Replace letter *s* with letter *l*. What word did you make? (lap)
8. Add letter *e* in front of letter *a*. What word did you make? (leap) *Leap* means "to jump."

A Systematic instruction in **sound/symbol correspondences** (phonics) in the early levels teaches **strong decoding skills** to facilitate comprehension.

B Every lesson includes **Direct Instruction** and **Guided Practice**, with boldfaced scripting that models appropriate directions and explanations.

C **Independent practice** is provided in the *Workbook*. *Workbook* pages are reproduced at point of use for easy reference.

D *Practice Masters* are an option for **additional practice**.

E ✳ **Reteach** signals an opportunity to reteach **tested skills** as needed. These activities are in the **Reteaching and Extending** section at the end of the lesson, and they are cross-referenced within the lesson at appropriate points of use.

F **Word-Building** activities contribute to students' skill in blending sounds to form words and support the development of independent decoding.

G **Letter-substitution exercises** help students realize the word power they acquire as they learn sound/letter relationships.

I, T Vocabulary: word meaning

Note: Each story in *Snapshots* provides pupils with an opportunity to apply learned sound/symbol correspondences to a related text. Most words in each selection are decodable, in that they are comprised of sound/symbol correspondences that pupils have learned in this program. In addition, pupils learn "special" words. Special words are not yet decodable, but are the high-frequency function words and story-useful words that are present in interesting and meaningful selections.

In this part of the lesson plan, special words and decodable words are introduced in context sentences. Such practice is helpful to the development of fluent word recognition and reinforces pupils' understanding of the meanings of these words.

DIRECT INSTRUCTION Tell pupils that they are going to talk about some words they will read in the next story. Print the following words and sentences on the chalkboard, omitting the underlining.

IC
1

> away   don't   girl   home
>
> 1. The girl had a cat.
> 2. "I don't like dogs," she said.
> 3. "Keep the dog away from my cat."
> 4. I sent my dog home.
>
> aren't   beat   bring   feel   leap
> legs   let   let's   lick   lost   lot
> stick   still   tell

Read the first sentence and identify the word *girl*.

ASK What kind of pet did the girl have? (a cat) **Let's read the sentence together.** (The girl had a cat.) **Who can find and read the word *girl* in this sentence?**

Read the second sentence and point to the word *don't*. Explain that *don't* is made by putting the words *do* and *not* together. Ask if the girl likes dogs. (no) Have pupils read the sentence with you and then ask a pupil to find and read the word *don't*.

Read Sentence 3 and point to the word *away*. Ask if the girl wants the dog to play with her cat. (no) Have pupils read the sentence with you. Then have a pupil point to the word *away* and read it.

Read Sentence 4. Point to the word *home* and read it. Ask if the dog will bother the cat now and why. (No, because it has gone home.) Have pupils read the sentence with you. Then ask a pupil to point to the word *home* and read it.

T16   *Snapshots*, Level 5

The words in the second set are new words that contain known phonic elements. You may wish to ask pupils to read the words, using what they know about letters and sounds.

GUIDED PRACTICE Print the following sentences on the chalkboard, omitting the underlining.

IC
2

> 1. The girl has a dog that likes to leap.
> 2. She let it stand on its back legs to lick her hand.
> 3. Do you feel like running?
> 4. Don't run away and get lost!
> 5. You beat me, but I still like you.
> 6. Aren't you going to bring me the stick?
> 7. Let's go home.
> 8. I have a lot to tell my mom.

Provide opportunities for pupils to practice reading the new special words and the new decodable words in these sentences by following the suggestions below.

Sentence 1: Have the sentence read aloud. Ask pupils what the dog likes to do. (leap) Call on volunteers to find and read the word *girl*.

Sentence 2: Have the sentence read. Ask what the girl let the dog do. (stand on its back legs to lick her hand) Have the words with the /l/ sound read. (*let, legs, lick*)

Sentences 3–4: Ask pupils to read the sentences. Ask who is speaking in the sentences. (the girl) Ask to whom she is speaking. (the dog)

Sentence 5: Have the sentence read and ask how the dog beat the girl. (It ran faster than she did.) Ask if the girl is angry with the dog. (No, she still likes it.)

Sentence 6: Read the sentence and ask what the girl wants the dog to do. (bring her the stick) Tell pupils that *aren't* is a contraction made from the words *are* and *not*.

Sentences 7–8: Have the sentences read. Have pupils read the words *Let's, lot, tell*. Explain that *Let's* stands for *Let us*.

Provide each pupil with an opportunity to read one of the sentences aloud.

WB
2   **INDEPENDENT PRACTICE**   *Workbook* page 2 may be used to practice reading story vocabulary.

PM
3   **ADDITIONAL PRACTICE**   *Practice Masters* page 3 may be used as an optional practice for reading story vocabulary. (See page T30 for reduced pages with answers.)

✱ **RETEACH** For those pupils who need additional instruction, see "Reaching Lesson Skills," page T28, under "Reteaching and Extending."

WORKBOOK   Decoding/Vocabulary
                                Use with "Go Away,
                                Dog," Lesson 1.

Name _____

Print the word.

> lost   don't   girl   home   away

1 Pam is a ___girl___

2 Will she find the pen like ___lost___?

3 She went ___away___ to look for it.

4 I ___don't___ think she will find the pen.

5 I bet she left it at ___home___

2   *Snapshots*
    Level 5

• **Vocabulary:** word meaning
Directions: Print the word from the box that completes each sentence.
To the Parent: Have your child use the words in the box in sentences.

COMPREHENSION/THINKING

Focus
I, T Inferential: drawing conclusions

Note: Learning to read is a process that involves interaction among pupils, text, and instructional factors. The Comprehension/Thinking Focus skill, which is developed throughout the lesson plan, helps pupils identify the what, how, and why of reading and then apply this knowledge in a variety of reading situations. In Step 1, the teacher identifies **what** the Focus skill is. In Step 2, pupils discuss **how** the Focus skill applies to the story just read. In Step 3, pupils use the Focus skill for reading and thinking about related materials. In doing so, pupils begin to understand **why** they learned this skill.

DIRECT INSTRUCTION Tell pupils to listen carefully as you read a short story. Then ask the questions that follow.

READ The children were playing tag in the park. One of the children looked up at the sky. "I think we should go home," she said.

ASK Why might the children need to go home? (Possible answers include: It is getting dark; it is going to rain.) **What clue made you think this?** (One child looked at the sky.)

SAY When we read stories, we often use what we already know and what the story tells us to help us draw conclusions. When you guessed why the children should go home, you were drawing a conclusion. You used what you know about the sky to explain why one of the children thought it was time to go home.

GUIDED PRACTICE Read the following story. Tell pupils that when you finish, you will ask them to draw a conclusion about the story.

READ Tad was excited. It was the day before his birthday. He was hoping for a special gift. He had seen just what he wanted in the store window. It was red and shiny with two wheels. He knew he was big enough to ride it by himself. On the day of his birthday, Tad ran downstairs. He was thrilled to see on the porch exactly what he wanted.

ASK What do you think was Tad's birthday present? (a new bike) **What facts from the story made you think that it was a new bike?** (It was red and shiny; it had two wheels; he could ride it by himself.)

SAY Our next story is called "Go Away, Dog." What do you know about dogs that would explain why someone might want a dog to go away? (Possible answers include: Some people don't like dogs; some people are afraid of dogs.)

Lesson 1 "Go Away, Dog" (pages 2–9)   T17

H **Direct Instruction** focuses on the lesson's "special words" — new words that are not yet completely decodable on the basis of sound/letter knowledge.

I IC 1 signals a chalkboard presentation that is also available in the *Instructional Charts*.

J The sound/symbol correspondence taught in Step 1 is always reflected in new words from the lesson's reading selection. In this lesson, the sound/symbol correspondence taught in Step 1 is initial /l/*l*, and seven of the new words begin with *l*. Thus, what students learn is immediately applied.

K **Guided Practice** provides opportunities for students to practice reading the new "special" words and new decodable words in sentences.

L WB 2 and PM 3 signal references to *Workbook* and *Practice Master* pages that offer additional practice with new story vocabulary.

M *Workbook* practice focuses on the "special" words — those that are not yet completely decodable.

N Every lesson has a **Comprehension/Thinking Focus skill** that is introduced in Step 1 and applied in each subsequent step. Both Direct Instruction and Guided Practice give students an awareness of a skill that has high utility in the upcoming reading selection.

O Instruction focuses students on how they construct meaning as they combine what they already know with new information.

Step 2 Reading for Comprehension

Step 2 concentrates on students understanding, enjoying, and learning from the selection.

2 READING FOR COMPREHENSION

A Background for the Teacher

SUMMARY A girl who doesn't like dogs meets a dog and tries to get it to go away. The dog continues to play and do tricks until it finally wins the girl's affection.

INFORMATION This story is told entirely in dialog. The girl in the story is speaking to the dog. No quotation marks are used to indicate that the words are spoken by the girl.

B Using Prior Knowledge

Note: Prior knowledge, or background experience brought to the text, provides a framework that helps pupils understand and remember new information. The oral discussion suggested in this section of the lesson plan is designed to help the teacher find out what pupils already know and what they need to know for comprehending the upcoming text.

Explain that the story pupils are going to read is about girl and a dog. The girl in the story wants the dog to go away. Continue by asking questions such as those that follow.

1. **Some people like to have dogs for pets. What are some things that people can do with a dog?** (Possible answers include: play with it; take it for a walk; teach it tricks.)
2. **Some people don't like dogs. Why do you think some people don't like dogs?** (Possible answers include: They may be afraid a dog will bite; they may not like dogs to lick them or to jump on them.)

C Setting a Purpose for Reading

Note: Having a purpose for reading helps pupils construct the meaning of a text, resulting in a better comprehension of both literal meanings and implied ideas. Establishing a purpose also provides a model for pupils to use later in determining what they may expect to learn from their reading.

Have pupils open their books to page 2. Explain that the title of this story is "Go Away, Dog." Ask pupils why the girl might want the dog to go away. (Possible answers include: The dog is bothering her; she doesn't like dogs.)

Point out the headnote at the top of page 2. Explain that this is a note that will help pupils think about the story they are going to read. Have the headnote read aloud. Ask pupils to predict whether the girl will get the dog to go away.

D Reading Silently

Some pupils may be able to read this story independently. Direct them to read the whole story to find out more about the little girl and her new-found friend. For those pupils who need more guidance, suggestions for directed reading follow.

"Big dogs, little dogs.
I <u>don't</u> like dogs."
the little <u>girl</u> said.
Will she get the dog to go <u>away</u>?

Go Away, Dog

Go away, you bad dog.
Go away from me.
I don't like you, dog.
I don't like dogs.
Big dogs, little dogs.
I don't like dogs at all.

2

Don't <u>bring</u> that <u>stick</u> to me.
If I toss the stick,
will you go away?

There, go away with your stick.

Are you <u>still</u> here?
Why did you bring the stick back?

Let me have the stick.
Let go of the stick, dog.

3

E Before reading page 2

SAY One day a friendly dog ran up to a little girl. The girl was not happy. Read page 2 to see why the girl wanted the dog to go away.

F After reading page 2

Why did she want the dog to go away? (She didn't like dogs at all.) Literal

Before reading page 3

SAY Do you think the dog will go away? Read page 3 to yourself.

After reading page 3

1. **Did the dog go away?** (no) **How do you know?** (because it brought the stick back) Inferential
2. **What did the dog do to try to get the girl's attention?** (It brought her a stick.) Inferential
3. **What did the girl do with the stick?** (She threw the stick to get the dog to go away.) **What did the dog do?** (It brought the stick back.) Literal

G

A **Background for the Teacher** provides a summary of the selection and information that will be useful in helping students prepare for reading.

B **Using Prior Knowledge** promotes discussion to help teachers assess students' prior knowledge of the selection's topic and content, and provides suggestions for building additional readiness for interacting with the story.

C **Setting a Purpose for Reading** encourages students to make predictions and set purposes for reading.

D **Reading Silently** suggests that some students may be able to read the selection independently, while others may benefit from the directed reading that follows.

E **Before Reading** questions and statements encourage students to make predictions about what will happen or what they will learn.

F **After Reading** questions focus on ideas and events of central importance to the story as students review previous predictions and prepare to make new ones.

G Questions are labeled *literal, inferential,* or *critical,* and suggested answers are given.

H Reproductions of the *Pupil's Edition* pages are annotated to show the first appearance of each new vocabulary word. **Decodable words** are underlined once in red. **Special words** are underlined twice.

Ⓘ Discussing the Selection   Ⓜ Using Language

Note: Comprehension is promoted through construction of a story map. A story map is the logical organization of events and ideas of central importance to a story. You can help pupils construct a story map by asking the questions provided. The questions are both literal and inferential in nature, since basic understanding of a story requires recalling specific events as well as making inferences. Critical thinking questions are included to expand pupils' understanding of the selection.

Ⓙ PURPOSE Ask pupils to read to themselves the question at the bottom of page 9. Remind them that at the beginning of the story they wanted to find out if the girl would get the dog to go away. Then ask pupils to answer the question on page 9. (She didn't get the dog to go away because she started to like this dog; she decided to take it home with her.)

Ⓚ STORY MAPPING Tell pupils to think about what the girl and the dog did in the story and the way they did it. Then ask the questions that follow.

1. **What problem did the girl have in the story?** (She wanted the dog to go away; she didn't like dogs.) Literal
2. **What are some of the ways the girl tried to get the dog to go away?** (She told it to go away; she tossed a stick at it; she tried to run with it.) Inferential
3. **What did the dog do to make the girl change her mind?** (The dog brought her a stick; it tugged the stick away; it stood on its back legs; it ran with her.) Inferential

Ⓛ CRITICAL THINKING

1. **Do you think the girl changed her mind about not liking dogs?** (Answers will vary. Possible answers include: Yes, since she found a dog she liked; no, just because she liked this dog doesn't mean that she would like all dogs.)
2. **What do you think the girl's mother might have said about the dog?** (Answers will vary. Possible answers include: She might have said that they would look in the paper to see if anyone lost the dog or that they would run an ad saying that they had found the dog.)

Note: Throughout the program, there are activities directed to the development of all the language arts—reading, writing, speaking, and listening—as well as to their integration. One of the places that this is consistently done is in the "Using Language" section of the lesson plan, in which the reading selection is used as a springboard for a variety of language activities. In this level, oral reading is emphasized because it provides a window on pupils' development as readers. Oral reading can also help develop pupils' sense of the structure and rhythm of language. Pupils listen as the teacher models the tone, stress, and pauses of sentences. Then opportunities are provided for pupils to incorporate the model in their reading. Early composition abilities also are developed as pupils discuss and write about shared experiences.

ORAL READING: EXPRESSION Have pupils turn to page 2. Ask who was talking throughout this story. (the girl) Point out that this whole story was told as if we were listening to what the girl told the dog. Remind pupils that the girl did not like dogs. Have volunteers read page 2 the way the girl might have sounded.

Follow a similar procedure for the remaining pages.

Page 3: Ask a pupil to read the first four lines the way the girl might have said them. Then have other pupils read the last four lines the way the girl might have said them.

Page 4: Have the lines read that tell what the girl thought was fun. (You got the stick away from me.) Then ask pupils to read the lines that tell what the girl did not like. (That was fun, dog, but don't leap on me. I don't like that.) Ask what lines show that the girl might have been beginning to change her mind. (You aren't bad for a dog, but I don't like dogs.)

Page 5: Ask a pupil to read the sentences that tell what the girl said after the dog stood on its back legs. (Say, I like that dog. I will pet you, dog.)

Page 6: Ask pupils to read the first question the girl asked the dog. (If I run with you, will you go away?)

Page 7: Ask pupils to read the sentence that showed the girl was starting to like the dog. (You are a lot of fun, but I have to go home.)

Page 8: Have the first three sentences read in the way the girl might have said them. Then have pupils read the last four sentences in the way the girl might have said them.

Page 9: Ask volunteers to read the sentence that tells what the girl's mother would do. (My mom will find out if you are lost.) Then ask volunteers to read the last three sentences the way the girl might have said them.

SPEAKING: ROLE PLAYING Remind pupils that the girl was going to take the dog home to her mother. Ask what the girl might have told her mother about the dog and have pupils share their ideas with the class. Then ask what the mother might have said. (Answers will vary.)

Call on a volunteer to pretend to be the girl and a volunteer to pretend to be her mother. Have the volunteers act out what the girl and her mother might have said to each other. Give other pairs of pupils a chance to act out the scene.

Ⓝ Applying the Focus Skill

INFERENTIAL: DRAWING CONCLUSIONS Remind pupils that sometimes they can use what they know from a story to tell how a character feels or what might happen. This is called drawing a conclusion.

SAY In the beginning of our story, the girl said she didn't like big dogs and she didn't like small dogs. What can you conclude about the way she feels about *all* dogs? (She doesn't like them.)

At the end of the story, the girl said, "If you don't have a home, you can stay with me." What can you conclude about the way she feels about this dog? (She likes this dog.)

Evaluating Comprehension

WB 3 INDEPENDENT PRACTICE *Workbook* page 3 may be used for an informal evaluation of story comprehension.

Ⓞ

Fill in the circle.

1. ● The girl did not like dogs.
   ○ The girl needed a pet dog.
2. ○ The dog lost the stick.
   ● The dog got the stick.
3. ○ The girl ran away from the dog.
   ● The girl ran with the dog.
4. ● The dog had fun with the girl.
   ○ The dog did not like the girl.
5. ○ The dog went back to its home.
   ● The dog went to the girl's home.

Ⓟ HOW AM I DOING?

Many pupils need time to establish or improve their self-confidence in reading. To help improve children's self-confidence, ask the following questions to gauge your teaching effectiveness in this area.

	Yes	No	Sometimes
1. Have I made a wide selection of picture books available?	☐	☐	☐
2. Have I encouraged pupils to look through books even if they may be unable to read the words?	☐	☐	☐
3. Have I provided time to permit individuals to tell about the books they have read and enjoyed?	☐	☐	☐
4. Have I praised pupils for reading?	☐	☐	☐

Lesson 1 "Go Away, Dog" (pages 2–9)   T23

T24   *Snapshots,* Level 5

Ⓘ **Discussing the Selection** questions appear in the *Pupil's Edition*, Levels 6 — 15, and in the *Teacher's Edition* at all levels.

Ⓙ Questioning begins with the **purpose-setting question** established before the story was read. This one question is printed in the *Pupil's Edition* in Level 5.

Ⓚ Next, a series of questions helps students construct a **story map** — that is, a logical organization of events of central importance to the story. The questions require students to recall specific details and make inferences.

Ⓛ Finally, **critical-thinking** questions invite students to react to what they have read as they draw conclusions, make judgments, seek solutions to problems, and relate text information to their prior knowledge. (Following nonfiction selections, questions focus on main idea, important supporting details, and the relationship of the selection's topic to the unit theme and to other selections in the unit.)

Ⓜ The **Using Language** feature at the end of each selection uses the reading as a springboard for a variety of language activities. Many **Using Language** activities encourage student writing (particularly in Levels 7 — 15) and involve appropriate steps of the writing process. Others encourage oral language development. In the early levels, oral reading is emphasized because it provides a window on students' development as readers and helps develop students' sense of the structure and rhythm of language.

Ⓝ **Applying the Focus Skill** leads students to see how the lesson's Focus Skill applies to the selection they just read.

Ⓞ A *Workbook* page provides a means of informally **evaluating comprehension.**

Ⓟ **How Am I Doing?** is a feature that provides occasional reminders to teachers of behaviors, materials, and features of the classroom environment that promote growth in reading, writing, listening, speaking, and thinking.

Step 3 Developing Reading and Thinking Skills

Step 3 offers a variety of strategies for introducing skills, particularly those from the language and study skills strands. Step 3 also provides for reinforcing skills taught earlier in the level and for maintaining skills taught in previous levels.

---

3 DEVELOPING READING AND THINKING SKILLS

DECODING/VOCABULARY

R Accumulated elements: phonograms -ell, -ill

> **Note:** Direct instruction in blending teaches pupils how to put together sounds to make words. As phonic elements in this program accumulate, blending is done with phonograms and consonant clusters to encourage pupils to use units larger than single letters. This aids decoding automaticity.

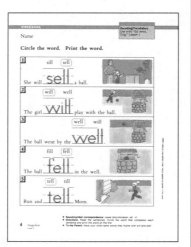

DIRECT INSTRUCTION Place *Word Card fill* under *Word Card still* in the *Pocket Chart* and have them read. Ask what is alike about these words. (They rhyme; they end with *ill*.) Point to the letters *ll* and remind pupils that when two of the same letters are together in a word, they usually stand for one sound.

Place *Word Cards tell* and *bell* next to *still* and *fill*. Have pupils read the two new words. Ask pupils to tell what is the same about the words *tell* and *bell*. (They rhyme; they end with *ell*.)

GUIDED PRACTICE Read each of the following words and call on pupils to tell if the word ends with /ill/ or /ell/: *well, smell, bill, fell, mill, skill, spell.*

WB **INDEPENDENT PRACTICE** *Workbook*
4 page 4 may be used to practice identifying the phonograms *-ell, -ill.*

M Vocabulary: antonyms

DIRECT INSTRUCTION Print the following sets of sentences on the chalkboard, omitting the words in parentheses.

> **IC**
> **3**
> 1. The dog will go up.
> 2. The dog will go down.
>
> 3. The kitten is <u>big</u>. (little)
> 4. The bed is too <u>soft</u>. (hard)
> 5. The food is <u>hot</u>. (cold)
> 6. The dog will <u>go</u> home. (come)

Have Sentences 1 and 2 read aloud and ask which word is different in each sentence. (*up, down*)

SAY Look up. Now look down. *Up* and *down* are opposite directions. We call the words *up* and *down* "opposites." What is the opposite of *in*? (out) What is the opposite of *big*? (little)

GUIDED PRACTICE Direct pupils' attention to the remaining sentences on the chalkboard.

Have each sentence read. Ask what word is the opposite of the underlined word. Then have the sentence read again, substituting the opposite for the underlined word.

Lesson 1 "Go Away, Dog" (pages 2–9) T25

WB **INDEPENDENT PRACTICE** *Workbook*
5 page 5 may be used to practice recognizing antonyms.

PM **ADDITIONAL PRACTICE** *Practice Masters*
4 page 4 may be used as an optional practice for recognizing antonyms. (See page T31 for reduced pages with answers.)

T26 *Snapshots, Level 5*

COMPREHENSION/THINKING

Focus
I, T Inferential: drawing conclusions

DIRECT INSTRUCTION Remind pupils that they can use what they know from a story to draw a conclusion. Tell them that you will read a story and will ask them to draw a conclusion about the story.

READ Tara looked at her dog Spunky. "How did you ever get so dirty?" she asked. "There's only one thing left to do," said Tara, as she poured water into the tub.

ASK What do you think will happen to Spunky? (Tara will give Spunky a bath.) What clues helped you to decide? (The dog is very dirty; Tara filled the tub with water.)

Tell pupils that when they decided Tara would give Spunky a bath, they were drawing a conclusion.

GUIDED PRACTICE Have pupils listen as you read the following paragraph. Ask pupils to use clues from the paragraph to answer the questions that follow.

READ Adam finished his cereal and juice. Then he picked up his books and headed for the bus stop.

ASK What time of day was it? (morning) What clues helped you to decide? (He finished his cereal and juice, which are usually eaten at breakfast.) Where was Adam going? (to school) What clues helped you to decide? (He picked up his books and headed for the bus stop.)

Explain that drawing conclusions can help you understand what is happening in the stories you read. Sometimes the author may not tell you everything that is happening. In "Go Away, Dog" the author never said, "Now the girl has changed her mind." You had to draw the conclusion that the girl had changed her mind about the dog.

WB **INDEPENDENT PRACTICE** *Workbook*
6 page 6 may be used to practice drawing conclusions.

A Direct Instruction in **blending** emphasizes putting sounds together to make words. As phonic elements accumulate, blending is done with phonograms and consonant clusters (**accumulated elements**) to encourage students to recognize units of sound/letter correspondence that are larger than single letters.

B Each *Workbook* page includes a note **to the parent** that offers a suggestion for parents to use in sharing their child's learning experience.

C Understanding of the lesson's **Focus skill** is further reinforced as students apply the skill with new material.

Reteaching and Extending

Reteaching and Extending activities are intended for use as needed to provide for individual differences.

✳ RETEACHING AND EXTENDING

Reteaching Lesson Skills

The activities that follow provide reteaching of skills developed in this lesson. Not every pupil needs to complete these activities. Choose only the activities that are needed to provide for the individual differences in your classroom.

DECODING/VOCABULARY

I, T   Sound/symbol correspondence: consonant /l/l, ll (initial, medial, final)

✳ **RETEACH** Display *Letter Card l*.

SAY   This is letter *l*. Letter *l* stands for the /l/ sound. The word *lion* has the /l/ sound at the beginning. Say *lion* with me: *lion*. Now say *lemon* with me: *lemon*. Do you hear the /l/ sound at the beginning of the word *lemon*? (yes) Say the word *leg* with me: *leg*. Do you hear the /l/ sound at the beginning of *leg*? (yes)

Some words have the /l/ sound at the end. Say the word *bell* with me: *bell*. Where do you hear the /l/ sound in *bell*? (at the end) Some words have the /l/ sound in the middle. Say the word *yellow* with me: *yellow*. Where do you hear the /l/ sound in *yellow*? (in the middle)

Read the following words and ask pupils to tell where the /l/ sound is heard in the word. Use these words: *ball, like, will, sail, pal, meal, leap*.

RM 1   Distribute *Reteach Masters* page 1 and explain the directions on the page.

I, T   Vocabulary: word meaning

✳ **RETEACH** Print the following words and sentences on the chalkboard, omitting the underlining.

IC 1

away don't girl home
1. The <u>girl</u> had a cat.
2. "I <u>don't</u> like dogs," she said.
3. "Keep the dog <u>away</u> from my cat."
4. I sent my dog <u>home</u>.
aren't beat bring feel leap
legs let let's lick lost lot
stick still tell

Point to the first sentence and have it read. Ask who had a cat. (the girl) Call on pupils to point to and read the word *girl*.

Follow a similar procedure with the remaining sentences, calling attention to the underlined words.

Display *Word Cards* for each of the underlined words. Ask pupils to hold up and read the words that answer the following questions:

1. **Which word means "do not"?** (*don't*)
2. **Which word names a person?** (*girl*)
3. **Which word means "far from"?** (*away*)
4. **Which word names the place where you live?** (*home*)

Ask pupils to read the second set of words and to make up sentences using each word.

RM 2   Distribute *Reteach Masters* page 2 and explain the directions on the page.

COMPREHENSION/THINKING

I, T   Inferential: drawing conclusions

✳ **RETEACH** Remind pupils that they can use the information in a story to figure out what will happen. This is called drawing a conclusion. Tell pupils that you will read a paragraph and then you will ask them what conclusion they can draw.

READ   Anna loved stuffed animals. She had teddy bears and rabbits and other animals all over her bed and on the floor of her room. "Anna," said her mother, "we need to find a place for you to put your stuffed animals." So Anna's mom bought some boards and some nails.

ASK   What will Anna's mother do with the boards and nails? (Possible answer: She will build shelves for the stuffed animals.)

Extending Selection Concepts

Note: A total reading program must provide for the deliberate development of interest in reading. This is most effectively done by making books readily available and by helping pupils see reading as an important and enjoyable part of their daily lives. This section of the lesson plan suggests activities that expand the theme of the selection and that relate reading to various content areas.

LANGUAGE ARTS

INDEPENDENT READING: VOCABULARY WORDS Have pupils make Word Banks. (See page T13 for instructions.) Distribute the cards to pupils to place in their Word Banks. The word cards may be used as flash cards with a partner, or pupils may use them to make up sentences such as *Let's go home*. You may use blank word cards to add any words you feel pupils need to practice or to make sentences.

Pupils may add more words to their Word Banks as they read each story in *Snapshots*. (See the word list on pages 151–154 in *Snapshots*.)

WRITING: STORIES (Cooperative Learning) Have pupils work in small groups to write a story in which some things happen that are the opposite of what happened in "Go Away, Dog." Their story will be called "Come Here, Dog." Have pupils use the story in their books to help them write an "opposite" story. For example, the child in the "Come Here, Dog" story will like dogs and will want the dog to bring the stick and play. The story can end the same way "Go Away, Dog" ends. Provide drawing paper for pupils to illustrate their stories.

LITERATURE

LISTENING: POETRY Remind pupils that the little girl in "Go Away, Dog" wanted the dog to go away. Tell pupils that you have a poem about another dog. Tell them to listen to see how this dog is different from the one in "Go Away, Dog." Read aloud "My Dog."

My Dog
His feet are big,
His ears are floppy.
When he eats
He's very sloppy.
He can't do tricks—
Jump over sticks
Or anything that's clever.
But he's my own,
My very own,
And I'll love him
Forever!
Helen Lorraine

Have pupils tell how this dog is different from the one in the story. Have pupils talk about some of their experiences with dogs or some of the things their pet dogs can do.

LISTENING: FICTION Choose a story about dogs and read it aloud to the class.

Bridwell, Norman. *Clifford's Pals*. Scholastic, 1985. This is one of a series of books about Emily Elizabeth's big red dog, Clifford.
Gackenbach, Dick. *Dog for a Day*. Clarion, 1987. This is a hilarious tale of a boy turned into a dog for a day.
Griffith, Helen V. *Alex and the Cat*. Greenwillow, 1982. Three short stories tell about Alex the puppy trying to be a cat, trying to be a wild animal, and getting into trouble because of a lost chick.
Oxenbury, Helen. *Our Dog*. Dial Press, 1984. A boy tells about the adventures he and his family have with their dog.
Schwartz, Amy. *Oma and Bobo*. Bradbury, 1987. Grandmother Oma helps Bobo the dog learn to do some tricks.

D **Reteaching Lesson Skills** provides for reteaching the lesson's new words and all tested skills covered in the lesson.

E RM 2 signals the use of a *Reteach Master* as a part of the reteaching activity.

F **Extending Selection Concepts** offers listening, speaking, reading, and writing activities to expand interest and understanding, and to relate reading to the content areas.

G Some activities are suitable for **independent** projects; others are ideal **cooperative-learning** situations.

H Annotated **bibliographies** of books related to the content of the lesson's selection offer teachers a variety of good stories and nonfiction selections to **read aloud** to children.

COMPONENTS
INSTRUCTION, PRACTICE, AND TEACHING SUPPORT

INSTRUCTIONAL MATERIALS

PUPIL'S EDITIONS
The *Pupil's Editions* include a write-in text for Readiness (Level 1), soft-bound Preprimers (Levels 2–4), and hard-bound books from the Primer through Grade 8 (Levels 5–15). Each grade level contains poetry, fiction, and nonfiction by recognized authors of quality literature for children.

TEACHER'S EDITIONS
The *Teacher's Editions* (Levels K–15) contain easy-to-follow lesson plans for presenting selections, developing and reteaching skills, and extending lesson concepts. Reduced reproductions of the pupil's pages and the *Workbook* pages are included at the point of use. Reduced reproductions of the *Practice Masters* and the *Reteach Masters* are also included at the end of the lesson plan.

KINDERGARTEN KIT
The *Kindergarten Kit* includes *Big Books* for shared-reading activities and for teacher modeling, a *Teacher's Edition, Practice Masters,* and *Reteach Masters.* The kit also contains story booklets, puppets, a *Teacher's Idea Book,* and audio-cassettes of stories that provide additional opportunities for students to experience good literature.

ADDITIONAL PRACTICE MATERIALS

WORKBOOKS
The four-color *Workbooks* (Levels 2–15) provide independent practice of skills, including vocabulary, comprehension Focus Skills, study skills, and the conventions of language and writing. In addition, the *Workbooks* provide for informal evaluation of selection comprehension. The *Workbooks* are also available in a copying-master version, and the annotated *Teacher's Edition* provides answers for both formats.

PRACTICE MASTERS/RETEACH MASTERS
The *Practice Masters* (Levels K–15) provide additional review of all skills presented in a unit. The *Reteach Masters* (Levels K–15) offer alternative instruction and practice for selected tested skills. The *Practice* and *Reteach Masters* are in copying-master form, with answers provided on reduced reproductions of the student pages.

TEACHER'S IDEA BOOK

The *Teacher's Idea Books* for Kindergarten through Grade 8 (Levels K–15) contain teacher information and resource materials to meet individual classroom needs. Materials include pacing information and informal reading inventories; reproducible word and picture cards; pattern masters; bibliography of books, audio-visual media; and computer software suggested for each unit; and classroom ideas for bulletin boards, activity centers, and independent reading activities. The school-home connection is supported with parent letters (in English and in Spanish), monthly calendars suggesting daily reading activities, and certificates of book completion. Adapted lesson strategies for pupils with limited English proficiency are also included.

TEACHER'S RESOURCE ORGANIZER

The *Teacher's Resource Organizer* is a handy storage device that provides convenient filing and access for the following copying-master materials:

Workbook	Placement Test
Practice Masters	End-of-Unit Tests, Form A
Reteach Masters	End-of-Book Test, Skills Mastery
Instructional Charts	End-of-Book Test, Assessment of
Teacher's Idea Book	Reading Comprehension

RESOURCE BOX

The *Resource Box* for Readiness through Grade 1 (Levels 1–6) contains picture cards, letter and pattern cards, word cards, inflectional-ending cards, and punctuation cards called for in the *Teacher's Edition*. Alternate suggestions for making these cards may also be found in the *Teacher's Edition*. The card material specific to Level 1 is available in a separate package.

INSTRUCTIONAL CHARTS

The *Instructional Charts* (Levels 2–15) are large presentations of the chalkboard activities recommended in the *Teacher's Edition*. The charts are available in display size (25″ × 25″) and in copying masters, from which transparencies may be made.

POCKET CHART

The Pocket Chart (36″ × 24″) for Levels K–6 enables the teacher to model lesson responses using the variety of cards contained in the *Resource Box*.

WORD BUILDER AND WORD BUILDER CARDS

The *Word Builder* allows every student to take an active part in responding to lesson activities. These small individual pocket charts are used by each child at his or her own desk and provide hands-on experiences in putting letters together and then blending the sounds into words. The *Word Builder* is used in Levels 1 through 4.

BIG BOOKS

Big Books (17″ × 22″) for shared-reading activities and teacher modeling are available from Kindergarten through Grade 3 (Levels K–10). The *Big Books* for Kindergarten include a shared-reading book and a book for discussion activities and skills practice. The *Big Books* for Readiness and the Preprimers (Levels 1–4) are enlarged forms of the *Pupil's Editions*. The *Big Books* for Primer through Grade 3 include selected stories and poems for shared-reading experiences.

COMPONENTS
TESTING, SOFTWARE, AND MEDIA

TESTING AND MANAGEMENT MATERIALS

PLACEMENT TESTS

The *Primary Placement Test* (Levels 1–10) and the *Intermediate Placement Test* (Levels 11–15) are designed to help place students entering the program for the first time. Students read passages from typical grade-level selections so that the teacher may assess their current reading ability and determine an appropriate placement. The placement tests are available in classroom sets of 35 booklets or in copying-master form.

END-OF-UNIT TESTS

The *End-of-Unit Tests* (Levels 5–15) are designed to evaluate a student's mastery of the skills and vocabulary presented in a unit of study. To accommodate pre- and post-testing or post-testing and retesting, each unit test is available in two forms, Form A and Form B. Each form of tests is packaged by level, in sets of 35 booklets. A copying-master version is also available.

END-OF-BOOK TESTS

The End-of-Book Tests are available in two forms: *Skills Mastery* and *Assessment of Reading Comprehension*. The *Skills Mastery* tests (Levels 1–15) may be used to assess students' mastery and retention of reading skills and vocabulary presented within a particular unit. The *Assessment of Reading Comprehension* tests (Levels 2–15; one test for Levels 2–4) are holistic evaluations of comprehension that provide comprehensive measurements of a student's total reading achievement. Each test is available as copying masters or prepackaged in sets of 35 booklets.

INDIVIDUAL RECORD FOLDERS

The *Individual Record Folders* (Levels 1–15) accommodate an on-going record of each student's scores on the *End-of-Unit Tests* and *End-of-Book Tests* throughout the program.

CLASS II COMPUTER MANAGEMENT SYSTEM

The *CLASS II Computerized Learning and Scoring System* automatically scores all tests and monitors mastered and nonmastered objectives. The system will provide individualized or summary analyses of students' strengths and weaknesses. *CLASS II* is available for the Apple® II +, IIe, and IIc. computers. Machine-scorable answer cards, purchased separately, may be used with the Chatsworth OMR 500, 1000, 2000; True Data Micro Mark I and II; Mountain 1100A; SCAN-TRON 1200; and NCS Sentry 3000.

Apple® is the registered trademark of Apple Computer Inc.

STORY BRANCHES

Story Branches is a reading skills practice program for Grades 3–8 (Levels 9–15) that offers students activities related to the theme and content of each unit. The program focuses on vocabulary, comprehension, thinking, study, and language skills. Students read short selections and then decipher a puzzle as they complete a set of post-reading comparision and contrast questions. *Story Branches* is available for Apple®II +, IIe, and IIc.

WRITER'S NOTEBOOK II

Writer's Notebook II is an easy-to-use word processing program for Grades 3–8 (Levels 9–15). Once students have entered their compositions, they may edit and rearrange copy until they are completely satisfied with their efforts. The Spell-Check feature is an added bonus that makes proofreading simpler and more satisfying. The *Writer's Notebook II* is available for the Apple® family of computers.

Apple® is a registered trademark of Apple Computer Inc.

STORIES ON TAPE

Stories on Tape are audio-cassette tapes that feature stories and poems from each book, narrated by character voices and accompanied with appropriate music. All selections—except some Bonus Selections and short poems—are recorded in Levels 1–10. For Levels 11–15, major selections in each level have been recorded. The audio-cassettes for Level K are in the *Kindergarten Kit,* but they may also be purchased separately.

The *Stories on Tape* are packaged in durable plastic containers with *A Note to the Teacher* that provides suggestions for using the tapes.

HRW LITERATURE LIBRARIES

The *HRW Literature Libraries* (Levels K–15) are sets of soft-bound books chosen from the best of children's literature. Each set provides a variety of reading suited to the vocabulary and interests of that grade-level student.

WRITING FOLDER

The *Writing Folder* provides convenient and accessible storage for each student's writing projects.

SKILLS CHART

This Skills Chart provides an overview of the skills taught in **HRW READING: Reading Today and Tomorrow.** In each *Teacher's Edition,* Book Overviews (Levels 1–4) and Unit Overviews (Levels 5–15) offer detailed information regarding the scope and sequence of instruction. The Index of Skills in the back of each *Teacher's Edition* provides page references for all skills instruction.

T = tested at this level

★ = Introduction of phonic elements is completed by the end of Level 8.
Phonics instruction in Level 9 is for review and maintenance only.

SKILL	1	2	3	4	5	6	7	8	9	10	11	12	13	14	15
READINESS CONCEPTS															

DECODING/VOCABULARY

Phonics (Sound/Symbol Correspondence)

SKILL	1	2	3	4	5	6	7	8	9	10	11	12	13	14	15
consonants (initial, medial, final)	T	T	T	T	T	T	T	T							
consonant digraphs		T	T	T			T	T							
consonant clusters			T	T	T			T	★						
short vowels	T	T	T	T											
long vowels	T		T		T	T	T	T	★						
r-controlled vowels						T	T	T	★						
diphthongs and variant vowel forms							T	T	★						
phonograms															
word building (blending)															
word identification using phonics and context clues															

Word Structure

SKILL	1	2	3	4	5	6	7	8	9	10	11	12	13	14	15
base words and spelling changes		T				T	T								
contractions			T	T	T	T	T								
compound words					T					T					
inflected forms		T	T		T	T	T	T							
prefixes and suffixes						T	T	T	T	T	T	T	T	T	T
Greek and Latin roots														T	T

Vocabulary (Word Meaning)

SKILL	1	2	3	4	5	6	7	8	9	10	11	12	13	14	15
lesson vocabulary	T	T	T	T	T	T	T	T	T	T	T	T	T	T	T
meaning from context						T	T	T	T	T	T	T	T	T	T
multiple meanings		T		T		T							T		
synonyms and antonyms				T	T	T									
homophones and homographs					T			T			T				
abbreviations							T								
acronyms													T		
connotation and denotation															
appositives												T		T	
compound words						T				T					
analogies												T		T	
word origins													T		T

COMPREHENSION/THINKING

Literal

SKILL	1	2	3	4	5	6	7	8	9	10	11	12	13	14	15
cause and effect	T			T				T		T			T		
main idea/topic	T				T			T		T					
details/specific information		T		T			T			T			T	T	
pronoun referents		T				T				T					
sequence	T		T		T					T		T			

SKILL / LEVEL

SKILL	1	2	3	4	5	6	7	8	9	10	11	12	13	14	15
Inferential															
cause and effect							T		T						
comparison and contrast								T						T	
drawing conclusions			T		T		T		T		T		T	T	
main idea (unstated)							T			T		T			
predicting outcomes			T			T		T		T		T			T
sequence (inferred story events)														T	
Critical															
alternatives															
author's purpose										T			T		
evaluations and judgments															
fact and opinion									T			T	T		
generalizations													T		
persuasion and propaganda													T		T
prior knowledge															
slanted writing and bias													T		
problem solving															
Story Structure															
characters				T		T		T			T	T		T	T
mood												T		T	
plot								T		T		T		T	T
point of view									T		T		T		
setting					T		T		T		T		T		
story mapping															
theme											T		T		
Nonfiction Structure															
cause and effect															T
comparison and contrast												T		T	T
description								T		T		T			
main idea and details									T			T		T	
problem and solution													T		
temporal sequence								T		T		T			
Elements of Style															
alliteration and repetition													T		
allusion															T
descriptive words															
dialect/jargon/slang														T	
dialogue							T			T			T		
figurative language							T				T		T		T
flashback and foreshadowing													T	T	
elements of poetry															
other literary elements (puns, parody, symbolism, humor, imagery, etc.)											T			T	T
Forms of Literature		T			T					T	T	T	T	T	

STUDY SKILLS

SKILL	1	2	3	4	5	6	7	8	9	10	11	12	13	14	15
Book Features		T			T				T	T	T	T	T	T	T
Graphic Aids							T	T	T	T	T	T		T	T
References															
types											T	T	T	T	T
dictionary/glossary usage					T			T		T		T	T	T	T
encyclopedia usage										T		T		T	
evaluating reference sources														T	

SKILL

STUDY SKILLS (continued)

Skill	1	2	3	4	5	6	7	8	9	10	11	12	13	14	15
Content-Area Reading									▓	▓	▓	▓	▓	▓	▓
Study Aids															
determining purpose and rate									▓	▓	▓	▓	▓	▓	▓
question-answer relationships							▓	▓	▓	▓	▓	▓	▓	▓	▓
rereading to clarify								▓	▓	▓	▓	▓	▓	▓	▓
skimming and scanning										▓	▓	▓	▓	▓	▓
summarizing				▓	▓	▓	▓	T	▓	▓	T	▓	▓	▓	▓
Locating/Organizing Information															
alphabetical order		T	▓	▓	T	▓	T	▓	T	▓	T				
card catalog								T	T	T			T	▓	▓
cross-references													T		
note taking									▓	▓	▓	▓	▓	▓	▓
classification	T	▓			T	▓		T	▓				T	▓	
outlines								T	▓		T	▓	T	▓	T
reports								▓	▓	▓	▓	▓	▓	▓	▓
test-taking							▓	▓	▓	▓	▓	▓	▓	▓	▓
written directions				▓	▓	▓	▓	▓	▓	▓	▓	▓	▓	▓	▓
Functional Skills															
forms and applications									▓	▓	▓	▓	T	▓	▓
labels											▓	▓	▓	▓	▓
banking											▓	▓	▓	▓	▓
menus, signs, symbols, schedules, directories							▓	▓	▓	▓	▓	▓	▓	▓	▓

LANGUAGE

Skill	1	2	3	4	5	6	7	8	9	10	11	12	13	14	15
Listening															
to follow directions	▓	▓	▓	▓	▓	▓									
for specific information	▓	▓	▓	▓	▓	▓	▓	▓	▓	▓	▓	▓	▓	▓	▓
to stories, poems, and nonfiction read aloud	▓	▓	▓	▓	▓	▓	▓	▓	▓	▓	▓	▓	▓	▓	▓
Speaking (including oral reading, descriptions, directions, explanations, interviews, reports, paraphrasing, storytelling and retelling, persuasion)	▓	▓	▓	▓	▓	▓	▓	▓	▓	▓	▓	▓	▓	▓	▓
Writing															
language - experience stories	▓	▓	▓	▓	▓	▓	▓	▓							
sentences, stories, story endings, paragraphs		▓	▓	▓	▓	▓	▓	▓	▓	▓	▓	▓	▓	▓	▓
specific types of fiction										▓			▓	▓	▓
specific types of nonfiction										▓			▓	▓	▓
poems (verse)				▓	▓	▓	▓	▓	▓	▓	▓	▓	▓	▓	▓
Conventions of Language															
punctuation	▓	▓	▓	▓	▓	▓	▓	▓	▓	▓	▓	▓	▓		
capitalization	▓	▓	▓	▓	▓	▓	▓	▓	▓	▓	▓	▓	▓		
sentence construction	▓	▓	▓	▓	▓	▓	▓	▓	▓	▓	▓	▓	▓	▓	▓
paragraph construction				▓	▓	▓	▓	▓	▓	▓	▓	▓	▓	▓	▓

SPOTLIGHTS

BOOK INTRODUCTION

Introducing *Spotlights*
(T2–T5)

Materials

Spotlights, Level 6
Teacher's Idea Book

Special Populations

See *Teacher's Idea Book* for additional suggestions to help pupils with limited English proficiency.

Using Prior Knowledge

Display a copy of *Spotlights* and tell pupils that this is their new reading book. Read the title and ask what spotlights are. (Spotlights are bright lights that shine on actors and actresses in a play or in a circus. Sometimes spotlights are used to draw attention to places, such as sporting events or grand openings.) Tell pupils that when a play is acted out on a stage, the characters in the play are said to be "in the spotlight." When you read a story, you might say that the characters in the story are "in the spotlight."

READING TODAY AND TOMORROW
SPOTLIGHTS
LEVEL 6

READING TODAY AND TOMORROW
SPOTLIGHTS
LEVEL 6

Isabel Beck, Senior Author

Bonnie Armbruster   Taffy Raphael
Margaret McKeown   Lenore Ringler
Donna Ogle

HOLT, RINEHART AND WINSTON, INC.
Austin   New York   Chicago   San Diego   Toronto   Montreal

Using the Title Page

Distribute copies of *Spotlights* and encourage pupils to look through the books. Then help pupils find the title page. Tell them that the first page of a book is called the title page because it has the title of the book on it.

Requests for permission to make copies of any part of the work should be mailed to:

Permissions
Holt, Rinehart and Winston, Inc.
1627 Woodland Drive
Austin, Texas 78741

Printed in the United States of America
ISBN 0-15-718050-6
78901 061 7654321

Acknowledgments

For permission to reprint copyrighted material, grateful acknowledgment is made to the following sources:

Aileen Fisher: "Houses" from *Up the Windy Hill* by Aileen Fisher, Abelard Press, N.Y. 1953. Copyright renewed 1981.

Harcourt Brace Jovanovich, Inc.: "Wheels and Wings" from *Magpie Lane* by Nancy Byrd Turner. Copyright © 1927 by Harcourt Brace Jovanovich, Inc.; renewed 1955 by Nancy Byrd Turner.

Harper & Row, Publishers, Inc.: "Trains" from *I Go A-Traveling* by James S. Tippett. Copyright © 1929 by Harper & Row, Publishers, Inc.

Henry Holt and Company, Inc.: Adapted from *Mr. Gumpy's Outing* by John Burningham. Illustrations by John Burningham. Copyright © 1970 by John Burningham.

Holiday House: Adapted from *Happy Mother's Day!* by Steven Kroll. Copyright © 1985 by Steven Kroll. Adapted from *The Biggest Pumpkin Ever* by Steven Kroll. Copyright © 1984 by Steven Kroll. Adapted from *Toot! Toot!* by Steven Kroll. Copyright © 1983 by Steven Kroll.

Parents Magazine Press, a division of Gruner + Jahr USA Publishing: Adaptation of text of *Aren't You Forgetting Something, Fiona?* Copyright © 1984 by Joanna Cole.

G.P. Putnam's Sons: "Hiding" from *Everything and Anything* by Dorothy Aldis. Copyright © 1925-1927. Copyright renewed 1953-1955 by Dorothy Aldis.

Contents

1 Neighbors

Adapted from stories by Lilian Moore

v

2 Great Ideas

Adapted from stories by Joanna Cole

vi

Using the Table of Contents

Ask pupils to turn to the Table of Contents. Call on a pupil to tell what the Table of Contents contains. (the names of the stories and the pages on which each story begins) Explain that this book has three groups of stories and that each group is listed on a different page.

Have pupils look at the first page of the Table of Contents. Tell them that the title of the first story is "Day Comes to Dilly Street." Call on a pupil to tell on which page the first story begins. (page 4) Follow a similar procedure with several additional story titles.

3 Surprises

Adapted from stories by Steven Kroll

Idea Center

LETTER CARDS, PATTERN CARDS, AND WORD CARDS

If you do not have the *Resource Box,* you can make your own *Letter Cards, Pattern Cards,* and *Word Cards* by printing each letter, letters, or word on an index card.

PICTURE CARDS

If you do not have the *Resource Box,* you can make your own *Picture Cards.* Color and cut apart the pictures from the *Teacher's Idea Book* and paste each on a card. Or, you may prefer to find pictures in magazines or workbooks to paste on cards.

PUNCTUATION CARDS AND INFLECTIONAL ENDING CARDS

If you do not have the *Resource Box,* you can make your own *Punctuation Cards* and *Inflectional Ending Cards* by printing each punctuation mark or inflectional ending on an index card.

POCKET CHART

If you do not have a *Pocket Chart,* you can make your own. Use a sheet of tagboard that is approximately 24 by 18 inches. Mark and score a line 4 inches from the top of the tagboard and another line 5 inches from the top. Accordion-fold along the lines to make a pocket. Staple the ends. Follow a similar procedure for other pockets. Then attach the Pocket Chart to a piece of corrugated cardboard cut to fit, approximately 18 by 18 inches, and tape the edges.

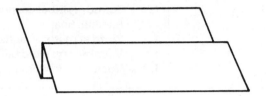

UNIT 1 OVERVIEW

TITLE	DECODING/VOCABULARY		COMPREHENSION/THINKING	
Day Comes to Dilly Street pages 4–9 (T12–T29)	M	**Sound/symbol correspondence:** consonant /l/*l*, *ll* (initial, medial, final)	M	**Story structure:** setting
	I, T	**Sound/symbol correspondence:** vowel /ē/*y* (final)		
	M	**Sound/symbol correspondence:** vowel /ō/*oa*, *ow* (medial, final)		
	I	**Word structure:** suffix -*y*		
	I	**Vocabulary:** word building		
	I, T	**Vocabulary:** word meaning		
Wake Up, Shadows pages 10–11 (T30–T31)			Ⓘ	**Forms of literature:** poetry
Pesty! pages 12–13 (T32–T33)	R, T	**Sound/symbol correspondence:** vowel /ē/*y* (final)		
	R	**Word structure:** suffix -*y*		
Minx and Jinx pages 14–21 (T34–T55)	I, T	**Sound/symbol correspondence:** consonant /j/*j* (initial)	Ⓘ, **T**	**Inferential:** predicting outcomes
	M	**Sound/symbol correspondence:** vowel /ā/*a-e*		
	M	**Accumulated elements:** consonant clusters *sw*, *tw* (initial)		
	I	**Vocabulary:** word building		
	I, T	**Vocabulary:** word meaning		
Who Wants a Kitten? pages 22–31 (T56–T77)	R, T	**Sound/symbol correspondence:** consonant /j/*j* (initial)	I, T	**Story structure:** plot (problems and solutions)
	R, T	**Sound/symbol correspondence:** vowel /ē/*y* (final)		
	I, T	**Word structure:** inflectional endings -*er*, -*est*		
	I, T	**Word structure:** suffix -*er*		
	R	**Word structure:** suffix -*y*		
	I, T	**Vocabulary:** word meaning		

Ⓘ Expanded treatment of skill introduced at a previous level

Key to Symbols

I Introduced in this lesson
R Reinforced from an earlier lesson in this level
M Maintained from previous levels
T Tested in this level

STUDY SKILLS	LANGUAGE	LANGUAGE APPLICATIONS
I **Functional reading**: signs and symbols (safety)	Ⓘ **Listening**: oral directions (multiple–step)	**Oral reading**: answering questions **Listening**: safety speaker, information, fiction **Speaking**: telling about a picture (Cooperative Learning); making comparisons **Writing**: making a safety book
I, T **References**: dictionary (entry words and definitions)	Ⓘ **Conventions of language**: capitalization	**Oral reading**: answering questions **Speaking**: role playing **Writing**: making a poster (Cooperative Learning) **Listening**: poetry, fiction, information
R **Functional reading**: signs and symbols (safety)	**M** **Speaking**: telephone communication	**Oral reading**: expression **Writing**: thank-you notes **Listening**: fiction

TITLE	DECODING/VOCABULARY		COMPREHENSION/THINKING	
Bear Trouble pages 32–43 (T78–T101)	M	**Sound/symbol correspondence:** consonant /l/*le* (final)	R, T	**Story structure:** plot (problems and solutions)
	I, T	**Sound/symbol correspondence:** vowel /ī/*i-e*		
	R, T	**Word structure:** inflectional endings *-er, -est*		
	R, T	**Word structure:** suffix *-er*		
	I	**Vocabulary:** word building		
	I, T	**Vocabulary:** word meaning		
Mike's Slide pages 44–45 (T102–T103)	R, T	**Sound/symbol correspondence:** vowel /ī/*i-e*		
Things in the Pool pages 46–47 (T104–T105)			R	**Forms of literature:** poetry
The Chili Pot pages 48–57 (T106–T127)	R, T	**Sound/symbol correspondence:** vowel /ī/*i-e*	R, T	**Inferential:** predicting outcomes
	R	**Sound/symbol correspondence:** vowel discrimination /ĭ/, /ī/		
	I, T	**Word structure:** contractions (with *'re*)		
	M	**Vocabulary:** compound words		
	M	**Vocabulary:** multiple meanings		
	I	**Vocabulary:** word building		
	I, T	**Vocabulary:** word meaning		
End-of-Unit Review (T128–T133) NOTE–These skills are tested in *End-of-Unit 1 Test*	R, T	**Sound/symbol correspondence:** consonant /j/*j* (initial)	*R, T	**Inferential:** predicting outcomes
	*R, T	**Sound/symbol correspondence:** vowel /ē/*y* (final)	R, T	**Story structure:** plot (problems and solutions)
	*R, T	**Sound/symbol correspondence:** vowel /ī/*i-e*		
	*R, T	**Word structure:** inflectional endings *-er, -est*		
	*R, T	**Word structure:** suffix *-er*		
	*R, T	**Vocabulary:** word meaning		

* Tested in *End-of-Book Test*

Key to Symbols
I   Introduced in this lesson
R   Reinforced from an earlier lesson in this level
M   Maintained from previous levels
T   Tested in this level

STUDY SKILLS	LANGUAGE	LANGUAGE APPLICATIONS
M **Locating information:** alphabetical order	**I** **Speaking:** paraphrasing **R** **Conventions of language:** capitalization	**Oral reading:** answering questions **Critical thinking:** problem solving (Cooperative Learning) **Speaking/Writing:** using vocabulary words **Listening:** fiction
R, T **References:** dictionary (entry words and definitions)	**R** **Listening:** oral directions (multiple–step)	**Oral reading/Speaking:** dialogue **Writing:** stories **Listening:** fiction
*R, T **References:** dictionary (entry words and definitions)		

Materials

Spotlights, Level 6: pages 2–3
Teacher's Idea Book

Special Populations

See *Teacher's Idea Book* for additional suggestions to help pupils with limited English proficiency.

Using Prior Knowledge

Have pupils turn to pages 2 and 3 of *Spotlights.* Point to the title on page 3 and tell them that the name of the first unit in *Spotlights* is "Neighbors." Ask pupils to tell who neighbors are. (Neighbors are people who live near each other.)

SAY Many people live in neighborhoods in the city where the houses are close together, so neighbors live nearby. Out in the country, the houses may be very far apart, and people might have to drive in a car to visit a neighbor.

Ask pupils to tell who or what might be neighbors in the picture on page 2 (the cats). Point out that the cats are sitting together on a grocery store sign. Explain that "corner" grocery stores are very common in city neighborhoods. Then ask what neighbors might do with and for each other. (Possible answers include: They might play or work together.)

Direct pupils' attention to page 3 and tell them that this page has a list of the stories that are in this unit. Each of these stories tells about neighbors in some way. Choose several story titles to read. As you read each title, ask pupils to predict how the story might tell about neighbors.

Tell pupils that the stories in this unit were written by Lilian Moore. You may want to share the following information about the author.

Lilian Moore has written many children's stories. She has also written several books of poetry for children. She was a teacher and a reading specialist for the New York City schools. She also served as editor of the Arrow Book Club for children. She now lives and writes on a farm in Kerhonkson, New York. Ms. Moore has received several awards for her books and was named Poet of the Year for 1986.

NEIGHBORS

adapted from stories
by Lilian Moore
"Day Comes to Dilly Street"
"Minx and Jinx"
"Who Wants a Kitten?"
"Bear Trouble"
"The Chili Pot"

2

3

LESSON 1 "Day Comes to Dilly Street"
pages 4–9 (T12–T29)

Skill Strands

DECODING/VOCABULARY

M **Sound/symbol correspondence:** consonant /l/*l*, *ll* (initial, medial, final)

I, T **Sound/symbol correspondence:** vowel /ē/*y* (final)

M **Sound/symbol correspondence:** vowel /ō/*ow, oa* (medial, final)

I **Word structure:** suffix -*y*

I **Vocabulary:** word building

I, T **Vocabulary:** word meaning

COMPREHENSION/THINKING

Focus

M **Story structure:** setting

STUDY SKILLS

I **Functional reading:** signs and symbols (safety)

LANGUAGE

I **Listening:** oral directions (multiple–step)

Lesson Vocabulary

Decodable words: *Billy, bus, Candy, Dilly, fresh, hurry, milk, purr, sunny, toast, Tommy, trucks, yet*

Special words: *cars, hello, people, neighbors*

Materials

Spotlights, Level 6: pages 4–9
Workbook: pages 1–7

Practice Masters: pages 1–4
Instructional Charts: pages 1–4
Resource Box: Letter Cards b/ B, f, h, i, l(2), n(2), r(2), s, u, y
    Word Cards boat, cars, coat, grow, hello, neighbors, people, slow, snow, toast
Pocket Chart
Teacher's Idea Book
Reteach Masters: pages 1–2

Language Applications

USING LANGUAGE

Oral reading: answering questions
Speaking: making comparisons

EXTENDING SELECTION CONCEPTS

Listening: safety speaker
Listening: information
Speaking: telling about a picture (Cooperative Learning)
Writing: making a safety book
Listening: fiction

Special Populations

See the *Teacher's Idea Book* for additional suggestions to help pupils with limited English proficiency.

Key to Symbols

I Introduced in this lesson
R Reinforced from an earlier lesson in this level
M Maintained from previous levels
T Tested in this level

Idea Center

BIBLIOGRAPHY

Set up a reading corner or reading table where books will be available throughout the year. Encourage pupils to use the books and to take care of them. For this story, display various books about signs and neighborhoods. A suggested bibliography follows. Suggestions for reading aloud and annotations appear in the lesson plan.

Hasler, Eveline. *Winter Magic.* William Morrow, 1984.

Hoban, Tana. *I Read Signs.* Greenwillow, 1983.

———. *I Read Symbols.* Greenwillow, 1983.

McPhail, David. *Farm Morning.* Harcourt Brace Jovanovich, 1985.

Paul, Ann Whitford. *Owl at Night.* Putnam, 1985.

Provensen, Alice and Martin. *Town & Country.* Crown, 1984.

Planning Chart

		Instruction	Written Practice	Extending
Step 1 Preparing for the Selection	I, T	**Sound/symbol correspondence:** vowel /ē/ *y* (final)	*Workbook* page 1 *Practice Masters* page 1 *Reteach Masters* page 1	**Speaking:** telling about a picture (Cooperative Learning)
	I	**Word structure:** suffix *–y*		
	I	**Vocabulary:** word building		
	I, T	**Vocabulary:** word meaning	*Workbook* page 2 *Practice Masters* page 2 *Reteach Masters* page 2	
	M	**Story structure:** setting		**Listening:** fiction
Step 2 Reading for Comprehension		**Oral reading:** answering questions		
		Speaking: making comparisons		
		Story structure: setting		**Listening:** safety speaker
		Story comprehension	*Workbook* page 3	
Step 3 Developing Reading and Thinking Skills	M	**Sound/symbol correspondence:** vowel /ō/ *oa, ow* (medial, final)	*Workbook* page 4	
	M	**Sound/symbol correspondence:** consonant /l/ *l, ll* (initial, medial, final)	*Workbook* page 5	**Listening:** information
	M	**Story structure:** setting	*Workbook* page 6 *Practice Masters* page 3	
	I	**Functional reading:** signs and symbols (safety)	*Workbook* page 7 *Practice Masters* page 4	**Writing:** making a safety book
	I	**Listening:** oral directions (multiple-step)		

DECODING/VOCABULARY

I, T **Sound/symbol correspondence:** vowel /ē/γ (final)

I **Word structure:** suffix -γ

Note: Learning to read requires understanding the alphabetic principle. This principle is that a written symbol—a letter or letters—is associated with a unit of speech—a sound. Direct teaching of sound/symbol correspondences makes gaining understanding of the alphabetic principle easier. Associating a sound with a letter (or letters) helps pupils to quickly gain independent decoding strategies.

DIRECT INSTRUCTION Print the following sentences and words on the chalkboard:

> 1. I see a silly bunny.
> 2. Patty went out to play on a sunny day.
>
>   hurry   Tommy
>   silly   funny
>   happy   chilly

Read the first sentence aloud. Point to the words *silly* and *bunny* and read them. Ask what is the same about these words. (They end with γ; they end with /ē/.)

SAY The word *silly* has two parts. Listen as I say each part: *sil ly.* Now say *sil ly* with me: *sil ly.* When a word has two parts and the last letter is γ, the γ usually stands for the /ē/ sound.

Now say *bun ny* with me: *bun ny.* How many word parts do you hear in *bunny*? (two) What sound does γ stand for in *bunny*? (/ē/)

Read the second sentence and call attention to the words *Patty* and *sunny.*

SAY The words *Patty* and *sunny* end with the /ē/ sound. What letter do you see at the end of *Patty* and *sunny*? (γ) The letter γ in *Patty* and *sunny* stand for the /ē/ sound. The word *Patty* was made by doubling the

consonant *t* and adding *y. Patty* is a nickname for *Pat.* **How was the word *sunny* made?** (The word *sunny* was made by doubling the consonant *n* in sun and adding *y.*) **If the sun is out, we say that the day is *sunny.***

Have pupils read the sentence with you.

GUIDED PRACTICE Direct pupils' attention to the two columns of words on the chalkboard.

Tell pupils that the γ at the end of each word stands for the /ē/ sound. Point to each word and have it read.

Then call on pupils to point to the words on the chart and to read them.

WB 1 **INDEPENDENT PRACTICE** *Workbook* page 1 may be used to practice identifying sound/symbol correspondence /ē/γ.

PM 1 **ADDITIONAL PRACTICE** *Practice Masters* page 1 may be used as an optional practice for identifying sound/symbol correspondence /ē/y. (See page T28 for reduced pages with answers.)

✳ **RETEACH** For those pupils who need additional instruction, see "Reteaching Lesson Skills," page T27, under "Reteaching and Extending."

I Vocabulary: word building

> **Note:** The word building activity that is provided in this section of the lesson plan contributes strongly to the development of pupils' blending skills. The consistent use of the word building activity supports the development of independent decoding.

DIRECT INSTRUCTION Use *Letter Cards* to make the word *sunny* in the *Pocket Chart* and have the word read. Ask what sound letter *y* at the end of *sunny* stands for. (/ē/) Change *Letter Card s* to *b* and have the new word read. (*bunny*)

GUIDED PRACTICE Display *Letter Cards B, f, h, i, l, l, r, r.* Tell pupils that you will ask them to use the cards to make new words in the *Pocket Chart.*

1. **Change the *b* in *bunny* to *f*. What is the new word?** (*funny*)
2. **Change the *nn* to *rr*. What is the new word?** (*furry*)
3. **Change the *f* to *h*. What is the new word?** (*hurry*)
4. **Change the *urr* to *ill*. What is the new word?** (*hilly*)
5. **Take off the *y*. What is the new word?** (*hill*) **How many parts are in *hill*?** (one)
6. **Change the *h* to capital *b*. What is the new word?** (*Bill*) **How many parts are in *Bill*?** (one)
7. **Add *y* to the end of the word. What is the new word?** (*Billy*) **How many parts are in *Billy*?** (two)

I, T Vocabulary: word meaning

> **Note:** Each story in *Spotlights* provides pupils with an opportunity to apply learned sound/symbol correspondences to a related text. Most new words in each selection are decodable, in that they are comprised of sound/symbol correspondences that pupils have learned in this program. In addition, pupils learn "special" words. Special words are not yet decodable, but are the high-frequency function words and story-useful words that are present in interesting and meaningful selections.
>
> In this part of the lesson plan, special words and decodable words are introduced in context sentences. Such practice is helpful to the development of fluent word recognition and reinforces pupils' understanding of the meanings of these words.

DIRECT INSTRUCTION Print the following words and sentences on the chalkboard, omitting the underlining.

> **cars hello people neighbors**
>
> 1. My <u>neighbors</u> have a big dog.
> 2. The dog likes to ride in <u>cars</u>.
> 3. It wags its tail at <u>people</u>.
> 4. The dog wags its tail to say <u>hello</u>.
>
> **Billy Candy Dilly hurry milk sunny toast Tommy**

Tell pupils that they are going to talk about some words they will read in the next story.

Read the first sentence. Point to the word *neighbors* and read it. Ask who neighbors are. (Neighbors are people who live near you.) Ask what the neighbors have. (a big dog) Have the sentence read. Then call on a pupil to find and read the word *neighbors*.

Read Sentence 2. Point to the word *cars* and read it. Have pupils read the sentence with you. Then ask pupils to find and read the word *cars*.

Read Sentence 3 aloud. Point to the word *people* and read it. Ask at whom the dog wags its tail. (people) Have the sentence read. Then ask pupils to find and read the word *people*.

Read Sentence 4 aloud. Point to the word *hello* and read it. Ask why the dog wags its tail. (It wags its tail to say hello.) Have pupils read the sentence with you. Then ask them to find and read the word *hello*.

The words in the second set are new words that contain known phonic elements. You may wish to ask pupils to read the words, using what they know about letters and sounds.

GUIDED PRACTICE Print the following sentences on the chalkboard, omitting the underlining.

IC 3

1. Jimmy's house is on <u>Dilly</u> Street.
2. <u>Cars</u> and <u>people</u> <u>hurry</u> up and down the street.
3. <u>Billy</u> and <u>Tommy</u> are my <u>neighbors</u>.
4. They like to eat <u>toast</u>.
5. Their cat, <u>Candy</u>, likes fresh <u>milk</u>.
6. On <u>sunny</u> days, they say <u>hello</u> to people.

Provide opportunities for pupils to practice reading the new special words and some of the new decodable words in these sentences by following the suggestions below.

Sentence 1: Have the sentence read and ask pupils to tell where Jimmy lives. (on Dilly Street) Have pupils find and read the word *Dilly*.

Sentence 2: Have pupils find and read the words *cars* and *people*. Then have the sentence read aloud. Ask what the cars and people do. (They hurry up and down the street.)

Sentences 3–4: Have a pupil find and read the word *neighbors*. Then have sentences 3 and 4 read aloud. Ask who Billy and Tommy are. (neighbors) Ask what they like to eat. (*toast*)

Sentence 5: Call on a pupil to find and read the word *Candy*. Ask who or what is named *Candy*. (Candy is the cat's name.) Ask how pupils know it is a name. (It starts with a capital *c*.) Ask what the cat likes. (fresh milk) Explain that *fresh* means "not spoiled." Then have the sentence read.

Sentence 6: Have the sentence read aloud and ask pupils to find and read the word *hello*.

INDEPENDENT PRACTICE *Workbook* page 2 may be used to practice reading story vocabulary.

WB 2

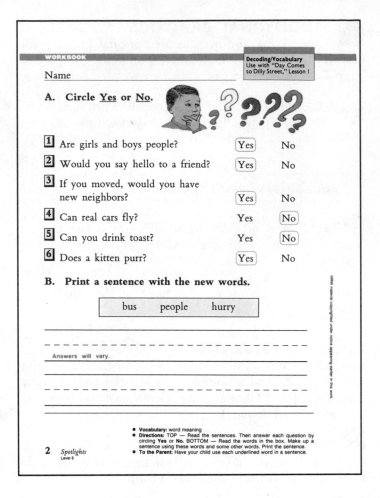

ADDITIONAL PRACTICE *Practice Masters* page 2 may be used as an optional practice for reading story vocabulary. (See page T28 for reduced pages with answers.)

PM 2

RETEACH For those pupils who need additional instruction, see "Reteaching Lesson Skills," page T27, under "Reteaching and Extending."

COMPREHENSION/THINKING

Focus ——————————————————————
M   Story structure: setting
——————————————————————

Note: Learning to read is a process that involves interaction among pupils, text, and instructional factors. The Comprehension/Thinking Focus skill, which is developed throughout the lesson plan, helps pupils identify the what, how, and why of reading and then apply this knowledge in a variety of reading situations. In Step 1, the teacher identifies **what** the Focus skill is. In Step 2, pupils discuss **how** the Focus skill applies to the story just read. In Step 3, pupils use the Focus skill for reading and thinking about related materials. In doing so, pupils begin to understand **why** they learned this skill.

DIRECT INSTRUCTION Ask pupils to look around the room.

| SAY | **We are in school. The place where we are is called our setting. Our setting is this classroom. Each story you read has a setting. The setting of a story is where and when the story takes place. Where would you expect a story called "Lost in the Zoo" to take place?** (in a zoo) **Where would you expect a story called "The Seals of Alaska" to take place?** (in Alaska) |

GUIDED PRACTICE Remind pupils that sometimes during a story the setting changes. Ask them to listen as you read the following story.

| READ | **Sally looked under her bed and in her closet. She wanted to find her kite. Finally, she looked behind her bookcase. There was the kite, all rolled up, just the way she had put it away last summer. Sally pulled the kite out carefully and ran to the park. Jimmy was flying his kite by the pond. He was waiting for Sally to arrive.** |

| ASK | **Where was Sally at the beginning of the story?** (She was at home, looking for her kite.) **Where was Sally at the end of the story?** (She was at the park.) |

2 READING FOR COMPREHENSION

Background for the Teacher

SUMMARY   This selection chronicles the things that happen in a city neighborhood as a new day begins.

INFORMATION   This is an informational selection. The imaginary Dilly Street is used to symbolize a street in a city neighborhood. Pupils will read what happens as the day begins on Dilly Street and will be asked to compare it to other neighborhoods in the morning.

Using Prior Knowledge

Note: Prior knowledge, or background experience brought to the text, provides a framework that helps pupils understand and remember new information. The oral discussion suggested in this section of the lesson plan is designed to help the teacher find out what pupils already know and what they need to know for comprehending the upcoming text.

Ask if pupils have ever been awake early in the morning, before anyone else was awake. Ask how the house sounds when everyone is asleep. (very quiet) Then ask what noises might be heard as people start to get up and get ready to go to work or to school. (Possible answers include: pots and pans clanging, showers running, people brushing their teeth and getting dressed.) Develop a discussion by asking questions such as those that follow:

1. **If you went outside, how do you think your neighborhood would sound before anyone got up in the morning?** (very quiet) **What sounds might you hear as people leave for work or school?** (Possible answers include: people saying good-by, cars starting, children walking to the bus stop or to school.)
2. **What are some things that boys and girls might do before they go to school in the morning?** (Possible answers include: eat breakfast, get dressed, fix a lunch, walk the dog.)

Setting a Purpose for Reading

Note: Having a purpose for reading helps pupils construct the meaning of a text, resulting in better comprehension of both literal meanings and implied ideas. Establishing a purpose also provides a model for pupils to use later in determining what they may expect to learn from their reading.

Have pupils open their books to page 4 and call on a volunteer to read the title of the selection.

Point out the headnote at the top of the page. Tell pupils that this note will help them think about the story they are going to read. Have the headnote read aloud. Then ask what kinds of things the neighbors on Dilly Street might do as day begins.

Reading Silently

Some pupils may be able to read this story independently. Direct them to read the whole story to find out more about what happened on Dilly Street as the day began. For those pupils who need more guidance, suggestions for directed reading follow.

What do the neighbors on Dilly Street do when day comes?

Day Comes to Dilly Street

The sun has not yet come up on Dilly Street.

People are sleeping. All is still.

4

Then it is sunup.
The birds sing.
The dogs yip, and the cats purr.

"Get up!" the moms say.
"Don't go back to sleep."
In all the houses, people wake up.

Toast and eggs are on the plates.
Cold, fresh milk fills the glasses.

"Hurry," the dads say.
"Let's eat."

It's going to be a sunny day on Dilly Street.

5

Before reading pages 4–5

| SAY | **A new day is about to begin on Dilly Street. What kind of day do you think it will be? Read pages 4 and 5 to yourself.** |

After reading pages 4–5

1. **What kind of day is it going to be on Dilly Street?** (sunny) Literal
2. **Why do you think the dads say "hurry"?** (Possible answers include: They don't want breakfast to get cold; they don't want the children to be late for school; they don't want to be late for work.) Critical

Noise fills the street.
People hurry out of the houses.
<u>Cars</u> and <u>trucks</u> rush
down the streets and roads.

Lots of cars!
Lots of trucks!

6

People stand at the bus stop.
They wait for buses to take them
to work.

Lots of people!
"<u>Hello</u>," they say to one another.
"Looks like a sunny day."

7

Before reading pages 6–7

SAY **What do you think is happening outside the homes on Dilly Street? Read pages 6 and 7 to yourself.**

After reading pages 6–7

1. **What is happening outside the homes on Dilly Street?** (Cars and trucks are rushing down the streets; people are hurrying out of their homes; some people are waiting at the bus stop.) Inferential
2. **What are some things people say to each other?** ("Hello! Looks like a sunny day.") Literal
3. **If you were waiting for the bus, what are some things you might say to the people that you know at the bus stop?** (Possible answers include: "How are you today? I wonder if the bus will be on time.") Critical

T20 *Spotlights,* Level 6

Boys and girls come out
of the houses.

They are happy it is a sunny day
on Dilly Street.

"Hello, Billy."

"Hello, Candy."

"Hello, Tommy," the friends say
to one another.

Day has come to Dilly Street.

8

1. What do the neighbors on Dilly
   Street do when day comes?
2. How do the people on Dilly Street
   get to work?
3. How are the people on Dilly Street
   like your neighbors?
4. How do neighbors help one another?

9

Before
reading
page
8

| SAY | **What do you think the children in the neighborhood do in the morning? Read page 8 to yourself.** |

After
reading
page
8

1. **What do the children do in the
   morning?** (They come out of their
   houses and say hello to one another.)
   Literal
2. **Where do you think the children are
   going?** (to school) **How can you tell?**
   (They are carrying books and lunch
   boxes; there is a school crossing guard in
   the picture.) Inferential

Discussing the Selection

Questions 1–4 below may be used for developing and
evaluating pupils' comprehension of the selection.
Questions preceded by a number appear in *Spotlights*
after the selection. Questions preceded by a bullet are
additional questions for extending discussion.

MAIN IDEA

1. **What do neighbors on Dilly Street do when day
   comes?** (Possible answers include: They wake up;
   they eat breakfast; they leave for school or work.)
   Literal

• **How does everyone on Dilly Street feel? Why?**
  (They seem happy because it is a sunny day.) Critical

SUPPORT

2. **How do the people on Dilly Street get to work?**
   (Some ride buses; some probably drive cars or walk.)
   Inferential

• **What do people on Dilly Street have for breakfast?** (toast, eggs, milk) Literal

3. How are the people on Dilly Street like your neighbors? (Answers will vary.) Critical

4. How do neighbors help one another? (Possible answers include: babysit, take in the mail when a neighbor is on vacation, take care of a neighbor's pet.) Critical

• **How do you think the rest of the stories in this unit will be like this selection?** (Answers will vary. Possible answers include: The stories will be about neighbors, too.) Critical

Using Language

Note: Throughout the program, there are activities directed to the development of all the language arts—reading, writing, speaking, and listening—as well as to their integration. One of the places that this is consistently done is in the "Using Language" section of the lesson plan, in which the reading selection is used as a springboard for a variety of language activities. In this level, oral reading is emphasized because it provides a window on pupils' development as readers. Oral reading can also help develop pupils' sense of the structure and rhythm or language. Pupils listen as the teacher models the tone, stress, and pauses of sentences. Then opportunities are provided for pupils to incorporate the model in their reading. Early composition abilities also are developed as pupils discuss and write about shared experiences.

ORAL READING: ANSWERING QUESTIONS
Remind pupils that the selection "Day Comes to Dilly Street" told about things that happened early in the morning. Explain that you will ask some questions that pupils can answer by reading parts of the selection aloud. Have pupils turn to page 4 in their books. Ask what is happening on Dilly Street before the sun comes up. (The sun has not yet come up on Dilly Street. People are sleeping. All is still.)

Follow a similar procedure for the remaining pages.

Page 5: Ask pupils to tell what the moms say. ("Get up!" the moms say. "Don't go back to sleep.") Ask what the dads say. ("Hurry," the dads say. "Let's eat.")

Page 6: Ask a pupil to read the first sentence aloud. Then ask what kind of noise fills the streets. (People hurry out of the houses. Cars and trucks rush down the streets and roads. Lots of cars! Lots of trucks!)

Page 7: Ask pupils to read why people are standing at the bus stop. (They wait for buses to take them to work.)

Page 8: Call on a pupil to read what the children say to one another. ("Hello, Billy." "Hello, Candy." "Hello, Tommy," the friends say to one another.)

SPEAKING: MAKING COMPARISONS Suggest that Dilly Street may be similar to other neighborhoods. Ask pupils to suggest how all neighborhoods may be alike. (Possible answers include: The children play together; neighbors borrow things from each other; neighborhoods do things together.) Then have pupils suggest ways that one neighborhood may be different from another. (Possible answers include: Houses may be far apart or close together; streets may be quiet or busy.)

Applying the Focus Skill

STORY STRUCTURE: SETTING Remind pupils that the setting is where or when a story takes place. Ask where this selection took place. (on Dilly Street) Ask if Dilly Street was in the country or in the city. (in the city) Ask how pupils can tell. (There were many houses, buses, trucks, cars; there was not much open space.) Ask what time of day the selection took place. (morning)

Evaluating Comprehension

WB 3 **INDEPENDENT PRACTICE** *Workbook* page 3 may be used for an informal evaluation of story comprehension.

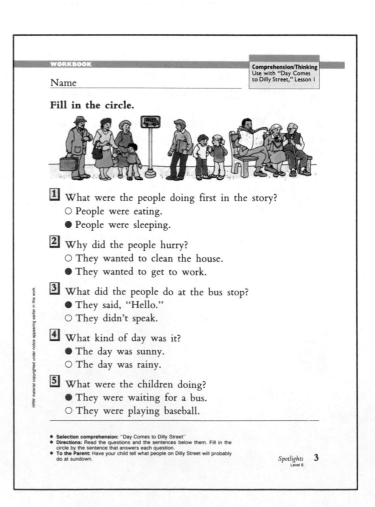

3 DEVELOPING READING AND THINKING SKILLS

DECODING/VOCABULARY

M   Sound/symbol correspondence: vowel /ō/ *oa, ow* (medial, final)

DIRECT INSTRUCTION   Place *Word Card toast* in the *Pocket Chart* and place *Word Card grow* under it. Point to each word and have it read aloud.

Ask what vowel sound is heard in *toast* and *grow.* (/ō/) Ask what letters stand for /ō/ in *toast.* (*oa*) Then ask what letters stand for /ō/ in *grow.* (*ow*) Remind pupils that the letter pairs *oa* and *ow* can both stand for the /ō/ sound.

GUIDED PRACTICE   Display *Word Cards boat, snow, slow, coat* and have them read. Call on pupils to find the two pairs of rhyming words and to place each pair in the *Pocket Chart.* (*boat, coat; snow, slow*) Have each pair of rhyming words read aloud. Ask what two letters stand for /ō/ in each pair of rhyming words. (*oa, ow*)

WB 4   INDEPENDENT PRACTICE   *Workbook* page 4 may be used to practice identifying sound/symbol correspondence /ō/ *oa, ow.*

M   Sound/symbol correspondence: consonant /l/*l, ll* (initial, medial, final)

DIRECT INSTRUCTION Print the following sentence and words on the chalkboard:

> My pal Billy was last.
>
> left   fellow   fill
> hello   lots   tail

Have the sentence read. Call on a pupil to find and read each word in the sentence that has the /l/ sound. When *pal, Billy,* and *last* are read, ask where the /l/ sound is heard. (beginning, middle, end) Point out that the /l/ sound in *Billy* is spelled with two *l*'s. Remind pupils that the /l/ sound can be at the beginning, in the middle, or at the end of a word.

GUIDED PRACTICE Direct pupils' attention to the words on the chalkboard. Call on a pupil to read a word and to tell where the /l/ sound is heard in the word. Continue until each word has been read.

WB 5   INDEPENDENT PRACTICE *Workbook* page 5 may be used to practice identifying sound/symbol correspondence /l/*l, ll*.

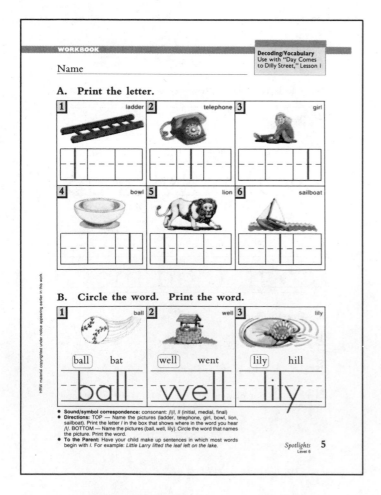

COMPREHENSION/THINKING

Focus

M   Story structure: setting

DIRECT INSTRUCTION Have pupils turn to page 4 in their books and look at the picture. Call on a pupil to describe where the story takes place. (on a city street with apartment buildings as well as houses) Ask the time of day. (early morning) Have pupils look at page 5. Call on a pupil to tell what this picture shows. (people inside a house) Ask if this story shows what is happening now, a long time ago, or sometime in the future. (now)

SAY   When and where a story takes place is called the setting. You can often figure out the setting of a story by looking at the pictures and by reading about what the characters in the story do.

GUIDED PRACTICE Read the following sentences. After each sentence, ask where the characters mentioned in the sentences might be.

1. **Mary and Bob ran across the hot sand into the cool water.** (Mary and Bob are at the beach or seashore.)
2. **The boys and girls put their math books on their desks and began to work.** (The boys and girls are at school.)
3. **Jenny and Billy saw the trained lions and the man walk a tightrope.** (Jenny and Billy are at a circus.)
4. **Tom and Peter took their books up to the desk and gave the man their library cards.** (Tom and Peter are at the library.)

WB 6   INDEPENDENT PRACTICE *Workbook* page 6 may be used to practice identifying setting.

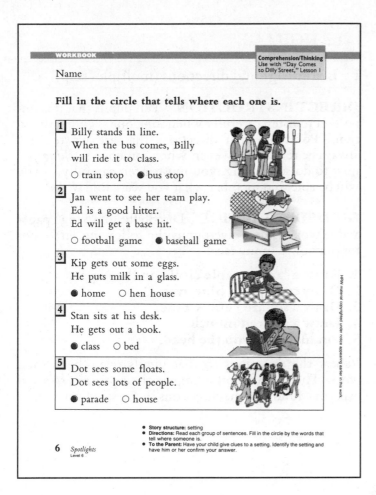

Name

Comprehension/Thinking
Use with "Day Comes
to Dilly Street," Lesson 1

Fill in the circle that tells where each one is.

1 Billy stands in line.
When the bus comes, Billy
will ride it to class.
○ train stop ● bus stop

2 Jan went to see her team play.
Ed is a good hitter.
Ed will get a base hit.
○ football game ● baseball game

3 Kip gets out some eggs.
He puts milk in a glass.
● home ○ hen house

4 Stan sits at his desk.
He gets out a book.
● class ○ bed

5 Dot sees some floats.
Dot sees lots of people.
● parade ○ house

● **Story structure:** setting
● **Directions:** Read each group of sentences. Fill in the circle by the words that tell where someone is.
● **To the Parent:** Have your child give clues to a setting. Identify the setting and have him or her confirm your answer.

6 *Spotlights*
Level 6

PM 3 **ADDITIONAL PRACTICE** *Practice Masters* page 3 may be used as an optional practice for identifying setting. (See page T29 for reduced pages with answers.)

STUDY SKILLS

I Functional reading: signs and symbols (safety)

DIRECT INSTRUCTION Draw a picture of a stop sign and a stoplight on the chalkboard. Point to the stop sign and ask what someone driving a car would do if he or she were to see this sign. (The person would stop.)

Tell pupils that all signs do not have words. A stoplight is one example of a sign without words. A sign without words is a symbol. Point to the stoplight and ask what a stoplight tells us. (It tells us when to stop and go.)

Call on pupils to tell some other kinds of safety signs or symbols they might see on their way to school. (Possible answers include: "Walk" and "Do Not Walk" signs, railroad crossing signs, speed limit signs.)

GUIDED PRACTICE Have pupils open their books to page 6 of "Day Comes to Dilly Street." Call on pupils to point out the signs and symbols illustrated in this story and to tell the meaning of each one. (stop signs, stoplights, crossing guard) Ask pupils to explain how each sign helps to keep people safe from accidents. (Possible answers include: Each of these signs or symbols tells drivers when to stop so that people or other cars may safely cross the street.)

WB 7 **INDEPENDENT PRACTICE** *Workbook* page 7 may be used to practice recognizing signs and symbols.

Name _____

Print a word.

| go | stop |

1 Billy is walking.
He sees this:
It is red.

Billy will **stop**.

2 Billy is walking.
He sees this:
It is green.

Billy will **go**.

3 Candy walks to the end
of the street.
She sees this:

She will **go**.

4 Candy walks to the end
of the street.
She sees this:

She will **stop**.

5 A crossing guard
shows this
to Tom:

Tom will **stop**.

6 A crossing guard
shows this
to cars:

They will **stop**.

- **Functional reading:** signs and symbols
- **Directions:** Read each story. Choose the word from the box that completes the last sentence in each story. Print the word.
- **To the Parent:** Have your child design safety signs for the following: *Do not drive here; Walk, do not run.*

Spotlights **7**
Level 6

LANGUAGE

I Listening: oral directions (multiple–step)

DIRECT INSTRUCTION   Tell pupils that it is important to listen carefully when someone is giving directions. Point out that directions that are written can always be reread. However, when someone is *telling* you how to do something, you must listen carefully so you will be able to remember what you were told to do.

GUIDED PRACTICE Distribute drawing paper and crayons. Then give pupils the following directions for drawing a funny face.

1. **Draw a large purple circle on the paper.**
2. **Draw two round blue eyes.**
3. **Draw a square yellow nose.**
4. **Draw a sad red mouth.**
5. **Put black hair on the head.**

Repeat the directions so that pupils may check their work. Then have pupils compare their pictures to see if everyone followed the directions in the same way.

PM 4 ADDITIONAL PRACTICE   *Practice Masters* page 4 may be used as an optional practice for recognizing signs and symbols. (See page T29 for reduced pages with answers.)

HOW AM I DOING?

Most pupils are filled with creative ideas. Ask yourself the following questions to gauge your teaching effectiveness in this area.

	Yes	No	Some-times
1. Have I encouraged pupils to share their ideas with others?	☐	☐	☐
2. Have I provided a time for pupils to respond to one another's ideas?	☐	☐	☐
3. Have I provided an opportunity for pupils to organize their ideas before asking them to speak before a group?	☐	☐	☐

Reteaching Lesson Skills

The activities that follow provide reteaching of skills developed in this lesson. Not every pupil needs to complete these activities. Choose only the activities that are needed to provide for the individual differences in your classroom.

DECODING/VOCABULARY

I, T **Sound/symbol correspondence:** vowel /ē/y (final)

※ **RETEACH** Write the words *penny* and *hurry* on the chalkboard. Point to the words and read them. Ask what letter is at the end of both words. (*y*)

> **SAY** **The word *penny* has two parts. Listen as I say each part: *pen ny*. Now say *pen ny* with me: *pen ny*. When a word has two parts and the last letter is *y*, the *y* usually stands for the /ē/ sound.**

Follow a similar procedure with *hurry*.

RM 1 Distribute *Reteach Masters* page 1 and explain the directions on the page.

I, T **Vocabulary:** word meaning

※ **RETEACH** Print the following words and sentences on the chalkboard, omitting the underlining.

> **cars   hello   people   neighbors**
>
> 1. My <u>neighbors</u> have a big dog.
> 2. The dog likes to ride in <u>cars</u>.
> 3. It wags its tail at <u>people</u>.
> 4. The dog wags its tail to say <u>hello</u>.
>
> **Billy   Candy   Dilly   hurry   milk
> sunny   toast   Tommy**

Read the first sentence and ask who has a big dog. (my neighbors) Call on a pupil to point to and read the word *neighbors*. Then have the sentence read.

Continue in the same manner with the remaining sentences, calling attention to the underlined words.

Display *Word Cards* for each of the underlined words. Have pupils hold up and read the card that answers each of the following questions:

1. **Which word tells what friendly people say to each other when they meet?** (*hello*)
2. **Which word means "more than one person"?** (*people*)
3. **Which word is another name for people who live near you?** (*neighbors*)
4. **Which word is another name for automobiles?** (*cars*)

RM 2 Distribute *Reteach Masters* page 2 and explain the directions on the page.

Extending Selection Concepts

LANGUAGE ARTS

LISTENING: SAFETY SPEAKER   Invite a crossing guard or traffic officer to discuss with the group the importance of safety signs and symbols.

SOCIAL STUDIES

LISTENING: INFORMATION   Choose a book about safety signs and symbols to share with the class.

Hoban, Tana. *I Read Signs.* Greenwillow, 1983. Photographs effectively introduce signs and symbols frequently seen along the street.
———. *I Read Symbols.* Greenwillow, 1983. This book also shows familiar symbols.

SPEAKING: TELLING ABOUT A PICTURE (Cooperative Learning) Encourage small groups of pupils to discuss the things that might happen in their neighborhoods on a Saturday afternoon. Then have each group work together to produce a large composite picture that shows the activities. Invite each group to show and explain their picture to the class.

WRITING: MAKING A SAFETY BOOK   Invite pupils to draw a safety sign. Help pupils write the meaning of the sign on the page. Collect the pictures and put them together into a book. Display the book where pupils can look at it on their own. Encourage pupils to add pictures to the book as they learn about additional safety signs and symbols.

LITERATURE

LISTENING: FICTION   Choose a story about a neighborhood and read it aloud to the class. Encourage pupils to compare the setting of the story with that of "Day Comes to Dilly Street."

Hasler, Eveline. *Winter Magic.* William Morrow, 1984. Peter's cat takes him out into a snow-covered world to show him the secrets of winter.
McPhail, David. *Farm Morning.* Harcourt Brace Jovanovich, 1985. A father and his daughter share a special morning as they feed the animals.
Paul, Ann Whitman. *Owl at Night.* Putnam, 1985. This book describes the daily ritual of day turning into night and night changing back to day.
Provensen, Alice and Martin. *Town & Country.* Crown, 1984. This book describes life in a big city and on a farm near a village.

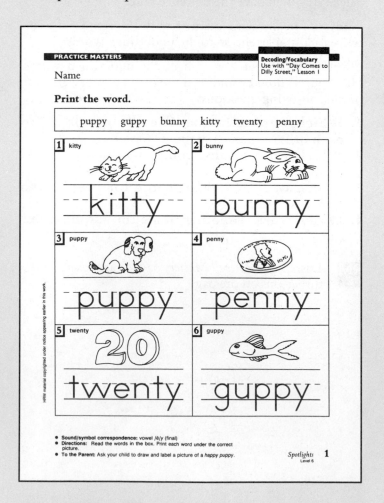

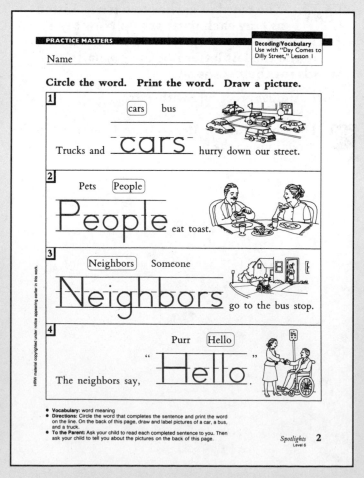

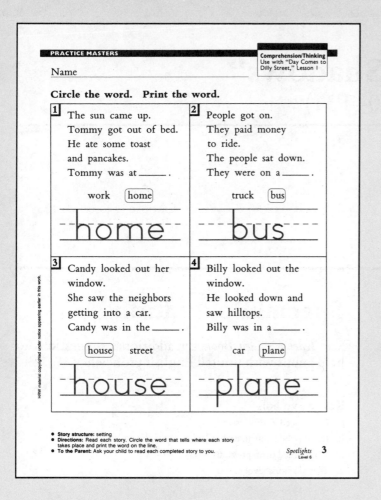

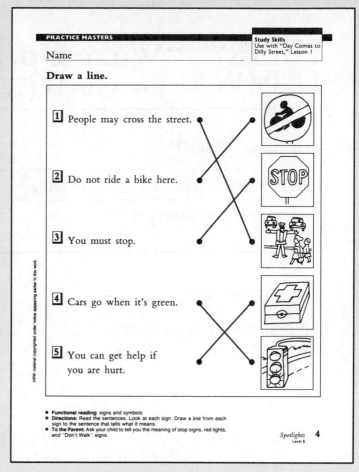

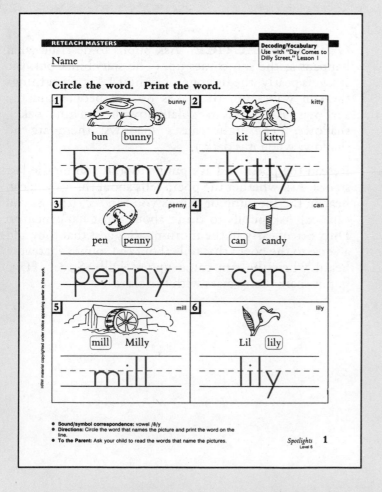

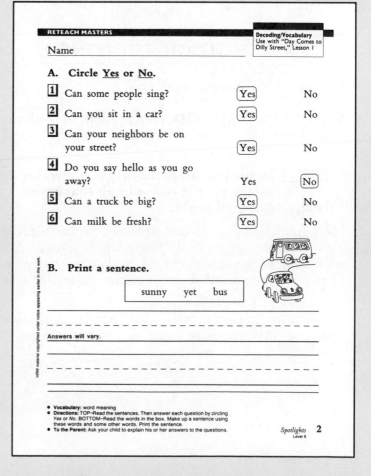

POETRY LESSON
"Wake Up, Shadows"
pages 10–11 (T30–T31)

Skill Strands

> COMPREHENSION/THINKING

I **Forms of literature:** poetry

Materials

Spotlights, Level 6: pages 10–11
Teacher's Idea Book

Special Populations

See *Teacher's Idea Book* for additional suggestions to help pupils with limited English proficiency.

Key to Symbols
I Introduced in this lesson
R Reinforced from an earlier lesson in this level
M Maintained from previous levels
T Tested in this level

> COMPREHENSION/THINKING

I **Forms of literature:** poetry

DIRECT INSTRUCTION Ask pupils to recall the time of day that the story "Day Comes to Dilly Street" took place. (morning)

SAY In the morning, the bright sun wakes up the people and animals that have been sleeping all night.

Have pupils find page 10 in their books. Explain that the poem on this page is called "Wake Up, Shadows." Ask what time of day this poem might describe and why. (The poem might tell about morning because the title says "Wake Up.")

Explain that the poem tells what happens as the sun comes up. Ask pupils to listen as you read the poem aloud.

GUIDED PRACTICE Ask pupils to describe what happens as the sun comes up. (The stars blink out, the sky gets pearly, the light gets brighter.) Ask what things the sun wakes up. (It wakes up the people and the shadows.) Ask pupils to explain how the sun can "wake" shadows. (The light causes shadows; there are no shadows when it is dark.)

Reread the poem and ask pupils to join you on the last stanza. Ask whether the poem tells about things you can hear in the morning or things you can see. (things you can see) Ask pupils to think about what happened on Dilly Street early in the morning. Suggest that they add a verse to the poem that tells about the sounds that were heard when the sun came up on Dilly Street. Have pupils share their verses with the class.

(To be read by the teacher)

Wake Up, Shadows

The stars wink out.
They blink out
one by one.

The sky is pearly
now that night
is done.

The lights get bold,
grows gold—
here comes the sun!

Wake up, people.
Wake up, shadows.
Day's begun.

Lilian Moore

10

11

SKILLS LESSON

"Pesty!"
pages 12–13 (T32–T33)

Skill Strands

DECODING/VOCABULARY

R, T   **Sound/symbol correspondence:** vowel /ē/y (final)

R   **Word structure:** suffix -y

Materials

Spotlights, Level 6: pages 12–13

Resource Box: Word Cards candy, funny, happy, hurry muddy, rainy, sunny

Teacher's Idea Book

Special Populations

See *Teacher's Idea Book* for additional suggestions to help pupils with limited English proficiency.

Key to Symbols

I   Introduced in this lesson

R   Reinforced from an earlier lesson in this level

M   Maintained from previous levels

T   Tested in this level

DECODING/VOCABULARY

R, T   **Sound/symbol correspondence:** vowel /ē/y (final)

R   **Word structure:** suffix -y

DIRECT INSTRUCTION   Place *Word Card happy* in the *Pocket Chart* and have the word read. Ask what letter stands for the /ē/ sound at the end of *happy*. (*y*) Have pupils say the word *happy* with you as you clap the parts. Point out that the word *happy* has two parts, or syllables. Explain that when the letter *y* is at the end of a word that has two parts, the letter *y* stands for the /ē/ sound.

Tell pupils that you will hold up some *Word Cards* and will call on one of them to read each word and to make up a sentence with the word. Hold up the *Word Cards funny, sunny, hurry, candy, muddy, rainy* one at a time.

GUIDED PRACTICE   Have pupils find page 12 in their books. Call on a pupil to read the title of the story. Ask what letter stands for the /ē/ sound at the end of *Pesty*. (letter *y*) Have pages 12 and 13 read aloud. Call on pupils to tell what words in the story end with the letter *y* that stands for /ē/. (*Renny, rainy, Shaggy, Milly, muddy, dirty, Pesty, funny*)

Call on pupils to answer each of the following questions with a word from the story that ends with the /ē/ sound.

1. **What are two girls' names?** (*Milly, Renny*)
2. **Which word tells about the weather?** (*rainy*)
3. **What is the opposite of *clean*?** (*dirty*)
4. **What is the dog's name?** (*Shaggy*)
5. **Which word means "a lot of fun"?** (*funny*)
6. **What name might you call a pet that is a pest?** (*Pesty*)
7. **Which word means "full of mud"?** (*muddy*)

Pesty!

Read the sentences.
Tell the story.

"We'll have to <u>play</u> <u>inside</u>,"
said <u>Renny</u>.
"Look at that <u>rain</u>.
What a rainy day!"

"Here comes <u>Shaggy</u>," said <u>Milly</u>.
"My dog was playing
in the <u>mud</u> again.
Look at how muddy he is."

12

"Down, boy!" said Renny.
"You'll get dirt on my <u>slacks</u>.
I don't want dirty slacks."

Milly grinned at Shaggy.
"You can be a <u>real</u> pest!" she said.
"Maybe we will <u>name</u> you Pesty."

"I like your dog," said Renny.
"He's lots of fun.
I wish I had a funny dog."

13

LESSON 2 "Minx and Jinx"
pages 14–21 (T34–T55)

Skill Strands

DECODING/VOCABULARY

I, T **Sound/symbol correspondence:** consonant /j/*j* (initial)

M **Sound/symbol correspondence:** vowel /ā/*a-e*

M **Accumulated elements:** consonant clusters *sw, tw* (initial)

I **Vocabulary:** word building

I, T **Vocabulary:** word meaning

COMPREHENSION/THINKING

Focus
I, T **Inferential:** predicting outcomes

STUDY SKILLS

I, T **References:** dictionary (entry words and definitions)

LANGUAGE

I **Conventions of language:** capitalization

Lesson Vocabulary

Decodable words: *anyone, dish, drink, Dusty, every, everywhere, gray, Jack, jeep, Jet, jump, just, lap, mail, mother, nodded, problem, Tabby, twin, weeks*

Special words: *Jinx, Minx, surprise, Their*

Materials

Snapshots, Level 6: pages 14–21
Workbook: pages 8–13

Practice Masters: pages 5–9
Instructional Charts: pages 5–11
Resource Box: Letter Cards a, c, e (2), g, j, J, m, n, p, s, t, u
    Word Cards Jack, jeep, jet, Jinx, jump, just, Minx, surprise, sweep, swift, swim, swing, their, tweet, twig, twin, twist

Pocket Chart
Teacher's Idea Book
Reteach Masters: pages 3–4

Language Applications

USING LANGUAGE

Oral reading: answering questions
Speaking: role playing

EXTENDING SELECTION CONCEPTS

Writing: making a poster (Cooperative Learning)
Listening: poetry
Listening: fiction
Listening: information

Special Populations

See the *Teacher's Idea Book* for additional suggestions to help pupils with limited English proficiency.

Key to Symbols
I Introduced in this lesson
R Reinforced from an earlier lesson in this level
M Maintained from previous levels
T Tested in this level

Idea Center

BIBLIOGRAPHY

Add to your reading corner or reading table various books about cats. A suggested bibliography follows. Suggestions for reading aloud and annotations appear in the lesson plan.

Corbin, William. *The Everywhere Cat.* Coward, McCann & Geoghegan, 1970.

Hurd, Edith Thacher. *Catfish and the Kidnapped Cat.* Harper & Row, 1974.

Keats, Ezra Jack. *Pet Show!* Macmillan, 1972.

Selsam, Millicent E. *How Kittens Grow.* Four Winds Press, 1973.

Stein, Sara Bonnett. *Cat.* Harcourt Brace Jovanovich, 1985.

Wheeler, Cindy. *Marmalade's Christmas Present.* Alfred A. Knopf, 1984.

Planning Chart

		Instruction	Written Practice	Extending
Step 1 Preparing for the Selection	I, T	**Sound/symbol correspondence:** consonant /j/*j* (initial)	*Workbook* page 8 *Practice Masters* page 5 *Reteach Masters* page 3	
	I	**Vocabulary:** word building		
	I, T	**Vocabulary:** word meaning	*Workbook* page 9 *Practice Masters* page 6 *Reteach Masters* page 4	**Writing:** making a poster (Cooperative Learning)
	I, T	**Inferential:** predicting outcomes		
Step 2 Reading for Comprehension		**Oral reading:** answering questions		**Listening:** information
		Speaking: role playing		
		Inferential: predicting outcomes		
		Story comprehension	*Workbook* page 10	
Step 3 Developing Reading and Thinking Skills	M	**Sound/symbol correspondence:** vowel /ā/*a-e*		**Listening:** poetry
	M	**Accumulated elements:** consonant clusters *sw, tw* (initial)		
	I, T	**Inferential:** predicting outcomes	*Workbook* page 11 *Practice Masters* page 7	
	I, T	**References:** dictionary (entry words and definitions)	*Workbook* page 12 *Practice Masters* page 8	**Listening:** fiction
	I	**Conventions of language:** capitalization	*Workbook* page 13 *Practice Masters* page 9	

DECODING/VOCABULARY

I, T   Sound/symbol correspondence: consonant /j/j (initial)

DIRECT INSTRUCTION Tell pupils that you will say a tongue twister and then you will ask them to repeat it.

> **SAY** **Jill juggles jam and jelly.**

Have pupils repeat the sentence with you. Then ask what Jill juggles. (jam and jelly) Hold up *Letter Card j.*

> **SAY** **This is letter *j*. The word *jam* begins with letter *j*. Letter *j* stands for the /j/ sound. Say *jam* with me: *jam*. Now say *jelly*: *jelly*. Does the word *jelly* begin with the /j/ sound? (yes) What letter stands for the beginning sound in *jelly*? (*j*)**

Place *Letter Card j* and *Letter Card J* in the *Pocket Chart.* Point to capital *J*.

> **SAY** **This is capital *J*. Capital *J* stands for the /j/ sound in names such as *Jack* and *Jill*.**

GUIDED PRACTICE Print the following tongue twisters on the chalkboard, omitting the underlining.

> 1. Jenny's jelly jiggles.
> 2. Jimmy's jam jumps.
> 3. Jam and jelly jump and jiggle.

Have each sentence read. Have the words beginning with *j* underlined and read again. Then invite pupils to read all three sentences as quickly as they can.

WB 8 INDEPENDENT PRACTICE *Workbook* page 8 may be used to practice identifying sound/symbol correspondence /j/j.

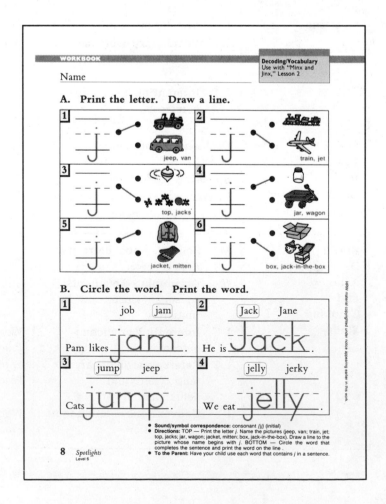

✻ **RETEACH** For those pupils who need additional instruction, see "Reteaching Lesson Skills," page T51, under "Reteaching and Extending."

I Vocabulary: word building

DIRECT INSTRUCTION Use *Letter Cards* to make the word *jump* in the *Pocket Chart* and have the word read. Ask what sound the letter *j* stands for at the beginning of *jump*. (/j/) Take out the *j* and replace it with *st*. Have the new word read. (*stump*)

GUIDED PRACTICE Display *Letter Cards a, e, e, g, j,* and *t.* Tell pupils that you will call on them to use the cards to make new words in the *Pocket Chart.*

1. **Take the *mp* out of *stump*. Put the *st* after the *u* and put *j* at the beginning. What word did you make?** (*just*)
2. **Take out the *st* and put *g* at the end. What word did you make?** (*jug*)
3. **Take out the *ug* and replace it with *et*. What word did you make?** (*jet*)
4. **Take out the *j* and replace it with *m*. What word did you make?** (*met*)
5. **Take out the *m* and put back the *j*. What word did you make?** (*jet*)
6. **Take out the *et* and replace it with *am*. What word did you make?** (*jam*)
7. **Replace the *a* with *u*. Put *p* at the end. What word did you make?** (*jump*)
8. **Take out the *um* and replace it with *ee*. What word did you make?** (*jeep*)

I, T Vocabulary: word meaning

DIRECT INSTRUCTION Print the following words and sentences on the chalkboard, omitting the underlining.

Jinx   Minx   surprise   Their
1. Our neighbors had a <u>surprise</u>.
2. <u>Their</u> cat had kittens.
3. <u>Jinx</u> is the tan kitten.
4. <u>Minx</u> is the black kitten.
Jack   jeep   Jet   jump   just   twin

Tell pupils that they are going to talk about some words they will read in the next story.

Read the first sentence. Point to the word *surprise* and read it. Ask who had a surprise. (our neighbors) Have pupils read the sentence with you. Then ask them to find and read the word *surprise.*

Read Sentence 2. Point to the word *Their* and read it. Ask whose cat had kittens. (the neighbor's) Ask what word in the second sentence means "the neighbor's." (*Their*) Have pupils read the sentence with you. Then ask them to find and read the word *Their.*

Read Sentence 3. Point to the word *Jinx* and read it. Ask pupils what the tan kitten was named. (*Jinx*) Explain that *Jinx* is a name. Have pupils read the sentence with you. Then have them point to the word *Jinx* and read it.

Read Sentence 4. Point to the word *Minx* and read it. Ask which kitten was named *Minx*. (the black one) Have pupils read the sentence with you. Then have them point to the word *Minx* and read it.

The words in the second set are new words that contain known phonic elements. You may wish to ask pupils to read the words, using what they know about letters and sounds.

GUIDED PRACTICE Print the following sentences on the chalkboard, omitting the underlining.

> 1. <u>Jack</u> <u>just</u> put the kittens in the <u>jeep</u>.
> 2. He nodded when his <u>twin</u> asked if he could go along.
> 3. <u>Their</u> kittens were a <u>surprise</u> for the neighbors.
> 4. <u>Minx</u>, <u>Jinx</u>, and <u>Jet</u> go <u>everywhere</u> with Jack.
> 5. They <u>jump</u> and play all day.

Provide opportunities for pupils to practice reading the new special words and some of the new decodable words by following the suggestions below.

Sentence 1: Have the sentence read. Ask where Jack put the kittens. (in the jeep) Explain that a jeep is like a small car. Have pupils find and read the words *jeep* and *just*.

Sentence 2: Ask who wanted to go along with Jack. (Jack's twin) Tell pupils that twins are children born on the same day in the same family. Ask why Jack nodded. (to let his twin know he could go along)

Sentence 3: Have the sentence read. Ask if the neighbors knew the kittens were coming. (No, they were a surprise.) Have pupils find and read the words *surprise* and *their*.

Sentence 4: Call on a pupil to read the sentence. Then ask if Jack takes the kittens to a lot of places. (Yes, he takes them everywhere.) Have pupils find and read the word *everywhere*.

Sentence 5: Have the sentence read. Then ask what the kittens do. (They jump and play all day.) Have pupils find and read the word *jump*.

Invite pupils to select a sentence to read aloud. Ask pupils to point to and read the words that begin with *j*. (*Jack, just, jeep, Jinx, jet, jumped*)

WB 9 **INDEPENDENT PRACTICE** *Workbook* page 9 may be used to practice reading story vocabulary.

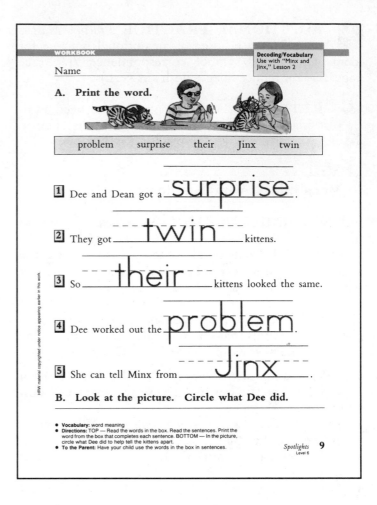

ADDITIONAL PRACTICE *Practice Masters* page 6 may be used as an optional practice for reading story vocabulary. (See page T54 for reduced pages with answers.)

RETEACH For those pupils who need additional instruction, see "Reteaching Lesson Skills," page T51, under "Reteaching and Extending."

COMPREHENSION/THINKING

Focus

I, T   Inferential: predicting outcomes

DIRECT INSTRUCTION Read the following story and ask pupils to tell what they think will happen.

READ Jan's dog liked to chase things. It ran after balls, rabbits, and flying leaves. One day, Jan put the dog out in the backyard. A squirrel was running along the back fence.

ASK What do you think the dog will do? (The dog will chase the squirrel.) What clues in the story make you think this will happen? (The story says that the dog liked to chase things.)

GUIDED PRACTICE Print the following story on the chalkboard. Have pupils read the story and predict what may happen next.

> Jake's cat was missing.
> Jake looked and looked for her.
> Then Jake peeked in a basket
> under the steps.
> There was his cat!
> She had three little surprises for Jake.

Ask what surprises the cat may have had for Jake. (kittens) Ask why pupils think this. (The story said that she had three little surprises.)

Point out that pupils used the information in the story and what they already knew to make a prediction.

Background for the Teacher

SUMMARY Jack's cat has kittens. Jack has fun watching the kittens grow. He is sad when his mother tells him that they must find homes for the kittens.

INFORMATION This is a realistic story about a boy, his pet cat, and the problems that arise as kittens grow and change.

Using Prior Knowledge

Ask if any pupils have cats at home and invite these pupils to tell some things that their cats like to do. Ask if any pupils have seen newborn kittens, puppies, or other animals. Develop a discussion by asking the questions that follow:

1. **When kittens or puppies are just born, can you play with them?** (No, they are too little.)
2. **Who takes care of the new kittens or puppies?** (The mother takes care of her babies.)
3. **What would you do if you had to find homes for kittens or puppies?** (Possible answers include: ask your friends if they want one; put an ad in the paper; ask people in the neighborhood.)

Setting a Purpose for Reading

Have pupils turn to page 14 in their books and look at the pictures. Tell pupils that the title of this story is "Minx and Jinx." Ask who Jinx and Minx are. (Answers will vary.)

Point out the headnote at the top of page 14 and call on a pupil to read it aloud. Then ask what Jack's problem might be.

Reading Silently

Some pupils may be able to read this story independently. Direct them to read the whole story to find out more about what Jack's problem might be. For those pupils who need more guidance, suggestions for directed reading follow.

Neighbors can help when someone has a problem.
In this story, Jack has a problem.
Read to find out what he must do.

Minx and Jinx

"I have a surprise for you,"
said Jack's mother.

"A surprise for me?" asked Jack.
"I know!
I sent away for a little jeep
with some box tops.
Did the jeep come in the mail?"

14

"This surprise didn't come
in the mail," said Jack's mother.
"Come and see."

"Tabby had kittens!" Jack said.
"Look how little they are.
Hooray for my cat!"

15

Before reading pages 14–15 **SAY** **Jack's mother had a surprise for him. What do you think it may be? Read pages 14 and 15 to yourself.**

After reading pages 14–15 1. **What did Jack guess the surprise might be?** (a little jeep) Literal
2. **What was the surprise?** (Jack's cat had kittens.) Literal

One kitten was all gray.
"I'll name that one Dusty,"
said Jack.
One kitten was all black.
"That one will be Jet," said Jack.

The other two kittens looked
just like Tabby, their mother.
"I'll name them Minx and Jinx,"
Jack said.
"Twin names for twin kittens."

16

Every day, Jack came to look
at the kittens.
At first, all they did was sleep
or eat.

"I wish they would do something
that is fun," he said.
"Kittens take too long to grow."

17

Before reading pages 16–17

SAY **Jack couldn't wait to play with the kittens. Do you think he will play with them right away? Read pages 16 and 17.**

After reading pages 16–17

1. **Did Jack play with the kittens right away?** (no) **Why not?** (At first, all the kittens did was sleep and eat.) Inferential
2. **What was the first thing Jack did for each kitten?** (He gave each kitten a name.) Inferential
3. **What did Jack want the kittens to do?** (He wanted them to grow so they would do something fun.) Inferential

Then one day, the kittens sat up
and looked at Jack.
"Hello, Dusty!
Hello, Jet!
Hello, Minx and Jinx!
I'm Jack," he said.

18

The kittens grew and grew.
They could <u>drink</u> milk from a <u>dish</u>.
They could run after a ball.
They could <u>jump</u> into Jack's <u>lap</u>.

The kittens followed Jack
<u>everywhere</u> he went.
What fun they were!

19

Before reading pages 18–19

SAY **What do you think the kittens will do as they grow? Read pages 18 and 19 to see.**

After reading pages 18–19

1. **What did the kittens learn to do as they grew bigger?** (They could drink from a dish; they could run after a ball; they could jump into Jack's lap.) Literal
2. **Do you think the kittens liked Jack? How can you tell?** (The kittens liked Jack because they followed him everywhere he went.) Inferential

The <u>weeks</u> passed.

One day, Jack's mother was waiting for him when he got off the bus.

"Jack, the kittens are getting too big for us to keep," she said.

"We'll have to find other homes for them."

20

Jack <u>nodded</u>.

"I'll ask my friends if <u>anyone</u> wants a kitten," he said.

"I'll find good homes for them."

Discussing the Selection

1. What must Jack do?
2. Why did Jack's mother think that the kittens were too big to keep?
3. Why will Jack ask his friends to help?
4. When did you find out what Jack's problem was?
5. How would you feel if you were Jack?

21

Before reading pages 20–21

SAY At the beginning of the story, we were told that Jack had a problem. What do you think his problem might be? Read pages 20 and 21 to yourself.

After reading pages 20–21

1. **What was Jack's problem?** (The kittens were getting too big to keep; he had to find other homes for them.) Inferential
2. **Why was this a problem for Jack?** (He loved the kittens and probably wanted to keep them.) Inferential
3. **Why didn't Jack beg his mother to let him keep the kittens?** (Possible answers include: Jack knew it would be too much trouble to have five cats as pets.) Critical

Discussing the Selection

PURPOSE

1. **What must Jack do?** (find homes for the kittens) Literal

STORY MAPPING

2. **Why did Jack's mother think that the kittens were too big to keep?** (Possible answers include: They were getting big enough to take care of themselves; they were old enough to leave their mother.) Critical

- **Why did Jack have to wait to play with the kittens until they got older?** (At first, they needed lots of sleep and only got up to eat.) Inferential

3. **Why will Jack ask his friends to help?** (Possible answers include: Jack's friends may want the kittens; they may know people who want the kittens.) Critical

- **How did Jack know the kittens were ready to play with him?** (They sat up and looked at him.) Inferential

4. **When did you find out what Jack's problem was?** (at the end of the story) Inferential

CRITICAL THINKING

5. **How would you feel if you were Jack?** (Answers will vary. Possible answers include: upset because he had to give away his kittens.)

Using Language

ORAL READING: ANSWERING QUESTIONS

Have pupils answer the following questions by reading sentences from the story.

Page 14: **What did Jack think the surprise might be? Read what Jack said.** ("I know! I sent away for a little jeep with some box tops. Did the jeep come in the mail?")

Page 15: **What was Jack's surprise? Read the sentences that tell what the surprise was.** ("Tabby had kittens!" Jack said. "Look how little they are. Hooray for my cat!")

Page 16: **Why did Jack name two kittens Minx and Jinx? Read the sentences that tell why.** ("I'll name them Minx and Jinx," Jack said. "Twin names for twin kittens.")

Page 17: **What did the kittens do at first?** (At first, all they did was sleep or eat.) **How did Jack feel about this? Read the sentences that tell how Jack felt.** ("I wish they would do something that is fun," he said. "Kittens take too long to grow.")

Page 19: **Read the sentences that tell what the kittens could do when they got bigger.** (They could drink milk from a dish. They could run after a ball. They could jump into Jack's lap. The kittens followed Jack everywhere he went.)

Page 20: **What was the bad news that Jack's mother told him?** ("Jack, the kittens are getting too big for us to keep," she said. "We'll have to find other homes for them.")

Page 21: **What did Jack promise to do?** ("I'll ask my friends if anyone wants a kitten," he said. "I'll find good homes for them.")

SPEAKING: ROLE PLAYING Invite pupils to pretend to be Jack and one of his friends. Have the pupils act out what Jack and his friend might have said to one another when Jack asked the friend to take a kitten.

Applying the Focus Skill

INFERENTIAL: PREDICTING OUTCOMES
Remind pupils that when they guess what might happen, they are making a prediction. Tell them that they can often use the information in a story to make a prediction about what will happen.

Ask pupils to predict whether Jack will be able to find homes for the kittens. (Answers will vary.)

Evaluating Comprehension

WB 10   **INDEPENDENT PRACTICE**   *Workbook* page 10 may be used for an informal evaluation of story comprehension.

WORKBOOK

Comprehension/Thinking
Use with "Minx and Jinx," Lesson 2

Name _____

Fill in the circle.

1
  ○ Jack's surprise was a little jeep.
  ● Jack's surprise was Tabby's new kittens.

2
  ● One kitten was black, and one kitten was gray.
  ○ All the kittens were black.

3
  ● Minx and Jinx looked just the same.
  ○ Minx and Jinx were twin boys.

4
  ○ The kittens never grew.
  ● The kittens grew and grew.

5
  ● Jack had to find homes for the kittens.
  ○ Jack was going to keep the kittens.

6
  ○ Jack was happy to give away the kittens.
  ● Jack was sad to give away the kittens.

● **Story comprehension:** "Minx and Jinx"
● **Directions:** Read the sentences. Fill in the circles by the sentences that tell about the story "Minx and Jinx."
● **To the Parent:** Have your child retell the story.

10   *Spotlights*
Level 6

3 DEVELOPING READING AND THINKING SKILLS

DECODING/VOCABULARY

M   Sound/symbol correspondence: vowel /ā/a-e

DIRECT INSTRUCTION Use *Letter Cards* to make the word *tap* in the *Pocket Chart* and have the word read. Ask what sound the letter *a* stands for in *tap.* (/a/) Place *Letter Card e* at the end of the word and have the new word read. (*tape*) Ask what sound the *a* stands for in *tape.* (/ā/, long *a*) Ask why *a* stands for /ā/ in *tape.* (because the word *tape* has an *a,* followed by a consonant, and ends with letter *e*)

Follow a similar procedure with the words *can* and *cane.*

GUIDED PRACTICE Print the following sentences on the chalkboard, omitting the underlining.

> 1. Jane will be in the game with Fran.
> 2. I will bake a cake for lunch.
> 3. Jake can swing on the gate.
> 4. Kate can take a plate.

Call on pupils to read each sentence. Then have pupils find and read the words in which letter *a* stands for the /ā/ sound.

M   Accumulated elements: consonant clusters *sw, tw* (initial)

> **Note:** Direct instruction of a blending strategy teaches pupils how to blend sounds into words. As phonic elements in this program accumulate, attention is focused on phonograms and consonant clusters. Pupils have previously been introduced to the individual letters and sounds that make up these accumulated elements.

DIRECT INSTRUCTION Place *Word Card twin* under *Word Card twist* in the *Pocket Chart* and have the words read. Ask what two letters are at the beginning of the word *twist.* (*tw*) Ask what two letters are at the beginning of the word *twin.* (*tw*) Remind pupils that the letters *tw* make up a consonant cluster because the letters are together and are consonants.

Place *Word Card swim* under *Word Card swing* in the *Pocket Chart* and have the words read. Ask pupils to tell what two letters make up the consonant cluster at the beginning of each word. (*sw*)

GUIDED PRACTICE Tell pupils that you will hold up some words that begin with the consonant clusters *sw* and *tw.* Call on a pupil to read each word and to name the two letters that make up the consonant cluster at the beginning of the word. Hold up *Word Cards sweep, twig, swift, twist, twin, swing, tweet.*

COMPREHENSION/THINKING

Focus

I, T **Inferential:** predicting outcomes

DIRECT INSTRUCTION Remind pupils that when they read a story, they may try to guess what is going to happen. When they guess what might happen, they are making a prediction.

Read the following story and have pupils predict what may happen.

> **READ** Jerry knocked on the door. When Mrs. Smith opened the door, Jerry said, "This little kitten is named Princess. Mom says I have to find her a good home. Would you like to have a kitten?"
>
> "Princess is a lovely kitten," said Mrs. Smith. "She is such a pretty color, and her fur is nice and soft. I love to watch kittens play."

> **ASK** What do you think will happen next? (Mrs. Smith will take the kitten.) **Why do you predict that she will take the kitten?** (She thinks it is a pretty kitten, and she loves to watch kittens play.)

GUIDED PRACTICE Print the following story on the chalkboard and ask pupils to read it.

> Penny liked to run.
> Every day she would put on her running shoes.
> Then she would go for a long run.
> One day, Jimmy said, "I can run faster than anyone."
> "I will run with you," said Penny.

Ask pupils to predict what will happen when Penny and Jimmy race. (Penny will win.) Ask why they think this will happen. (Penny will probably win because she runs every day.)

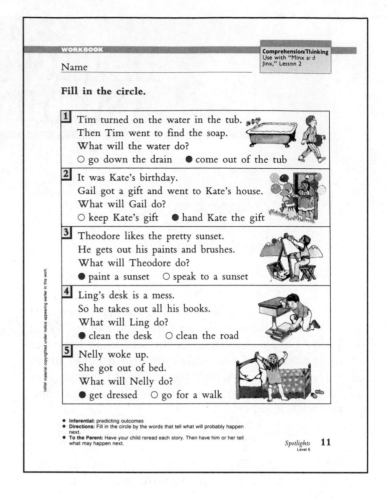

INDEPENDENT PRACTICE *Workbook* page 11 may be used to practice predicting outcomes.

ADDITIONAL PRACTICE *Practice Masters* page 7 may be used as an optional practice for predicting outcomes. (See page T54 for reduced pages with answers.)

RETEACH For those pupils who need additional instruction, see "Reteaching Lesson Skills," page T52, under "Reteaching and Extending."

STUDY SKILLS

I, T   References: dictionary (entry words and definitions)

DIRECT INSTRUCTION Print the following on the chalkboard:

> Jack sent for a jeep.
>
> **jeep**   an open car
> **pit 1**   a deep hole   **2** a
> seed, like in a plum
>
> muffin
> jug
> bundle

Have the sentence read.

SAY **Suppose that you did not know what a jeep was. Where could you look to find out the meaning of the word *jeep*?** (in a dictionary)

Display a dictionary and tell pupils that a dictionary contains words and their meanings.

SAY **The words in a dictionary are listed in alphabetical order. What is the first letter of the word *jeep*?** (*j*) **To find the word *jeep*, you would look in the dictionary where the words that begin with *j* are located.**

Direct pupils' attention to the definition for *jeep* on the chalkboard. Explain that this is the way the word *jeep* might be listed in a dictionary. Point to the word *jeep*.

SAY **First, you will find the word you are looking for. After the word, you will find the definition. A definition tells you what a word means. The definition for *jeep* is "an open car."**

Call attention to the word *pit* and ask how many definitions are given for the word. (two) Have both definitions read. Then ask pupils to tell the meaning of *pit* in the sentence *I threw away the cherry pit.* ("a seed, like in a plum")

GUIDED PRACTICE Direct pupils' attention to the words on the chalkboard.

Remind pupils that words in a dictionary are listed in alphabetical order. Ask which word would come first in a dictionary and why. (*bundle*, because it begins with a *b* which comes before *j* and *m* in the alphabet) Ask which word would come next. (*jug*) Ask which word would come last. (*muffin*)

Demonstate how to find the words in a dictionary and read the definitions aloud.

WB 12 **INDEPENDENT PRACTICE** *Workbook* page 12 may be used to practice using a dictionary.

PM 8 **ADDITIONAL PRACTICE** *Practice Masters* page 8 may be used as an optional practice for using a dictionary. (See page T54 for reduced pages with answers.)

✳ **RETEACH** For those pupils who need additional instruction, see "Reteaching Lesson Skills," page T52, under "Reteaching and Extending."

WORKBOOK

Study Skills
Use with "Minx and Jinx," Lesson 2

Name _____

Read the sentences.   Print the number.

> **dust 1** little specks of dirt
>   **2** to clean by brushing off dirt
> **guard 1** someone who looks
>   after things   **2** to look after
>   a thing
> **pit 1** a deep hole   **2** a seed, like
>   in a plum

1. The lion fell into the deep pit.   1
2. The dogs will guard the house.   2
3. Gail got a rag to dust the books.   2
4. The worktable had dust on it.   1
5. Cherries have pits in them.   2
6. The guard looks after the money.   1

• **References:** dictionary
• **Directions:** Read the words and the definitions. Read each sentence. Print the number that shows the meaning of each underlined word.
• **To the Parent:** Have your child use each meaning for the listed words in sentences.

12   *Spotlights*
Level 6

Lesson 2 "Minx and Jinx" (pages 14–21)   T49

I Conventions of language: capitalization

DIRECT INSTRUCTION Print the following sentences on the chalkboard.

 IC 11

> 1. Dusty is gray.
> 2. Jet is black.
> 3. Jinx and Minx are tan.
>
> 4. jack's cat tabby had kittens.
> 5. pam and jenny came to see the kittens.
> 6. "The black kitten is jet," said jack.

Have the first three sentences read aloud. Ask what Dusty, Jet, Jinx, and Minx are. (They are the names of kittens from the story.) Ask how pupils know that the words *Dusty, Jet, Jinx,* and *Minx* are names. (They each begin with a capital letter.)

GUIDED PRACTICE Direct pupils' attention to Sentences 4–6 on the chalkboard. Call on a pupil to read each sentence aloud. Then have pupils tell which words in the sentence are names. Have pupils point to each name and tell what needs to be done to make the name correct. (Each name should begin with a capital letter.)

WB 13 **INDEPENDENT PRACTICE** *Workbook* page 13 may be used to practice capitalizing names.

PM 9 **ADDITIONAL PRACTICE** *Practice Masters* page 9 may be used as an optional practice for capitalizing names. (See page T55 for reduced pages with answers.)

✳ RETEACHING AND EXTENDING

Reteaching Lesson Skills

The activities that follow provide reteaching of skills developed in this lesson. Not every pupil needs to complete these activities. Choose only the activities that are needed to provide for the individual differences in your classroom.

DECODING/VOCABULARY

I, T Sound/symbol correspondence: consonant /j/*j* (initial)

✳ **RETEACH** Hold up *Letter Card j.*

> **SAY** **This is letter *j*. Letter *j* stands for the /j/ sound at the beginning of *jar*. Say *jar* with me: *jar*. Say *jump*: *jump*. Does *jump* begin with the same sound as *jar*? (yes) What letter stands for the beginning sound in *jump*? (*j*)**

Place *Word Cards jump, just, jeep, jet, Jack* in the *Pocket Chart*. Point to each word and ask a pupil to read it.

 Distribute *Reteach Masters* page 3 and explain the directions on the page.

I, T Vocabulary: word meaning

✳ **RETEACH** Print the following words and sentences on the chalkboard, omitting the underlining.

Jinx Minx surprise Their
1. Our neighbors had a <u>surprise</u>.
2. <u>Their</u> cat had kittens.
3. <u>Jinx</u> is the tan kitten.
4. <u>Minx</u> is the black kitten.
Jack jeep Jet jump just twin

Point to the first sentence and have it read. Ask what the neighbors had. (a surprise) Call on pupils to point to and read the word *surprise*. Continue in the same manner with the remaining sentences, calling attention to the underlined words.

Display the *Word Cards* for each of the underlined words. Have pupils hold up and read the word that answers each of the following questions:

1. **Which word means "something that belongs to them"?** (*Their*)
2. **Which words are names?** (*Jinx, Minx*) **How can you tell that these words are names?** (They begin with capital letters.)
3. **Which word means "something that was not expected"?** (*surprise*)

Ask pupils to read the second set of words and to use them in sentences.

 Distribute *Reteach Masters* page 4 and explain the directions on the page.

Focus

I, T Inferential: predicting outcomes

✳ **RETEACH**   Read the following story and ask pupils to predict what might happen.

READ **James put some popcorn in the pan. It did not look like much corn, so he added more. Then he put in more, just to be sure there was enough. Soon the corn began to pop.**

ASK **What do you think will happen?** (Possible answers include: The popcorn will pop out of the pan because James put in too much.) **Why do you think this will happen?** (The story said that he added more and more corn.) **What do you know about popcorn that helped you make the prediction?** (Possible answers include: If there is too much popcorn in the pan, it will push up the lid and pop out.)

Point out that pupils used the information in the story and what they knew about popcorn to make a prediction.

I, T References: dictionary (entry words and definitions)

✳ **RETEACH** Print the following dictionary entry and definition on the chalkboard:

IC 10

shoemaker	someone who makes shoes

SAY **This is what you might find if you were to look up the word** *shoemaker* **in a dictionary.**

Call on a pupil to read the definition of *shoemaker* and to use the word in a sentence.

Then help pupils locate the following words and their meanings in a dictionary: *cat, home, friend, neighbor.*

HOW AM I DOING?

Many pupils need encouragement to do independent reading. Ask yourself the following questions to gauge your teaching effectiveness in this area.

	Yes	No	Some-times
1. Have I taken pupils to the library?	☐	☐	☐
2. Have I provided time for independent silent reading?	☐	☐	☐
3. Have I encouraged and praised children for their independent reading efforts?	☐	☐	☐
4. Have I suggested guidance for reading at home such as finding a special time and place to read?	☐	☐	☐

Extending Selection Concepts

WRITING: MAKING A POSTER (Cooperative Learning) Ask what Jack's mother told him to do at the end of the story. (She told him to find homes for his kittens.) Explain that one way to find homes for kittens might be to make a poster and put it where people will see it. Have small groups of pupils discuss what they might want people to know about the kittens. Ask a member of the group to list the things the group might want to say on a poster. Then provide each group with a large piece of paper and have the group make a poster to advertise Jack's kittens. Invite each group to share its poster with the class.

LITERATURE

LISTENING: POETRY Tell pupils that Jack's friends might want one of Jack's kittens. Explain that you will read a poem about choosing a kitten. Read aloud "Choosing a Kitten."

Choosing a Kitten

A black-nosed kitten will slumber all day;
A white-nosed kitten is ever glad to play;
A yellow-nosed kitten will answer to your call;
And a gray-nosed kitten I like best of all.

Anonymous

Have pupils tell what kind of kitten they would choose and why.

LISTENING: FICTION Choose a story about cats or kittens and read it aloud to the class.

Corbin, William. *The Everywhere Cat.* Coward, McCann & Geoghegan, 1970. This book shows all the places where you might find a cat.

Hurd, Edith Thacher. *Catfish and the Kidnapped Cat.* Harper & Row, 1974. Catfish, the cat, comes to the rescue of a kidnapped cat and earns a big reward.

Keats, Ezra Jack. *Pet Show!* Macmillan, 1972. Archie needs a pet to bring to school for the pet show. He goes out looking for his cat and when he can't find it, he brings a very unusual pet to school.

Wheeler, Cindy. *Marmalade's Christmas Present.* Alfred A. Knopf, 1984. Marmalade, the orange cat, receives a kitten as a Christmas present. This story tells how Marmalade learns to accept the interloper.

SCIENCE

LISTENING: INFORMATION Choose an informational book about cats to read to the class.

Selsam, Millicent E. *How Kittens Grow.* Four Winds Press, 1973. A photographic essay describing four kittens' first eight weeks of life.

Stein, Sara Bonnett. *Cat.* Harcourt Brace Jovanovich, 1985. This book shows the characteristics, habits, and daily activities of a cat.

PRACTICE MASTERS

Decoding/Vocabulary
Use with "Minx and Jinx," Lesson 2

Name _____

Circle the word.   Print the word.

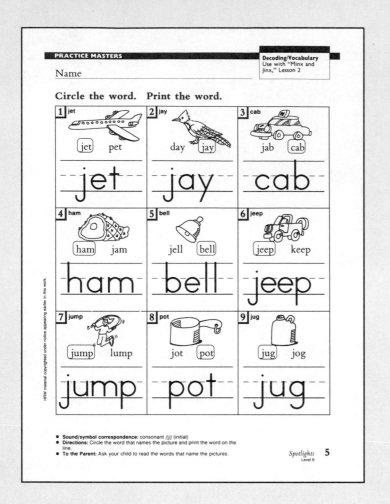

1 jet	2 jay	3 cab
(jet) pet	day (jay)	jab (cab)
jet	**jay**	**cab**

4 ham	5 bell	6 jeep
(ham) jam	jell (bell)	(jeep) keep
ham	**bell**	**jeep**

7 jump	8 pot	9 jug
(jump) lump	jot (pot)	(jug) jog
jump	**pot**	**jug**

- **Sound/symbol correspondence:** consonant /j/ (initial)
- **Directions:** Circle the word that names the picture and print the word on the line.
- **To the Parent:** Ask your child to read the words that name the pictures.

Spotlights Level 6   **5**

PRACTICE MASTERS

Decoding/Vocabulary
Use with "Minx and Jinx," Lesson 2

Name _____

Circle the word.   Print the word.   Draw a picture.

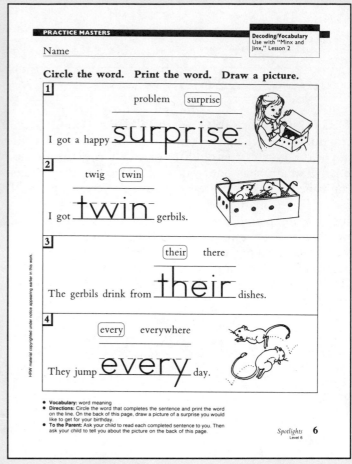

1	problem (surprise)
	I got a happy **surprise**

2	twig (twin)
	I got **twin** gerbils.

3	(their) there
	The gerbils drink from **their** dishes.

4	(every) everywhere
	They jump **every** day.

- **Vocabulary:** word meaning
- **Directions:** Circle the word that completes the sentence and print the word on the line. On the back of this page, draw a picture of a surprise you would like to get for your birthday.
- **To the Parent:** Ask your child to read each completed sentence to you. Then ask your child to tell you about the picture on the back of this page.

Spotlights Level 6   **6**

PRACTICE MASTERS

Comprehension/Thinking
Use with "Minx and Jinx," Lesson 2

Name _____

Print the word.   Draw Minx and Jinx.

run   sleep   drink   eat

1	My kittens see food.
	They will **eat** .

2	Minx and Jinx see a bowl of fresh milk.
	They will **drink** .

3	A big mean dog runs after Minx and Jinx.
	They will **run** .

4	Minx and Jinx are in their bed.
	They will **sleep** .

- **Inferential:** predicting outcomes
- **Directions:** Read the sentences. Print the word from the box that tells what will probably happen next. Then draw a picture of Minx and Jinx to show what is happening in each story.
- **To the Parent:** Ask your child to read each completed story to you and tell you about what is happening in the picture next to each story.

Spotlights Level 6   **7**

PRACTICE MASTERS

Study Skills
Use with "Minx and Jinx," Lesson 2

Name _____

Print the word.

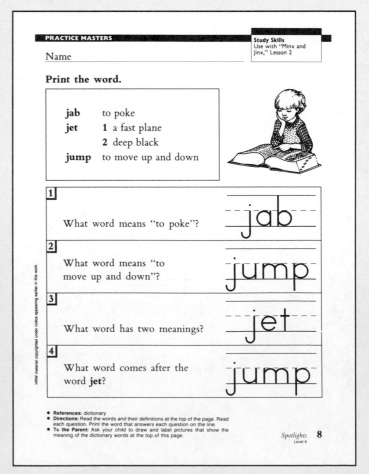

jab	to poke
jet	1 a fast plane
	2 deep black
jump	to move up and down

1	What word means "to poke"?	**jab**
2	What word means "to move up and down"?	**jump**
3	What word has two meanings?	**jet**
4	What word comes after the word **jet**?	**jump**

- **References:** dictionary
- **Directions:** Read the words and their definitions at the top of the page. Read each question. Print the word that answers each question on the line.
- **To the Parent:** Ask your child to draw and label pictures that show the meaning of the dictionary words at the top of this page.

Spotlights Level 6   **8**

T54   *Spotlights*, Level 6

Language
Use with "Minx and Jinx," Lesson 2

Name _____

Circle the word.   Print the sentence.

1 My name is bill.

My name is Bill.

2 jay is my friend.

Jay is my friend.

3 stan is my dog.

Stan is my dog.

4 minx is a cat.

Minx is a cat.

- **Conventions of language:** capitalization
- **Directions:** Read each sentence. Circle the word in each sentence that begins with a small letter, but should begin with a capital letter. Then print the complete sentence correctly on the line. Be sure that each name and the first word in each sentence begin with a capital letter.
- **To the Parent:** Ask your child to read each sentence to you. Then ask your child to tell you all the words that begin with a capital letter.

Spotlights
Level 6

9

Decoding/Vocabulary
Use with "Minx and Jinx," Lesson 2

Name _____

A. Print the letter.   Circle the picture.

| 1 jack, sack | 2 jug, bug | 3 beans, jeans |
| 4 car, jar | 5 jam, ham | 6 jay, hay |

B. Print the word.

jog   jeep   jump

1 jeep — jeep
2 jump — jump
3 jog — jog

- **Sound/symbol correspondence:** consonant /j/ (initial)
- **Directions:** TOP–Print the letter *j* on each line. Name each picture (jack, sack; jug, bug; beans, jeans; car, jar; jam, ham; jay, hay). Circle each picture whose name begins with the /j/ sound. BOTTOM–Read the words that begin with the /j/ sound. Print each word under the correct picture.
- **To the Parent:** Ask your child to name the pictures that begin with *j*.

Spotlights
Level 6

3

Decoding/Vocabulary
Use with "Minx and Jinx," Lesson 2

Name _____

Fill in the circle.

1 Jack just got two _____ kittens.
○ grow   ● gray   ○ grab

2 His kittens, Jinx and Minx, are ten _____ old.
○ weeps   ● weeks   ○ went

3 Has _____ seen Jack's twin kittens?
● anyone   ○ any   ○ anyway

4 Jack looked _____ for Minx and Jinx.
○ ever   ● everywhere   ○ every

5 They were not jumping on _____ bed.
○ then   ● their   ○ them

6 They were not _____ milk from their dish.
○ grinning   ○ drink   ● drinking

7 Then Jack got a happy _____ .
○ problem   ○ sudden   ● surprise

8 His kittens were sleeping on his dad's _____ .
● lap   ○ leap   ○ last

- **Vocabulary:** word meaning
- **Directions:** Fill in the circle in front of the word that completes each sentence.
- **To the Parent:** Ask your child to read each completed sentence to you.

Spotlights
Level 6

4

LESSON 3

"Who Wants a Kitten?"
pages 22–31 (T56–T77)

Skill Strands

DECODING/VOCABULARY

R, T **Sound/symbol correspondence:** consonant /j/*j* (initial)

R, T **Sound/symbol correspondence:** vowel /ē/*y* (final)

I, T **Word structure:** inflectional endings *-er, -est*

I, T **Word structure:** suffix *-er*

R **Word structure:** suffix *-y*

I, T **Vocabulary:** word meaning

COMPREHENSION/THINKING

Focus

I, T **Story structure:** plot (problems and solutions)

STUDY SKILLS

R **Functional reading:** signs and symbols (safety)

LANGUAGE

M **Speaking:** telephone communication

Lesson Vocabulary

Decodable words: *alike, bell, bet, blackest, Faith, furry, Jane, Jean, jumpers, Kim, least, Patty, pleaded, rang, runners, softest, Turner, yelled*

Special words: *both, live, Mr., Mrs., next, telephone*

Materials

Snapshots, Level 6: pages 22–31
Workbook: pages 14–20

Practice Masters: pages 10–13
Instructional Charts: pages 12–18
Resource Box: Letter Cards a, e, f, j, m, p, s, t, u
  Inflectional Ending Cards -er, -est
  Word Cards both, bunny, furry, happy, jail, Jane, jeep, jet, jiggle, Jinx, jump, jumper, just, live, Mr., Mrs., next, penny, saw, telephone
  Punctuation Card period
Pocket Chart
Teacher's Idea Book
Reteach Masters: page 5

Language Applications

USING LANGUAGE

Oral reading: expression

EXTENDING SELECTION CONCEPTS

Writing: thank-you notes
Listening: fiction

Special Populations

See *Teacher's Idea Book* for additional suggestions to help pupils with limited English proficiency.

Key to Symbols
I Introduced in this lesson
R Reinforced from an earlier lesson in this level
M Maintained from previous levels
T Tested in this level

Idea Center

BIBLIOGRAPHY

Add to your reading corner or reading table various books about kittens and caring for pets. A suggested bibliography follows. Suggestions for reading aloud and annotations appear in the lesson plan.

de Paola, Tomie. *The Kids' Cat Book.* Holiday House, 1979.

Pfloog, Jan. *Kittens Are Like That.* Random House, 1976.

Slate, Joseph. *Lonely Lula Cat.* Harper & Row, 1985.

Taylor, Mark. *The Case of the Missing Kittens.* Atheneum, 1978.

Planning Chart

	Instruction	Written Practice	Extending
Step 1 Preparing for the Selection	I, T **Word structure:** inflectional endings -er, -est I, T **Word structure:** suffix -er I, T **Vocabulary:** word meaning I, T **Story structure:** plot (problems and solutions)	*Workbook* page 14 *Practice Masters* page 10 *Workbook* page 15 *Practice Masters* page 11 *Reteach Masters* page 5	**Writing:** thank-you notes
Step 2 Reading for Comprehension	**Oral reading:** expression **Story structure:** plot (problems and solutions) **Story comprehension**	*Workbook* page 16	
Step 3 Developing Reading and Thinking Skills	R, T **Sound/symbol correspondence:** consonant /j/j (initial) R, T **Sound symbol correspondence:** vowel /ē/y (final) R **Word structure:** suffix -y I, T **Story structure:** plot (problems and solutions) R **Functional reading:** signs and symbols (safety) M **Speaking:** telephone communication	*Workbook* page 17 *Practice Masters* page 12 *Workbook* page 18 *Workbook* page 19 *Practice Masters* page 13 *Workbook* page 20	**Listening:** fiction

DECODING/VOCABULARY

I, T **Word structure:** inflectional endings *-er,*
-est

I, T **Word structure:** suffix *-er*

DIRECT INSTRUCTION Print the following
words and sentences on the chalkboard:

> soft   softer   softest
>
> 1. Minx has soft fur.
> 2. Jet has softer fur than Minx.
> 3. Dusty has the softest fur of all.
>
> jump   camp
> jumper   camper

Point to the words *soft, softer, softest* and have pupils read
them with you. Then point to the first two sentences
and have them read. Ask pupils to tell which cat's fur
was softer. (Jet's) Ask what ending was added to *soft* to
make *softer.* (*-er*) Have the third sentence read. Ask
which kitten had the softest fur of all. (Dusty) Call on a
pupil to tell what ending was added to *soft* to make *softest.*
(*-est*)

SAY **These are three words that describe
the kittens' fur.** (Point to the word *soft.*)
**This word tells what Minx's fur was like. It
was soft.** (Point to the word *softer.*) **This word
tells what Jet's fur was like when compared to
Minx's fur. Jet's fur was softer than Minx's
fur. The letters *-er* were added to the end of
soft to make the word *softer.* The word *softer*
was used to compare Jet's fur with Minx's fur.**
(Point to the word *softest.*) **This word tells that
Dusty's fur was the softest of all. The letters
-est were added to the end of *soft* to make the
word *softest.* The word *softest* was used to
compare Dusty's fur with both Jet's and
Minx's fur.**

Direct pupils' attention to the words remaining on the
chalkboard.

SAY **A person who jumps is called a
jumper. What letters were added to
the word *jump* to make the word *jumper.***
(letters *-er*) **Sometimes we add the letters *-er* to
a word to mean "a person who does some-
thing or a thing that does something." What
would you call a person who likes to camp?**
(camper) **What letters were added to *camp* to
make *camper?*** (*-er*)

GUIDED PRACTICE Print the following set of
sentences on the chalkboard and have the first set read
aloud.

> 1. Minx is fast.
> 2. Jinx is faster.
> 3. Dusty is the fastest of all.
>
> 4. Joan can sing.
> 5. Joan is a good singer.

Have pupils pretend that Minx, Jinx, and Dusty were in
a race. Call on pupils to answer the following questions.

1. **Which cat cannot run as fast as the others?**
(Minx)
2. **Read the sentence that tells why Dusty would
probably win the race.** (*Dusty is the fastest of all.*)
3. **What ending was added to *fast* to make *fastest?***
(*-est*)
4. **Which cat can run faster than Minx, but not as
fast as Dusty?** (Jinx)
5. **What ending was added to *fast* to make *faster?***
(*-er*)

Ask a pupil to read the second set of sentences. Ask what
Joan can do. (sing) Call on a pupil to find a word in the
second sentence that is another word for a person who
sings. (*singer*)

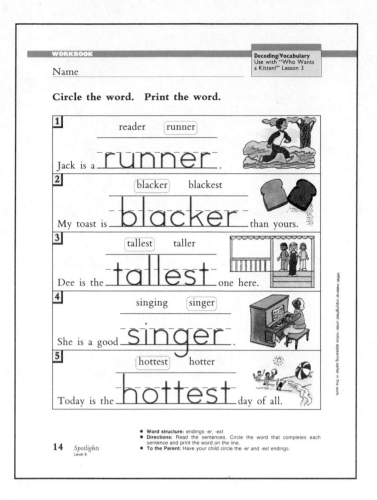

WORKBOOK

Decoding/Vocabulary
Use with "Who Wants
a Kitten?" Lesson 3

Name _____

Circle the word. Print the word.

1 reader | runner

Jack is a _runner_ .

2 blacker | blackest

My toast is _blacker_ than yours.

3 tallest | taller

Dee is the _tallest_ one here.

4 singing | singer

She is a good _singer_ .

5 hottest | hotter

Today is the _hottest_ day of all.

• **Word structure:** endings -er, -est
• **Directions:** Read the sentences. Circle the word that completes each sentence and print the word on the line.
• **To the Parent:** Have your child circle the -er and -est endings.

14 *Spotlights*
Level 6

WB 14 **INDEPENDENT PRACTICE** *Workbook* page 14 may be used to practice identifying inflectional endings *-er, -est.*

PM 10 **ADDITIONAL PRACTICE** *Practice Masters* page 10 may be used as an optional practice for identifying inflectional endings *-er, -est.* (See page T76 for reduced pages with answers.)

❋ **RETEACH** For those pupils who need additional instruction, see "Reteaching Lesson Skills," page T74, under "Reteaching and Extending."

I, T Vocabulary: word meaning

DIRECT INSTRUCTION Print the following words and sentences on the chalkboard, omitting the underlining.

IC 14

> **both live Mr. Mrs. next telephone**
>
> 1. <u>Mr.</u> and <u>Mrs.</u> Black are our neighbors.
> 2. They <u>live</u> in a big house.
> 3. Mr. and Mrs. Black <u>both</u> like to fish.
> 4. My <u>telephone</u> rang.
> 5. Mr. Black asked me to go fishing <u>next</u> week.
>
> **blackest   furry**
> **Jane   Jean   jumpers**
> **Patty   runners   softest   Turner**

Tell pupils that they are going to talk about some words they will read in the next story.

Read the first sentence. Point to the words *Mr.* and *Mrs.* and read them aloud. Ask what were the names of the neighbors. (Mr. and Mrs. Black) Have pupils read the sentence with you. Then ask them to find and read the words *Mr.* and *Mrs.*

Read Sentence 2. Point to the word *live* and read it. Ask where Mr. and Mrs. Black live. (in a big house) Have pupils read the sentence with you. Then ask them to find and read the word *live.*

Read Sentence 3. Point to the word *both* and read it. Ask if Mr. *and* Mrs. Black like to fish. (Yes, they both like to fish.) Have pupils read the sentence with you. Then have them point to the word *both* and read it.

Read Sentence 4. Point to the word *telephone* and read it. Have pupils read the sentence with you. Then ask them to point to the word *telephone* and read it.

Read Sentence 5. Ask who called on the telephone. (Mr. Black) Ask why Mr. Black called. (He asked the person to go fishing next week.) Point to the word *next* and read it. Ask when they were going fishing. (next week) Have pupils read the sentence with you. Then ask them to point to the word *next* and read it.

The words in the second set are new words that contain known phonic elements. You may wish to ask pupils to read the words, using what they know about letters and sounds.

GUIDED PRACTICE Print the following sentences on the chalkboard, omitting the underlining.

> 1. <u>Mr.</u> and <u>Mrs.</u> <u>Turner</u> are <u>both</u> <u>runners</u>.
> 2. They have the <u>softest</u>, <u>blackest</u> kitten in the neighborhood.
> 3. The kitten is a good <u>jumper</u>.
> 4. The Turners <u>live</u> <u>next</u> to <u>Jane</u>, <u>Jean</u>, and <u>Patty</u>.
> 5. "Can we pet your <u>furry</u> kitten?" the girls pleaded.
> 6. The <u>telephone</u> rang so the girls went home.

Provide opportunities for pupils to practice reading the new special words and some of the new decodable words in these sentences by following the suggestions below.

Have the first sentence read. Ask if Mrs. Turner runs, too. (Yes, Mr. and Mrs. Turner are both runners.)

Sentences 2–3: Have the sentences read. Then ask what the kitten looks like. (It is soft and black.) Ask what other word describes the kitten. (*jumper*) Call on pupils to find and read the words that have the ending *-est*. (*softest, blackest*)

Sentence 4: Call on a pupil to read the sentence. Ask if the Turners live near Jane, Jean, and Patty. (Yes, they live next to them.) Have pupils read the three names in the sentence. (*Jane, Jean, Patty*)

Sentence 5: Have the sentence read. Ask what the girls pleaded to do. (pet the furry kitten) Have pupils find and read the word *furry*.

Sentence 6: Call on a pupil to read the sentence. Then ask why the girls went home. (because the telephone rang) Have pupils point to and read the word *telephone*.

Invite volunteers to select a sentence to read aloud.

INDEPENDENT PRACTICE *Workbook* page 15 may be used to practice reading story vocabulary.

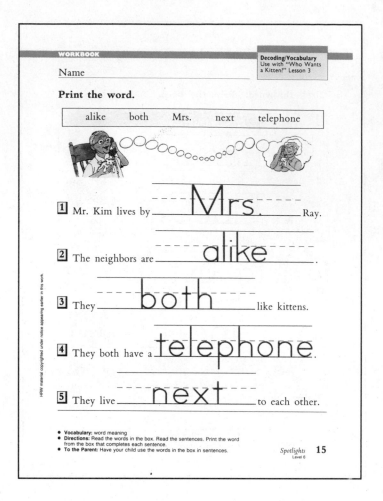

ADDITIONAL PRACTICE *Practice Masters* page 11 may be used as an optional practice for reading story vocabulary. (See page T76 for reduced pages with answers.)

✳ **RETEACH** For those pupils who need additional instruction, see "Reteaching Lesson Skills," page T75, under "Reteaching and Extending."

COMPREHENSION/THINKING

Focus

I, T   **Story structure:** plot (problems and solutions)

DIRECT INSTRUCTION   Ask pupils to listen as you read the following story:

READ Jim felt sad. Today was his mother's birthday, and he did not have enough money to buy her a nice present.

"A present doesn't have to come from a store," said Jim's dad. "Doing something nice for someone can be a present, too."

Jim thought and thought. His mother liked him to keep his room clean. She was happy when he took out the trash and watered the garden. Jim got some paper and crayons.

After dinner, Jim gave his mom a big envelope. Inside the envelope was a piece of paper. Jim had written "Mom, I promise to keep my room clean. I will take out the trash every week. I will water the garden all summer. Love, Jim"

"This is the best present of all," said Jim's mom.

SAY What was Jim's problem at the beginning of the story? (He did not have enough money to buy his mother a birthday present.) **Did Jim solve his problem?** (yes) **How did he solve his problem?** (He gave his mom a note that said that he would do nice things for her.)

In most stories that you read, a character has some kind of problem. At the end of the story, the problem is usually solved. The problem and the way it is solved make up the *plot* of the story.

GUIDED PRACTICE   Ask pupils to name a favorite story. Then have them tell what the problem and the solution was in the story. Encourage pupils to suggest stories that others in the class may know. (Answers will vary. Possible answers include: Cinderella couldn't go to the ball because she had nothing to wear. Her fairy godmother came and made Cinderella beautiful so she could go to the ball; Little Red Riding Hood was going to be eaten by a wolf. A woodsman came and saved her.)

Background for the Teacher

SUMMARY   Jack must find homes for the four kittens. He quickly finds homes for all but Minx and Jinx. Jack wants the two kittens to stay together, but no one wants two kittens. Finally, Jack finds the perfect home for the twin kittens with twin girls.

INFORMATION   This is the conclusion of the story that was begun in "Minx and Jinx."

Using Prior Knowledge

Ask pupils to recall the problem Jack had at the end of "Minx and Jinx." (He had to find homes for his kittens.) Ask what Jack said he would do. (He would ask his friends to help.) Ask how Jack's friends might have helped him. (They might have taken one of the kittens for a pet; they might have known someone who wanted a kitten.)

Setting a Purpose for Reading

Have pupils open their books to page 22. Tell pupils to look at the picture and ask them what they see. (Jack showing the black kitten to a girl.) Ask pupils why they think Jack is showing the kitten to the girl. (He wants her to take it home.)

Call on a pupil to read aloud the headnote at the top of the page. Ask pupils how they think Jack's neighbors will help him find homes for the kittens.

Reading Silently

Some pupils may be able to read this story independently. Direct them to read the whole story to find out more about Jack and if he found homes for the kittens. For those pupils who need more guidance, suggestions for directed reading follow.

How do you think Jack's neighbors
will help him find homes for
the kittens?

Who Wants a Kitten?

Jack had to find homes for his
kittens.

"Do you want a kitten?" he asked
his friends on Dilly Street.

"No," said <u>Faith</u>.

"No," said <u>Kim</u>, "but my
grandmother wants a black kitten."

"Then she may have Jet," said Jack.
"He's <u>blackest</u> of all."

22

The <u>next</u> to go was Dusty.
Jack's friend <u>Patty</u> wanted Dusty.

"You do like kittens, don't you?"
Jack asked her.

Patty nodded and said,
"Kittens are so <u>furry</u> and soft."

"Well, Dusty is the <u>softest</u> one
of all," said Jack,
"so she's the one for you."

So the little gray kitten went to
<u>live</u> with Patty.

23

Before
reading
pages
22–23

SAY **Jack needed to find homes for
the kittens. Do you think he
will have any luck? Read pages 22 and
23.**

After
reading
pages
22–23

1. **Who took the first kitten?** (Kim took
Jet for her grandmother.) Literal
2. **How do you think Jack felt when the
first kitten left his house?** (Answers
will vary. Possible answers include: He
was sad because he would miss the
kitten; he was happy because he had
found the kitten a good home.) Critical
3. **Who took the next kitten?** (Patty took
Dusty.) Literal

Just Minx and Jinx were left.
"Minx and Jinx are a lot <u>alike</u>,"
Jack said.
"They are <u>both</u> good <u>runners</u>, and
they are both good <u>jumpers</u>.
Minx and Jinx are the best
of friends, too.
How can I take one away
from the other?"

24

One day, Jack's mother said,
"<u>Mrs</u>. Little will take Minx or Jinx."

"Oh, Mom," said Jack, "I can't
take Minx away from Jinx."

"Mrs. Little doesn't want two
cats," Jack's mother said.

"Can I look for one home
for them?" Jack <u>pleaded</u>.

"If you work fast," Mother said.

25

Before reading pages 24–25

SAY **How many kittens were left?
Do you think Jack will have a
problem finding homes for Jinx and
Minx? Read pages 24 and 25 to
yourself.**

After reading pages 24–25

**Why was finding homes for Jinx and
Minx a problem for Jack?** (Jinx and Minx
were so much alike that Jack wanted them
to stay together.) Inferential

Jack went to every house on Dilly Street.

No one wanted two kittens.

"Minx or Jinx," the people said, "but not Minx and Jinx."

Jack's mother was upset.

"Jack," she said, "Mrs. Little will take one kitten, and <u>Mr.</u> Wells said he will take the other. What do you say?"

"Minx and Jinx will miss each other," said Jack.

"I know," said Mother, "but at <u>least</u> they will both have good homes."

26

Just then the <u>telephone</u> rang.

"Hello," said a girl.
"My name is <u>Jane</u> <u>Turner</u>.
Are you the boy who is looking for a home for some kittens?"

"Yes," said Jack.
"Yes, I am."

27

Before reading pages 26–27

SAY **Poor Jack. Do you think he will have to give Jinx and Minx to two different people? Read pages 26 and 27 to yourself.**

After reading pages 26–27

1. **Did Jack have any luck finding one owner for Jinx and Minx?** (No, no one wanted two kittens.) Inferential
2. **What happened while Jack was trying to figure out what to do?** (He got a telephone call.) Literal
3. **Why do you think the girl was calling Jack?** (Answers will vary. Possible answers include: She was interested in the kittens.) Critical

"Well," said the girl,
"Mrs. Little said you have
two kittens left.
Will you let me have both of them?"

"You mean you want two kittens?"
asked Jack.

"Yes," said the girl.
"Can I come and get them?"

"You <u>bet</u>!" said Jack.
"I'll tell you where I live."

28

Putting down the telephone,
Jack ran to find his mother.
"Mom! Mom!" he <u>yelled</u>.
"Some girl on the telephone said
she is going to come for Minx and Jinx.
She wants them both!"

"Why would she want two kittens?"
asked Jack's mother.

"Who knows?" said Jack.
"I'm just glad Minx and Jinx
can still live with each other."

29

Before reading pages 28–29
Do you think Jane Turner will help Jack solve his problem? Read pages 28 and 29 to find out.

After reading pages 28–29
1. **Was Jack's problem solved?** (Yes, Jane Turner wanted both kittens.) Inferential
2. **How did Jack feel when he got off the telephone?** (happy, relieved that Jinx and Minx would be together) Inferential

Jack waited and waited.
At last the <u>bell</u> rang.
What a surprise!
Jack saw not one girl, but two.

"Hello," said one girl.
"I'm Jane."

"I'm <u>Jean</u>," said the other.

30

Jack could not tell Jane from Jean.
The girls were twins!
"I have just the kittens for you,"
said Jack.
"Minx and Jinx for Jean and Jane!"

Discussing the Selection
1. How did Jack's neighbors help him find homes for his kittens?
2. Why did Jack want Minx and Jinx to stay with each other?
3. Why didn't a lot of the people want two kittens?
4. When did you find out that Minx and Jinx were just the kittens for Jean and Jane?
5. Do you think Jack will see <u>any</u> of the kittens again?

31

Before reading pages 30–31

SAY **Why do you think the girl wanted two kittens? Read pages 30 and 31 to yourself.**

After reading pages 30–31

1. **Why did the girl want two kittens?** (She had a twin sister; they could each have a pet.) Inferential
2. **Why did Jack think that his kittens were the perfect pets for the girls?** (He had twin cats for the twin girls.) Inferential

Discussing the Selection

Questions preceded by a number appear in *Spotlights* after the selection. Questions preceded by a bullet are additional questions for extending discussion.

PURPOSE

1. **How did Jack's neighbors help him find homes for his kittens?** (Some of them took kittens as pets; others found people who wanted kittens; Mrs. Little told the twin girls that Jack had two kittens.) Inferential

STORY MAPPING

2. **Why did Jack want Minx and Jinx to stay with each other?** (They were so much alike and were best friends.) Inferential

• **Why didn't Jack want Mrs. Little to have just Minx or Jinx?** (because he wanted Minx and Jinx to stay with each other) Inferential

3. **Why didn't a lot of the people want two kittens?** (Answers will vary. Possible answers include: They only wanted to have to take care of one pet.) Critical

• **How did Jack feel when he got the phone call from Jane Turner?** (happy, excited, relieved) Inferential

4. **When did you find out that Minx and Jinx were just the kittens for Jean and Jane?** (when Jack opened the door and saw that the girls were twins) Critical

CRITICAL THINKING

5. **Do you think Jack will see any of the kittens again?** (Answers will vary. Possible answers include: Yes, since he gave them to people in the neighborhood.)

• **Do you think Jack did a good job trying to find homes for the kittens? Why or why not?** (Answers will vary. Possible answers include: Yes, he worked very hard to find just the right home for each kitten.)

Using Language

ORAL READING: EXPRESSION Have pupils turn to page 22 in their books. Remind them that Jack needed to find good homes for his kittens. Call on a pupil to read what Kim said to Jack. ("No," said Kim, "but my grandmother wants a black kitten.") Ask pupils to read what Jack said to Kim. ("Then she may have Jet," said Jack. "He's blackest of all.")

Follow a similar procedure for the remaining pages, using the suggestions below.

Page 23: Ask pupils to read the conversation between Jack and Patty.

Page 24: Ask pupils to read the sentences that explain why Jack wanted to keep Jinx and Minx together. ("Minx and Jinx are a lot alike," Jack said. "They are both good runners, and they are both good jumpers. Minx and Jinx are the best of friends, too. How can I take one away from the other?")

Page 25: Remind pupils that Jack pleaded with his mother not to separate Minx and Jinx. Have pupils read what Jack told his mother when she said that Mrs. Little would take either Jinx or Minx. ("Oh, Mom," said Jack, "I can't take Minx away from Jinx.")

Pages 27–28: Have two pupils pretend to be on the telephone and read the conversation between Jane Turner and Jack.

Page 29: Ask how Jack felt after the telephone call. (excited) Call on pupils to read what Jack and his mother said to each other.

Pages 30–31: Ask a pupil to read what Jack said to Jane and Jean. ("I have just the kittens for you," said Jack. "Minx and Jinx for Jean and Jane!")

Applying the Focus Skill

STORY STRUCTURE: PLOT Remind pupils that in a story, a character often has a problem. Ask what Jack's problem was. (He needed to find homes for his kittens, but he wanted to find one home for the last two kittens.) Ask how Jack's problem was solved in the end. (Twin girls took the twin kittens.)

Evaluating Comprehension

WB 16 **INDEPENDENT PRACTICE** *Workbook* page 16 may be used for an informal evaluation of story comprehension.

WORKBOOK

Comprehension/Thinking
Use with "Who Wants a Kitten?" Lesson 3

Name _____

A. Fill in the circle.

1 Jack had to find ____.
● homes for the kittens
○ food for the kittens

2 Dusty and Jet were the ____.
○ last kittens to find homes
● first kittens to find homes

3 Jack wanted to find ____.
○ two homes for Minx and Jinx
● one home for Minx and Jinx

4 At last, a girl called to say she wanted ____.
● both kittens
○ one of the kittens

5 When the girl came, Jack saw twin girls for ____!
○ twin dogs
● twin kittens

B. Print a sentence that tells how Jack felt.

Answers will vary.

● Story comprehension: "Who Wants a Kitten?"
● Directions: TOP — Read the sentences. Fill in the circle by the words that complete each sentence so that it tells about "Who Wants a Kitten?" BOTTOM — Tell how Jack felt at the end of the story.
● To the Parent: Have your child retell the story.

16 *Spotlights* Level 6

HOW AM I DOING?

Many pupils need encouragement to do outside writing. Ask yourself the following questions to gauge your teaching effectiveness in encouraging creativity.

	Yes	No	Some-times
1. Have I suggested to pupils that they write outside of class?	☐	☐	☐
2. Have I encouraged them to write notes to take home?	☐	☐	☐
3. Have I suggested that pupils keep a list of ideas for things that they would like to write about in the future?	☐	☐	☐
4. Have I shared good examples of writing with them?	☐	☐	☐
5. Have I shared examples of my writing with them?	☐	☐	☐

3 DEVELOPING READING AND THINKING SKILLS

DECODING/VOCABULARY

R, T **Sound/symbol correspondence:** consonant /j/j (initial)

DIRECT INSTRUCTION Use *Word Cards* and *Punctuation Card period* to make the sentence *Jane just saw Jinx jump.* in the *Pocket Chart.* Have the sentence read aloud. Then have pupils remove the words that begin with letter *j* and place them one under the other. (*Jane, just, Jinx, jump*) Point to each word and have pupils read it with you. Ask what sound the letter *j* stands for. (/j/)

GUIDED PRACTICE Tell pupils that you will hold up some *Word Cards* and that you will call on them to read the word on each card. Hold up *Word Cards jump, just, jiggle, jumper, jeep, jet, jail* one at a time. Then display the *Word Cards* and invite pupils to select a *Word Card* and read the word.

WB 17 **INDEPENDENT PRACTICE** *Workbook* page 17 may be used to practice identifying sound/symbol correspondence /j/j.

PM 12 **ADDITIONAL PRACTICE** *Practice Masters* page 12 may be used as an optional practice for identifying sound/symbol correspondence /j/j. (See page T77 for reduced pages with answers.)

✱ **RETEACH** For those pupils who need additional instruction, see "Reteaching Lesson Skills," page T74, under "Reteaching and Extending."

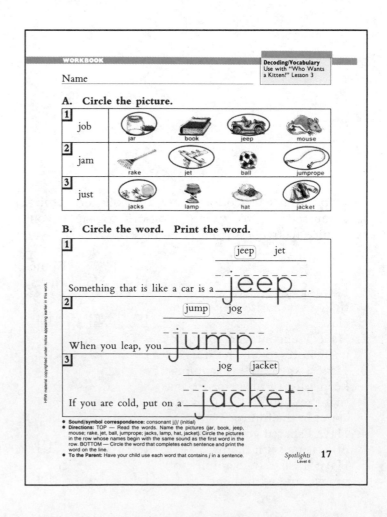

R, T   **Sound/symbol correspondence:** vowel /ē/ γ (final)

R   **Word structure:** suffix -γ

DIRECT INSTRUCTION Print the following words and sentences on the chalkboard, omitting the underlining.

> 1. Taffy said, "Don't be so silly."
>
>   snowy   windy   dirty
>
> 2. Danny saw a bunny.
> 3. Peggy had a happy grin.
> 4. Jenny said, "Pass the jelly."
> 5. Jimmy put the penny in the piggy bank.

Read the sentence. Then point to and read the words *Taffy* and *silly.* Ask how these two words are alike. (They both end with γ; they both end with the /ē/ sound.)

SAY	**The words *Taffy* and *silly* each have two parts. Say *Taf fy* with me: *Taf fy.* Say *sil ly* with me: *Sil ly.* The letter *y* at the end of *Taffy* and *silly* stands for the /ē/ sound. When the letter *y* is at the end of a word with two parts, *y* usually stands for the /ē/ sound.**

Have pupils read the sentence with you.

Point to and read the words *snowy, windy, dirty.* Tell pupils that these words all end with γ. Ask which sound is at the end of each word. (/ē/)

SAY	**If we wanted to talk about a day when it was snowing, we would say it was a "snowy" day. What would we say if we wanted to talk about a day when the wind was blowing?** (It was a windy day.)

Have pupils think of sentences using the word *dirty.* Then point to each word and have pupils read it with you.

GUIDED PRACTICE Indicate Sentences 2–5 on the chalkboard. Call on pupils to read each sentence and to tell which words in each sentence have letter *y* that stands for the /ē/ sound at the end of the word.

INDEPENDENT PRACTICE *Workbook* page 18 may be used to practice identifying sound/symbol correspondence /ē/γ.

RETEACH For those pupils who need additional instruction, see "Reteaching Lesson Skills," page T74, under "Reteaching and Extending."

COMPREHENSION/THINKING

Focus

I, T   Story structure: plot (problems and solutions)

DIRECT INSTRUCTION   Explain that in most stories one of the characters has a problem and tries to find a way to solve the problem. At the end of the story, the problem is usually solved. The problem and solution in a story make up the plot of the story.

GUIDED PRACTICE   Print the following story on the chalkboard and ask pupils to read it to themselves.

> Penny could not find her kitten.
> She looked everywhere, but she did not see Fluffy.
> Then Penny's mom said, "Look up, Penny."
> There was Fluffy, sitting in the oak tree.
> "You silly kitty," said Penny.

ASK   **What was Penny's problem?** (She could not find her kitten, Fluffy.) **How was Penny's problem solved?** (Her mother told her to look up, and then Penny saw the kitten in a tree.) **What was the plot of the story?** (At first, Penny couldn't find her kitten; then her mother showed her where it was.)

WORKBOOK

Comprehension/Thinking
Use with "Who Wants
a Kitten?" Lesson 3

Name _____

Fill in the circle.

Kim got a little dog for her birthday.
Kim made a little doghouse for the dog.
As the weeks passed, the dog got bigger.
Then the dog got too big to fit
in the doghouse.
Kim was sad.
So, Dad got some planks.
He made a new doghouse for Kim's dog.
Kim was happy.
The dog was happy, too.

1 What did Kim get?
○ a cat
● a dog
○ a bird

2 What was the problem?
○ Kim got a little dog for her birthday.
○ Kim made a doghouse for her dog to live in.
● Kim's dog got too big for the doghouse.

3 How did Dad help Kim?
○ He made another little doghouse.
● He made a bigger doghouse.
○ He got a new little dog for Kim.

4 Then how did Kim feel?
○ upset
● happy
○ sad

- **Story structure:** plot
- **Directions:** Read the story. Then read each question about the story. Fill in the circle in front of the answer to each question.
- **To the Parent:** Ask your child to draw a picture to illustrate Kim's problem.

Spotlights **19**
Level 6

INDEPENDENT PRACTICE   *Workbook* page 19 may be used to practice identifying problems and solutions.

ADDITIONAL PRACTICE   *Practice Masters* page 13 may be used as an optional practice for identifying problems and solutions. (See page T77 for reduced pages with answers.)

✳ RETEACH   For those pupils who need additional instruction, see "Reteaching Lesson Skills," page T75, under "Reteaching and Extending."

R   Functional reading: signs and symbols (safety)

DIRECT INSTRUCTION   Ask what a person in a car or a person walking must do when a traffic light turns red. (stop) Explain that a red light is a symbol that means "stop." Ask what the walker or driver may do when the light turns green. (go) Traffic lights are symbols that help keep people safe.

GUIDED PRACTICE   Ask pupils what they must do before crossing a street. (look both ways to make sure no cars are coming) Ask what the white or yellow lines on streets at a corner mean. (People should walk between the lines to cross the street.) Tell pupils that a crosswalk is a symbol to help keep people safe.

Ask pupils to name some other signs or symbols that they may see as they walk or ride to school. Ask them to explain what each sign or symbol means.

WB 20   **INDEPENDENT PRACTICE**   *Workbook* page 20 may be used to practice recognizing signs and symbols.

M   Speaking: telephone communication

DIRECT INSTRUCTION   Ask how Jack found out that someone wanted both kittens. (A girl called on the telephone.) Ask pupils to look at page 27 in their books and to read the page to themselves.

SAY   **When the telephone rang, Jack answered it. Page 27 does not tell what Jack said when he picked up the phone. Who can tell us what Jack might have said?** (Possible answers include: "Hello"; "hello, this is Jack speaking.")

When you answer a telephone, it is polite to tell your name to the person who is calling. What was the first thing that the girl told Jack? (She told him her name.) **When you call someone on the telephone, it is polite to tell your name to the person who answers the phone.**

GUIDED PRACTICE   Have pupils work together in pairs. One pupil should pretend to have kittens to give away. The other pupil should pretend to want a kitten. Encourage each pair of pupils to act out a telephone call in which a person asks about a kitten. Remind pupils to tell their names when they answer the phone and when they make the phone call.

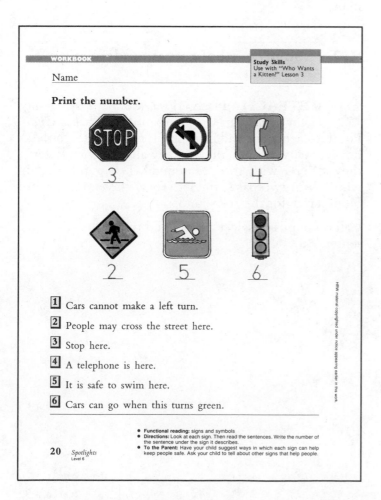

WORKBOOK

Study Skills
Use with "Who Wants a Kitten?" Lesson 3

Name _____

Print the number.

3   1   4

2   5   6

1 Cars cannot make a left turn.

2 People may cross the street here.

3 Stop here.

4 A telephone is here.

5 It is safe to swim here.

6 Cars can go when this turns green.

• Functional reading: signs and symbols
• **Directions:** Look at each sign. Then read the sentences. Write the number of the sentence under the sign it describes.
• **To the Parent:** Have your child suggest ways in which each sign can help keep people safe. Ask your child to tell about other signs that help people.

20   *Spotlights* Level 6

Reteaching Lesson Skills

The activities that follow provide reteaching of skills developed in this lesson. Not every pupil needs to complete these activities. Choose only the activities that are needed to provide for the individual differences in your classroom.

DECODING/VOCABULARY

I, T   Word structure: inflectional endings *-er, -est*

I, T   Word structure: suffix *-er*

❋   **RETEACH**   Write the following words in a column on the chalkboard:

fast	help
faster	helper
fastest	

Have pupils read the first column of words. Call on pupils to choose the word that best completes each of the following sentences:

1. **Jim's bike is _____ than my bike.** (*faster*) **What was added to the word *fast* to make the word *faster*?** (*-er*)
2. **Sue has the _____ bike of all.** (*fastest*) **What was added to the word *fast* to make the word *fastest*?** (*-est*)

Direct pupils' attention to the words *help* and *helper* on the chalkboard. Have pupils read the words. Ask which word means "a person who helps"? (*helper*) Ask what was added to the word *help* to change the word to mean "a person who helps"? (*-er*) Have pupils use each word in a sentence.

R, T   Sound/symbol correspondence: consonant /j/*j* (initial)

❋   **RETEACH**   Display Word Card *jet* and have pupils read the word with you. Ask what letter is at the beginning of the word *jet* and what sound the letter stands for. (*j*, /j/)

Print the following sentences on the chalkboard, omitting the underlining.

1. Janet jiggled the jelly.
2. Jack and Jill are in the jeep.
3. Jim has a job on a jet plane.
4. Justin likes jam and jelly.

Have the sentences read. Then call on pupils to find and read the words in the sentences that begin with the /j/ sound.

R, T   Sound/symbol correspondence: vowel /ē/*y* (final)

❋   **RETEACH**   Place *Word Cards furry, penny, bunny, happy* in a column in the *Pocket Chart.* Point to each word and have pupils read it with you. Ask how these words are alike. (They all end with letter *y*; they all end with the /ē/ sound.) Tell pupils that in words with two parts, the letter *y* at the end of a word often stands for the /ē/ sound.

Call on pupils to select a word and to use the word in a sentence.

I, T   Vocabulary: word meaning

 RETEACH Print the following words and sentences on the chalkboard, omitting the underlining.

> **both   live   Mr.   Mrs.   next   telephone**
>
> 1. <u>Mr.</u> and <u>Mrs.</u> Black are our neighbors.
> 2. They <u>live</u> in a big house.
> 3. Mr. and Mrs. Black <u>both</u> like to fish.
> 4. My <u>telephone</u> rang.
> 5. Mr. Black asked me to go fishing <u>next</u> week.
>
> blackest   furry
> Jane   Jean   jumpers
> Patty   runners   softest   Turner

Point to and read the words *Mr.* and *Mrs.* Call on a pupil to find and read the sentence that contains the words *Mr.* and *Mrs.* Ask why the neighbors are called Mr. and Mrs. Black. (because they are married)

Follow a similar procedure for the remaining sentences, calling attention to the underlined words.

Display *Word Cards* for each underlined word. Have pupils hold up and read the *Word Card* that answers each of the following questions.

1. **Which word means "two"?** (*both*)
2. **Which word names something you can use to talk to people?** (*telephone*)
3. **Which word means "a man"?** (*Mr.*)
4. **Which word means "a woman"?** (Mrs.)
5. **Which word rhymes with *give?*** (*live*)
6. **Which word means "the one after this one"?** (*next*)

RM 5 Distribute *Reteach Masters* page 5 and explain the directions on the page.

Focus

I, T   Story structure: plot (problems and solutions)

 RETEACH Read aloud the following story. Then ask pupils what the problem was and how it was solved.

READ Today was the day of the big softball game. Matt's team had been practicing every day. They all had matching shirts and caps.

Matt's father was going to drive him to the park, but when they got in the car, it wouldn't start. Matt knew he was going to miss the game. Just then the city bus came to a stop at the corner. Matt and his father jumped on the bus and made it to the game just in time.

Ask what the problem in the story was. (The car wouldn't start on the day of the big game.) Ask how the problem was solved. (A bus came along and took Matt and his father to the park.)

Extending Selection Concepts

WRITING: THANK-YOU NOTES Ask if Jane and Jean were happy with their kittens. (Yes, they were happy to have their kittens.) Remind pupils that when someone gives you something, it is polite to send that person a thank-you note. Tell pupils to think about what Jane or Jean may have said in a thank-you note to Jack. Then have them write a thank-you note to Jack. Or pupils may wish to write and mail a thank-you note to someone who has done something nice for them. The note may be a thank-you for a present or it may be a note to a parent or a teacher to thank him or her for doing something special. Remind pupils to begin the note with a salutation and to end it with a closing. Encourage pupils to read their notes to the class.

LISTENING: FICTION Choose a story about caring for a kitten and read it aloud to the class.

de Paola, Tomie. *The Kids' Cat Book.* Holiday House, 1979. Patrick goes to Granny Twinkle's for a free kitten and learns all about cats.

Pfloog, Jan. *Kittens Are Like That.* Random House, 1976. Who can resist lovable, playful kittens, even when they get into mischief?

Slate, Joseph. *Lonely Lula Cat.* Harper & Row, 1985. While searching for her old friends who now live far away, lonely Lula Cat discovers new friends close by.

Taylor, Mark. *The Case of the Missing Kittens.* Atheneum, 1978. Where are the kittens? Angus the dog solves the mystery.

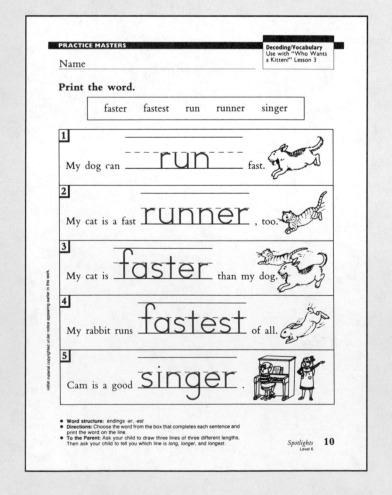

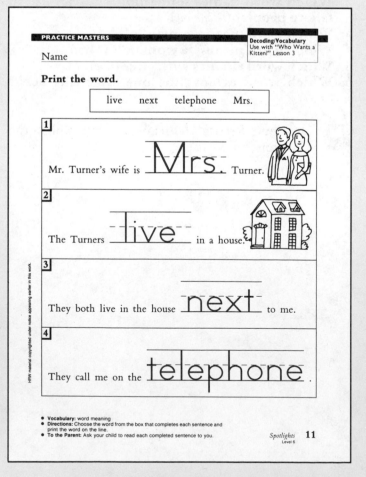

Name

Print the word. Circle the words.

| jet | Jane | jack | jumped |

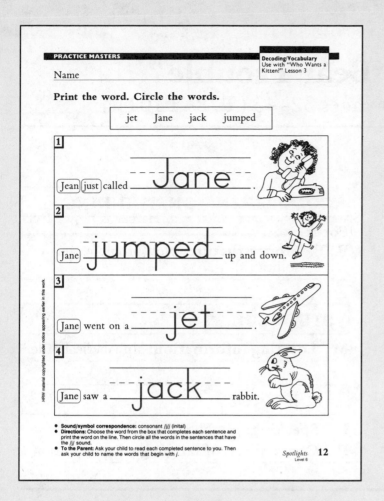

1 [Jean] [just] called ___Jane___ .

2 [Jane] ___jumped___ up and down.

3 [Jane] went on a ___jet___ .

4 [Jane] saw a ___jack___ rabbit.

- **Sound/symbol correspondence:** consonant /j/j (inital)
- **Directions:** Choose the word from the box that completes each sentence and print the word on the line. Then circle all the words in the sentences that have the /j/ sound.
- **To the Parent:** Ask your child to read each completed sentence to you. Then ask your child to name the words that begin with j.

Spotlights **12**
Level 6

Name

Circle the problem.   Draw a line.

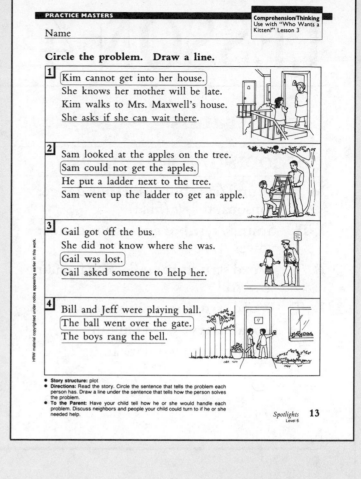

1 [Kim cannot get into her house.]
She knows her mother will be late.
Kim walks to Mrs. Maxwell's house.
<u>She asks if she can wait there.</u>

2 Sam looked at the apples on the tree.
[Sam could not get the apples.]
<u>He put a ladder next to the tree.</u>
<u>Sam went up the ladder to get an apple.</u>

3 Gail got off the bus.
She did not know where she was.
[Gail was lost.]
<u>Gail asked someone to help her.</u>

4 Bill and Jeff were playing ball.
[The ball went over the gate.]
<u>The boys rang the bell.</u>

- **Story structure:** plot
- **Directions:** Read the story. Circle the sentence that tells the problem each person has. Draw a line under the sentence that tells how the person solves the problem.
- **To the Parent:** Have your child tell how he or she would handle each problem. Discuss neighbors and people your child could turn to if he or she needed help.

Spotlights **13**
Level 6

Name

Circle the word.   Print the word.

1 Mr.   [Mrs.]

Mr. and ___Mrs.___ Turner have two birds.

2 like   [live]

The birds ___live___ in a birdhouse.

3 [next]   nest

The birdhouse is ___next___ to a big tree.

4 [Both]   Bet

___Both___ birds are black.

- **Vocabulary:** word meaning
- **Directions:** Circle the word that completes the sentence and print the word on the line.
- **To the Parent:** Ask your child to read each completed sentence to you.

Spotlights **5**
Level 6

LESSON 4 "Bear Trouble"
pages 32–43 (T78–T101)

Skill Strands

DECODING/VOCABULARY

M   **Sound/symbol correspondence:** consonant /l/*le* (final)

I, T   **Sound/symbol correspondence:** vowel /ī/*i-e*

R, T   **Word structure:** inflectional endings *-er, -est*

R, T   **Word structure:** suffix *-er*

I   **Vocabulary:** word building

I, T   **Vocabulary:** word meaning

COMPREHENSION/THINKING

Focus

R, T   **Story structure:** plot (problems and solutions)

STUDY SKILLS

M   **Locating information:** alphabetical order

LANGUAGE

I   **Speaking:** paraphrasing

R   **Conventions of language:** capitalization

Lesson Vocabulary

Decodable words: *dropped, fine, met, nap, pine, rid, side, smile, sneak, spells, spent, sunrise, swim, tickle, time*

Special words: *bear, began, chipmunk, Ha, place, squirrel, trouble, woods*

Materials

Spotlights, Level 6: pages 32–43
Workbook: pages 21–27

Practice Masters: pages 14–17
Instructional Charts: pages 19–26
Resource Box: Letter Cards d, e, f, h, i, l, m, n, r, t
             Word Cards a, Bear, began, Chipmunk, Dog, fin, fine, fish, Ha, has, place, Rabbit, Squirrel, The, trouble, woods
             Punctuation Cards period
Pocket Chart
Teacher's Idea Book
Reteach Masters: pages 6–7

Language Applications

USING LANGUAGE

Oral reading: answering questions
Critical thinking: problem solving (Cooperative Learning)

EXTENDING SELECTION CONCEPTS

Speaking/Writing: using vocabulary words
Listening: fiction

Special Populations

See *Teacher's Idea Book* for additional suggestions to help pupils with limited English proficiency.

Key to Symbols
I   Introduced in this lesson
R   Reinforced from an earlier lesson in this level
M   Maintained from previous levels
T   Tested in this level

Idea Center

BIBLIOGRAPHY

Add to your reading corner or reading table various books about bears, squirrels, or chipmunks. A suggested bibliography follows. Suggestions for reading aloud and annotations appear in the lesson plan.

Delton, Judy. *Two Good Friends.* Crown, 1974.
Gage, Wilson. *Cully, Cully and the Bear.* Greenwillow, 1983.
Sharmat, Marjorie Weinman. *The Trip and Other Sophie and Gussie Stories.* Macmillan, 1976.

Planning Chart

		Instruction	Written Practice	Extending
Step 1 Preparing for the Selection	I, T	**Sound/symbol correspondence:** vowel /ī/i-e	*Workbook* page 21 *Practice Masters* page 14 *Reteach Masters* page 6	
	I	**Vocabulary:** word building		
	I, T	**Vocabulary:** word meaning	*Workbook* page 22 *Practice Masters* page 15 *Reteach Masters* page 7	
	R, T	**Story structure:** plot (problems and solutions)		
Step 2 Reading for Comprehension		**Oral reading:** answering questions		
		Critical thinking: problem solving (Cooperative Learning)		
		Story structure: plot (problems and solutions)		
		Story comprehension	*Workbook* page 23	
Step 3 Developing Reading and Thinking Skills	M	**Sound/symbol correspondence:** consonant /l/le (final)	*Practice Masters* page 16	**Speaking/Writing:** using vocabulary words
	R, T	**Word structure:** inflectional endings -er, -est	*Workbook* page 24	
	R, T	**Word structure:** suffix -er		
	R, T	**Story structure:** plot (problems and solutions)	*Workbook* page 25 *Practice Masters* page 17	**Listening:** fiction
	M	**Locating information:** alphabetical order	*Workbook* page 26	
	I	**Speaking:** paraphrasing		
	R	**Conventions of language:** capitalization	*Workbook* page 27	

DECODING/VOCABULARY

I, T   Sound/symbol correspondence: vowel /ī/*i-e*

DIRECT INSTRUCTION   Use *Word Cards* and *Punctuation Card* period to make the sentence *The fish has a fine fin.* in the *Pocket Chart*. Read the sentence aloud. Then ask what the fish has. (a fine fin) Remove the words *fine* and *fin* from the sentence and place them one on top of the other in the *Pocket Chart*. Point to each word and have pupils read it with you.

SAY   Say *fin: fin.* The letter *i* in the word *fin* stands for the /i/ sound. Now say *fine: fine.* Do you hear the /i/ sound in *fine*? (no) The word *fine* has the /ī/ sound. When a word has an *i*, followed by a consonant, and ends with letter *e*, *i* usually stands for the /ī/ sound. We call the /ī/ sound the long sound of letter *i*. Read *fine* with me: *fine.* Read each word when I point to it.

Point to *fin* and *fine* several times.

GUIDED PRACTICE   Print the following pairs of words on the chalkboard:

1. pin	pine
2. rid	ride
3. kit	kite

Have pupils read each pair of words and explain why the letter *i* in the second word stands for the long sound of letter *i*. (Each word has *i*, followed by a consonant, and ends with the letter *e*.)

Call on pupils to read the word on the chalkboard that goes with each of the following clues. Then have them tell if the word has the long or short sound of letter *i*.

1. **This is a kind of tree.** (*pine* - long)
2. **This can fly on the end of a string.** (*kite* - long)
3. **This has a sharp point.** (*pin* - short)
4. **This is what you do in a car.** (*ride* - long)

Call on pupils to select and read a pair of words from the chalkboard.

WB 21   INDEPENDENT PRACTICE   *Workbook* page 21 may be used to practice identifying sound/symbol correspondence /ī/*i-e*.

PM 14   ADDITIONAL PRACTICE   *Practice Masters* page 14 may be used as an optional practice for identifying sound/symbol correspondence /ī/*i-e*. (See page T100 for reduced pages with answers.)

✳ RETEACH   For those pupils who need additional instruction, see "Reteaching Lesson Skills," page T97, under "Reteaching and Extending."

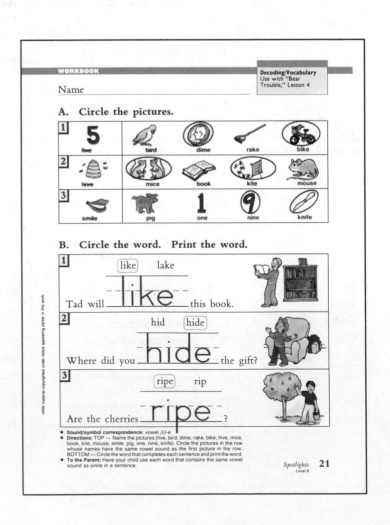

I Vocabulary: word building

DIRECT INSTRUCTION Place *Letter Cards* in the *Pocket Chart* to make the word *fine.* Have pupils read the word. Ask what sound *i* stands for in *fine.* (/ī/) Ask why the letter *i* stands for the /ī/ sound. (The word *fine* has an *i,* followed by a consonant, and ends with the letter *e.*) Take away the *e* and have the word read. (*fin*) Replace the *e* and have the word read. (*fine*)

GUIDED PRACTICE Display *Letter Cards d, h, l, m, r, t.* Tell pupils that you will call on them to use the *Letter Cards* to make new words in the *Pocket Chart.* Have a pupil replace letter *f* with letter *m* and read the new word. (*mine*) Continue by giving the following directions:

1. **Replace the *n* with *l*. What word did you make?** (*mile*)
2. **Place letter *s* in front of the word. What word did you make?** (*smile*)
3. **Trade places with the *m* and the *l*. What word did you make?** (*slime*)
4. **Take off the *e*. What word did you make?** (*slim*)
5. **Replace the *sl* with *t*. Put *e* at the end. What word did you make?** (*time*)
6. **Replace the *t* with *d*. What word did you make?** (*dime*)
7. **Take off the *e*. What word did you make?** (*dim*)
8. **Replace the *d* with *r*. What word did you make?** (*rim*)
9. **Replace the *m* with *d*. What word did you make?** (*rid*)
10. **Add *e* at the end. What word did you make?** (*ride*)

I, T Vocabulary: word meaning

DIRECT INSTRUCTION Print the following words and sentences on the chalkboard, omitting the underlining.

> **Bear began Chipmunk Ha place Squirrel trouble woods**
>
> 1. <u>Bear</u> <u>began</u> his day in the <u>woods</u>.
> 2. He went to eat some of <u>Squirrel</u>'s food.
> 3. <u>Chipmunk</u> began to eat some nuts, too.
> 4. "Get away from this <u>place</u>, or there will be <u>trouble</u>!" said Squirrel.
> 5. Bear and Chipmunk giggled, "<u>Ha</u>, ha, ha," and went away.
>
> **fine pine side smile
> sunrise tickle time**

Tell pupils that they are going to talk about some words they will read in the next story.

Read the first sentence aloud. Point to the word *Bear* and read it. Ask what time of day it was. (It was probably morning because Bear had just begun his day.) Have the sentence read with you. Then call on pupils to find and read the words *Bear* and *woods.*

Read Sentences 2 and 3 aloud. Then point to and read the words *Squirrel's* and *Chipmunk.* Ask who ate Squirrel's food with *Bear.* (Chipmunk) Have pupils read the sentences with you.

Read Sentence 4 aloud. Point to the word *place* and read it. Then point to the word *trouble* and read it. Ask what Squirrel told Bear and Chipmunk. (*"Get away from my place, or there will be trouble."*) Have pupils read the sentence with you. Then ask pupils to find and read the words *place* and *trouble.*

Read Sentence 5 aloud. Point to the word *Ha* and read it. Ask why Bear and Chipmunk giggled. (because they had taken some of Squirrel's nuts) Have pupils read the sentence with you and have the words *Ha, ha, ha* read.

The words in the second set are new words that contain known phonic elements. You may wish to ask pupils to read the words, using what they know about letters and sounds.

GUIDED PRACTICE Print the following sentences on the chalkboard, omitting the underlining.

> 1. Bear got up at <u>sunrise</u>.
> 2. "What a <u>fine</u> day!" Bear said with a <u>smile</u>.
> 3. He went to the <u>woods</u> to nap by a <u>pine</u> tree.
> 4. <u>Chipmunk</u> and <u>Squirrel</u> wanted to sneak up and <u>tickle</u> Bear.
> 5. Then the <u>trouble</u> <u>began</u>.
> 6. Bear turned on his <u>side</u> and yelled, "Get away from this <u>place</u>."
> 7. "Ha, ha," they giggled as they ran.
> 8. Then they <u>spent</u> some time by the pond.

Provide opportunities for pupils to practice reading the new special words and some of the new decodable words in these sentences by following the suggestions below.

Have the first sentence read. Then have pupils find and read the word *sunrise*. Ask what two words make up this compound word. (*sun, rise*) Have pupils find and read *Bear*.

Sentences 2–3: Call on pupils to read the sentences. Then ask if it will be a nice day. (Yes, it will be a fine day.) Ask what Bear was going to do. (take a nap in the woods) Ask if that makes him happy. (Yes, he's smiling.) Have pupils find and read the word *smile*.

Sentence 4: Have the sentence read. Then ask what Chipmunk and Squirrel wanted to do. (sneak up and tickle Bear) Have pupils find and read the words *sneak* and *tickle*.

Sentences 5–6: Have the sentences read. Ask what happened. (Bear woke up.) Have pupils find and read the word *trouble*.

Sentence 7: Call on a pupil to read the sentence. Ask if Chipmunk and Squirrel were sorry for waking up Bear. (No, they giggled.) Have pupils say "Ha, ha, ha" as Chipmunk and Squirrel might have said it.

Sentence 8: Have the sentence read. Ask what Squirrel and Chipmunk did next. (They spent time by the pond.) Have pupils find and read the word *spent*.

Call on pupils to find and read the words in which letter *i* stands for the /ī/ sound. (*sunrise, pine, fine, side, smile, time*)

Invite pupils to select a sentence to read aloud.

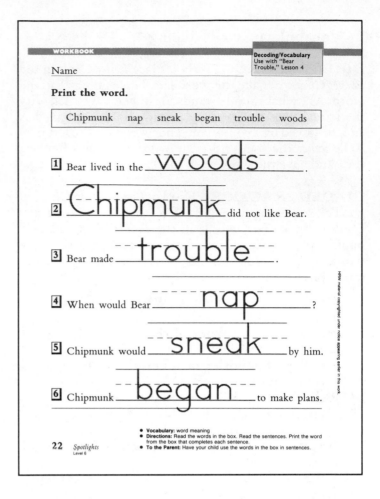

INDEPENDENT PRACTICE *Workbook* page 22 may be used to practice reading story vocabulary.

ADDITIONAL PRACTICE *Practice Masters* page 15 may be used as an optional practice for reading story vocabulary. (See page T100 for reduced pages with answers.)

RETEACH For those pupils who need additional instruction, see "Reteaching Lesson Skills," page T98, under "Reteaching and Extending."

COMPREHENSION/THINKING

Focus

R, T Story structure: plot (problems and solutions)

DIRECT INSTRUCTION   Remind pupils that in many stories, a character has a problem that needs to be solved. Then read the following story and ask what the character's problem is.

| READ | Joe and his friends were playing ball in the park. The park was next to Mrs. Simon's house. When it was Joe's turn to hit the ball, he swung as hard as he could. Smack! The ball went up and up. Then down it came. Crash! The ball went through the window into Mrs. Simon's kitchen. "Oh, no!" said Joe. "What should I do?"

| ASK | What was Joe's problem? (He hit the ball through Mrs. Simon's window and broke the window.) **Listen as I read more of the story.**

| READ | Joe knocked on Mrs. Simon's door. "I broke your window," he said. "It was an accident, and I'm sorry. I will rake your lawn or do other work for you to earn money to pay for the window."

| ASK | How Did Joe solve his problem? (He offered to work for Mrs. Simon to pay for fixing the window.)

GUIDED PRACTICE   Tell pupils that you will read a story and ask questions about the story.

| READ | Alan walked slowly home from the library. His arms were full of books. He couldn't decide which books to leave for another day, so he had checked out seven books. He was excited about reading the stories, but he had forgotten about the long walk home. His arms were getting tired. Just then Alan saw his neighbor, Kenny, coming down the sidewalk. Kenny was pulling a wagon.

"Hey, Alan," said Kenny. "Why don't you put those books in my wagon, and we can pull them home?"

| ASK | What was Alan's problem? (He had too many books to carry home.) **How was Alan's problem solved?** (His neighbor came along and offered to take home the books in his wagon.)

Lesson 4 "Bear Trouble" (pages 32–43)   T83

Background for the Teacher

SUMMARY The little animals that live in the woods like to go to the pond. Then one day a big bear comes to sleep by the pond. He comes back each day and the little animals are afraid to play by the pond. Chipmunk and Squirrel decide to find a way to get the bear to go away.

INFORMATION This is a fantasy story in which the animals think and act like people.

Using Prior Knowledge

Explain that the story pupils are going to read is about the trouble a big bear causes for some little animals. Ask why a big bear might be a problem for little animals. (Possible answers include: Little animals might be afraid of a big bear; the big bear might be mean.) Develop a discussion by asking the questions that follow:

1. **What would you do if you saw a bear?** (Answers will vary.)
2. **What would you need to do if a bear decided to nap in your backyard?** (Answers will vary.)

Setting a Purpose for Reading

Ask pupils to turn to page 32 in their books and tell them that the title of this story is "Bear Trouble." Ask what kind of trouble a bear might cause. (Possible answers include: A bear might scare someone; it might eat people's food.)

Point out the headnote at the top of page 32 and tell pupils that this note will help them think about the story they are going to read. Have the headnote read aloud. Then ask what little animals might be able to do about a big bear.

Reading Silently

Some pupils may be able to read this story independently. Direct them to read the whole story to find out more about a bear and the trouble it causes for the little animals. For those pupils who need more guidance, suggestions for directed reading follow.

Big Bear spells trouble for his neighbors in the <u>woods</u>.

Read to find out what the little animals do.

Bear Trouble

Deep in the green woods was a little pond.

All the little animals came to the pond.

They came to fish.

They came to drink.

They came to <u>swim</u>.

The pond was a happy <u>place</u>.

32

Little <u>Squirrel</u> and Little <u>Chipmunk</u> lived by the pond.

They were best friends.

From <u>sunrise</u> to sunset, they played in the woods.

They <u>spent</u> much of the <u>time</u> at the pond.

They would hide under the <u>pine</u> trees, or they would just play by the <u>side</u> of the pond.

One day, trouble came to the pond.

The trouble was Big Bear.

All he wanted to do was sleep.

33

Before reading pages 32–33

SAY **The little animals were happy in the woods. Then something happened. Read pages 32 and 33 to see what happened.**

After reading pages 32–33

1. **What happened at the pond?** (A big bear came to sleep at the pond.) Literal
2. **What did the little animals like to do at the pond?** (They liked to fish, to drink, to swim, and to play.) Inferential
3. **What animals were best friends?** (Little Chipmunk and Little Squirrel) Literal

Big Bear looked at the pine trees
and the soft grass next to the pond.
"This is a <u>fine</u> place to <u>nap</u>,"
said Big Bear with a <u>smile</u>.
So he did.

Big Bear came to the pond each day
to sleep.
When Big Bear was at the pond,
the little animals couldn't go there.
Big Bear was too mean!
The trouble was that Big Bear was
at the pond much of the time.

34

The animals had a meeting.
"How can we get <u>rid</u> of Big Bear?"
they asked.
They turned to wise Grandfather
Chipmunk for his help.
He did not know what to do.

The next day, Little Squirrel and
Little Chipmunk <u>met</u> in the woods.
"How can we make Big Bear
go away?" asked Little Squirrel.
"We must think of a way."

35

Before reading pages 34–35

SAY **Why do you think a sleeping bear could be such a problem? Read pages 34 and 35.**

After reading pages 34–35

1. **Why was the bear such a big problem?** (He was mean, and he came to the pond each day.) Inferential
2. **What did the little animals do?** (They had a meeting to try to think of a way to get rid of the bear.) Literal
3. **Why do you think the little animals asked Grandfather Chipmunk for help?** (They asked Grandfather Chipmunk because he was wise and because he might know how to solve the problem.) Inferential

"Let's <u>sneak</u> up to the pond
and take a look at Big Bear,"
said Little Chipmunk.

"No!" said Little Squirrel.
"What if Big Bear wakes up?"

"We'll take just one little look,"
said Little Chipmunk.

So off they went to the pond.

Wise Grandfather Chipmunk saw the
little animals as they ran to the pond.
"What if Big Bear wakes up?
They will be in trouble.
I must go for help."

36

Squirrel and Chipmunk hid in a tree
by the pond.
   They looked down and saw
Big Bear sleeping.

   Just then, a green bug <u>dropped</u>
on Big Bear's ear.

<u>Tickle</u>, tickle, tickle.

"<u>Ha</u>, ha, ha!" said Big Bear.

Tickle, tickle, tickle.

"Ha, ha, ha," said Big Bear.

Then the bug moved away, and
Big Bear fell back to sleep.

37

Before reading pages 36–37

SAY **Little Squirrel and Little Chipmunk wanted to do something about the bear. What do you think they will do? Read pages 36 and 37 to yourself.**

After reading pages 36–37

1. **What did Little Squirrel and Little Chipmunk do?** (They went to the pond to look at the bear.) Literal
2. **What did Grandfather Chipmunk think when he saw Little Squirrel and Little Chipmunk on their way to the pond?** (He was afraid the squirrel and the chipmunk would be in trouble with the bear, so he went to get help.) Inferential
3. **What did Little Squirrel and Little Chipmunk see at the pond?** (They saw a bug tickle the bear's ear and bother the bear.) Literal

Squirrel and Chipmunk were both thinking the same thing.

They got a twig and began to tickle the sleeping bear.

Tickle, tickle, tickle.

"Ha, ha, ha," went Big Bear.

Tickle, tickle, tickle.

"Ha, ha!" said Big Bear. "Stop! Stop!"

Squirrel and Chipmunk did not stop.

At last, Big Bear could no longer stand it.
Up he jumped, and away he ran. He ran as fast as he could.

Squirrel and Chipmunk ran to tell the others.

38

39

Before reading pages 38–39

SAY **Little Squirrel and Little Chipmunk got an idea. What do you think they will do? Read pages 38 and 39.**

After reading pages 38–39

What did Little Squirrel and Little Chipmunk do? (They tickled the bear until the bear ran away.) Literal

All of a sudden, Squirrel stopped.
"What's that noise?" he asked.
"Is it Big Bear?"

Both friends ran
up a pine tree to hide.
It wasn't Big Bear.
It was Grandfather Chipmunk and
the other animals running to the pond.

"We must help the little ones,"
said Grandfather Chipmunk.

40

"We are fine!"
yelled Squirrel and Chipmunk as they
jumped from the tree.

"You ran away from Big Bear!"
the other animals said.

"No, we did not!" said Squirrel.
"Big Bear is the one who
ran away."

"What made him go away?"
asked Grandfather Squirrel.

"We did!" said Squirrel.

"How could little animals like you
do that?" asked Mother Squirrel.

"We did it with a tickle!"
said Chipmunk.

41

Before reading pages 40–41

| SAY | **Little Squirrel and Little Chipmunk thought the problem was solved. What do you think? Read pages 40 and 41 to yourself.** |

After reading pages 40–41

1. **Why did Little Squirrel and Little Chipmunk hide in a tree?** (They heard a noise and thought it was Big Bear.) Inferential
2. **What was the noise?** (The little animals were coming to the pond to help Little Squirrel and Little Chipmunk.) Literal
3. **What did the animals think when they saw Little Squirrel and Little Chipmunk up in the tree?** (They thought that Little Squirrel and Little Chipmunk had run away from the bear.) Inferential

So that day, the animals went back
to the pond.

They went to fish.

They went to drink.

They went to swim.

They had a good time,
but Chipmunk and Squirrel
had the best time of all.

They got big bear hugs
from all their friends and neighbors
at the pond!

42

Discussing the Selection

1. What did the little animals do to
   get rid of Big Bear?
2. Why did the animals want Big Bear
   to go away?
3. What made Chipmunk and Squirrel
   tickle Big Bear?
4. When did you find out that
   Chipmunk and Squirrel's plan
   worked?
5. What will happen if Big Bear comes
   back to the pond?

43

Before reading page 42

SAY **How do you think the animals will feel when they find out that Little Squirrel and Little Chipmunk got rid of the bear? Read page 42 to yourself.**

After reading page 42

How did the animals feel when they found out that Little Squirrel and Little Chipmunk had gotten rid of the bear? How can you tell? (The animals were happy because they hugged Little Squirrel and Little Chipmunk.) Inferential

Discussing the Selection

Questions preceded by a number appear in the *Spotlights* after the selection. Questions preceded by a bullet are additional questions for extending discussion.

PURPOSE

1. **What did the little animals do to get rid of Big Bear?** (They tickled the bear until the bear ran away.) Literal

STORY MAPPING

2. **Why did the animals want Big Bear to go away?** (The bear was at the pond so the little animals could no longer go there to fish, play, swim, and drink.) Inferential

• **Why did Big Bear come to the pond each day?** (to sleep) Literal

3. **What made Chipmunk and Squirrel tickle Big Bear?** (They got the idea from watching a bug that had tickled the bear's ear.) Inferential

• **Why did Grandfather Chipmunk go for help?** (He thought Big Bear would wake up and harm Little Squirrel and Little Chipmunk.) Inferential

4. When did you find out that Chipmunk and Squirrel's plan worked? (on page 38, when Big Bear got up and ran away and the little animals returned to the pond) Literal

CRITICAL THINKING

5. What will happen if Big Bear comes back to the pond? (Answers will vary. Possible answers include: The animals will be frightened and will have to stay away until they get rid of the bear again.)

Using Language

ORAL READING: ANSWERING QUESTIONS Have pupils open their books to page 33. Explain that you will ask a question about the story that they can answer by reading sentences from the story. When everyone has found the answer, have them read it together.

Page 33: **What did Little Squirrel and Little Chipmunk do each day?** (From sunrise to sunset, they played in the woods.) **What happened to make trouble at the pond?** (One day, trouble came to the pond. The trouble was Big Bear. All he wanted to do was sleep.)

Page 34: **Read the sentences that tell why Big Bear was a problem at the pond.** (When Big Bear was at the pond, the little animals couldn't go there. Big Bear was too mean!)

Page 36: **What did Grandfather Chipmunk say when he saw the little animals go to the pond?** ("What if Big Bear wakes up? They will be in trouble. I must go for help.")

Page 37: **What did Little Squirrel and Little Chipmunk see happen at the pond?** (Just then, a green bug dropped on Big Bear's ear. Tickle, tickle, tickle. "Ha, ha, ha!" said Big Bear. Tickle, tickle, tickle. "Ha, ha, ha," said Big Bear. Then the bug moved away, and Big Bear fell back to sleep.)

Page 40: **What frightened Little Squirrel and Little Chipmunk on their way back from the pond?** ("What's that noise?" he asked. "Is it Big Bear?")

Page 42: **What did the animals do when they found out Big Bear was gone?** (So that day, the animals went back to the pond.)

CRITICAL THINKING: PROBLEM SOLVING (Cooperative Learning) Have pupils work in small groups to discuss alternate ways that the animals might have gotten Big Bear to leave the pond. Have each group select the best solution and write it down. Encourage members of the group to illustrate the solution. Have each group share its solution with the class.

Applying the Focus Skill

STORY STRUCTURE: PLOT Remind pupils that most stories have a problem that gets solved in some way. Ask what the problem was in the story "Bear Trouble." (Big Bear came to the pond every day to sleep and scared away the little animals.) Ask how the problem was solved. (Little Squirrel and Little Chipmunk tickled Big Bear and disturbed his sleep so he went away.)

Evaluating Comprehension

WB 23 **INDEPENDENT PRACTICE** *Workbook* page 23 may be used for an informal evaluation of story comprehension.

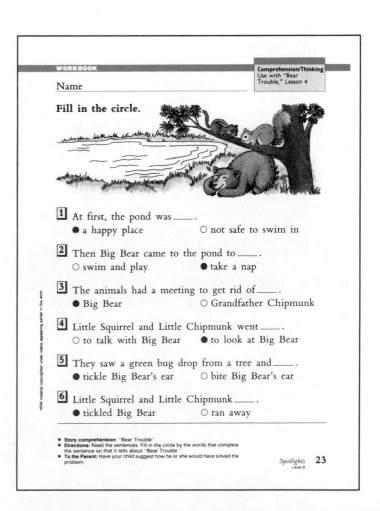

3 DEVELOPING READING AND THINKING SKILLS

DECODING/VOCABULARY

M Sound/symbol correspondence: consonant/l/*le* (final)

DIRECT INSTRUCTION Print the following nonsense rhyme and words on the chalkboard:

> Can you tickle
> A little green pickle?
>
> wiggle juggle trouble
> puddle jiggle giggle

Have the rhyme read. Ask what letters at the end of the word *tickle* stand for the /l/ sound. (*le*) Have pupils point to and read the other two words in the rhyme that end like *tickle*. (*little, pickle*)

GUIDED PRACTICE Call attention to the words on the chalkboard. Have each word read and ask which letters stand for the /l/ sound in the word.

PM 16 ADDITIONAL PRACTICE *Practice Masters* page 16 may be used as an optional practice for identifying sound/symbol correspondence /l/*le.* (See page T100 for reduced pages with answers.)

R, T Word structure: inflectional endings *-er, -est*

R, T Word structure: suffix *-er*

DIRECT INSTRUCTION Print the following words and sentences on the chalkboard:

> fast faster fastest
>
> 1. Chipmunk runs fast.
> 2. Squirrel runs faster than Chipmunk.
> 3. Rabbit runs the fastest of all.
>
> sleep sleeper
>
> 4. The bear likes to sleep.
> 5. The bear is a good sleeper.

Have the first set of words and sentences read.

SAY **Let's pretend that Squirrel, Chipmunk, and Rabbit wanted to have a race. Who can find and read the sentence that tells who would probably win the race?** (*Rabbit runs the fastest of all.*) **What word in that sentence tells you that Rabbit would probably win?** (*fastest*) **What letters were added to *fast* to make *fastest*?** (*-est*) **What sentence tells who would come in second in the race?** (*Squirrel runs faster than Chipmunk.*) **What letters were added to *fast* to make *faster*?** (*-er*) **Who do you think would lose the race?** (Chipmunk) **How do you know?** (Help pupils understand that, even though Chipmunk runs fast, Squirrel can run faster. Rabbit would probably win the race because Rabbit is the fastest of all.)

Have the second set of words and sentences read. Ask what the bear likes to do. (sleep) Point to the word *sleeper* in Sentence 5.

SAY **In this sentence, the word *sleeper* means "someone who sleeps." The letters *-er* were added to *sleep* to make the word *sleeper*. Sometimes when we add the letters *-er* to a word, we make a new word that means "someone who does something." Someone who sleeps is a sleeper. What would you call a person who sings?** (a singer) **What would you call a person who helps?** (a helper)

GUIDED PRACTICE Print the following words and sentences on the chalkboard, omitting the words in parentheses.

> big   bigger   biggest
>
> 1. Mary has a _____ book. (*big*)
> 2. Tim has a _____ book than Mary. (*bigger*)
> 3. Candy has the _____ book of all. (*biggest*)
>
> run   runner
>
> 4. Chang likes to _____. (*run*)
> 5. He is a good _____. (*runner*)

Have the first set of words and sentences read. Then call on a pupil to choose the word that best completes each sentence and have it read.

Follow a similar procedure for the second set of words and sentences.

WB 24 **INDEPENDENT PRACTICE** *Workbook* page 24 may be used to practice identifying inflectional endings *-er, -est.*

✳ **RETEACH** For those pupils who need additional instruction, see "Reteaching Lesson Skills," page T97, under "Reteaching and Extending."

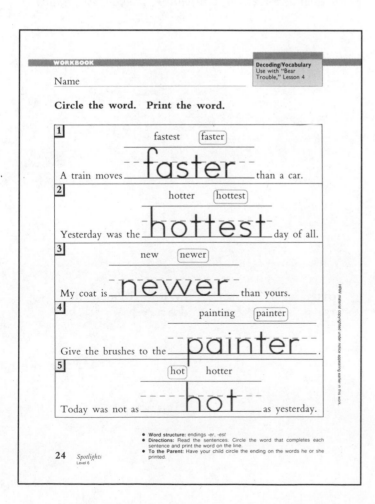

COMPREHENSION/THINKING

Focus

R, T **Story structure:** plot (problems and solutions)

DIRECT INSTRUCTION Remind pupils that in "Bear Trouble," the animals had a problem. At the end of the story, they found a way to solve their problem. Explain that the characters in most stories have problems that need to be solved.

GUIDED PRACTICE Read the following story and ask the questions that follow.

READ **A little toad wanted to go to the other side of the pond.**

"I will carry you across on my back," said the alligator.

"No, you will eat me," said the toad. "How can I get across the pond?"

"I will carry you across in my beak," said the hawk.

"No, you will eat me," said the toad.

Just then, the toad saw a log that had fallen across the pond.

"Good-by," said the toad. "Now I can get across the pond."

ASK **What was the little toad's problem?** (It wanted to get to the other side of a pond.) **How was the toad's problem solved?** (A log had fallen across the pond; the toad would hop along the log to get to the other side of the pond.) **Why didn't the toad let the alligator or the hawk carry it across the pond?** (The toad was afraid that they would eat it.)

WB 25 **INDEPENDENT PRACTICE** *Workbook* page 25 may be used to practice recognizing problems and solutions.

WORKBOOK

Name _____

Draw a line under the problem. Fill in the circle.

1

Billy needs a gift for Mom.
He knows Mom likes birds.
Billy sees his paints.

What will Billy do?

● He will paint a bird.
○ He will get a pet bird.

2

The book was on the shelf.
Jill could not get it.
Just then Mom came.

What will Jill do?

● She will ask for help.
○ She will scream.

3

Dog and Lion were friends.
A thorn was stuck in Lion.
He could not get it out.

What will Dog do?

○ She will run away.
● She will help Lion.

4

Dad wants to make a cake.
He does not know how.
Then he sees a book.

What will Dad do?

● He will read the book.
○ He will throw the book.

- **Story structure:** plot
- **Directions:** Read the story. Underline the problem the person has. Then fill in the circle by the solution.
- **To the Parent:** Have your child tell what clues in the story led him or her to the answer.

Spotlights **25**
Level 6

ADDITIONAL PRACTICE *Practice Masters* page 17 may be used as an optional practice for recognizing problems and solutions. (See page T100 for reduced pages with answers.)

✳ **RETEACH** For those pupils who need additional instruction, see "Reteaching Lesson Skills," page T98, under "Reteaching and Extending."

STUDY SKILLS

M Locating information: alphabetical order

DIRECT INSTRUCTION Place *Word Cards Squirrel, Bear, Chipmunk* in the *Pocket Chart* and have them read.

SAY Pretend that we have an animal telephone book. If we wanted to call Bear, we would have to look up his telephone number. The names in a telephone book are listed in alphabetical order. That means that the names that begin with *a* are listed first, the names that begin with *b* are next, and so on. Which of these animals would come first in the animal phone book? (*Bear*) Why? (*Bear* begins with *B*; letter *b* comes before *c* and *s* in the alphabet.)

Place *Word Card Bear* in the *Pocket Chart*. Have pupils tell which animal would come next (*Chipmunk*) and place the word under *Bear*. Then have pupils tell which animal would come last (*Squirrel*) and place the word at the end of the list.

GUIDED PRACTICE Remove the *Word Cards* from the *Pocket Chart* and display them with *Word Cards Dog, Rabbit*. Have pupils place the animal names in alphabetical order. (*Bear, Chipmunk, Dog, Rabbit, Squirrel*)

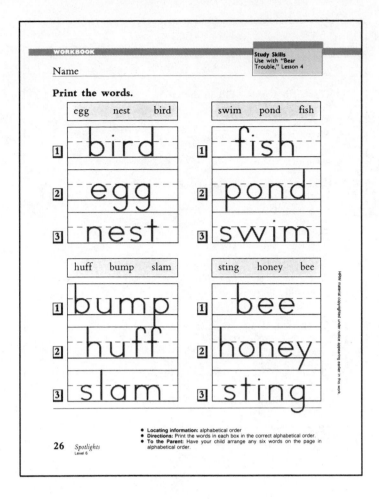

Name

Study Skills
Use with "Bear Trouble," Lesson 4

Print the words.

egg	nest	bird

1 bird
2 egg
3 nest

swim	pond	fish

1 fish
2 pond
3 swim

huff	bump	slam

1 bump
2 huff
3 slam

sting	honey	bee

1 bee
2 honey
3 sting

HRW material copyrighted under notice appearing earlier in this work.

● **Locating information:** alphabetical order
● **Directions:** Print the words in each box in the correct alphabetical order.
● **To the Parent:** Have your child arrange any six words on the page in alphabetical order.

26 *Spotlights*
Level 6

WB 26 **INDEPENDENT PRACTICE** *Workbook* page 26 may be used to practice putting words in alphabetical order.

LANGUAGE

I Speaking: paraphrasing

DIRECT INSTRUCTION   Ask pupils to open their books to page 32.

SAY **The little animals liked to fish, to drink, and to swim at the pond. Read the words from page 32 that tell what the animals did at the pond.** (All the little animals came to the pond. They came to fish. They came to drink. They came to swim.)

SAY **When I said that the animals liked to fish, drink, and swim at the pond, I was not using the exact words that are written in the story. I was telling part of the story in my own words. This is called paraphrasing. Look at page 33 in your books. I will paraphrase part of this page. Then I will ask you to read the exact words from the story.**

One day, Big Bear caused a problem at the pond.

Call on pupils to read the part of the story that tells that the bear caused a problem at the pond. (*One day, trouble came to the pond. The trouble was Big Bear.*) Point out that when you paraphrase you tell what happened using your own words.

GUIDED PRACTICE   Call on a pupil to select and read several sentences from the story. Then have another pupil paraphrase what was read.

R Conventions of language: capitalization

DIRECT INSTRUCTION Call on a pupil to print his or her name on the chalkboard. Ask what kind of letter is at the beginning of the pupil's name. (a capital letter) Explain that a name always begin with a capital letter.

GUIDED PRACTICE Print the following sentences on the chalkboard, omitting the underlining.

> 1. bob named his dog sam.
> 2. I had scott and tammy to my house.
> 3. Did you see jimmy at the shop?
> 4. Put samson back in his doghouse.

Call on a pupil to read each sentence and tell which word or words in the sentence are names. Have another pupil print the names with a capital letter at the beginning of each.

WB 27 INDEPENDENT PRACTICE *Workbook* page 27 may be used to practice capitalizing names.

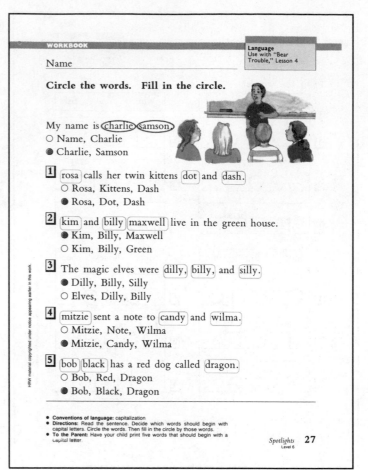

✳ RETEACHING AND EXTENDING

Reteaching Lesson Skills

The activities that follow provide reteaching of skills developed in this lesson. Not every pupil needs to complete these activities. Choose only the activities that are needed to provide for the individual differences in your classroom.

DECODING/VOCABULARY

I, T   Sound/symbol correspondence: vowel /ī/i-e

✳ **RETEACH**   Print the following pairs of words on the chalkboard:

IC 19

1.	dim	dime
2.	hid	hide
3.	slid	slide
4.	spin	spine

Point to the first pair of words and read them.

SAY   The letter *i* in *pin* stands for the /i/ sound. The letter *i* in *pine* stands for the /ī/ sound because *pine* has an *i*, followed by a consonant, and ends with letter *e*. Read each word as I point to it.

Point to each word several times.

Point to each remaining pair of words and have pupils read them with you. Call on pupils to identify the sound of letter *i* in each word. Explain that the *i* in *ride*, *kite*, and *fine* stands for the /ī/ sound because each word has *i*, followed by a consonant, and ends in *e*.

RM 6   Distribute *Reteach Masters* page 6 and explain the directions on the page.

R, T   Word structure: inflectional endings *-er*, *-est*

R, T   Word structure: suffix *-er*

✳ **RETEACH**   Print the following words and sentences on the chalkboard. Have the first set of words and the sentences read.

IC 26

big   bigger   biggest

1. Bill has a big dog.
2. Shana has a bigger dog than Bill.
3. Tammy has the biggest dog of all.

sing   play
singer   player

SAY   When we talk about the size of just one dog, as the first sentence does, we say that the dog is big. What word do we use when we compare the size of one dog to another? (*bigger*) We double the final consonant *g* before adding an ending to *big*. What ending was added to *big* to make *bigger*? (*-er*) When we compare the size of one dog to two or more dogs, what word do we use? (*biggest*) What ending was added to *big* to make *biggest*? (*-est*)

Have *sing* and *singer* read. Ask what a singer is. (someone who sings) Ask pupils what new word was made when the ending *-er* was added to *sing*. (*singer*) Ask what *singer* means. ("someone who sings")

Have *play* and *player* read. Ask what a player is. (someone who plays) Explain that the ending *-er* was added to *play* to make a new word that means "someone who plays."

I, T   Vocabulary: word meaning

 RETEACH Print the following words and sentences on the chalkboard, omitting the underlining.

IC 20

> **Bear began Chipmunk Ha place Squirrel trouble woods**
>
> 1. <u>Bear</u> <u>began</u> his day in the <u>woods</u>.
> 2. He went to eat some of <u>Squirrel</u>'s food.
> 3. <u>Chipmunk</u> began to eat some nuts, too.
> 4. "Get away from this <u>place</u>, or there will be <u>trouble</u>!" said Squirrel.
> 5. Bear and Chipmunk giggled, "<u>Ha</u>, ha, ha," and went away.
>
> **fine   pine   side   smile**
> **sunrise   tickle   time**

Point to the word *Bear* and read the word. Call on a pupil to find and read a sentence that contains the word *Bear.* Continue in the same manner with the remaining sentences.

Display *Word Cards* for the underlined words. Call on pupils to hold up and read the word that answers each of the following questions.

1. **Which words name animals?** (*Bear, Chipmunk, Squirrel*)
2. **Which word means "started"?** (*began*)
3. **Which word tells what you say when you laugh?** (*Ha*)
4. **Which word rhymes with *face*?** (*place*)
5. **Which word means "forest"?** (*woods*)
6. **Which word means "a problem"?** (*trouble*)

 RM 7 Distribute *Reteach Masters* page 7 and explain the directions on the page.

Focus

R, T   Story structure: plot (problems and solutions)

RETEACH Read the following story and then ask pupils what the problem was and how it was solved.

READ **Freckles the Clown was not happy. She could not find one of her giant red shoes. "Oh dear!" groaned Freckles. "How can I go out on stage with only one shoe? People will laugh at me."**

Suddenly, Freckles smiled the biggest smile she could. "How silly of me," she said. "People are supposed to laugh at me. Maybe I will be funnier if I only wear one shoe."

Ask what problem Freckles had (She couldn't find one of her red shoes.) and how Freckles solved her problem. (She decided to go out on stage with only one shoe because people were supposed to laugh at clowns.)

Extending Selection Concepts

LANGUAGE ARTS

SPEAKING/WRITING: USING VOCABULARY WORDS Place *Word Cards Bear, began, Chipmunk, Ha, place, Squirrel, trouble, woods* in a container. Invite a pupil to select two words from the container, to read the words, and to use both words in one sentence. Then have the pupil return the cards to the container and ask another pupil to complete the activity. Pupils may perform this activity in pairs or in small groups. Encourage pupils to write and illustrate the sentence they made.

LITERATURE

LISTENING: FICTION Choose a story about bears, squirrels, or chipmunks. Ask pupils to listen as you read the story. Ask what the problem was in the story and how the problem was solved.

Delton, Judy. *Two Good Friends.* Crown, 1974. A bear and a duck, two unlikely animals to be friends, demonstrate their friendship.

Gage, Wilson. *Cully, Cully and the Bear.* Greenwillow, 1983. An old codger and an angry bear chase each other around and around a tree.

Sharmat, Marjorie Weinman. *The Trip and Other Sophie and Gussie Stories.* Macmillan, 1976. These four short stories show the problems and delights of friendship between two squirrels.

HOW AM I DOING?

Many pupils need help in clarifying their ideas so they can begin establishing a well-organized approach to creative writing. Ask yourself the following questions to gauge your teaching effectiveness in this area.

	Yes	No	Some-times
1. Do I respond positively to pupils' questions?	☐	☐	☐
2. Did I help them understand the importance of writing clear descriptions?	☐	☐	☐
3. Do I share well written articles or books with the class?	☐	☐	☐
4. As I read aloud, do I point out good examples of descriptive writing as models for them to emulate?	☐	☐	☐

Name

Print the word.

kite	bike	fire	tire
pine	nine	smile	slide

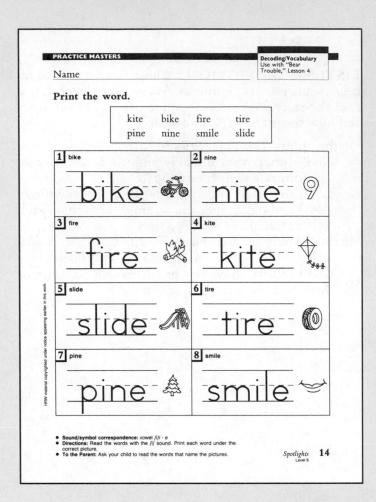

1 bike — bike

2 nine — nine

3 fire — fire

4 kite — kite

5 slide — slide

6 tire — tire

7 pine — pine

8 smile — smile

• **Sound/symbol correspondence:** vowel /ī/ - e
• **Directions:** Read the words with the /ī/ sound. Print each word under the correct picture.
• **To the Parent:** Ask your child to read the words that name the pictures.

Name

Draw a line.

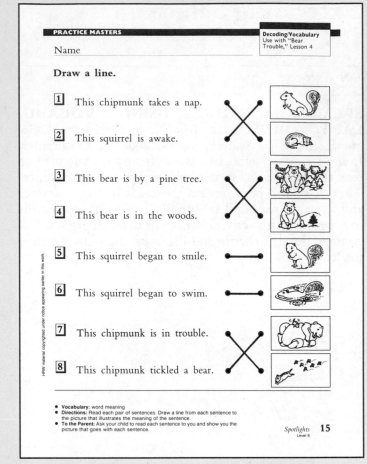

1 This chipmunk takes a nap.

2 This squirrel is awake.

3 This bear is by a pine tree.

4 This bear is in the woods.

5 This squirrel began to smile.

6 This squirrel began to swim.

7 This chipmunk is in trouble.

8 This chipmunk tickled a bear.

• **Vocabulary:** word meaning
• **Directions:** Read each pair of sentences. Draw a line from each sentence to the picture that illustrates the meaning of the sentence.
• **To the Parent:** Ask your child to read each sentence to you and show you the picture that goes with each sentence.

Name

Print the word. Circle the words.

cuddle	beagle	puddle	apple

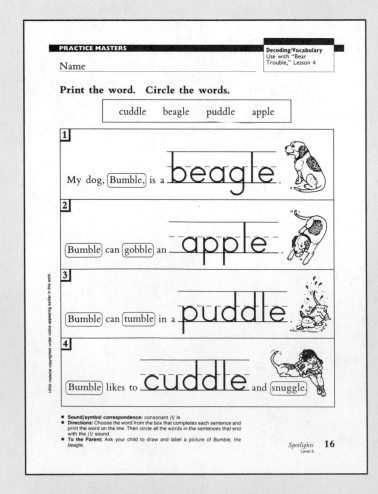

1 My dog, (Bumble,) is a beagle.

2 (Bumble) can (gobble) an apple.

3 (Bumble) can (tumble) in a puddle.

4 (Bumble) likes to cuddle and (snuggle).

• **Sound/symbol correspondence:** consonant /l/ le
• **Directions:** Choose the word from the box that completes each sentence and print the word on the line. Then circle all the words in the sentences that end with the /l/ sound.
• **To the Parent:** Ask your child to draw and label a picture of *Bumble, the beagle.*

Name

Print the sentence.

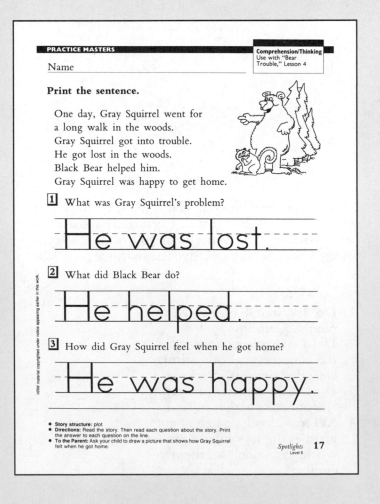

One day, Gray Squirrel went for a long walk in the woods. Gray Squirrel got into trouble. He got lost in the woods. Black Bear helped him. Gray Squirrel was happy to get home.

1 What was Gray Squirrel's problem?

He was lost.

2 What did Black Bear do?

He helped.

3 How did Gray Squirrel feel when he got home?

He was happy.

• **Story structure:** plot
• **Directions:** Read the story. Then read each question about the story. Print the answer to each question on the line.
• **To the Parent:** Ask your child to draw a picture that shows how Gray Squirrel felt when he got home.

Name

Circle the word. Print the word.

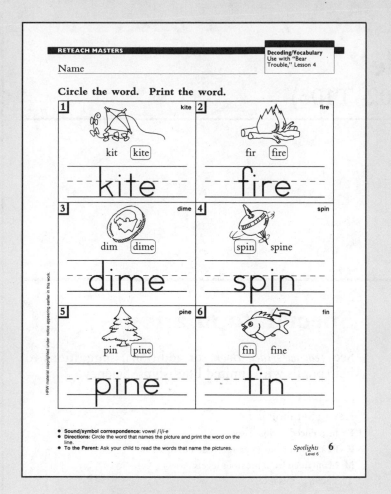

1 kite
kit kite
kite

2 fire
fir fire
fire

3 dime
dim dime
dime

4 spin
spin spine
spin

5 pine
pin pine
pine

6 fin
fin fine
fin

- **Sound/symbol correspondence:** vowel /i/i-e
- **Directions:** Circle the word that names the picture and print the word on the line.
- **To the Parent:** Ask your child to read the words that name the pictures.

Spotlights
Level 6   **6**

Name

Print the word.

began   trouble   woods   place

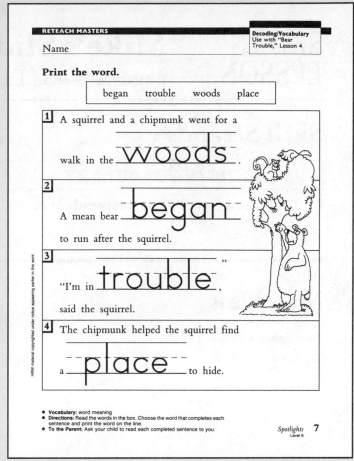

1 A squirrel and a chipmunk went for a
walk in the **woods** .

2 A mean bear **began**
to run after the squirrel.

3 "I'm in **trouble** ,"
said the squirrel.

4 The chipmunk helped the squirrel find
a **place** to hide.

- **Vocabulary:** word meaning
- **Directions:** Read the words in the box. Choose the word that completes each sentence and print the word on the line.
- **To the Parent:** Ask your child to read each completed sentence to you.

Spotlights
Level 6   **7**

"Mike's Slide"
pages 44–45 (T102–T103)

Skill Strands

DECODING/VOCABULARY

R, T **Sound/symbol correspondence:**
vowel /ī/i-e

Materials

Spotlights, Level 6: pages 44–45
Teacher's Idea Book

Special Populations

See *Teacher's Idea Book* for additional suggestions to help pupils with limited English proficiency.

Key to Symbols
I Introduced in this lesson
R Reinforced from an earlier lesson in this level
M Maintained from previous levels
T Tested in this level

DECODING/VOCABULARY

R, T **Sound/symbol correspondence:** vowel /ī/i-e

DIRECT INSTRUCTION Ask pupils to solve the following riddle:

 **I am at a playground.
You climb up my ladder
And zip back down.
What am I?** (a slide)

When pupils guess the word *slide,* print the word on the chalkboard. Point to the word and have pupils read it with you. Ask what letter stands for the /ī/ sound in *slide.* (letter *i*) Ask pupils to explain why letter *i* stands for the /ī/ sound. (It is followed by a consonant and letter *e.*)

GUIDED PRACTICE Have pupils find page 44 in *Spotlights.* Have the title read. ("Mike's Slide") Explain that many words in this story have letter *i,* followed by a consonant, with letter *e* at the end. Have pupils read pages 44 and 45 to themselves.

Ask what Mike built. (a slide) Ask what he used to make the slide. (pine) Ask why Mike was filled with pride. (He had made people smile.) Invite pupils to name the words on pages 44 and 45 in which letter *i* stands for the /ī/ sound. (*Mike's, slide, pine, fine, Mike, smile, wide, pile, side, glide, mile, pride*)

Mike's Slide

Read the sentences.
Tell the story.

"This pine is fine
To make a slide,"
Said Big Mike with a smile.

"It's not too thin.
It's not too wide."
He put the pine in a pile.

Mike made the side
Where people glide
Go on and on for a mile.

Mike looked at the slide
And was filled with pride.
He had made the people smile.

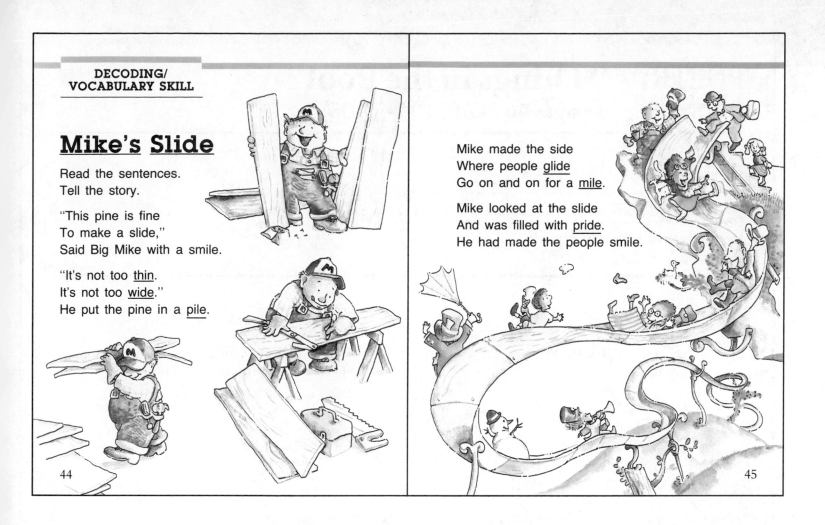

44

45

POETRY LESSON

"Things in the Pool"
pages 46–47 (T104–T105)

Skill Strands

COMPREHENSION/THINKING

R **Forms of literature:** poetry

Materials

Spotlights, Level 6: pages 46–47
Teacher's Idea Book

Special Populations

See *Teacher's Idea Book* for additional suggestions to help pupils with limited English proficiency.

Key to Symbols
I Introduced in this lesson
R Reinforced from an earlier lesson in this level
M Maintained from previous levels
T Tested in this level

COMPREHENSION/THINKING

R **Forms of literature:** poetry

DIRECT INSTRUCTION Ask where the little animals liked to go in "Bear Trouble." (They liked to go to the pond.) Explain that a small pond can also be called a pool. Tell pupils that there is a poem in their books about a quiet pool.

Have pupils find pages 46 and 47 in their books and read the title "Things in the Pool." Ask what kinds of things might be found in a pool. (Possible answers include: fish, frogs, bugs, turtles.) Have pupils listen as you read the poem to see what things are found in this pool. Read aloud the poem "Things in the Pool."

GUIDED PRACTICE Ask what things were in the quiet pool. (fish, bugs, snakes, turtles) Ask what the poet meant by the words "I see me looking up, my eyes, my face." (When you look into a pool of water, you can see yourself reflected in the water just as if you were looking into a mirror.)

Reread the poem and ask pupils to join you. Encourage pupils to read the poem on their own.

(To be read by the teacher)

Things in the Pool

In this quiet pool
fish
glide
bugs
ride
snakes
slide
turtles
hide

And in this quiet place
I
see
Me
looking up,
my
eyes
my
face.

Lilian Moore

46

47

LESSON 5

"The Chili Pot"
pages 48–57 (T106–T127)

Skill Strands

DECODING/VOCABULARY

R, T   **Sound/symbol correspondence:** vowel /ī/*i-e*

R   **Sound/symbol correspondence:** vowel discrimination: /i/, /ī/

I, T   **Word structure:** contractions (with *'re*)

M   **Vocabulary:** compound words

M   **Vocabulary:** multiple meanings

I   **Vocabulary:** word building

I, T   **Vocabulary:** word meaning

COMPREHENSION/THINKING

Focus

R, T   **Inferential:** predicting outcomes

STUDY SKILLS

R, T   **References:** dictionary (entry words and definitions)

LANGUAGE

R   **Listening:** oral directions (multiple-step)

Lesson Vocabulary

Decodable words: *bite, bowls, different, everyone, land, please, plenty, pot, table, these, they're, we're, you're*

Special words: *been, chili, even, Maria, Tina*

Materials

Spotlights, Level 6: pages 48–57
Workbook: pages 28–33

Practice Masters: pages 18–22
Instructional Charts: pages 27–34
Resource Box: Letter Cards a, b, e, f, i, k, m, n, t
          Word Cards been, bit, chili, even, fin, hid, Maria, pin, rid, Tina

Pocket Chart
Teacher's Idea Book
Reteach Masters: page 8

Language Applications

USING LANGUAGE

Oral reading/Speaking: dialogue

EXTENDING SELECTION CONCEPTS

Writing: stories
Listening: fiction

Special Populations

See *Teacher's Idea Book* for additional suggestions to help pupils with limited English proficiency.

Key to Symbols

I   Introduced in this lesson
R   Reinforced from an earlier lesson in this level
M   Maintained from previous levels
T   Tested in this level

Idea Center

BIBLIOGRAPHY

Add to your reading corner or reading table folk tales about cooking pots or about magic spells that go awry. A suggested bibliography follows. Suggestions for reading aloud and annotations appear in the lesson plan.

Galdone, Joanna. *The Magic Porridge Pot.* The Seabury Press, 1976.

Galdone, Paul. *The Table, the Donkey, and the Stick.* McGraw-Hill, 1976.

Planning Chart

	Instruction	Written Practice	Extending
Step 1 Preparing for the Selection	**R, T** **Sound/symbol correspondence:** vowel /ī/*i-e* **I, T** **Word structure:** contractions (with *'re*) **I** **Vocabulary:** word building **I, T** **Vocabulary:** word meaning **R, T** **Inferential:** predicting outcomes	 *Workbook* page 28 *Practice Masters* page 18 *Workbook* page 29 *Practice Masters* page 19 *Reteach Masters* page 8	
Step 2 Reading for Comprehension	**Oral reading/Speaking:** dialogue **Inferential:** predicting outcomes **Story comprehension**	 *Workbook* page 30	
Step 3 Developing Reading and Thinking Skills	**R** **Sound/symbol correspondence:** vowel discrimination: /i/, /ī/ **M** **Vocabulary:** compound words **M** **Vocabulary:** multiple meanings **R, T** **Inferential:** predicting outcomes **R, T** **References:** dictionary (entry words and definitions) **R** **Listening:** oral directions (multiple-step)	*Workbook* page 31 *Practice Masters* page 20 *Workbook* page 32 *Practice Masters* page 21 *Workbook* page 33 *Practice Masters* page 22	**Writing:** stories **Listening:** fiction

DECODING/VOCABULARY

R, T Sound/symbol correspondence: vowel /ī/i-e

DIRECT INSTRUCTION Print the following words on the chalkboard. Read aloud the words in the first row.

hide	nine	file	like
mile	dine	ride	bike
slide	pile	hike	pine

Ask what is alike about the four words. (Possible answers include: They have four letters; they have the /ī/, or long i, sound; they have the letters i and e.)

> **SAY** In the words *hide, nine, file,* and *like,* letter *i* stands for the /ī/ sound. Each word has an *i,* followed by a consonant, and ends with *e*. In words like these, *i* usually stands for the /ī/ sound.

GUIDED PRACTICE Direct pupils' attention to the last two rows of words on the chalkboard and have each word read. Ask pupils to explain what sound letter *i* stands for in each word and why. (Letter *i* stands for the /ī/, or long i, sound because each word has an *i,* followed by a consonant, and ends with *e*.)

✳ RETEACH For those pupils who need additional instruction, see "Reteaching Lesson Skills," page T124, under "Reteaching and Extending."

I, T Word structure: contractions (with *'re*)

DIRECT INSTRUCTION Print the following sentences on the chalkboard:

1. You are tops.	
2. You're tops.	
1. we are	a. they're
2. you are	b. we're
3. they are	c. you're

Have pupils read the first sentence with you.

> **SAY** **We can put the words *you* and *are* together to make one word.** (Read the second sentence aloud and point to *You're.*) **This is the word *You're.* The words *you* and *are* were put together to make the word *you're.* What letter was left out of *you are* to make *you're?*** (*a*) **What does the apostrophe in *you're* mean?** (The apostrophe shows that letter *a* has been left out.)

Have pupils read each sentence aloud.

GUIDED PRACTICE Direct pupils' attention to the columns of words on the chalkboard.

Call on a pupil to read the words by number 1. Then ask the pupil to match the two words with the contraction that has the same meaning. Continue in the same manner with the remaining sets of words and contractions. (1-b, 2-c, 3-a)

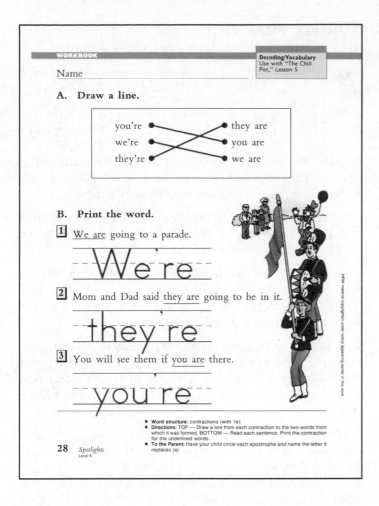

Name _____

A. Draw a line.

you're ●   ● they are
we're ●   ● you are
they're ●   ● we are

B. Print the word.

1 We are going to a parade.

$$We're$$

2 Mom and Dad said they are going to be in it.

$$they're$$

3 You will see them if you are there.

$$you're$$

- Word structure: contractions (with 're)
- Directions: TOP — Draw a line from each contraction to the two words from which it was formed. BOTTOM — Read each sentence. Print the contraction for the underlined words.
- To the Parent: Have your child circle each apostrophe and name the letter it replaces (a).

28   *Spotlights*
Level 6

WB 28   **INDEPENDENT PRACTICE**   *Workbook* page 28 may be used to practice identifying contractions with *'re*.

PM 18   **ADDITIONAL PRACTICE**   *Practice Masters* page 18 may be used as an optional practice for identifying contractions with *'re*. (See page T126 for reduced pages with answers.)

✳   **RETEACH**   For those pupils who need additional instruction, see "Reteaching Lesson Skills," page T124, under "Reteaching and Extending."

I   Vocabulary: word building

DIRECT INSTRUCTION Use *Letter Cards* to make the word *mine* in the *Pocket Chart* and have it read. Ask what sound the letter *i* stands for in *mine* and why. (Letter *i* stands for the /ī/ sound in *mine* because *mine* has an *i*, followed by a consonant, and an *e* is at the end of the word.) Replace the *i* with *a* and have the new word read. (*mane*) Ask what sound the letter *a* stands for in *mane* and why. (Letter *a* stands for the /ā/ sound in *mane* because *a* is followed by a consonant and an *e* is at the end of the word.) Remove the letter *e* and have the new word read. (*man*)

GUIDED PRACTICE   Display *Letter Cards b, e, f, i, k, t*. Ask a pupil to change the word *man* to *mane*. Have the new word read. Continue by giving the following instructions:

1. **Change the *n* to *k*. What word did you make?** (*make*)
2. **Change *make* to *bake*. Read the new word.**
3. **Change the *a* to *i*. What word did you make?** (*bike*)
4. **Change the *k* to *t*. What word did you make?** (*bite*)
5. **Change *bite* to *bit*. Read the new word.**
6. **Change the *i* to *a*. What word did you make?** (*bat*)
7. **Change the *b* to *f*. What word did you make?** (*fat*)
8. **Change the *a* to *i*. What word did you make?** (*fit*)
9. **Change the *t* to *n*. What word did you make?** (*fin*)
10. **Change *fin* to *fine*. Read the new word.**

I, T Vocabulary: word meaning

DIRECT INSTRUCTION Print the following words and sentences on the chalkboard, omitting the underlining.

> been chili even Maria Tina
>
> 1. <u>Maria</u> has not <u>been</u> happy.
> 2. She made some <u>chili</u>.
> 3. <u>Tina</u> did not like the chili.
> 4. She would not <u>even</u> taste it.
>
> **bite different**
> **they're we're you're**

Tell pupils that they are going to talk about some words they will read in the next story.

Read the first sentence. Point to the word *Maria* and read it. Ask who has not been happy. (Maria) Have pupils read the sentence with you. Then ask them to find and read the word *been*.

Read Sentence 2. Point to the word *chili* and read it. Ask what Maria made. (some chili) Have pupils read the sentence with you. Then ask them to find and read the word *chili*.

Read Sentence 3. Point to the word *Tina* and read it. Ask how Tina felt about chili. (She did not like it.) Have pupils read the sentence with you. Then ask them to find and read the word *Tina*.

Read Sentence 4. Point to the word *even* and read it. Ask how you can tell that Tina *really* did not like chili. (She would not even taste it.) Have pupils read the sentence with you. Then ask them to find and read the word *even*.

The words in the second set are new words that contain known phonic elements. You may wish to ask pupils to read the words, using what they know about letters and sounds.

GUIDED PRACTICE Print the following sentences on the chalkboard, omitting the underlining.

> 1. This chili is <u>different</u> from Mom's.
> 2. <u>You're</u> not going to like it.
> 3. <u>They're</u> not even going to take a <u>bite</u>.
> 4. Everyone thinks <u>we're</u> silly.

Provide opportunities for pupils to practice reading the new special words and some of the new decodable words in these sentences by following the suggestions below.

Sentence 1: Have the sentence read. Then have pupils find and read the word *different*. Ask if this chili is like the chili that Mom makes. (No, it is different.)

Sentence 2: Have the sentence read aloud. Ask who is not going to like the chili. (you) Have pupils find and read the contraction *you're*. Then ask what two words make up the contraction. (*you are*)

Sentence 3: Ask pupils to find and read the word *even*. Have the sentence read aloud. Ask if they will try the chili. (No, they're not even going to take a bite.) Ask what two words make up the contraction *They're*. (They are)

Sentence 4: Have the sentence read aloud. Ask why someone might think the people in the story are silly. (because they won't even taste the chili) Call on a pupil to find and read the contraction *we're*. Then ask for what letter the apostrophe in *we're* stands. (*a*)

Invite pupils to select a sentence to read aloud.

Name _____

Decoding/Vocabulary
Use with "The Chili Pot," Lesson 5

Print the word.

| chili | different | even | Maria | pot |

1. Maria _____ wanted to eat.

2. "I want something different _____."

3. Mom took out a big pot _____.

4. Then she made some chili _____.

5. Everyone liked it, even _____ Dad.

● **Vocabulary:** word meaning
● **Directions:** Read the words in the box. Read the sentences. Print the word from the box that completes each sentence.
● **To the Parent:** Have your child use the words in the box in sentences.

Spotlights **29**
Level 6

WB 29 **INDEPENDENT PRACTICE** *Workbook* page 29 may be used to practice reading story vocabulary.

PM 19 **ADDITIONAL PRACTICE** *Practice Masters* page 19 may be used as an optional practice for reading story vocabulary. (See page T126 for reduced pages with answers.)

✳ **RETEACH** For those pupils who need additional instruction, see "Reteaching Lesson Skills," page T124, under "Reteaching and Extending."

Focus

R, T Inferential: predicting outcomes

DIRECT INSTRUCTION Tell pupils that you will read a story. Then you will ask what might happen next.

READ Patty wanted to take some toys to her friend's house. She put her doll, some books, her teddy bear, and her roller skates into a box. Then she tried to pick up the box. It was too heavy for her to lift.

ASK What do you think Patty will do? (Possible answers include: She will take some things out of the box.)

SAY When you guess what might happen, you are making a prediction. What did you know about Patty and the box that helped you predict what she would do? (You knew that she put too many toys into the box.) You used the information in the story to help you make a prediction.

GUIDED PRACTICE Read the following story and ask pupils to predict what might happen next.

READ Maggie was hungry when she got home from school. She looked in the cupboard. She saw cookies, some bread, and a jar of peanut butter. She knew that her mother did not like her to eat cookies for a snack.

ASK What do you think Maggie will do? (She will make a peanut butter sandwich.) What do you know from listening to the story that helped you predict that she would eat a sandwich? (The story said that she saw peanut butter and some bread; it also said that her mother did not like her to eat cookies.)

Lesson 5 "The Chili Pot" (pages 48–57)   T111

Background for the Teacher

SUMMARY   Maria buys a pot that will make chili when she says some magic words. She must say different magic words when she wants the pot to stop making chili. Maria's friend Tina finds out the secret for making chili, but she does not know how to stop the pot.

INFORMATION   This story is a folk tale much like "The Sorcerer's Apprentice" or "The Magic Stick." It teaches the moral that someone who is greedy will be taught a lesson.

Using Prior Knowledge

Ask pupils to think about the people who fix school lunches or cook meals at home. Ask how the cooks might feel if they found a magic pot that would make meals all by itself. (Possible answers include: They might be happy.) Develop a discussion by asking questions such as those that follow:

1. **Have you ever heard a story about something that is "magic"? What do the people in the stories usually have to say to make the magic work?** (Possible answers include: They have to say magic words.)
2. **Pretend that your friend left a magic wand at your house. What might you do?** (Possible answers include: try to use the magic wand; take the wand back to the friend.)

Setting a Purpose for Reading

Have pupils turn to pages 48 and 49 in their books and look at the pictures. Explain that the title of this story is "The Chili Pot." Ask what would be made in a chili pot. (chili)

Point out the headnote at the top of page 48. Explain that the note will help pupils think about the story they are going to read. Have the headnote read aloud. Then ask pupils to predict what they think will happen when a neighbor wants to make chili.

Reading Silently

Some pupils may be able to read this story independently. Direct them to read the whole story to find out more about what happened when Maria tried to make chili in her new pot. For those pupils who need more guidance, suggestions for directed reading follow.

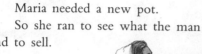
Maria's chili pot is different
from other pots.

Read to find out what happens when
a neighbor wants to make chili.

The Chili Pot

A long time ago, there lived a girl
by the name of Maria.

One day a man came by,
selling pots.

Maria needed a new pot.

So she ran to see what the man
had to sell.

48

People came from miles away
to look at the pots.

"Why, they're not even new pots,"
everyone said.

They walked away.

49

Before
reading
pages
48–49

SAY **One day, a man came along
selling pots. Do you think the
people will be interested in the pots?
Read pages 48 and 49 to yourself.**

After
reading
pages
48–49

1. **How did the people feel about the
   pots the man had to sell? Why?** (They
   were disappointed because the pots were
   not new pots.) Inferential
2. **Why did Maria go to see the pots?**
   (because she needed one) Literal

"Don't go away," the man said to Maria.

"These pots do things other pots can't do."

"Like what?" asked Maria.

"What do you like to eat?"

"Chili," said Maria.

"Then take this one," said the man as he picked up a little gray pot.

"Say, **Chili I want**, and the pot will make chili.

Say, **Chili stop**, and the pot will stop.

You're going to like the chili that it makes."

50

Maria ran home.

She put the little gray pot on the table.

"Chili I want," she said.

The pot began to make chili.

When Maria said, "Chili stop," the pot stopped.

Maria ate the chili.

"This is fine chili!

I will make some for all my neighbors," she said.

After that, Maria's neighbors had all the chili they wanted.

51

Before reading pages 50–51

SAY Do you think Maria will stay and look at the pots? Read pages 50 and 51 to find out.

After reading pages 50–51

1. **How did the man get Maria to look at the pots?** (He told her that the pots would do things other pots would not do.) Inferential
2. **What was special about the pot Maria bought?** (It would make chili when she said, "Chili I want"; it would stop when she said, "Chili stop.") Inferential
3. **Do you think Maria believed the man? Why or why not?** (yes, because she went home to make chili) Critical

Tina was Maria's neighbor.
"This chili is the best I have ever had," said Tina.
"How can you make so much in just a little bit of time?"

Maria would not tell her.

Day after day, Tina ate Maria's chili.

Day after day, Tina asked Maria how she made the chili, but Maria would not tell.

52

"I'll hide by Maria's window," Tina said to herself.
"Then I will find out how she makes all that fine chili."

So the next day, Tina hid by Maria's window.

Tina saw Maria put the gray pot on the table.

Then Maria said, "Chili I want."
The pot began to make chili.

"So that's how she does it," Tina said, and she ran back to her house.

Tina was not by the window when Maria said, "Chili stop."

53

Before reading pages 52–53

| SAY | **Maria shared her chili with her neighbors. What did the neighbors think about Maria and her chili? Read page 52 and 53 to yourself.**

After reading pages 52–53

1. **What did Tina think about Maria's chili?** (She thought it was the best chili; she wanted Maria to tell her how she made it.) Inferential
2. **What did Tina do?** (She hid and watched Maria make the chili.) Literal
3. **What didn't Tina hear Maria say?** ("Chili stop.") **What do you think will happen?** (Answers will vary. Possible answers include: Tina will not know how to get the pot to stop making chili.) Critical

The following day, Tina went to Maria's house.

Maria was not home.

"Today I will be the one to make fine chili," she said as she put the pot on the table.

"Chili I want," said Tina, and the pot began to make chili.

In no time, the chili filled the pot and flowed down the sides.

The chili ran out of the house and out into the street.

Maria was on her way home when she saw the chili . . . miles of chili!

"Help! Help, Maria!" yelled Tina. "Make the chili pot stop!"

54

Maria ran into the house. "Chili stop," she said, and the pot stopped.

"<u>Please</u> do not be mad, Maria," pleaded Tina.

"I did not mean to make this mess. I will clean it up."

"We'll get the neighbors to help," said Maria.

"<u>We're</u> going to have <u>plenty</u> of chili to eat."

55

Before reading page 54

SAY **What do you think Tina will do? Read page 54 to yourself.**

After reading page 54

What happened when Tina tried to make chili? (The pot kept making chili; the chili overflowed and went everywhere.) **Why?** (Tina did not know to say "Chili stop.") Inferential

Before reading pages 55–57

SAY **What do you think will happen when Maria comes home? Read pages 55 to 57 to yourself.**

So the neighbors came.

They put chili in big <u>bowls</u>, and they put chili in little bowls.

Then they sat down to eat.

They ate <u>bite</u> after bite of the best chili in the <u>land</u>.

56

After that, Maria still made chili for all her friends.

However, no one ever again asked how she did it.

Discussing the Selection

1. How was Maria's pot different from other pots?
2. How did Tina find out how the chili was made?
3. What happened when Tina made the chili?
4. Find the sentence in the story that tells why Tina could not stop the chili pot.
5. If you were Maria, would you have <u>been</u> upset with Tina? Why?

57

After reading pages 55–57

1. **What was the first thing Maria did when she got home?** (She yelled, "Chili stop.") Literal
2. **Do you think Maria was angry with Tina? Why or why not?** (Possible answers include: yes, because Tina had made a mess; no, because Maria knew she could get help from the neighbors.) Inferential
3. **Why didn't anyone ever again ask Maria to tell how the chili was made?** (Possible answers include: Maria always shared the chili, so no one needed to know; everyone had learned a lesson from helping clean up the chili.) Critical

Discussing the Selection

Questions preceded by a number appear in *Spotlights* after the selection. Questions preceded by a bullet are additional questions for extending discussion.

PURPOSE

1. **How was Maria's pot different from other pots?** (It would make chili when Maria said, "Chili I want"; it would stop when Maria said, "Chili stop.") Inferential

• **Where did Maria get her special chili pot?** (She bought it from a man selling pots.) Literal

STORY MAPPING

2. **How did Tina find out how the chili was made?** (She hid by Maria's window and watched Maria.) Literal

3. **What happened when Tina made chili?** (She didn't know how to stop the pot, so chili overflowed and went everywhere.) Inferential

• **Where in the story did Maria first know that something was wrong?** (when she saw chili flowing into the street) Inferential

4. **Find the sentence in the story that tells why Tina could not stop the chili pot.** (Page 53: Tina was not by the window when Maria said, "Chili stop.") Literal

CRITICAL THINKING

5. **If you were Maria, would you have been upset with Tina? Why?** (Answers will vary. Possible answers include: yes, because Tina should not have sneaked into Maria's house and used her things; no, because Tina was sorry for what she had done.)

• **How did Maria show that she was a good neighbor?** (Possible answers include: She always shared her chili with the neighbors; she did not seem to get upset when her neighbor tried to make chili.)

Using Language

ORAL READING/SPEAKING: DIALOGUE
Tell pupils that when the characters in a story talk to each other, the words they say are called dialogue. Ask pupils to tell what marks are around the words someone says in a story. (quotation marks)

Have pupils turn to page 49 and find the words in quotation marks. Call on pupils to tell who is speaking. (the people who looked at the pots) Have what the people said read. ("Why, they're not even new pots," everyone said.)

Follow a similar procedure for the remaining pages, using the suggestions below.

Page 50: Have pupils take the parts of the man and Maria and read the conversation on this page.

Page 51: Ask a pupil to read what Maria said after she ate the chili. ("This is fine chili! I will make some for all my neighbors," she said.)

Page 54: Remind pupils that Tina had made a mess. Ask one of them to read what Tina said when Maria came home. ("Help! Help, Maria!" yelled Tina. "Make the chili pot stop!")

Page 55: Ask pupils to find the word that tells how Tina sounded when she spoke to Maria. (*pleaded*) Then have pupils read what Tina and Maria said to each other.

Applying the Focus Skill

INFERENTIAL: PREDICTING OUTCOMES
Remind pupils that they can use what they know, along with the information in a story, to make predictions. Ask pupils to tell what they knew about Tina and the chili pot that helped them predict that Tina would have trouble with the chili pot. (The story said that Tina did not see Maria tell the pot to stop, so Tina did not know how to stop the pot.)

Evaluating Comprehension

WB 30 **INDEPENDENT PRACTICE** *Workbook* page 30 may be used for an informal evaluation of story comprehension.

Comprehension/Thinking
Use with "The Chili Pot," Lesson 5

Name _____

Fill in the circle.

1. ● One day a man came by selling pots.
   ○ One day a man came by selling chili.

2. ○ The man gave Maria a new pot.
   ● The man gave Maria a pot that made chili.

3. ○ The pot made chili all day long.
   ● The pot made chili when Maria said, "Chili I want."

4. ● Maria said, "Chili stop," to make the pot stop.
   ○ Maria could not make the chili pot stop.

5. ● Tina wanted to make chili like Maria.
   ○ Tina wanted to take the chili pot.

6. ○ Tina made a little bowl of chili.
   ● Tina could not stop the pot.

7. ● Maria stopped the pot and gave everyone chili.
   ○ Maria would not speak to Tina.

● Story comprehension: "The Chili Pot"
● **Directions:** Read the sentences. Fill in the circle by the sentences that tell about the story "The Chili Pot."
● **To the Parent:** Have your child retell the story.

30 *Spotlights* Level 6

HOW AM I DOING?

Many pupils are not familiar with folklore. Ask yourself the following questions to make sure pupils have the opportunity to explore this form of literature.

	Yes	No	Sometimes
1. Have I read any folklore selections aloud to the pupils?	☐	☐	☐
2. Have I utilized other sources of media to expose folklore to the pupils such as filmstrips or movies?	☐	☐	☐
3. Have I made a wide selection of folklore reading material available?	☐	☐	☐
4. Have I taken the pupils to the library?	☐	☐	☐

DEVELOPING READING AND THINKING SKILLS

DECODING/VOCABULARY

R Sound/symbol correspondence: vowel discrimination: /i/, /ī/

DIRECT INSTRUCTION Print the following words on the chalkboard:

pin	pine	
pin	bite	like
fish	spin	fine
bike	kite	ship

Call on a pupil to read the first word. Ask what sound the letter *i* stands for in *pin.* (/i/) Have the second word read. Ask what sound the letter *i* stands for in *pine.* (/ī/) Ask why the letter *i* stands for the long sound in the word *pine.* (The word *pine* has an *i*, followed by a consonant, and ends with *e*.)

GUIDED PRACTICE Direct pupils' attention to the remaining words on the chalkboard. Call on pupils to read a word and to tell what sound the letter *i* stands for in the word and why. (Letter *i* stands for the short *i* sound in *pin, fish, spin,* and *ship; i* stands for the /ī/ sound in the rest of the words because each word has an *i*, followed by a consonant, and ends with *e*.)

WB 31 INDEPENDENT PRACTICE *Workbook* page 31 may be used to practice discriminating /i/ and /ī/.

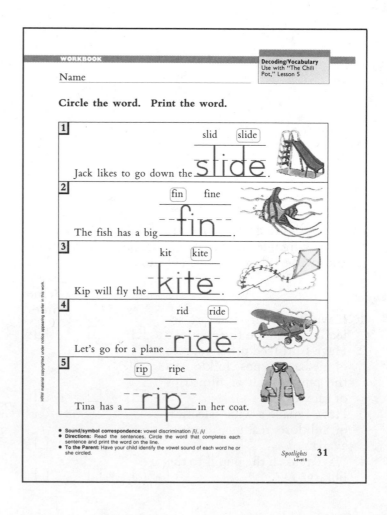

WORKBOOK

Name _____

Decoding/Vocabulary
Use with "The Chili Pot," Lesson 5

Circle the word. Print the word.

1. slid (slide)
   Jack likes to go down the **slide**.

2. (fin) fine
   The fish has a big **fin**.

3. kit (kite)
   Kip will fly the **kite**.

4. rid (ride)
   Let's go for a plane **ride**.

5. (rip) ripe
   Tina has a **rip** in her coat.

- Sound/symbol correspondence: vowel discrimination /i/, /ī/
- **Directions:** Read the sentences. Circle the word that completes each sentence and print the word on the line.
- **To the Parent:** Have your child identify the vowel sound of each word he or she circled.

Spotlights Level 6   **31**

M   Vocabulary: compound words

DIRECT INSTRUCTION   Print the following sentences on the chalkboard, omitting the underlining. Have the first sentence read.

> 1. <u>Everyone</u> ate chili.
>
> 2. The book is in your <u>backpack</u>.
> 3. Taffy's <u>doghouse</u> is red.
> 4. They like to jump on the <u>haystack</u>.
> 5. Tim hit the <u>baseball</u>.
> 6. The <u>bookshelf</u> is dusty.

Point to the word *Everyone* and tell pupils that this word is made by putting two words together. Remind pupils that a word that is made from two words is called a compound word. Call on a pupil to name the two words in *everyone.* (*every, one*)

GUIDED PRACTICE   Indicate the remaining sentences on the chalkboard. Call on a pupil to read each sentence and to tell which word is a compound word. Ask what two words make up each compound word. (*back, pack; dog, house; hay, stack; base, ball; book, shelf*)

ADDITIONAL PRACTICE   *Practice Masters* page 20 may be used as an optional practice for recognizing compound words. (See page T127 for reduced pages with answers.)

M   Vocabulary: multiple meanings

DIRECT INSTRUCTION   Write the following sentences on the chalkboard, omitting the definitions in parentheses.

> 1. Tim will <u>plant</u> the seed.
> 2. He will need to water the <u>plant</u>.
>
> 3. He <u>left</u> to go home. (went away from)
> 4. The park is on the <u>left</u> side of the street. (a side of the body)
>
> 5. The dog had a <u>litter</u> of puppies. (bunch)
> 6. There is a lot of <u>litter</u> in the park. (trash on the ground)

Have the first two sentences read. Call attention to the underlined words in each sentence. (*plant*) Remind pupils that sometimes the same word can have more than one meaning.

ASK   **In which sentence does the word** *plant* **mean "something that has leaves and grows from a seed"?** (Sentence 2) **In which sentence does** *plant* **mean "to place in the ground"?** (Sentence 1)

Remind pupils that you can often tell what a word means by reading the rest of the sentence in which the word appears.

GUIDED PRACTICE   Direct pupils' attention to Sentences 3–6.

Have Sentences 3 and 4 read aloud. Then have pupils read the underlined word in each sentence and tell what the word means. Follow a similar procedure with the remaining pair of sentences.

COMPREHENSION/THINKING

Focus
R, T Inferential: predicting outcomes

DIRECT INSTRUCTION Remind pupils that when they read a story, they can try to guess what is going to happen. This is called making a prediction.

GUIDED PRACTICE Read the following story and ask pupils to predict what will happen.

> **READ** **Jenny took her new kite to the park. The wind was blowing just right. Last night, Dad had helped Jenny tie a tail and some string to the kite. Jenny ran with the kite behind her. Up, up went the kite. Jenny was so excited that she never noticed the big oak tree.**

Ask pupils what they think might happen. (Jenny's kite will get tangled in the oak tree; Jenny will run into the tree.) Ask what information in the story helped them make the prediction. (Jenny never noticed the oak tree.) Ask what pupils had to know about kites to make the prediction. (They had to know that kites and kite strings can become tangled in tree branches.)

WB 32 INDEPENDENT PRACTICE *Workbook* page 32 may be used to practice predicting outcomes.

PM 21 ADDITIONAL PRACTICE *Practice Masters* page 21 may be used as an optional practice for predicting outcomes. (See page T127 for reduced pages with answers.)

✳ RETEACH For those pupils who need additional instruction, see "Reteaching Lesson Skills," page T125, under "Reteaching and Extending."

Comprehension/Thinking
Use with "The Chili Pot," Lesson 5

Name _____

Fill in the circle.

1
Maria ran out of her house. It looked like it would rain. But Maria had no umbrella.

What will happen?

○ Maria will slip.
● Maria will get wet.

2
Tina dropped her milk. She didn't have any money. Pat had some money.

What will Pat do?

● He'll lend money to her.
○ He'll go home.

3
Billy Bear moved. He wanted a new friend. He saw a girl with a ball.

What will Billy do?

● Billy will play.
○ Billy will go away.

4
Tom and Tim like snow. They put on coats and hats. They grabbed their sled.

What will the boys do?

● They will play outside.
○ They will play inside.

● **Inferential:** predicting outcomes
● **Directions:** Read each story. Fill in the circle by the sentence that tells what will probably happen next.
● **To the Parent:** Have your child read one story and explain his or her answer.

32 *Spotlights* Level 6

R, T   References: dictionary (entry words and definitions)

DIRECT INSTRUCTION   Ask pupils where they might look to find the meaning of a word. (in a dictionary)

Print the following words and definitions on the chalkboard:

chili	a food made with meat and beans
rabbit	an animal that hops
rest	to sleep or nap
road	a wide path

Read the first sample dictionary entry aloud. Ask what chili is. (a food made with meat and beans) Tell pupils that in a dictionary the definition comes after the entry word.

GUIDED PRACTICE   Indicate the remaining entry words and definitions.

Have the word *rabbit* read. Then ask what a rabbit is. (an animal that hops) Ask which word means "a wide path." (*road*) Ask what the word *rest* means. ("to sleep or nap")

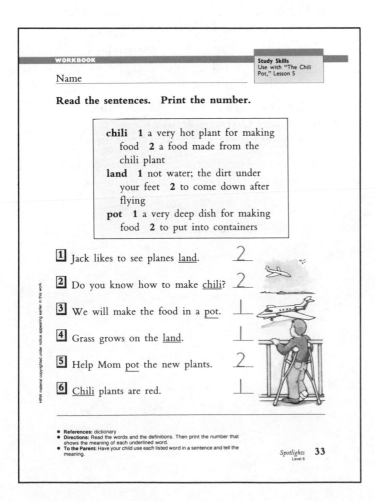

INDEPENDENT PRACTICE   *Workbook* page 33 may be used to practice using a dictionary.

ADDITIONAL PRACTICE   *Practice Masters* page 22 may be used as an optional practice for using a dictionary. (See page T127 for reduced pages with answers.)

❋ **RETEACH**   For those pupils who need additional instruction, see "Reteaching Lesson Skills," page T125, under "Reteaching and Extending."

LANGUAGE

R   Listening: oral directions (multiple-step)

DIRECT INSTRUCTION   Remind pupils that Maria knew how to make the chili pot work because she listened when the man gave her directions. Ask why the pot did not work for Tina. (It did not work because she did not know how to use it.) Point out that Tina did not hear all the directions.

SAY   When a person is giving directions, it is important to listen very carefully. You need to listen so you will know what you need to do.

GUIDED PRACTICE   Have pupils carry out the following directions:

1. **Raise both hands over your head. Clap three times. Nod your head twice.**
2. **Tap your right foot three times. Tap your left foot two times. Clap your hands once.**
3. **Clap your hands four times. Nod your head. Tap your feet three times.**
4. **Clap once. Stamp your feet once. Nod your head twice.**

Reteaching Lesson Skills

The activities that follow provide reteaching of skills developed in this lesson. Not every pupil needs to complete these activities. Choose only the activities that are needed to provide for the individual differences in your classroom.

DECODING/VOCABULARY

R, T   Sound/symbol correspondence: vowel /ī/*i-e*

❋   **RETEACH** Display *Word Cards pin, rid, bit, fin,* and *hid.* Call on a pupil to read a word and to tell what sound the letter *i* stands for in the word. (/i/) Then have another pupil place *Letter Card e* at the end of the word and read the new word. Ask what sound the letter *i* stands for now. (/ī/) Continue in the same manner with the remaining words.

I, T   Word structure: contractions (with *'re*)

❋   **RETEACH** Print the following words on the chalkboard:

we are	you are	they are
we're	you're	they're

Have *we are* and *we're* read. Tell pupils that we sometimes put two words together into one word. Point to the word *we're* and read it. Tell pupils that the word *we're* was made from the words *we are.* Ask what letter was left out of *we are* to make *we're.* (letter *a*) Tell pupils that in *we're,* the apostrophe takes the place of the letter *a.* Continue in the same manner with the remaining words.

I, T   Vocabulary: word meaning

❋   **RETEACH** Print the following words and sentences on the chalkboard, omitting the underlining.

IC 29

been   chili   even   Maria   Tina

1. <u>Maria</u> has not <u>been</u> happy.
2. She made some <u>chili</u>.
3. <u>Tina</u> did not like the chili.
4. She would not <u>even</u> taste it.

bite   different
they're   we're   you're

Point to the word *Maria* and read it. Have a pupil find and read a sentence that contains the word *Maria.* Continue in the same manner with the remaining sentences, calling attention to the underlined words.

Display *Word Cards* for each of the underlined words. Then have a pupil hold up and read the word that answers each of the following questions.

1. **Which words are names?** (*Maria, Tina*)
2. **Which word names a kind of soup?** (*chili*)
3. **Which word means "used to be"?** (*been*)

Ask pupils to read the second set of words and to use them in senences.

 Distribute *Reteach Masters* page 8 and explain the directions on the page.

COMPREHENSION/THINKING

Focus

R, T   Inferential: predicting outcomes

✳ **RETEACH** Tell pupils that people often try to predict what the weather will be. They look at maps, watch storms grow, and check the temperatures to make predictions. In other words, they make predictions based on what they know about the weather and weather patterns.

Tell pupils that they can make predictions about what will happen in a story. Remind them that when they make a prediction, they are guessing what may happen, using the information in the story and what they already know. Read the following story and ask what will happen next.

READ Bradley had a bright, red balloon. He held on to the string as he ran down the sidewalk. He was so busy looking up at the balloon that he did not see the rock in the middle of the sidewalk.

ASK What do you think might happen? (Bradley will trip.) **Why did you make that prediction?** (because a person usually trips when his or her foot hits a rock unexpectedly)

STUDY SKILLS

R, T   References: dictionary (entry words and definitions)

✳ **RETEACH** Print the following words and meanings on the chalkboard and have them read.

hen	a chicken that lays eggs
hive	a home for bees
house	a place to live

Point out that in a dictionary, words and meanings are found listed something like this. Then ask the following questions.

1. **Which word means "a place to live"?** (*house*)
2. **Which word names a home for bees?** (*hive*)
3. **Which word means "a chicken that lays eggs"?** (hen)

R   Listening: oral directions

✳ **RETEACH** Ask who told Maria how to use the chili pot. (the man who sold it to her) Ask if the pot would have worked if Maria had not listened to the man. (No, it would not have worked.) Tell pupils that it is important to listen when someone gives directions.

Call on pupils to tell what they would be doing if they were to follow the directions below.

1. **First, take out two slices of bread. Spread peanut butter on one slice. Spread jelly on the other slice.** (making a peanut butter and jelly sandwich)
2. **Tie a string on a pole. Tie a hook on the string. Put bait on the hook.** (going fishing)
3. **Put on your bathing suit. Get your pail and shovel. Take a towel to sit on.** (going to the beach)

Extending Selection Concepts

LANGUAGE ARTS

WRITING: STORIES Have pupils pretend that they have found a pot or pan that will cook by itself. Ask them to think about what they would like the pan to cook and how they would make the pan work. Then have pupils write about their magic pot or pan. Remind them that it is important to have a way to stop the pan. Encourage pupils to share their stories with the class.

LITERATURE

LISTENING: FICTION Choose another story about a magic pot or a magic spell gone awry and read it aloud. Ask pupils to compare the story with "The Chili Pot."

Galdone, Joanna. *The Magic Porridge Pot.* The Seabury Press, 1976. The porridge pot makes porridge with just a word.

Galdone, Paul. *The Table, the Donkey, and the Stick.* McGraw-Hill, 1976. Three brothers are sent out into the world to make their fortunes. They meet someone who gives each of them a gift.

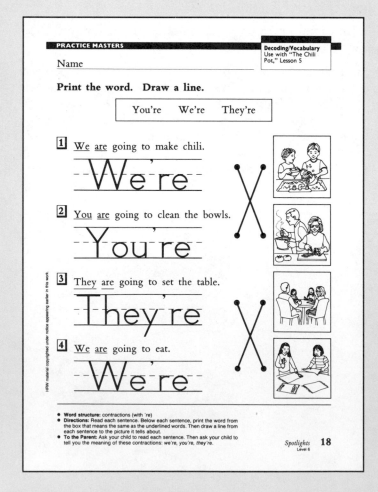

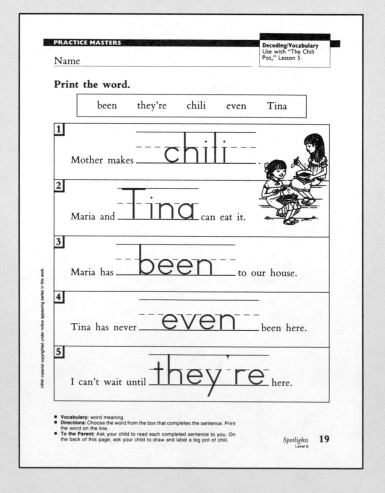

Name

Circle the word. Print the words.

1 Red Robin likes ⟨sunshine.⟩

sun _shine_

2 Red Robin got up at ⟨sunrise.⟩

sun _rise_

3 She looked ⟨everywhere⟩ for her friends.

every _where_

4 "Where is ⟨everyone?"⟩ she asked.

every _one_

5 She found her friends at the ⟨birdhouse.⟩

bird _house_

- **Vocabulary:** compound words
- **Directions:** Read each sentence and circle the compound word. Print on the lines the two words that make up each compound word.
- **To the Parent:** Ask your child to draw and label a picture of a *birdhouse*.

Spotlights
Level 6 **20**

Name

Fill in the circle.

1

Tina made a pot of chili.
She went to get a bowl.
The bowl had a hole in it.
What did Tina do next?

● She got a new bowl.

○ She went out to play.

2

Tina made a pot of chili.
She put some chili in a bowl.
She put the bowl on the table.
Then Tina sat down at the table.
What did Tina do next?

○ She ate an apple.

● She ate the chili.

- **Inferential:** predicting outcomes
- **Directions:** Read each story and the question at the end of the story. Fill in the circle by the sentence that answers the question.
- **To the Parent:** Ask your child to read each story to you and tell you what Tina did next.

Spotlights
Level 6 **21**

Name

Print the words.

bowl	a deep dish
chili	a hot food
pot	**1** a deep pan to put food in
	2 a deep pan to put plants in
sunrise	the time when the sun comes up

1 What word means "a hot food"?

chili

2 What word means "a deep dish"?

bowl

3 What two things can you put in a pot?

food and plants

4 What does the sun do at sunrise?

comes up

- **References:** dictionary
- **Directions:** Read the words and meanings at top of the page. Read each question. Print the answer to each question on the line.
- **To the Parent:** Ask your child to draw and label pictures of the dictionary words at the top of this page.

Spotlights
Level 6 **22**

Name

A. Circle Yes or No.

1 Are things that are different just the same? Yes ⟨No⟩

2 Can a bean be fat even if it is thin? Yes ⟨No⟩

3 Can bowls be on a table? ⟨Yes⟩ No

4 Can you're mean "you are"? ⟨Yes⟩ No

5 Does everyone like chili? Yes ⟨No⟩

B. Print a sentence.

we're	plenty	these

Answers will vary.

- **Vocabulary:** word meaning
- **Directions:** TOP –Read the sentences. Then answer each question by circling Yes or No. BOTTOM – Read the words in the box. Make up a sentence using these words and some other words. Print the sentence.
- **To the Parent:** Ask your child to explain his or her answers to the questions.

Spotlights
Level 6 **8**

Lesson 5 "The Chili Pot" (pages 48–57) T127

END-OF-UNIT 1 REVIEW
(T128–T133)

Skill Strands

DECODING/VOCABULARY

R, T **Sound/symbol correspondence:** consonant /j/*j* (initial)

R, T **Sound/symbol correspondence:** vowel /ē/*y* (final)

R, T **Sound/symbol correspondence:** vowel /ī/*i-e*

R, T **Word structure:** inflectional endings -*er*, -*est*

R, T **Word structure:** suffix -*er*

R, T **Vocabulary:** word meaning

COMPREHENSION/THINKING

R, T **Inferential:** predicting outcomes

R, T **Story structure:** plot (problems and solutions)

STUDY SKILLS

R, T **References:** dictionary (entry words and definitions)

Materials

Workbook: pages 34–37
Practice Masters: pages 23–24
Instructional Charts: pages 35–37
Resource Box: Letter Card *e, j*
           Word Cards *a, Billy, bit, bite, bunny, Candy, fin, fine, happy, has, kit, kite, pin, rid, ride, sunny*
           Punctuation Card period
Pocket Chart
Teacher's Idea Book
End-of-Unit 1 Test

Special Populations

See *Teacher's Idea Book* for additional suggestions to help pupils with limited English proficiency.

Key to Symbols
I Introduced in this lesson
R Reinforced from an earlier lesson in this level
M Maintained from previous levels
T Tested in this level

DECODING/VOCABULARY

R, T   Sound/symbol correspondence: vowel /ē/y (final)

GUIDED PRACTICE   Use *Word Cards* and *Punctuation Card period* to make the sentence *Candy has a happy bunny.* in the *Pocket Chart* and have the sentence read. Then place *Word Cards Candy, happy, bunny* in a column and have them read. Ask what is the same about these words. (They end with letter *y;* they have the /ē/ sound at the end.) Ask what letter stands for the /ē/ sound at the end of each word. (*y*) Remind pupils that when a word that ends with *y* has two parts, the *y* usually stands for the /ē/ sound.

PM 23   ADDITIONAL PRACTICE   *Practice Masters* page 23 may be used as an optional practice for identifying sound/symbol correspondence /ē/y. (See page T133 for reduced pages with answers.)

R, T   Sound/symbol correspondence: vowel /ī/i-e

GUIDED PRACTICE   Display *Word Card pin* and have it read. Ask what sound the letter *i* stands for in *pin.* (/i/) Ask what you would add to the end of the word *pin* to make the letter *i* stand for the /ī/ sound. (Add *e* to the end of the word.) Add *e* to the end of *pin* and have the new word read. (*pine*)

Display the following pairs of *Word Cards: rid, ride; bit, bite; kit, kite; fin, fine.*

Point to each word and have it read. Then shuffle the *Word Cards* and place them in a pile. Show one card at a time and have pupils read it and tell what sound the *i* stands for in the word.

WB 34   INDEPENDENT PRACTICE   *Workbook* page 34 may be used to practice identifying sound/symbol correspondence /ī/i-e.

WORKBOOK

Decoding/Vocabulary
Use with End-of-Unit 1
Review

Name _____

Fill in the circle.

1 Dee got a new ____ for her birthday. ○ bake ○ bit ● bike	**2** The boys and girls stand in a ____. ○ lean ● line ○ lint
3 Tad wants to fly his new ____. ● kite ○ kick ○ kit	**4** Kim's coat is red, and ____ is yellow. ● mine ○ mane ○ mint
5 The boys and girls went on a long ____. ○ hide ○ hint ● hike	**6** You can pick the cherries if they are ____. ○ rip ● ripe ○ ride
7 Look at the clock to see what ____ it is. ● time ○ tip ○ team	**8** The bees make honey in their ____. ○ have ○ hid ● hive

34 *Spotlights*
Level 6

● **Sound/symbol correspondence:** vowel /ī/i-e
● **Directions:** Read each sentence and the words under it. Fill in the circle by the word that completes the sentence.
● **To the Parent:** Have your child put consonant letters at the beginning of *-ide* to form words.

End-of-Unit 1 Review   T129

R, T Sound/symbol correspondence: consonant /j/j (initial)

GUIDED PRACTICE Omitting the underlining, print the following sentences on the chalkboard and have them read.

> 1. Jack has jelly in a jar.
> 2. Jan jumps in the jeep.
> 3. The jeep jiggles in the jungle.
> 4. John has a job making jam.

Call on pupils to read the words in each sentence that begin with the /j/ sound.

R, T Word structure: inflectional endings -er, -est

R, T Word structure: suffix -er

GUIDED PRACTICE Print the following sentences on the chalkboard and have them read.

> 1. Tim is a fast runner.
> 2. Jack is a faster runner.
> 3. Billy is the fastest runner.

Point to the first sentence and have it read aloud. Ask which word means "a person who runs"? (runner) Ask what ending was added to run to make the word runner. (-er)

ASK **Who does not run as fast as Jack?** (Tim) **Which boy would probably win a running race?** (Billy) **Why?** (because he runs fastest) **Which boy would probably lose the race?** (Tim) **Why?** (because Jack and Billy both run faster)

PM 24 ADDITIONAL PRACTICE *Practice Masters* page 24 may be used as an optional practice for identifying inflectional endings -er, -est. (See page T133 for reduced pages with answers.)

R, T Vocabulary: word meaning

GUIDED PRACTICE Make a list of vocabulary words from this unit. (See page T395.) Have pupils choose words from the list, use them in sentences, and illustrate the sentences. Compile the pages into a classroom "Picture Dictionary." Display the dictionary in a place where pupils can use it to find the meanings of words.

COMPREHENSION/THINKING

R, T Inferential: predicting outcomes
R, T Story structure: plot (problems and solutions)

GUIDED PRACTICE Print the following story on the chalkboard and ask pupils to read it.

> Jeff wanted a pet.
> At the pet shop he saw soft, fluffy kittens and a shaggy puppy.
> Jeff felt sad.
> His mother said their house was too little for a cat or a dog.
> Then Jeff saw something at the back of the pet shop.
> "I know what to do," said Jeff.
> "I can't have a dog or a cat, but I can still have a pet."

Remind pupils that in most stories the character has a problem. Ask what problem Jeff had in this story. (He wanted a pet, but his house was too small.)

ASK **Do you think Jeff found a way to solve his problem?** (yes) **What makes you think so?** (Jack said he could still have a pet.) **What do you predict Jeff will do?** (Possible answers include: He will get a fish, or a gerbil, or a guinea pig, or some other small animal.)

Print the last part of the story on the chalkboard and ask pupils to read it.

> Jeff got a bowl and some rocks.
> "You will need this little box of food," said the man.
> Then the man handed Jeff his pet in a little bag.
> Jeff couldn't wait to see his new pet swim in the glass bowl.

ASK How did Jeff solve his problem? (He got a fish for a pet.) **Was your prediction correct?** (yes)

Point out that the story had a problem and a solution. Tell pupils that they used the information in the story to predict what might happen. At the end of the story, they found out if their prediction was correct.

WB 35 **INDEPENDENT PRACTICE** *Workbook* page 35 may be used to practice predicting outcomes.

WB 36 **INDEPENDENT PRACTICE** *Workbook* page 36 may be used to practice recognizing problems and solutions.

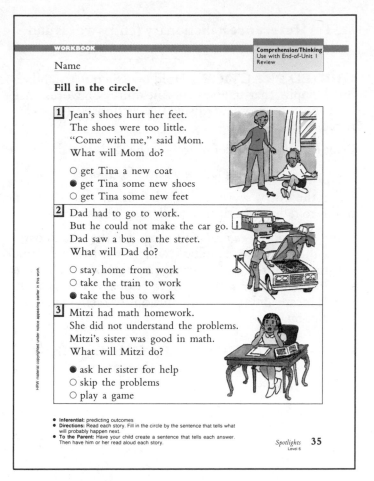

Name _____

Fill in the circle.

1 Jean's shoes hurt her feet.
The shoes were too little.
"Come with me," said Mom.
What will Mom do?

○ get Tina a new coat
● get Tina some new shoes
○ get Tina some new feet

2 Dad had to go to work.
But he could not make the car go.
Dad saw a bus on the street.
What will Dad do?

○ stay home from work
○ take the train to work
● take the bus to work

3 Mitzi had math homework.
She did not understand the problems.
Mitzi's sister was good in math.
What will Mitzi do?

● ask her sister for help
○ skip the problems
○ play a game

● **Inferential:** predicting outcomes
● **Directions:** Read each story. Fill in the circle by the sentence that tells what will probably happen next.
● **To the Parent:** Have your child create a sentence that tells each answer. Then have him or her read aloud each story.

Spotlights **35**
Level 6

Name _____

Draw a line. Fill in the circle.

1 Dean was waiting for Mom.
It was raining.
Dean could see a shop.

How will he work out his problem?
● Dean will wait in the shop.
○ Dean will wait in the rain.

2 Gail was at her grandmother's house.
Grandmother fell and could not get up.
Gail was too little to lift Grandmother.

How will Gail work out her problem?
○ She will wait for help to come.
● She will ask for help on the telephone.

3 Beth was in math class.
She did not feel well.
She wanted to go home.

How will she work out her problem?
● She'll tell someone she's sick.
○ She'll play a game.

● **Story structure:** plot
● **Directions:** Read the story. Draw one line under the problem each person has. Fill in the circle by the solution.
● **To the Parent:** Have your child tell how he or she would handle each problem. Discuss with your child the way you would want him or her to react in a similar situation.

36 *Spotlights*
Level 6

End-of-Unit 1 Review   T131

R, T References: dictionary (entry words and definitions)

GUIDED PRACTICE Hold up a dictionary and remind pupils that it gives the meanings of words. Ask how the entry words are listed in a dictionary. (They are in alphabetical order.)

Print the following definition on the chalkboard:

dish a plate or a bowl for food

Have the entry word and its definition read. Call on pupils to tell what a dish is. (a plate or a bowl for food)

Print the words *camper* and *every* on the chalkboard. Have the words read and ask which word would come before *dish* in the dictionary. (*camper*) Ask which word would come after *dish* in the dictionary. (*every*) Help pupils locate and read the definitions of *camper* and *every* in a dictionary.

WB 37 INDEPENDENT PRACTICE *Workbook* page 37 may be used to practice using a dictionary.

WORKBOOK

Study Skills
Use with End-of-Unit 1
Review

Name _____

Read the sentences. Print the number.

> **dish** 1 something to put food on
>   2 a meal
> **mail** 1 a note or gift that comes
>   to your home   2 to send a
>   note or gift
> **smile** 1 a happy look, like a grin
>   2 to make a happy look or grin

1 A gift came for me in the <u>mail</u>. ⊥

2 Dad put the toast on a <u>dish</u>. ⊥

3 This funny book made me <u>smile</u>. 2

4 I will <u>mail</u> Dee a thank-you note. 2

5 Grandmother's <u>smile</u> makes me happy. ⊥

6 Billy's chili <u>dish</u> tastes very good. 2

● **References:** dictionary
● **Directions:** Read the words and the definitions. Then print the number that shows the meaning of each underlined word.
● **To the Parent:** Have your child use each listed word in a sentence and tell its meaning.

Spotlights
Level 6 **37**

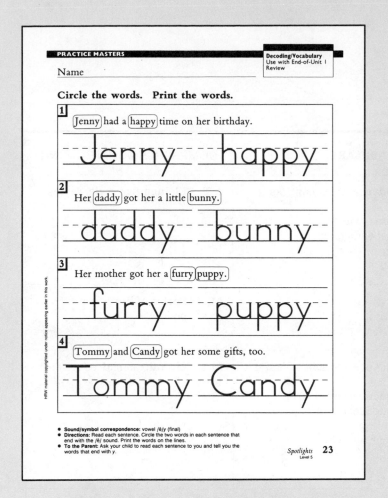

Name

Circle the words.   Print the words.

1 Jenny had a happy time on her birthday.

Jenny   happy

2 Her daddy got her a little bunny.

daddy   bunny

3 Her mother got her a furry puppy.

furry   puppy

4 Tommy and Candy got her some gifts, too.

Tommy   Candy

- **Sound/symbol correspondence:** vowel /ē/y (final)
- **Directions:** Read each sentence. Circle the two words in each sentence that end with the /ē/ sound. Print the words on the lines.
- **To the Parent:** Ask your child to read each sentence to you and tell you the words that end with y.

Spotlights **23**
Level 5

Name

Print the word.

| hunt | hunters | biggest | bigger |

1 This bear is big.

That bear is **bigger** .

2 These bears are big.

The gray bear is **biggest** of all.

3 The bears **hunt** for food.

4 They are good **hunters** .

- **Word structure:** endings -er, -est
- **Directions:** Choose the word from the box that completes each sentence and print the word on the line.
- **To the Parent:** Ask your child to draw a picture of three different-size bears. Then ask your child to tell you which bear is *big*, *bigger*, and *biggest*.

Spotlights **24**
Level 6

UNIT 2 OVERVIEW

TITLE	DECODING/VOCABULARY		COMPREHENSION/THINKING	
Fun on Wheels pages 60–67 (T140–T159)	I, T	**Sound/symbol correspondence:** consonant /ks/*x* (final)	I, T	**Elements of style:** rhyme
	R, T	**Word structure:** contractions (with *'re*)		
	M	**Word structure:** inflectional ending *-es*		
	I	**Vocabulary:** word building		
	I, T	**Vocabulary:** word meaning		
Wheels and Wings pages 68–69 (T160–T161)			M	**Forms of literature:** poetry
A Place for Babies pages 70–75 (T162–T181)	R, T	**Sound/symbol correspondence:** consonant /ks/*x* (final)	M	**Literal:** main idea (stated)
	R, T	**Sound/symbol correspondence:** vowel /ī/*i-e*		
	I, T	**Sound/symbol correspondence:** *r*-controlled vowel /är/*ar*		
	M	**Word structure:** contractions (with *'ll, 's*)		
	I	**Vocabulary:** word building		
	I, T	**Vocabulary:** word meaning		
This is the Place for Me pages 76–87 (T182–T205)	I, T	**Sound/symbol correspondence:** vowel /ō/*o-e*	(I), T	**Story structure:** characters (major and minor)
	R, T	**Sound/symbol correspondence:** *r*-controlled vowel /är/*ar*	R, T	**Inferential:** predicting outcomes
	R, T	**Sound/symbol correspondence:** vowel /ē/*y* (final)		
	I, T	**Word structure:** base changes (drop final *e* and add *–ed*)		
	R	**Word structure:** suffix *-y*		
	I	**Vocabulary:** word building		
	I, T	**Vocabulary:** word meaning		
The Mole's Home pages 88–89 (T206–T207)	R, T	**Sound/symbol correspondence:** vowel /ō/*o-e*		

(I) Expanded treatment of skill introduced at a previous level

STUDY SKILLS	LANGUAGE	LANGUAGE APPLICATIONS
M **Graphic aids:** illustrations	**M** **Writing:** language-experience stories	**Choral reading:** rhymes **Writing:** rhymes **Speaking:** reciting rhymes (Cooperative Learning) **Listening:** fiction; information
R, T **References:** dictionary (entry words and definitions)		**Oral reading/Speaking:** answering questions **Writing:** animal reports (Cooperative Learning) **Listening:** information
	M **Writing:** sentences	**Oral reading:** descriptions **Listening:** fiction; poetry

TITLE	DECODING/VOCABULARY		COMPREHENSION/THINKING	
Houses pages 90–91 (T208–T209)			M	**Forms of literature:** poetry
Aren't You Forgetting Something, Fiona? pages 92–101 (T210–T231)	R, T R R, T R, T R, T I I, T	**Sound/symbol correspondence:** vowel /ō/o-e **Sound/symbol correspondence:** vowel discrimination /o/, /ō/ **Word structure:** base changes (drop final e and add -ed) **Word structure:** inflectional endings -er, -est **Word structure:** suffix -er **Vocabulary:** word building **Vocabulary:** word meaning	R, T	**Story structure:** characters (major and minor)
Peach Boy pages 102–111 (T232–T251)	M I, T R, T I I, T	**Sound/symbol correspondence:** consonant /y/y (initial) **Sound/symbol correspondence:** consonant digraph /ch/ch, tch (initial, medial, final) **Sound/symbol correspondence:** r-controlled vowel /är/ar **Vocabulary:** word building **Vocabulary:** word meaning	I M	**Forms of literature:** folklore (folk tales and fairy tales) **Forms of literature:** fantasy and realism
Remember When pages 112–113 (T252–T253)	I, T	**Vocabulary:** word meaning	M	**Literal:** sequence
End-of-Unit Review (T254–T259) NOTE: These skills are tested in *End-of-Unit 2 Test.*	R, T *R, T *R, T *R, T R, T *R, T	**Sound/symbol correspondence:** consonant /ks/x (final) **Sound/symbol correspondence:** r-controlled vowel /är/ar **Sound/symbol correspondence:** vowel /ō/o-e **Word structure:** base changes (drop final e and add -ed) **Word structure:** contractions (with 're) **Vocabulary:** word meaning	*R, T *R, T	**Story structure:** characters (major and minor) **Elements of style:** rhyme

Ⓘ Expanded treatment of skill introduced at a previous level
* Tested in the *End-of-Book Test*

Key to Symbols
I Introduced in this lesson
R Reinforced from an earlier lesson in this level
M Maintained from previous levels
T Tested in this level

STUDY SKILLS	LANGUAGE	LANGUAGE APPLICATIONS
	(I) **Conventions of language:** sentence construction (word order)	**Oral reading:** expression **Speaking:** role playing **Writing:** sentences; notes **Listening:** poetry; fiction
	R **Conventions of language:** sentence construction (word order)	**Oral reading:** answering questions **Speaking:** telling stories (Cooperative Learning) **Listening:** fiction

Materials

Spotlights, Level 6: pages 58–59
Teacher's Idea Book

Special Populations

See *Teacher's Idea Book* for additional suggestions to help pupils with limited English proficiency.

Using Prior Knowledge

Tell pupils that the next unit in *Spotlights* is called "Great Ideas."

> **SAY** **Many things that we have today, we have because someone had a great idea. Thomas Edison had the idea that electricity could be used to make light. He kept working until he invented the electric light bulb. Before we had electric lights, people had to burn candles or oil lamps. Electric lights were a great idea!**

Ask pupils to tell about other inventions or happenings that they think were great ideas. (Possible answers include: airplanes, cars, pizza.) Then have pupils open their books to page 58. Ask them to look at the picture and tell what is happening. (A girl is learning to ride a bicycle.) Have pupils suggest why the bicycle was a great idea. (Possible answers include: The bicycle helps us get from one place to another; riding is fun.) Then ask why learning to ride a bicycle might be a great idea for the girl. (Possible answers include: A bicycle is fun to ride; she might be able to ride her bicycle to school; she might be able to do errands for her mother.) Call on pupils to tell how traveling by bicycle might be better than walking. (A bicycle is faster than walking; you can go farther on a bicycle than you can walk.)

Direct pupils' attention to page 59 and point out that each of the stories in this unit tells about a great idea or about someone who had a great idea. Choose several story titles to read. As you read each title, ask how the story might tell about great ideas. (Possible answers include: "Fun on Wheels" is probably about inventions that have wheels; "Aren't . . . Fiona?" might be about an idea that helps people remember things.)

Tell pupils that the stories in this unit were written by Joanna Cole. You may want to share the following information about the author.

Joanna Cole worked for a time as a school librarian. She later became an editor of children's books for Doubleday & Co. As an editor for Doubleday, Miss Cole helped to compile a book of folk tales and a book of children's poetry.

Miss Cole has written many books of fiction and nonfiction for children. Her nonfiction books are noted for combining factual observation with simple, concise explanations. Her works are considered to be outstanding additions to any science collection.

Several of Miss Cole's books have been listed in *Children's Choices* by the International Reading Council/Children's Book Council Joint Committee, including *A Calf Is Born, A Chick Hatches,* and *Get Well, Clown Arounds.* She is also a regular contributor to Parents' Magazine.

GREAT IDEAS

adapted from stories
by Joanna Cole

"Fun on Wheels"

"A Place for Babies"

"This Is the Place for Me"

"Aren't You Forgetting Something, Fiona?"

"Peach Boy"

58

59

LESSON 6 "Fun on Wheels"
pages 60–67 (T140–T159)

Skill Strands

DECODING/VOCABULARY

I, T **Sound/symbol correspondence:** consonant /ks/ *x* (final)

R, T **Word structure:** contractions (with *'re*)

M **Word structure:** inflectional ending *-es*

I **Vocabulary:** word building

I, T **Vocabulary:** word meaning

COMPREHENSION/THINKING

Focus _____

I, T **Elements of style:** rhyme

STUDY SKILLS

M **Graphic aids:** illustrations

LANGUAGE

M **Writing:** language-experience stories

Lesson Vocabulary

Decodable words: *ax, bats, boats, dip, fix, floats, fox, life, Max, mix, rip, six, three, win, whoever*

Special words: *five, four, great, idea, invented, more, seven, wheel*

Materials

Spotlights, Level 6: pages 60–67
Workbook: pages 38–43

Practice Masters: pages 25–29
Instructional Charts: pages 38–43
Resource Box: Letter Cards *a, b, f, i, m/M, o, s, x*
             Word Cards *ax, five, four, fox, great, idea, invented, mix, more, ox, seven, six, They're, We're, wax, wheel, You're*

Pocket Chart
Teacher's Idea Book
Reteach Masters: pages 9–10

Language Applications

USING LANGUAGE
Choral reading: rhymes

EXTENDING SELECTION CONCEPTS
Writing: rhymes
Speaking: reciting rhymes (Cooperative Learning)
Listening: fiction
Listening: information

Special Populations

See *Teacher's Idea Book* for additional suggestions to help pupils with limited English proficiency.

Key to Symbols

I   Introduced in this lesson
R Reinforced from an earlier lesson in this level
M Maintained from previous levels
T Tested in this level

Idea Center

BIBLIOGRAPHY

Add to your reading corner or reading table various books about wheels. You may also wish to include some stories written in rhyme. A suggested bibliography follows. Suggestions for reading aloud and annotations appear in the lesson plan.

Barton, Byron. *Wheels*. Crowell, 1979.
Carlstrom, Nancy White. *Jesse Bear, What Will You Wear?* Macmillan, 1986.
Cole, Joanna. *Cars and How They Go*. Thomas Y. Crowell, 1983.
Degen, Bruce. *Jamberry*. Harper & Row, 1983.
Perkins, Al. *Hand, Hand, Fingers, Thumb*. Random House, 1969.
Seuss, Dr. *And To Think That I Saw It on Mulberry Street*. Hale, 1937.
Shaw, Nancy. *Sheep in a Jeep*. Houghton Mifflin, 1986.

Planning Chart

	Instruction	Written Practice	Extending
Step 1 Preparing for the Selection	**I, T** **Sound/symbol correspondence:** consonant /ks/*x* (final) **I** **Vocabulary:** word building **I, T** **Vocabulary:** word meaning **I, T** **Elements of style:** rhyme	*Workbook* page 38 *Practice Masters* page 25 *Reteach Masters* page 9 *Workbook* page 39 *Practice Masters* page 26 *Reteach Masters* page 10	**Writing:** rhymes
Step 2 Reading for Comprehension	**Choral reading:** rhymes **Elements of style:** rhyme **Story comprehension**	*Workbook* page 40	
Step 3 Developing Reading and Thinking Skills	**R, T** **Word structure:** contractions (with *'re*) **M** **Word structure:** inflectional ending *-es* **I, T** **Elements of style:** rhyme **M** **Graphic aids:** illustrations **M** **Writing:** language-experience stories	*Workbook* page 41 *Practice Masters* page 27 *Workbook* page 42 *Practice Masters* page 28 *Workbook* page 43 *Practice Masters* page 29	**Speaking:** reciting rhymes (Cooperative Learning) **Listening:** fiction **Listening:** information

DECODING/VOCABULARY

I, T Sound/symbol correspondence: consonant /ks/ *x* (final)

DIRECT INSTRUCTION Print the following words and sentences on the chalkboard:

fox	box
fix	six
Max	ax

1. Max has an ax.
2. I will fix six dinners.
3. The mix is in a box.
4. The fox ate six eggs.

Read the words in the first row and ask what is the same about the words. (They end with *ox*.)

SAY	The letter *o* stands for the /o/ sound in *fox* and *box*. The letter *x* stands for the sound you hear at the end of *fox* and *box*. Read each word as I point to it.

Read the words in the second row and ask what is the same about the words. (They end with *ix*.)

SAY	The letter *i* stands for the /i/ sound in *fix* and *six*. The letter *x* stands for the sound you hear at the end of *fix* and *six*. Read each word as I point to it.

Read the words in the third row and ask pupils what is the same about the words. (They end with *ax*.)

SAY	The letter *a* stands for the /a/ sound in *Max* and *ax*. The letter *x* stands for the sound you hear at the end of *Max* and *ax*.

Call on pupils to read all the words.

GUIDED PRACTICE Direct pupils' attention to the numbered sentences on the chalkboard. Have each sentence read and then ask which words end with the sound of the letter *x*.

WB 38 INDEPENDENT PRACTICE *Workbook* page 38 may be used to practice identifying sound/symbol correspondence /ks/ *x*.

PM 25 ADDITIONAL PRACTICE *Practice Masters* page 25 may be used as an optional practice for identifying sound/symbol correspondence /ks/ *x*. (See page T158 for reduced pages with answers.)

✳ RETEACH For those pupils who need additional instruction, see "Reteaching Lesson Skills," page T156, under "Reteaching and Extending."

I Vocabulary: word building

DIRECT INSTRUCTION Use *Letter Cards* to make the word *mix* in the *Pocket Chart* and have the word read. Replace letter *m* with *f* and have the new word read. (*fix*)

GUIDED PRACTICE Display *Letter Cards a, b, m/M, o,* and *s.* Tell pupils that you will ask them to use the *Letter Cards* to make new words in the *Pocket Chart.*

1. **Replace the *i* in *fix* with *o*. What is the new word?** (*fox*)
2. **Replace the *f* with *b*. What is the new word?** (*box*)
3. **Remove the *b*. What is the new word?** (*ox*)
4. **Change the *o* to *a*. What is the new word?** (*ax*)
5. **Put capital *M* in front of *a*. What is the new word?** (*Max*) **How can you tell that *Max* is a name?** (It begins with a capital letter.)
6. **Take out the *Ma* and put *si* in front of *x*. What is the new word?** (*six*)
7. **Replace the *s* with *m*. What is the new word?** (*mix*)
8. **Replace the *m* with *f*. What is the new word?** (*fix*)
9. **Replace the *i* with *o*. What is the new word?** (*fox*)

I, T Vocabulary: word meaning

DIRECT INSTRUCTION Tell pupils that they are going to talk about some words they will read in the next story. Print the following words and sentences on the chalkboard, omitting the underlining.

> five four great idea invented
> more seven wheel
>
> 1. Ben's wagon lost a <u>wheel</u>.
> 2. Ben had a <u>great</u> <u>idea</u>.
> 3. He went to the dump to look for <u>more</u> wheels.
> 4. He saw <u>seven</u> wheels.
> 5. <u>Five</u> of them were no good, but he only needed one.
> 6. Now his wagon has <u>four</u> good wheels.
> 7. Ben was glad the wheel had been <u>invented</u>.
>
> ax fix fox
> Max mix six

Read Sentence 1. Point to the word *wheel* and read it. Ask what is wrong with Ben's wagon. (It lost a wheel.) Have pupils read the sentence with you. Then have a pupil find and read the word *wheel*.

Read Sentence 2. Point to the words *great* and *idea* and read them. Have pupils read the sentence with you. Then call on pupils to find and read the words *great* and *idea*.

Read Sentence 3. Point to the word *more* and read it. Ask what Ben's great idea was. (He would look for more wheels at the dump.) Have pupils read the sentence with you. Then ask them to find and read the word *more*.

Read Sentence 4. Point to the word *seven* and read it. Ask how many wheels Ben found. (seven) Have pupils read the sentence with you. Then ask them to find and read the word *seven*.

Read Sentence 5. Point to the word *five* and read it. Ask what was wrong with some of the wheels. (They were no good.) Have pupils read the sentence with you. Then call on a pupil to find and read the word *five*.

Read Sentence 6. Point to the word *four* and read it. Ask what Ben did with one wheel. (He fixed his wagon.) Have pupils read the sentences with you. Then ask them to find and read the word *four*.

Read the last sentence. Point to the word *invented* and read it. Tell pupils that when someone *invents* something, he or she builds or makes something that has never been built or made before. Ask why Ben was glad. (He was glad that the wheel had been invented.) Have pupils read the sentence with you. Then ask them to find and read the word *invented*.

The words in the second set are new words that contain known phonic elements. You may wish to ask pupils to read the words, using what they know about letters and sounds.

GUIDED PRACTICE Print the following sentences on the chalkboard, omitting the underlining.

> 1. <u>Max</u> had a <u>great</u> <u>idea</u> for his camping trip.
> 2. He would <u>fix</u> a cake in the shape of a <u>wheel</u>.
> 3. He <u>was</u> glad the cake <u>mix</u> had been <u>invented</u>.
> 4. The mix said to use <u>five</u> eggs, but Max used one <u>more</u> and put in <u>six</u>.
> 5. Max left for his trip with his <u>ax</u>, his cake, and <u>seven</u> friends.
> 6. He saw a <u>fox</u> and <u>four</u> bears.

Provide opportunities for pupils to practice reading the new special words and some of the new decodable words by following the suggestions below.

Sentence 1: Have the sentence read. Ask what Max had. (a great idea) Have pupils find and read the words *great idea.*

Sentence 2: Have the sentence read. Ask if Max was going to make a cake. (Yes, he would fix one in the shape of a wheel.) Call on pupils to point to and read the words *fix* and *wheel.*

Sentence 3: Call on a pupil to read the sentence. Then ask why Max was glad. (because the cake mix had been invented) Have pupils find and read the word *invented.*

Sentence 4: Have pupils find and read the number words in the sentence. (*five, six*) Then have the sentence read. Have pupils find and read the word *more.*

Sentence 5: Call on a pupil to read the sentence. Then ask what Max took on his trip. (his ax, his cake, seven friends) Have pupils find the two words that rhyme in the sentence. (*Max, ax*)

Sentence 6: Have pupils read the sentence to themselves. Then ask what Max saw on his trip. (a fox and four bears) Have pupils find and read the words *fox* and *four.*

Invite pupils to select a sentence to read aloud.

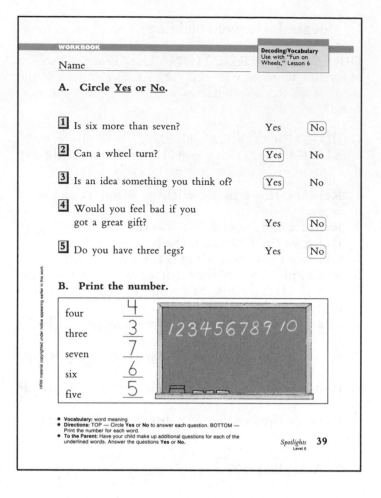

INDEPENDENT PRACTICE *Workbook* page 39 may be used to practice reading story vocabulary.

ADDITIONAL PRACTICE *Practice Masters* page 26 may be used as an optional practice for reading story vocabulary. (See page T158 for reduced pages with answers.)

RETEACH For those pupils who need additional instruction, see "Reteaching Lesson Skills," page T156, under "Reteaching and Extending."

COMPREHENSION/THINKING

Focus

I, T   Elements of style: rhyme

DIRECT INSTRUCTION Print the following rhyme on the chalkboard and ask pupils to read it.

> I have a dog, and his name is Wags.
> His dog food comes in great big bags.
> When I put dog food in his dish,
> He wags his tail—swish, swish, swish.

Tell pupils that rhyming words are words that end with the same sounds. Call on a pupil to read the first two lines. Then ask what words in these lines rhyme. (*Wags, bags*) Have the next two lines read aloud and ask pupils to name the rhyming words. (*dish, swish*)

GUIDED PRACTICE Explain that you are going to read some rhymes. After each rhyme, you will ask pupils to name the rhyming words.

1. **I can fix,
   I can mix,
   I can do things,
   'Cause I'm six.** (*fix, mix, six*)

2. **I can dig,
   and dance a jig,
   I can do them
   'Cause I'm big!** (*dig, jig, big*)

Lesson 6 "Fun on Wheels" (pages 60–67)   T145

Background for the Teacher

SUMMARY This selection shows some of the numerous ways wheels are used.

INFORMATION This selection, from a book of the same title, is written in rhyme and is intended to show the importance of the wheel in a humorous manner.

Using Prior Knowledge

Explain that this selection is about wheels. Develop a discussion by asking questions such as those that follow.

1. **What are some things with wheels that people can ride in?** (Possible answers include: cars, trucks, trains, wagons.)
2. **What are some things with wheels that you can play with?** (Possible answers include: toy cars, roller skates, bicycles, toy trains.)

Setting a Purpose for Reading

Have pupils find page 60 in their books. Tell them that the title of this story is "Fun on Wheels." Ask if they think this might be a funny story and why. (Possible answers include: Yes, the word *fun* is in the title; the pictures are funny-looking.) Tell pupils that this selection is written with rhyming words. Then ask pupils to name some of the things that have wheels in the pictures on page 60. (unicycle, motorcycle, tricycle, wagon) Point out the headnote at the top of page 60. Tell pupils that this note will help them think about the selection they are going to read. Ask a pupil to read it aloud.

Reading Silently

Some pupils may be able to read this story independently. Direct them to read the whole story to find out more about wheels and why they are great ideas. For those pupils who need more guidance, suggestions for directed reading follow.

Whoever invented the wheel had a great idea. Read to find out why.

Fun on Wheels

One wheel,
Two wheels,
Three wheels,
Four.

Five wheels,
Six wheels,
Seven wheels,
More.

60

61

Before reading pages 60–61

SAY **Lots of things with wheels are pictured here. What do people use wheels for? Read pages 60 and 61 to yourself.**

After reading pages 60–61

1. **What has one wheel?** (the unicycle) **What is a unicycle used for?** (for riding; for fun) Inferential
2. **Who or what has five wheels?** (the clown) **What is the clown using wheels for?** (to juggle) Inferential
3. **What has seven wheels?** (the circus wagon) **What is a circus wagon used for?** (to carry animals) Inferential

Fox on wheels,
Box on wheels,

Coats,
Boats,
Floats on wheels.

Max on wheels,
Ax on wheels,

Cats,
Hats,
Bats on wheels.

62

63

Before reading pages 62–63

SAY **Wheels help us carry many things. Read pages 62 and 63 to yourself to find out how.**

After reading pages 62–63

1. **How are coats on wheels?** (The coat rack has wheels.) Inferential
2. **What kind of floats are on wheels?** (floats in a parade) Inferential
3. **How are cats, hats, and bats on wheels?** (A cat baseball team is on a float in a parade.) Inferential

Wheels that <u>mix</u>,
Wheels that spin.

Wheels that <u>fix</u>,
Wheels that <u>win</u>!

House on wheels,
Mouse on wheels.

64

65

Before reading pages 64–65

SAY **Read pages 64 and 65 to yourself to find out how wheels can do work.**

After reading pages 64–65

1. **What things with wheels are used for working?** (the mixer, the steam roller) Inferential
2. **What things with wheels are used for having fun?** (the Ferris wheel, the race cars) Inferential
3. **Which picture shows something that is make-believe?** (the one with the mouse on a bicycle) Inferential

Dip,
Slip,
Rip on wheels!

Skip on wheels,
Skate on wheels,
Everyone feels
Great on wheels!

Discussing the Selection

1. Why was inventing the wheel a great idea?
2. How can people have fun on wheels?
3. How do wheels help people?
4. What in this story could happen in real <u>life</u>?
5. What are other ways we can have fun on wheels?

66

67

Before reading pages 66–67

SAY **Read pages 66 and 67 to yourself to find out how everyone feels on wheels.**

After reading pages 66–67

How does everyone feel on wheels? (great) **Why?** (Possible answers include: Everyone in the pictures seems to be having fun on wheels.) Critical

Discussing the Selection

Questions preceded by a number appear in *Spotlights* after the selection. Questions preceded by a bullet are additional questions for extending discussion.

PURPOSE

1. **Why was inventing the wheel a great idea?** (Possible answers include: The wheel can be used to carry things; it can do work; it can be used to have fun.) Critical

STORY MAPPING

2. **How can people have fun on wheels?** (Possible answers include: People can ride bikes, motorbikes, roller skates, Ferris wheels.) Inferential

3. **How do wheels help people?** (Possible answers include: Wheels can help carry heavy loads; they can do work, such as mixing things.) Inferential

4. **What in this story could happen in real life?** (Possible answers include: People could ride bicycles, tricycles, motorcycles, roller skates, Ferris wheels; things such as boat trailers, mobile homes, egg beaters, and steam rollers can be used by people.) Inferential

CRITICAL THINKING

5. **What are other ways we can have fun on wheels?** (Answers will vary. Possible answers include: by going for a train ride, riding in a taxi, riding on a bicycle built for two.)

Using Language

CHORAL READING: RHYMES Have pupils turn to pages 60 and 61 and remind them that the selection was written in rhyme. Read pages 60 and 61 aloud, emphasizing the rhythm and the rhyming words. Then have pupils choral read the pages with you.

Follow a similar procedure for the remaining pages.

Applying the Focus Skill

ELEMENTS OF STYLE: RHYME Ask pupils to name some of the rhyming words on page 62 of the story. (*fox, box; coats, boats, floats*) Invite pupils to read the page, emphasizing the rhythm. Have them suggest some lines that could be added to the page. (Possible answers include: Ox on wheels.) Then have them draw pictures to illustrate the added lines.

Follow a similar procedure for the remaining pages.

Evaluating Comprehension

WB 40 **INDEPENDENT PRACTICE** *Workbook* page 40 may be used for an informal evaluation of story comprehension.

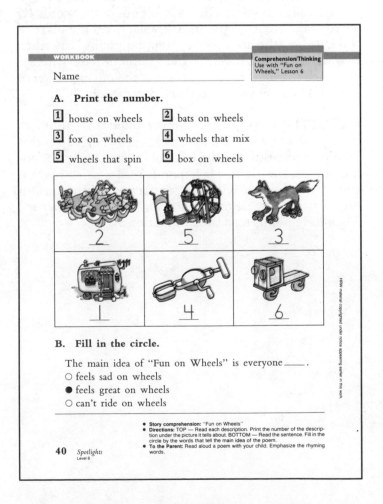

3 DEVELOPING READING AND THINKING SKILLS

DECODING/VOCABULARY

R, T   Word structure: contractions (with *'re*)

DIRECT INSTRUCTION Print the following sentence and words on the chalkboard:

> We are great.
>
> We're
>
> we are •   • they're
> you are •   • we're
> they are •   • you're

Have the sentence read aloud. Point to the words *We are* and remind pupils that these words can be put together to make one word. Point to and read the word *We're.* Have pupils tell what letter was left out of the words *We are* to make *We're.* (letter *a*) Ask what takes the place of the letter *a.* (the apostrophe) Remind pupils that when two words are put together and a letter or letters are left out, an apostrophe takes the place of the missing letter or letters. The new word is called a contraction.

GUIDED PRACTICE Direct pupils' attention to the two sets of words on the chalkboard. Tell pupils that each pair of words on the left can be matched to a contraction on the right. Have pupils read a pair of words and match the pair with the contraction that stands for the pair. (*we are, we're; you are, you're; they are, they're*) Then have pupils read the contractions.

WB 41   INDEPENDENT PRACTICE *Workbook* page 41 may be used to practice identifying contractions with *'re.*

PM 27   ADDITIONAL PRACTICE *Practice Masters* page 27 may be used as an optional practice for identifying contractions with *'re.* (See page T158 for reduced pages with answers.)

✳ RETEACH For those pupils who need additional instruction, see "Reteaching Lesson Skills," page T156, under "Reteaching and Extending."

WORKBOOK

Decoding/Vocabulary
Use with "Fun on Wheels" Lesson 6

Name _____

A. Print the words.

1 they're   they are

2 you're   you are

3 we're   we are

B. Fill in the circle.

1 Grandma said that ____ a good friend.
   ● you're   ○ we're

2 " ____ twins," said Mom about the two new neighbors.
   ○ We're   ● They're

3 Dee and Dean said to Jen, " ____ happy to meet you."
   ○ You're   ● We're

- **Word structure:** contractions (with *'re*)
- **Directions:** TOP — Read the contraction. Print the words it stands for on the line. BOTTOM — Read the sentences and the words. Fill in the circle by the word that completes each sentence.
- **To the Parent:** Have your child use each contraction in a sentence.

Spotlights Level 6   **41**

M Word structure: inflectional ending -es

DIRECT INSTRUCTION Print the following sentences and words on the chalkboard:

> 1. A fox ran up the hill.
> 2. Three foxes can play.
>
> 3. Dad and Tom fix the car.
> 4. Dad fixes the car.
>
> fox   fix   ax   mix
> foxes fixes axes mixes

Point to the first sentence and have it read. Ask how many foxes ran up the hill. (one) Then have the second sentence read. Ask how many foxes can play. (three) Point to the word *foxes*. Tell pupils that the ending *-es* was added to *fox* to mean "more than one fox." Remind pupils that the ending *-es* can be added to the end of a word to make a new word that means "more than one."

Point to the third sentence and have it read. Ask what Dad and Tom do. (They fix the car.) Have the fourth sentence read aloud. Ask what Dad does. (He fixes the car.) Point to the words *fix* and *fixes*. Remind pupils that the letters *es* can sometimes be added to the end of a word to make a new word that means "what someone does."

GUIDED PRACTICE Have each word pair on the chalkboard read. Call on pupils to choose a word from the chalkboard to complete each sentence you will read.

1. **Three _____ ran in the woods.** *(foxes)*
2. **Mom can _____ the broken toy.** *(fix)*
3. **The cook _____ everything together.** *(mixes)*
4. **They cut down the tree with one _____.** *(ax)*
5. **A _____ has a bushy tail.** *(fox)*
6. **We will _____ up the batter.** *(mix)*

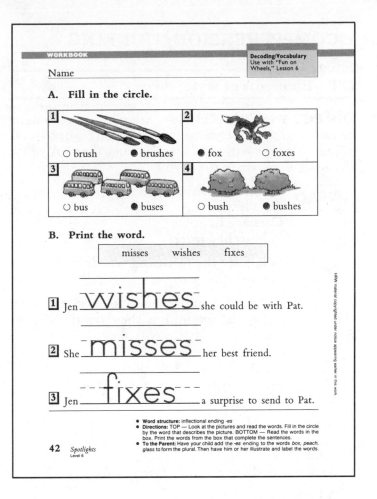

INDEPENDENT PRACTICE *Workbook* page 42 may be used to practice identifying words with inflectional ending *-es*.

ADDITIONAL PRACTICE *Practice Masters* page 28 may be used as an optional practice for identifying words with inflectional ending *-es*. (See page T159 for reduced pages with answers.)

COMPREHENSION/THINKING

Focus
I, T   Elements of style: rhyme

DIRECT INSTRUCTION   Ask why a poem might be called a rhyme. (because it has rhyming words) Tell pupils that you will read a rhyme and then ask what rhyming words are in the rhyme.

READ   **Cats have whiskers,**
Cats have fur,
Cats are happy
When they purr.

ASK   **What are the rhyming words in the rhyme?** (*fur, purr*)

Repeat the rhyme and then ask pupils to say it with you. Have pupils clap the rhythm as they say the rhyme again.

GUIDED PRACTICE   Tell pupils that you will read some rhymes with missing words. Then you will ask pupils to guess what the missing words are.

1. **In the bathtub**
   Where it will float,
   I can play
   with my little toy _____. (*boat*)

2. **A little frog**
   All spotted green
   Hides in the pond,
   So it can't be _____. (*seen*)

3. **Little seeds fly**
   When the wind blows.
   Where will they land?
   Nobody _____. (*knows*)

Call on pupils to recite some lines from a favorite nursery rhyme. Ask them to name the rhyming words in the rhyme.

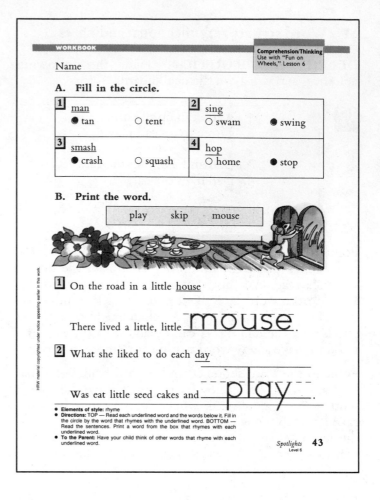

INDEGPENDENT PRACTICE   *Workbook* page 43 may be used to practice recognizing rhyme.

ADDITIONAL PRACTICE   *Practice Masters* page 29 may be used as an optional practice for recognizing rhyme. (See page T159 for reduced pages with answers.)

❋   **RETEACH**   For those pupils who need additional instruction, see "Reteaching Lesson Skills," page T157, under "Reteaching and Extending."

STUDY SKILLS

M Graphic aids: illustrations

DIRECT INSTRUCTION Remind pupils that when they read, they can get information from both words *and* pictures. Sometimes pictures make a story easier to understand. Remind pupils that the pictures in a story are called illustrations.

Have pupils open their books to page 60 and call on a pupil to read the page aloud.

| SAY | The words "One wheel, two wheels, three wheels, four" probably would |

not have made much sense without the pictures. What can you find in the picture that has one wheel? (the unicycle) **What has two wheels?** (the motorcycle) **What has three wheels?** (the tricycle) **What has four wheels?** (the wagon)

GUIDED PRACTICE Ask pupils to read page 62 aloud. Then ask what is meant by "Fox on wheels." (the fox on roller skates) Ask what is meant by "Box on wheels." (The box is a crate that has been made into a scooter.) Ask what is meant by "Coats, Boats, Floats on wheels." (The coats are on a rolling coat rack; the boat is on a trailer; the floats are in a parade.)

Have other pages from "Fun on Wheels" read aloud and ask pupils to explain how the artist illustrated the words.

LANGUAGE

M Writing: language-experience stories

DIRECT INSTRUCTION Display chart paper and tell pupils that they will work together to make up a story about wheels. Tell pupils that you will write their story on the chart paper for them. Help organize the story by asking pupils to answer questions such as the following:

> **How should our story start?**
> **What kinds of uses for wheels should we include?**
> **How should our story end?**

GUIDED PRACTICE As pupils dictate, write the sentences on the chart. Read back each sentence and invite pupils to join you. When the story is finished, have it read several times. Have pupils illustrate their favorite part of the story. Display the illustrations near the chart paper, where pupils can enjoy the story on their own.

HOW AM I DOING?

Pupils need time to express their opinions and to listen to others. Ask yourself the following questions to gauge your teaching effectiveness in this area.

	Yes	No	Some-times
1. Have I encouraged pupils to respect each other's opinions?	☐	☐	☐
2. Have I provided enough time for pupils to share ideas?	☐	☐	☐
3. Have I provided feedback about pupils ideas?	☐	☐	☐
4. Have I presented activities in which pupils can express their opinions?			

Lesson 6 "Fun on Wheels" (pages 60–67) T155

✳ RETEACHING AND EXTENDING

Reteaching Lesson Skills

The activities that follow provide reteaching of skills developed in this lesson. Not every pupil needs to complete these activities. Choose only the activities that are needed to provide for the individual differences in your classroom.

DECODING/VOCABULARY

I, T   Sound/symbol correspondence: consonant ks/*x* (final)

✳   **RETEACH**   Use *Word Cards* to make the following pairs of words in the *Pocket Chart: ox, fox; ax, wax; six, mix.*

Point to *ox* and *fox* and read them aloud. Ask what is alike about these words. (They rhyme; they end with letters *ox.*) Tell pupils that letter *x* stands for the sound at the end of *ox* and *fox.* Follow a similar procedure for the remaining word pairs.

Remove the *Word Cards* from the *Pocket Chart,* shuffle them, and hold up one card at a time. Have pupils read each word. Then display *Word Cards* and ask pupils to find the rhyming words and put them together in the *Pocket Chart.* Have the pairs of rhyming words read aloud.

  Distribute *Reteach Masters* page 9 and explain the directions on the page.

R, T   Word structure: contractions (with *'re*)

✳   **RETEACH**   Print the following sentences on the chalkboard and have them read.

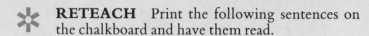

1. We are playing tag.
2. You are It!
3. They are running away.

Display *Word Cards We're, They're, You're* and have them read. Ask what two words were put together to make each contraction. (*we are, they are, you are*) Have pupils read the sentences as they are written and then with the contractions in place.

I, T   Vocabulary: word meaning

✳   **RETEACH**   Print the following words and sentences on the chalkboard, omitting the underlining.

five   four   great   idea   invented **more   seven   wheel**
1. Ben's wagon lost a <u>wheel</u>.
2. Ben had a <u>great</u> <u>idea</u>.
3. He went to the dump to look   for <u>more</u> wheels.
4. He saw <u>seven</u> wheels.
5. <u>Five</u> of them were no good,   but he only needed one.
6. Now his wagon has <u>four</u> good wheels.
7. Ben was glad the wheel had been   <u>invented</u>.
ax   fix   fox **Max   mix   six**

Point to the word *wheel* and read it. Call on a pupil to find and read a sentence that contains the word *wheel.* Continue in the same manner with the remaining sentences, calling attention to the underlined words.

Display *Word Cards* for the underlined words. Call on pupils to hold up and read the word that answers each of the following questions:

1. **Which words name numbers?** (*five, four, seven*)
2. **Which words mean "very good plan"?** (*great idea*)
3. **Which word means "discovered or made"?** (*invented*)
4. **Which word means "something round that turns"?** (*wheel*)

Ask pupils to read the second set of words and to use them in sentences.

 Distribute *Reteach Masters* page 10 and explain the directions on the page.

COMPREHENSION/THINKING

Focus
I, T   Elements of style: rhyme

 RETEACH Print the following rhyme and words on the chalkboard:

> I saw a _____.
> Sit on a _____.
>
> box   cat   frog
> hat   log   fox

Call on a pupil to select two rhyming words from the chalkboard. Have pupils repeat the rhyme, using the pair of rhyming words. Follow a similar procedure with the remaining pairs of rhyming words. Then ask pupils to suggest other pairs of rhyming words that might complete the rhyme.

Extending Selection Concepts

LANGUAGE ARTS

WRITING: RHYMES Print the following incomplete sentences on the chalkboard.

> Here is a _____.
> It has a _____.

Have pupils read the lines and suggest rhyming words that might complete the sentences. (Possible answers include: *goat, coat; cat, hat; mouse, house.*) Invite pupils to copy the sentences, putting the rhyming words of their choice in the blanks. Ask pupils to illustrate their rhymes. Display the rhymes and illustrations where pupils can read and share each other's work.

SPEAKING: RECITING RHYMES (Cooperative Learning) Let small groups of pupils work together to present a nursery rhyme or other simple poem to the class. Encourage them to practice reciting the rhyme until they can recite it together. Then have them pantomime the rhyme by putting motions to the words. Have each group present its choral recitation of the rhyme with motions or actions to the class.

LITERATURE

LISTENING: FICTION Choose a story that is told in rhyme and read it aloud to the class. If the story has a repeating rhyme, ask pupils to join in each time the rhyme repeats.

Carlstrom, Nancy White. *Jesse Bear, What Will You Wear?* Macmillan, 1986. This is the story of Jesse Bear's day told in verse and paintings.

Degen, Bruce. *Jamberry.* Harper & Row, 1983. This is the story of a rhyme-spouting bear who takes a boy on an adventure through the fantastic world of berries.

Perkins, Al. *Hand, Hand, Fingers, Thumb.* Random House, 1969. The repeating rhyme pattern of this book will have pupils clapping and reciting as you read.

Dr. Seuss. *And To Think That I Saw It on Mulberry Street.* Hale, 1937. This classic story of a boy's wild imagination is told in rhyme.

Shaw, Nancy. *Sheep in a Jeep.* Houghton Mifflin, 1986. This children's favorite tells the hilarious story of a group of sheep that goes riding in a jeep.

SCIENCE

LISTENING: INFORMATION Choose a book that explains some of the many uses of wheels and read it to the class.

Barton, Byron. *Wheels.* Crowell, 1979. This is a picture book about wheels. It highlights the invention of the wheel and its importance and uses.

Cole, Joanna. *Cars and How They Go.* Thomas Y. Crowell, 1983. With clear language and logical sequence, this book explains how wheels help make cars go.

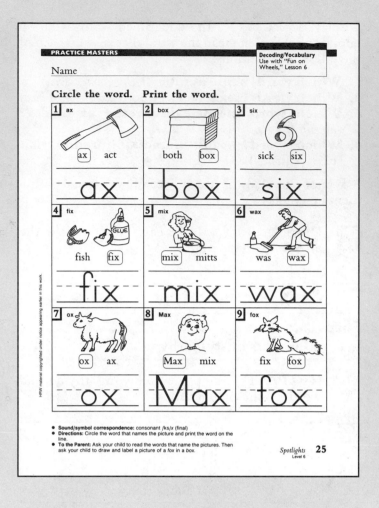

Name _____

Circle the word.   Print the word.

1. ax / act — ax
2. box / both — box
3. sick / six — six
4. fish / fix — fix
5. mix / mitts — mix
6. was / wax — wax
7. ox / ax — ox
8. Max / mix — Max
9. fix / fox — fox

- **Sound/symbol correspondence:** consonant /ks/x (final)
- **Directions:** Circle the word that names the picture and print the word on the line.
- **To the Parent:** Ask your child to read the words that name the pictures. Then ask your child to draw and label a picture of a *fox* in a *box*.

Spotlights Level 6   **25**

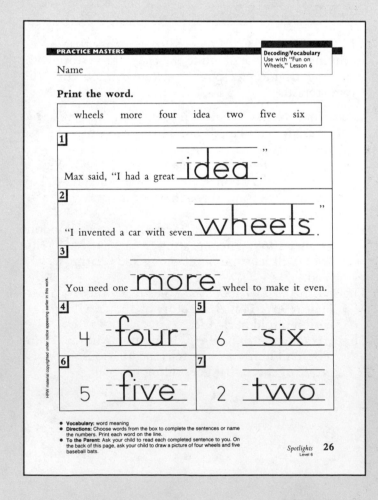

Name _____

Print the word.

| wheels | more | four | idea | two | five | six |

1. Max said, "I had a great **idea**."
2. "I invented a car with seven **wheels**."
3. You need one **more** wheel to make it even.
4. 4 **four**
5. 6 **six**
6. 5 **five**
7. 2 **two**

- **Vocabulary:** word meaning
- **Directions:** Choose words from the box to complete the sentences or name the numbers. Print each word on the line.
- **To the Parent:** Ask your child to read each completed sentence to you. On the back of this page, ask your child to draw a picture of four wheels and five baseball bats.

Spotlights Level 6   **26**

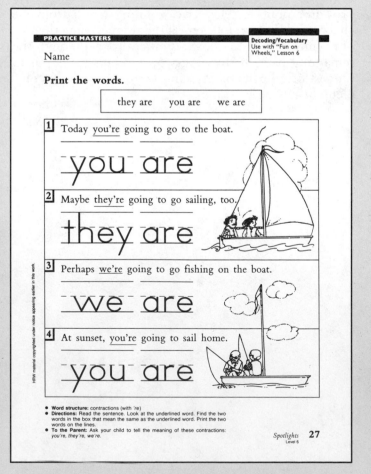

Name _____

Print the words.

| they are | you are | we are |

1. Today you're going to go to the boat. — **you are**
2. Maybe they're going to go sailing, too. — **they are**
3. Perhaps we're going to go fishing on the boat. — **we are**
4. At sunset, you're going to sail home. — **you are**

- **Word structure:** contractions (with 're)
- **Directions:** Read the sentence. Look at the underlined word. Find the two words in the box that mean the same as the underlined word. Print the two words on the lines.
- **To the Parent:** Ask your child to tell the meaning of these contractions: *you're, they're, we're.*

Spotlights Level 6   **27**

Name _____

Print the word.

1 A big red <u>fox</u> ran in the woods.

Six little ___foxes___ followed it.

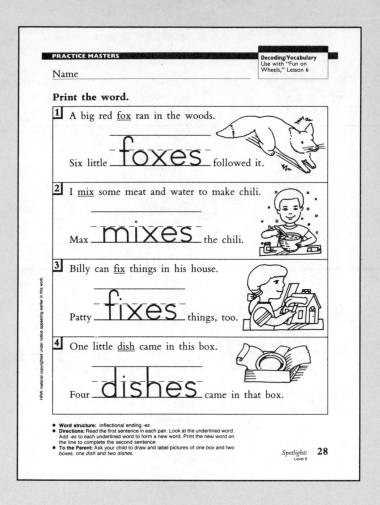

2 I <u>mix</u> some meat and water to make chili.

Max ___mixes___ the chili.

3 Billy can <u>fix</u> things in his house.

Patty ___fixes___ things, too.

4 One little <u>dish</u> came in this box.

Four ___dishes___ came in that box.

- **Word structure:** inflectional ending *-es*
- **Directions:** Read the first sentence in each pair. Look at the underlined word. Add *-es* to each underlined word to form a new word. Print the new word on the line to complete the second sentence.
- **To the Parent:** Ask your child to draw and label pictures of one *box* and two *boxes*, one *dish* and two *dishes*.

Spotlights
Level 6 **28**

Name _____

Print the word.

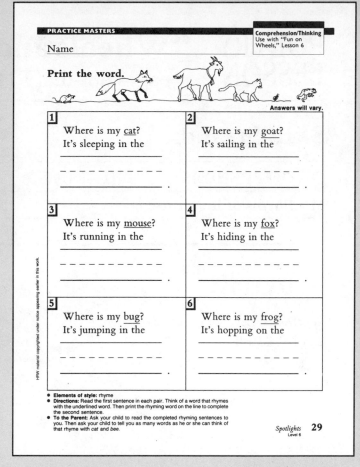

Answers will vary.

1 Where is my <u>cat</u>?
It's sleeping in the _____
_____ .

2 Where is my <u>goat</u>?
It's sailing in the _____
_____ .

3 Where is my <u>mouse</u>?
It's running in the _____
_____ .

4 Where is my <u>fox</u>?
It's hiding in the _____
_____ .

5 Where is my <u>bug</u>?
It's jumping in the _____
_____ .

6 Where is my <u>frog</u>?
It's hopping on the _____
_____ .

- **Elements of style:** rhyme
- **Directions:** Read the first sentence in each pair. Think of a word that rhymes with the underlined word. Then print the rhyming word on the line to complete the second sentence.
- **To the Parent:** Ask your child to read the completed rhyming sentences to you. Then ask your child to tell you as many words as he or she can think of that rhyme with *cat* and *bee*.

Spotlights
Level 6 **29**

Name _____

Print the word. Circle the words.

six	Max
ox	fix

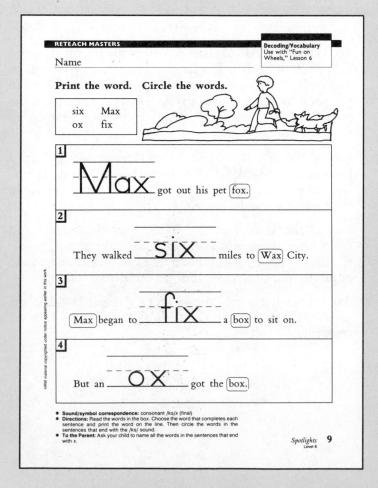

1 ___Max___ got out his pet (fox).

2 They walked ___six___ miles to (Wax) City.

3 (Max) began to ___fix___ a (box) to sit on.

4 But an ___ox___ got the (box).

- **Sound/symbol correspondence:** consonant /ks/*x* (final)
- **Directions:** Read the words in the box. Choose the word that completes each sentence and print the word on the line. Then circle the words in the sentences that end with the /ks/ sound.
- **To the Parent:** Ask your child to name all the words in the sentences that end with *x*.

Spotlights
Level 6 **9**

Name _____

Print the words.

great	Five	four	seven	invented	idea

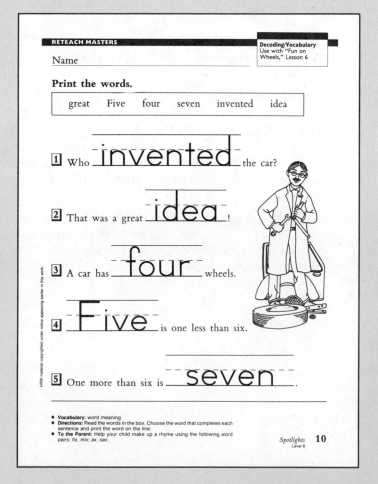

1 Who ___invented___ the car?

2 That was a great ___idea___ !

3 A car has ___four___ wheels.

4 ___Five___ is one less than six.

5 One more than six is ___seven___ .

- **Vocabulary:** word meaning
- **Directions:** Read the words in the box. Choose the word that completes each sentence and print the word on the line.
- **To the Parent:** Help your child make up a rhyme using the following word pairs: *fix, mix; ax, sax.*

Spotlights
Level 6 **10**

POETRY LESSON

"Wheels and Wings"
pages 68–69 (T160–T161)

Skill Strands

COMPREHENSION/THINKING

M   Forms of literature: poetry

Materials

Spotlights, Level 6: pages 68–69
Teacher's Idea Book

Special Populations

See *Teacher's Idea Book* for additional suggestions to help pupils with limited English proficiency.

Key to Symbols
I   Introduced in this lesson
R   Reinforced from an earlier lesson in this level
M   Maintained from previous levels
T   Tested in this level

COMPREHENSION/THINKING

M   Forms of literature: poetry

DIRECT INSTRUCTION   Ask pupils to name some things with wheels that they might ride on when they play. (Possible answers include: bicycles, skateboards, roller skates.) Point out that riding on things with wheels can be lots of fun.

Have pupils find page 68 in their books and read the title of the poem. ("Wheels and Wings") Ask pupils to listen as you read the poem to see how the poet feels about riding on wheels. Read aloud the poem on pages 68–69.

GUIDED PRACTICE   Ask how the poet feels about riding on wheels. (The poet thinks riding is fun, as much fun as flying.) Ask to whom or what the person in the poem is speaking. (birds) Ask what the person in the poem is telling the birds. (Riding fast and gliding on wheels is like flying.)

Reread the first stanza. Then read the second and third lines again and ask which words rhyme. (*wings, things*) Read the fourth and fifth lines and ask pupils to name the rhyming words. (*wheels, heels*)

Reread the second stanza. Then read the second and third lines again and ask pupils to name the rhyming words. (*rise, skies*) Read the fourth and fifth lines and ask pupils to name the rhyming words. (*sliding, gliding*)

Ask why wheels are compared to wings. (Possible answers include: Wheels let us go fast so we feel like we are flying.)

(To be read by the teacher)

Wheels and Wings

Ahoy and ahoy, birds!
We cannot have wings
And feathers and things,
But dashing on wheels
With the wind at our heels
Is almost like flying—
Such joy, birds!

Oho and oho, birds!
Of course we can't rise
Up and up to the skies;
But skimming and sliding
On rollers, and gliding,
Is almost as jolly,
You know, birds!

Nancy Byrd Turner

68

69

LESSON 7 "A Place for Babies"
pages 70–75 (T162–T181)

Skill Strands

DECODING/VOCABULARY

R, T **Sound/symbol correspondence:** consonant /ks/x (final)

R, T **Sound/symbol correspondence:** vowel /ī/i-e

I, T **Sound/symbol correspondence:** r-controlled vowel /är/ar

M **Word structure:** contractions (with 'll, 's)

I **Vocabulary:** word building

I, T **Vocabulary:** word meaning

COMPREHENSION/THINKING

Focus

M **Literal:** main idea (stated)

STUDY SKILLS

R, T **References:** dictionary (entry words and definitions)

Lesson Vocabulary

Decodable words: *cannot, dart, father, frog, harm, piggyback, pocket, ride, safe, until, wet, wiggle*

Special words: *babies, baby, carried, carry*

Materials

Spotlights, Level 6: pages 70–75
Workbook: pages 44–49

Practice Masters: pages 30–33
Instructional Charts: pages 44–51
Resource Box: Letter Cards a, c, d, e, f, m, r, s, t (2)
Word Cards ax, babies, baby, bit, box, carried, carry, fin, fix, fox, mix, ox, pin, rip, six, slid, wax

Pocket Chart
Teacher's Idea Book
Reteach Masters: pages 11–12

Language Applications

USING LANGUAGE

Oral reading/Speaking: answering questions

EXTENDING SELECTION CONCEPTS

Writing: animal reports (Cooperative Learning)
Listening: information

Special Populations

See *Teacher's Idea Book* for additional suggestions to help pupils with limited English proficiency.

Key to Symbols
I Introduced in this lesson
R Reinforced from an earlier lesson in this level
M Maintained from previous levels
T Tested in this level

Idea Center

BIBLIOGRAPHY

Add to your reading corner or reading table various books about animals and animal babies. A suggested bibliography follows. Suggestions for reading aloud and annotations appear in the lesson plan.

Cole, Joanna. *Large as Life: Daytime Animals.* Knopf, 1985.

———. *Large as Life: Nightime Animals.* Knopf, 1985.

Hewett, Joan. *Watching Them Grow: Inside a Zoo Nursery.* Little, Brown, 1979.

Yabuuchi, Masayuki. *Whose Baby?* Philomel, 1985.

Planning Chart

		Instruction	Written Practice	Extending
Step 1 Preparing for the Selection	I, T	**Sound/symbol correspondence:** *r*-controlled vowel /är/*ar*	*Workbook* page 44 *Practice Masters* page 30 *Reteach Masters* page 11	
	I	**Vocabulary:** word building		
	I, T	**Vocabulary:** word meaning	*Workbook* page 45 *Practice Masters* page 31 *Reteach Masters* page 12	
	M	**Literal:** main idea (stated)		
Step 2 Reading for Comprehension		**Oral reading/Speaking:** answering questions **Literal:** main idea (stated) **Story comprehension**	*Workbook* page 46	**Writing:** animal reports (Cooperative Learning)
Step 3 Developing Reading and Thinking Skills	R, T	**Sound/symbol correspondence:** consonant /ks/*x* (final)	*Workbook* page 47	
	R, T	**Sound/symbol correspondence:** vowel /ī/*i-e*		**Listening:** information
	M	**Word structure:** contractions (with *'ll, 's*)	*Workbook* page 48 *Practice Masters* page 32	
	M	**Literal:** main idea (stated)	*Workbook* page 49 *Practice Masters* page 33	
	R, T	**References:** dictionary (entry words and definitions)		

1 PREPARING FOR THE SELECTION

DECODING/VOCABULARY

I, T Sound/symbol correspondence: *r*-controlled vowel /är/*ar*

DIRECT INSTRUCTION Print the following rhyme and words on the chalkboard:

IC 44

> I want to ride in a rocket.
> I want to go so far.
> I will put into my pocket
> Star after star after star.
>
>   star
>   far
>
>   farm   dart   harm
>   arm   car   park

Read the rhyme and ask what the poet wants to put in his or her pocket. (star after star after star) Point to the word *star* below the rhyme.

SAY Here is the word *star*. Read *star* with me: *star*. (Point to the word *far*.) Here is the word *far*. Read *far* with me: *far*. What is the same about the words *star* and *far*? (They rhyme; they end with letters *ar*.) The letters *ar* together can stand for the /är/ sound.

GUIDED PRACTICE Refer pupils to the three pairs of words on the chalkboard. Have each word read and ask how the words are alike. (They each have *ar*; they have the /är/ sound.) Then call on a pupil to read the word from the chalkboard that answers each of the following questions:

1. **What did Old MacDonald have?** *(farm)*
2. **Which word means the same as *hurt*?** *(harm)*
3. **Which word names a part of your body?** *(arm)*
4. **Which word means "to move very fast"?** *(dart)*
5. **Which word names a place where children might play?** *(park)*
6. **Which word names something you can ride in?** *(car)*

WB 44 **INDEPENDENT PRACTICE** *Workbook* page 44 may be used to practice identifying sound/symbol correspondence /är/*ar*.

PM 30 **ADDITIONAL PRACTICE** *Practice Masters* page 30 may be used as an optional practice for identifying *r*-controlled vowel /är/*ar*. (See page T180 for reduced pages with answers.)

✳ RETEACH For those pupils who need additional instruction, see "Reteaching Lesson Skills," page T178, under "Reteaching and Extending."

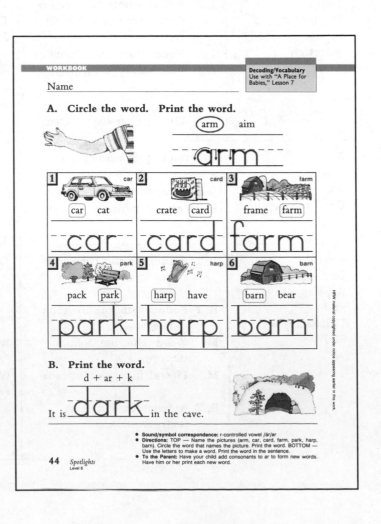

I Vocabulary: word building

DIRECT INSTRUCTION Place *Letter Cards* in the *Pocket Chart* to make the word *star* and have pupils read it. Ask what letters stand for the /är/ sound (*ar*) and where the /är/ sound is heard in *star*. (at the end) Place *Letter Card t* at the end of the word and have the new word read. (*start*)

GUIDED PRACTICE Display *Letter Cards c, d, f, m.* Call on pupils to use the letters to change the word in the *Pocket Chart.*

1. **Take away *st* from the beginning of *start*. What is the new word?** (*art*)
2. **Take away *t* and put *m* at the end. What is the new word?** (*arm*)
3. **Put *f* in front of the word. What is the new word?** (*farm*)
4. **Take away *m*. What is the new word?** (*far*)
5. **Replace the *f* with *c*. What is the new word?** (*car*)
6. **Put *t* at the end of the word. What is the new word?** (*cart*)
7. **Replace the *c* with *d*. What is the new word?** (*dart*)
8. **Replace *d* with *st*. What is the new word?** (*start*)

I, T Vocabulary: word meaning

DIRECT INSTRUCTION Tell pupils that they are going to talk about some words they will read in the next story. Print the following words and sentences on the chalkboard, omitting the underlining.

> **babies   baby   carried   carry**
>
> 1. Jim has a <u>baby</u> sister.
> 2. <u>Babies</u> can't walk.
> 3. So Jim has to <u>carry</u> his sister.
> 4. He <u>carried</u> her in his arms.
>
> **dart   harm   ride**

Read the first sentence. Point to the word *baby* and read it. Ask if Jim's sister was younger than he was. (Yes, she was a baby sister.) Have pupils read the sentence with you. Ask them to find and read the word *baby*.

Read the first sentence. Point to the word *baby* and read it. Ask if Jim's sister was younger than he was. (Yes, she was a baby sister.) Have pupils read the sentence with you. Ask them to find and read the word *baby*.

Read Sentence 2. Point to the word *babies* and read it. Tell pupils that this word means "more than one baby." Ask what the sentence says babies can't do. (walk) Have pupils read the sentence with you. Then have them find and read the word *babies*.

Read Sentence 3. Point to the word *carry* and read it. Ask how Jim's sister went from place to place. (Jim had to carry her.) Have pupils read the sentence with you. Then have them point to the word *carry* and read it. (Some pupils may notice that the letters *ar* in *carry* do not stand for the /är/ sound. Explain that this word does not follow the /är/*ar* correspondence.)

Read Sentence 4. Point to the word *carried* and read it. Ask how Jim carried his sister. (in his arms) Have pupils read the sentence with you. Then ask them to point to the word *carried* and read it.

The words in the second set are new words that contain known phonic elements. You may wish to ask pupils to read the words, using what they know about letters and sounds.

GUIDED PRACTICE Print the following sentences on the chalkboard, omitting the underlining.

1. Tim and three <u>babies</u> went for a <u>ride</u>.
2. He could not <u>carry</u> more than one <u>baby</u>.
3. He was afraid he would <u>harm</u> them.
4. They would <u>dart</u> away from him.
5. He put them in a wagon that <u>carried</u> all three.

Provide opportunities for pupils to practice reading the new special words and some of the new decodable words in these sentences by following the suggestions below.

Sentence 1: Have the sentence read. Ask if more than one baby went for a ride. (Yes, three babies went.) Call on pupils to find and read the word *ride*.

Sentence 2: Call on a pupil to read the sentence. Ask pupils to find and read the word *carry*.

Sentence 3: Have the sentence read. Ask why Tim didn't want to carry all three babies. (He was afraid he would harm them.) Have pupils find and read the word *harm*.

Sentence 4: Call on a pupil to read the sentence. Ask if the babies could get away quickly. (Yes, they could dart away.) Have pupils find and read the word *dart*.

Sentence 5: Have pupils read the sentence together. Then ask how Tim carried all three babies. (in a wagon) Have pupils find and read the word *carried*.

Invite pupils to select a sentence to read aloud.

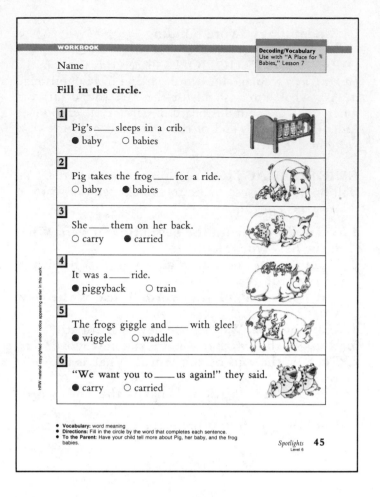

INDEPENDENT PRACTICE *Workbook* page 45 may be used to practice reading story vocabulary.

ADDITIONAL PRACTICE *Practice Masters* page 31 may be used as an optional practice for reading story vocabulary. (See page T180 for reduced pages with answers.)

RETEACH For those pupils who need additional instruction, see "Reteaching Lesson Skills," page T179, under "Reteaching and Extending."

COMPREHENSION/THINKING

Focus

M   Literal: main idea (stated)

DIRECT INSTRUCTION   Ask pupils to explain what the main idea of a paragraph or story is. (The main idea is what the story or paragraph is about.) Remind pupils that there is often a sentence in the story that tells the main idea. Have pupils listen as you read the following paragraph:

READ   **Many things happen in the spring. The animals that sleep through the long winter wake up. Little flowers start to bloom. New leaves grow on the trees, and birds begin to build new nests.**

ASK   **What is this paragraph about?** (springtime) **What does the paragraph tell you about springtime?** (It tells about the things that happen in the spring.) **This paragraph tells about things that happen in the spring. I will read the paragraph again. Listen for the sentence that tells the main idea.** *(Many things happen in the spring.)*

GUIDED PRACTICE   Print the following story on the chalkboard and ask pupils to read it.

> Marsha was a great baby sitter.
> She would fix good snacks.
> She would read books.
> She would tell a bedtime story.

ASK   **What is the main idea of this story?** (Marsha was a great baby sitter.) **What are some things that Marsha would do?** (She would fix good snacks, read books, and tell bedtime stories.) **The first sentence of this story tells the main idea. Read the first sentence with me:** *Marsha was a great baby sitter.*

Have a pupil read the second, the third, and the fourth sentences. Point out that each sentence tells why Marsha was a great baby sitter.

Background for the Teacher

SUMMARY   Animals carry their babies in many different ways. In addition to kangaroos, some frogs, fish, and chameleons have unusual ways to carry their young.

INFORMATION   This article presents factual information about how animal babies are transported from place to place. The animals presented include the kangaroo, the poison arrow frog, the African mouth brooder fish, the chameleon, the baboon, the tiger, and the swan.

Using Prior Knowledge

Explain that the selection pupils are going to read is about animal babies. Ask if anyone has ever seen a mother dog with puppies, a mother cat with kittens, or other animal mothers with babies. Ask what the mother does to take care of her babies. (Possible answers include: She feeds them; she protects them; she carries them from place to place.) Develop a discussion by asking questions such as those that follow.

1. **When you were a baby, you couldn't walk. How did you get from one place to another?** (Possible answers include: Someone had to carry you; you crawled on your hands and knees.)
2. **When baby animals are born, many of them cannot walk. How do you think they get from place to place?** (Possible answers include: The mother and father animals carry the babies.)

Setting a Purpose for Reading

Have pupils find page 70 in their books. Tell pupils that the title of this story is "A Place for Babies." Point out the headnote at the top of page 70. Explain that this note will help pupils think about the story they are going to read. Have the headnote read. Then ask pupils to predict what kinds of baby animals they will read about.

Reading Silently

Some pupils may be able to read this story independently. Direct them to read the whole story to find out more about some baby animals and how they get from one place to another. For those pupils who need more guidance, suggestions for directed reading follow.

Babies go from one place to another in different ways.

Read to find out what these ways are.

A Place for Babies

There are different ways to take a baby from one place to another.

When you were a baby, you were carried in someone's arms.

70

Most animals cannot carry babies in their arms.

They have other ways to take their babies from one place to another.

This mother is carrying her baby in a pocket.

71

SAY **Many animals need to carry their babies. How do you think they do it? Read pages 70 and 71 to yourself.**

1. **How are human babies carried?** (in someone's arms) Literal
2. **How are baby kangaroos carried?** (in the mother kangaroo's pocket) Inferential
3. **Why do you think most animals cannot carry babies in their arms?** (Possible answers include: because they walk on all four feet, because they don't have arms or hands.) Critical

This <u>father frog</u> keeps
the frog eggs <u>safe</u> <u>until</u> they hatch.
Then the babies <u>wiggle</u>
onto the father's back.

To keep them <u>wet</u>, the father frog
takes the babies for a swim!

72

Some mother fish carry their eggs
inside their <u>throats</u>.
There the eggs are safe from <u>harm</u>.

When the little ones hatch,
they swim next to their mother.
If they are in trouble,
they will <u>dart</u> back inside their
mother's throat.

73

Before
reading
pages
72–73

SAY Not all animals have pockets.
The illustration on page 72 is of
a poison arrow frog, and the illustration on page 72 is of an African mouth
brooder fish. Read pages 72 and 73 to
learn how they carry their babies.

After
reading
pages
72–73

1. **How does this father frog carry his babies?** (He carries them on his back.) Literal
2. **How does this mother fish take care of her baby fish?** (She carries them inside her throat.) Literal
3. **What do the baby fish do if they see danger?** (They dart back inside the mother's throat.) Inferential

This baby is being carried on its father's horns!

This baby is getting a piggyback ride!
It likes to be carried on its mother's back.

74

Look at these animals.
See the different ways they're carrying their babies.

Discussing the Selection
1. What are some ways babies go from one place to another?
2. How do some father frogs keep their frog eggs safe?
3. Why is carrying fish eggs inside the mother fish's throat a good idea?
4. How do the animals shown here carry their babies?

75

Before reading pages 74–75

SAY Read pages 74 and 75 to yourself to learn more ways that animals carry their babies.

After reading pages 74–75

1. **This lizard is called a chameleon. How is the baby chameleon being carried?** (on its father's horns) Literal
2. **This animal is called a baboon. How does the mother baboon carry her baby?** (She gives it a piggyback ride.) Inferential
3. **Which animal carries its baby the most like a human baby?** (the baboon) Inferential
4. **Which animal do you think has the most unusual way of carrying its baby?** (Answers will vary. Possible answers include: the chameleon, because the baby is carried on its father's horns; the brooder fish, because the mother carries her babies in her throat.) Critical

Discussing the Selection

Questions preceded by a number appear in *Spotlights* after the selection. Questions preceded by a bullet are additional questions for extending discussions.

MAIN IDEA

1. **What are some ways babies go from one place to another?** (in mother's or father's arms, on mother's or father's back, in mother's throat, on horns, in a pocket) Inferential

SUPPORT

2. **How do some father frogs keep their frog eggs safe?** (They carry them on their backs.) Literal

THEME-RELATED

3. **Why is carrying fish eggs inside the mother fish's throat a good idea?** (Possible answers include: The mother fish always has them with her and can protect them from enemies.) Critical

- **What do the little fish do when they hatch?** (They swim next to their mother and dart into her throat if they are in trouble.) Inferential

SELECTION-RELATED

4. **How do the animals shown here carry their babies?** (The swan carries the babies on its back; the tiger carries its babies in its mouth.) Critical

- **The selection says that human babies are carried in someone's arms. What are some other ways they go from place to place?** (Possible answers include: in a carriage or stroller, in a knapsack or a backpack worn by an adult.)

Using Language

ORAL READING/SPEAKING: ANSWERING QUESTIONS Have pupils to turn to page 70 in their books. Ask if this story was about make-believe animals or if it told about real animals. (It was about real animals.) Ask how pupils could tell. (The pictures were photographs of real animals; the animals did not talk or wear clothes.) Explain that people often read about real things because they want to learn something. Ask pupils what they learned from reading this story. (They learned how different animals carry their babies.)

Tell pupils that you will ask some questions from the following pages that can be answered by reading parts of the selection.

Page 70: **How were you carried when you were a baby?** (When you were a baby, you were carried in someone's arms.)

Page 71: **How does a kangaroo carry her baby?** (This mother is carrying her baby in a pocket.)

Page 72: **How does this father frog take care of its babies?** (This father frog keeps the frog eggs safe until they hatch. Then the babies wiggle onto the father's back. To keep them wet, the father frog takes the babies for a swim!)

Page 73: **How do some mother fish keep their eggs safe from harm?** (Some mother fish carry their eggs inside their throats.)

Page 74: **How does the father chameleon carry his baby?** (This baby is being carried on its father's horns!) **How does the mother baboon carry her baby?** (This baby is getting a piggyback ride!)

Applying the Focus Skill

LITERAL: MAIN IDEA Remind pupils that the main idea of a selection is what the selection is about. Have pupils turn to page 70. Ask them to find the sentence on this page that tells the main idea of the selection. *(There are different ways to take a baby from one place to another.)* Ask if each part of the selection told about different ways to take a baby from one place to another. (yes)

Then ask if a sentence about a squirrel hiding acorns would belong in this selection. (Possible answers include: No, a squirrel hiding nuts does not tell about the main idea of the selection.) Ask what the sentence would have to tell about the squirrel to belong in this selection. (It would have to tell how a baby squirrel goes from place to place.)

Evaluating Comprehension

WB 46 **INDEPENDENT PRACTICE** *Workbook* page 46 may be used for an informal evaluation of selection comprehension.

Name _____

A. Draw a line.

1️⃣ This baby gets carried in a pocket.

2️⃣ This baby hides in its mother's throat.

3️⃣ This baby rides in someone's arms.

4️⃣ This baby gets a piggyback ride.

B. Fill in the circle.

"A Place for Babies" tells how _____ .
- ○ babies walk with help
- ● babies get from place to place with help
- ○ babies grow

- Selection comprehension: "A Place for Babies"
- Directions: TOP — Read the sentences. Draw a line from the sentence to the picture it describes. BOTTOM — Fill in the circle by the words that complete the sentence.
- To the Parent: Have your child tell why the selection was titled "A Place for Babies."

46 *Spotlights* Level 6

HOW AM I DOING?

Many pupils need encouragement to participate in group reading activities. Ask yourself the following questions to check your effectiveness in getting pupils involved.

	Yes	No	Some- times
1. Do I ask pupils questions to focus their attention on key lesson concepts?	☐	☐	☐
2. Do I systematically select pupils for reading or answering questions to insure that all pupils participate?	☐	☐	☐
3. Do I allow enough "wait time" for a pupil to think about the answer before I ask someone else?	☐	☐	☐
4. Do I monitor individual pupils by giving immediate feedback on their answers to my questions?	☐	☐	☐

3 DEVELOPING READING AND THINKING SKILLS

DECODING/VOCABULARY

R, T Sound/symbol correspondence: consonant /ks/x (final)

DIRECT INSTRUCTION Place *Word Cards fox, ax, six* in the *Pocket Chart*, one under the other. Point to each word and have it read. Ask what letter stands for the sound heard at the end of each word. (*x*)

GUIDED PRACTICE Display *Word Cards mix, box, wax, fix, ox.* Call on a pupil to select a card, to read the word, and to place the word next to its rhyming word in the *Pocket Chart.* When all the words have been placed in the *Pocket Chart* have pupils read each row of rhyming words. (*fox, box, ox; ax, wax; six, mix, fix*)

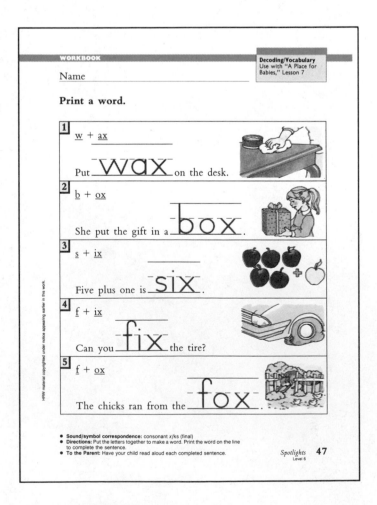

WB 47 INDEPENDENT PRACTICE *Workbook* page 47 may be used to practice identifying sound/symbol correspondence /ks/x.

✳ **RETEACH** For those pupils who need additional instruction, see "Reteaching Lesson Skills," page T178 under "Reteaching and Extending."

R, T Sound/symbol correspondence: vowel /ī/i-e

DIRECT INSTRUCTION Print the following words on the chalkboard:

bit	rid	fin
bite	ride	fine
spin	bite	fish
ship	stripe	pine
mine	slip	lip

Call attention to the first three pairs of words. Read the first pair and ask what is different about them. (*Bit* has the /i/ sound; *bite* has the /ī/ sound; *bite* ends with *e.*)

Tell pupils that the sound of letter *i* followed by a consonant can be changed by adding *e* to the end of a word. Ask what sound the letter *i* stands for in *bit.* (/i/) Ask what sound the letter *i* stands for in *bite.* (/ī/) Follow a similar procedure for the remaining word pairs.

GUIDED PRACTICE Direct pupils' attention to the second set of words. Call on pupils to read the words and to tell what sound the letter *i* stands for in each word. (/ī/: *bite, stripe, pine, mine;* /i/: *spin, fish, ship, slip, lip*)

✳ **RETEACH** For those pupils who need additional instruction, see "Reteaching Lesson Skills," page T178, under "Reteaching and Extending."

M Word structure: contractions (with *'ll, 's*)

DIRECT INSTRUCTION Print the following sentences and words on the chalkboard, omitting the lines connecting the bullets.

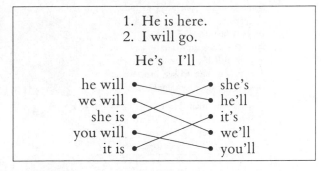

1. He is here.
2. I will go.

He's   I'll

he will ●   ● she's
we will ●   ● he'll
she is ●   ● it's
you will ●   ● we'll
it is ●   ● you'll

Have each sentence read aloud. Point to the first sentence and remind pupils that the words *He is* can be put together to make one word. Ask what the one word is. (*He's*) Point to the word *He's* and ask pupils to read it. Then ask them to tell what letter was left out of the words *He is* to make *He's*. (*i*) Remind pupils that the apostrophe takes the place of the letters missing from the words that make contractions.

Follow a similar procedure with the second sentence and the contraction *I'll*.

GUIDED PRACTICE Direct pupils' attention to the remaining sets of words. Call on a pupil to read the first two words on the left and to find the corresponding contraction on the right. Ask the pupil to draw a line from the words to the contraction. Continue in the same manner with the remaining words and contractions.

WB 48 INDEPENDENT PRACTICE *Workbook* page 48 may be used to practice identifying contractions with *'ll,* and *'s.*

PM 32 ADDITIONAL PRACTICE *Practice Masters* page 32 may be used as an optional practice for identifying contractions with *'ll,* and *'s.* (See page T181 for reduced pages with answers.)

COMPREHENSION/THINKING

Focus

M Literal: main idea (stated)

DIRECT INSTRUCTION Ask what is meant by the main idea of a story or a paragraph. (The main idea is what the story or paragraph is about. Sometimes one sentence in the story tells the main idea.) Remind pupils that each sentence of a story or paragraph should tell something about the main idea.

GUIDED PRACTICE Print the following paragraph on the chalkboard:

> A mother cat will look
> after her baby kittens.
>   She will feed them
> and will keep them clean.
>   She will carry them
> to a safe place.
>   She will stay by them
> to keep them from harm.

Have the paragraph read and ask what it tells about. (It tells how a mother cat will look after her kittens.) Ask which senence tells the main idea of the pragraph. (the first sentence)

Have each of the next sentences read. After each sentence, ask if the sentence tells how the mother cat will look after her baby kittens. When all the sentences have been read, point out that every sentence in the paragraph tells something about the main idea.

WB 49 INDEPENDENT PRACTICE *Workbook* page 49 may be used to practice identifying the main idea.

PM 33 ADDITIONAL PRACTICE *Practice Masters* page 33 may be used as an optional practice for identifying the main idea. (See page T181 for reduced pages with answers.)

WORKBOOK

Name _____

Comprehension/Thinking
Use with "A Place for Babies," Lesson 7

Fill in the circle.

1
Some animals have ways to hide.
A deer can hide in the woods.
Its coat blends in
with the grass and trees.
A rock fish looks just like a rock.
The fish is hard to see in the water.
A snow rabbit's coat looks like snow.

What is the main idea?
● Some animals have ways to hide.
○ Some animals cannot see.
○ Some animals have coats.

2
Not all birds live in trees.
Some live in barns on farms.
Still others make their homes
in bushes or in the grass.
You can find seagulls at the beach.

What is the main idea?
○ Not all birds can fly.
○ Not all birds like caves for homes.
● Not all birds live in trees.

● **Literal:** main idea
● **Directions:** Read each paragraph. Fill in the circle by the sentence that tells the main idea.
● **To the Parent:** Have your child tell why he or she selected each answer.

Spotlights
Level 6 **49**

STUDY SKILLS

R, T **References:** dictionary (entry words and definitions)

DIRECT INSTRUCTION Ask pupils where they might look if they wanted to find the meaning of a word. (dictionary)

Print the following words and definitions on the chalkboard:

piggyback	to ride on the back of something or someone
carry	to take from one place to another
frog	a small animal that is a good jumper
safe	**1** free from harm **2** a box that locks

Read the first sample dictionary entry aloud. Remind pupils that words in a dictionary are listed in alphabetical order. Ask under which letter *piggyback* would be found. (*p*) Ask what *piggyback* means. ("to ride on the back of something or someone") Ask which word has more than one meaning. *(safe)* Read the sentence *I kept my jewelry in the safe.* and ask what *safe* means in the sentence. (a box that locks)

GUIDED PRACTICE Direct pupils' attention to the dictionary entries for *carry, frog,* and *safe.*

Have each entry word read aloud. Ask what *safe* means. ("free from harm") Ask which word tells what you might do with a baby. (*carry*) Ask under what letter the word *frog* would be found. (*f*)

✱ RETEACH For those pupils who need additional instruction, see "Reteaching Lesson Skills," page T179, under "Reteaching and Extending."

Reteaching Lesson Skills

The activities that follow provide reteaching of skills developed in this lesson. Not every pupil needs to complete these activities. Choose only the activities that are needed to provide for the individual differences in your classroom.

> DECODING/VOCABULARY

R, T Sound/symbol correspondence: consonant /ks/ *x* (final)

✻ **RETEACH** Print the following sentences on the chalkboard:

1. Max and Rex fix a cake.
2. The mix is in a box.

Tell pupils that the letter *x* stands for the sound heard at the end of *fox*. Ask them to repeat *fox* after you. Then have the sentences on the chalkboard read. Call on pupils to point to and read the words in the sentences in which *x* stands for the sound heard at the end of the word *ax*. (*Max, Rex, fix, mix, box*)

I, T Sound/symbol correspondence: *r*-controlled vowel /är/ *ar*

✻ **RETEACH** Print the following words on the chalkboard:

farm   dart   harm
arm   car   park

Point to each word and read it aloud. Tell pupils that in each word, the letters *ar* together stand for the /är/ sound.

Call on pupils to read a word at random and to tell which letters stand for the /är/ sound.

RM 11 Distribute *Reteach Masters* page 11 and explain the directions on the page.

R, T Sound/symbol correspondence: vowel /ī/ *i-e*

✻ **RETEACH** Place *Word Cards pin, rip, fin, bit, slid* in the *Pocket Chart*. Call on a pupil to read each word and to tell what sound the letter *i* stands for in the word. (/i/) Then have another pupil place *Letter Card e* at the end of the word and read the new word. Ask how adding letter *e* changes the sound of letter *i*. (It makes the sound of letter *i* long; it makes it stand for the /ī/ sound.) Remind pupils that when a word has an *i*, followed by a consonant, and ends with *e*, the *i* stands for the /ī/ sound.

Continue in the same manner with the remaining words.

I, T Vocabulary: word meaning

 RETEACH Print the following words and sentences on the chalkboard, omitting the underlining.

---

babies baby carried carry

1. Jim had a <u>baby</u> sister.
2. <u>Babies</u> can't walk.
3. So Jim had to <u>carry</u> his sister.
4. He <u>carried</u> her in his arms.

dart harm ride

Point to the word *baby* and read it. Call on a pupil to find and read the sentence that contains the word *baby*. Continue in the same manner with the remaining sentences, calling attention to the underlined words.

Display *Word Cards* for each of the underlined words. Have pupils hold up and read the *Word Card* that answers each of the following questions:

1. **Which word means "more than one baby"?** (*babies*)
2. **Which word means "to take from one place to another"?** (*carry*)
3. **Which word names a newborn animal or person?** (*baby*)
4. **Which word means "taken from one place to another place"?** (*carried*)

RM 12 Distribute *Reteach Masters* page 12 and explain the directions on the page.

STUDY SKILLS

R, T References: dictionary (entry words and definitions)

Display a dictionary and allow pupils to look through it. Discuss that the words in a dictionary are listed in alphabetical order and that the definition comes after the word. Ask pupils under what letter they would look to find the word *wet*. (*w*) Then help pupils find and read the meaning of *wet*. Allow pupils to look up other words and read the definitions, providing help as needed.

Extending Selection Concepts

WRITING: ANIMAL REPORTS (Cooperative Learning) Have pupils work in small groups to write a report about one of the animals in "A Place for Babies." Have pupils make a list of questions they would like to answer about the animal, such as *Where does it live? What does it eat? How does it protect itself? What are its enemies?* Help each group find information about the animal in an encyclopedia or a book about animals. Provide drawing paper for pupils to illustrate their reports. When the group has answered its questions, invite the group to present its report to the class. Display the reports and illustrations where they can be seen and read by all pupils.

LISTENING: INFORMATION Choose an informational book about animals to read to the class. Invite pupils to tell about their favorite animal in the book.

Cole, Joanna. *Large as Life: Daytime Animals.* Knopf, 1985.

———. *Large as Life: Nightime Animals.* Knopf, 1985. The text and the life-size illustrations in these two books present the characteristics of daytime and nightime animals.

Hewett, Joan. *Watching Them Grow: Inside a Zoo Nursery.* Little, Brown, 1979. This book explains how baby animals are cared for in a zoo nursery.

Yabuuchi, Masayuki. *Whose Baby?* Philomel, 1985. Colorful illustrations add to the text of this informational book about animals and their offspring.

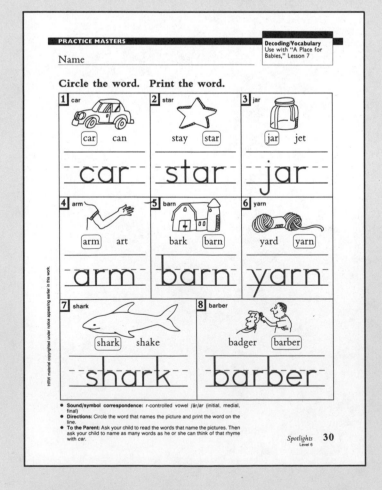

Name

Print the word.

| He's | She's | He'll | She'll |

1 He is going to carry the baby in his arms. — He's

2 He will keep the baby safe from harm. — He'll

3 She is going to carry the baby on her back — She's

4 She will take the baby for a piggyback ride. — She'll

- **Word structure:** contractions (with 's and 'll)
- **Directions:** Read each sentence. Beside the sentence, print the contraction from the box that means the same as the underlined words.
- **To the Parent:** Ask your child to read the sentences, substituting the contractions for the underlined words.

Spotlights Level 6 **32**

Name

Fill in the circle.

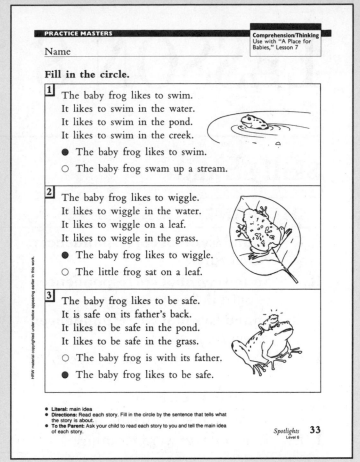

1
The baby frog likes to swim.
It likes to swim in the water.
It likes to swim in the pond.
It likes to swim in the creek.
● The baby frog likes to swim.
○ The baby frog swam up a stream.

2
The baby frog likes to wiggle.
It likes to wiggle in the water.
It likes to wiggle on a leaf.
It likes to wiggle in the grass.
● The baby frog likes to wiggle.
○ The little frog sat on a leaf.

3
The baby frog likes to be safe.
It is safe on its father's back.
It likes to be safe in the pond.
It likes to be safe in the grass.
○ The baby frog is with its father.
● The baby frog likes to be safe.

- **Literal:** main idea
- **Directions:** Read each story. Fill in the circle by the sentence that tells what the story is about.
- **To the Parent:** Ask your child to read each story to you and tell the main idea of each story.

Spotlights Level 6 **33**

Name

Print the word. Circle the words.

| harm | starfish | darted | sharp |

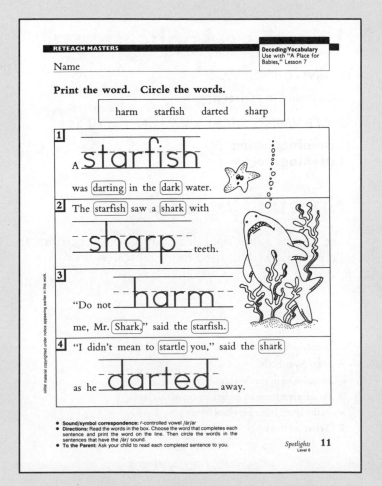

1 A starfish was (darting) in the (dark) water.

2 The (starfish) saw a (shark) with sharp teeth.

3 "Do not harm me, Mr. (Shark,)" said the (starfish.)

4 "I didn't mean to (startle) you," said the (shark) as he darted away.

- **Sound/symbol correspondence:** *r*-controlled vowel /är/ar
- **Directions:** Read the words in the box. Choose the word that completes each sentence and print the word on the line. Then circle the words in the sentences that have the /är/ sound.
- **To the Parent:** Ask your child to read each completed sentence to you.

Spotlights Level 6 **11**

Name

Circle the word. Print the word.

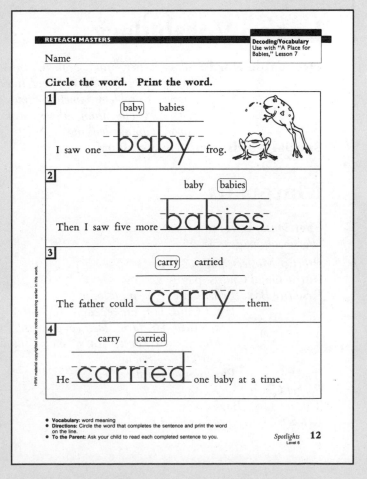

1 (baby) babies — I saw one baby frog.

2 baby (babies) — Then I saw five more babies.

3 (carry) carried — The father could carry them.

4 carry (carried) — He carried one baby at a time.

- **Vocabulary:** word meaning
- **Directions:** Circle the word that completes the sentence and print the word on the line.
- **To the Parent:** Ask your child to read each completed sentence to you.

Spotlights Level 6 **12**

LESSON 8 "This Is the Place for Me"

pages 76–87 (T182–T205)

Skill Strands

DECODING/VOCABULARY

I, T   **Sound/symbol correspondence:** vowel /ō/o-e

R, T   **Sound/symbol correspondence:** r-controlled vowel /är/ar

R, T   **Sound/symbol correspondence:** vowel /ē/y (final)

I, T   **Word structure:** base changes (drop final e and add -ed)

R   **Word structure:** suffix -y

I   **Vocabulary:** word building

I, T   **Vocabulary:** word meaning

COMPREHENSION/THINKING

Focus

I, T   **Story structure:** characters (major and minor)

R, T   **Inferential:** predicting outcomes

LANGUAGE

M   **Writing:** sentences

Lesson Vocabulary

Decodable words: *alone, better, broke, broken, cannot, evening, hungry, Morty, kept, liked, named, problem, smelled, smoke, snack, snow, than, those, woke, upon, yummy-looking*

Special words: *gone, now, over, scary*

Materials

Spotlights, Level 6: pages 76–87
Workbook: pages 50–55

Practice Masters: pages 34–36
Instructional Charts: pages 52–58
Resource Box: Letter Cards e, h, m, n, o, p, t
               Word Cards bed, broke, came, car, cat, disappeared, far, farm, fast, gone, house, in, Morty, now, over, scary, snow, stand, start, the, window
               Punctuation Card period
Pocket Chart
Teacher's Idea Book
Reteach Masters: pages 13–14

Language Applications

USING LANGUAGE

Oral reading: descriptions

EXTENDING SELECTION CONCEPTS

Listening: fiction
Listening: poetry

Special Populations

See *Teacher's Idea Book* for additional suggestions to help pupils with limited English proficiency.

Key to Symbols

I   Introduced in this lesson
R   Reinforced from an earlier lesson in this level
M   Maintained from previous levels
T   Tested in this level

Idea Center

BIBLIOGRAPHY

Add to your reading corner or reading table various books about houses and homes. A suggested bibliography follows. Suggestions for reading aloud and annotations appear in the lesson plan.

Alexander, Sue. *Dear Phoebe.* Little, Brown, 1984.
Frasconi, Antonio. *The House That Jack Built.* Harcourt, Brace & World, 1958.
Grifalconi, Ann. *The Village of Round and Square Houses.* Little, Brown, 1986.
Maynard, Joyce. *New House.* Harcourt Brace Jovanovich, 1987.
Mendoza, George. *Need a House? Call Ms. Mouse.* Grosset & Dunlap, 1981.

Planning Chart

		Instruction	Written Practice	Extending
Step 1 Preparing for the Selection	I, T	**Sound/symbol correspondence:** vowel /ō/o-e	*Workbook* page 50 *Practice Masters* page 34 *Reteach Masters* page 13	
	I	**Vocabulary:** word building		
	I, T	**Word structure:** base changes (drop final e and add -ed)	*Workbook* page 51 *Practice Masters* page 35	
	I, T	**Vocabulary:** word meaning	*Workbook* page 52 *Practice Masters* page 36 *Reteach Masters* page 14	
	I, T	**Story structure:** characters (major and minor)		
Step 2 Reading for Comprehension		**Oral reading:** descriptions		**Listening:** fiction
		Story structure: characters (major and minor)		
		Story comprehension	*Workbook* page 53	
Step 3 Developing Reading and Thinking Skills	R, T	**Sound/symbol correspondence:** r-controlled vowel /är/ar	*Workbook* page 54	
	R, T	**Sound/symbol correspondence:** vowel /ē/y (final)		**Listening:** poetry
	R	**Word structure:** suffix -y		
	I, T	**Story structure:** characters (major and minor)	*Workbook* page 55	
	R, T	**Inferential:** predicting outcomes		
	M	**Writing:** sentences		

DECODING/VOCABULARY

I, T Sound/symbol correspondence: vowel /ō/o-e

DIRECT INSTRUCTION Print the following words on the chalkboard:

joke	rose	nose
poke	nose	stone
rob	rod	cod
robe	rode	code

Read the words in the first column and have pupils repeat them.

ASK **What is alike about these words?** (They rhyme; they end with *oke.*)

SAY **Letter *o* stands for the /ō/ sound in *joke* and *poke.***

Follow a similar procedure using the word pairs *rod/rode* and *cod/code.*

Read aloud each word on the chalkboard emphasizing the /ō/ sound and have pupils repeat the words after you.

SAY **Each of these words has letter *o* followed by a consonant, and ends with letter *e.* When a word has letter *o,* followed by a consonant, and ends with letter *e,* *o* usually stands for the /ō/ sound.**

Have pupils read each word as you point to it.

GUIDED PRACTICE Direct pupils' attention to the remaining word pairs on the chalkboard. Have the first pair of words read. Ask which word in the pair has the /ō/ sound. *(robe)* Ask why the *o* in *robe* stands for /ō/. *(because robe has an o, followed by a consonant, and ends with e)*

Continue in the same manner with the remaining word pairs.

 INDEPENDENT PRACTICE *Workbook* page 50 may be used to practice identifying sound/symbol correspondence /ō/o-e.

PM 34 ADDITIONAL PRACTICE *Practice Masters* page 34 may be used as an optional practice for identifying sound/symbol correspondence /ō/o-e. (See page T204 for reduced pages with answers.)

✳ RETEACH For those pupils who need additional instruction, see "Reteaching Lesson Skills," page T201, under "Reteaching and Extending."

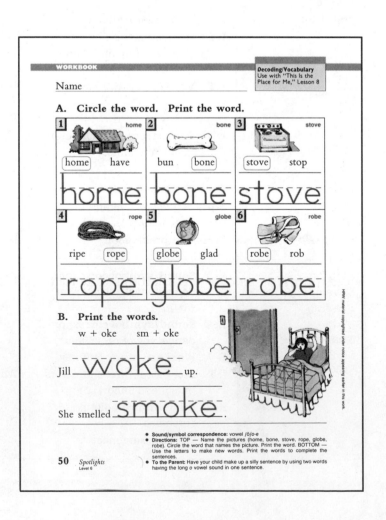

I Vocabulary: word building

DIRECT INSTRUCTION Use *Letter Cards* to make the word *home* in the *Pocket Chart*. Have pupils read the word. Change the letter *m* to *p* and have the new word read. (*hope*) Ask why the letter *o* stands for the /ō/ sound in *hope*. (because it is followed by a consonant and the letter *e*) Remove the letter *e* and have the new word read. (*hop*)

GUIDED PRACTICE Display *Letter Cards e, n, t.* Tell pupils that they will use these letters to make new words in the *Pocket Chart*.

1. **Change the *p* in *hop* to *t*. What is the new word?** (*hot*)
2. **Change the *h* to *n*. What is the new word?** (*not*)
3. **Put letter *e* at the end of the word. What is the new word?** (*note*)
4. **Exchange places with the *n* and the *t*. What is the new word?** (*tone*)
5. **Take out the *n* and the *e*. Put *p* after *o*. What is the new word?** (*top*)
6. **Replace the *t* with *h*. What is the new word?** (*hop*)
7. **Put *e* at the end of the word. What is the new word?** (*hope*)
8. **Take the *e* away. What is the new word?** (*hop*)

I, T Word structure: base changes (drop final *e* and add -*ed*)

DIRECT INSTRUCTION Print the following sentences and word pairs on the chalkboard:

> **IC 53**
>
> 1. Jim looked for a new hat.
> 2. He liked the red one.
> 3. He hoped it would fit.
>
> | look | like | hope |
> | looked | liked | hoped |
>
> | joke | hunt | name |
> | joked | hunted | named |

Read the first sentence aloud. Ask if this sentence tells if Jim is looking for a new hat right now or if he looked for a new hat in the past. (It tells what Jim did in the past.) Point out that the -*ed* ending added to a word indicates that the action took place in the past.

Read the second sentence aloud. Ask which word tells us that something was done in the past. (*liked*)

Read the third sentence aloud. Ask which word tells us that something happened in the past. (*hoped*)

Point to and read the words *look* and *looked*. Ask what letters were added to *look* to make the word *looked*. (-*ed*) Tell pupils that the letters -*ed* were added to *look* to tell us that someone looked in the past.

Then point to and read the words *like* and *liked*. Tell pupils that when a word ends with *e*, as *like* does, we drop *e* before adding -*ed*. Ask what word we get when we drop the *e* in *like* and add -*ed*. (*liked*)

Continue in the same manner with *hope* and *hoped*.

GUIDED PRACTICE Direct pupils' attention to the remaining pairs of words on the chalkboard. Have pupils read each pair of words and tell how the first word in the pair was changed to make the second word. (The final *e* was dropped and -*ed* was added to *joke* and *name*; -*ed* was added to *hunt*.)

WB 51 **INDEPENDENT PRACTICE** *Workbook* page 51 may be used to practice dropping final *e* before adding the -*ed* ending.

PM 35 **ADDITIONAL PRACTICE** *Practice Masters* page 35 may be used as an optional practice for dropping the final *e* before adding the -*ed* ending. (See page T204 for reduced pages with answers.)

 RETEACH For those pupils who need additional instruction, see "Reteaching Lesson Skills," page T202, under "Reteaching and Extending."

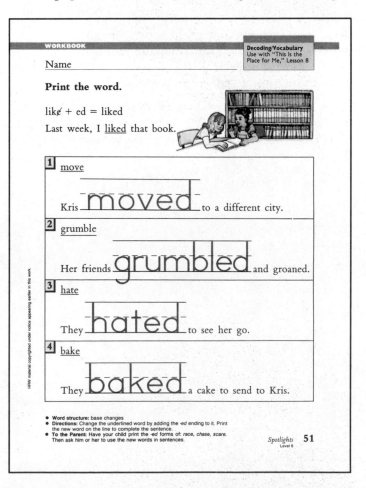

I, T   Vocabulary: word meaning

DIRECT INSTRUCTION   Tell pupils that they are going to talk about some words they will read in the next story. Print the following words and sentences on the chalkboard, omitting the underlining.

gone   Now   over   scary
1. Maria rode <u>over</u> the hill to see her friend.
2. Then they saw a <u>scary</u> show.
3. <u>Now</u> Maria does not want to go home.
4. If only she had not <u>gone</u> to the show!
alone   broken   hungry **Morty   smoke   those** **woke   yummy-looking**

Read the first sentence. Point to the word *over* and read it. Ask how Maria got to her friend's house. (She rode over the hill.) Have pupils read the sentence with you. Then ask them to find and read the word *over.*

Read Sentence 2. Point to the word *scary* and read it. Ask what Maria and her friend did. (They saw a scary show.) Have pupils read the sentence with you. Then ask them to find and read the word *scary.*

Read Sentence 3. Point to the word *Now* and read it. Ask why Maria does not want to go home. (because the scary show frightened her) Have pupils read the sentence with you. Then have them point to the word *Now* and read it.

Read Sentence 4. Point to the word *gone* and read it. Ask what Maria now wished. (that she had not gone to the show) Have pupils read the sentence with you. Then have them point to the word *gone* and read it.

The words in the second set are new words that contain known phonic elements. You may wish to ask pupils to read the words, using what they know about letters and sounds.

GUIDED PRACTICE   Print the following sentences on the chalkboard, omitting the underlining.

1. <u>Morty</u> <u>woke</u> up in his room.
2. His brother was <u>gone</u> <u>now</u>.
3. It was <u>scary</u> to be <u>alone</u>.
4. Morty was <u>hungry</u>.
5. He wanted one of <u>those</u>   <u>yummy-looking</u> snacks.
6. Then he smelled <u>smoke</u>.
7. It was coming from a <u>broken</u> lamp that   had tipped <u>over</u>.

Provide opportunities for pupils to practice reading the new special words and some of the new decodable words in these sentences by following the suggestions below.

Sentence 1: Have the sentence read. Ask pupils to find and read the word *woke.*

Sentence 2: Call on a pupil to read the sentence. Ask if Morty's brother was there. (No, he was gone.) Have pupils find and read the word *gone.*

Sentence 3: Have the sentence read. Ask how Morty felt being alone. (scared) Have pupils find and read the word *alone.*

Sentences 4–5: Have the sentences read. Ask why Morty wanted a snack. (He was hungry.) Have pupils find and read the word *those.*

Sentences 6–7: Have pupils read the sentences. Ask what Morty smelled. (smoke) Have pupils find and read the words *broken* and *over.*

Encourage pupils to select a sentence to read aloud.

WB 52   INDEPENDENT PRACTICE   *Workbook* page 52 may be used to practice reading story vocabulary.

Name _____

Decoding/Vocabulary
Use with "This Is the
Place for Me," Lesson 8

Print the word.

| snack | over | vanished | now | scary |

1 Greg was hungry.

He made a yummy-looking _____ **snack** .

2 He put the food on the table.

Then it _____ **vanished** .

3 He looked here and there.

He looked all _____ **over** .

4 "My food is gone!" said Greg.

"This is _____ **scary** ."

5 Then someone giggled.

Who isn't hungry _____ **now** ?

52 *Spotlights*
Level 6

● **Vocabulary:** word meaning
● **Directions:** Read the words in the box. Read the sentences. Print the word from the box that completes each sentence.
● **To the Parent:** Have your child continue the story about the ghost and Greg.

PM 36 **ADDITIONAL PRACTICE** *Practice Masters* page 36 may be used as an optional practice for reading story vocabulary. (See page T204 for reduced pages with answers.)

✳ **RETEACH** For those pupils who need additional instruction, see "Reteaching Lesson Skills," page T202, under "Reteaching and Extending."

COMPREHENSION/THINKING

Focus

I, T **Story structure:** characters (major and minor)

DIRECT INSTRUCTION Remind pupils that the people or animals in a story are called characters. Help pupils recall the characters in the story "The Chili Pot," from the first unit of *Spotlights*. (Maria, Tina, Maria's neighbors, the man selling pots) Maria and Tina could be called the major characters in the story because the story was mostly about them. The man who sold the pots and the neighbors were not as important in the story. Characters that are not as important are called minor characters.

GUIDED PRACTICE Read the following story and then call on pupils to identify the major and minor characters.

READ Ann was playing in the park. She heard a loud clap and looked up at the gray sky. "I think I should go home," thought Ann. When she got home, Ann told her mom how frightened she was of the thunder. Ann and Mom drank hot chocolate and sat by the window, talking about the storm. In no time at all, Ann felt much better.

SAY This story had two characters. Who was the major character, the person that the story told about the most? (Ann) Who was the minor character? (Ann's mother)

Tell pupils that most stories have both major and minor characters.

Background for the Teacher

SUMMARY Morty the bear wants to find a new house. Each house that he discovers has a problem. Finally, Morty finds the perfect house—his old one.

INFORMATION This story, from a book of the same title, has a main character who is dissatisfied with what he has until he tries other things. Then he discovers that what he had in the beginning was really the best. Many stories and folk tales are about animals or people who wish for something other than what they have. The same lesson—be content with what you have—is taught in all variations.

Using Prior Knowledge

Tell pupils that they will read a make-believe story about a bear. Have pupils tell what they might expect a make-believe bear to do. (Possible answers include: wear clothing, talk, act like a human.) Develop a discussion by asking questions such as those that follow.

1. **What kind of problems do you think a big bear might have if his house was too small?** (Possible answers include: He would be too crowded; he would bump into things.)
2. **What do you think people might do if their family was too big for their house?** (They might move to a bigger house; they might build rooms onto the house to make it bigger.)

Setting a Purpose for Reading

Have pupils find page 76 in their books and read the title of the story. ("This Is the Place for Me") Point out the headnote at the top of the page. Tell pupils that this note will help them think about what is going to happen in the story. Have the note read and then ask pupils to predict how a bear might find a new house.

Reading Silently

Some pupils may be able to read this story independently. Direct them to read the whole story to find out more about a bear who goes house-hunting.

For those pupils who need more guidance, suggestions for directed reading follow.

A bear named Morty is looking
for a new house.
How will he find one?

This Is the Place for Me

Morty the bear broke things
in his house all the time.

He was so big that he kept
crashing into things.

He broke his bed, and
he broke his table.
One day, he even broke a window.

76

When Morty woke up at sunrise,
there was snow all over his bed.
There was snow all over his table.
There was snow all over the place.

"This house is a mess!"
said Morty.
"I need to find a new one."

77

Before
reading
pages
76–77

SAY **Morty the bear had a problem
with his house. What do you
think his problem was? Read pages 76
and 77 to yourself.**

After
reading
pages
76–77

1. **What was Morty's problem?** (His
   house was too small; he kept crashing
   into things and breaking them.) Literal
2. **How will Morty try to solve his
   problem?** (He will look for a new
   house.) Inferential

Morty packed his bag, and he set out to find a new home.

He walked and he walked.
He came upon a hole in the side of a hill.
"This is the place for me!" said Morty, and he moved in.

He liked it there, but the next day, he smelled smoke.
"I can't live here!" said Morty.
"I have to find another house."

78

Morty walked and walked.
He came upon a yummy-looking house.
"This is the place for me!" said Morty.
So he moved in.

He liked it there.

Late that same evening, Morty woke up.
He was hungry for a snack.

79

Before reading pages 78–79

SAY Do you think it will be easy to find a new house? Read pages 78 and 79 to yourself.

After reading pages 78–79

1. **What was wrong with the first house that Morty found?** (The house he found had a dragon living in it.) Inferential
2. **What did Morty do next?** (He went looking for another house.) Literal
3. **What house did he find?** (He found a gingerbread house.) Literal
4. **Did Morty like the gingerbread house?** (yes) **Do you think he will stay there?** (Answers will vary. Possible answers include: Yes, he will if he likes it.) Critical

In no time at all, the house was <u>gone</u>.

"That was a great house, but <u>now</u> I need to find another one," said Morty.

80

Morty walked and walked.
He came upon a house floating on the water.

"I like this house," he said.

81

Before reading pages 80–81

SAY **Morty was hungry for a snack. What do you think he will eat? Read pages 80 and 81 to yourself.**

After reading pages 80–81

1. **Why didn't Morty stay in the ginger-bread house?** (He ate it.) Literal
2. **What house did he find next?** (He found a houseboat.) Literal

The problem was that Morty was too big.

"This is not the place for me," he said as he went looking for a house again.

82

He came upon three more houses.
One was too little.
One was too thin.
One was too scary!

"I cannot live in those," said Morty as he walked away.

83

Before reading pages 82–83

SAY **Morty has had a problem with every house he has found. What more could go wrong? Read pages 82 and 83 to yourself.**

After reading pages 82–83

1. **What went wrong with the house-boat?** (Morty was too big, so it sank.) Inferential
2. **What problems did Morty find with the other houses he saw?** (One was too little; one was too thin; one was too scary.) Inferential

Morty was sad.
He was all <u>alone</u> with no place
to live.

84

Just then he stopped.

There was a house.
The windows were <u>broken</u>, so he
looked inside.

The bed was broken, and the table
was broken.

85

Before
reading
pages
84–85

SAY How do you think poor Morty
felt now? Read pages 84 and 85
to find out.

After
reading
pages
84–85

1. **How did Morty feel?** (sad) **Why?** (He
   was all alone with no place to live.)
   Literal
2. **What kind of house did Morty see
   next?** (one with broken windows, table,
   and bed) Literal
3. **Who do you think owned this house?**
   (Answers will vary, but should reflect
   some recognition that the house had been
   Morty's house.) Critical

However . . .
it did not have a dragon.
It was not too little.
It was not too thin.
Morty could not sink it.
He could not eat it,
and it was not scary.

Morty got to work and fixed
the house, so it was as good as new.

86

"This is the place for me,"
said Morty.
"It is much <u>better</u> <u>than</u> my
other house."

It was, wasn't it?

Discussing the Selection
1. How did Morty find a place
   to live?
2. Why did Morty need to go from
   house to house?
3. What was Morty thinking when he
   saw the last house?
4. At what place in the story did you
   know that Morty was back in his
   first house?
5. Did Morty know that his new house
   was the house he had left?

87

Before reading pages 86–87

SAY **Morty saw a house with many broken things. Do you think there was anything good about the house? Read pages 86 and 87.**

After reading pages 86–87

1. **What made this house perfect for Morty?** (It did not have a dragon; it was not too little; it was not too thin; Morty could not sink it; he could not eat it; and it was not scary.) Inferential
2. **Why did Morty think this house was better than his first house?** (He thought it was better because he fixed up the house so it was as good as new, and his old house had been a mess.) Critical

Discussing the Selection

Questions preceded by a number appear in *Spotlights* after the selection. Questions preceded by a bullet are additional questions for extending discussion.

PURPOSE

1. **How did Morty find a place to live?** (He went from house to house looking for one that he liked.) Inferential

STORY MAPPING

2. **Why did Morty need to go from house to house?** (Every house he found had some kind of problem.) Inferential

   • **Why did Morty need to find a new house?** (His house was a mess; everything was broken.) Literal

3. **What was Morty thinking when he saw the last house?** (He thought that the house was perfect for him because it did not have any of the problems that the other houses had.) Inferential

4. **At what place in the story did you know that Morty was back in his first house?** (The picture on page 85 shows his old house.) Inferential

   • **Why did Morty think his "new" house was much better than his first house?** (It was better because he worked and fixed it up until it was as good as new.) Inferential

CRITICAL THINKING

5. **Did Morty know that his new house was the house he had left?** (Answers will vary. Possible answers include: No, Morty didn't seem to have any idea that this house was the house he had left.)

   • **What do you think Morty would do if his house became a mess once again?** (Possible answers include: He would stay in the house, but would fix it up; he would build a new house that would be just perfect for him.)

Using Language

ORAL READING: DESCRIPTIONS Have pupils find page 76 in their books. Point out that this page describes what happened to Morty the bear. Call on pupils to read the page aloud.

Follow a similar procedure for the remaining pages.

Page 77: **Read the sentences that describe what happened to Morty because his window was broken.** (When Morty woke up at sunrise, there was snow all over his bed. There was snow all over his table. There was snow all over the place.)

Page 78: **Read the sentences that describe what Morty did to find a new home.** (Morty packed his bag, and he set out to find a new home. He walked and he walked.)

Page 79: **Read the word that tells how the next house looked.** (*yummy-looking*)

Page 81: **Read the sentence that describes where Morty found the next house.** (He came upon a house floating on the water.)

Page 83: **Read the sentences that describe what was wrong with the next three houses Morty found.** (One was too little. One was too thin. One was too scary!)

Page 84: **Read the page aloud to find out how Morty felt.** (Morty was sad. He was all alone with no place to live.)

Page 85: **Read the sentences that describe the house that Morty found at last.** (The windows were broken, so he looked inside. The bed was broken, and the table was broken.)

Page 86: **Read the sentences that tell what Morty did to the house.** (Morty got to work and fixed the house, so it was as good as new.)

Applying the Focus Skill

STORY STRUCTURE: CHARACTERS Ask what was the name of the character in the story "This Is the Place for Me." (Morty) Ask if there were any other characters in the story. (the dragon) Point out that Morty was the major character of the story because the story told about Morty's hunt for a new house.

Tell pupils that the dragon was a minor character because it did not have much to do with the story.

Evaluating Comprehension

WB 53 **INDEPENDENT PRACTICE** *Workbook* page 53 may be used for an informal evaluation of story comprehension.

WORKBOOK

Comprehension/Thinking
Use with "This Is the
Place for Me," Lesson 8

Name _____

Fill in the circle.

1 What didn't Jerome like?
● He didn't like his house.
○ He didn't like his food.
○ He didn't like his friends.

2 What was Jerome's house like?
○ It was so neat.
● It was a mess.
○ It was too little.

3 What did Jerome set out to find?
○ a cave
○ a snack
● a new house

4 How did Jerome feel without a house?
○ happy and alone
● sad and alone
○ sad and hungry

5 What did Jerome end up doing?
● He fixed his broken-down house.
○ He moved to a cave.
○ He rented a houseboat.

● **Story comprehension:** "This Is the Place for Me"
● **Directions:** Read each question. Fill in the circle by the words that answer each question.
● **To the Parent:** Have your child tell how Jerome felt as he found each house and then found out something was wrong with each one.

Spotlights **53**
Level 6

3 DEVELOPING READING AND THINKING SKILLS

DECODING/VOCABULARY

R, T **Sound/symbol correspondence:** *r-controlled vowel /är/ar*

DIRECT INSTRUCTION Remind pupils that the letters *ar* together can stand for the /är/ sound. Then place *Word Cards far* and *farm* in the *Pocket Chart* and have each word read. Ask what letters stand for the /är/ sound in *far* and *farm.* (*ar*)

GUIDED PRACTICE Display *Word Cards stand, start, car, cat, fast* with *Word Cards far* and *farm.* As you read each word, call on a pupil to hold up and read the corresponding *Word Card.* Then have pupils separate the *Word Cards* into one group that contains the /är/ sound and one group that does not contain the /är/ sound. Have the words in each group read.

WB 54 **INDEPENDENT PRACTICE** *Workbook* page 54 may be used to practice identifying sound/symbol correspondence /är/*ar.*

✳ **RETEACH** For those pupils who need additional instruction, see "Reteaching Lesson Skills," page T201, under "Reteaching and Extending."

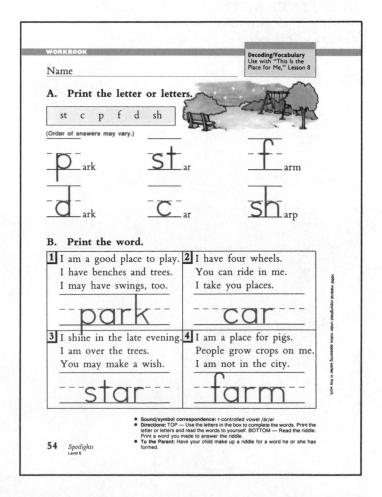

R, T   Sound/symbol correspondence: vowel /ē/ɣ (final)

R   Word structure: suffix -ɣ

DIRECT INSTRUCTION   Write the following words on the chalkboard:

bunny	penny
sun	Tim
sunny	Timmy

hurry   penny   snowy   Billy   snappy

Point to the words *bunny* and *penny* and read them. Ask what sound is at the end of both words. (/ē/) Tell pupils that the letter ɣ stands for the /ē/ sound at the end of words that have two parts like *penny* and *bunny.* Have pupils read the words with you.

Point to and read the words *sun* and *sunny.* Ask what is different about them. (*Sunny* has double *n* and a ɣ at the end.) Tell pupils that the ɣ at the end of *sunny* stands for the /ē/ sound. We would use the word *sunny* to tell about a day when the sun was shining. *Sunny* was made by doubling the consonant *n* in *sun* and adding ɣ.

Follow a similar procedure for *Tim* and *Timmy,* telling pupils that *Timmy* is a nickname for *Tim.*

GUIDED PRACTICE   Call on pupils to read the words in the bottom row and to tell what sound the ɣ stands for at the end of each word. (/ē/)

✳   **RETEACH**   For those pupils who need additional instruction, see "Reteaching Lesson Skills," page T201, under "Reteaching and Extending."

COMPREHENSION/THINKING

Focus

I, T   Story structure: characters (major and minor)

DIRECT INSTRUCTION   Ask what we call the people or animals in a story. (characters) Point out that many stories have a major character that is the "star" of the story. The other characters in the story are called the minor characters.

GUIDED PRACTICE   Print the following story on the chalkboard and ask pupils to read it.

Rose was a hermit crab.
A hermit crab lives in a sea shell.
The shell that Rose lived in was too little.

"Have you seen a bigger shell?"
Rose asked Seagull and Turtle.

"Yes," said Seagull.

"You will find a bigger shell
by that stone," said Turtle.

Rose went and got the fine, big shell.
Now Rose had a new home.

Ask pupils to name the characters from the story. (Rose, Turtle, and Seagull) Then ask which character was the major character and why. (Rose was the major character because the entire story was about Rose and her problem.) Have pupils tell which characters were minor characters and why. (Turtle and Seagull were minor characters because they each had only a small part in the story.)

Comprehension/Thinking
Use with "This Is the Place for Me," Lesson 8

Name _____

Fill in the circle.

1
Jane wanted to get a new bike.
But she needed some money.
Dad gave her ideas for jobs.
Mrs. Jones paid Jane to walk her dog.
Jane worked for others, too.
In no time, Jane had her new bike!

This selection tells mainly about ___.
● Jane
○ Dad
○ Mrs. Jones

2
Pat left his house to go fishing.
He nodded to some neighbors.
Mrs. Hill wished him good luck.
Pat fished at the lake.
He got seven fish.
Pat packed up the fish and went home.
He was happy to have fish to eat.

This selection tells mainly about ___.
○ Mrs. Hill
● Pat
○ some neighbors

● **Story structure:** characters
● **Directions:** Read the story. Then fill in the circle by the words that tell who the stories were about.
● **To the Parent:** Name a favorite story of your child's. Ask him or her to tell who the story is about.

Spotlights
Level 6   **55**

WB 55 **INDEPENDENT PRACTICE** *Workbook* page 55 may be used to practice identifying major and minor characters.

✳ **RETEACH** For those pupils who need additional instruction, see "Reteaching Lesson Skills," page T203, under "Reteaching and Extending."

R, T Inferential: predicting outcomes

DIRECT INSTRUCTION Ask pupils if they try to guess what will happen when they read a story. Tell them that when they make guesses what will happen, they are making a prediction.

Read the following story and then have pupils predict what will happen next.

READ **Susan was packing her trunk with all the things she would need. She had to take clothes for both daytime and nighttime, her sleeping bag, and a flashlight. She would be gone for two weeks so she had to make sure she took enough of everything.**
"It's time to go," Susan's mother called. "The bus will be leaving soon."

ASK **What do you think Susan will do next?** (She will leave the house to go to the bus.) **Why did you make that prediction?** (Susan's mother said that the bus would be leaving and that it was time to go.)

GUIDED PRACTICE Print the following story on the chalkboard and ask pupils to read it.

IC 58
Grandfather and Hal went to the park.
They were having fun
on the swing.
All of a sudden, it got dark,
and the sun went away.
The wind began to blow hard.

Ask pupils to predict what Grandfather and Hal will do next. (They will go home.) Ask why they think this will happen. (If it rains when you're at the park, you usually go home.)

✳ **RETEACH** For those pupils who need additional instruction, see "Reteaching Lesson Skills," page T203, under "Reteaching and Extending."

M Writing: sentences

DIRECT INSTRUCTION Use *Word Cards* and *Punctuation Card period* to make the sentence *Morty broke the bed.* in the *Pocket Chart.* Have the sentence read aloud. Ask how pupils know that this group of words is a sentence. (It begins with a capital letter; it ends with a period; it tells a complete idea.)

GUIDED PRACTICE Display *Word Cards snow, came, in, window, house* along with the cards that are already in the *Pocket Chart.* Have the words read aloud. Tell pupils that the back of each *Word Card* has the same word beginning with a capital letter. Then ask a pupil to make a sentence using some of the *Word Cards* in the *Pocket Chart.* Have the new sentence read. (Possible sentences include: *Snow came in the house; Snow came in the window.*) Have other pupils make sentences in the *Pocket Chart* and read them.

✳ RETEACHING AND EXTENDING

Reteaching Lesson Skills

The activities that follow provide reteaching of skills developed in this lesson. Not every pupil needs to complete these activities. Choose only the activities that are needed to provide for the individual differences in your classroom.

DECODING/VOCABULARY

I, T   Sound/symbol correspondence: vowel /ō/*o-e*

 RETEACH   Print the following words on the chalkboard:

pin	cap	hop
pine	cape	hope

rope	stone	broke	cone	home

Point to *pin* and *pine* and have them read. Ask what sound letter *i* stands for in *pin*. (/i/, short *i*) Ask what sound letter *i* stands for in *pine*. (/ī/, long *i*) Remind pupils that *pine* has the /ī/ sound because the word has an *i* followed by a consonant, and ends with *e*.

Follow a similar procedure for *cap/cape* and *hop/hope*.

Then have pupils read the last row of words on the chalkboard and tell what sound letter *o* stands for in each word and why. (Letter *o* stands for /ō/ because it is followed by a consonant and *e*.).

 Distribute *Reteach Masters* page 13 and explain the directions on the page.

R, T   Sound/symbol correspondence: *r*-controlled vowel /är/*ar*

✳ **RETEACH**   Place *Word Cards far, farm, start, car* in the *Pocket Chart*. Point to each word and read it aloud. Tell pupils that each word contains the /är/ sound. Ask what two letters stand for the /är/ sound in each word. (*ar*) Tell pupils that letters *ar* together often stand for the /är/ sound.

Remove the *Word Cards* and shuffle them. Hold up one card at a time and call on pupils to read each word.

R, T   Sound/symbol correspondence: vowel /ē/*y* (final)

✳ **RETEACH**   Write the words *happy, hurry, penny* on the chalkboard. Point to each word and read it aloud. Ask what is alike about the three words. (They all end with *y*; they all end with the /ē/ sound; they all have two parts.) Tell pupils that when a word ends with *y* and has two parts, the *y* usually stands for the /ē/ sound. Call on pupils to point to and read each word.

I, T   Word structure: base changes (drop final *e* and add *-ed*)

 RETEACH   Print the following word pairs on the chalkboard:

hunt	like	bake
hunted	liked	baked

Point to and read the first word pair.

SAY   **I hunt today. I hunted yesterday. The word *hunted* tells us that the hunting happened in the past. The ending *-ed* was added to the word *hunt* to make the word *hunted*.**

Point to the second pair of words and read it aloud.

SAY   **I like something today. I liked it yesterday, too. The word *liked* tells us that something happened in the past. Drop *e* from *like* before adding *-ed* to make *liked*.**

Have the last pair of words read. Ask how *bake* was changed to make *baked*. (The *e* in *bake* was dropped and the ending *-ed* was added.)

I, T   Vocabulary: word meaning

 RETEACH   Print the following words and sentences on the chalkboard, omitting the underlining.

> **gone   Now   over   scary**
>
> 1. Maria rode <u>over</u> the hill to see her friend.
> 2. Then they saw a <u>scary</u> show.
> 3. <u>Now</u> Maria does not want to go home.
> 4. If only she had not <u>gone</u> to the show!
>
> **alone   broken   hungry
> Morty   smoke   those
> woke   yummy-looking**

Point to the word *over* and read it. Call on a pupil to find and read the sentence that contains the word *over*. Continue in the same manner with the remaining sentences, calling attention to the underlined words.

Display *Word Cards* for each of the underlined words. Have pupils hold up and read the card with the word that answers each of the following questions.

1. **Which word means "at this time"?** (*now*)
2. **Which word is the opposite of *under*?** (*over*)
3. **Which word means "frightening"?** (*scary*)
4. **Which word tells that someone already went somewhere?** (*gone*)

RM 14   Distribute *Reteach Masters* page 14 and explain the directions on the page.

COMPREHENSION/THINKING

Focus

I, T Story structure: characters (major and minor)

✳ **RETEACH** Tell pupils that the characters are the people or animals in a story. Point out that a story usually has one character that is more important than the others. This character is called the major character of the story. Ask pupils to think of some major characters from the stories they have read in *Spotlights*. (Possible answers include: Morty, Maria, Jack.)

Tell pupils that many stories have more than one character. The other characters that are not as important in a story are called the minor characters. Ask pupils to name some minor characters from the stories in *Spotlights*. (Possible answers include: Jane Turner in "Minx and Jinx," the neighbors in "The Chili Pot," Grandfather Chipmunk in "Bear Trouble.")

R, T Inferential: predicting outcomes

✳ **RETEACH** Read the following story and ask pupils to predict what will happen.

READ **Chris and Amy were going to the circus with their families on the same night. They hoped they would see each other there. When Amy got to the circus, she saw Chris sitting with his family. There were some empty seats next to them.**

ASK **What do you think will happen?** (Possible answers include: Amy's family will sit next to Chris and his family.) **Why do you think this will happen?** (Chris and Amy had looked forward to seeing each other at the circus; there were seats available so they could sit together.)

Extending Selection Concepts

LITERATURE

LISTENING: FICTION Select a story about a house or finding a home and read it aloud. Ask pupils to compare the house or houses in the book with the houses that Morty found in "This Is the Place for Me."

Alexander, Sue. *Dear Phoebe.* Little, Brown, 1984. Phoebe Dormouse wants to be independent, but winds up finding out that it's not so great to be alone.

Frasconi, Antonio. *The House That Jack Built.* Harcourt, Brace & World, 1958. This well-known tale is a cumulative rhyme about Jack building a house.

Grifalconi, Ann. *The Village of Round and Square Houses.* Little, Brown, 1986. A grandmother explains the importance in her village of round and square houses.

Maynard, Joyce. *New House.* Harcourt Brace Jovanovich, 1987. Andy uses the scrap material from the new house being built down the street to build a treehouse.

Mendoza, George. *Need a House? Call Ms. Mouse.* Grosset & Dunlap, 1981. Ms. Mouse designs the perfect house for each of her animal friends.

LISTENING: POETRY Tell pupils that you will read a poem about an animal that never has to worry about finding a home.

A House for One
The turtle children,
Sister and brother,
Do not live in one house
With their father and mother.
Each baby turtle
Is happy alone
In a snug little house
Of his very own.

Laura Arlon

Ask in what kind of houses turtles live. (shells) Ask why turtles never have to worry about finding a home. (because they always have their shells with them)

HOW AM I DOING?

Many pupils need encouragement to read and to write poetry. Ask yourself the following questions to gauge your teaching effectiveness in this area.

	Yes	No	Some-times
1. Have I made a wide selection of poetry books available for pupils to read or browse through?	☐	☐	☐
2. Do I take time to read aloud poetry to pupils?	☐	☐	☐
3. Do I help pupils understand the meaning of the poetry that is read aloud in class?	☐	☐	☐
4. Do I encourage pupils to write poetry of their own?	☐	☐	☐
5. Do I allow time for pupils to read their poems to the class?	☐	☐	☐

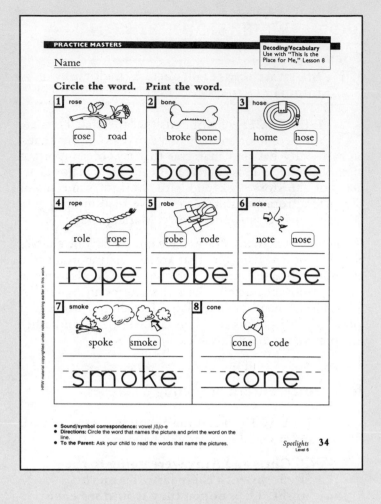

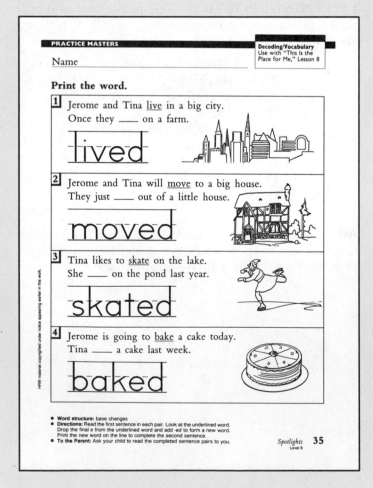

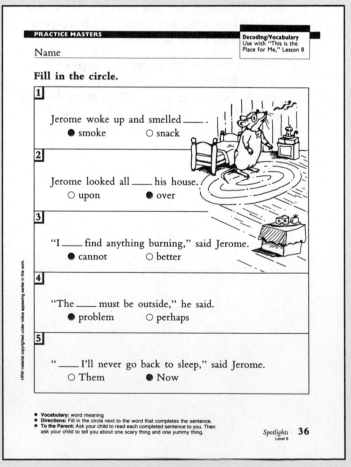

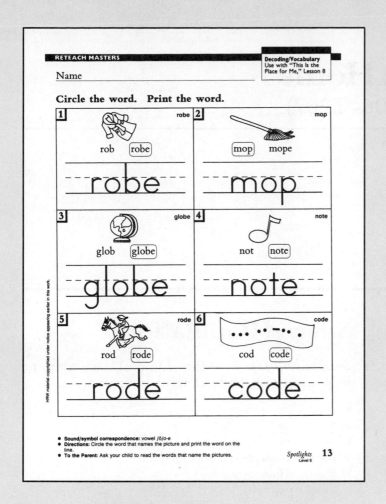

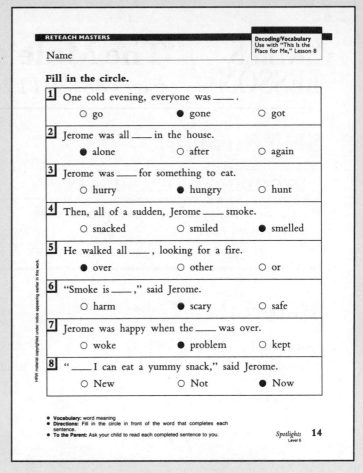

"The Mole's Home"
pages 88–89 (T206–T207)

Skill Strands

DECODING/VOCABULARY

R, T **Sound/symbol correspondence:**
vowel /ō/o-e

Materials

Spotlights, Level 6: pages 88–89
Resource Box: Word Cards drop, hop, hope, mole, pond, rope, stone
Teacher's Idea Book

Special Populations

See *Teacher's Idea Book* for additional suggestions to help pupils with limited English proficiency.

Key to Symbols
I Introduced in this lesson
R Reinforced from an earlier lesson in this level
M Maintained from previous levels
T Tested in this level

DECODING/VOCABULARY

R, T **Sound/symbol correspondence:** vowel /ō/o-e

DIRECT INSTRUCTION Place *Word Cards hop* and *hope* in the *Pocket Chart* and have the words read. Ask why the letter *o* in *hope* stands for the long sound of *o*. (because the word *hope* has an *o*, followed by a consonant, and ends with letter *e*)

Display *Word Cards rope, mole, pond, drop, stone.* Call on pupils to hold up a word card and read the word. Then have the word placed in the *Pocket Chart* under *hop* if the letter *o* has the same sound as in *hop* or under *hope* if the letter *o* has the same sound as in *hope.* Have the list of long *o* words read. (*hope, rope, mole, stone*)

GUIDED PRACTICE Have pupils find page 88 in their books and read the title at the top of the page. ("The Mole's Home") Tell pupils that the mole is trying to find his way home and that they can find the path the mole should travel by reading the directions. Have pupils read the directions and use their fingers to follow the path the mole should take.

Call on pupils to find and read the words on page 88 that contain the long sound of letter *o.* (*Mole's, Home, mole, hole, rope, pole, rose, stones*)

The <u>Mole's</u> Home

Help the mole find his home.

<u>Start</u> with the mole.
Go past the hole.
Next, go to the <u>rope</u>.
Then <u>scamper</u> up the <u>pole</u>.
Look for the <u>rose</u>.
Jump over the four <u>stones</u>.
There's the mole's home!

88

89

"Houses"
pages 90–91 (T208–T209)

Skill Strands

COMPREHENSION/THINKING

M **Forms of literature:** poetry

Materials

Spotlights, Level 6: pages 90–91
Teacher's Idea Book

Special Populations

See *Teacher's Idea Book* for additional suggestions to help pupils with limited English proficiency.

Key to Symbols

I Introduced in this lesson
R Reinforced from an earlier lesson in this level
M Maintained from previous levels
T Tested in this level

COMPREHENSION/THINKING

M **Forms of literature:** poetry

DIRECT INSTRUCTION Ask pupils to tell what Morty was looking for in "This Is the Place for Me." (a new house) Point out that Morty was a make-believe bear and that he did not live in the same kind of home in which a real bear might live. Ask who usually lives in a house with windows and doors and a roof. (people, humans)

Have pupils find page 90 in their books and tell them that this is a poem about houses. The poet, or the person who wrote the poem, thinks that a house looks like a face. Ask pupils to listen to see if they agree with the poet. Read the poem "Houses" aloud.

GUIDED PRACTICE Ask pupils to tell what part of a house might be its hat. (the roof) Ask what parts of a house make the eyes, nose, and mouth of the face. (Windows are noses and eyes; the door is the mouth.) Ask what the poet says a porch seems to be. (a mustache) Ask pupils to listen as you reread the poem. Invite them to draw a picture of a house that looks like a face.

Houses

Houses are faces
(haven't you found?)
with their hats in the air,
and their necks in the ground.

Windows are noses,
windows are eyes,
and doors are the mouths
of a suitable size.

And a porch—or the place
where porches begin—
is just like a mustache
shading the chin.

Aileen Fisher

90

91

LESSON 9

"Aren't You Forgetting Something, Fiona?"
pages 92–101 (T210–T231)

Skill Strands

DECODING/VOCABULARY

R, T	**Sound/symbol correspondence:** vowel /ō/o-e
R	**Sound/symbol correspondence:** vowel discrimination /o/, /ō/
R, T	**Word structure:** base changes (drop final e and add -ed)
R, T	**Word structure:** inflectional endings -er, -est
R, T	**Word structure:** suffix -er
I	**Vocabulary:** word building
I, T	**Vocabulary:** word meaning

COMPREHENSION/THINKING

Focus

R, T	**Story structure:** characters (major and minor)

LANGUAGE

I	**Conventions of language:** sentence construction (word order)

Lesson Vocabulary

Decodable words: *backward, cartwheels, class, date, everything, family, flips, forgetting, forgot, handstands, hope, joke, outside, party, present, simple, sister, Tammy, tennis, workout, yourself*

Special words: *about, else, except, Fiona*

Materials

Spotlights, Level 6: pages 92–101
Workbook: pages 56–62

Practice Masters: pages 37–41
Instructional Charts: pages 59–66
Resource Box: Letter Cards a, d, e, h, i, l, m, n, o, p, r
             Word Cards about, else, except, Fiona, like

Pocket Chart
Teacher's Idea Book
Reteach Masters: page 15

Language Applications

USING LANGUAGE

Oral reading: expression
Speaking: role playing

EXTENDING SELECTION CONCEPTS

Writing: sentences
Writing: notes
Listening: poetry
Listening: fiction

Special Populations

See *Teacher's Idea Book* for additional suggestions to help pupils with limited English proficiency.

Key to Symbols

I Introduced in this lesson
R Reinforced from an earlier lesson in this level
M Maintained from previous levels
T Tested in this level

Idea Center

SENTENCE SCRAMBLE GAME

Make the "Sentence Scramble Game," using the page from the *Teacher's Idea Book*. Or print on a sheet of tagboard some mixed-up sentences that can be cut apart and made into complete sentences. Examples follow.

liked cartwheels Fiona to do.
Hope flips like Did do to?
fix could Father things.
lots of sing songs Grandmother would.
Mother put Can away things?

Pupils will need a copy of the page, scissors, and an envelope in which to store their "Sentence Scramble Games." (See page T230 for directions.)

BIBLIOGRAPHY

Add to your reading corner or reading table various books about forgetfulness. A suggested bibliography follows. Suggestions for reading aloud and annotations appear in the lesson plan.

Aliki. *Use Your Head, Dear.* Greenwillow, 1983.
Weinberg, Lawrence. *The Forgetful Bears.* Clarion, 1981.

Planning Chart

		Instruction	Written Practice	Extending
Step 1 Preparing for the Selection	R, T	**Sound/symbol correspondence:** vowel /ō/o-e	*Workbook* page 56 *Practice Masters* page 37	
	I	**Vocabulary:** word building		
	I, T	**Vocabulary:** word meaning	*Workbook* page 57 *Practice Masters* page 38 *Reteach Masters* page 15	**Writing:** sentences
	R, T	**Story structure:** characters (major and minor)		
Step 2 Reading for Comprehension		**Oral reading:** expression **Speaking:** role playing **Story structure:** characters (major and minor)		
		Story comprehension	*Workbook* page 58	
Step 3 Developing Reading and Thinking Skills	R	**Sound/symbol correspondence:** vowel discrimination /o/, /ō/	*Workbook* page 59 *Practice Masters* page 39	**Writing:** notes
	R, T	**Word structure:** base changes (drop final *e* and add *-ed*)	*Workbook* page 60 *Practice Masters* page 40	**Listening:** poetry
	R, T	**Word structure:** inflectional endings *-er, -est*		
	R, T	**Word structure:** suffix *-er*		
	R, T	**Story structure:** characters (major and minor)	*Workbook* page 61 *Practice Masters* page 41	**Listening:** fiction
	I	**Conventions of language:** sentence construction (word order)	*Workbook* page 62	

DECODING/VOCABULARY

R, T **Sound/symbol correspondence:** vowel /ō/o-e

DIRECT INSTRUCTION Print the following words and sentences on the chalkboard, omitting the underlining.

> rob
> robe
>
> 1. The dog dug a <u>hole</u> for its <u>bone</u>.
> 2. <u>Hope</u> and Don jump <u>rope</u>.
> 3. Tom has a <u>joke</u> book.
> 4. Bob tripped on a <u>stone</u> and dropped his <u>cone</u>.

Call attention to the words *rob* and *robe*. Read the words and ask what sound the letter *o* stands for in the word *rob*. (/o/) Ask what sound the letter *o* stands for in the word *robe*. (/ō/) Have pupils tell why the *o* in *robe* stands for the long sound of *o*. (because the *o* in *robe* is followed by a consonant and the letter *e*) Have pupils point to and read *rob* and *robe*.

GUIDED PRACTICE Call attention to the sentences on the chalkboard and have each one read. Call on pupils to find and read the words from the sentences that have the long *o* sound.

WB 56 **INDEPENDENT PRACTICE** *Workbook* page 56 may be used to practice identifying sound/symbol correspondence /ō/o-e.

PM 37 **ADDITIONAL PRACTICE** *Practice Masters* page 37 may be used as an optional practice for identifying sound/symbol correspondence /ō/o-e. (See page T230 for reduced pages with answers.)

✱ **RETEACH** For those pupils who need additional instruction, see "Reteaching Lesson Skills," page T228, under "Reteaching and Extending."

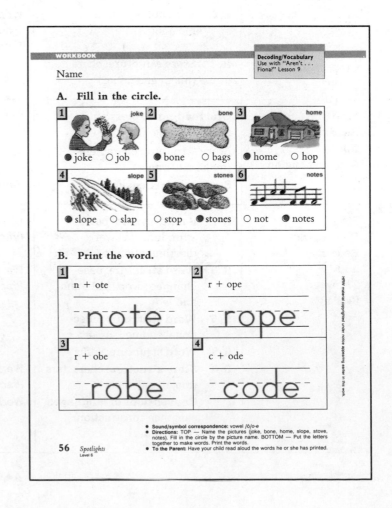

I Vocabulary: word building

DIRECT INSTRUCTION Use *Letter Cards* to make the word *hop* in the *Pocket Chart* and have the word read. Hold up *Letter Card e* and ask how to change *hop* to *hope*. (Place letter *e* at the end.) Place *e* at the end of *hop* and ask pupils to read the new word. (*hope*) Remove *e* and replace it several times, asking pupils to read the word each time.

GUIDED PRACTICE Display *Letter Cards a, d, e, i, l, m, n, r*. Tell pupils that you will call on them to use the cards to make new words in the *Pocket Chart*.

1. **Change the *h* in *hope* to *r*. What is the new word?** (*rope*)
2. **Change the *p* to *d*. What is the new word?** (*rode*)
3. **Change the *o* to *i*. What is the new word?** (*ride*)
4. **Change the *r* to *h*. What is the new word?** (*hide*)
5. **Take off the *e*. What is the new word?** (*hid*)
6. **Change the *i* to *a*. What is the new word?** (*had*)
7. **Change the *h* to *m*. What is the new word?** (*mad*)
8. **Add letter *e* to the end of the word. What is the new word?** (*made*)
9. **Change the *d* to *n*. What is the new word?** (*mane*)
10. **Take away the *e*. What is the new word?** (*man*)
11. **Put *e* after *n*. What is the new word?** (*mane*)
12. **Change the *a* to *i*. What is the new word?** (*mine*)
13. **Change the *m* to *l*. What is the new word?** (*line*)
14. **Change the *i* to *o*. What is the new word?** (*lone*)

I, T Vocabulary: word meaning

DIRECT INSTRUCTION Print the following words and sentences on the chalkboard, omitting the underlining.

about else except Fiona
1. <u>Fiona</u> will not eat peas.
2. She will eat anything <u>else</u>.
3. She ate everything for dinner <u>except</u> the peas.
4. What will Mom do about <u>Fiona</u>?
hope joke party present sister tennis workout

Read the first sentence. Point to the name *Fiona* and read it. Explain that *Fiona* is a girl's name. Have pupils read the sentence with you. Then ask them to find and read the name *Fiona*.

Read Sentence 2. Point to the word *else* and read it. Ask if Fiona will eat broccoli. (Yes, she will eat anything except peas.) Have pupils read the sentence with you. Then have them find and read the word *else*.

Read Sentence 3. Point to the word *except* and read it. Ask what Fiona ate for dinner. (everything except the peas) Have pupils read the sentence with you. Then ask them to find and read the word *except*.

Read Sentence 4. Point to the word *about* and read it. Then have pupils read the question with you. Ask what Mom should do about Fiona. (Answers will vary.) Have pupils find and read the word *about*.

The words in the second set are new words that contain known phonic elements. You may wish to ask pupils to read the words, using what they know about letters and sounds.

GUIDED PRACTICE Print the following sentences on the chalkboard, omitting the underlining.

> 1. <u>Fiona</u> went to her <u>sister</u> Tammy's birthday <u>party</u>.
> 2. "I <u>hope</u> you like my <u>present</u>," said Fiona.
> 3. Everyone <u>else</u> <u>except</u> Tammy knows the present is a <u>joke</u>.
> 4. The present is a book <u>about</u> <u>tennis</u>, and Tammy doesn't even like tennis.
> 5. She likes to go to <u>workout</u> class.

Provide opportunities for pupils to practice reading the new special words and some of the new decodable words in these sentences by following the suggestions below.

Sentence 1: Ask volunteers to find and read the name *Fiona* and sister. Ask who are sisters. (Fiona and Tammy) Then have the sentence read.

Sentence 2: Have the sentence read. Ask pupils to find and read the word *hope*. Ask what Fiona hopes. (She hopes Tammy will like her birthday present.) Ask pupils to find and read the word present.

Sentence 3: Have the sentence read. Ask who knew the present was a joke. (everyone else except Tammy) Have pupils find and read the words *else* and *except*.

Sentence 4: Have the sentence read aloud. Ask pupils to tell what Fiona gave Tammy for her birthday. (a book about tennis) Ask pupils what tennis is. (a game played with a racquet and balls on a court with a net) Have pupils find and read the word *about*.

Sentence 5: Have the sentence read. Ask what Tammy likes to do. (She likes to go to workout class.) Have pupils find and read the word *workout*.

INDEPENDENT PRACTICE *Workbook* page 57 may be used to practice reading story vocabulary.

ADDITIONAL PRACTICE *Practice Masters* page 38 may be used as an optional practice for reading story vocabulary. (See page T230 for reduced pages with answers.)

RETEACH For those pupils who need additional instruction, see "Reteaching Lesson Skills," page T229, under "Reteaching and Extending."

COMPREHENSION/THINKING

Focus

R, T **Story structure:** characters (major and minor)

DIRECT INSTRUCTION Tell pupils to listen as you read the following story to find out who are the major and minor characters.

READ John and his friends were roller skating. John skated around the block alone. He found a wallet someone had dropped. John showed the wallet to his friends. Then he looked for the owner's name.

ASK Who are the characters in this story? (John and his friends) Who is the major character? (John) Why? (Most of the story tells about what John did.) John's friends are the minor characters because they play only a small part in the story.

GUIDED PRACTICE Point out that sometimes there is more than one major character in a story. Tell pupils that you are going to read another story and you will ask them to name the major and minor characters.

READ Kevin and Sue wanted to surprise their mom. Kevin carefully poured a jar of spaghetti sauce in a pan and heated it. Sue put the spaghetti in a pan to boil. Then they both set the table. When Mom came home, she was happy to find dinner on the table.

ASK Who are the major characters? (Kevin and Sue) Who is the minor character? (their mother)

2 READING FOR COMPREHENSION

Background for the Teacher

SUMMARY An elephant named Fiona has trouble remembering simple things. Her family tries to help her find ways to remember things, but she still gets confused. Finally, something happens that Fiona is able to remember.

INFORMATION The light-hearted story of Fiona's forgetfulness was taken from a book of the same title and is all the more humorous because Fiona is an elephant. The elephant is reputed to "never forget."

Using Prior Knowledge

Tell pupils that the story they are going to read is about an elephant named Fiona. Fiona has trouble remembering things. Develop a discussion by asking questions such as those that follow.

1. **Sometimes people forget things. What are some things people might forget?** (Possible answers include: to return books to the library; to do chores at home; what time a favorite TV program begins.)
2. **What can people do that might help them remember things?** (Possible answers include: ask someone to remind them; write themselves a note; leave something by the door so they will see it when they leave the house.)

Setting a Purpose for Reading

Ask pupils to find page 92 in their books. Tell them that the title of this story is "Aren't You Forgetting Something, Fiona?" Ask what Fiona might be forgetting. (Possible answers include: to do chores at home; to brush her teeth; to do her homework.)

Point out the headnote at the top of page 92. Tell pupils that this note will help them think about the story they are going to read. Have the note read. Ask pupils to predict if Fiona's family will be able to help her.

Reading Silently

Some pupils may be able to read this story independently. Direct them to read the whole story to find out more about Fiona and her family and if they can help her.

For those pupils who need more guidance, suggestions for directed reading follow.

Fiona has trouble remembering.
Will her family's ideas help her?

Aren't You Forgetting
Something, Fiona?

In Fiona's family, everyone
remembered things . . .
everyone except Fiona.

Fiona's mother remembered where
she put things.

Fiona's father remembered how to
do things.

Fiona's grandmother remembered
the words to songs.

Even Fiona's sister Tammy
remembered things.

92

93

Before reading pages 92–93

SAY **Everyone forgets things now and then. Why was forgetting such a problem for Fiona? Read pages 92 and 93 to yourself.**

After reading pages 92–93

Why do you think forgetting things was such a problem for Fiona? (Possible answers include: Everyone else in her family could remember things; Fiona probably felt bad because she kept forgetting things.) Critical

Fiona, on the other hand, had trouble remembering even <u>simple</u> things.

If her mother asked her to get one thing, she came back with something <u>else</u>.

When she went to play <u>tennis</u>, she would forget her tennis shoes.

It was no <u>joke</u> . . .
Fiona <u>forgot</u> a lot.

94

One day, Fiona planned to take a <u>workout class</u> with her best friend, Hope.

The week the class was to start, Fiona got upset.
What if she forgot her workout bag?
What if she forgot to go to class at all?

Fiona asked her family for help.

95

Before reading pages 94–95

SAY **Poor Fiona had a problem. What do you think she will do to solve her problem? Read pages 94 and 95 to yourself.**

After reading pages 94–95

1. **What did Fiona do to try to solve her problem?** (She asked her family for help.) Literal
2. **Why was Fiona so worried?** (She was going to take a workout class, and she did not want to forget anything.) Inferential

"Make a big X on that <u>date</u>,"
said Tammy.

"Put up a note telling <u>yourself</u>
to go to class," said Grandmother.

"Put your bag where you'll see
it," said Father.

"Put a ribbon on your trunk,"
said Fiona's mother.

"When you see the ribbon, you'll
know there's something to remember."

Fiona did it all.

96

On the day of the class, Fiona saw
the X and the note.

She picked up her bag and went
<u>outside</u>, but it was too good to last.

Fiona forgot where she was going.
She went up one street and down
the other.

97

Before
reading
pages
96–97

| SAY | What do you think Fiona's family will tell her to do? Read pages 96 and 97 to yourself.

After
reading
pages
96–97

1. **What were some things that Fiona's family suggested to help her remember?** (She should put a big X on the date; she should put up a note; she should put her bag where she'll see it; she should put a ribbon on her trunk.) Inferential
2. **Which suggestion did Fiona try?** (She tried them all.) Literal
3. **Did the suggestions help Fiona?** (No, she saw the X and the note; she got her bag and went outside, but then she forgot where she was going.) Inferential

Then Fiona saw the ribbon on her trunk.

"If I have on a ribbon, I must be going to a party," she said.
"I'll bet it's Hope's birthday."

So Fiona ran to get a present.

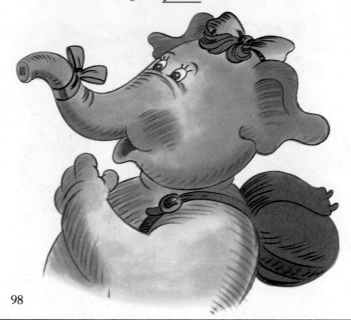

98

On Fiona's way to the party, she saw Hope looking out a window.

It was then that Fiona remembered the workout class.

"That's what the ribbon was for!" said Fiona.

Fiona wanted Hope to have the present anyway.

"Today isn't my birthday, but thank you, Fiona," said Hope.
"We can take turns with the jump rope in class."

99

Before reading pages 98–99

SAY **Fiona forgot again! Do you think she will remember the workout class? Read pages 98 and 99 to yourself.**

After reading pages 98–99

1. **What made Fiona remember the workout class?** (She saw her friend Hope looking out a window of a building that had a sign that said "Jean's Workout Class.") Literal
2. **Why did Fiona think she was going to a party?** (She thought the ribbon on her trunk meant that she should go to a party.) Literal
3. **Why did Fiona want Hope to have the present anyway?** (so they could use the jump rope in workout class) Literal

At home, Fiona showed her family what she did in class that day.

She showed them how to do <u>handstands</u> and jumping jacks.

She showed them how to do <u>cartwheels</u> and <u>backward</u> <u>flips</u>.

Fiona remembered <u>everything</u>!

It had been a fine day—one Fiona would remember for a long time.

100

Discussing the Selection

1. How did Fiona's family help her?
2. Why was Fiona so upset <u>about</u> not remembering things?
3. Why did Fiona get a birthday present for Hope?
4. When did you find out that Fiona remembered what the ribbon was for?
5. Do you think Fiona will still have trouble remembering things?

101

Before reading pages 100–101

SAY **Do you think Fiona will ever be able to remember anything? Read pages 100 and 101 to yourself.**

After reading pages 100–101

1. **What did Fiona remember?** (She remembered everything she did in the workout class.) Literal
2. **Why do you think Fiona said she would remember that day for a long time?** (Possible answers include: She had so much fun; she was able to remember everything she did in class.) Critical

Discussing the Selection

Questions preceded by a number appear in *Spotlights* after the selection. Questions preceded by a bullet are additional questions for extending discussion.

PURPOSE

1. **How did Fiona's family help her?** (Fiona's family suggested ways that Fiona could remind herself to do things.) Literal

STORY MAPPING

2. **Why was Fiona so upset about not remembering things?** (She was the only one in her family who could not remember things; she was afraid that she would forget to take her bag to the workout class or that she would even forget to go.) Inferential

• **What are some things that Fiona forgot?** (She forgot what her mother asked her to get; she forgot her tennis shoes when she went to play tennis.) Literal

3. **Why did Fiona get a birthday present for Hope?** (When Fiona saw the ribbon on her trunk, she thought she must be going to a birthday party for Hope.) Inferential

• **What did Fiona do with the birthday present?** (She gave it to Hope anyway; she and Hope used it in class.) Literal

4. **When did you find out that Fiona remembered what the ribbon was for?** (On page 99, the sentences said: On Fiona's way to the party, she saw Hope looking out a window. It was then that Fiona remembered the workout class.)

CRITICAL THINKING

5. **Do you think Fiona will still have trouble remembering things?** (Answers will vary. Possible answers include: no, because Fiona remembered what happened at the class so she will probably start remembering things that are important to her; yes, she won't remember any better than before.)

Using Language

ORAL READING: EXPRESSION Have pupils turn to page 92 in their books and ask them to find the sentence that has three dots in it.

SAY **These three dots are called points of ellipsis and tell the reader to pause for a moment before finishing the sentence. Let's read the sentence together, pausing at the three dots.** (Point out that the word *except* is emphasized as the sentence is read.)

Have pupils read sentences from each page of the story by following the suggestions below.

Page 93: **Read the sentences that tell what Fiona's father and mother were able to remember.** (Fiona's mother remembered where she put things. Fiona's father remembered how to do things.)

Page 94: **Read the sentences as though you are telling someone about poor Fiona's problem.**

Page 95: **Read what worried Fiona.** (What if she forgot her workout bag? What if she forgot to go to class at all?)

Page 96: **Read what each member of Fiona's family suggested she should do.**

Page 97: **Read the sentences that tell what Fiona did when she went outside.** (Fiona forgot where she was going. She went up one street and down the other.)

Page 98: **Read what Fiona said when she thought she remembered where she was going.** ("If I have on a ribbon, I must be going to a party," she said. "I'll bet it's Hope's birthday.")

Page 99: **Read what Fiona said when she discovered what the ribbon was really for.** ("That's what the ribbon was for!" said Fiona.)

Page 100: **Fiona was excited about her workout class. Read the page in a way that shows how excited she was.**

SPEAKING: ROLE PLAYING Have pupils reread the part on page 96 where Fiona's family suggests ways Fiona can remember. Then have several pupils pretend to be Fiona and the members of her family. Ask them to act out, in their own words, what Fiona said to her family and the suggestions her family gave.

Applying the Focus Skill

STORY STRUCTURE: CHARACTERS Ask who was the major character in the story "Aren't You Forgetting Something, Fiona?" (Fiona) Ask pupils to name the minor characters in the story. (Fiona's mother, father, sister, grandmother, and Fiona's friend Hope)

Evaluating Comprehension

WB 58 **INDEPENDENT PRACTICE** *Workbook* page 58 may be used for an informal evaluation of story comprehension.

Comprehension/Thinking
Use with "Aren't . . .
Fiona!" Lesson 9

Name _____

Fill in the circle.

1 Fiona's problem was that she ___ things.
● forgot   ○ lost

2 The rest of the family ___ everything.
○ forgot   ● remembered

3 Fiona asked for some ___ .
○ presents   ● help

4 Everyone gave her ___ .
● ideas   ○ ribbons

5 Seeing ___ made Fiona remember.
○ Tammy   ● Hope

6 Fiona ___ her family all the things she did.
● showed   ○ twisted

7 She didn't ___ one thing!
● forget   ○ remember

58 *Spotlights* Level 6

● **Story comprehension:** "Aren't You Forgetting Something, Fiona?"
● **Directions:** Read the sentences. Fill in the circle by the word that completes each sentence so it tells about "Aren't You Forgetting Something, Fiona?"
● **To the Parent:** Have your child read the completed story summary.

HOW AM I DOING?

Many pupils need to establish or improve their self-confidence in reading. To help improve children's self-confidence, ask yourself the following questions to gauge your teaching effectiveness in this area.

	Yes	No	Some-times
1. Have I made a wide selection of picture books available?	☐	☐	☐
2. Have I encouraged pupils to look through books even if they may be unable to read the words?	☐	☐	☐
3. Have I provided time to permit individuals to tell about the books they have read and enjoyed?	☐	☐	☐
4. Have I praised pupils for reading?	☐	☐	☐

DECODING/VOCABULARY

R   Sound/symbol correspondence: vowel discrimination /o/, /ō/

DIRECT INSTRUCTION   Print the following sentences and words on the chalkboard:

> 1. I hope I can hop.
>
>   hope   hop
>
> 2. The stone is hot.
> 3. I have a mop at home.
> 4. The note is not for Sam.
> 5. The dog will not drop the bone.

Have the first sentence read. Then point to the words *hope* and *hop*. Ask which word has the long sound of letter *o* and why. (*Hope* has the long sound of *o* because *hope* has an *o*, followed by a consonant, and letter *e* is at the end.)

GUIDED PRACTICE   Direct pupils' attention to the numbered sentences. Have each sentence read. Then have pupils read the words with *o* and tell if the *o* in each word stands for /o/ or /ō/. (2. *stone* /ō/, *hot* /o/; 3. *mop* /o/, *home* /ō/; 4. *note* /ō/, *not* /o/; 5. *dog, drop* /o/, *bone* /ō/)

WB 59   INDEPENDENT PRACTICE   *Workbook* page 59 may be used to practice discriminating /o/ and /ō/.

PM 39   ADDITIONAL PRACTICE   *Practice Masters* page 39 may be used as an optional practice for discriminating /o/ and /ō/. (See page T231 for reduced pages with answers.)

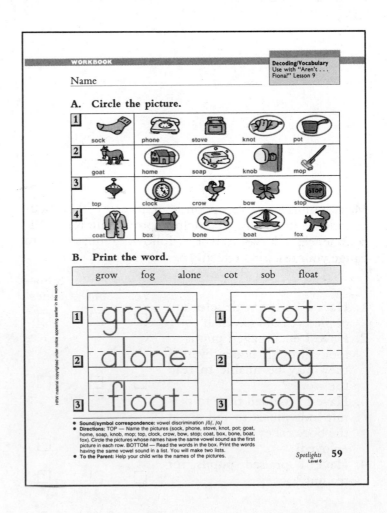

R, T Word structure: base changes (drop final *e* and add *-ed*)

DIRECT INSTRUCTION Print the following sentences and words on the chalkboard:

> 1. Fiona asked for help.
> 2. Her family will help her.
> 3. Fiona liked the class.
>
> | hope | bake | name |
> |------|------|------|
> | hoped | baked | named |

Have pupils read the first two sentences. Ask which sentence tells something that happened in the past. (Sentence 1) Point to the word *asked* and remind pupils that the ending *-ed* is added to a word to make the word mean that something happened in the past.

Have the third sentence read. Then call on pupils to tell which word has the *-ed* ending. (*liked*) Hold up *Word Card like*. Point out that the *e* at the end of *like* was dropped before the ending *-ed* was added.

GUIDED PRACTICE Direct pupils' attention to *hope* and *hoped* and have each word read. Then call on a pupil to tell which word shows something that happened in the past. Ask how *hope* was changed to *hoped*. (The *e* was dropped before adding *-ed*.)

Follow a similar procedure with *bake/baked* and *name/named*.

INDEPENDENT PRACTICE *Workbook* page 60 may be used to practice dropping the final *e* before adding *-ed*.

ADDITIONAL PRACTICE *Practice Masters* page 40 may be used as an optional practice for dropping the final *e* before adding *-ed*. (See page T231 for reduced pages with answers.)

RETEACH For those pupils who need additional instruction, see "Reteaching Lesson Skills," page T228, under "Reteaching and Extending."

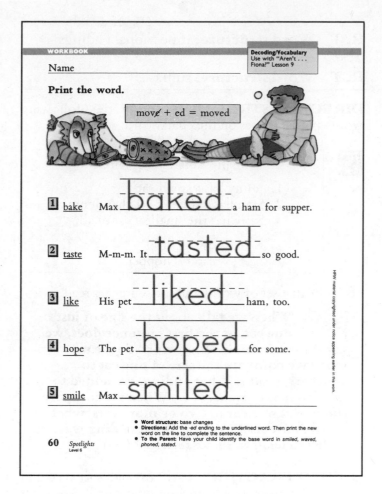

R, T **Word structure:** inflectional endings -*er*, -*est*

R, T **Word structure:** suffix -*er*

DIRECT INSTRUCTION Print the following words and sentences on the chalkboard:

> small   smaller   smallest
>
> 1. Jenny has a small cat.
> 2. Stan has a smaller cat than Jenny.
> 3. Sally has the smallest cat of all.
>
> eat   hop
> eater   hopper

Have the first set of words and the sentences read.

SAY **When we talk about the size of just one cat, as the first sentence does, we say the cat is small. What word do we use when we compare the size of one cat to another?** (*smaller*) **What ending was added to *small* to make *smaller*?** (-*er*) **When we compare the size of one cat to two or more cats, what word do we use?** (*smallest*) **What ending was added to *small* to make *smallest*?** (-*est*)

GUIDED PRACTICE Have *eat* and *eater* read and ask what an eater is. ("someone who eats") Ask what letters were added to *eat* to make *eater*. (-*er*)

Follow a similar procedure for *hop* and *hopper,* calling attention to the fact that the *p* in *hop* was doubled before the -*er* ending was added.

✳ **RETEACH** For those pupils who need additional instruction, see "Reteaching Lesson Skills," page T229, under "Reteaching and Extending."

Focus

R, T **Story structure:** characters (major and minor)

DIRECT INSTRUCTION Remind pupils that the most important character in a story is called the major character. The other characters in the story are called the minor characters.

GUIDED PRACTICE Print the following story on the chalkboard and ask pupils to read it.

> Hope waited and waited.
>   At last, she went to the workout
> class alone.
>   She wished Fiona would come.
>   Hope looked out the window.
>   Where could Fiona be?

Ask who is the major character in this story and why. (Hope is the major character because the story tells mostly about her.)

WB 61 **INDEPENDENT PRACTICE** *Workbook* page 61 may be used to practice identifying major and minor characters.

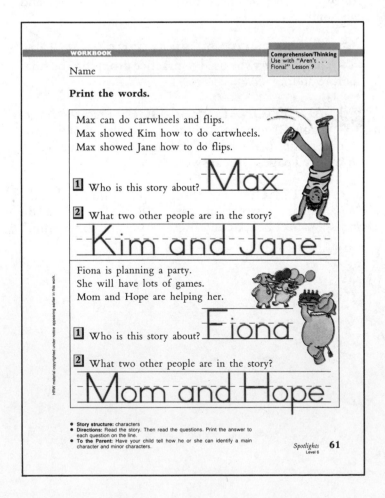

PM
41 **ADDITIONAL PRACTICE** *Practice Masters* page 41 may be used as an optional practice for identifying major and minor characters. (See page T231 for reduced pages with answers.)

 RETEACH For those pupils who need additional instruction, see "Reteaching Lesson Skills," page T229, under "Reteaching and Extending."

LANGUAGE

I   Conventions of language: sentence construction (word order)

DIRECT INSTRUCTION Print the following sentences and mixed-up sentences on the chalkboard:

IC
66

> forgot everything Fiona.
> Fiona forgot everything.
>
> 1. class Workout fun is.
> 2. Hope looked out the window.
> 3. upset got Fiona.
> 4. ask she help for Did?
> 5. Fiona remembered everything.

Have pupils read the first two lines. Then ask them to tell which line makes sense. *(Fiona forgot everything.)* Tell pupils that the line that makes sense is a sentence. It begins with a capital letter, and it ends with a period.

GUIDED PRACTICE Have pupils look at Lines 1–5 and read each line. After each line is read, ask if the group of words makes sense. Invite pupils to put the words that do not make sense in order to make a sentence. (1. *Workout class is fun;* 3. *Fiona got upset;* 4. *Did she ask for help?*)

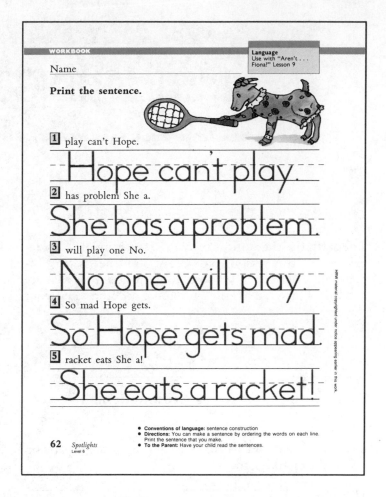

WB
62 **INDEPENDENT PRACTICE** *Workbook* page 62 may be used to practice constructing sentences.

✳ RETEACHING AND EXTENDING

Reteaching Lesson Skills

The activities that follow provide reteaching of skills developed in this lesson. Not every pupil needs to complete these activities. Choose only the activities that are needed to provide for the individual differences in your classroom.

DECODING/VOCABULARY

R, T   Sound/symbol correspondence: vowel /ō/o-e

 RETEACH   Print the following word pairs on the chalkboard:

not	rob	hop
note	robe	hope

Point to the words *not* and *note* and have them read. Point out that adding letter *e* to the end of the word *not* changed the sound of letter *o* from /o/ to /ō/. The *o* in *note* stands for the /ō/ sound because *o* is followed by a consonant and the letter *e*.

Have pupils read the remaining words. Ask how adding an *e* to *rob* and *hop* changed the sound letter *o* stands for. (The *e* changed the sound that *o* stands for from /o/ to /ō/.) Ask why the *o* in *robe* and *hope* stands for the /ō/ sound. (because each word has *o*, followed by a consonant, and ends with *e*)

R, T   Word structure: base changes (drop final *e* and add *-ed*)

 RETEACH   Print the following word pairs on the chalkboard:

hunt	like	hope
hunted	liked	hoped

Point to the first pair of words and have it read. Ask what was added to *hunt* to make the word *hunted*. (the ending *-ed*) Ask which word tells something that happened in the past. (*hunted*)

Then point to the next pair of words and have it read. Tell pupils that the word *liked* was made by dropping the *e* in *like* and adding *-ed*. *Liked* tells that something happened in the past.

Point to the last pair of words and have it read. Ask pupils to explain what ending was added to *hope* to make *hoped* and how it was added. (The final *e* in *hope* was dropped before adding *-ed*.)

R, T   Word structure: inflectional endings *-er, -est*

R, T   Word structure: suffix *-er*

 RETEACH   Print the following words on the chalkboard:

> slow   hunt
> slower   hunter
> slowest

Have the first group of words read. Ask what is different about the words. (*Slower* has *-er* at the end; *slowest* has *-est* at the end.) Tell pupils that the endings *-er* and *-est* are added to words when we want to compare things. The word *slower* would be used to compare one thing with another. The word *slowest* would be used to compare one thing with two or more things. Have pupils make up sentences using each word. (Possible answers include: *The red car is slower than the blue one; The green car was the slowest car in the race.*)

Direct pupils' attention to *hunt* and *hunter*. Ask what is different about the two words. (*Hunter* has *-er* at the end.) Tell pupils that sometimes the letters *-er* are added to the end of a word to make a new word that means "someone who does something." A hunter is "someone who hunts."

Have pupils think of other words to which the letters *-er* can be added to mean "someone who does something." (Possible answers include: *runner, skipper, jumper.*)

I, T   Vocabulary: word meaning

 RETEACH   Print the following words and sentences on the chalkboard, omitting the underlining.

> **about   else   except   Fiona**
>
> 1. Fiona will not eat peas.
> 2. She will eat anything else.
> 3. She ate everything for dinner except the peas.
> 4. What will Mom do about Fiona?
>
> **joke   hope   party   present
> sister   tennis   workout**

Point to the word *Fiona* and read it. Tell pupils that *Fiona* is a girl's name. Call on a pupil to find and read a sentence that contains the word *Fiona*.

Continue in the same manner with the remaining sentences, calling attention to the underlined words.

Display *Word Cards* for each of the underlined words. Have pupils hold up and read the word that answers each of the following questions:

1. **Which word rhymes with *shout*?** (*about*)
2. **Which word tells us that something is not like the others?** (*except*)
3. **Which word means "other or different"?** (*else*)
4. **Which word is a name?** (*Fiona*)

Have pupils read the second set of words and use them in sentences.

 Distribute *Reteach Masters* page 15 and explain the directions on the page.

COMPREHENSION/THINKING

Focus

R, T   Story structure: characters (major and minor)

 RETEACH   Print the following story on the chalkboard and have it read.

> It was a perfect day for a picnic.
> Bill put some food in a basket.
> He got his ball and bat.
> Then he rushed to the park.
> Betty was waiting at the gate.

Ask pupils to name the two characters in the story. (Bill and Betty) Ask which character was more important in the story. (Bill) Tell pupils that Bill is the major character in the story. Point out that Betty is a minor character because the story does not tell much about her.

Extending Selection Concepts

WRITING: SENTENCES Distribute copies of the "Sentence Scramble Game." (See page T211.) Invite pupils to cut apart the words that are on the page. Pupils may then put the cards in order to make sentences. On a piece of paper, have each pupil copy a sentence and illustrate it. Remind pupils to capitalize the first letter of the first word in the sentence and to end the sentence with a period or a question mark. Encourage them to read their sentences and show their illustrations to the class. Pupils may store their cards in envelopes and add words as they wish. Encourage pupils to play the game on their own or in pairs.

WRITING: NOTES Invite pupils to compose a note to Fiona that tells her what she must do to get to the workout class. The note should include taking her bag, going to the gym, meeting Hope. Have pupils read their notes aloud.

LISTENING: POETRY Tell pupils that you will read a nursery rhyme about someone who is forgetful. Ask them to listen to find out what this person forgets. Read aloud "Diddle Diddle Dumpling."

Diddle Diddle Dumpling
Diddle, diddle, dumpling, my son John,
Went to bed with his stockings on;
One shoe off, and one shoe on,
Diddle, diddle, dumpling, my son John.
Mother Goose

Ask what John forgot to do. (He forgot to take off his socks and one shoe before he went to bed.) Reread the rhyme and ask pupils to join you.

LISTENING: FICTION Choose a story about a forgetful character and read it aloud to the class. Ask pupils to compare the character to Fiona.

Aliki. *Use Your Head, Dear.* Greenwillow, 1983. An alligator learns to use his head with the help of some friends.

Weinberg, Lawrence. *The Forgetful Bears.* Clarion, 1981. An absent-minded bear family forgets where they're going.

PRACTICE MASTERS — Decoding/Vocabulary — Use with "Aren't . . . , Fiona!" Lesson 9

Name _____

Print the word. Circle the words.

| hole   close   mole   woke |

1 A (mole) woke up in his (home).

2 The (mole) stuck his (nose) out of a hole.

3 The mole (spoke) to me.

4 Do not put the (hose) too close to my (hole).

● Sound/symbol correspondence: vowel /ō/o-e
● **Directions:** Choose the word from the box that completes each sentence and print the word on the line. Then circle all the words in the sentences that have the /ō/ sound.
● **To the Parent:** Ask your child to read each sentence to you and tell you the words that have the same vowel sounds as *hope.*

Spotlights Level 6 **37**

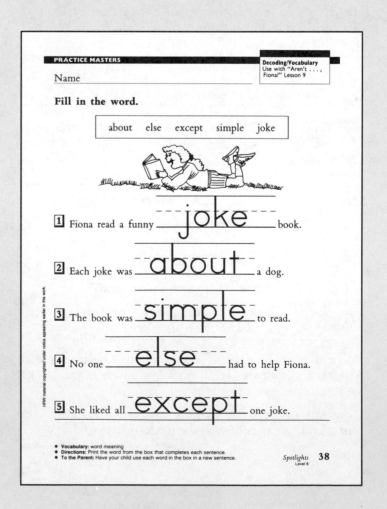

PRACTICE MASTERS — Decoding/Vocabulary — Use with "Aren't . . . , Fiona!" Lesson 9

Name _____

Fill in the word.

| about   else   except   simple   joke |

1 Fiona read a funny joke book.

2 Each joke was about a dog.

3 The book was simple to read.

4 No one else had to help Fiona.

5 She liked all except one joke.

● Vocabulary: word meaning
● **Directions:** Print the word from the box that completes each sentence.
● **To the Parent:** Have your child use each word in the box in a new sentence.

Spotlights Level 6 **38**

Name

Circle the words. Print the words.

1 Mom [rode] in the car with Rod [Robe].

rode   Robe

2 "I can't find my top and [rope]," said [Hope].

rope   Hope

3 Dot didn't mail a [note] to Todd's [home].

note   home

4 I [hope] the frog will hop out of its [hole].

hope   hole

- **Sound/symbol correspondence:** vowel discrimination /ō/, /o/
- **Directions:** Read each sentence. Circle the two words in each sentence that have the /ō/ sound and print the words on the lines.
- **To the Parent:** Ask your child to read each sentence to you and tell you the words that have the same vowel sound as *hope*.

Spotlights Level 6 **39**

Name

Print the word.

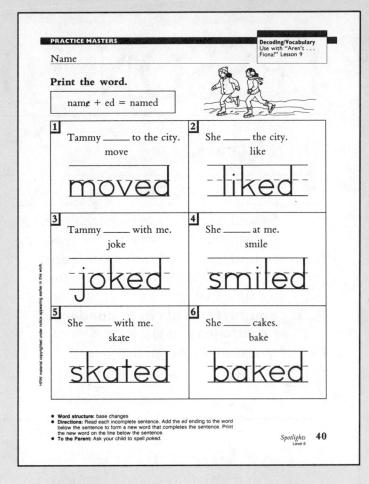

| name + ed = named |

1 Tammy ____ to the city.
move

moved

2 She ____ the city.
like

liked

3 Tammy ____ with me.
joke

joked

4 She ____ at me.
smile

smiled

5 She ____ with me.
skate

skated

6 She ____ cakes.
bake

baked

- **Word structure:** base changes
- **Directions:** Read each incomplete sentence. Add the *ed* ending to the word below the sentence to form a new word that completes the sentence. Print the new word on the line below the sentence.
- **To the Parent:** Ask your child to spell *poked*.

Spotlights Level 6 **40**

Name

Fill in the circle.

1 Gail likes to work out.
Sometimes she meets Kate at the club.
Gail likes to run, jump rope, and swim.
After the hard work, Gail rests.
Then she walks home to have lunch.

Who is the selection mainly about?

○ the family   ○ Kate   ● Gail

2 Mrs. Hopewell looked up at the sky.
Then she ran to get the food.
"Hurry, everyone!" she said.
Mr. Marx helped everyone get inside.
No one wanted to get soaked in the rain.
Now Mrs. Hopewell's picnic would be inside.

Who is the selection mainly about?

○ Mr. Marx   ○ the neighbors   ● Mrs. Hopewell

- **Story structure:** characters
- **Directions:** Read each story. Then read the question about the story. Fill in the circle by the words that answer the question.
- **To the Parent:** Ask your child to tell how he or she can identify the main character in a story.

Spotlights Level 6 **41**

Name

A. Circle <u>Yes</u> or <u>No</u>.

1 When you remember to take something,
do you have it with you?   [Yes]   No

2 Can you take a present you forgot
to get?   Yes   [No]

3 Is anyone else with you if you are alone?   Yes   [No]

4 If something is hard, can it be simple?   Yes   [No]

5 If you know all about basketball,
can you understand the game?   [Yes]   No

6 If everyone is happy except you,
are you sad?   [Yes]   No

B. Print a sentence.

| except   hope   else |

_____

Answers will vary.

_____

_____

- **Vocabulary:** word meaning
- **Directions:** TOP–Read the sentences. Then answer each question by circling *Yes* or *No*. BOTTOM–Read the words in the box. Make up a sentence using these words and some other words. Print the sentence.
- **To the Parent:** Ask your child to explain his or her answers to the questions.

Spotlights Level 6 **15**

Lesson 9 "Aren't You Forgetting Something, Fiona?" (pages 92–101)   T231

LESSON 10

"Peach Boy"
pages 102–111 (T232–T251)

Skill Strands

DECODING/VOCABULARY

M	**Sound/symbol correspondence:** consonant /y/*y* (initial)
I, T	**Sound/symbol correspondence:** consonant digraph /ch/*ch, tch* (initial, medial, final)
R, T	**Sound/symbol correspondence:** *r*-controlled vowel /är/*ar*
I	**Vocabulary:** word building
I, T	**Vocabulary:** word meaning

COMPREHENSION/THINKING

Focus

I	**Forms of literature:** folklore (folk tales and fairy tales)
M	**Forms of literature:** fantasy and realism

LANGUAGE

R	**Conventions of language:** sentence construction (word order)

Lesson Vocabulary

Decodable words: *army, bark, branches, chattered, chirped, far, fetch, fire, hillside, hut, luck, match, nuts, outsmart, peach, reaching, riches, ripe, scratch, stole, stream, swam, treat, watched*

Special words: *giant, woman*

Materials

Spotlights, Level 6: pages 102–111
Workbook: pages 63–69

Practice Masters: pages 42–45
Instructional Charts: pages 67–71
Resource Box: Letter Cards a, i, l, n, p, r, u
  Pattern Card ch
  Word Cards army, bark, branch, champ, chatter, chick, chin, far, farm, giant, hatch, march, peach, scratch, smart, woman, yard, yarn, yell, yellow, yes, yet

Pocket Chart
Teacher's Idea Book
Reteach Masters: pages 16–17

Language Applications

USING LANGUAGE

Oral reading: answering questions

EXTENDING SELECTION CONCEPTS

Speaking: telling stories (Cooperative Learning)
Listening: fiction

Special Populations

See *Teacher's Idea Book* for additional suggestions to help pupils with limited English proficiency.

Key to Symbols
I Introduced in this lesson
R Reinforced from an earlier lesson in this level
M Maintained from previous levels
T Tested in this level

Idea Center

BIBLIOGRAPHY

Add to your reading corner or reading table various folk tales and fairy tales. A suggested bibliography follows. Suggestions for reading aloud and annotations appear in the lesson plan.

Briggs, Raymond. *Jim and the Beanstalk.* Coward McCann, 1970.

Rogasky, Barbara. *Rapunzel.* Holiday House, 1982.

Zelinsky, Paul O. *Rumpelstiltskin.* E. P. Dutton, 1986.

Planning Chart

	Instruction		Written Practice	Extending
Step 1 Preparing for the Selection	I, T	**Sound/symbol correspondence:** consonant digraph /ch/*ch, tch* (initial, medial, final)	*Workbook* page 63 *Practice Masters* page 42 *Reteach Masters* page 16	**Listening:** fiction
	I	**Vocabulary:** word building		
	I, T	**Vocabulary:** word meaning	*Workbook* page 64 *Practice Masters* page 43 *Reteach Masters* page 17	
	I	**Forms of literature:** folklore (folk tales and fairy tales)		
Step 2 Reading for Comprehension		**Oral reading:** answering questions		
		Forms of literature: folklore (folk tales and fairy tales)		
		Story comprehension	*Workbook* page 65	
Step 3 Developing Reading and Thinking Skills	R, T	**Sound/symbol correspondence:** *r*-controlled vowel /är/*ar*	*Workbook* page 66 *Practice Masters* page 44	**Speaking:** telling stories (Cooperative Learning)
	M	**Sound/symbol correspondence:** consonant /y/*y* (initial)	*Workbook* page 67 *Practice Masters* page 45	
	I	**Forms of literature:** folklore (folk tales and fairy tales)	*Workbook* page 68	
	M	**Forms of literature:** fantasy and realism		
	R	**Conventions of language:** sentence construction (word order)	*Workbook* page 69	

DECODING/VOCABULARY

I, T Sound/symbol correspondence: consonant digraph /ch/*ch, tch* (initial, medial, final)

DIRECT INSTRUCTION Print the following rhyme and words on the chalkboard:

> I am a baby chick.
> Out of an egg I hatch.
> In the yard, I cheep, cheep, cheep,
> And scratch and scratch and scratch.
>
>   rich   chin   catch   peach
>   march   champ   reach   fetch

Point to each line as you read the rhyme aloud. Have pupils tell what animal the rhyme tells about. (a chick) Point to the word *chick*.

> **SAY** **Here is the word *chick*. Read *chick* with me: *chick*. The word *chick* begins with the letters *ch*. When the letters *ch* are together, they usually stand for the /ch/ sound.**

Call on pupils to find and read three other words in the rhyme that begin with *ch*. (*cheep, cheep, cheep*) Ask what sound the letters *ch* stand for in *cheep*. (/ch/)

Ask what the chick does when it comes out of an egg. (It hatches.) Point to the word *hatch*.

> **SAY** **Here is the word *hatch*. The /ch/ sound is at the end of the word *hatch*. When the /ch/ sound is at the end of a word, a letter *t* is often with the letters *ch*. The letters *tch* stand for the /ch/ sound at the end of *hatch*.**

Ask a pupil to find and read three other words that end with the /ch/ sound. (*scratch, scratch, scratch*)

Have pupils read the rhyme with you.

GUIDED PRACTICE Direct pupils' attention to the words on the chalkboard. Call on pupils to read the words and to tell which letters in each word stand for the /ch/ sound.

WB 63 INDEPENDENT PRACTICE *Workbook* page 63 may be used to practice identifying consonant digraph /ch/*ch, tch*.

PM 42 ADDITIONAL PRACTICE *Practice Masters* page 42 may be used as an optional practice for identifying consonant digraph /ch/*ch, tch*. (See page T250 for reduced pages with answers.)

✳ RETEACH For those pupils who need additional instruction, see "Reteaching Lesson Skills," page T248, under "Reteaching and Extending."

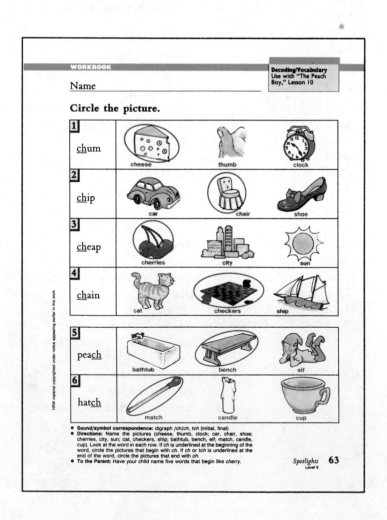

I Vocabulary: word building

DIRECT INSTRUCTION Use *Letter Cards* and *Pattern Card ch* to make the word *chip* in the *Pocket Chart*. Have the word read. Replace the *p* with *n* and have the new word read. (*chin*)

GUIDED PRACTICE Display *Letter Cards a, l, p, r, u*. Tell pupils that they will use these letters to make new words in the *Pocket Chart*.

1. **Take *ch* away from *chin*. What is the new word?** (*in*)
2. **Put *ch* at the end of the word. What is the new word?** (*inch*)
3. **Put *p* at the beginning of the word. What is the new word?** (*pinch*)
4. **Replace *i* with *u*. What is the new word?** (*punch*)
5. **Replace *p* with *l*. What is the new word?** (*lunch*)
6. **Replace *lu* with *ra*. What is the new word?** (*ranch*)
7. **Take out *an*. Put letter *i* in the middle. What is the new word?** (*rich*)

I, T Vocabulary: word meaning

DIRECT INSTRUCTION Tell pupils that they are going to talk about some words they will read in the next story. Print the following words and sentences on the chalkboard, omitting the underlining.

> **giant   woman**
>
> 1. Jack went to see a giant.
> 2. A woman said, "Go away, Jack."
>
> **branches chattered chirped fetch
> match peach reaching riches
> scratch watched**

Read the first sentence. Point to the word *giant* and read it. Ask what a giant is. (A giant is a very big person; giants are characters in some fairy tales.) Have pupils find and read the word *giant*. Then have the sentence read.

Read the second sentence aloud. Point to the word *woman* and read it. Ask what the woman told Jack. (She told him to go away.) Have pupils read the sentence with you. Then ask them to find and read the word *woman*.

The words in the second set are new words that contain known phonic elements. You may wish to ask pupils to read the words, using what they know about letters and sounds.

GUIDED PRACTICE Print the following sentences on the chalkboard, omitting the underlining.

> 1. I <u>watched</u> the birds as they sat on the <u>branches</u> of my <u>peach</u> tree.
> 2. They liked to <u>scratch</u> at the bark.
> 3. One day, I went to <u>fetch</u> some peaches.
> 4. As I was <u>reaching</u> for one, the birds <u>chirped</u> and <u>chattered</u>.
> 5. They acted as if the peaches were their <u>riches</u>.
> 6. The birds were no <u>match</u> for a <u>woman</u> like me.
> 7. I looked like a <u>giant</u> and scared them away.

Provide opportunities for pupils to practice reading the new special words and some of the new decodable words in these sentences by following the suggestions below.

Sentence 1: Have the sentence read. Ask where the birds sat. (on the branches of my peach tree) Have pupils find and read the words with the /ch/ sound. (*watched, branches, peach*)

Sentence 2: Have the sentence read. Ask what the birds liked to do. (scratch at the bark) Have pupils point to and read the word *scratch*.

Sentences 3–4: Call on a pupil to read the sentences. Ask if the woman wanted some peaches. (Yes, she went to fetch some; she was reaching for one.) Ask what words tell that the birds were noisy. (*chirped* and *chattered*)

Sentence 5: Have the sentence read. Tell pupils that *riches* are treasures. Have pupils find and read *riches*.

Sentence 6: Have the sentence read. Ask if the woman was afraid of the birds. (No, they were no match for her.) Have pupils find and read the words *match* and *woman*.

Sentence 7: Have a pupil find and read the word *giant*. Then have the sentence read aloud.

Ask volunteers to find and read the words that have the /ch/ sound. (*watched, branches, peach, chirped, chattered, reaching, fetch, scratch, riches, match*) Then invite pupils to choose a sentence to read aloud.

WB 64 **INDEPENDENT PRACTICE** *Workbook* page 64 may be used to practice reading story vocabulary.

Name _____

Decoding/Vocabulary
Use with "The Peach Boy," Lesson 10

Print the word.

| giant | riches | woman | gone | fetch |

1 An elf is little.

A _giant_ is big.

2 The peach is not where you put it.

It is _gone_.

3 I will get a pail of water.

I will _fetch_ some water.

4 Dad is a man.

Mom is a _woman_.

5 A giant guarded the treasure.

No one could get his _riches_!

64 *Spotlights*
Level 6

• **Vocabulary:** word meaning
• **Directions:** Read the words in the box. Print the word from the box that completes each sentence.
• **To the Parent:** Have your child use the words in the box to make up a story.

PM 43 **ADDITIONAL PRACTICE** *Practice Masters* page 43 may be used as an optional practice for reading story vocabulary. (See page T250 for reduced pages with answers.)

✳ **RETEACH** For those pupils who need additional instruction, see "Reteaching Lesson Skills," page T248, under "Reteaching and Extending."

COMPREHENSION/THINKING

Focus

I **Forms of literature:** folklore (folk tales and fairy tales)

DIRECT INSTRUCTION Tell pupils that folk tales are stories that were first told long ago. No one knows who made up the stories. At first, most of the stories were not written down in books, but were passed on by storytellers. Ask what stories pupils might know that have magical or make-believe characters, such as witches, giants, elves, and fairies. (Possible answers include: *Jack and the Beanstalk, Sleeping Beauty, Cinderella.*) Fairy tales were first told long ago and then written down by people like the Brothers Grimm and Hans Christian Andersen.

GUIDED PRACTICE: Read a familiar fairy tale, such as *Jack and the Beanstalk* by Beatrice de Regniers (Atheneum, 1985). If you do not have a book, help pupils recall a familiar story. Then ask questions such as the following:

1. **What was magical in the story?**
2. **Was there a giant or a witch?**
3. **What did it do?**
4. **How did the story end?**

2 READING FOR COMPREHENSION

Background for the Teacher

SUMMARY A man and woman find a peach that has a boy inside. They name him Peach Boy. When Peach Boy is grown, he sets out to drive away a mean giant that has been stealing from the people. He accomplishes this feat with cleverness rather than with strength.

INFORMATION This story, based on a very old oriental fairy tale, has a kind and clever major character who triumphs over an evil giant.

Using Prior Knowledge

Tell pupils that they are going to read a fairy tale about a character named Peach Boy. Ask why a character might be named Peach Boy. (Possible answers include: He eats peaches; he grows peaches; he looks like a peach.) Develop a discussion by asking questions such as those that follow.

1. **Do you know any stories where a nice character who is not very strong tries to get rid of a big, mean character?** (Possible answers include: *Little Red Riding Hood, Hansel and Gretel, The Three Little Pigs.*)
2. **Which character usually wins?** (the nice character)

Setting a Purpose for Reading

Have pupils find page 102 in their books and have the title read. Point out the headnote at the top of the page. Remind pupils that this note will help them think about the story they are going to read. Have the headnote read. Then ask why Peach Boy might want to outsmart a giant. (Answers will vary. Possible answers include: because the giant is mean.)

Reading Silently

Some pupils may be able to read this story independently. Direct them to read the whole story to find out more about Peach Boy and how he outsmarts a giant.

For those pupils who need more guidance, suggestions for directed reading follow.

You need good ideas to <u>outsmart</u> a <u>giant</u>!
Find out how <u>Peach</u> Boy does it.

Peach Boy

Long ago, a man and a <u>woman</u> lived in a little <u>hut</u>.

On one side of the hut was a <u>stream</u>.

On the other side was a hill.

One day, the man went up the <u>hillside</u> to gather some <u>branches</u> for a <u>fire</u>.

102

The woman went down to the stream to <u>fetch</u> some water.

Now, when she was there, she saw a fine, <u>ripe</u> peach floating down the stream.

"I'm in <u>luck</u> today," said the woman, <u>reaching</u> into the water.

103

Before reading pages 102–104

SAY **Who do you think Peach Boy was? Read pages 102 to 104 to yourselves.**

That evening, when the man came home, the woman set the peach on his plate.

"What a fine treat!" said the man with a smile.

All of a sudden, the peach broke in two, and what was inside but a little boy!

"We will name him Peach Boy," the woman said to the man.

They watched Peach Boy grow into a fine man.

104

Now, in those days, there was a giant.

This giant lived on some land in the middle of the sea.

The giant was mean and scary and stole riches from the people.

One day, Peach Boy said, "I will go to the place where the giant lives.

I will bring back all the riches that he stole."

So the man and the woman fetched some cakes for Peach Boy to take along with him.

105

After reading pages 102–104

1. **Who was Peach Boy?** (He was a boy that the man and woman found inside a peach.) Literal
2. **Do you think Peach Boy could be a real boy? Why or why not?** (Possible answers include: No, a real boy would not be inside a peach.) Critical

Before reading page 105

After reading page 105

SAY **What special thing do you think Peach Boy wanted to do? Read page 105 to yourself.**

1. **What special thing did Peach Boy want to do?** (He wanted to bring back the riches the giant stole from the people.) Inferential
2. **Was the giant a good giant or a bad giant? Why?** (He was a bad giant because he was mean and stole from people.) Inferential
3. **What did the man and woman give the Peach Boy to take with him?** (They gave him some cakes.) Literal

Peach Boy hadn't gone far when he met a spotted dog.

"Here is a cake for you, Dog," said Peach Boy.

"Will you come to the giant's house with me?"

"I will!" said the dog.

So he ate the cake and went with Peach Boy.

106

Peach Boy and the dog hadn't gone far when they came upon a monkey.

The monkey was sitting in a tree and tossed nuts upon them.

"Here is a cake for you, Monkey," said Peach Boy.

"Will you come to the giant's house with us?"

"I will!" chattered the monkey.

So the monkey ate the cake and went with them.

107

Before reading pages 106–108

SAY **Do you think Peach Boy was able to get the riches from the mean giant all by himself? Read pages 106 to 108 to yourself.**

Just then a big green bird was flying over the trees.

"Bird! Bird!" said Peach Boy.
"Here is a cake for you.
Will you come with us to the giant's house?"

"Yes!" chirped the bird.

So he ate the cake and went with them.

In time, the four came to the sea.
Peach Boy made a boat, and they sailed to the giant's house.

108

"Bird," said Peach Boy.
"Fly over the house and tell me what you see."

The bird did just that.

"The giant is sleeping," said the bird.

"Good," said Peach Boy.

Then Peach Boy said, "Dog, run to the back of the giant's house. Bark and scratch by the window.

Monkey, you toss lots of nuts at the giant's house."

The dog and the monkey did as they were asked.
The noise woke up the sleeping giant.

109

After reading pages 106–108

1. **Did Peach Boy go to the giant's house alone?** (No, he took a dog, a monkey, and a bird with him.) Inferential
2. **Why did the dog, the monkey, and the bird go with Peach Boy?** (He gave them each a cake and asked them to come along.) Literal
3. **Why did Peach Boy want his friends to go to the giant's house?** (He needed their help to outsmart the giant.) Inferential

Before reading page 109

SAY **What did Peach Boy and his friends do when they got to the giant's house? Read page 109.**

After reading page 109

1. **Why did Peach Boy tell Bird to fly over the giant's house?** (because Bird could see everything that was happening from up in the sky) Inferential
2. **Why did Peach Boy have Dog and Monkey make a lot of noise?** (so they would wake up the giant) Inferential

Peach Boy yelled, "Run, Giant, run!
An <u>army</u> is on its way here.
You will be no <u>match</u> for it."

With that, the giant jumped into
the sea and <u>swam</u> far away.

110

Peach Boy and his friends gathered
up the riches and carried them home.
All the people in the land
were happy.
The scary, mean giant was never
seen again.

Discussing the Selection
1. How did Peach Boy outsmart the giant?
2. Why did Peach Boy go to the giant's home?
3. How did the animals help Peach Boy?
4. When did you find out what Peach Boy's plan was?
5. In what ways was Peach Boy different from the others in the story?

111

Before reading pages 110–111

SAY **What do you think happened next? Read pages 110 and 111 to yourself.**

After reading pages 110–111

1. **What did Peach Boy say to the giant?** ("Run, Giant, run! An army is on its way here. You will be no match for it.") Literal
2. **What did the giant do?** (The giant jumped into the sea and swam far away.) Inferential
3. **What did Peach Boy and his friends do then?** (They gathered up the riches and took them home to the people.) Literal
4. **Why do you think the giant believed Peach Boy?** (because he probably thought the noise Dog and Monkey made was an army coming) Critical

Discussing the Selection

Questions preceded by a number appear in *Spotlights* after the selection. Questions preceded by a bullet are additional questions for extending discussion.

PURPOSE

1. **How did Peach Boy outsmart the giant?** (He had his friends make a lot of noise; then he told the giant that an army was on its way, and the frightened giant ran away.) Inferential

STORY MAPPING

2. **Why did Peach Boy go to the giant's home?** (He went to get the riches the giant had stolen from the people.) Literal

• **How did Peach Boy get his name?** (A woman cut open a peach and found him inside.) Inferential

3. **How did the animals help Peach Boy?** (The bird found out that the giant was sleeping; the dog barked and scratched at the window; the monkey threw nuts at the house.) Inferential

• **How did Peach Boy get the animals to help him?** (He fed them cakes.) Literal

4. **When did you find out what Peach Boy's plan was?** (On page 109, Peach Boy told the animals to make a lot of noise; on page 110, Peach Boy told the giant that an army was on its way.) Inferential

CRITICAL THINKING

5. **In what ways was Peach Boy different from the others in the story?** (Possible answers include: He was magical because he was found in a peach; he was very smart because he knew how to outsmart the giant.)

• **What did you think of Peach Boy's plan to outsmart the giant?** (Possible answers include: The plan was a good one because it worked; the plan wasn't very clever, but it worked because the giant was stupid.)

Using Language

ORAL READING: ANSWERING QUESTIONS
Tell pupils that you will ask some questions about "Peach Boy" that they can answer by reading sentences from the story. Ask pupils to turn to page 102 in their books and tell where the man went one day. (One day, the man went up the hillside to gather some branches for a fire.)

Follow a similar procedure for the remaining pages.

Page 103: Ask what the woman found at the stream. (Now, when she was there, she saw a fine, ripe peach floating down the stream.)

Page 104: Ask what happened to the peach. (All of a sudden, the peach broke in two, and what was inside but a little boy!)

Page 105: Have the sentences read that tell about the giant. (Now, in those days there was a giant. This giant lived on some land in the middle of the sea. The giant was mean and scary and stole riches from the people.)

Pages 106–108: Have a pupil read what Peach Boy said to each animal and have a different pupil read what each animal said.

Page 109: Have pupils read what Peach Boy and the bird said to each other. Then have the sentence read that tells what happened when the animals did as they were told. (The noise woke up the sleeping giant.)

Page 110: Ask a pupil to read the sentence that means "An army is coming." (An army is on its way here.) Then have the sentence read that means "You will not be able to fight it." (You will be no match for it.)

Page 111: Ask pupils to read the sentences that tell that the story had a happy ending. (All the people in the land were happy. The scary, mean giant was never seen again.)

Applying the Focus Skill

FORMS OF LITERATURE: FOLKLORE Remind pupils that fairy tales have characters that could not be real. Ask which characters in "Peach Boy" were not real people or animals and why. (Peach Boy was not real because a real boy could not be inside a peach; the animals were not real because they could talk; the giant was not real.) Ask what happened in this story that was magical. (The peach broke in two, and Peach Boy was inside.)

Evaluating Comprehension

WB 65 **INDEPENDENT PRACTICE** *Workbook* page 65 may be used for an informal evaluation of story comprehension.

Comprehension/Thinking
Use with "The Peach Boy," Lesson 10

Name _____

Fill in the circle.

1 The tale "Peach Boy" takes place _____.
○ now
● long ago
○ last week

2 Some people in the story were _____.
○ a dog, a bird, a giant
● a man, a woman, a boy
○ a man, a boy, a peach

3 Peach Boy asked for cakes to take with him so he could _____.
○ feed a giant
● eat when he was hungry
○ throw into the sea

4 Peach Boy handed cakes to _____.
○ a giant, a bird, and a fish
○ a man, a woman, a dog
● a bird, a dog, a monkey

5 Peach Boy, the dog, the monkey, and the bird _____.
○ worked as a team to make the giant yell.
● worked as a team to chase away the giant
○ worked as a team to bring back the giant

• **Story comprehension:** "The Peach Boy"
• **Directions:** Read the incomplete sentences. Fill in the circle by the words that complete each sentence so it tells about "The Peach Boy."
• **To the Parent:** Have your child tell what might have happened to the giant after he swam away.

Spotlights **65**
Level 6

3 DEVELOPING READING AND THINKING SKILLS

DECODING/VOCABULARY

R, T Sound/symbol correspondence: *r*-controlled vowel /är/*ar*

DIRECT INSTRUCTION Place *Word Card bark* in the *Pocket Chart* and have it read. Place *Word Card far* under the word *bark* and have it read. Ask what is alike about these words. (They have the /är/ sound in the middle.) Point to the letters *ar* and remind pupils that the letters *ar* usually stand for the /är/ sound.

GUIDED PRACTICE Call on pupils to read the words as you hold up the following *Word Cards: smart, farm, march, army.*

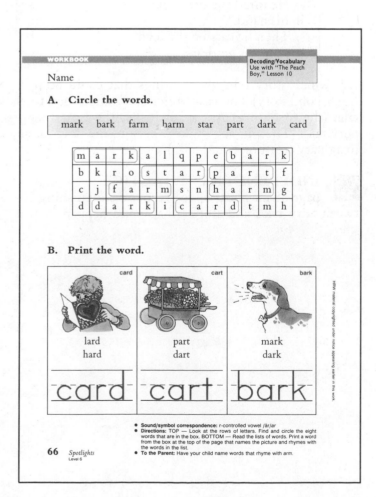

WORKBOOK

Decoding/Vocabulary
Use with "The Peach Boy," Lesson 10

Name _____

A. Circle the words.

| mark | bark | farm | harm | star | part | dark | card |

m	a	r	k	a	l	q	p	e	b	a	r	k
b	k	r	o	s	t	a	r	p	a	r	t	f
c	j	f	a	r	m	s	n	h	a	r	m	g
d	d	a	r	k	i	c	a	r	d	t	m	h

B. Print the word.

card · cart · bark

lard / hard

part / dart

mark / dark

card   cart   bark

● Sound/symbol correspondence: r-controlled vowel /är/ar
● Directions: TOP — Look at the rows of letters. Find and circle the eight words that are in the box. BOTTOM — Read the lists of words. Print a word from the box at the top of the page that names the picture and rhymes with the words in the list.
● To the Parent: Have your child name words that rhyme with arm.

66 *Spotlights* Level 6

INDEPENDENT PRACTICE *Workbook* page 66 may be used to practice identifying sound/symbol correspondence /är/*ar*.

ADDITIONAL PRACTICE *Practice Masters* page 44 may be used as an optional practice for identifying sound/symbol correspondence /är/*ar*. (See page T250 for reduced pages with answers.)

✱ RETEACH For those pupils who need additional instruction, see "Reteaching Lesson Skills," page T248, under "Reteaching and Extending."

M Sound/symbol correspondence: consonant /y/*y* (initial)

DIRECT INSTRUCTION Place *Word Card yes* in the *Pocket Chart* and have it read. Ask what letter is at the beginning of the word *yes* and what sound it stands for. (Letter *y* stands for the /y/ sound.)

GUIDED PRACTICE Place *Word Cards yell, yard, yarn, yet, yellow* in the *Pocket Chart* and have them read. Call on pupils to read the word from the *Pocket Chart* that correctly completes each of the following sentences:

1. **I like to play in the back** _____. *(yard)*
2. **I think** _____ **is a bright color.** *(yellow)*
3. **The kitten likes to play with** _____. *(yarn)*
4. **You must not** _____ **in the house.** *(yell)*
5. **It is not time to go home** _____. *(yet)*

INDEPENDENT PRACTICE *Workbook* page 67 may be used to practice identifying sound/symbol correspondence /y/*y*.

Name _____

Decoding/Vocabulary
Use with "The Peach
Boy," Lesson 10

Fill in the circle.

1 Maria's dress was _____.
○ yes   ● yellow

2 Don't _____ the dog's leash.
○ yak   ● yank

3 One kind of food is a _____.
● yam   ○ yell

4 Dad has not come home _____.
● yet   ○ yes

5 The puppy _____, so I held it.
○ yard   ● yipped

6 My hat is made from _____.
● yarn   ○ yippy

7 My big sister does not _____ at me.
● yell   ○ yard

8 Let's play in the front _____.
○ yoke   ● yard

- **Sound/symbol correspondence:** consonant /y/y (initial)
- **Directions:** Read the sentences and the words below them. Fill in the circle by the word that completes each sentence.
- **To the Parent:** Have your child say all the picture names and words that begin with y.

Spotlights **67**
Level 6

PM 45 **ADDITIONAL PRACTICE** *Practice Masters* page 45 may be used as an optional practice for identifying sound/symbol correspondence /y/y. (See page T250 for reduced pages with answers.)

Focus

I Forms of literature: folklore (folk tales and fairy tales)

M Forms of literature: fantasy and realism

DIRECT INSTRUCTION Remind pupils that fairy tales often have make-believe characters to which magical things happen. Ask what was magical in the story "The Chili Pot." (The pot made chili by itself.)

GUIDED PRACTICE Print the following stories on the chalkboard and ask pupils to read them.

IC 70
> Sandy ran away from the party and sat down on a bench.
> She was very upset.
> Someone said, "Why are you sad, little pig?"
> Sandy saw a dragon standing by the bench.
>
> Willy bent down and peeked under the log.
> He saw a little toad in the shade.
> He lifted the little toad in his hand.
> Then he carried the toad back to his garden.

Ask which story tells about things that could be real. (the second story) Then ask which story might be a fairy tale. (the first story) Ask what makes the first story a fairy tale. (The pig acted like a person; the dragon, an imaginary creature, could talk.)

WB 68 **INDEPENDENT PRACTICE** *Workbook* page 68 may be used to practice distinguishing between fairy tales and stories that could happen in real life.

Comprehension/Thinking
Use with "The Peach Boy," Lesson 10

Name _____

A. Circle what could happen.

1 Jack planted a magic seed.

2 Every day, Jack went to work.

3 The magic plant grew bigger than a house.

4 Jack went up the plant.

5 Jack's mother fixed supper for him.

B. Finish the story.

Answers will vary.

- **Forms of literature:** folk literature
- **Directions:** TOP — Read the sentences. Circle the sentences that could happen. BOTTOM — Read the sentences you did not circle. The sentences tell a story. Print an ending to the story.
- **To the Parent:** Have your child tell how a fairy tale is different from a real-life story.

68 *Spotlights* Level 6

GUIDED PRACTICE Direct pupils' attention to the next group of words on the chalkboard. Have pupils put the sentence in order. Then ask what must follow the last word to make the sentence complete. (a punctuation mark) Have the sentence read. *(She saw a peach.)*

Follow a similar procedure for the remaining groups of words. (3. *The giant is sleeping;* 4. *Peach Boy made a boat.*)

WB 69 **INDEPENDENT PRACTICE** *Workbook* page 69 may be used to practice putting words in order to construct sentences.

LANGUAGE

R Conventions of language: sentence construction (word order)

DIRECT INSTRUCTION Print the following groups of words on the chalkboard:

IC 71

> 1. ran giant The away.
> 2. saw She a peach.
> 3. sleeping is The giant.
> 4. a boat made Peach Boy.

Have pupils read the first group of words. Point out that these words can be arranged to make a sentence, but they are not in the correct order. Ask which word is the first word of the sentence and why. (The first word is *The* because it begins with a capital letter.) Then ask which word should come next. Continue until the sentence has been constructed. *(The giant ran away.)*

Language
Use with "The Peach Boy," Lesson 10

Name _____

Print a sentence.

house	car	cat	is	ran
a	moved	giggled	on	in
fast	slow	soft	sudden	the

A cat ran fast.

1 Answers will vary.

2

- **Conventions of language:** sentence construction
- **Directions:** Read the words in the box. Then read the sentence that is made up with words from the box. Print two sentences using some of the words.
- **To the Parent:** Have your child read the sentences. Then ask him or her to make word substitutions to form silly sentences. For example, "The house ran quickly."

Spotlights Level 6 **69**

Lesson 10 "Peach Boy" (pages 102–111) T247

Reteaching Lesson Skills

The activities that follow provide reteaching of skills developed in this lesson. Not every pupil needs to complete these activities. Choose only the activities that are needed to provide for the individual differences in your classroom.

DECODING/VOCABULARY

I, T **Sound/symbol correspondence:** consonant digraph /ch/ *ch, tch* (initial, medial, final)

✳ **RETEACH** Display *Word Card chick* and read the word.

> **SAY** The word *chick* begins with the /ch/ sound. The letters *ch* together can stand for the /ch/ sound. I will hold up some more words that begin with the /ch/ sound. Read each word to me.

Hold up *Word Cards chatter, champ, chin* one at a time.

Display *Word Card scratch* and read the word. Ask where the letters *ch* appear in *scratch*. (at the end) Point out the letter *t* in front of the *ch* and explain that the letters *tch* stand for the /ch/ sound at the end of *scratch*.

Call on pupils to read the words as you hold up the following *Word Cards: branch, peach, hatch.*

Then shuffle all the *Word Cards* and have them read as you hold up one card at a time.

RM 16 Distribute *Reteach Masters* page 16 and explain the directions on the page.

R, T **Sound/symbol correspondence:** *r*-controlled vowel /är/ *ar*

✳ **RETEACH** Print *far* on the chalkboard and read it. Tell pupils that the letters *ar* can stand for the /är/ sound. Print *park, farm, party, bark, smart* on the chalkboard. Point to each word and have it read. Ask what two letters stand for the /är/ sound in each word. (*ar*)

I, T **Vocabulary:** word meaning

✳ **RETEACH** Print the following words and sentences on the chalkboard, omitting the underlining.

> **giant   woman**
>
> 1. Jack went to see a <u>giant</u>.
> 2. A <u>woman</u> said, "Go away, Jack."
>
> **branches chattered chirped fetch
> match peach reaching riches
> scratch watched**

Point to the word *giant* and read it. Call on a pupil to find and read a sentence that contains the word *giant*. Follow a similar procedure with the word *woman*.

Display *Word Cards giant* and *woman*. Call on a pupil to hold up and read the *Word Card* that answers each of the following questions:

1. Which word means "a very big person"? (*giant*)
2. Which word means "a grown-up girl"? (*woman*)

Call on pupils to read the second set of words and to use them in sentences.

RM 17 Distribute *Reteach Masters* page 17 and explain the directions on the page.

Extending Selection Concepts

LANGUAGE ARTS

SPEAKING: TELLING STORIES (Cooperative Learning) Have pupils work together in groups. Invite each group to retell a fairy tale of its choice. Have members of the group draw pictures to illustrate different parts of the fairy tale. Then help pupils tape their pictures together in the order that the events take place in the story. Use an opaque projector to show one picture at a time, inviting each member of the group to tell their part of the fairy tale. You may then place the pictures into a book.

LISTENING: FICTION Choose a fairy tale and read it to the class. Ask pupils to compare the fairy tale to "Peach Boy."

Briggs, Raymond. *Jim and the Beanstalk.* Coward McCann, 1970. This is a delightful sequel to *Jack and the Beanstalk.*

Rogasky, Barbara. *Rapunzel.* Holiday House, 1982. This is the classic Grimms' story of a girl who is locked in a tower and raised by a witch until she is rescued by a handsome prince.

Zelinsky, Paul O. *Rumpelstiltskin.* E. P. Dutton, 1986. One of Grimms' most popular tales is retold in a fresh way and accented with beautiful illustrations by the author.

HOW AM I DOING?

Many pupils need encouragement to establish better self-discipline for independent reading. Ask yourself the following questions to gauge your teaching effectiveness in this area.

	Yes	No	Some-times
1. Have I taken pupils to the library?	☐	☐	☐
2. Have I provided time for independent silent reading?	☐	☐	☐
3. Have I encouraged an independent reading program for pupils that praises children for their efforts?	☐	☐	☐
4. Have I suggested guidance for reading at home, such as finding a special time and place to read?	☐	☐	☐

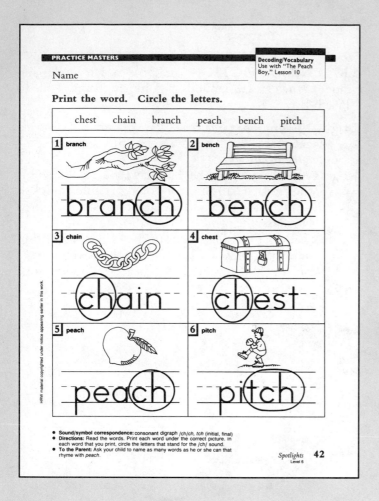

Name _____

Print the word. Circle the letters.

| chest | chain | branch | peach | bench | pitch |

1 branch

bran(ch)

2 bench

ben(ch)

3 chain

(chain)

4 chest

(ch)est

5 peach

pea(ch)

6 pitch

pi(tch)

- **Sound/symbol correspondence:** consonant digraph /ch/ch, tch (initial, final)
- **Directions:** Read the words. Print each word under the correct picture. In each word that you print, circle the letters that stand for the /ch/ sound.
- **To the Parent:** Ask your child to name as many words as he or she can that rhyme with *peach*.

Spotlights
Level 6   **42**

Name _____

Fill in the circle.

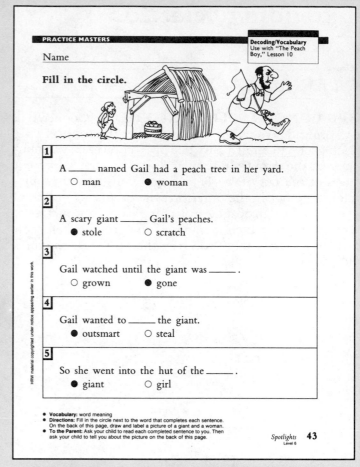

1 A _____ named Gail had a peach tree in her yard.
○ man   ● woman

2 A scary giant _____ Gail's peaches.
● stole   ○ scratch

3 Gail watched until the giant was _____.
○ grown   ● gone

4 Gail wanted to _____ the giant.
● outsmart   ○ steal

5 So she went into the hut of the _____.
● giant   ○ girl

- **Vocabulary:** word meaning
- **Directions:** Fill in the circle next to the word that completes each sentence. On the back of this page, draw and label a picture of a giant and a woman.
- **To the Parent:** Ask your child to read each completed sentence to you. Then ask your child to tell you about the picture on the back of this page.

Spotlights
Level 6   **43**

Name _____

Print the word. Circle the words.

| Art | bark | arms | farm |

1 Mark lives on a **farm** .

2 Mark has a dog named **Art** .

3 Art likes to **bark** at cars.

4 Art darts into Mark's **arms**

- **Sound/symbol correspondence:** r-controlled vowel /är/ar (initial, medial)
- **Directions:** Choose the word from the box that completes each sentence and print the word on the line. Then circle the words in the sentences that have the /är/ sound.
- **To the Parent:** Ask your child to read each completed sentence to you. Then ask your child to name the words that have the same vowel sound as *car*.

Spotlights
Level 6   **44**

Name _____

Print the word. Circle the words.

| you | yourself | yellow | yelped |

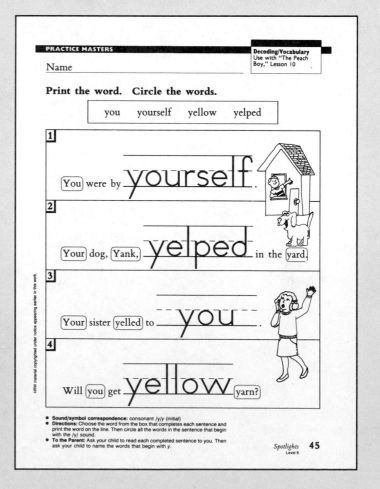

1 You were by **yourself** .

2 Your dog, Yank, **yelped** in the yard.

3 Your sister yelled to **you** .

4 Will you get **yellow** yarn?

- **Sound/symbol correspondence:** consonant /y/y (initial)
- **Directions:** Choose the word from the box that completes each sentence and print the word on the line. Then circle all the words in the sentence that begin with the /y/ sound.
- **To the Parent:** Ask your child to read each completed sentence to you. Then ask your child to name the words that begin with *y*.

Spotlights
Level 6   **45**

Name _____

Circle the word. Print the word.

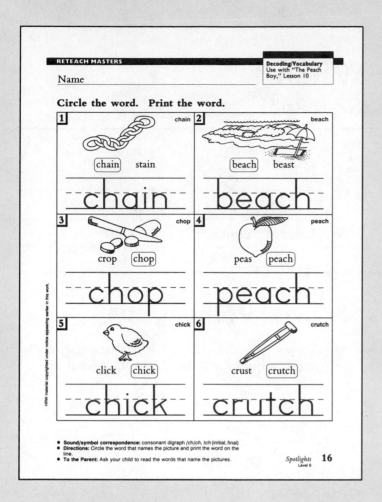

1 chain

chain stain

chain

2 beach

beach beast

beach

3 chop

crop chop

chop

4 peach

peas peach

peach

5 chick

click chick

chick

6 crutch

crust crutch

crutch

- **Sound/symbol correspondence:** consonant digraph /ch/ch, tch (initial, final)
- **Directions:** Circle the word that names the picture and print the word on the line.
- **To the Parent:** Ask your child to read the words that name the pictures.

Spotlights **16**
Level 6

Name _____

Print the word.

giant woman fetch reached

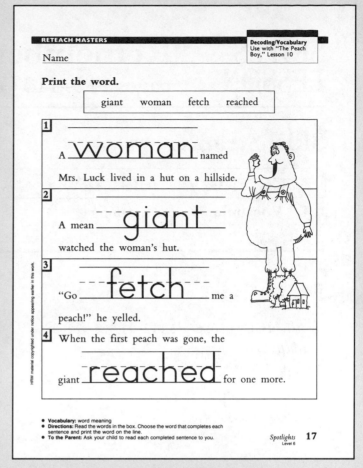

1

A **woman** named

Mrs. Luck lived in a hut on a hillside.

2

A mean **giant**

watched the woman's hut.

3

"Go **fetch** me a

peach!" he yelled.

4 When the first peach was gone, the

giant **reached** for one more.

- **Vocabulary:** word meaning
- **Directions:** Read the words in the box. Choose the word that completes each sentence and print the word on the line.
- **To the Parent:** Ask your child to read each completed sentence to you.

Spotlights **17**
Level 6

SKILLS LESSON

"Remember When"
pages 112–113 (T252–T253)

Skill Strands

DECODING/VOCABULARY
I, T   **Vocabulary:** word meaning

COMPREHENSION/THINKING
M   **Literal:** sequence

Materials

Spotlights, Level 6: pages 112–113
Instructional Charts: page 72–73
Teacher's Idea Book

Special Populations

See *Teacher's Idea Book* for additional suggestions to help pupils with limited English proficiency.

Key to Symbols
I   Introduced in this lesson
R   Reinforced from an earlier lesson in this level
M   Maintained from previous levels
T   Tested in this level

DECODING/VOCABULARY

I, T   **Vocabulary:** word meaning

DIRECT INSTRUCTION Print the following words and sentences on the chalkboard:

> **pictures**
> There are a lot of <u>pictures</u> in this book.
>
> **row**
> The <u>pictures</u> were lined up in a <u>row</u>.

Read the first sentence aloud. Point to the word *pictures* and read it. Ask what the book has. (a lot of pictures) Have pupils read the sentence with you.

Call attention to the word *row* and give pupils a chance to identify it, using what they know about sounds and letters.

GUIDED PRACTICE Have the second sentence read. Ask pupils if the pictures were lined up next to one another. (Yes, they were in a row.) Ask pupils to find and read the word *row*.

Remember When

Look at each <u>row</u> of <u>pictures</u>.
Tell what happens first.
Tell what happens next.
Tell what happens last.

1

112

113

COMPREHENSION/THINKING

M   Literal: sequence

DIRECT INSTRUCTION Print the following sentences on the chalkboard, omitting the answers in parentheses.

 IC 73

(3)	The animals made a lot of noise.
(1)	A little boy was in the peach.
(2)	Peach Boy left for the giant's house.
(4)	The giant ran away.

Have the sentences read. Explain that these sentences tell some things that happened in the story "Peach Boy." Ask which sentence tells what happened first. (*A little boy was in the peach.*) Have a pupil print number 1 in front of this sentence.

Continue by having the other sentences numbered in order. Then have the sentences read in order. Tell pupils that remembering the order of events can make it easier to remember the story.

GUIDED PRACTICE Have pupils find pages 112 and 113 in their books and tell them that this page is called "Remember When." Ask pupils why they think the pages are called "Remember When." (Possible answers include: They are recalling the events of the story they just read; they are remembering when things happened.) Tell pupils to listen as you read the directions, calling attention to the word *pictures.* Then ask pupils to read aloud the directions with you.

Have pupils look at the first row of pictures and describe what happened first, next, and last. First, the woman found a peach floating down the stream; next, the man was happy about having a peach for dinner; last, the peach broke in two, and a little boy was inside.)

Follow a similar procedure with the remaining rows of pictures. As pupils describe what is happening in each picture, they will be retelling the story in their own words.

End-of-Unit 2 Review

(T254–T259)

Skill Strands

DECODING/VOCABULARY

R, T   **Sound/symbol correspondence:** consonant /ks/x (final)

R, T   **Sound/symbol correspondence:** r-controlled vowel /är/ar

R, T   **Sound/symbol correspondence:** vowel /ō/o-e

R, T   **Word structure:** base changes (drop final e and add –ed)

R, T   **Word structure:** contractions (with 're)

R, T   **Vocabulary:** word meaning

COMPREHENSION/THINKING

R, T   **Story structure:** characters (major and minor)

R, T   **Elements of style:** rhyme

Materials

Workbook: pages 70–74

Practice Masters: pages 46–48

Instructional Charts: page 74–77

Resource Box: Word Cards bag, barn, car, far, fast, flat, march, park, ranch, smashed, star

Pocket Chart

Teacher's Idea Book

End-of-Unit 2 Test

Special Populations

See *Teacher's Idea Book* for additional suggestions to help pupils with limited English proficiency.

Key to Symbols

I   Introduced in this lesson

R   Reinforced from an earlier lesson in this level

M   Maintained from previous levels

T   Tested in this level

DECODING/VOCABULARY

R, T   Sound/symbol correspondence: consonant /ks/ *x* (final)

GUIDED PRACTICE   Print the following words and sentences on the chalkboard, omitting the underlining.

> fox
> six
> ax
>
> 1. The <u>fox</u> is in the <u>box</u>.
> 2. Mom can <u>fix</u> the <u>mixer</u>.
> 3. Dad has <u>six</u> nails and one <u>ax</u>.

Point to each word and have it read. Ask what letter is at the end of each word. (*x*) Tell pupils that letter *x* stands for the sound heard at the end of *fox, six,* and *ax.*

Direct pupils' attention to the sentences and have each sentence read. Then call on pupils to point to and read the two words in each sentence that end with the sound of letter *x.*

WB 70   INDEPENDENT PRACTICE   *Workbook* page 70 may be used to practice identifying sound/symbol correspondence /ks/ *x.*

PM 46   ADDITIONAL PRACTICE   *Practice Masters* page 46 may be used as an optional practice for identifying sound/symbol correspondence /ks/ *x.* (See page T259 for reduced pages with answers.)

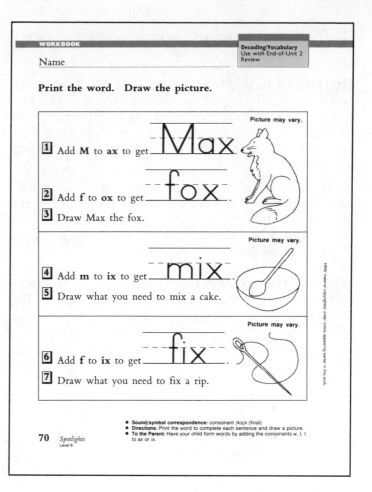

R, T Sound/symbol correspondence: *r-con-trolled vowel /är/ar*

R, T Sound/symbol correspondence: *vowel /ō/o-e*

GUIDED PRACTICE Place *Word Card star* in the *Pocket Chart* and have it read. Display *Word Cards far, fast.* Call on pupils to read each word and to tell which word has the same vowel sound as *star.* (*far*) Place *Word Card far* under *star.* Ask which two letters stand for the /är/ sound. (*ar*)

Display *Word Cards barn, bag, car, park, ranch, march.* Call on a pupil to read a word and to place the card in the *Pocket Chart* under *far* and *star* if the word contains the /är/ sound. Have pupils read the words in the *Pocket Chart.* (*star, far, barn, car, park, march*)

WB 71 INDEPENDENT PRACTICE *Workbook* page 71 may be used to practice identifying sound/symbol correspondence /är/ar.

GUIDED PRACTICE Print the following words on the chalkboard:

hop	rob	not
hope	robe	note
bone	lock	rope	smoke	pond

Point to the words *hop* and *hope* and have them read. Ask what vowel sound can be heard in *hop.* (/o/) Ask what vowel sound can be heard in *hope.* (/ō/) Ask why the letter *o* stands for the long sound of *o* in *hope.* (because *hope* has an *o*, followed by a consonant, and letter *e* is at the end of the word) Point to each of the remaining word pairs and have them read.

Call pupils' attention to the bottom row of words. Have a pupil read each word and tell if *o* stands for the short or the long sound of *o.* Then randomly point to each word on the chalkboard and have it read. (short *o: lock, pond;* long *o: bone, rope, smoke*)

WB 72 INDEPENDENT PRACTICE *Workbook* page 72 may be used to practice identifying sound/symbol correspondence /ō/o-e.

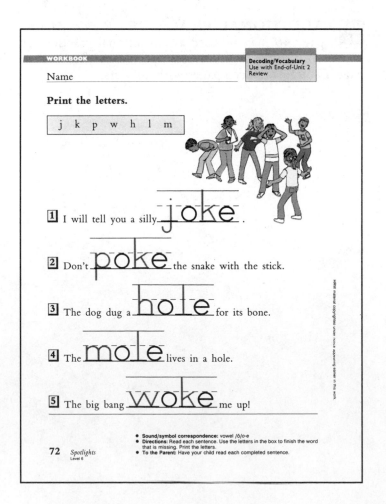

R, T Word structure: base changes (drop final *e* and add *–ed*)

GUIDED PRACTICE Print the following word pairs on the chalkboard:

IC 75

march	bake	hope	smile
marched	baked	hoped	smiled

Point to the first pair of words and have it read. Ask what was added to *march* to make *marched*. (*–ed*) Tell pupils that the ending *-ed* changes a word to mean that something happened in the past.

Point to the second pair of words and have it read. Ask which word tells that something happened in the past. (*baked*) Point out that the word *bake* has an *e* at the end. Tell pupils that to make the word *baked*, the *e* in *bake* was dropped, and the ending *–ed* was added. When a word ends with *e,* the *e* must be dropped before the *–ed* ending is added.

Follow a similar procedure with the remaining word pairs.

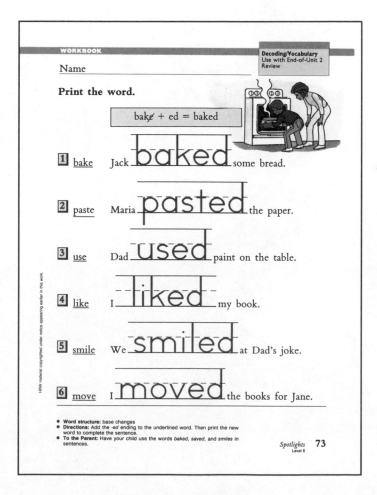

WORKBOOK

Decoding/Vocabulary Use with End-of-Unit 2 Review

Name _____

Print the word.

bak*e* + ed = baked

1. bake Jack **baked** some bread.

2. paste Maria **pasted** the paper.

3. use Dad **used** paint on the table.

4. like I **liked** my book.

5. smile We **smiled** at Dad's joke.

6. move I **moved** the books for Jane.

• **Word structure:** base changes
• **Directions:** Add the *-ed* ending to the underlined word. Then print the new word to complete the sentence.
• **To the Parent:** Have your child use the words *baked, saved,* and *smiles* in sentences.

Spotlights Level 6 **73**

WB 73 INDEPENDENT PRACTICE *Workbook* page 73 may be used to practice dropping the final *e* before adding *-ed*.

PM 48 ADDITIONAL PRACTICE *Practice Masters* page 48 may be used as an optional practice for dropping the final *e* before adding *-ed.* (See page T259 for reduced pages with answers.)

R, T Word structure: contractions (with *'re*)

GUIDED PRACTICE Print the following sentences on the chalkboard and have Sentences 1 and 2 read.

IC 75

1. You are a fast runner.
2. You're a fast runner.

3. We are happy.
4. We're happy.

5. They are in a hurry.
6. They're in a hurry.

Ask what is different about the sentences. (Sentence 2 has the contraction *you're*.) Ask how *You are* was changed to make *You're*. (The two words were put together, and letter *a* was replaced with an apostrophe.) Make sure pupils understand that the contraction *You're* has the same meaning as *You are.*

Follow a similar procedure with Sentences 3–4 and Sentences 5–6.

R, T Vocabulary: word meaning

List vocabulary words from the unit on the chalkboard. (See pages 183–184 in *Spotlights*.) Have pupils write and illustrate rhymes in which some of the words are used. Put the rhymes together in a book and invite pupils to take turns reading their favorite rhymes.

R, T   Story structure: characters (major and minor)

GUIDED PRACTICE   Print the following story on the chalkboard:

> Max has a bike.
> He likes to go fast.
> He puts on a helmet and arm pads
> and rides his bike on a track.
> His friend, Billy, comes
> to watch Max ride.

Ask pupils to read the story and to tell the names of the characters. (Max, Billy) Have pupils identify the major character (Max) and the minor character. (Billy)

INDEPENDENT PRACTICE   *Workbook* page 74 may be used to practice identifying major and minor characters.

R, T   Elements of style: rhyme

GUIDED PRACTICE   Print the following rhymes on the chalkboard:

> 1. Milly had a hat.
>   On it she sat.
>   Now the hat is _____.
>
> 2. Of sweets and treats and such,
>   I sometimes eat too _____.
>
> 3. The dog went to the park.
>   It liked to run and _____.
>
> 4. The giant's skin is green.
>   He is big and _____.

Ask pupils to read the first rhyme. Then display *Word Cards smashed, flat* and ask which word belongs at the end of the rhyme and why. (*Flat* belongs because it rhymes with *hat* and *sat*.)

Call on a pupil to read each remaining rhyme aloud. Then have pupils suggest a word to complete the rhyme and have the completed rhyme read. (Possible answers include: *much, bark, mean.*)

* Administer *End-of-Unit 2 Test.*

WORKBOOK

Comprehension/Thinking
Use with End-of-Unit 2 Review

Name _____

Fill in the circle.

1
Kim likes to sail in her boat.
She has fun sailing and fishing.
Sometimes Kim takes Linda along.

Who is the selection mainly about?
● Kim   ○ Jerome   ○ Linda

2
Pam had a birthday party.
The children at the party gave Pam gifts.
Tommy made her a birthday cake.

Who is the selection mainly about?
○ Tommy   ○ the children   ● Pam

3
Grandfather made a birdhouse.
Grandfather put the seed in the birdhouse.
Then he and Billy watched the birds.

Who is the selection mainly about?
○ Billy   ● Grandfather   ○ birds

● **Story structure:** characters
● **Directions:** Read the stories. Fill in the circle next to the words that answer the questions.
● **To the Parent:** Have your child identify another character in each of the selections.

74   *Spotlights*
     Level 6

Name _____

Circle the words. Print the words.

1 [Max] saw a [fox] in an oak tree.

Max   fox

2 [Max] cut down the oak tree with an [ax].

Max   ax

3 Then [Max] went fishing and got [six] fish.

Max   six

4 He put the [six] fish in a big [box].

six   box

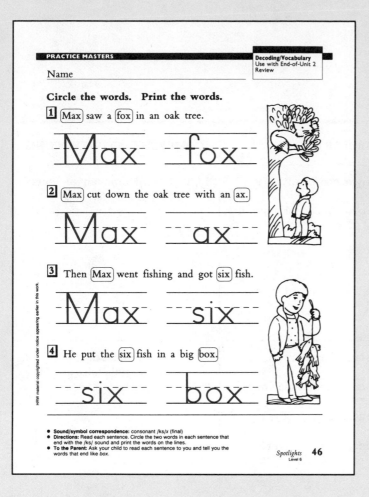

* **Sound/symbol correspondence:** consonant /ks/x (final)
* **Directions:** Read each sentence. Circle the two words in each sentence that end with the /ks/ sound and print the words on the lines.
* **To the Parent:** Ask your child to read each sentence to you and tell you the words that end like *box*.

Spotlights
Level 6   **46**

Name _____

Circle the words. Print the words.

1 Dot's house is [close] to my [home].

close   home

2 One day, I [woke] up and [rode] to Dot's house.

woke   rode

3 A [spoke] on the wheel of my bike [broke].

spoke   broke

4 I [hope] we can fix it with [rope].

hope   rope

* **Sound/symbol correspondence:** vowel /ō/o-e
* **Directions:** Read each sentence. Circle the two words in each sentence that have the /ō/ sound. Print the words on the lines.
* **To the Parent:** Ask your child to read each sentence to you and tell you the words that have the same vowel sound as *hope*.

Spotlights
Level 6   **47**

Name _____

Print the word.

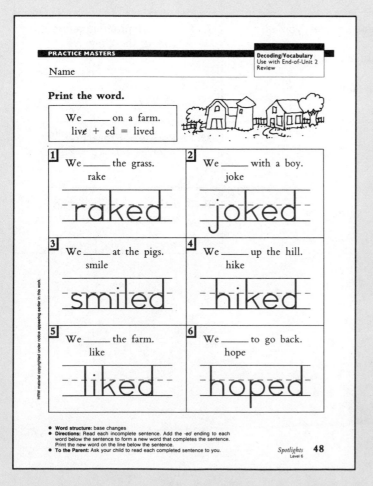

We _____ on a farm.
liv~~e~~ + ed = lived

1 We _____ the grass.
rake

raked

2 We _____ with a boy.
joke

joked

3 We _____ at the pigs.
smile

smiled

4 We _____ up the hill.
hike

hiked

5 We _____ the farm.
like

liked

6 We _____ to go back.
hope

hoped

* **Word structure:** base changes
* **Directions:** Read each incomplete sentence. Add the *-ed* ending to each word below the sentence to form a new word that completes the sentence. Print the new word on the line below the sentence.
* **To the Parent:** Ask your child to read each completed sentence to you.

Spotlights
Level 6   **48**

UNIT 3
OVERVIEW

TITLE	DECODING/VOCABULARY		COMPREHENSION/THINKING	
The Biggest Pumpkin Ever pages 116–125 (T266–T287)	I, T	**Sound/symbol correspondence:** consonant /v/v (initial, medial, final)	(I), T	**Literal:** pronoun referents (*he, it, she, they, we*)
	R, T	**Sound/symbol correspondence:** consonant digraph /ch/ch, tch (initial, final)		
	I	**Vocabulary:** word building		
	I, T	**Vocabulary:** word meaning		
Save the Day! pages 126–127 (T288–T289)	R, T	**Sound/symbol correspondence:** consonant /v/v (initial, final)		
Thumbelina pages 128–137 (T290–T311)	I, T	**Sound/symbol correspondence:** consonant /m/mb (final)	R	**Forms of literature:** folklore (folk tales and fairy tales)
	R, T	**Sound/symbol correspondence:** r-controlled vowel /är/ar		
	I, T	**Sound/symbol correspondence:** vowel /yo͞o/, /o͞o/u–e		
	R	**Sound/symbol correspondence:** vowel discrimination/är/, /ûr/		
	I	**Vocabulary:** word building		
	I, T	**Vocabulary:** word meaning		
Toot! Toot! pages 138–147 (T312–T333)	R, T	**Sound/symbol correspondence:** vowel /yo͞o/, /o͞o/u–e	R, T	**Literal:** pronoun referents (*he, it, she, they, we*)
	R, T	**Word structure:** contractions (with *'re*)		
	I, T	**Word structure:** suffix *-ly*		
	(I), T	**Vocabulary:** antonyms and synonyms		
	I, T	**Vocabulary:** word meaning		
Trains pages 148–149 (T334–T335)			M	**Forms of literature:** poetry
Going to Grandma's pages 150–151 (T336–T337)			R, T	**Inferential:** predicting outcomes

(I) Expanded treatment of skill introduced at a previous level

Key to Symbols
I Introduced in this lesson
R Reinforced from an earlier lesson in this level
M Maintained from previous levels
T Tested in this level

STUDY SKILLS	LANGUAGE	LANGUAGE APPLICATIONS
M Organizing information: written directions **M Study aids:** summarizing	**M Conventions of language:** commas in direct address	**Oral reading:** expression **Writing:** recipes (Cooperative Learning) **Listening:** fiction; poetry
M Graphic aids: maps	**I Writing:** descriptive sentences	**Oral reading:** readers theater **Speaking:** acting out a play; role playing **Listening:** poetry; fiction
	R Writing: descriptive sentences	**Oral reading:** details **Writing:** descriptive sentences (Cooperative Learning) **Speaking:** role playing **Listening:** fiction

UNIT 3 OVERVIEW (Continued)

TITLE	DECODING/VOCABULARY	COMPREHENSION/THINKING
Happy Mother's Day pages 152–161 (T338–T357)	**I, T** **Sound/symbol correspondence:** consonant /kw/ *qu* (initial, medial) **M** **Accumulated elements:** consonant clusters *bl, cl, fl, gl, sl* (initial); *ld, lk, lp, lt* (final) **R, T** **Word structure:** suffix *-ly* **R, T** **Vocabulary:** antonyms and synonyms **I** **Vocabulary:** word building **I, T** **Vocabulary:** word meaning	**M** **Inferential:** drawing conclusions
Hiding pages 162–163 (T358–T359)		**R, T** **Forms of literature:** poetry
Gifts to Make pages 164–169 (T360–T377)	**R, T** **Sound/symbol correspondence:** consonant /kw/ *qu* (initial, medial) **I, T** **Sound/symbol correspondence:** consonant /z/z, *zz* (initial, medial, final) **M** **Vocabulary:** homophones **I** **Vocabulary:** word building **I, T** **Vocabulary:** word meaning	**M** **Literal:** details
End-of-Unit Review (T378–T385) NOTE: These skills are tested in the *End-of-Unit 3 Test*.	*R, T **Sound/symbol correspondence:** consonant /m/*mb* (final) *R, T **Sound/symbol correspondence:** consonant /kw/ *qu* (initial, medial) *R, T **Sound/symbol correspondence:** consonant /v/v (initial) *R, T **Sound/symbol correspondence:** consonant /z/z, *zz* (initial, medial) *R, T **Sound/symbol correspondence:** consonant digraph /ch/*ch, tch* (initial, final) *R, T **Sound/symbol correspondence:** vowel /yōo/, /ōo/u-e *R, T **Word structure:** suffix *–ly* *R, T **Vocabulary:** antonyms and synonyms *R, T **Vocabulary:** word meaning	*R, T **Literal:** pronoun referents

Ⓘ Expanded treatment of skill introduced at a previous level
* Tested in *End-of-Book Test*

Key to Symbols

I Introduced in this lesson
R Reinforced from an earlier lesson in this level
M Maintained from previous levels
T Tested in this level

STUDY SKILLS	LANGUAGE	LANGUAGE APPLICATIONS
M Organizing information: classification	**R Speaking:** paraphrasing	**Oral reading:** expression **Writing:** stories (Cooperative Learning) **Listening:** fiction
M Graphic aids: illustrations	**M Writing:** language–experience stories	**Oral reading:** directions **Independent reading:** following written directions (Cooperative Learning)

Materials

Spotlights, Level 6: pages 114–115
Teacher's Idea Book

Special Populations

See *Teacher's Idea Book* for additional suggestions to help pupils with limited English proficiency.

Using Prior Knowledge

Have pupils turn to pages 114 and 115 of *Spotlights.* Tell pupils that the last unit in *Spotlights* is called "Surprises." Ask them what a surprise is. (something you don't expect) Ask what might surprise someone. (Answers will vary. Possible answers include: a present, a special party.) Have pupils look at the picture on page 114. Ask what kinds of surprises this picture reminds them of. (Possible answers include: birthdays, presents, surprise parties.)

Direct pupils' attention to page 115. Indicate the list of stories that are in this unit and tell pupils that each of these stories has to do with the idea of a surprise. Read the name of each story and ask how the story might tell about a surprise. (Possible answers include: "Happy Mother's Day" might tell about a Mother's Day surprise; "The Biggest Pumpkin Ever" might tell about a Halloween surprise.) Encourage pupils to share their ideas with the class. Point out that they will learn if their guesses are right or wrong as they read the stories.

Tell pupils that the stories in this unit were written by Steven Kroll. You may want to share the following information about the author.

Steven Kroll believes that he is able to write for children because he is in touch with his own childhood and is still able to appreciate the wonder that a child feels with each new experience. His stories communicate this childhood wonder in a light-hearted way. Mr. Kroll enjoys writing children's stories because they allow him to stretch his imagination and to explore the fanciful as well as the real.

Several of Steven Kroll's books have been listed in *Children's Choices* by the International Reading Council/Children's Book Council Joint Committee, including *Amanda and the Giggling Ghost, If I Could Be My Grandmother, The Tryannosaurus,* and *The Biggest Pumpkin Ever.*

114

SURPRISES

adapted from stories
by Steven Kroll

"The Biggest Pumpkin Ever"

"Thumbelina"

"Toot! Toot!"

"Happy Mother's Day"

"Gifts to Make"

115

LESSON 11

"The Biggest Pumpkin Ever"
pages 116–125 (T266–T287)

Skill Strands

DECODING/VOCABULARY

I, T   **Sound/symbol correspondence:** consonant /v/*v* (initial, medial, final)

R, T   **Sound/symbol correspondence:** consonant digraph /ch/*ch,tch* (initial, final)

I   **Vocabulary:** word building

I, T   **Vocabulary:** word meaning

STUDY SKILLS

M   **Organizing information:** written directions

M   **Study aids:** summarizing

COMPREHENSION/THINKING

Focus

I, T   **Literal:** pronoun referents (*he, it, she, they, we*)

LANGUAGE

M   **Conventions of language:** commas in direct address

Lesson Vocabulary

Decodable words: *become, blanket, Clayton, contest, cover, crept, dark, deal, Desmond, explained, fact, fed, frost, garden, gave, hummed, hundred, jack-o'-lantern, pumpkin, shrugged, skill, tracks, van, vine, within*

Special words: *carved, field, love, mice, sure, very, village*

Materials

Spotlights, Level 6: pages 116–125
Workbook: pages 75–80
Practice Masters: pages 49–51
Instructional Charts: pages 78–84
Resource Box: Letter Cards: *a, b, e, i, n, s, t, v*
           Word Cards: *carved, champ, chase, chimp, chip, field, itch, love, match, mice, much, patch, sure, very, village*
Pocket Chart
Teacher's Idea Book
Reteach Masters: page 18

Language Applications

USING LANGUAGE

Oral reading: expression

EXTENDING SELECTION CONCEPTS

Writing: recipes (Cooperative Learning)
Listening: fiction
Listening: poetry

Special Populations

See *Teacher's Idea Book* for additional suggestions to help pupils with limited English proficiency.

Key to Symbols

I   Introduced in this lesson
R   Reinforced from an earlier lesson in this level
M   Maintained from previous levels
T   Tested in this level

Idea Center

BIBLIOGRAPHY

Add to your reading corner or reading table various books about pumpkins. A suggested bibliography follows. Suggestions for reading aloud and annotations appear in the lesson plan.

Johnston, Tony. *The Vanishing Pumpkin.* Putnam, 1983.

Titherington, Jeanne. *Pumpkin, Pumpkin.* Greenwillow, 1986.

Tudor, Tasha. *Pumpkin Moonshine.* Walck, 1962.

Planning Chart

	Instruction	Written Practice	Extending
Step 1 Preparing for the Selection	**I, T Sound/symbol correspondence:** consonant /v/v (initial, medial, final) **I Vocabulary:** word building **I, T Vocabulary:** word meaning **I, T Literal:** pronoun referents (*he, it, she, they, we*)	*Workbook* page 75 *Practice Masters* page 49 *Workbook* page 76 *Practice Masters* page 50 *Reteach Masters* page 18	
Step 2 Reading for Comprehension	**Oral reading:** expression **Literal:** pronoun referents (*he, it, she, they, we*) **Story comprehension**	*Workbook* page 77	
Step 3 Developing Reading and Thinking Skills	**R, T Sound/symbol correspondence:** consonant digraph /ch/ch, tch (initial, final) **I, T Literal:** pronoun referents (*he, it, she, they, we*) **M Organizing information:** written directions **M Study aids:** summarizing **M Conventions of language:** commas in direct address	*Workbook* page 78 *Workbook* page 79 *Practice Masters* page 51 *Workbook* page 80	**Writing:** recipes (Cooperative Learning) **Listening:** fiction **Listening:** poetry

1 PREPARING FOR THE SELECTION

DECODING/VOCABULARY

I, T   Sound/symbol correspondence: consonant /v/*v* (initial, medial, final)

DIRECT INSTRUCTION   Print the following sentence and words on the chalkboard:

In Val's vase are seven vines.
gave   carve
van   vest   ever   visit
gave   vote   vet   never

Read the sentence. Ask what is in the vase. (*seven vines*) Point to the word *vase* and read it.

> **SAY**   **The word *vase* begins with the letter *v*. Letter *v* stands for the /v/ sound. Can you find other words in this sentence that begin with the /v/ sound?** (*Val's, vase*) **What letter stands for the /v/ sound?** (*v*)

Point out that one word in the sentence has the letter *v* in the middle. Call on a pupil to find and read the word that has the letter *v* in the middle. (*seven*) Then have the sentence read aloud.

> **SAY**   **Say the word *gave* with me: *gave*. Where do you hear the /v/ sound in *gave*?** (*at the end*) **Say the word *carve* with me: *carve*. Where do you hear the /v/ sound in *carve*?** (*at the end*)

Indicate the words *gave* and *carve* on the chalkboard. Explain that the /v/ sound is heard at the end of *gave* and *carve* because the letter *e* is silent.

GUIDED PRACTICE   Direct pupils' attention to the rows of words on the chalkboard. Point to each word and have it read. Then have pupils read the words as you point to them at random.

Read the following incomplete sentences and have pupils select from the chalkboard the word that belongs in each sentence. The answers in parentheses are provided for your convenience.

1. **An animal doctor is a _____.** (*vet*)
2. **We like to ride in the _____.** (*van*)
3. **Sandy likes to _____ her grandparents.** (*visit*)
4. **The princess lived happily _____ after.** (*ever*)
5. **The man wore a _____ over his shirt.** (*vest*)
6. **Mr. Smith _____ the dog a bone.** (*gave*)
7. **We will _____ for the one we like best.** (*vote*)
8. **The school bus is _____ late.** (*never*)

WB 75   INDEPENDENT PRACTICE   *Workbook page 75 may be used to practice identifying sound/symbol correspondence /v/v.*

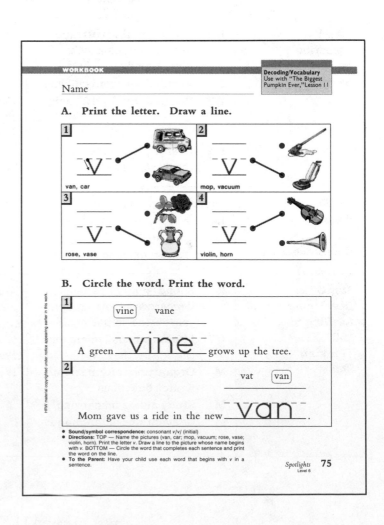

PM 49 **ADDITIONAL PRACTICE** *Practice Masters* page 49 may be used as an optional practice for identifying sound/symbol correspondence /v/v. (See page T286 for reduced pages with answers.)

✱ **RETEACH** For those pupils who need additional instruction, see "Reteaching Lesson Skills," page T283, under "Reteaching and Extending."

I Vocabulary: word building

DIRECT INSTRUCTION Place *Letter Cards* in the *Pocket Chart* to make the word *van*. Ask pupils to name the beginning letter and to tell what sound it stands for. (*v*; /v/) Then have the word read. Ask how a van might be used. (Possible answers include: People can ride in it; it can hold camping equipment.)

GUIDED PRACTICE Display *Letter Cards b, e, i, s, t*. Tell pupils that you will call on them to use the letter cards to change the word in the *Pocket Chart*.

1. **Take away *v* from *van*. What is the new word?** (*an*)
2. **Replace *a* with *i*. What word did you make?** (*in*)
3. **Put *v* at the beginning of the word and put *e* at the end. What word did you make?** (*vine*)
4. **Replace *in* with *as*. What is the new word?** (*vase*)
5. **Replace *e* with *t*. What is the new word?** (*vast*) *Vast* means "very big."
6. **Replace *a* with *e*. What is the new word?** (*vest*)
7. **Replace *v* with *b* What is the new word?** (*best*)
8. **Replace *b* with *n*. What is the new word?** (*nest*)
9. **Replace *n* with *v*. What word did you make?** (*vest*)

I, T Vocabulary: word meaning

DIRECT INSTRUCTION Tell pupils that they are going to talk about some words they will read in the next story. Print the following words and sentences on the chalkboard, omitting the underlining.

> **carved   field   love   mice**
> **sure   very   village**
>
> 1. One mouse lived in a <u>village</u>.
> 2. One mouse lived in a <u>field</u>.
> 3. The <u>mice</u> were <u>very</u> good friends.
> 4. "Come see what I <u>carved</u>!" said the field mouse.
> 5. "That pumpkin <u>sure</u> is funny," said his friend.
> 6. "I <u>love</u> it!"
>
> **cover   crept   gave**
> **jack-o'-lantern   van   vine**

Read Sentence 1. Then point to the word *village* and read it. Ask what a village is. (A village is a town.) Ask what lived in this village. (a mouse) Call on pupils to find and read *village* and then have the sentence read aloud.

Read Sentence 2. Then point to the word *field* and read it. Explain that a field is a large, open space with no buildings. Parks have fields, and farms have fields. Ask what lives in this field. (a mouse) Call on pupils to find and read *field* and then have the sentence read aloud.

Read Sentence 3. Then point to the word *mice* and read it. Explain that *mice* means "more than one mouse." Point to the word *very* and read it. Ask if the village mouse and the field mouse knew each other. (Yes, they were very good friends.) Have pupils point to and read *mice* and *very*. Then have the sentence read aloud.

Read Sentence 4 aloud. Then point to the word *carved* and read it. Ask what is used to carve something. (a knife) Ask pupils to find and read *carved*. Then have the sentence read aloud.

Read Sentence 5. Then point to the word *sure* and read it. Ask what the field mouse carved. (a pumpkin) Ask how someone might carve a pumpkin. (Someone might carve a face in a pumpkin to make a jack-o'-lantern.) Ask pupils to find and read *sure*. Have the sentence read aloud.

Read Sentence 6. Then point to the word *love* and read it. Ask what the mouse loved. (the funny pumpkin) Ask pupils to find and read the word *love* and then have the sentence read aloud.

The words in the second set are new words that contain known phonic elements. You may wish to ask pupils to read the words, using what they know about letters and sounds.

GUIDED PRACTICE Print the following sentences on the chalkboard, omitting the underlining.

> 1. Clayton <u>carved</u> the <u>very</u> big pumpkin on the <u>vine</u>.
> 2. "I <u>sure</u> <u>love</u> to carve a <u>jack-o'-lantern!</u>" he <u>explained</u> to his dad.
> 3. Clayton's dad <u>gave</u> him the <u>van</u> to go into the <u>village</u>.
> 4. Clayton hummed as he loaded the pumpkin into the van.
> 5. Just then, a hundred <u>field</u> <u>mice</u> <u>crept</u> into the garden.
> 6. "I'll <u>cover</u> my pumpkin so they don't see it!" said Clayton.

Provide opportunities for pupils to practice reading the new special words and some of the new decodable words in these sentences by following the suggestions below.

Sentences 1–2: Have the sentences read. Call on pupils to find and read the words with the /v/ sound. *(carved, very, vine, love, carve)* Ask what a jack-o'-lantern is. (a pumpkin that has a face carved into it)

Sentences 3–4: After the sentences have been read, ask if Clayton was happy. (Yes, he hummed.) Then ask where Clayton was going. (into the village)

Sentences 5–6: Have the sentences read aloud. Call on a pupil to find and read the word *field*. Ask what went into the garden. (a hundred field mice) Ask which word means "sneaked." *(crept)* Call on pupils to tell what Clayton did so the field mice would not see the pumpkin. (He covered it.)

Invite pupils to read a sentence, to name the words that have the /v/ sound, and to tell where the /v/ sound is heard in each word.

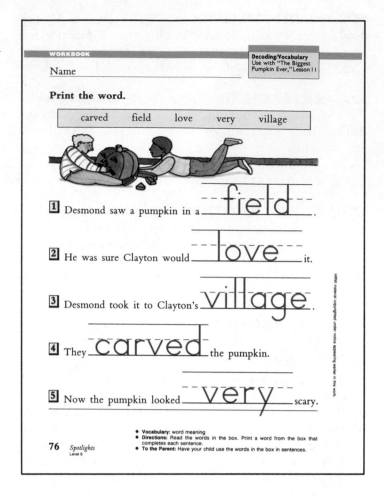

INDEPENDENT PRACTICE *Workbook* page 76 may be used to practice reading story vocabulary.

ADDITIONAL PRACTICE *Practice Masters* page 50 may be used as an optional practice for reading story vocabulary. (See page T286 for reduced pages with answers.)

RETEACH For those pupils who need additional instruction, see "Reteaching Lesson Skills," page T284, under "Reteaching and Extending."

COMPREHENSION/THINKING

Focus

I, T **Literal:** pronoun referents (*he, it, she, they, we*)

DIRECT INSTRUCTION Print the following sentences on the chalkboard and have them read.

1. Timmy saw a pumpkin.
2. It was very big.
3. He carried it home.

4. Chuck and Carla planted pumpkin seeds.
5. They put water on the seeds.

6. Then a little vine started to grow.
7. One day, little pumpkins were on it.

8. Chuck and Carla each picked a pumpkin.
9. She will make a jack-o'-lantern.
10. He will make pumpkin muffins.

ASK **What was very big?** (the pumpkin) **Which word in the second sentence takes the place of *pumpkin*?** (*It*) **The word *It* is called a pronoun. A pronoun is a word that can be used instead of the name of a person or a thing. In the second sentence, the word *It* is used instead of the word *pumpkin*.**

Point to the word *He* in the third sentence and tell pupils that *He* is also a pronoun. Ask who carried something home. (Timmy) Explain that the word *He* is used instead of the name *Timmy*. Point to the word *it* in the third sentence and ask which word *it* stands for. (*pumpkin*)

GUIDED PRACTICE Direct pupils' attention to Sentences 4–10 on the chalkboard.

Have Sentences 4–5 read. Then ask which word in Sentence 5 is underlined. (*They*) Ask which word or words *They* replaces. (*Chuck and Carla*)

Have each remaining group of sentences read and ask pupils to tell which word or words each underlined word replaces. (*it—vine; She—Carla; He—Chuck*)

Background for the Teacher

SUMMARY   Clayton the field mouse finds a pumpkin growing in a garden and decides to care for it. Desmond, unknown to Clayton, is caring for the same pumpkin. When the pumpkin becomes huge, each mouse has a different plan for it. However, they come to a compromise that makes them both happy.

INFORMATION   This story was adapted from the book of the same title. The story contains narrative prose and dialogue by which the reader is able to understand the plans and thoughts of two field mice.

Using Prior Knowledge

Tell pupils that the next story in *Spotlights* is about two mice and one big pumpkin. Develop a discussion by asking questions such as those that follow.

1. **Sometimes two people like the same stuffed animal or toy. What might people do when this happens?** (Possible answers include: share it, take turns playing with it.)
2. **When two people disagree about the way to do something, what should they do?** (Encourage pupils to suggest that the people should talk about their problem and find a way that they can both agree.)

Setting a Purpose for Reading

Have pupils look at the picture on page 116. Have the title of the story read. Tell pupils that a pumpkin grows on a vine. Then ask pupils to tell how people can help a plant grow. (Possible answers include: water and care for it; give it plant food.)

Point out the headnote at the top of page 116. Tell pupils that this note will help them think about the story they are about to read. Have the note read aloud. Encourage pupils to predict what might surprise the mice. (Answers will vary. Possible answers include: a jack-o'-lantern, a cat.)

Reading Silently

Some pupils may be able to read this story independently. Direct them to read the whole story to find out more about Clayton and Desmond and a very big pumpkin. For those pupils who need more guidance, suggestions for directed reading follow.

Clayton and Desmond are two mice who are in for some surprises.
Read to find out what happens.

The Biggest Pumpkin Ever

One day, two mice fell in love with the same pumpkin.

Clayton, the village mouse, saw it on the vine in his mother's garden.

It was still little and green, but Clayton was sure he could make it grow very big.

Maybe it could get so big that it could win the ribbon at the pumpkin contest.

116

Desmond, the field mouse, happened upon the same pumpkin on the same day.

He was sure that if he helped it grow, it could become the biggest jack-o'-lantern he ever carved.

117

Before reading pages 116–117

SAY **Clayton was a mouse that lived in a village, and Desmond was a mouse that lived in a field. Read pages 116 and 117 to yourself to see what they both found.**

After reading pages 116–117

1. **What did Clayton and Desmond both find?** (They both found the same pumpkin.) Literal
2. **What did each mouse want to do with the pumpkin?** (Clayton wanted to win a ribbon at the pumpkin contest; Desmond wanted to carve a big jack-o'-lantern.) Inferential
3. **What did each mouse decide to do?** (Each one wanted to help the pumpkin grow.) Literal

So that day, Clayton watered the pumpkin.

Then he put plant food in the dirt by the pumpkin vine.

After <u>dark</u>, Desmond <u>crept</u> into the garden.

He watered the pumpkin and <u>gave</u> it some plant food, too.

The next day, Clayton watered and <u>fed</u> the pumpkin.

The next evening, Desmond did the same thing.

The pumpkin started to grow.

118

Clayton's mother went to see the pumpkin.

"My word!" she said.

"All I do is water and feed it," Clayton said.

That evening, Desmond's dad went to see the pumpkin, too.

"That's some pumpkin!"

"All I do is water and feed it," Desmond said.

<u>Within</u> two weeks, the pumpkin was the biggest one Clayton had ever seen.

All his friends in the village came to see it.

119

Before reading pages 118–119

SAY **Both mice wanted to take care of the pumpkin. What do you think will happen? Read pages 118 and 119 to find out.**

After reading pages 118–119

1. **What happened to the pumpkin?** (The pumpkin grew and grew because Clayton and Desmond were both watering and feeding it.) Inferential

2. **Why didn't Clayton and Desmond know that they both were feeding the pumpkin?** (Clayton worked in the day, and Desmond worked at night.) Inferential

That evening, Desmond and his dad spent a long time looking at the pumpkin.

"How do you think it got so big?" Desmond asked.

His dad <u>shrugged</u>.
"A little luck, a little <u>skill</u>."

"I can't wait to carve it!" said Desmond.

The pumpkin was growing fast. In <u>fact</u>, it was even bigger than Clayton's house.

How would he get it to the village for the contest?

"It's even too big to fit in my dad's <u>van</u>!" he said.
"I'll have to think of something."

120

Late one evening, it got very cold.

Thinking there was going to be a <u>frost</u>, Clayton rushed out to <u>cover</u> the pumpkin.

One <u>blanket</u> wouldn't cover the pumpkin, so he went back for all the blankets he could find.

As he worked, he <u>hummed</u>. Then he stopped. Someone else was humming. Someone else was covering the pumpkin, too!

121

Before reading pages 120–121

| SAY | **What problems do you think Clayton and Desmond will have with such a big pumpkin? Read pages 120 and 121 to yourself.**

After reading pages 120–121

1. **What was Clayton worried about?** (He was worried about how he would get the pumpkin to the village for the contest.) Literal
2. **Why were Clayton and Desmond both in the garden at the same time?** (They both wanted to cover the pumpkin to protect it from the frost.) Inferential

Desmond stopped humming. Someone else was covering the pumpkin, too.

Clayton put down his blankets and peeked on the other side of the pumpkin.

Desmond put down his blankets and peeked on the other side of the pumpkin.

The two mice bumped into one another and fell down.

122

"You have been feeding the pumpkin," said Clayton.

"You have been feeding the pumpkin," said Desmond.

"That's why it got so big," said Clayton.

"That's why it got so big," said Desmond.

Clayton <u>explained</u> that he wanted to win the pumpkin contest.
"I know I'll win if I can just get the pumpkin to the village," he said.

"I'll help you," said Desmond.
"Just let me carve the pumpkin into a jack-o'-lantern when the contest is over."

"It's a <u>deal</u>," said Clayton.

123

Before reading pages 122–123

Do you think Clayton and Desmond will see each other? Read pages 122 and 123.

After reading pages 122–123

1. **How did the mice find each other?** (Each mouse heard the other one humming; they both peeked around the pumpkin; and they bumped into each other.) Inferential
2. **Were Clayton and Desmond upset when they discovered each other? Why or why not?** (No, they knew that the pumpkin was so big because they had both been feeding it; they could both use the pumpkin in the way they wanted if they took turns.) Inferential
3. **How were the mice going to help each other?** (Desmond would help Clayton take the pumpkin to the village for the contest; then Clayton would let Desmond carve the pumpkin into a jack-o'-lantern.) Inferential

On the day of the contest, mice came from all over.

Some came in cars, and some came in trucks.

All of a sudden, everyone stopped in their <u>tracks</u>.

Over the fields came the biggest pumpkin anyone had ever seen.

It was being pulled by a <u>hundred</u> field mice.

Everyone went into the fields to see the pumpkin.

Clayton's pumpkin got the ribbon!

124

When the contest was over, the hundred field mice pulled the pumpkin back to the garden.

Then Desmond carved the best jack-o'-lantern ever.

That evening, its smile could be seen glowing for miles!

Discussing the Selection

1. In what ways were Clayton and Desmond surprised?
2. What did each mouse want to do with the pumpkin?
3. Why did the pumpkin grow so big?
4. When did you know that Clayton and Desmond both got what they wanted?
5. In this story, what could have happened in real life?

125

Before reading pages 124–125

What happened at the pumpkin contest? Read pages 124 and 125 to find out.

After reading pages 124–125

1. **What happened at the contest?** (Clayton won.) Literal
2. **How did Clayton get the pumpkin to the contest?** (A hundred field mice pulled it.) Literal
3. **Did everything work out for Clayton and Desmond?** (Yes, Clayton won the blue ribbon, and Desmond carved the best jack-o'-lantern ever.) Inferential

Discussing the Selection

Questions preceded by a number appear in *Spotlights* after the selection. Questions preceded by a bullet are additional questions for extending discussion.

PURPOSE

1. **In what ways were Clayton and Desmond surprised?** (They were surprised that the pumpkin grew so big; they were each surprised to find that someone else was taking care of the pumpkin.) Inferential

STORY MAPPING

2. **What did each mouse want to do with the pumpkin?** (Clayton wanted to win a blue ribbon for the biggest pumpkin; Desmond wanted to carve the pumpkin into a jack-o'-lantern.) Inferential

3. **Why did the pumpkin grow so big?** (Clayton was giving the pumpkin water and plant food every day, and Desmond was giving it water and plant food every night.) Inferential

4. **When did you know that Clayton and Desmond both got what they wanted?** (Possible answers include: at the bottom of page 123, where the two mice made a deal; at the end of the story, when Clayton won the prize and Desmond carved the pumpkin.) Inferential

CRITICAL THINKING

5. **In this story, what could have happened in real life?** (Possible answers include: Two people might care for the same pumpkin; there are contests for the biggest and best vegetables; many people really do carve pumpkins into jack-o'-lanterns.)
- **How would the ending of this story have been different if Clayton and Desmond had not made a deal?** (Answers will vary. Possible answers include: They would not have both gotten their own way.)

Using Language

ORAL READING: EXPRESSION Have pupils turn to page 116 and ask who the major characters in the story were. (two mice named Clayton and Desmond) Have pupils read the lines on page 116 that tell what Clayton thought he could do with the pumpkin. (It was still little and green, but Clayton was sure he could make it grow very big. Maybe it could get so big that it could win the ribbon at the pumpkin contest.)

Follow a similar procedure with the remaining pages by having pupils read parts from the story that answer the questions below.

Page 117: Ask pupils to read the lines that tell what Desmond thought he could do with the pumpkin. (He was sure that if he helped it grow, it could become the biggest jack-o'-lantern he ever carved.)

Page 118: Ask one pupil to read the lines that tell how Clayton cared for the pumpkin. (So that day, Clayton watered the pumpkin. Then he put plant food in the dirt by the pumpkin vine.) Ask another pupil to read the lines that tell how Desmond cared for it. (He watered the pumpkin and gave it some plant food, too.)

Page 119: Ask a pupil to read what Clayton's mother said. ("My word!" she said.) Then have a pupil read what Desmond's father said. ("That's some pumpkin!")

Page 120: Ask a pupil to read what Desmond asked his dad. ("How do you think it got so big?") Then have his dad's answer read. ("A little luck, a little skill.")

Pages 121 and 122: Call on pupils to read aloud the pages.

Page 123: Have pupils play the parts of Clayton and Desmond and read the lines on the page as the characters may have said them.

Page 124: Have pupils read the sentence that tells how the mice came to the contest. (Some came in cars, and some came in trucks.)

Page 125: Have pupils read the sentences that tell what happened to the pumpkin after the contest. (When the contest was over, the hundred field mice pulled the pumpkin back to the garden. Then Desmond carved the best jack-o'-lantern ever.)

Applying the Focus Skill

LITERAL: PRONOUN REFERENTS Remind pupils that some words can take the place of the name of a person or the name of a thing. These words are called pronouns.

Ask pupils to turn to page 116 in their books and have the first two sentences read. Ask what was on the vine. (the pumpkin) Ask what word in the second sentence takes the place of the word *pumpkin*. (*it*) Have the third sentence read aloud and ask who could make the pumpkin grow. (Clayton) Ask what word in the third sentence takes the place of Clayton's name. (*he*)

Have pupils turn to page 119 and ask who said "My word!" (Clayton's mother) Ask what word in the second sentence takes the place of the words *Clayton's mother*. (*she*)

Evaluating Comprehension

WB 77 **INDEPENDENT PRACTICE** *Workbook* page 77 may be used for an informal evaluation of story comprehension.

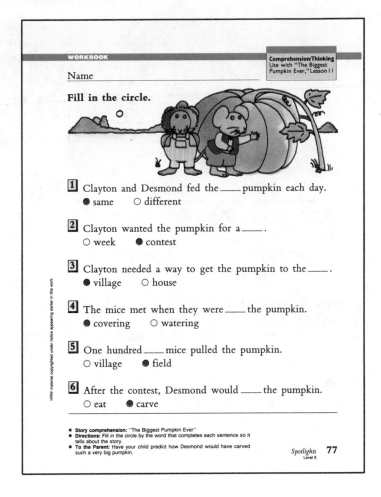

WORKBOOK

Comprehension/Thinking
Use with "The Biggest
Pumpkin Ever," Lesson 11

Name _____

Fill in the circle.

1 Clayton and Desmond fed the ____ pumpkin each day.
● same   ○ different

2 Clayton wanted the pumpkin for a ____.
○ week   ● contest

3 Clayton needed a way to get the pumpkin to the ____.
● village   ○ house

4 The mice met when they were ____ the pumpkin.
● covering   ○ watering

5 One hundred ____ mice pulled the pumpkin.
○ village   ● field

6 After the contest, Desmond would ____ the pumpkin.
○ eat   ● carve

- **Story comprehension:** "The Biggest Pumpkin Ever"
- **Directions:** Fill in the circle by the word that completes each sentence so it tells about the story.
- **To the Parent:** Have your child predict how Desmond would have carved such a very big pumpkin.

Spotlights **77**
Level 6

3 DEVELOPING READING AND THINKING SKILLS

DECODING/VOCABULARY

R, T   Sound/symbol correspondence: consonant digraph /ch/ch,tch (initial, final)

DIRECT INSTRUCTION   Place *Word Card chip* in the *Pocket Chart* and have it read. Point out that the word *chip* begins with the /ch/ sound. Ask what two letters together stand for the /ch/ sound in *chip*. (*ch*)

Place *Word Card patch* in the *Pocket Chart* and have it read. Ask where the /ch/ sound is heard in *patch*. (at the end) Point out that letter *t* is in front of the *ch* in *patch*. Remind pupils that the letters *tch* stand for the /ch/ sound at the end of some words.

GUIDED PRACTICE   Hold up the following *Word Cards* that contain the /ch/ sound and ask pupils to read each word and tell what letters stand for the /ch/ sound: *champ, much, chase, match, itch, chimp.*

WB 78   INDEPENDENT PRACTICE   *Workbook* page 78 may be used to practice identifying consonant digraph /ch/ch, tch.

✳ RETEACH   For those pupils who need additional instruction, see "Reteaching Lesson Skills," page T283, under "Reteaching and Extending."

COMPREHENSION/THINKING

Focus

I, T   Literal: pronoun referents (*he, it, she, they, we*)

DIRECT INSTRUCTION   Print the following words and sentences on the chalkboard:

Marsha	it
jack-o'-lantern	he
Billy	they
Jack and Jill	she

1. <u>Jim</u> had a garden.
2. <u>The garden</u> was hard work.
3. One day, <u>Betty</u> came to help Jim.
4. <u>Jim and Betty</u> worked together.

Remind pupils that a pronoun takes the place of the name of a person or a thing. Have the two columns of words read. Point to the word *Marsha.* Ask which pronoun on the right could take the place of the name *Marsha.* (*she*)

Continue in the same manner with the remaining names and pronouns. (*jack-o'-lantern–it, Billy–he, Jack and Jill–they*)

WORKBOOK

Name _____

Decoding/Vocabulary
Use with "The Biggest Pumpkin Ever," Lesson 11

A.   Circle the pictures.

1. chest | cherry | car | chick | sock
2. coach | van | peach | cat | bench
3. match | watch | duck | mop | patch

B.   Circle the word.   Print the word.

1. chat | [catch]
   Can you **catch** the ball?
2. [cheek] | check
   Mom kissed me on the **cheek**.
3. batch | [beach]
   I like to play at the **beach**.

- Sound/symbol correspondence: consonant digraph /ch/ch, tch (initial, final)
- **Directions:** TOP — Name the pictures (chest, cherry, car, chick, sock; coach, van, peach, cat, bench; match, watch, duck, mop, patch). Circle the pictures in the row whose names contain /ch/. BOTTOM — Circle the word that completes each sentence and print the word on the line.
- **To the Parent:** Say pairs of words. Have your child identify the word that has the same beginning or ending sound as *cherry*.

78   *Spotlights* Level 6

GUIDED PRACTICE Indicate the sentences on the chalkboard. Have the first sentence read and ask which pronoun could be used to take the place of the underlined word. (*he*) Have the sentence reread, using the pronoun instead of the name.

Follow a similar procedure with the remaining sentences (2. *It*, 3. *she*, 4. *they*)

WB 79 **INDEPENDENT PRACTICE** *Workbook* page 79 may be used to practice identifying pronoun referents.

PM 51 **ADDITIONAL PRACTICE** *Practice Masters* page 51 may be used as an optional practice for identifying pronoun referents. (See page T287 for reduced pages with answers.)

✱ **RETEACH** For those pupils who need additional instruction, see "Reteaching Lesson Skills," page T284, under "Reteaching and Extending."

M Organizing information: written directions

DIRECT INSTRUCTION Print the following sets of directions on the chalkboard, omitting the answers in parentheses.

IC 83

> Put some dirt in a cup.
> Put some seeds in the dirt.
> Sprinkle water in the cup each day.
>
> (2) ___ Catch a bug.
> (1) ___ First, get a jar and punch holes in the lid.
> (3) ___ Then put the bug in the jar.

Have the first set read aloud. Ask what would happen if pupils were to follow the directions. (A plant would grow in the cup.)

ASK **Should you put the seed in the cup before you fill it with dirt?** (no) **Would a plant grow if you watered an empty cup every day?** (no) **It is important that you follow directions in the right order.**

GUIDED PRACTICE Direct pupils' attention to the second set of directions and have the directions read. Explain that they are not in the right order. Ask which direction should come first. (*First, get a jar and punch holes in the lid.*) Have a pupil print number 1 in front of the sentence.

Continue having the sentences numbered in order. Then have the directions read in the correct order.

WB 80 **INDEPENDENT PRACTICE** *Workbook* page 80 may be used to practice following written directions.

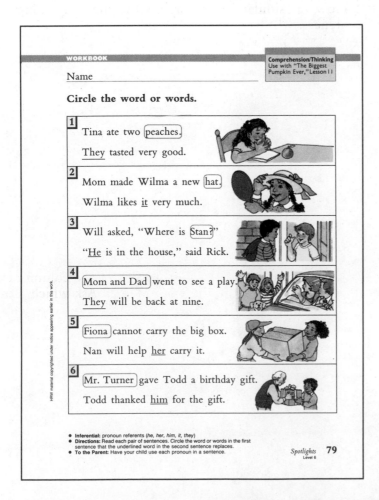

WORKBOOK

Comprehension/Thinking
Use with "The Biggest Pumpkin Ever," Lesson 11

Name _____

Circle the word or words.

1. Tina ate two (peaches.)
   They tasted very good.

2. Mom made Wilma a new (hat.)
   Wilma likes it very much.

3. Will asked, "Where is (Stan?)"
   "He is in the house," said Rick.

4. (Mom and Dad) went to see a play.
   They will be back at nine.

5. (Fiona) cannot carry the big box.
   Nan will help her carry it.

6. (Mr. Turner) gave Todd a birthday gift.
   Todd thanked him for the gift.

• **Inferential:** pronoun referents (*he, her, him, it, they*)
• **Directions:** Read each pair of sentences. Circle the word or words in the first sentence that the underlined word in the second sentence replaces.
• **To the Parent:** Have your child use each pronoun in a sentence.

Spotlights Level 6 **79**

Name _____

Study Skills
Use with "The Biggest Pumpkin Ever," Lesson 11

Draw a picture.

Picture may vary.

1 Make a big pumpkin on a vine.

2 Draw four little pumpkins on the vine, too.

3 Put green stems on each pumpkin.

4 Place a mouse in a red hat in the picture.

5 Draw another mouse beside the first one.

80 *Spotlights*
Level 6

● **Organizing information:** written directions
● **Directions:** Read the sentences. Do what each sentence tells you.
● **To the Parent:** Have your child tell about his or her picture.

M   Study aids: summarizing

DIRECT INSTRUCTION Remind pupils that when they tell someone about a story, they do not have to include every little thing that happened. They only have to include the most important events. This is called summarizing.

GUIDED PRACTICE Tell pupils that together you are going to write a summary of "The Biggest Pumpkin Ever." Call on pupils to tell important things that happened in the story. Make a list of the events on the chalkboard in the order in which they happened. Remind pupils that they should not tell everything that happened in the story. They should only tell the most important things. When the summary is completed, have it read. (Answers will vary. Possible answers include: Clayton helped the pumpkin grow, so he could win a contest; Desmond helped the pumpkin grow, so he could carve a jack-o'-lantern; Clayton and Desmond met and made a deal to help each other; Clayton got the ribbon at the contest; Desmond carved the best jack-o'-lantern ever.)

LANGUAGE

M   Conventions of language: commas in direct address

DIRECT INSTRUCTION Print the following sentences on the chalkboard and have the first sentence read.

IC 84

> 1. "Clayton, water the garden."
> 2. "Desmond, carve the pumpkin."
> 3. "My pumpkin won a ribbon, Mom!"
> 4. "Dad, look at my big jack-o'-lantern."

Ask who is being told to water the garden. (Clayton) Point out the comma after the name Clayton.

SAY **This is a comma. The comma after Clayton's name shows that someone is speaking to Clayton.**

Call on several pupils to read the sentence, pausing at the comma.

GUIDED PRACTICE Have Sentence 2 read and ask to whom someone is speaking. (Desmond) Have another pupil come to the chalkboard and point to the name of the person being spoken to and the comma that separates the name from the rest of the sentence.

Follow a similar procedure with the remaining sentences.

✳ RETEACHING AND EXTENDING

Reteaching Lesson Skills

The activities that follow provide reteaching of skills developed in this lesson. Not every pupil needs to complete these activities. Choose only the activities that are needed to provide for the individual differences in your classroom.

DECODING/VOCABULARY

I, T **Sound/symbol correspondence:** consonant /v/*v* (initial, medial, final)

✳ **RETEACH** Print the following words on the chalkboard:

IC 78	van	vest	ever	visit
	gave	vote	vet	never

Point to the word *van* and read it. Explain that the word *van* begins with letter *v*. Letter *v* stands for the /v/ sound. Have pupils find and read the words that begin with letter *v*. (*vest, visit, vote, vet*)

Tell pupils that sometimes the /v/ sound is in the middle of a word. Have pupils find and read the words that have the /v/ sound in the middle. (*ever, never*)

Point to the word *gave* and read it. Ask where the /v/ sound is heard in *gave*. (at the end) Explain that the /v/ sound is heard at the end of the word *gave* because the letter *e* is silent.

Point to each word at random and have it read.

R, T **Sound/symbol correspondence:** consonant digraph /ch/*ch, tch* (initial, final)

✳ **RETEACH** Display *Word Cards champ, chase, chimp, chip, itch, match, much, patch* in random order. Explain that each of these words contains the /ch/ sound. Call on pupils to select and read the words that begin with the /ch/ sound. Have the words placed in the *Pocket Chart. (champ, chase, chimp, chip)*

Then call on pupils to select and read the words that end with the /ch/ sound. Have these words placed in the *Pocket Chart. (itch, match, much, patch)* Point out the words *itch, match, patch* and tell pupils that the letters *tch* stand for the /ch/ sound. Have both groups of words read.

I, T   Vocabulary: word meaning

 RETEACH Print the following words and sentences on the chalkboard, omitting the underlining.

> **carved   field   love   mice**
> **sure   very   village**
>
> 1. One mouse lived in a village.
> 2. One mouse lived in a field.
> 3. The mice were very good friends.
> 4. "Come see what I carved!" said the field mouse.
> 5. "That pumpkin sure is funny," said his friend.
> 6. "I love it!"
>
> **cover   crept   gave**
> **jack-o'-lantern   van   vine**

Read the first sentence. Then point to the word *village* and read it. Ask where a mouse lived. (in a village) Call on a pupil to read the sentence.

Follow a similar procedure with the remaining sentences, calling attention to the underlined words.

Display *Word Cards* for the underlined words. Then ask pupils to hold up the *Word Card* that answers each of the following questions:

1. **Which word means "more than one mouse"?** (*mice*)
2. **Which word names a large open area with no buildings?** (*field*)
3. **Which word names a small town?** (*village*)
4. **Which word means "to like something very, very much"?** (*love*)
5. **Which word means "cut with a knife"?** (*carved*)

Have pupils read the second set of words and use them in sentences.

 Distribute *Reteach Masters* page 18 and explain the directions on the page.

Focus

I, T   Literal: pronoun referents (*he, it, she, they, we*)

 RETEACH: Ask pupils to listen as you read the following sentences:

1. **Jack got on a bus.**
2. **Jack went to a movie.**
3. **Then Jack went home.**

Point out that in every sentence you said Jack's name. Ask pupils to listen as you read another set of sentences.

1. **Jack got on a bus.**
2. **He went to a movie.**
3. **Then he went home.**

Ask what was different about the second set of sentences. (Jack's name was not in every sentence; the word *he* was used instead of Jack's name.) Tell pupils that we sometimes use words that take the place of names and these words are called pronouns.

Print the following sentences on the chalkboard:

> 1. Kate sat on the step.
> 2. Bob and Jean are on the team.
> 3. My mom baked a roast.
> 4. My dad and I play chess.
> 5. The book is on the bed.

Have each sentence read. Then ask a pupil to replace the underlined word or words with a pronoun. (1. *She*, 2. *They*, 3. *She*, 4. *They*, 5. *It*)

Extending Selection Concepts

Clayton and Desmond had fun with a pumpkin. Tell pupils that you will read a poem about the fun they can have with pumpkins.

LANGUAGE ARTS

WRITING: RECIPES (Cooperative Learning) Ask pupils to suggest some things they may have eaten that were made with pumpkin. (Possible answers include: pumpkin pie, pumpkin bread, pumpkin muffins.) Have small groups of pupils discuss what they would like to make from a pumpkin. When the group has chosen something, have the group write a recipe for the food. Remind them that when writing the directions, they should include how to mix the ingredients, what kind of pan to use, and how long to cook the ingredients. Encourage each group to illustrate their finished product. Collect the recipes into a "Pumpkin Cookbook."

LITERATURE

LISTENING: FICTION Select a story about pumpkins and read it to the class. Ask pupils to compare the pumpkins in the book to the pumpkin in "The Biggest Pumpkin Ever."

Johnston, Tony. *The Vanishing Pumpkin.* Putnam, 1983. The repetitive phrases and charming de Paola illustrations make this story of a madcap Halloween fun for all.

Titherington, Jeanne. *Pumpkin, Pumpkin.* Greenwillow, 1986. Beautifully illustrated with soft pencil drawings, this story follows the growth of a child's pumpkin from seed to full-grown.

Tudor, Tasha. *Pumpkin Moonshine.* Walck, 1962. A young girl wants to find the biggest pumpkin to make a jack-o'-lantern.

A Pumpkin Seed

A pumpkin seed's a little thing,
When it is planted in the spring,
But, oh, the fun that it can bring!

At Halloween it turns into
A pumpkin pie for me and you,
Or jack-o'-lantern that says "Boo!"
Alice Crowell Hoffman

Ask what kinds of fun you can have with a pumpkin. (You can make a jack-o'-lantern or a pumpkin pie; you can plant the seeds and watch them grow.)

HOW AM I DOING

Many pupils need encouragement to read and to write poetry. Ask yourself the following questions to gauge your teaching effectiveness in this area.

	Yes	No	Some-times
1. Have I made poetry books available for pupils to look at?	☐	☐	☐
2. Do I take time to read aloud poetry to pupils?	☐	☐	☐
3. Do I help pupils understand the meaning of the poetry that is read aloud in class?	☐	☐	☐
4. Do I encourage pupils to write poetry of their own?	☐	☐	☐
5. Do I allow time for pupils to read their poems to the class?	☐	☐	☐

Name _____

Print the word.

van	vase	vine	cave	hive
five	beaver	drive		

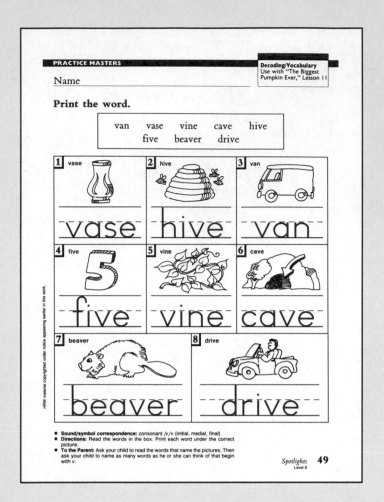

1 vase

vase

2 hive

hive

3 van

van

4 five

five

5 vine

vine

6 cave

cave

7 beaver

beaver

8 drive

drive

- **Sound/symbol correspondence:** consonant /v/v (initial, medial, final)
- **Directions:** Read the words in the box. Print each word under the correct picture.
- **To the Parent:** Ask your child to read the words that name the pictures. Then ask your child to name as many words as he or she can think of that begin with *v*.

Spotlights **49**
Level 6

Name _____

Fill in the circle. Draw a picture.

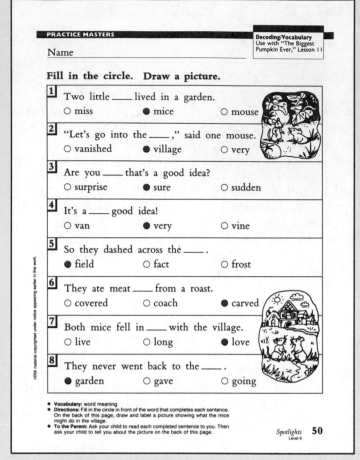

1 Two little ____ lived in a garden.
○ miss   ● mice   ○ mouse

2 "Let's go into the ____ ," said one mouse.
○ vanished   ● village   ○ very

3 Are you ____ that's a good idea?
○ surprise   ● sure   ○ sudden

4 It's a ____ good idea!
○ van   ● very   ○ vine

5 So they dashed across the ____ .
● field   ○ fact   ○ frost

6 They ate meat ____ from a roast.
○ covered   ○ coach   ● carved

7 Both mice fell in ____ with the village.
○ live   ○ long   ● love

8 They never went back to the ____ .
● garden   ○ gave   ○ going

- **Vocabulary:** word meaning
- **Directions:** Fill in the circle in front of the word that completes each sentence. On the back of this page, draw and label a picture showing what the mice might do in the village.
- **To the Parent:** Ask your child to read each completed sentence to you. Then ask your child to tell you about the picture on the back of this page.

Spotlights **50**
Level 6

Name _____

Circle the word.   Print the word.

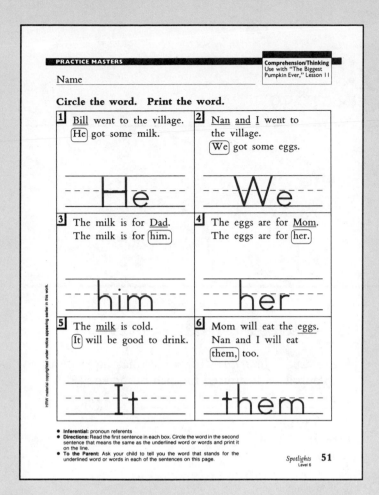

1 <u>Bill</u> went to the village.
[He] got some milk.

H e

2 <u>Nan</u> <u>and</u> <u>I</u> went to
the village.
[We] got some eggs.

W e

3 The milk is for <u>Dad</u>.
The milk is for [him.]

h i m

4 The eggs are for <u>Mom</u>.
The eggs are for [her.]

h e r

5 The <u>milk</u> is cold.
[It] will be good to drink.

I t

6 Mom will eat the <u>eggs</u>.
Nan and I will eat
[them,] too.

t h e m

- **Inferential:** pronoun referents
- **Directions:** Read the first sentence in each box. Circle the word in the second sentence that means the same as the underlined word or words and print it on the line.
- **To the Parent:** Ask your child to tell you the word that stands for the underlined word or words in each of the sentences on this page.

Spotlights **51**
Level 6

Name _____

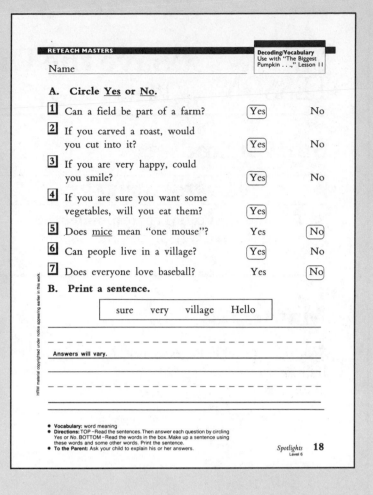

A.   Circle <u>Yes</u> or <u>No</u>.

1 Can a field be part of a farm?   [Yes]   No

2 If you carved a roast, would
you cut into it?   [Yes]   No

3 If you are very happy, could
you smile?   [Yes]   No

4 If you are sure you want some
vegetables, will you eat them?   [Yes]

5 Does <u>mice</u> mean "one mouse"?   Yes   [No]

6 Can people live in a village?   [Yes]   No

7 Does everyone love baseball?   Yes   [No]

B.   Print a sentence.

| sure   very   village   Hello |

_____

Answers will vary.

_____

_____

- **Vocabulary:** word meaning
- **Directions:** TOP – Read the sentences. Then answer each question by circling Yes or No. BOTTOM – Read the words in the box. Make up a sentence using these words and some other words. Print the sentence.
- **To the Parent:** Ask your child to explain his or her answers.

Spotlights **18**
Level 6

"Save the Day!"
Pages 126–127 (T288–T289)

Skill Strands

DECODING/VOCABULARY

R, T **Sound/symbol correspondence:**
consonant /v/*v* (initial, medial, final)

Materials

Spotlights, Level 6: Pages 126–127
Instructional Charts: page 85
Teacher's Idea Book

Special Populations

See *Teacher's Idea Book* for additional suggestions to help pupils with limited English proficiency.

Key to Symbols
I Introduced in this lesson
R Reinforced from an earlier lesson in this level
M Maintained from previous levels
T Tested in this level

DECODING/VOCABULARY

R, T **Sound/symbol correspondence:** consonant /v/*v* (initial, medial, final)

DIRECT INSTRUCTION Print the following words and sentences on the chalkboard, omitting the underlining.

> van   vine   vest   very
> give   cave   save   drive
>
> 1. Val can drive the van.
> 2. The vet can save the dog.
> 3. The cave is very dark.
> 4. Pat will give the vine some water.

Point to the word *van* and read it. Ask what letter stands for the /v/ sound at the beginning of *van*. (*v*)

Point to the word *give*. Ask where the /v/ sound is heard in *give*. (at the end) Tell pupils that the /v/ sound is heard at the end of *give* because the letter *e* is silent.

Have the remaining words read. Ask a pupil to point to and read a word that begins with the /v/ sound. (*van, vine, vest, very*) Then ask another pupil to point to and read a word that ends with the /v/ sound. (*give, cave, save, drive*) Continue until each word has been read.

Ask a pupil to read each sentence and to tell which words in the sentence contain the /v/ sound.

Save the Day!

The mice need help getting
to the top of the pumpkin.
Show them the way.
Follow the vine and
read each word.

very

vet

save

dive

vest

vote

cave

vase

wave

126

127

GUIDED PRACTICE Ask pupils to find pages 126
and 127 in their books. Have the title and the directions
read. Then call on pupils to read the words on the leaves
that answer each of the following questions:

1. **Which word tells what you might do with your
   hand as you say good-by?** (*wave*)
2. **Which word tells what a swimmer might do
   into a pool?** (*dive*)
3. **Which word names the kind of a doctor who
   takes care of animals?** (*vet*)
4. **Which word means "a lot"?** (*very*)
5. **Which word names a hole in the side of a hill?**
   (*cave*)
6. **Which word names something in which
   flowers may be placed?** (*vase*)
7. **Which word names something to wear?** (*vest*)
8. **Which word tells what people do in an election?**
   (*vote*)

LESSON 12 "Thumbelina"
pages 128–137 (T290–T311)

Skill Strands

DECODING/VOCABULARY

I, T   **Sound/symbol correspondence:** consonant /m/*mb* (final)

R, T   **Sound/symbol correspondence:** *r*-controlled vowel /är/*ar*

I, T   **Sound/symbol correspondence:** vowel /yo͞o/, /o͞o/*u-e*

R   **Sound/symbol correspondence:** vowel discrimination /är/, /ûr/

I   **Vocabulary:** word building

I, T   **Vocabulary:** word meaning

COMPREHENSION/THINKING

Focus

R   **Forms of literature:** folklore (folk tales and fairy tales)

STUDY SKILLS

M   **Graphic aids:** maps

LANGUAGE

I   **Writing:** descriptive sentences

Lesson Vocabulary

Decodable words: *asleep, bank, bride, crumbs, cute, faraway, felt, housework, numb, often, petals, rule, shell, sunshine, thumb, use, wed*

Special words: *Prince, Thumbelina*

Materials

Spotlights, Level 6: pages 128–137
Workbook: pages 81–87

Practice Masters: pages 52–56
Instructional Charts: pages 86–92
Resource Box: Letter Cards b, c, e, n, t, u
         Word Cards bark, cart, crumb, cub, cube, cut, cute, farm, flat, flute, harm, lamb, numb, Prince, thumb, Thumbelina, tub, tube, us, use

Pocket Chart
Teacher's Idea Book
Reteach Masters: pages 19–20

Language Applications

USING LANGUAGE

Oral reading: readers theater
Speaking: acting out a play (Cooperative Learning)

EXTENDING SELECTION CONCEPTS

Speaking: role playing
Listening: poetry
Listening: fiction

Special Populations

See *Teacher's Idea Book* for additional suggestions to help pupils with limited English proficiency.

Key to Symbols
I   Introduced in this lesson
R   Reinforced from an earlier lesson in this level
M   Maintained from previous levels
T   Tested in this level

Idea Center

BIBLIOGRAPHY

Add to your reading corner or reading table various folk tales or fairy tales, including some versions of "Thumbelina." A suggested bibliography follows. Suggestions for reading aloud and annotations appear in the lesson plan.

Andersen, Hans Christian (retold by Amy Ehrlich). *Thumbelina*. Dial, 1985.

Andersen, Hans Christian (translated by Richard and Clara Winston). *Thumbeline*. Morrow, 1980.

Galdone, Paul. *The Teeny-Tiny Woman*. Clarion, 1984.

Langton, Jane. *The Hedgehog Boy*. Harper & Row, 1985.

Morimoto, Junko. *The Inch Boy*. Viking, 1986.

Planning Chart

		Instruction	Written Practice	Extending
Step 1 Preparing for the Selection	I, T	**Sound/symbol correspondence:** consonant /m/*mb* (final)	*Workbook* page 81	
	I, T	**Sound/symbol correspondence:** vowel /yo͞o/, /o͞o/*u-e*	*Workbook* page 82 *Practice Masters* page 52 *Reteach Masters* page 19	
	I	**Vocabulary:** word building		
	I, T	**Vocabulary:** word meaning	*Workbook* page 83 *Practice Masters* page 53 *Reteach Masters* page 20	
	R	**Forms of literature:** folklore (folk tales and fairy tales)		
Step 2 Reading for Comprehension		**Oral reading:** readers theater		
		Speaking: acting out a play (Cooperative Learning)		**Speaking:** role playing
		Forms of literature: folklore (folk tales and fairy tales)		
		Story comprehension	*Workbook* page 84	
Step 3 Developing Reading and Thinking	R, T	**Sound/symbol correspondence:** *r*-controlled vowel /är/*ar*		
	R	**Sound/symbol correspondence:** vowel discrimination /är/, /ûr/	*Workbook* page 85 *Practice Masters* page 54	**Listening:** poetry
	R	**Forms of literature:** folklore (folk tales and fairy tales)	*Workbook* page 86 *Practice Masters* page 55	**Listening:** fiction
	M	**Graphic aids:** maps		
	I	**Writing:** descriptive sentences	*Workbook* page 87 *Practice Masters* page 56	

DECODING/VOCABULARY

I, T Sound/symbol correspondence: consonant /m/*mb* (final)

DIRECT INSTRUCTION Print the following words on the chalkboard and point to the word *thumb.*

thumb
crumb
numb
lamb

SAY This is the word *thumb.* **Read this word with me: *thumb.* What sound do you hear at the end of thumb?** (/m/) **What two letters are at the end of thumb?** *(mb)* **When a word ends with the letters *mb*, the *b* is silent. The letters *mb* at the end of a word stand for the /m/ sound.**

GUIDED PRACTICE Direct pupils' attention to the words on the chalkboard. Remind pupils that final *b* is silent in words that end with *mb.* Call on pupils to read the word that answers each of the following questions:

1. **Which word names a part of your body?** *(thumb)*
2. **Which word names a baby animal?** *(lamb)*
3. **Which word names a small bit of food?** *(crumb)*
4. **Which word means "not able to feel anything"?** *(numb)*

WB 81 INDEPENDENT PRACTICE *Workbook* page 81 may be used to practice identifying sound/symbol correspondence /m/*mb.*

✳ RETEACH For those pupils who need additional instruction, see "Reteaching Lesson Skills," page T308, under "Reteaching and Extending."

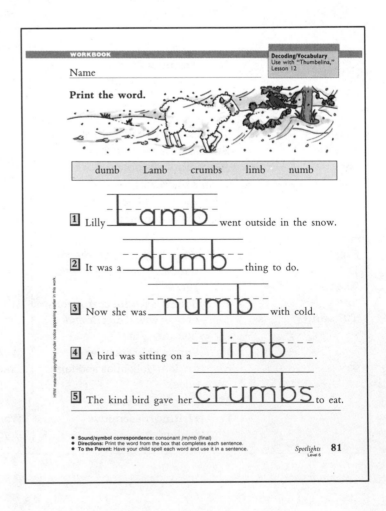

WORKBOOK — Decoding/Vocabulary Use with "Thumbelina," Lesson 12

Name _____

Print the word.

| dumb | Lamb | crumbs | limb | numb |

1 Lilly **Lamb** went outside in the snow.

2 It was a **dumb** thing to do.

3 Now she was **numb** with cold.

4 A bird was sitting on a **limb**.

5 The kind bird gave her **crumbs** to eat.

- Sound/symbol correspondence: consonant /m/mb (final)
- Directions: Print the word from the box that completes each sentence.
- To the Parent: Have your child spell each word and use it in a sentence.

Spotlights Level 6 **81**

I, T Sound/symbol correspondence: vowel /yo͞o/, /o͞o/u-e

DIRECT INSTRUCTION Place *Word Card tub* in the *Pocket Chart* and place *Word Card tube* under it. Point to each word as you read it.

SAY **The letter *u* in the word *tub* stands for the /u/ sound. Do you hear the /u/ sound in *tube*?** (no) **The vowel sound in *tube* is /o͞o/. We call this the long sound of letter *u*. What letter do you see at the end of the word *tube*?** (*e*) **When a word has letter *u*, followed by a consonant, and letter *e* is at the end of the word, the letter *u* can stand for the /o͞o/ sound. We call /o͞o/ the long sound of letter *u*.**

Have a pupil point to and read the word *tub*. Then ask another pupil to point to and read the word *tube*.

Place *Word Card cut* in the *Pocket Chart* and place *Word Card cute* under it. Point to each word as you read it.

SAY **What sound does the letter *u* stand for in *cut*?** (/u/) **Do you hear the /u/ sound in *cute*?** (no) **The vowel sound in *cute* is /yo͞o/. When a word has letter *u*, followed by a consonant, and ends with *e*, letter *u* can stand for the /yo͞o/ sound. We call the /yo͞o/ sound the long sound of letter *u*.**

Have a pupil point to and read the word *cut*. Then ask another pupil to point to and read *cute*.

GUIDED PRACTICE Have pupils raise their hands if they hear the long sound of letter *u* as you read each of the following words: *tube, rub, scrub, cute, flute, flat, sat, cube*.

Then place the following pairs of *Word Cards* in the *Pocket Chart*: *cub/cube, cut/cute, tub/tube, flat/flute*.

Call on pupils to read each pair of words. Then ask which word in the pair has the long *u* sound and why. (The second word has the long *u* sound because the letter *u* is followed by a consonant, and *e* is at the end of the word.)

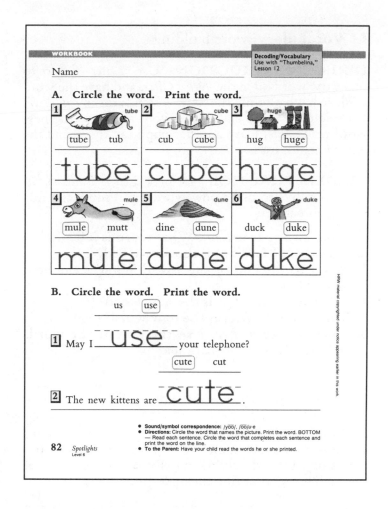

WB 82 **INDEPENDENT PRACTICE** *Workbook* page 82 may be used to practice identifying sound/symbol correspondence /yo͞o/,/o͞o/u-e.

PM 52 **ADDITIONAL PRACTICE** *Practice Masters* page 52 may be used as an optional practice for identifying sound/symbol correspondence /yo͞o/,/o͞o/ u-e. (See page T310 for reduced pages with answers.)

✱ **RETEACH** For those pupils who need additional instruction, see "Reteaching Lesson Skills," page T308, under "Reteaching and Extending."

I   Vocabulary: word building

DIRECT INSTRUCTION Use *Letter Cards* to make the word *cut* in the *Pocket Chart* and have the word read. Ask what sound the letter *u* stands for in *cut*. (/u/) Place letter *e* at the end of the word and have the new word read. (*cute*) Have another pupil say the sound the letter *u* stands for in *cute*. (/yoo/)

GUIDED PRACTICE Display *Letter Cards b, n*. Call on pupils to make new words by reading the following directions:

1. **Take away *e* from *cute*. What word is left?** (*cut*)
2. **Change *t* to *b*. What is the new word?** (*cub*)
3. **Add *e* to the end of the word. What is the new word?** (*cube*)
4. **Change *c* to *t*. What is the new word?** (*tube*)
5. **Take away *e*. What is the new word?** (*tub*)
6. **Change *b* to *n*. Add *e* to the end of the word. What is the new word?** (*tune*)

I, T   Vocabulary: word meaning

DIRECT INSTRUCTION Tell pupils that they are going to talk about some words they will read in the next story. Print the following words and sentences on the chalkboard, omitting the underlining.

> ### Prince   Thumbelina
>
> 1. The king's son is <u>Prince</u> James.
> 2. <u>Thumbelina</u> would like to meet Prince James.
>
> **crumbs   cute   numb**
> **rule   thumb   use**

Read the first sentence aloud. Point to the word *Prince* and read it. Ask who is the prince. (the king's son, James) Have pupils read the sentence with you. Then call on them to point to and read the word *Prince*.

Read the second sentence aloud. Point to and read the word *Thumbelina*. Explain that *Thumbelina* is a girl's name in the story they will read next. Ask pupils if they can find the name of a part of your hand in *Thumbelina*. (*thumb*) Have pupils read the sentence with you. Then ask pupils to find and read *Thumbelina* and *Prince*.

The words in the second set are new words that contain known phonic elements. You may wish to ask pupils to read the words, using what they know about letters and sounds.

GUIDED PRACTICE Print the following sentences on the chalkboard, omitting the underlining.

> 1. <u>Thumbelina</u> fed <u>crumbs</u> to the ducks in the river.
> 2. A <u>cute</u> duck kissed her <u>thumb</u>.
> 3. A <u>prince</u> from a faraway land came by.
> 4. "I could <u>use</u> some help," he said.
> 5. He asked her to be his bride and help <u>rule</u> his kingdom.
> 6. The girl was <u>numb</u> with surprise.

Provide opportunities for pupils to practice reading the new special words and some of the new decodable words in these sentences by following the suggestions below.

Sentence 1: Have the sentence read aloud. Ask what the girl was doing. (She was feeding crumbs to ducks.)

Sentence 2: Have the sentence read aloud. Ask what happened to the girl. (A duck kissed her thumb.) Ask what a river bank is. (It is the land at the side of the river.)

Sentence 3: Have a pupil find and read the word *prince*. Then have the sentence read aloud.

Sentence 4: Have the sentence read. Then ask if the prince needed help. (Yes, he could use some help.) Have pupils point to and read the word *use*.

Sentence 5: Have the sentence read aloud and ask what it means when someone is a bride. (It means that the person is getting or has just gotten married.) Explain that when a person rules a land, they make the laws for others to live by.

Sentence 6: Have the sentence read aloud and then ask what is meant by "numb with surprise." (The girl could hardly believe that the prince asked to marry her.) Explain that a person may also be numb from the cold, which means he or she cannot feel anything.

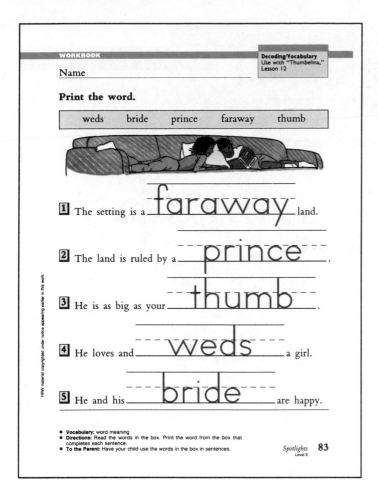

Name

Print the word.

| weds | bride | prince | faraway | thumb |

1 The setting is a <u>faraway</u> land.

2 The land is ruled by a <u>prince</u>

3 He is as big as your <u>thumb</u>.

4 He loves and <u>weds</u> a girl.

5 He and his <u>bride</u> are happy.

- **Vocabulary:** word meaning
- **Directions:** Read the words in the box. Print the word from the box that completes each sentence.
- **To the Parent:** Have your child use the words in the box in sentences.

Spotlights **83**
Level 6

HRW material copyrighted under notice appearing earlier in this work.

WB 83 **INDEPENDENT PRACTICE** *Workbook* page 83 may be used to practice reading story vocabulary.

PM 53 **ADDITIONAL PRACTICE** *Practice Masters* page 53 may be used as an optional practice for reading story vocabulary. (See page T310 for reduced pages with answers.)

✳ **RETEACH** For those pupils who need additional instruction, see "Reteaching Lesson Skills," page T309, under "Reteaching and Extending."

COMPREHENSION/THINKING

Focus

R **Forms of literature:** folklore (folk tales and fairy tales)

DIRECT INSTRUCTION Help pupils recall important events from the stories "The Chili Pot" and "Peach Boy." Ask what was magic in each story. ("The Chili Pot" had a magic pot; "Peach Boy" had a magic peach.) Then ask what other imaginary things were in the stories. (animals that could talk; a giant) Point out that folk tales and fairy tales are stories about make-believe things.

SAY **"The Chili Pot" and "Peach Boy" are very, very old stories and have been told to children for hundreds of years. Stories that are very old and that have something magical or have characters that do impossible things or are not real are called folk tales or fairy tales.**

GUIDED PRACTICE Print the following words on the chalkboard:

IC 89

| magic | rabbit | giant | prince |
| mother | dragon | farmer | fairy |

Have pupils read the words and tell which ones name something that could only be in a fairy tale or folk tale. (*magic, giant, dragon, fairy*)

Then ask pupils to tell what might happen in a folk tale or fairy tale about a giant rabbit and a farmer; a dragon and a prince. (Answers will vary.)

2 READING FOR COMPREHENSION

Background for the Teacher

SUMMARY Tiny Thumbelina is accidentally carried far from her home. She finds a new home with Mouse and makes friends with Mole and Bird. Mole wants to marry Thumbelina, but she is saddened because he lives underground and hates the sunlight. Before the wedding takes place, Bird carries Thumbelina off to a land of tiny people like herself. Thumbelina meets and marries a prince, and they live happily ever after.

INFORMATION The classic tale of "Thumbelina" is told here in the form of a play. Two readers narrate the actions of the characters of Thumbelina, Fish, Mouse, Mole, Bird, and Prince.

Using Prior Knowledge

Some pupils may be familiar with "Thumbelina." If so, ask why the girl is named "Thumbelina." (She is as small as a thumb.) Develop a discussion by asking questions such as those that follow.

1. **Could a real person be as small as your thumb?** (no) **This story is a fairy tale. What might animals in a fairy tale do that they cannot do in real life?** (Possible answers include: talk, wear clothes, do magic.)
2. **Thumbelina gets carried far from her home and cannot get back. What will she need to do?** (Possible answers include: find a new home, make new friends, try to find her way home.)

Setting a Purpose for Reading

Have pupils find page 128 in their books. Explain that "Thumbelina" is a play and that on page 128 is a list of the characters in the play. The characters in a play are called the cast. Point out that this play has two readers who will tell what is happening. Explain that the character's name appears first. The words the character is to read follow the punctuation mark called a colon.

Point out the headnote at the top of page 128. Tell pupils that this note will help them think about the play as they read it. Have the headnote read and ask pupils to suggest what kind of surprise Bird might have for Thumbelina. (Answers will vary. Possible answers include: Bird might have a nest and some baby birds.)

Reading Silently

Some pupils may be able to read this story independently. Direct them to read the whole story to find out more about the home Bird finds for Thumbelina. For those pupils who need more guidance, suggestions for directed reading follow.

Thumbelina wants a safe and happy home. What surprise does her friend Bird have for her?

Thumbelina

The Cast

Bird

Prince

Thumbelina

Mole

Mouse

Reader 1   Reader 2   Fish

128

ACT 1

Reader 1: *Some time ago, there lived a girl who was only as big as your thumb. Her name was Thumbelina.*

Reader 2: *Thumbelina's bed was an egg shell, and rose petals were her blankets.*

Reader 1: *One day, when Thumbelina fell asleep, the egg shell floated into the sea.*

129

Before reading page 128

The characters in a play are called the cast. Read page 128 to find out who the characters are in this play.

After reading page 128

Who are the characters in the play? *(Thumbelina, Bird, Prince, Mole, Mouse, Reader 1, Reader 2, Fish)*

Before reading page 129

SAY **Once upon a time, Thumbelina was very happy. Then something happened that changed her life. Read page 129 to yourself.**

After reading page 129

1. **What happened to Thumbelina?** (One day when she fell asleep, her eggshell bed floated into the sea.) Inferential
2. **How do you know that Thumbelina was very small?** (She was only as big as your thumb; her bed was an eggshell; her blankets were rose petals.) Inferential

Reader 2: *When Thumbelina woke up, she was far from home.*

Thumbelina: Help me! Someone, please help me!

Reader 1: *Just then, Fish swam along.*

Fish: I'll help you, little one. I will take you to the <u>bank</u>.

Thumbelina: Oh, thank you, Fish.

Reader 2: *Thumbelina made a home for herself on the bank. Everything was fine, until winter came.*

130

Reader 1: *Thumbelina, <u>numb</u> with cold, walked deep into the woods.*

Reader 2: *She saw an old mouse going into a <u>cute</u> little house.*

Thumbelina: May I stay here? I will work for my keep.

Mouse: Well, I could <u>use</u> some help with the <u>housework</u>.

Reader 1: *Thumbelina stayed. She cleaned and dusted, and she had plenty of <u>crumbs</u> to eat.*

131

Before reading pages 130–131

| SAY | **What do you think will happen to poor Thumbelina? Read pages 130 and 131 to yourself.** |

After reading pages 130–131

1. **How was Thumbelina saved?** (Fish took her to the bank.) Literal
2. **What happened to Thumbelina in the winter?** (She needed a place to stay warm; she went to stay with Mouse and helped with the housework.) Inferential

ACT 2

Reader 2: *Mouse and Thumbelina often visited Mole. He lived in a deep hole.*

Thumbelina: Don't you miss the sun, Mole?

Mole: I hate the sun!

Thumbelina: That's too bad. I like the sun very much.

132

Reader 1: *One day, when Mouse and Thumbelina were visiting Mole, a bird came crashing into the hole.*

Thumbelina: Oh, my! I must do something to help.

Reader 2: *So Thumbelina ran off to find a blanket.*

Thumbelina: Here, Bird. This will make you feel better.

Bird: Thank you, Thumbelina. Oh, if only I could fly.

Thumbelina: Stay until summer. By then, you will be well.

133

Before reading pages 132–133

SAY Act 2 is the second part of the play. Do you think Thumbelina will make friends if she stays with Mouse? Read pages 132 and 133 to yourself.

After reading pages 132–133

1. **How did Bird become Thumbelina's friend?** (Bird crashed into Mole's hole and could not fly; Thumbelina helped him and invited him to stay until summer.) Inferential

2. **How did Mole feel about the sunshine?** (He hated the sun.) Literal

Reader 1: *Mouse spoke to Thumbelina.*

Mouse: Mole wants you to be his <u>bride</u>.

Thumbelina: But I could never live in this dark hole.

Mouse: Mole is your friend. He will give you a good home.

Thumbelina: Tell Mole we will <u>wed</u> in the spring.

134

ACT 3

Reader 2: *Winter passed. The day of the wedding came.*

Bird: Thumbelina, come with me.

Thumbelina: I must stay.

Reader 1: *So Bird left.*

Mole: Today is the great day. There is even <u>sunshine</u>. I can't bear it myself.

Reader 2: *With that, Thumbelina ran off to see the sun for the last time. Looking up, she saw Bird.*

135

Before reading page 134
Mole asked Thumbelina a special question. How do you think she will answer. Read page 134 to find out.

After reading page 134
What did Thumbelina promise Mole?
(She said that they would be married in the spring.) Literal

Before reading pages 135–137
SAY **Soon the long winter was over. Then it was spring. What do you think Thumbelina will do? Read pages 135 to 137 to yourself.**

Bird: Jump on my back! I'll take you to a place where the sun shines all day, and where there are little people just like you.

Reader 1: *So Thumbelina hopped on Bird's back and waved to her two friends.*

Reader 2: *Thumbelina and Bird went to a <u>faraway</u> land. The prince of the land fell in love with Thumbelina. And she fell in love with him.*

Prince: Please be my bride and <u>rule</u> my kingdom with me.

136

Reader 1: *And so Thumbelina and the prince were happy ever after.*

Discussing the Selection
1. How did Bird surprise Thumbelina?
2. Why didn't she want to marry Mole?
3. Why did Bird want her to fly away with him?
4. When did you know Thumbelina would fly away with Bird?
5. How do you think Thumbelina's friends <u>felt</u> after she left?

137

After reading pages 135–137

1. **Why did Thumbelina run out to see the sun?** (She thought that after she married Mole, she would never see the sun again.) Inferential
2. **Where did Bird offer to take Thumbelina?** (Bird offered to take her to a place where the sun shines all day and where there are little people like herself.) Literal
3. **Do you think Thumbelina was always happy in her new home? Why or why not?** (Yes, she was happy because she married the prince, and they were happy ever after.) Critical

Discussing the Selection

Questions preceded by a number appear in *Spotlights* after the selection. Questions preceded by a bullet are additional questions for extending discussion.

PURPOSE

1. **How did Bird surprise Thumbelina?** (Bird surprised Thumbelina by taking her to a place where the sun shines all day and where she met people her own size.) Inferential

STORY MAPPING

2. **Why didn't she want to marry Mole?** (Mole lived underground, and Thumbelina would never see the sun.) Inferential

  • **Why do you think Mole liked living underground?** (Answers will vary. Possible answers include: because he didn't like the sun, because he had always lived underground.) Critical

3. **Why did Bird want her to fly away with him?** (Bird knew that Thumbelina would not be happy married to Mole.) Inferential

  • **Why did Thumbelina refuse to go with Bird at first?** (Mouse and Mole were her friends, and she did not want to hurt their feelings.) Inferential

4. **When did you know that Thumbelina would fly away with Bird?** (On page 136, Bird told Thumbelina that he would take her to a place where the sun shines all day and where there are little people.) Inferential

CRITICAL THINKING

5. **How do you think Thumbelina's friends felt after she left?** (Possible answers include: They probably were sad that she had gone; they were glad that she would be happy.)

  • **What do you think Thumbelina's life would have been like if she had married Mole?** (Answers will vary. Possible answers include: She would have been unhappy because she loved the sunshine.)

Using Language

ORAL READING: READERS THEATER Remind pupils that the story of Thumbelina was written as a play with parts to be acted out. Tell pupils they will read the play without acting it out. Have them turn to page 128 and read the names of the characters.

Select pupils to read the parts of Reader 1, Reader 2, Thumbelina, Fish, and Mouse. Then have pupils read aloud Act 1.

Select a new group of pupils to read the parts of Reader 1, Reader 2, Thumbelina, Mole, Mouse, and Bird. Then have the pupils read aloud Act 2.

Select a third group of pupils to read the parts of Reader 1, Reader 2, Thumbelina, Bird, Mole, and Prince. Then have Act 3 read aloud.

SPEAKING: ACTING OUT A PLAY (Cooperative Learning) Invite groups of pupils to act out the play "Thumbelina." Each group may perform one act or the entire play. The group may choose to let Reader 1 and Reader 2 read their parts, with the other characters, using their own words. Provide time for each group to practice and then to present their play.

Applying the Focus Skill

FORMS OF LITERATURE: FOLKLORE Ask why some stories are called folk tales or fairy tales. (Folk and fairy tales may have magic, animals that talk, and imaginary characters.) Ask why "Thumbelina" is a folk tale or fairy tale. (Possible answers include: A tiny person like Thumbelina could not be real; all the animals in the story could talk; the story ended by saying Thumbelina was happy forever.)

Evaluating Comprehension

WB 84 **INDEPENDENT PRACTICE** *Workbook* page 84 may be used for an informal evaluation of story comprehension.

WORKBOOK

Comprehension/Thinking
Use with "Thumbelina,"
Lesson 12

Name _____

Fill in the circle.

1 ● Thumbelina was very little.
○ Thumbelina was very big.

2 ● Thumbelina stayed with Mouse.
○ Thumbelina stayed with Mole.

3 ○ Mouse didn't need help with the housework.
● Mouse needed help with the housework.

4 ○ Mouse wanted to wed Thumbelina.
● Mole wanted to wed Thumbelina.

5 ● Mole hated the sunshine.
○ Thumbelina hated the sunshine.

6 ● Thumbelina wanted to be with people like herself.
○ Thumbelina stayed to wed Mole.

7 ● Thumbelina and the prince were happy.
○ Thumbelina became Mole's bride.

● **Story comprehension:** "Thumbelina"
● **Directions:** Read the sentences. Fill in the circle by the sentences that tell about "Thumbelina."
● **To the Parent:** Have your child choose one character from the play to illustrate and then caption with one or two sentences.

84 *Spotlights*
Level 6

3 DEVELOPING READING AND THINKING SKILLS

DECODING/VOCABULARY

R, T Sound/symbol correspondence: *r*-controlled vowel /är/*ar*

DIRECT INSTRUCTION Print the following sentence and words on the chalkboard:

> Mark went to start the car.
>
> star bark band tart same arm

Point to and read the sentence. Remind pupils that when the letters *ar* are together, they often stand for the /är/ sound. Call on pupils to point to and read the words in the sentence that have the /är/ sound. Then have the sentence read.

GUIDED PRACTICE Indicate the words on the chalkboard and have them read. Call on pupils to circle and read the words with the /är/ sound. (*star, bark, tart, arm*)

✳ **RETEACH** For those pupils who need additional instruction, see "Reteaching Lesson Skills," page T308, under "Reteaching and Extending."

R Sound/symbol correspondence: vowel discrimination /är/, /ûr/

DIRECT INSTRUCTION Print the following words and sentences on the chalkboard:

> far
> her
> sir
> fur
>
> 1. The bird can chirp.
> 2. Her kitten is a girl.
> 3. The lamb has curly fur.
> 4. The stars sparkle faraway.

Point to each word and have pupils read it. Point to the word *far* and ask what sound the letters *ar* stand for. (/är/) Point to the word *her* and ask what sound the letters *er* stand for. (/ûr/) Point to the word *sir* and ask what sound the letters *ir* stand for. (/ûr/) Point to the word *fur* and ask what sound the letters *ur* stand for. (/ûr/)

Remind pupils that *ar* stands for the /är/ sound and that *ir, er, ur* stand for the /ûr/ sound.

GUIDED PRACTICE Have a pupil read Sentence 1 aloud. Then ask another pupil to read the words that have the /ûr/ sound. (*bird, chirp*)

Follow a similar procedure with Sentences 2–3. (2. *Her, girl*; 3. *curly, fur*) After Sentence 4 has been read aloud, ask a pupil to identify the words with the /är/ sound.

Name _____

Decoding/Vocabulary
Use with "Thumbelina,"
Lesson 12

Fill in the circle.

1 The kitten's ___ is soft.
○ far ● fur ○ first

2 Did you ___ the chili?
○ sir ○ star ● stir

3 The horses live in the ___.
● barn ○ burn ○ burr

4 Pet the kitten to make it ___.
○ park ● purr ○ par

5 The dog helps ___ the sheep.
● herd ○ hard ○ her

6 That plant is a ___.
○ fan ○ farm ● fern

7 You have mud and ___ on your shoes.
○ duck ● dirt ○ dart

8 Wanda sent Kim a get-well ___.
● card ○ car ○ curb

- **Sound/symbol correspondence:** vowel discrimination /är/, /ûr/
- **Directions:** Read each sentence. Fill in the circle by the word that completes the sentences.
- **To the Parent:** Have your child list the *er* words in one column, the *ir* words in another, the *ur* words in a third, and the *ar* words in a fourth column.

Spotlights **85**
Level 6

COMPREHENSION/THINKING

Focus

R Forms of literature: folklore (fairy tales and folk tales)

DIRECT INSTRUCTION Remind pupils that some stories may have talking animals, imaginary characters such as giants, or magical characters such as elves. These stories are called fairy tales or folk tales because they tell about make-believe things.

GUIDED PRACTICE Print the following sentences on the chalkboard, omitting the answers in parentheses.

IC 89

> 1. The boy grabbed the giant's magic hen. (fairy tale)
> 2. The girl ate a sandwich for lunch. (fairy tale; real life)
> 3. The man was no bigger than my thumb. (fairy tale)
> 4. Riches fell out of the magic egg. (fairy tale)
> 5. The ant said, "You should work harder." (fairy tale)
> 6. The frog hopped to the bank of the pond. (fairy tale; real life)

Call on a volunteer to read each sentence and to tell if the sentence tells about something that could only happen in a fairy tale or if the sentence tells about something that could happen in both a fairy tale and real life.

WB 86 **INDEPENDENT PRACTICE** *Workbook* page 86 may be used to practice recognizing fairy tales.

WB 85 **INDEPENDENT PRACTICE** *Workbook* page 85 may be used to practice reading words with /är/ and /ûr/.

PM 54 **ADDITIONAL PRACTICE** *Practice Masters* page 54 may be used as an optional practice for reading words with /är/ and /ûr/. (See page T310 for reduced pages with answers.)

Name _____

Print fairy tale or real life.

1 A girl saw a toad by the road.
The toad was a prince under a
bad spell.
The girl kissed the toad.
The kiss turned the toad back
into a prince.
The prince made the girl his bride.

---- fairy tale ----

2 There were no apple trees
growing in Mr. King's yard.
Mr. King got lots of appleseeds
and planted them all over.
The seeds started to grow.
After a long time, there
were apple trees everywhere.

---- real life ----

● **Forms of literature:** folk literature
● **Directions:** Read the stories. Then print *fairy tale* if the things in the story could not really happen. Print *real life* if the things in the story could really happen.
● **To the Parent:** Have your child tell how and why he or she classified each story.

86 *Spotlights*
Level 6

PM 55 **ADDITIONAL PRACTICE** *Practice Masters* page 55 may be used as an optional practice for recognizing fairy tales. (See page T311 for reduced pages with answers.)

STUDY SKILLS

M **Graphic aids:** maps

DIRECT INSTRUCTION Remind pupils that a map is a special drawing of a certain area. It shows where places are located and how to get from one place to another.

GUIDED PRACTICE Help pupils recall the different places that Thumbelina went. List pupils' suggestions on the chalkboard. (Suggestions should include: the sea, the bank, the woods, Mouse's house, Mole's house, Prince's kingdom.)

Next, tell pupils that they can make a map of the places Thumbelina went. Remind them that a map looks like a picture taken from high above a place.

SAY **If you were up in a plane looking down, here is where Thumbelina began her trip.** (Make a star at the left side of a piece of chart paper to represent where Thumbelina was when she floated into the sea. Draw some wavy lines to represent the sea.)

Ask pupils where Thumbelina ended up next. (on the bank of the sea) Draw a line to indicate the other side of the sea. Then use pupils' suggestions to add other details to the map. Draw irregular circles for the trees in the woods; a box for Mouse's house; a circle for Mole's hole; and a faraway castle for Prince's kingdom. Point out that the map could be used by Mouse and Mole to visit Thumbelina and Prince in their kingdom.

LANGUAGE

I Writing: descriptive sentences

DIRECT INSTRUCTION Print the following sentences and words on the chalkboard, omitting the words in parentheses.

> 1. Thumbelina saw a big house.
> 2. Thumbelina saw a little house.
>
> 1. friend   pal   (synonyms)
> 2. sunny   dark   (antonyms)
> 3. asleep   awake   (antonyms)
> 4. hurry   rush   (synonyms)

Point to the first sentence and have it read. Point to the word *big* and ask pupils to tell some other words that mean the same thing as *big*. (Possible answers include: *huge, giant, large.*) Ask pupils to read the sentence, using words that mean the same thing as *big* in place of the word *big*. Explain that words that have almost the same meaning are called synonyms.

Point to the second sentence and have it read. Ask if *little* means almost the same thing as *big*. (no) Explain that *little* means the opposite of *big*. Words with opposite meanings are called antonyms.

Call on pupils to read the word pairs below the sentences. Have them tell if the words are synonyms or antonyms.

GUIDED PRACTICE Invite volunteers to choose a word pair of antonyms or a word pair of synonyms. Have pupils write and illustrate a sentence with each word.

WB 87 **INDEPENDENT PRACTICE** *Workbook* page 87 may be used to practice writing descriptive sentences with synonyms and antonyms.

PM 56 **ADDITIONAL PRACTICE** *Practice Masters* page 56 may be used as an optional practice for writing descriptive sentences with synonyms and antonyms. (See page T311 for reduced pages with answers.)

✳ RETEACHING AND EXTENDING

Reteaching Lesson Skills

The activities that follow provide reteaching of skills developed in this lesson. Not every pupil needs to complete these activities. Choose only the activities that are needed to provide for the individual differences in your classroom.

DECODING/VOCABULARY

I, T   Sound/symbol correspondence: consonant /m/*mb* (final)

✳ **RETEACH**   Display *Word Cards thumb, crumb, numb,* and *lamb.*

Point to and read *thumb.* Ask what letter is at the end of the word. (*b*) Ask what sound is heard at the end of the word *thumb.* (/m/) Tell pupils that when letters *mb* come together at the end of a word, the letter *b* is silent.

Point to each of the remaining *Word Cards* and have them read.

R, T   Sound/symbol correspondence: *r*-controlled vowel /är/*ar*

✳ **RETEACH**   Display *Word Cards farm, bark, harm, cart.* Point to each word and read it aloud. Tell pupils that each word contains the /är/ sound. Ask which two letters in each word stand for the /är/ sound. (*ar*) Tell pupils that the letters *ar* together often stand for the /är/ sound. Point to each word at random and have it read.

I, T   Sound/symbol correspondence: vowel /yo͞o/, /o͞o/*u-e*

✳ **RETEACH**   Place the following pairs of *Word Cards* in the *Pocket Chart: us/use, tub/tube, cut/cute, cub/cube.*

Indicate the *Word Cards us, use.* Have the first word read and the vowel sound of *u* identified /u/. Have the second word read and ask what is different about the word. (It ends with letter *e.*) Explain that the word *use* has the long sound of *u* because *u* is followed by a consonant and letter *e.* Then point to the words several times and have pupils read them.

Follow a similar procedure for the remaining pairs of words. Then have pupils hold up and read the words that contain the long sound of letter *u.* (*use, tube, cute, cube.*)

RM 19   Distribute *Reteach Masters* page 19 and explain the directions on the page.

I, T Vocabulary: word meaning

 RETEACH Print the following words and sentences on the chalkboard, omitting the underlining.

Prince   Thumbelina

1. The king's son is <u>Prince</u> James.
2. <u>Thumbelina</u> would like to meet Prince James.

crumbs   cute   numb
rule   thumb   use

Point to and read the word *Prince.* Ask a pupil to find and read a sentence that contains the word *Prince.* Continue in the same manner with the word *Thumbelina.*

Display *Word Cards Prince* and *Thumbelina.* Ask pupils to point to and read the word that names the son of a king and queen. (*Prince*) Then ask pupils to point to and read the word that is the name of a very small girl. (*Thumbelina*)

Ask pupils to read the second set of words and to use them in sentences.

RM 20 Distribute *Reteach Masters* page 20 and explain the directions on the page.

HOW AM I DOING?

Many pupils are not very familiar with folklore. Ask yourself the following questions to make sure pupils have the opportunity to explore this form of literature.

	Yes	No	Some- times
1. Have I read any folklore se- lections aloud to pupils?	☐	☐	☐
2. Have I utilized other sources of media to expose pupils to folklore, such as filmstrips, movies, or posters?	☐	☐	☐
3. Have I made a wide selection of folklore reading material available?	☐	☐	☐
4. Have I taken pupils to the library?	☐	☐	☐

Extending Selection Concepts

LANGUAGE ARTS

SPEAKING: ROLE PLAYING Help pupils recall the things that happened to Thumbelina. Encourage them to pretend to be Thumbelina and the prince and have Thumbelina tell the prince about her life before she met him.

LITERATURE

LISTENING: POETRY Remind pupils that Thumbelina got her name because she was no bigger than a person's thumb. Tell them that in some stories, little people are called fairies or elves. Read the following poem about a tiny elf and ask pupils to listen to see how the elf feels about being small.

The Little Elfman

I met a little elfman once,
    Down where the lilies blow,
I asked him why he was so small,
    And why he didn't grow.

He slightly frowned, and with his eyes
    He looked me through and through—
"I'm just as big for me," said he,
    "As you are big for you!"

John Kendrick Bangs

Ask if the elf was unhappy being small. (No, he felt that he was as big as he was supposed to be.)

LISTENING: FICTION Read aloud another version of the story "Thumbelina" (sometimes called "Thumbeline" or "Incheline") or another folk tale with a central character that is different from other people. Ask pupils to compare the story in their books with the other fairy tale.

Andersen, Hans Christian (retold by Amy Ehrlich). *Thumbelina*. Dial, 1985. The classic story of Thumbelina is retold.

Andersen, Hans Christian (translated by Richard and Clara Winston). *Thumbeline*. Morrow, 1980. This is a richly illustrated version of the story of Thumbelina.

Galdone, Paul. *The Teeny Tiny Woman*. Clarion, 1984. The classic story of the tiny woman in the tiny house in the tiny village is sure to entertain young readers.

Langton, Jane. *The Hedgehog Boy*. Harper & Row, 1985. This is a Latvian folk tale about a boy who is as prickly as a hedgehog and how he marries a princess.

Morimoto, Junko. *The Inch Boy*. Viking, 1986. This is a Japanese version of the story "Tom Thumb."

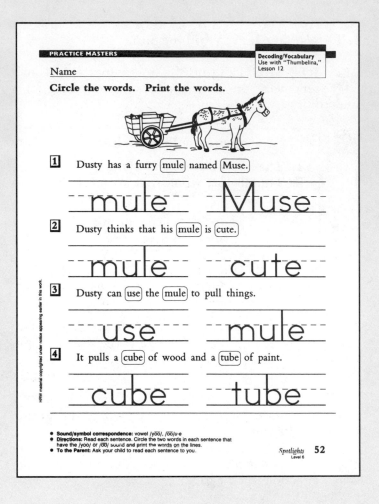

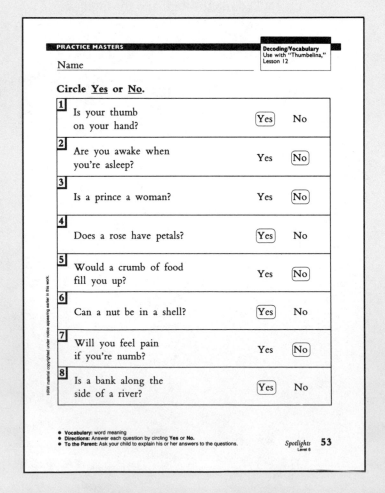

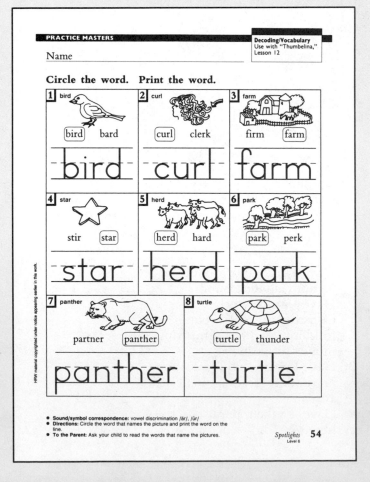

Name _____

Fill in the circle.

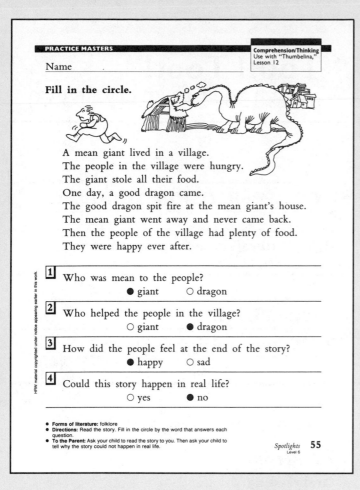

A mean giant lived in a village.
The people in the village were hungry.
The giant stole all their food.
One day, a good dragon came.
The good dragon spit fire at the mean giant's house.
The mean giant went away and never came back.
Then the people of the village had plenty of food.
They were happy ever after.

1 Who was mean to the people?
 ● giant ○ dragon

2 Who helped the people in the village?
 ○ giant ● dragon

3 How did the people feel at the end of the story?
 ● happy ○ sad

4 Could this story happen in real life?
 ○ yes ● no

● **Forms of literature:** folklore
● **Directions:** Read the story. Fill in the circle by the word that answers each question.
● **To the Parent:** Ask your child to read the story to you. Then ask your child to tell why the story could not happen in real life.

Name _____

**A. Circle the words that mean the opposite.
Print a sentence.**

fast [hot] [cold]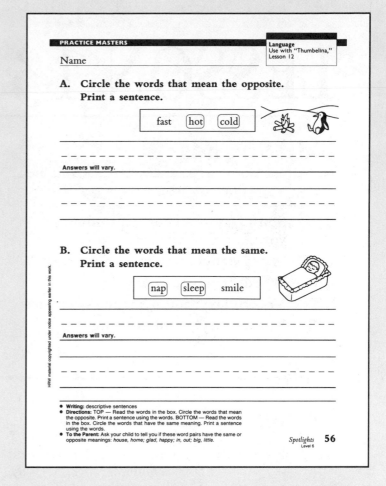

_____
Answers will vary.
_____
_____

**B. Circle the words that mean the same.
Print a sentence.**

[nap] [sleep] smile

_____
Answers will vary.
_____
_____

● **Writing:** descriptive sentences
● **Directions:** TOP — Read the words in the box. Circle the words that mean the opposite. Print a sentence using the words. BOTTOM — Read the words in the box. Circle the words that have the same meaning. Print a sentence using the words.
● **To the Parent:** Ask your child to tell you if these word pairs have the same or opposite meanings: *house, home; glad, happy; in, out; big, little.*

Name _____

Print the word. Circle the words.

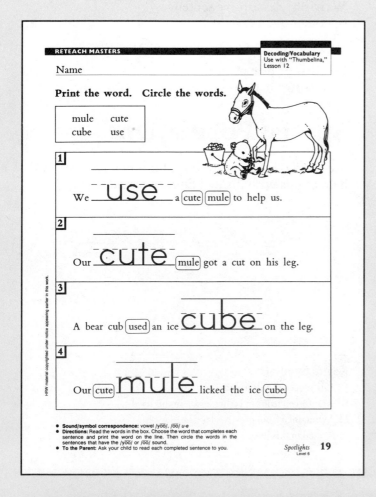

mule   cute
cube   use

1 _____
We **use** a [cute] [mule] to help us.

2 _____
Our **cute** [mule] got a cut on his leg.

3 _____
A bear cub [used] an ice **cube** on the leg.

4 _____
Our [cute] **mule** licked the ice [cube]

● **Sound/symbol correspondence:** vowel /yōō/, /ōō/ *u-e*
● **Directions:** Read the words in the box. Choose the word that completes each sentence and print the word on the line. Then circle the words in the sentences that have the /yōō/ or /ōō/ sound.
● **To the Parent:** Ask your child to read each completed sentence to you.

Name _____

Print the word.

faraway   wed   bride   asleep

1 Thumbelina fell
asleep in an eggshell.

2 She woke up in a
faraway land.

3 Mole asked her to be his
bride .

4 Thumbelina said she would
wed the Prince.

● **Vocabulary:** word meaning
● **Directions:** Read the words in the box. Choose the word that completes each sentence and print the word on the line.
● **To the Parent:** Ask your child to read each completed sentence to you.

LESSON 13

"Toot! Toot!"
pages 138–147 (T312–T333)

Skill Strands

DECODING/VOCABULARY

R, T   **Sound/symbol correspondence:** vowel /yo͞o/, /o͞o/u-e

R, T   **Word structure:** contractions (with 're)

I, T   **Word structure:** suffix -ly

I, T   **Vocabulary:** antonyms and synonyms

I, T   **Vocabulary:** word meaning

COMPREHENSION/THINKING

Focus

R, T   **Literal:** pronoun referents (*he, it, she, they, we*)

LANGUAGE

R   **Writing:** descriptive sentences

Lesson Vocabulary

Decodable words: *bench, cross, damp, dinner, Ferris, farm, finished, front, fondly, Grandma, hollered, OK, park, rapping, really, rode, slowly, speed, suddenly, suspect, sweetly, tickets, visit, weekend*

Special words: *calf, door, fair, horses, imagines, Larry, Toot*

Materials

Spotlights, Level 6: pages 138–147
Workbook: pages 88–93

Practice Masters: pages 57–59
Instructional Charts: pages 93–101
Resource Box: Word Cards calf, cold, door, end, fair, horses, imagines, Larry, pitch, toot

Pocket Chart
Teacher's Idea Book
Reteach Masters: pages 21–22

Language Applications

USING LANGUAGE

Oral reading: details
Writing: descriptive sentences
(Cooperative Learning)

EXTENDING SELECTION CONCEPTS

Speaking: role playing
Listening: fiction

Special Populations

See *Teacher's Idea Book* for additional suggestions to help pupils with limited English proficiency.

Key to Symbols

I   Introduced in this lesson

R   Reinforced from an earlier lesson in this level

M   Maintained from previous levels

T   Tested in this level

Idea Center

BIBLIOGRAPHY

Add to your reading corner or reading table various books about children who have active imaginations. A suggested bibliography follows. Suggestions for reading aloud and annotations for books appear in the lesson plan.

Berger, Barbara. *When the Sun Rose.* Philomel, 1986.
Carrick, Carol. *Patrick's Dinosaurs.* Clarion, 1983.
Heine, Helme. *The Pearl.* Atheneum, 1985.
Jonas, Ann. *The Trek.* Greenwillow, 1985.
Mayer, Mercer. *There's an Alligator Under My Bed.* Dial, 1987.
Spier, Peter. *Dreams.* Doubleday, 1986.

Planning Chart

	Instruction	Written Practice	Extending
Step 1 Preparing for the Selection	**I, T Word structure:** suffix *-ly*	*Workbook* page 88 *Practice Masters* page 57 *Reteach Masters* page 21	
	I, T Vocabulary: word meaning	*Workbook* page 89 *Practice Masters* page 58 *Reteach Masters* page 22	
	R, T Literal: pronoun referents *(he, it, she, they, we)*		
Step 2 Reading for Comprehension	**Oral reading:** details **Writing:** descriptive sentences (Cooperative Learning) **Literal:** pronoun referents *(he, it, she, they, we)* **Story comprehension**	*Workbook* page 90	
Step 3 Developing Reading and Thinking Skills	**R, T Sound/symbol correspondence:** vowel /yoo/, /oo/u-e	*Workbook* page 91 *Practice Masters* page 59	**Speaking:** role playing
	R, T Word structure: contractions (with *'re*)		
	I, T Vocabulary: antonyms and synonyms	*Workbook* page 92	
	R, T Literal: pronoun referents *(he, it, she, they, we)*	*Workbook* page 93	**Listening:** fiction
	R Writing: descriptive sentences		

DECODING/VOCABULARY

I, T   Word structure: suffix -*ly*

DIRECT INSTRUCTION Print the following sentences on the chalkboard and read the first sentence aloud.

> 1. The boy sang softly.
>
> 2. The candle glowed dimly.
> 3. Camels walk slowly.
> 4. The boy patted his dog fondly.
> 5. The team sadly walked home.

ASK   **Which word tells how the boy sang?** (*softly*) **What has been added to the word** *soft* **to make the word** *softly*? (-*ly*) **The ending** -*ly* **can be added to some words to form new words. When** -*ly* **is added to a word, the new word tells that something was done in a certain way. How did the boy sing?** (*softly*) **What other words describe how a boy might sing?** (Possible answers include: *loudly, sweetly.*)

GUIDED PRACTICE Direct pupils' attention to Sentences 2–5. Have Sentence 2 read.

ASK   **How did the candle glow?** (*dimly*) **What does** *dim* **mean?** (not very bright; dark) **What other words describe how a candle might glow?** (Possible answers include: *brightly, softly.*)

Follow a similar procedure with the remaining sentences, asking which word tells how something was done and then asking for other words that might describe that activity.

INDEPENDENT PRACTICE *Workbook* **WB 88** page 88 may be used to practice reading words with the suffix -*ly*.

ADDITIONAL PRACTICE *Practice Masters* **PM 57** page 57 may be used as an optional practice for reading words with the suffix -*ly*. (See page T332 for reduced pages with answers.)

✳ RETEACH For those pupils who need additional instruction, see "Reteaching Lesson Skills," page T330, under "Reteaching and Extending."

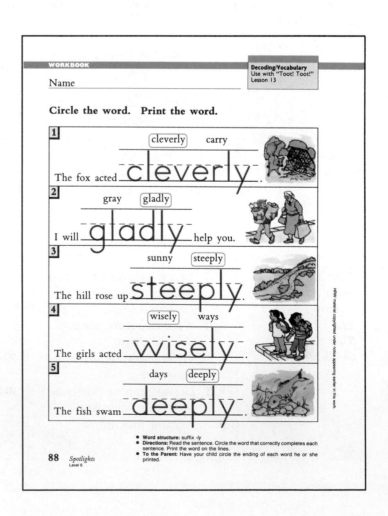

I, T Vocabulary: word meaning

DIRECT INSTRUCTION Tell pupils that they are going to talk about some words they will read in the next story. Print the following words and sentences on the chalkboard, omitting the underlining.

> **calf door fair horses**
> **imagines Larry toot**
>
> 1. Larry closes his <u>door</u>.
> 2. He <u>imagines</u> he is at a <u>fair</u>.
> 3. Then he imagines he is at a farm.
> 4. "<u>Toot</u>! Toot!" honks the tractor.
> 5. Larry sees a <u>calf</u> and some baby <u>horses</u>.
>
> **fondly hollered rapping really**
> **slowly suddenly suspect**
> **sweetly weekend**

Read Sentence 1 aloud. Point to the word *Larry* and read it. Explain that *Larry* is a name. Point to the word *door* and read it. Ask what Larry did. (closed his door) Have pupils read the sentence with you. Then ask them to find and read *Larry* and *door.*

Read Sentence 2 aloud. Point to the word *imagines* and read it. Ask what you do when you imagine something. (You pretend; you make-believe something.) Point to the word *fair* and read it. Ask what a fair is. (A fair is a gathering or celebration that usually has rides and entertainment.) Have pupils read the sentence with you. Then ask them to find and read *imagines* and *fair.*

Read Sentences 3–4 aloud. Have pupils read the sentences with you. Point to the word *Toot* and read it. Ask what makes a tooting sound. (the tractor) Then have pupils read *Toot* as the tractor may have sounded.

Read Sentence 5 aloud. Then point to the words *calf* and *horses* and read them. Explain that a calf is a baby cow. Have pupils read the sentence with you. Then call on pupils to point to and read the words *calf* and *horses.*

The words in the second set are new words that contain known phonic elements. You may wish to ask pupils to read the words, using what they know about letters and sounds. Ask pupils which word means the same as *knocking* (rapping); as *yelled* (hollered); and as *guess* or *figure out* (suspect).

GUIDED PRACTICE Print the following sentences on the chalkboard, omitting the underlining.

> 1. Larry <u>fondly</u> remembers his <u>weekend</u> visits at Grandma's farm.
> 2. "Who's that <u>rapping</u> on my <u>door</u>?" Grandma would <u>sweetly</u> say.
> 3. Last time he went, he walked <u>slowly</u> up to pet a new <u>calf</u>.
> 4. Larry is <u>really</u> happy when he sees the <u>horses</u>.
> 5. He always <u>imagines</u> the day when he will be a good rider.
> 6. He will ride at the <u>fair</u>.
> 7. <u>Suddenly</u>, the tractor went "<u>Toot</u>!"
> 8. "I <u>suspect</u> you're ready for <u>lunch</u>," <u>hollered</u> Grandpa.

Provide opportunities for pupils to practice reading the new special words and some of the new decodable words in these sentences by following the suggestions below.

Have the first sentence read and indicate the word *fondly.*

> **ASK** **Did Larry have nice visits at his Grandma's farm?** (yes) **How do you know?** (because he fondly remembers them) **If you are fond of something, you like it or love it very much. What is a weekend?** (Saturday and Sunday; the days of the week when there is no school or when many people are off work.)

Have pupils point to and read the words *Larry, fondly,* and *weekend.*

Follow a similar procedure for the remaining sentences by having each sentence read and asking the following questions. Then have the underlined words in each sentence read.

Sentence 2: **Which word means "knocking"?** *(rapping)* **Did Larry's grandma answer the door in a nice way?** (Yes, she answered it sweetly.)

Sentence 3: **What is a calf?** (a baby cow) **Why might Larry have walked slowly to pet the calf?** (So he wouldn't frighten it.)

Sentence 4: **Does Larry like to see the horses?** (Yes, he is really happy when he gets to see the horses.) **What is another word for *really*?** *(very, truly)*

Sentence 5: **Which word in the sentence means "dreams about"?** *(imagines)* **Does Larry think he is a good rider now?** (No, he imagines the day when he will be one.)

Sentence 6: **What will Larry do when he is a good rider?** (He will ride at the fair.) **What is a fair?** (A fair is a summer event where people show off their best animals and vegetables and compete in contests.)

Sentence 7: **Did the tractor surprise Larry?** (Yes, suddenly it tooted.) **What would toot on a tractor?** (a horn)

Sentence 8: **Which word in the sentence means "bet or guess"?** (suspect) **Why did Grandpa have to holler?** (because the tractor was probably noisy) **What is another word for *hollered*?** (shouted or yelled)

WB 89 **INDEPENDENT PRACTICE** *Workbook* page 89 may be used to practice reading story vocabulary.

PM 58 **ADDITIONAL PRACTICE** *Practice Masters* page 58 may be used as an optional practice for reading story vocabulary. (See page T332 for reduced pages with answers.)

✳ **RETEACH** For those pupils who need additional instruction, see "Reteaching Lesson Skills," page T330, under "Reteaching and Extending."

Focus

R, T **Literal:** pronoun referents (*he, it, she, they, we*)

DIRECT INSTRUCTION Print the following words and sentences on the chalkboard, omitting the answers in parentheses.

> We She It They He
> 1. Mike peeked in the box.
> 2. (He) saw a train set.
>
> 3. Kathy went to the bus stop.
> 4. (She) did not want to miss the bus.
>
> 5. Max had a new <u>lunch box</u>.
> 6. (It) was red.
>
> 7. Steve and Chuck went to the show.
> 8. (They) paid for their tickets.

Have the first two sentences read.

ASK **Who found a toy train?** (Mike) **Which word can be used in the second sentence to take the place of Mike's name?** (He)

Remind pupils that the word *he* is called a pronoun. A pronoun is a word that can be used instead of the name of a person or a thing.

GUIDED PRACTICE Have Sentences 3–4 read. Ask which word in Sentence 3 can be replaced with a pronoun in Sentence 4. (*Kathy* in Sentence 3 can be replaced with *she* in Sentence 4.)

Continue in the same manner with the remaining sentence pairs. (*It* replaces *lunch box*; *They* replaces *Steve and Chuck*.)

Background for the Teacher

SUMMARY As Larry plays with his train set, he imagines that he is taking the train to visit his grandparents. He becomes so lost in his imagination that he forgets to go to dinner. When at last he gets to the dinner table, he discovers that his grandparents are visiting. He is ecstatic when they ask him to spend some time at their house.

INFORMATION This story was adapted from the book of the same title. Part of the story takes place in a boy's imagination as he remembers his last visit with his grandparents. Some pupils may need help to discern what is happening in the boy's house and what is happening in the boy's imagination.

Using Prior Knowledge

Tell pupils that in the story they are about to read, a boy imagines that he is riding on his toy train and becomes so interested that he does not pay any attention to what is going on around him. Develop a discussion by asking questions such as those that follow.

1. **Have you ever been so busy playing that you forgot to do something your mother or father asked you to do?** (Answers will vary.)
2. **Where do you think someone might pretend to go on an imaginary trip?** (Answers will vary.)

Setting a Purpose for Reading

Have pupils find page 138 in their books and read the title. ("Toot! Toot!") Have pupils look at the picture and ask what might make the sound "Toot! Toot!" (the train)

Point out the headnote at the top of the page. Tell pupils that this note will help them think about the story as they read. Have the headnote read aloud and then ask what Larry might imagine. (Answers will vary. Possible answers include: He might imagine he's on a train or that he's the engineer.)

Reading Silently

Some pupils may be able to read this story independently. Direct them to read the whole story to find out more about the fun things Larry imagines. For those pupils who need more guidance, suggestions for directed reading follow.

Read to find out all the things that Larry imagines.

Toot! Toot!

One day, Larry went to play with his train set.

The train moved on the tracks. "Toot! Toot!" said Larry when the train passed in front of him.

Larry imagined speaking to his grandmother on the telephone.

"Hello?" said his grandmother from far away.

"Hello," said Larry. "May I come to visit?"

"Sure you may!"

Larry imagined standing and waiting for the train.

He imagined saying "Hello" to everyone and then jumping on the train.

138

139

Before reading pages 138–139

SAY **Larry liked to play with his toy train. What do you think he will do while he watches the train go around the tracks? Read pages 138 and 139 to yourself.**

After reading pages 138–139

1. **What did Larry do while he was playing with his train?** (He imagined that he called his grandmother and asked if he could come for a visit.) Literal

2. **How did Larry imagine that he would go to his grandmother's?** (He imagined that he would go on the train.) Inferential

Slowly the train moved out.
"Toot! Toot!" Larry said as it picked up speed.

He passed a row of shops and a little park with someone sitting on a bench.

Then the train passed a field. Larry saw a baby calf with her mother.
Next to them was another field with some horses in it.

140

Larry remembered the time he helped his grandfather feed the four horses on the farm.
The day had been cold and damp.
When they had finished feeding the horses, Grandma had hot drinks waiting for them.

141

Before reading pages 140–141

SAY **Larry was going on an imaginary trip. What things might he have seen? Read pages 140 and 141 to yourself.**

After reading pages 140–141

1. **What things did Larry imagine that he saw from the train?** (a row of shops, a park, a baby calf with her mother, a field with horses) Inferential
2. **What did Larry remember?** (He remembered that he helped his grandfather feed the horses on the farm and that his grandmother had hot drinks for them when they were finished.) Inferential

Bang! Bang!

Someone was <u>rapping</u> at Larry's <u>door</u>.

"Who's there?" he yelled over the noise.

"Time for <u>dinner</u>," said Mom.

"<u>OK</u>," said Larry, but then he was back on the train.

142

"Toot! Toot!" he <u>hollered</u> as the train slowed to <u>cross</u> a stream.

<u>Suddenly</u> there was a field filled with tents and a <u>Ferris</u> wheel.

The Ferris wheel made Larry think of the <u>fair</u> he had visited with his grandma and grandpa.

They <u>rode</u> the Ferris wheel and had a <u>really</u> fun day at that fair!

143

Before reading pages 142–143

SAY **Larry was so busy imagining that he forgot where he really was. What do you think will cause Larry to stop imagining? Read pages 142 and 143 to yourself.**

After reading pages 142–143

1. **What caused Larry to stop imagining?** (His mother knocked on his door and called him to dinner.) Literal
2. **Why didn't Larry go to dinner?** (He began to imagine he was back on the train again.) Inferential
3. **What did Larry think about this time?** (He remembered going to a fair with his grandparents.) Inferential

Bang! Bang! Bang!

Someone was rapping on the door again.

"Larry," said his mother, "your dinner is getting cold."

"Oh, I forgot about dinner," Larry said.

144

"Really, Larry!
How could you forget dinner?" said his mother.

"I was visiting Grandpa and Grandma on the train," explained Larry. "I kept thinking I was there."

"Then you're going to like dinner a lot," said Larry's mother.

"I am?" Larry asked.

"You are," said his mother very <u>sweetly</u>.

145

Before reading pages 144–145

SAY **Larry did not go down to dinner. What do you think will happen? Read pages 144 and 145 to yourself.**

After reading pages 144–145

1. **What happened when Larry did not go to dinner?** (His mother came back to get him.) Inferential
2. **What did Larry tell his mother that he was doing?** (He told her that he was pretending that he was visiting his grandparents.) Literal
3. **What did Larry's mother tell him about dinner?** (She said that he would like dinner a lot.) Literal

When Larry got to the table, Grandma and Grandpa were sitting there.

"Surprise!" they said.

"We want you to stay with us for the weekend," said Grandma fondly.

"You can help Grandpa feed all the horses.

Then we'll go to the fair and ride the Ferris wheel again."

"We have tickets for the train," said Grandpa.

"I love the train," said Larry, "and I love you!"

146

The next day, the train started down the tracks.

"Toot! Toot!" said Larry.

"Toot! Toot!"

Discussing the Selection

1. What things in this story did Larry imagine?
2. What things in this story were real?
3. What surprise did Larry have when he went for dinner?
4. When did you suspect that Grandma and Grandpa were at Larry's house?
5. How do you think Larry will pass the time on the train?

147

Before reading pages 146–147

SAY **What do you think will happen when Larry goes down to dinner? Read pages 146 and 147 to yourself.**

After reading pages 146–147

1. **What surprise did Larry find at the dinner table?** (His grandparents were there to take him home with them for the weekend.) Literal
2. **What did Larry's grandparents tell Larry?** (They told him that he could help feed the horses and that they would go to the fair again; they would ride on a train.) Literal
3. **Was Larry happy? How could you tell?** (Larry was happy because he said, "I love the train, and I love you.") Inferential

Discussing the Selection

Questions 1–5 appear in *Spotlights* after the selection. Questions preceded by a bullet are additional questions for extending discussion.

PURPOSE

1. **What things in this story did Larry imagine?** (He imagined that he called his grandmother on the phone; that he was riding on a train; that he was visiting his grandparents; that he was passing shops, fields, and a fair.) Inferential

STORY MAPPING

2. **What things in this story were real?** (Possible answers include: Larry's mother, the dinner, his grandparents, riding on the train at the end of the story.) Inferential

• **What did Larry imagine he would see on the train ride?** (a row of shops, a park, a field, a baby calf, some horses) Inferential

3. **What surprise did Larry have when he went for dinner?** (His grandparents were at the table.) Literal

• **What did Grandma and Grandpa ask Larry at dinner?** (They asked him to come stay with them for the weekend.) Literal

4. **When did you suspect that Grandma and Grandpa were at Larry's house?** (On page 145, when Larry's mother said that he would like dinner a lot.) Inferential

CRITICAL THINKING

5. **How do you think Larry will pass the time on the train?** (Answers will vary. Possible answers include: imagining what he will do at his grandparents' house; watching for the things he had imagined seeing when he had been in his bedroom.)

Using Language

ORAL READING: DETAILS Have pupils turn to page 138 and read the page to themselves. Then ask which words tell where the train moved. *(on the tracks)* Ask which words explain when Larry said "Toot! Toot!" *(when the train passed in front of him)* Tell pupils that these groups of words are details from the story. Details are bits of information that describe things and help make the story easy to understand.

Follow a similar procedure for the remaining pages, using the suggestions below.

Page 139: Ask a pupil to read the detail that tells where Larry's grandmother was. (far away) Then have the details read that describe what Larry imagined about getting on the train. (Larry imagined standing and waiting for the train. He imagined saying "Hello" to everyone and then jumping on the train.)

Page 140: Ask pupils to read the sentences that describe how the train moved. (Slowly the train moved out. "Toot! Toot!" said Larry as it picked up speed.) Then call on pupils to read the details that describe the fields. (Then the train passed a field. Larry saw a baby calf with her mother. Next to them was another field with some horses in it.)

Page 141: Ask a pupil to read the sentences that tell about the day Larry helped his Grandpa feed the horses. (The day had been cold and damp. When they had finished feeding the horses, Grandma had hot drinks waiting for them.)

Page 143: Have a pupil read the details that tell about the next field Larry imagined. (Suddenly there was a field filled with tents and a Ferris wheel.)

Page 145: Ask pupils to find the words that tell how Larry's mother spoke to him. (*very sweetly*) Then ask pupils to read the conversation between Larry and his mother.

Page 146: Ask which word tells how Larry's Grandmother spoke to him. (*fondly*) Ask what *fondly* means. (*Fondly* means that she spoke in a way that showed she loved Larry.) Then ask pupils to read what Larry and his grandparents said to one another in the way they might have spoken.

WRITING: DESCRIPTIVE SENTENCES (Co-operative Learning) Have pupils work in groups to make a book about a train ride. Tell pupils to discuss with one another where they might like to go on a train. Then have each member of the group write some sentences that describe something they might see from the window of the train. Encourage pupils to share their sentences with their group and then illustrate the sentences. Have the group work together to make a book that includes the sentences and pictures the group has made. Encourage each group to show their book about a train ride.

Applying the Focus Skill

LITERAL: PRONOUN REFERENTS Ask pupils to tell what a pronoun is. (A pronoun is a word used in place of a thing or a person's name.)

| SAY | **Larry liked to play with his train. He imagined that he went for a ride.** |

Who went for an imaginary train ride? (Larry) **When I said "He imagined that he went for an imaginary train ride," I used the word** *he* **instead of Larry's name. A word that can take the place of the name of a person or a thing is called a pronoun.**

Ask pupils to turn to page 146. Call on a pupil to read the first two sentences aloud. Then ask who said "Surprise!" (Larry's grandma and grandpa) Ask what word in the second sentence takes the place of the words *Grandma and Grandpa.* (*they*)

Then have the next sentence read aloud. Ask which names are replaced by the word *We.* (*Grandma and Grandpa*) Ask which name is replaced by the word *you.* (*Larry*)

Have the last two sentences read aloud. Ask who Larry was speaking about when he said *I.* (himself) Then ask who Larry meant when he said *you.* (his grandma and grandpa)

Evaluating Comprehension

WB 90 INDEPENDENT PRACTICE *Workbook* page 90 may be used for an informal evaluation of story comprehension.

WORKBOOK

Comprehension/Thinking
Use with "Toot! Toot!," Lesson 13

Name _____

Read the sentence. Fill in the circle.

1 Larry liked to ____ things.
● imagine   ○ make

2 Larry said "____" when the train went by.
● Toot! Toot!   ○ Bang! Bang!

3 Larry was playing with his ____.
○ book   ● train

4 Larry imagined going on a train to ____ Grandma.
○ play   ● visit

5 Grandma and Grandpa came for ____.
○ lunch   ● dinner

6 They had ____ for a real train ride.
● tickets   ○ wishes

• **Story comprehension:** "Toot! Toot!"
• **Directions:** Read the sentences. Circle the word that completes each sentence.
• **To the Parent:** Have your child describe some things he or she likes to imagine.

90 *Spotlights*
Level 6

DECODING/VOCABULARY

R, T   Sound/symbol correspondence: vowel /yo͞o/, /o͞o/u-e

DIRECT INSTRUCTION   Print the following words on the chalkboard:

IC 97

tub	cut	cub
tube	cute	cube
tune	bug	use
fun	flute	crumb

Point to the first pair of words and read them aloud. Remind pupils that *tube* has the long sound of the letter *u* because *u* is followed by a consonant and letter *e*. Have pupils read *tub* and *tube* as you point to each word.

Have each remaining word pair read and ask which word in each pair has the long sound of letter *u*. (*cute, cube*)

GUIDED PRACTICE   Direct pupils' attention to the second set of words on the chalkboard. Call on a pupil to read each word and to tell what sound is represented by letter *u*. (*tune /o͞o/, bug /u/, use /yo͞o/, fun /u/, flute /o͞o/, crumb /u/*)

Invite a pupil to read a word at random and have a second pupil point to the word. Continue until each word has been read.

INDEPENDENT PRACTICE   *Workbook* page 91 may be used to practice identifying sound/symbol correspondence /yo͞o/, /o͞o/u-e.
WB 91

ADDITIONAL PRACTICE   *Practice Masters* page 59 may be used as an optional practice for identifying sound/symbol correspondence /yo͞o/, /o͞o/ u-e. (See page T332 for reduced pages with answers.)
PM 59

✳ **RETEACH**   For those pupils who need additional instruction, see "Reteaching Lesson Skills," page T329, under "Reteaching and Extending."

WORKBOOK

Decoding/Vocabulary
Use with "Toot! Toot!," Lesson 13

Name _____

Print the word.

| cube | flute | use | mule | tube | rule |

1 A thing that looks like a block is a __cube__.

2 An animal with long ears is a __mule__.

3 A container for paints or creams is a __tube__.

4 Something you can play is a __flute__.

5 Something you must follow is a __rule__.

6 When you spend your money, you __use__ it.

HRW material copyrighted under notice appearing earlier in this work.

• Sound/symbol correspondence: vowel /yo͞o/, /o͞o/u-e
• **Directions:** Read the words in the box. Print the word from the box that completes each sentence.
• **To the Parent:** Have your child read the words he or she has printed.

Spotlights Level 6   **91**

R, T   Word structure: contractions (with *'re*)

DIRECT INSTRUCTION   Print the following words and sentences on the chalkboard:

> you are
> you're
>
> They're   We're   You're
>
> 1. <u>We are</u> going to visit Grandma.
> 2. <u>You are</u> eating an apple.
> 3. <u>They are</u> going swimming.

Have the words *you are* read. Tell pupils that sometimes we put these two words together into one word. Point to the word *you're* and read it. Explain that *you're* is called a contraction because it has an apostrophe where a letter was taken out. Ask what letter was left out of *you are* to make *you're.* (*a*) Tell pupils that in *you're,* the apostrophe takes the place of the letter *a.*

GUIDED PRACTICE   Direct pupils' attention to the three contractions and sentences on the chalkboard and have them read. Call on pupils to replace each underlined pair of words with a contraction. (1–*We're*; 2–*You're*; 3–*They're*) As each pair of words is replaced with a contraction, ask what letter the apostrophe in the contraction stands for. (*a*) Have the sentences with contractions read.

✳ RETEACH   For those pupils who need additional instruction, see "Reteaching Lesson Skills," page T329, under "Reteaching and Extending."

I, T   Vocabulary: antonyms and synonyms

DIRECT INSTRUCTION   Print the following sentences and words on the chalkboard, omitting the words in parentheses.

> 1. Larry was glad to see his grandma and grandpa.
> 2. Larry was happy to see his grandma and grandpa.
> 3. Larry was sad to see his grandma and grandpa.
>
> | | | |
> |---|---|---|
> | big | little | (antonyms) |
> | yell | holler | (synonyms) |
> | slow | fast | (antonyms) |
> | cut | carve | (synonyms) |
> | punch | hit | (synonyms) |
> | cold | hot | (antonyms) |

Call on a pupil to read the first sentence aloud. Then have pupils read the remaining sentences to themselves. Ask which sentence, 2 or 3, means almost the same thing as Sentence 1. (Sentence 1 and 2 mean almost the same because *happy* and *glad* have almost the same meaning.) Remind pupils that words that have almost the same meaning are called *synonyms.*

Have the third sentence read aloud. Ask if this sentence means almost the same thing as the first sentence. (no) Tell pupils that this sentence means the opposite of the first sentence. The word *sad* is the opposite of *glad.* Two words that have opposite meanings are called *antonyms.*

GUIDED PRACTICE   Direct pupils' attention to the word pairs on the chalkboard. Call on a pupil to read each pair of words and to tell if the words are antonyms or synonyms.

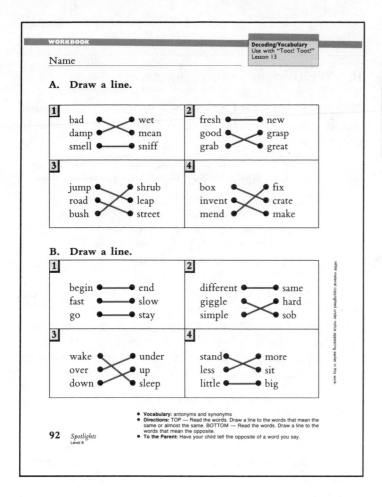

WORKBOOK

Decoding/Vocabulary
Use with "Toot! Toot!"
Lesson 13

Name _____

A. Draw a line.

1
bad — wet
damp — mean
smell — sniff

2
fresh — new
good — grasp
grab — great

3
jump — shrub
road — leap
bush — street

4
box — fix
invent — crate
mend — make

B. Draw a line.

1
begin — end
fast — slow
go — stay

2
different — same
giggle — hard
simple — sob

3
wake — under
over — up
down — sleep

4
stand — more
less — sit
little — big

• **Vocabulary:** antonyms and synonyms
• **Directions:** TOP — Read the words. Draw a line to the words that mean the same or almost the same. BOTTOM — Read the words. Draw a line to the words that mean the opposite.
• **To the Parent:** Have your child tell the opposite of a word you say.

92 *Spotlights*
Level 6

HRW material copyrighted under notice appearing earlier in this work

WB 92 **INDEPENDENT PRACTICE** Workbook page 92 may be used to practice recognizing antonyms and synonyms.

✳ **RETEACH** For those pupils who need additional instruction, see "Reteaching Lesson Skills," page T330, under "Reteaching and Extending."

COMPREHENSION/THINKING

Focus

R, T Literal: pronoun referents (*he, it, she, they, we*)

DIRECT INSTRUCTION Print the following sentences on the chalkboard:

 IC 100

> 1. The train started slowly.
> 2. Then it went faster.
> 3. The train passed by some farms.
> 4. It went, "Toot! Toot!"
> 5. The noise woke a little calf.
> 6. It ran to its mother.
> 7. She stayed with her baby.
> 8. They were happy again.

Have the first two sentences read. Ask what went faster. (the train) Ask which word in the second sentence takes the place of the words *the train*. (*it*) Tell pupils that *it* is a pronoun. A pronoun is a word that can take the place of the name of a person or a thing.

GUIDED PRACTICE Have Sentences 3 and 4 read. Ask which word in Sentence 4 takes the place of the words *the train*. (*It*) Have Sentences 5 and 6 read. Ask which word in Sentence 6 takes the place of the word *calf*. (*It*) Have Sentence 7 read. Ask which word takes the place of the words *its mother*. (*She*) Then have the last sentence read. Ask which words were replaced by the word *They*. (*the calf and its mother*)

WB 93 **INDEPENDENT PRACTICE** *Workbook* page 93 may be used to practice recognizing pronoun referents (*he, it, she, they, we*).

WORKBOOK

Name _____

Print the word.

He	it	She	They	them

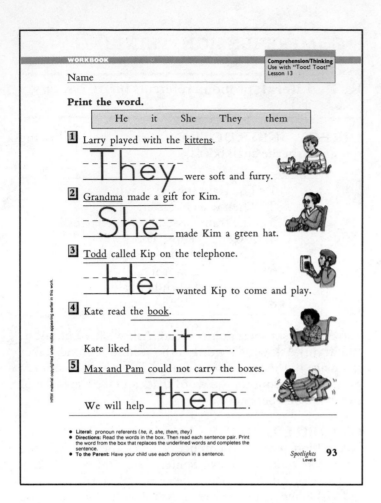

1 Larry played with the <u>kittens</u>.

They _____ were soft and furry.

2 <u>Grandma</u> made a gift for Kim.

She _____ made Kim a green hat.

3 <u>Todd</u> called Kip on the telephone.

He _____ wanted Kip to come and play.

4 Kate read the <u>book</u>.

Kate liked it _____ .

5 <u>Max and Pam</u> could not carry the boxes.

We will help them _____ .

- **Literal:** pronoun referents (*he, it, she, them, they*)
- **Directions:** Read the words in the box. Then read each sentence pair. Print the word from the box that replaces the underlined words and completes the sentence.
- **To the Parent:** Have your child use each pronoun in a sentence.

Spotlights **93**
Level 6

LANGUAGE

R **Writing:** descriptive sentences

DIRECT INSTRUCTION Print the following words on the chalkboard, omitting the words in parentheses.

IC 99

big	little	(antonyms)
yell	holler	(synonyms)
slow	fast	(antonyms)
cut	carve	(synonyms)
punch	hit	(synonyms)
cold	hot	(antonyms)

Call on a pupil to read the first two words. Ask if the words are antonyms or synonyms. (antonyms) Help pupils make up sentences by first asking questions such as: What animal is big? What animal is little? Then write a sentence using *big* and *little*. (Possible sentence includes: *The big dog barked at the little black kitten.*)

Continue in the same manner with the remaining pairs of words.

GUIDED PRACTICE Ask pupils to choose one pair of synonyms and one pair of antonyms. Have pupils write a sentence with each word and illustrate their sentences.

✳ RETEACH For those pupils who need additional instruction, see "Reteaching Lesson Skills," page T331, under "Reteaching and Extending."

✳ RETEACHING AND EXTENDING

Reteaching Lesson Skills

The activities that follow provide reteaching of skills developed in this lesson. Not every pupil needs to complete these activities. Choose only the activities that are needed to provide for the individual differences in your classroom.

> ### DECODING/VOCABULARY

R, T   Sound/symbol correspondence: vowel /yoo/, /oo/u-e

✳   **RETEACH** Print the following groups of words on the chalkboard:

tube	cut	cube
tub	cute	cub
tune	bug	use
fun	flute	crumb

Point to the first pair of words and read them aloud. Ask what is different about the words *tube* and *tub*. (The word *tube* has an *e* at the end; the letter *u* in *tube* stands for the long sound of *u*.) Follow a similar procedure with the next two pairs of words.

Then ask a pupil to point to and read a word from the second group of words that has the long sound of letter *u*. *(tune, use, flute)* Ask a pupil to point to and read a word that has the short sound of letter *u*. *(bug, fun, crumb)* Continue until each of the words has been read. Then call on pupils to read all the words.

R, T   Word structure: contractions (with *'re*)

✳   **RETEACH** Print the following sets of words on the chalkboard:

you are	we are	they are
you're	we're	they're

Point to and read the words *you are.* Tell pupils that we sometimes put two words together into one word called a contraction. Point to and read the word *you're.*

SAY	**The word *you're* was made by putting together the words *you are.* The**

apostrophe in *you're* takes the place of the *a* in *are.*

Have pupils read the remaining sets of words and tell what letter the apostrophe takes the place of in each contraction. *(a)*

I, T Word structure: suffix -ly

 RETEACH Put your fingers to your lips, say *shhh*, and ask what it means when you say *shhh*. (to be quiet) Then ask pupils to show how they would sit quietly or how they would talk quietly.

Print the following sentences on the chalkboard:

> 1. The girl sang sweetly.
> 2. My Mom fondly looked at the baby.
> 3. "I broke my wagon!" he said sadly.

Have the first sentence read aloud and ask how the girl sang. (*sweetly*) Tell pupils that the ending -*ly* was added to *sweet* to make a word that tells how something was done.

Follow a similar procedure with the remaining sentences.

RM 21 Distribute *Reteach Masters* page 21 and explain the directions on the page.

I, T Vocabulary: antonyms and synonyms

 RETEACH Display *Word Cards pitch, cold, end* in the *Pocket Chart.* Tell pupils that words that have almost the same meaning are called synonyms. Words that have opposite meanings are called antonyms.

Hold up each *Word Card* and ask a pupil to think of a word that is a synonym for the word. Ask another pupil to think of a word that is an antonym for the word. (Answers will vary. Possible answers include: synonyms—*pitch/toss, cold/chilly, end/finish;* antonyms—*pitch/catch, cold/hot, end/start.*)

I, T Vocabulary: word meaning

 RETEACH Print the following words and sentences on the chalkboard, omitting the underlining.

IC 94
> calf door fair horses
> imagines Larry toot
>
> 1. <u>Larry</u> closes his <u>door</u>.
> 2. He <u>imagines</u> he is at a <u>fair</u>.
> 3. Then he imagines he is at a farm.
> 4. "<u>Toot</u>! Toot!" honks the tractor.
> 5. Larry sees a <u>calf</u> and some baby <u>horses</u>.
>
> **fondly hollered rapping really
> slowly suddenly suspect
> sweetly weekend**

Point to the word *Larry* and read the word. Ask pupils to find a sentence that contains the word *Larry* and to read it aloud. Continue in the same manner with the remaining sentences, calling attention to the underlined words.

Display *Word Cards* for each of the underlined words. Have pupils hold up and read the word that answers each of the following questions.

1. **Which word names a baby cow?** (*calf*)
2. **Which word means the same thing as *pretends*?** (*imagines*)
3. **Which word is a boy's name?** (*Larry*)
4. **Which word is the sound a whistle makes?** (*toot*)
5. **Which word tells what you open and close to go into and out of a room?** (*door*)
6. **Which word names a place where you might find a Ferris Wheel?** (*fair*)
7. **Which word means "more than one horse"?** (*horses*)

Have pupils read the second set of words and use them in sentences.

RM 22 Distribute *Reteach Masters* page 22 and explain the directions on the page.

Focus

R, T **Literal:** pronoun referents (*he, it, she, they, we*)

✳ **RETEACH** Print the following sentences on the chalkboard, omitting the answers in parentheses. Have Sentences 1–2 read aloud.

IC 101

1. Max and Abby went to the fair.
2. (They) rode on the Ferris wheel.

3. A train is a fun way to go places.
4. (It) can go faster than a car.

5. Abby and I saw a calf in a field.
6. (We) didn't know if the calf could see us.

7. Abby had to hurry home.
8. (She) was late for dinner.

ASK **Where did Max and Abby go?** (to the fair) **Which word in the second sentence takes the place of the words *Max and Abby*?** (*They*) **The word *They* is a pronoun. A pronoun is a word that can take the place of the name of a person or a thing.**

Have Sentences 3 and 4 read aloud. Ask what word could be used in Sentence 4 to take the place of the words *A Train* in Sentence 3. (*It*)

Follow a similar procedure for the remaining sentences.

HOW AM I DOING?

Most pupils are filled with creative ideas. Ask yourself the following questions to gauge your teaching effectiveness in encouraging creativity.

	Yes	No	Some-times
1. Have I provided time for pupils to respond to a piece of literature?	☐	☐	☐
2. Do I foster new interests through literature?	☐	☐	☐
3. Have I encouraged pupils to share their ideas with others?	☐	☐	☐
4. Have I provided an opportunity to let pupils make a choice in what they would like to read?	☐	☐	☐

Extending Selection Concepts

LANGUAGE ARTS

SPEAKING: ROLE PLAYING Call on pupils to pretend to be Larry and to tell about the things he did on his visit to his grandparents' house. Pupils may look at page 146 to help them recall the things that Larry's grandparents had planned. Encourage pupils to use details to describe the visit.

LITERATURE

LISTENING: FICTION Choose a story about imagining or pretending and read it aloud. Ask pupils to compare the imagination of the character in the story with Larry's imagination.

Berger, Barbara. *When the Sun Rose.* Philomel, 1986. An imaginative little girl spends a happy day with her imaginary friend who arrives with a pet lion.

Carrick, Carol. *Patrick's Dinosaurs.* Clarion, 1983. Facts about prehistoric animals are interspersed in this story of a little boy with a big imagination.

Heine, Helme. *The Pearl.* Atheneum, 1985. Beaver is sure there is a pearl in the mussel he has found and dreams of what will happen to him because of his good fortune.

Jonas, Ann. *The Trek.* Greenwillow, 1985. City streets become a jungle, then a desert, as a girl trudges to school.

Mayer, Mercer. *There's an Alligator Under My Bed.* Dial, 1987. Fear is turned to fun as a little boy tries to trick the imaginary alligator under his bed into moving to the garage where alligators belong.

Spier, Peter. *Dreams.* Doubleday, 1986. Two children spend the day watching clouds change into many different scenes.

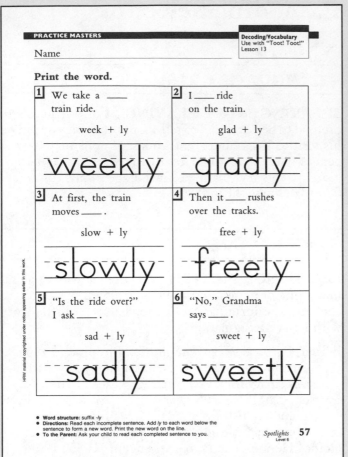

PRACTICE MASTERS

Decoding/Vocabulary
Use with "Toot! Toot!"
Lesson 13

Name _____

Print the word.

1 We take a ___ train ride.

week + ly

weekly

2 I ___ ride on the train.

glad + ly

gladly

3 At first, the train moves ___ .

slow + ly

slowly

4 Then it ___ rushes over the tracks.

free + ly

freely

5 "Is the ride over?" I ask ___ .

sad + ly

sadly

6 "No," Grandma says ___ .

sweet + ly

sweetly

- **Word structure:** suffix -ly
- **Directions:** Read each incomplete sentence. Add *ly* to each word below the sentence to form a new word. Print the new word on the line.
- **To the Parent:** Ask your child to read each completed sentence to you.

Spotlights
Level 6

57

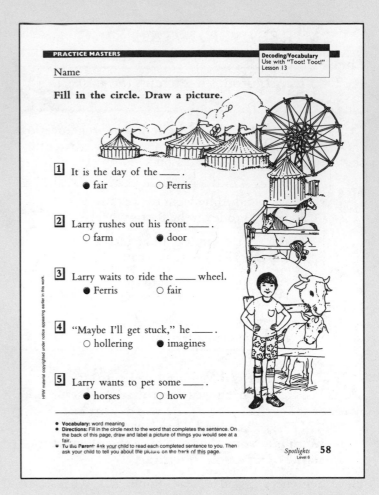

PRACTICE MASTERS

Decoding/Vocabulary
Use with "Toot! Toot!"
Lesson 13

Name _____

Fill in the circle. Draw a picture.

1 It is the day of the ___ .
- ● fair   ○ Ferris

2 Larry rushes out his front ___ .
- ○ farm   ● door

3 Larry waits to ride the ___ wheel.
- ● Ferris   ○ fair

4 "Maybe I'll get stuck," he ___ .
- ○ hollering   ● imagines

5 Larry wants to pet some ___ .
- ● horses   ○ how

- **Vocabulary:** word meaning
- **Directions:** Fill in the circle next to the word that completes the sentence. On the back of this page, draw and label a picture of things you would see at a fair.
- **To the Parent:** Ask your child to read each completed sentence to you. Then ask your child to tell you about the picture on the back of this page.

Spotlights
Level 6

58

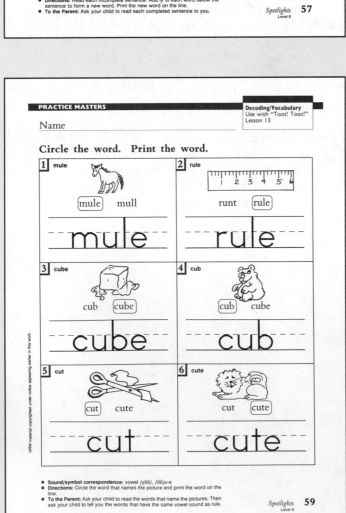

PRACTICE MASTERS

Decoding/Vocabulary
Use with "Toot! Toot!"
Lesson 13

Name _____

Circle the word. Print the word.

1 mule

mule   mull

mule

2 rule

runt   rule

rule

3 cube

cub   cube

cube

4 cub

cub   cube

cub

5 cut

cut   cute

cut

6 cute

cut   cute

cute

- **Sound/symbol correspondence:** vowel /yōō/, /ōō/u-e
- **Directions:** Circle the word that names the picture and print the word on the line.
- **To the Parent:** Ask your child to read the words that name the pictures. Then ask your child to tell you the words that have the same vowel sound as *rule*.

Spotlights
Level 6

59

RETEACH MASTERS

Decoding/Vocabulary
Use with "Toot! Toot!"
Lesson 13

Name

Circle the word. Print the word.

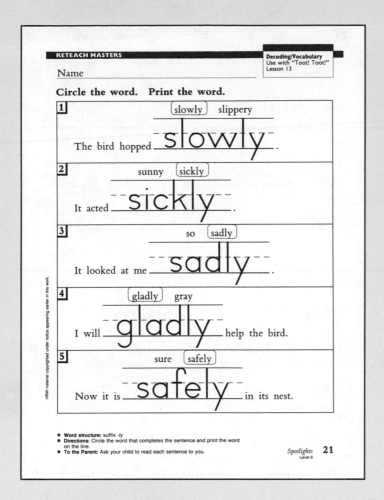

1 slowly slippery

The bird hopped slowly.

2 sunny sickly

It acted sickly.

3 so sadly

It looked at me sadly.

4 gladly gray

I will gladly help the bird.

5 sure safely

Now it is safely in its nest.

- **Word structure:** suffix -ly
- **Directions:** Circle the word that completes the sentence and print the word on the line.
- **To the Parent:** Ask your child to read each sentence to you.

Spotlights Level 6 **21**

RETEACH MASTERS

Decoding/Vocabulary
Use with "Toot! Toot!"
Lesson 13

Name

A. Circle Yes or No.

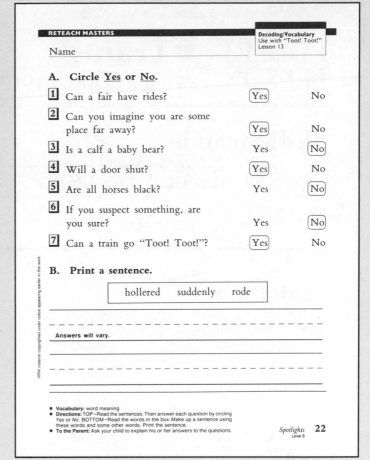

1 Can a fair have rides? | Yes | No

2 Can you imagine you are some place far away? | Yes | No

3 Is a calf a baby bear? | Yes | No

4 Will a door shut? | Yes | No

5 Are all horses black? | Yes | No

6 If you suspect something, are you sure? | Yes | No

7 Can a train go "Toot! Toot!"? | Yes | No

B. Print a sentence.

hollered   suddenly   rode

Answers will vary.

- **Vocabulary:** word meaning
- **Directions:** TOP – Read the sentences. Then answer each question by circling *Yes* or *No*. BOTTOM – Read the words in the box. Make up a sentence using these words and some other words. Print the sentence.
- **To the Parent:** Ask your child to explain his or her answers to the questions.

Spotlights Level 6 **22**

POETRY LESSON

"Trains"

pages 148–149 (T334–T335)

Skill Strands

COMPREHENSION/THINKING

M **Forms of literature:** poetry

Materials

Spotlights, Level 6: pages 148–149
Teacher's Idea Book

Special Populations

See *Teacher's Idea Book* for additional suggestions to help pupils with limited English proficiency.

Key to Symbols
I Introduced in this lesson
R Reinforced from an earlier lesson in this level
M Maintained from previous levels
T Tested in this level

COMPREHENSION/THINKING

M **Forms of literature:** poetry

DIRECT INSTRUCTION Remind pupils that Larry imagined that he was riding a train. Explain that people ride on passenger trains. Other trains, called freight trains, carry food, machinery, toys, automobiles, mail, and other products.

Have pupils find pages 148 and 149 in their books and tell them that this is a poem about trains. Ask pupils to listen to find out why the poet thinks trains are important. Read aloud "Trains."

GUIDED PRACTICE Ask why trains are important. (Possible answers include: They carry things over mountains, plains, and rivers; they bring their precious loads in without fail.) Read the second verse again and ask which word tells that the things on the train are important. (The word *precious* means "very valuable.") Reread the third verse and ask which words tell that the trains do not stop until they reach their destinations. ("Through day and darkness, Through dusk and dawn.")

Ask pupils to look at the first verse as you read it aloud. Then have them look at the last verse as you read it aloud. Ask what is special about these verses. (They are exactly alike.) Explain that poems and songs often repeat the same words. Each time the same words are repeated is called a "refrain."

Reread the first verse several times until pupils can recite it with you. Read the second and third verses and then have pupils recite the last verse with you.

(To be read by the teacher)

Trains

Over the mountains,
Over the plains,
Over the rivers,
Here come the trains.

Carrying passengers,
Carrying mail,
Bringing their precious loads
In without fail.

Thousands of freight cars
all rushing on
Through day and darkness,
Through dusk and dawn.

Over the mountains,
Over the plains,
Over the rivers,
Here come the trains.

James S. Tippett

148

149

"Going to Grandma's"
pages 150–151 (T336–T337)

Skill Strands

COMPREHENSION/THINKING

R, T   Inferential: predicting outcomes

Materials

Spotlights, Level 6: pages 150–151
Teacher's Idea Book

Special Populations

See *Teacher's Idea Book* for additional suggestions to help pupils with limited English proficiency.

Key to Symbols
I   Introduced in this lesson
R   Reinforced from an earlier lesson in this level
M   Maintained from previous levels
T   Tested in this level

COMPREHENSION/THINKING

R, T   Inferential: predicting outcomes

DIRECT INSTRUCTION Remind pupils that when you read a story, you can often guess what is going to happen. This is called making a prediction. Tell pupils that when you make a prediction, you use the information that is in the story and what you already know. Explain that you will read a story, and then you will ask pupils to make a prediction.

READ Mary planted flower seeds. Every day she watered the tiny plants. The plants grew bigger and bigger, but they did not have flowers. Mary did not think her garden would ever bloom. Then, one day, Mary was surprised when she went to water her garden.

ASK **What do you think happened in Mary's garden?** (The flowers started to bloom.) **What information in the story helped you make this prediction?** (The plants grew bigger and bigger; Mary was waiting for them to bloom; she was surprised one day.) **What did you already know about flowers that helped you make this prediction?** (Possible answers include: You knew that plants need to grow before they bloom.)

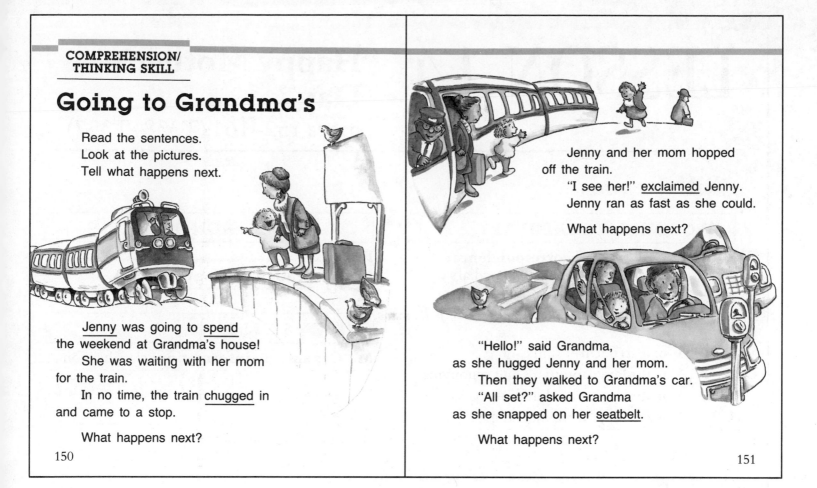

COMPREHENSION/ THINKING SKILL

Going to Grandma's

Read the sentences.
Look at the pictures.
Tell what happens next.

<u>Jenny</u> was going to <u>spend</u> the weekend at Grandma's house!
She was waiting with her mom for the train.
In no time, the train <u>chugged</u> in and came to a stop.

What happens next?

150

Jenny and her mom hopped off the train.
"I see her!" <u>exclaimed</u> Jenny.
Jenny ran as fast as she could.

What happens next?

"Hello!" said Grandma, as she hugged Jenny and her mom.
Then they walked to Grandma's car.
"All set?" asked Grandma as she snapped on her <u>seatbelt</u>.

What happens next?

151

GUIDED PRACTICE Have pupils turn to pages 150 and 151 in their books. Tell them that these pages tell about a trip that a girl takes to her grandma's house. Have the directions at the top of page 150 read aloud. Explain to pupils that they will be asked to read groups of sentences and to predict what they think might happen next.

Have the rest of page 150 read. Then call on pupils to predict what will happen next and why they think as they do. (Possible answers include: Jenny and her mom will get on the train to ride to Grandma's house.)

Have pupils read the top of page 151 to themselves. Then have them predict what will happen next. (Possible answers include: Jenny will hug or kiss her grandma.)

Have pupils read the top of page 151 to themselves. Then have them predict what will happen next. (Possible answers include: Jenny will hug or kiss her grandma.)

Ask if any information is included that might help them predict what Jenny will do at her grandma's. (no) Tell pupils that if they wanted to predict what Jenny might do at her grandma's, they would have to use what they already know about visiting grandparents.

LESSON 14 "Happy Mother's Day"

pages 152–161 (T338–T357)

Skill Strands

DECODING/VOCABULARY

I, T   **Sound/symbol correspondence:** consonant /kw/*qu* (initial, medial)

M   **Accumulated elements:** consonant clusters *bl, cl, fl, gl, sl* (initial); *ld, lk, lp, lt* (final)

R, T   **Word structure:** suffix *-ly*

R, T   **Vocabulary:** antonyms and synonyms

I   **Vocabulary:** word building

I, T   **Vocabulary:** word meaning

COMPREHENSION/THINKING

Focus

M   **Inferential:** drawing conclusions

STUDY SKILLS

M   **Organizing information:** classification

LANGUAGE

R   **Speaking:** paraphrasing

Lesson Vocabulary

Decodable words: *ashes, bathroom, bathtub, beside, bookshelf, children, cost, desk, drank, drapes, fireplace, job, kitchen, Lenny, Linda, member, neat, overflowing, P.S., queen, quickly, squashed, swept, washing*

Special words: *Laurie, Louise, room*

Materials

Spotlights, Level 6: pages 152–161
Workbook: pages 94–99

Practice Masters: pages 60–63
Instructional Charts: pages 102–108
Resource Box: Letter Cards a, c, i, k, l (2), *t*
              Pattern Card qu
              Word Cards Laurie, Louise, quarter, queen, quick, quilt, room, squeak
Pocket Chart
Teacher's Idea Book
Reteach Masters: page 23

Language Applications

USING LANGUAGE

Oral reading: expression

EXTENDING SELECTION CONCEPTS

Writing: stories (Cooperative Learning)
Listening: fiction

Special Populations

See *Teacher's Idea Book* for additional suggestions to help pupils with limited English proficiency.

Key to Symbols
I   Introduced in this lesson
R   Reinforced from an earlier lesson in this level
M   Maintained from previous levels
T   Tested in this level

Idea Center

BIBLIOGRAPHY

Add to your reading corner or reading table various books about mothers and Mother's Day gifts. A suggested bibliography follows. Suggestions for reading aloud and annotations appear in the lesson plan.

Bunting, Eve. *The Mother's Day Mice.* Clarion, 1986.

Kroll, Steven. *Happy Mother's Day.* Holiday House, 1985.

Thayer, Margorie. *A Mother for Mother's Day.* Childrens Press, 1980.

Williams, Vera B. *A Chair for My Mother.* Greenwillow, 1982.

Planning Chart

	Instruction	Written Practice	Extending
Step 1 Preparing for the Selection	I, T **Sound/symbol correspondence:** consonant /kw/ *qu* (initial, medial) I **Vocabulary:** word building I, T **Vocabulary:** word meaning M **Inferential:** drawing conclusions	*Workbook* page 94 *Practice Masters* page 60 *Workbook* page 95 *Practice Masters* page 61 *Reteach Masters* page 23	
Step 2 Reading for Comprehension	**Oral reading:** expression **Inferential:** drawing conclusions **Story comprehension**	*Workbook* page 96	
Step 3 Developing Reading and Thinking	R, T **Word structure:** suffix *-ly* M **Accumulated elements:** consonant clusters *bl, cl, fl, gl, sl* (initial); *ld, lk, lp, lt* (final) R, T **Vocabulary:** antonyms and synonyms M **Inferential:** drawing conclusions M **Organizing information:** classification R **Speaking:** paraphrasing	*Workbook* page 97 *Workbook* page 98 *Workbook* page 99 *Practice Masters* page 62 *Practice Masters* page 63	**Writing:** stories (Cooperative Learning) **Listening:** fiction

DECODING/VOCABULARY

I, T **Sound/symbol correspondence:** consonant /kw/ *qu* (initial, medial)

DIRECT INSTRUCTION Print the following sentence and columns of words on the chalkboard:

IC 102

The queen quickly quit quilting.	
queen	quack
quickly	quilt
quit	quarter
squash	quiz

Read the sentence and tell pupils that it is a tongue twister. Ask pupils to read the tongue twister with you.

SAY **This tongue twister has words that begin with the /kw/ sound. Say *queen* with me: *queen*.** (Point to the word *queen*.) **The word *queen* begins with letters *qu*. The letters *qu* together stand for the /kw/ sound.**

Point to and read each of the remaining words in the first column and have pupils repeat them. Ask what letters stand for the /kw/ sound in each word. (*qu*) After *squash* is read, remind pupils that the letter *a* in *squash* stands for the same sound as the letter *a* in *wash*.

GUIDED PRACTICE Have pupils repeat the word that has the /kw/ sound after you read each of the following word pairs: *quick, cat; green, queen; guilty, quilt; quack, black.*

Then call attention to the second column of words on the chalkboard and have them read. Ask pupils to point to and read the words from the second column that answer each of the following questions:

1. **Which word names a kind of blanket?** (*quilt*)
2. **Which word names a coin that is worth twenty-five cents?** (*quarter*)
3. **Which word means "a short test"?** (*quiz*)
4. **Which word names a sound a duck makes?** (*quack*)

WB 94 **INDEPENDENT PRACTICE** *Workbook* page 94 may be used to practice identifying sound/symbol correspondence /kw/ *qu.*

PM 60 **ADDITIONAL PRACTICE** *Practice Masters* page 60 may be used as an optional practice for identifying sound/symbol correspondence /kw/ *qu.* (See page T356 for reduced pages with answers.)

✳ RETEACH For those pupils who need additional instruction, see "Reteaching Lesson Skills," page T355, under "Reteaching and Extending."

I Vocabulary: word building

DIRECT INSTRUCTION Display *Pattern Card qu.* Explain that the letter *q* almost always has letter *u* after it. Add *Letter Cards* to make the word *quit* and have the word read. Place letter *l* between the *i* and the *t* and have the new word read. (*quilt*)

GUIDED PRACTICE Display *Letter Cards a, c, k, l.* Have pupils use the letters to make new words following the suggestions below.

1. **Take away *t* and place another *l* at the end. What is the new word?** (*quill*) **A porcupine has sharp quills.**
2. **Take away one *l*. Then put *a* between the *u* and the *i*. What is the new word?** (*quail*) **A quail is a bird.**
3. **Take away the *il* and place *ck* at the end of the word. What is the new word?** (*quack*)
4. **Change *a* to *i*. What is the new word?** (*quick*)
5. **Take away the *ck* and put *t* at the end. What is the new word?** (*quit*)

I, T Vocabulary: word meaning

DIRECT INSTRUCTION Print the following words and sentences on the chalkboard, omitting the underlining.

Laurie   Louise   room
1. <u>Laurie</u> made a card.
2. She hid the card in her <u>room</u>.
3. The card was for <u>Louise</u> on her birthday.
P.S.   queen   quickly   squashed

Read aloud the first sentence. Then point to the word *Laurie* and read it. Explain that *Laurie* is a girl's name. Have pupils read the sentence with you. Then ask pupils to find and read the word *Laurie*.

Read aloud the second sentence. Then point to the word *room* and read it. Ask what Laurie did with the card she made. (She hid it in her room.) Ask why she might hide the card. (Possible answers include: She did not want someone to see it.) Have pupils read the sentence with you. Then ask them to find and read the word *room*.

Read aloud the third sentence. Then point to the word *Louise* and read it. Ask what Laurie would do with the card. (She would give it to Louise on her birthday.) Have pupils read the sentence with you. Then ask them to find and read the word *Louise*.

The words in the second set are new words that contain known phonic elements. You may wish to ask pupils to read the words, using what they know about letters and sounds.

GUIDED PRACTICE Print the following sentences on the chalkboard, omitting the underlining.

1. <u>Laurie</u> made a fat sandwich for <u>Louise</u>.
2. "I feel like a <u>queen</u>!" Louise said.
3. She <u>squashed</u> the sandwich down to eat it.
4. After lunch, the girls <u>quickly</u> cleaned up the <u>room</u>.

5. They left the following note:
        Mom,
              We went to the park.
                    Love,
                    Laurie and Louise
<u>P.S.</u> We'll be back at 2:00.

Provide opportunities for pupils to practice reading the new special words and some of the new decodable words in these sentences by following the suggestions below.

Sentence 1: Ask pupils to find and read the names *Laurie* and *Louise.* Then have the sentence read aloud.

Sentences 2–3: Have the sentences read and ask why Louise felt like a queen. (because her sister had made a sandwich for her) Then ask pupils to find and read *squashed.* Ask why Laurie squashed the sandwich. (It was too fat to eat.)

Sentence 4: Have the sentence read aloud and ask what the girls did. (They cleaned up the room.) Ask how they worked. (*quickly*)

Sentence 5: Have the sentence read aloud. Then ask what the girls decided to add to their note after they had already signed their names. (a *P.S.*) Explain that a *P.S.* is added onto the end of a letter when the writer remembers something else he or she wishes to add. Have the *P.S.* read aloud.

Ask pupils to find and read *queen, squashed,* and *quickly.* Then invite each pupil to choose a sentence to read aloud.

INDEPENDENT PRACTICE *Workbook* page 95 may be used to practice reading story vocabulary.

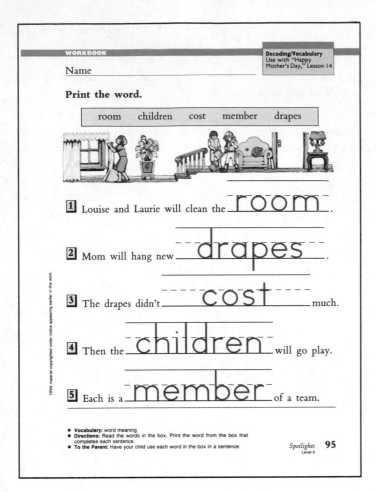

Name

Decoding/Vocabulary
Use with "Happy
Mother's Day," Lesson 14

Print the word.

| room | children | cost | member | drapes |

1 Louise and Laurie will clean the ___room___.

2 Mom will hang new ___drapes___.

3 The drapes didn't ___cost___ much.

4 Then the ___children___ will go play.

5 Each is a ___member___ of a team.

- **Vocabulary:** word meaning
- **Directions:** Read the words in the box. Print the word from the box that completes each sentence.
- **To the Parent:** Have your child use each word in the box in a sentence.

Spotlights
Level 6   **95**

PM 61 **ADDITIONAL PRACTICE** *Practice Masters* page 61 may be used as an optional practice for reading story vocabulary. (See page T357 for reduced pages with answers.)

✳ **RETEACH** For those pupils who need additional instruction, see "Reteaching Lesson Skills," page T355, under "Reteaching and Extending."

COMPREHENSION/THINKING

Focus

M Inferential: drawing conclusions

DIRECT INSTRUCTION Tell pupils that sometimes the author of the story does not tell you exactly what is happening. You have to use what you already know and clues from the story to help you figure out what is happening. When you do that, you are drawing a conclusion.

Tell pupils that you will ask them to draw a conclusion after they have listened to the following story.

READ **The bear looked and looked for the perfect place. The hollow tree was too small for him to crawl into it. The deep cave was too big to keep him warm. At last, he found a small cave. It would be just right for the long winter.**

ASK **What was the bear looking for?** (a place where he could sleep for the winter) **What clues in the story made you think this?** (The hollow tree was too small for him to crawl into it; the big cave would not keep him warm; the small cave was just right for the winter.) **What did you need to know about bears that helped you conclude that this bear needed a place to sleep for the winter?** (Bears sleep through the winter.)

GUIDED PRACTICE Ask pupils to listen to the following story and to be ready to draw a conclusion about it.

READ **Mark loved going to Hawaii. He had visited his grandmother when he was five, and he wanted to go back. When Mark got home on the last day of school, he saw airline tickets and a suitcase on his bed. He ran downstairs and hugged his mother.**

ASK **Where do you think Mark is going?** (Hawaii) **What facts from the story made you think that Mark was going to Hawaii?** (Mark loved to go there; he wanted to go back; airline tickets and a suitcase were on his bed; he ran and hugged his mother.)

Background for the Teacher

SUMMARY Each member of a family thinks of a special way to surprise Mom on Mother's Day. Mom is thrilled by all the surprises her family has in store for her.

INFORMATION This story was adapted from the book *Happy Mother's Day!* and resembles the format of a treasure hunt with one surprise leading to another.

Using Prior Knowledge

Tell pupils that they are going to read a story about a family celebrating Mother's Day in a special way. Continue by asking questions such as those that follow.

1. **What are some things that a family might do on Mother's Day?** (Possible answers include: cook dinner for Mother; buy flowers, candy, or another gift for her.)
2. **Some people make their own gifts. What kind of gift do you think people might make for Mother's Day?** (Possible answers include: cards, drawings, a special dinner.)

Setting a Purpose for Reading

Have pupils find page 152 in their books and read the title of the story.

Point out the headnote at the top of page 152. Explain that this note will help pupils think about the story they are going to read. Ask a pupil to read the note aloud and to predict what kind of surprises this mother might get on Mother's Day. (Answers will vary, but should include typical Mother's Day gifts, such as candy, clothes, cards.)

Reading Silently

Some pupils may be able to read this story independently. Direct them to read the whole story to find out more about the great Mother's Day gifts Mom gets.

For those pupils who need more guidance, suggestions for directed reading follow.

What are the surprises Mom gets on Mother's Day?

Happy Mother's Day

One day, when Mom got home, there was a note for her on the front door.

Mom dashed inside and ran to her room.

On the table <u>beside</u> the bed was a glass of milk and a snack.

Next to the milk was a note.

152

"What a surprise!" said Mom.

She <u>quickly</u> <u>drank</u> the milk and then looked under the bed.

"Surprise!" yelled <u>Lenny</u>, as he came out from under the bed.

"How lovely," Mom said.

"Now come with me," said Lenny.

153

Before reading pages 152–153

SAY **It was Mother's Day. What would have been a good surprise for Mother? Read pages 152 and 153 to find out what some of Mom's surprises were.**

After reading pages 152–153

1. **What was Mom's first surprise?** (a glass of milk and a snack) Literal
2. **How did Mom find out who left the surprise?** (There was a note from Lenny, and he yelled "Surprise!" from under the bed.) Inferential
3. **Where do you think Lenny was taking Mom?** (Possible answers include: to another room, to the kitchen.) Critical

Mom followed Lenny into
Linda's room.

The room was clean!

It hadn't looked that good
in weeks.

On the bookshelf was a note.

"Surprise!" Linda yelled.

"This looks great!" said Mom.

"Now come with us," said Linda.

Mom followed Linda and Lenny
to Laurie's room.

154

The windows that had needed
washing for so long were clean.

On one of them was a note.

"Surprise!" Laurie yelled, jumping
out from under her desk.

"I love it," said Mom as she gave
Laurie a kiss.

"Now come with us," said Laurie.

Mom went with Linda, Laurie, and
Lenny into Louise's room.

155

Before reading pages 154–155

 SAY

Mom.
Read pages 154 and 155 to find out where Lenny was taking

After reading pages 154–155

1. **Where did Lenny take Mom?** (to Linda's room) **Why?** (to show Mom that Linda had cleaned her room) Inferential
2. **What was special about Laurie's room?** (The windows were clean.) Literal
3. **What happened each time Mom found another surprise?** (She was led to the next one.) Inferential

The dirty <u>drapes</u> by the bed were no longer dirty.

On the bed was a note.

"Surprise!" yelled Louise, jumping out from in back of the door.

"I'm starting to feel like a queen," said Mom.

"You are a queen," said Louise. "Now come with us."

Mom followed the four <u>children</u> down to the family room.

156

The <u>fireplace</u> that had been <u>overflowing</u> with <u>ashes</u> was <u>swept</u> clean. On it was a note.

"Surprise!" yelled Larry as he came out from under a table.

"Thank you, Larry. You did a fine <u>job</u>!"

"Now come with us," said Larry.

157

Before reading pages 156–157

SAY **Mom was on her way into Louise's room. What do you think Louise's surprise will be? Read pages 156 and 157.**

After reading pages 156–157

1. **What did Mom see in Louise's room?** (The drapes were clean.) Literal
2. **Why do you think Mom was beginning to feel like a queen?** (Her children had done nice things for her to make her feel special.) Inferential
3. **What was Larry's gift to Mom?** (He had cleaned and swept the fireplace.) Literal

Mom followed Larry, Louise, Laurie, Linda, and Lenny into the <u>bathroom</u>.
It had been painted yellow.
On the sink was a note.

Yellow!
Like <u>sunshine</u>
Love, Dad

158

There was Dad <u>squashed</u> into the <u>bathtub</u>!
"Surprise!" he yelled.

"This is lovely!" said Mom.

"Now come with us!" said Dad.

"Surely there can't be more!" exclaimed Mom.

159

Before reading pages 158–159

SAY **Everyone had done something for Mother's Day except Dad. What do you think Dad's surprise will be? Read pages 158 and 159 to find out.**

After reading pages 158–159

1. **What was Dad's surprise?** (He had painted the bathroom yellow.) Inferential
2. **Why do you think Dad painted the bathroom?** (Possible answers include: It needed painting; Mom wanted it painted.) Critical

Mom followed Dad, Larry, Louise, Laurie, Linda, and Lenny into the <u>kitchen</u>.

Dinner was waiting.

In the middle of the table was a big cake.

On it were the words:

"Happy Mother's Day to the best Mom ever."

Mom hugged and kissed everyone.

"This is the best thing that has ever happened to me!" Mom said.

"You're the best thing that has ever happened to us!" said Dad, Larry, Louise, Linda, Laurie, and Lenny.

160

Discussing the Selection

1. What surprises did Mom get on Mother's Day?
2. How did Mom find her surprises?
3. How do you know Mom liked her gifts?
4. Find the places in the story that tell what each family <u>member</u> had for Mom.
5. Were the gifts from the family better than ones that <u>cost</u> money? Why or why not?

161

Before reading page 160 **Could there possibly have been any more surprises? Read page 160 to find out.**

After reading page 160
1. **What were Mom's last surprises?** (dinner and a cake) Literal
2. **How did Mom feel about everything her family had done?** (It was the best thing that had ever happened to her.) Inferential

Discussing the Selection

Questions preceded by a number appear in *Spotlights* after the selection. Questions preceded by a bullet are additional questions for extending discussion.

PURPOSE

1. **What surprises did Mom get on Mother's Day?** (Lenny had fixed her a snack; Linda had cleaned her room; Laurie had washed her windows; Louise had cleaned her drapes; Larry had cleaned the fireplace; Dad had painted the bathroom; the family had fixed dinner.) Inferential

• **How do you think each family member decided what his or her gift would be?** (Answers will vary, but should include that each thing the family did was probably something Mom had wanted to be done for a long time.) Critical

STORY MAPPING

2. **How did Mom find her surprises?** (The family wrote notes to tell her where to look; they took her from one place to another.) Literal

• **How do you think Mom felt as she went from room to room?** (excited, pleased, happy) Critical

3. **How do you know Mom liked her gifts?** (She smiled; she said she felt like a queen; she said that this was the best thing that had ever happened to her.) Inferential

- **Mom feels like a queen in this story. What do you think the expression "fit for a king" means?** (If something is fit for a king, it is very good.) Inferential

4. **Find the places in the story that tell what each family member had for Mom.** (page 152—Lenny made a snack for Mom; page 154—Linda cleaned her room; page 155—Laurie cleaned the windows; page 156—Louise cleaned the drapes; page 157—Larry swept the fireplace; pages 158–159—Dad painted the bathroom; page 160—the family fixed dinner and made a cake.) Inferential

CRITICAL THINKING

5. **Were the gifts from the family better than ones that cost money? Why or why not?** (Answers will vary. Many pupils will probably say that the gifts were better because they required time and effort on the part of each family member.)

- **What kind of gifts might this family give Dad on Father's Day?** (Answers will vary. Possible answers include: the same kinds of gifts they gave Mom.)

Using Language

ORAL READING: EXPRESSION Have pupils turn to page 152. Remind pupils that this story was written like a treasure hunt in that each note and gift led to another.

SAY **Let's read aloud the note that Mother found on the front door when she came home.** (Happy Mother's Day. There's a surprise waiting in your room.)

Follow a similar procedure for the remaining pages, using the following suggestions.

Page 153: **Read the note that Lenny wrote. Then read the line that tells what Mother said when she read the note in the way she may have said it.** ("What a surprise!" said Mom.)

Page 154: **Read the note that Mom found in Linda's room.** (Clean and neat, A Mother's Day treat. Love, Linda)

Page 155: **Read what Mom said when she noticed the clean windows.** ("I love it," said Mom as she gave Laurie a kiss.)

Page 156: **Read the note that Mom found in Louise's room.** (Today you're queen. I made them clean. Love, Louise) **Then read what Mom said when she saw the clean drapes.** ("I'm starting to feel like a queen," said Mom.)

Page 160: **Read the words that were on Mom's cake.** (Happy Mother's Day to the best Mom ever.) **Read what Mom said when she saw dinner and the cake.** ("This is the best thing that has ever happened to me!" Mom said.) **Then read what Mom's family said to her.** ("You're the best thing that has ever happened to us!" said Dad, Larry, Louise, Linda, Laurie, and Lenny.)

Applying the Focus Skill

INFERENTIAL: DRAWING CONCLUSIONS
Remind pupils that sometimes they can use clues from a story and what they already know to figure out what will happen. This is called drawing a conclusion.

SAY **In the beginning of our story, Mother saw a note that told her to go to her room. There she found a surprise. Then she was led to another room where she found another surprise. What did you conclude would happen each time Mom was led to another room?** (Mom would find another note and another gift.)

At the end of the story, Mom hugged and kissed everyone. What can you conclude about the way Mom felt about Mother's Day? (She was very happy; she was glad that her family had tried to please her.)

Evaluating Comprehension

WB 96 **INDEPENDENT PRACTICE** *Workbook* page 96 may be used for an informal evaluation of story comprehension.

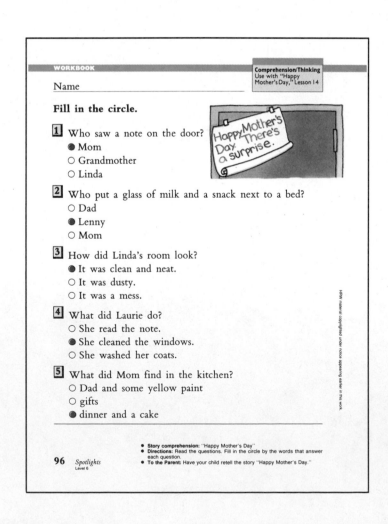

DECODING/VOCABULARY

R, T   Word structure: suffix *-ly*

DIRECT INSTRUCTION Print the following sentences on the chalkboard, omitting the underlining. Have the first sentence read.

> 1. Mom drank the milk <u>quickly</u>.
> 2. The king <u>slowly</u> cut the pie.
> 3. Blackbirds began to sing <u>badly</u>.
> 4. The queen <u>sadly</u> held her ears.
> 5. The blackbirds <u>quickly</u> quit singing.

ASK **Which word tells how Mom drank the milk?** (*quickly*) **The ending *-ly* was added to the word *quick* to make the word *quickly*. When *-ly* is added to a word, the new word describes how something is done.**

GUIDED PRACTICE Call on pupils to read the remaining sentences aloud. Ask pupils to find the *-ly* word in each sentence and to tell what the word means.

WB 97 **INDEPENDENT PRACTICE** *Workbook* page 97 may be used to practice reading words with the suffix *-ly*.

✱ **RETEACH** For those pupils who need additional instruction, see "Reteaching Lesson Skills," page T355, under "Reteaching and Extending."

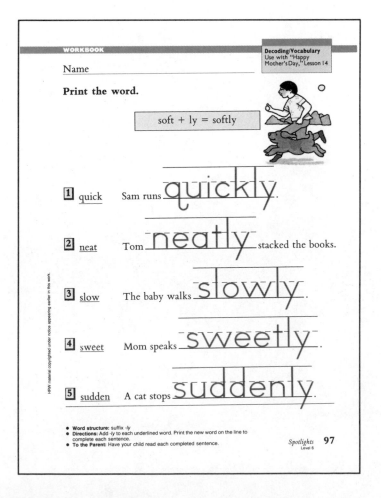

WORKBOOK

Decoding/Vocabulary
Use with "Happy
Mother's Day," Lesson 14

Name _____

Print the word.

> soft + ly = softly

1 <u>quick</u>   Sam runs quickly.

2 <u>neat</u>   Tom neatly stacked the books.

3 <u>slow</u>   The baby walks slowly.

4 <u>sweet</u>   Mom speaks sweetly.

5 <u>sudden</u>   A cat stops suddenly.

● **Word structure:** suffix -ly
● **Directions:** Add -ly to each underlined word. Print the new word on the line to complete each sentence.
● **To the Parent:** Have your child read each completed sentence.

Spotlights Level 6   **97**

M **Accumulated elements:** consonant clusters
bl, cl, fl, gl, sl (initial); *ld, lk, lp, lt* (final)

DIRECT INSTRUCTION Print the following
words on the chalkboard:

black	clean	fly	glow	sled
held	milk	melt	help	

slip	glass	flag
silk	cold	clap
blink	gulp	stilt

Point to the first row of words and have each word read.
Ask what two letters make up the consonant cluster at
the beginning of each word. *(bl, cl, fl, gl, sl)*

Point to the second row of words and have each word
read. Ask what two letters make up the consonant cluster at the end of each word. *(ld, lk, lt, lp)*

GUIDED PRACTICE Call attention to the second
set of words. Have a pupil read a word and call on a second pupil to point to the word that was read. Continue
this procedure until each word has been read.

WB 98 **INDEPENDENT PRACTICE** *Workbook*
page 98 may be used to practice reading words
with consonant clusters.

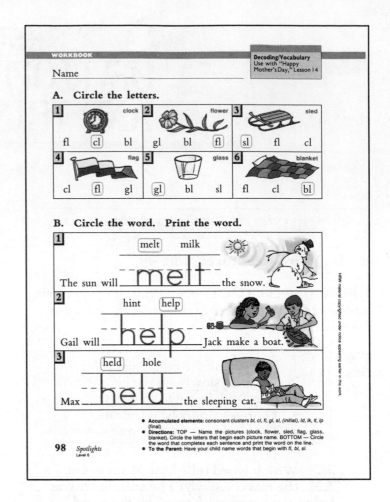

R, T **Vocabulary:** antonyms and synonyms

DIRECT INSTRUCTION Write the following
words on the chalkboard: *happy, glad, sad, stop, go, move.*
Have the words read. Remind pupils that words that
mean almost the same thing are called *synonyms.* Point to
the word *happy* and have a pupil point to and read the
word that is a synonym for *happy. (glad)* Have a pupil
point to and read the word that is the opposite of *happy.*
(sad) Remind pupils the words that are opposites are call
antonyms.

GUIDED PRACTICE Indicate the words *stop, go,
move.* Have a pupil point to and read the word that is a
synonym for *go (move)* and that is an antonym for *go.*
(stop)

✳ RETEACH For pupils who need additional
instruction, see "Reteaching Lesson Skills," page
T355, under "Reteaching and Extending."

COMPREHENSION/THINKING

Focus

M Inferential: drawing conclusions

DIRECT INSTRUCTION Tell pupils that authors of stories do not always tell readers exactly what is happening. Instead, authors may give clues that help readers figure out what is happening or readers may use what they already know to figure out what is happening. When readers do this, they are drawing conclusions.

GUIDED PRACTICE Print the following story on the chalkboard and have it read.

> Pam quickly gobbled her food.
> Then she grabbed her books and lunch box.
> She dashed out the door.
> She got to the bus stop just in time.

ASK **Do you think Pam was early or late?** (She was late.) **What clues helped you come to this conclusion?** (She gobbled her food; she grabbed her things and dashed out the door.) **Did Pam miss her bus?** (no) **What helped you come to this conclusion?** (the words *just in time*)

WB 99 INDEPENDENT PRACTICE *Workbook* page 99 may be used to practice drawing conclusions.

PM 62 ADDITIONAL PRACTICE *Practice Masters* page 62 may be used as an optional practice for drawing conclusions. (See page T357 for reduced pages with answers.)

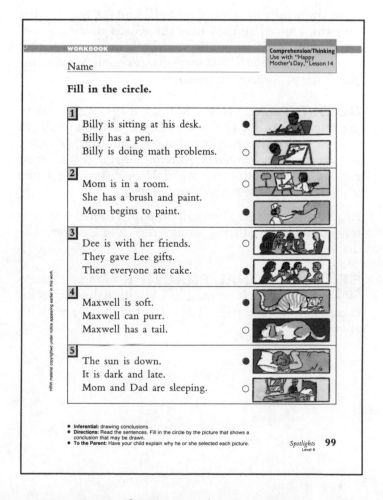

M   Organizing information: classification

DIRECT INSTRUCTION   Print the following diagram and words on the chalkboard:

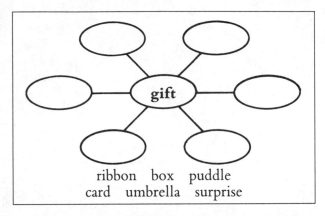

Point to the word *gift* in the chart and have it read. Then ask pupils to read the words below the diagram and to tell which words make them think of a gift. (*ribbon, box, card, surprise*) Write these words in the chart and explain that these words go together because they are all things that might be associated with a gift. Ask pupils to think of some other words that go with *gift* to complete the chart. (*birthday, bow, wrapping paper*) Print the additional words on the chart.

Read the words *puddle* and *umbrella* and ask pupils what they think of when they hear the words *puddle* and *umbrella*. (rain) Call on pupils to suggest other words that might go with *puddle* and *umbrella*. (Possible answers include: *storm, thunder, raincoat*.)

GUIDED PRACTICE   Make a diagram, similar to the one shown, for the word *Mother*. Call on pupils to suggest words that might tell about a mother. (Possible answers include: *nice, loving, cheerful, helpful, smart*.) Print each response around the word *Mother*, drawing a line from each response to the word *Mother*.

Read the responses. Then call on pupils to make up sentences about mothers, using the words from the diagram.

ADDITIONAL PRACTICE   *Practice Masters* page 63 may be used as an optional practice for classification. (See page T357 for reduced pages with answers.)

R   Speaking: paraphrasing

DIRECT INSTRUCTION   Ask pupils to find page 152 in their books.

SAY   **Mom found a note when she got home. Can you find and read the sentence on this page that tells that Mom found a note?** (*One day, when Mom got home, there was a note for her on the front door.*) **When I said "Mom found a note when she got home," I was not using the exact words that are written in the book. I was following the story, but I was telling it in my own words. When you tell someone else about a story, you use your own words and tell about only the important parts of the story.**

GUIDED PRACTICE   Have pupils look at pages 152–153 and tell in their own words what Lenny's note said and what surprises he had waiting for Mom. (Possible answers include: Lenny's note told his mom she was a good mom and to check under the bed; he had a glass of milk and a snack waiting for her.)

Follow a similar procedure for each child's surprise and for Dad's surprise.

✳ RETEACHING AND EXTENDING

Reteaching Lesson Skills

The activities that follow provide reteaching of skills developed in this lesson. Not every pupil needs to complete these activities. Choose only the activities that are needed to provide for the individual differences in your classroom.

DECODING/VOCABULARY

I, T Sound/symbol correspondence: /kw/*qu* (initial, medial)

✳ **RETEACH** Display *Word Card queen* and read the word.

> **SAY** *Queen* begins with the letters *qu*. The letters *qu* together stand for the /kw/ sound. Read this word with me: *queen.*

Hold up *Word Cards quick, quilt, squeak, queen, quarter* one at a time and ask pupils to read them.

I, T Vocabulary: word meaning

✳ **RETEACH** Print the following words and sentences on the chalkboard, omitting the underlining.

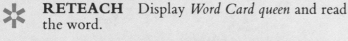

> **Laurie   Louise   room**
>
> 1. <u>Laurie</u> made a card.
> 2. She hid the card in her <u>room</u>.
> 3. The card was for <u>Louise</u> on her birthday.
>
> **P.S.   queen   quickly   squashed**

Point to the word *Laurie* and read it. Call on a pupil to find and read the sentence that contains the word *Laurie.* Follow a similar procedure with the remaining sentences, calling attention to the underlined words.

Display *Word Cards Laurie, Louise,* and *room.* Have a pupil hold up and read the words that are names. (*Laurie, Louise*) Have another pupil hold up and read the word that names a part of a house. (*room*)

Have pupils read the second set of words and use them in sentences.

 Distribute *Reteach Masters* page 23 and explain the directions on the page.

R, T Word structure: suffix *-ly*

✳ **RETEACH** Print the following sentences and words on the chalkboard:

> 1. He ran _____.
>   quick   quickly
> 2. The _____ boy sobbed.
>   sad   sadly
> 3. The hens sang _____.
>   bad   badly

Read the first sentence and the word choices below it. Explain that the ending *-ly* on the word *quickly* changes the word to tell how something was done. Ask how the boy ran. (*quickly*) Tell pupils that the word *quickly* belongs in the sentence. Print *quickly* in the blank and have the completed sentence read.

Call on pupils to fill in the remaining blanks and to read the completed sentences. (2—*The sad boy sobbed;* 3—*The hens sang badly.*)

R, T Vocabulary: antonyms and synonyms

✳ **RETEACH** Call on pupils to name a synonym as you read each of the following words: *fast (quick), hot (warm), sleepy (tired), scared (afraid).* Then call on pupils to name an antonym as you read each of the following words: *day (night), cold (hot), girl (boy), in (out).*

Extending Selection Concepts

LANGUAGE ARTS

WRITING: STORIES (Cooperative Learning) Have pupils work in small groups to write a story called "Happy Father's Day." Have pupils use the story in their books to help them write the story. For example, the family in "Happy Father's Day" might do things for Father that he would enjoy, just as Mother enjoyed her gifts. The story can end in a similar way to "Happy Mother's Day." You may wish to provide drawing paper for pupils to illustrate their stories.

LITERATURE

LISTENING: FICTION Choose a book about mothers and their families and read it aloud to the class.

Bunting, Eve. *The Mother's Day Mice.* Clarion, 1986. Three young mice search for special presents for Mother's Day.

Kroll, Steven. *Happy Mother's Day.* Holiday House, 1985. This is the original text that was adapted for the selection "Happy Mother's Day."

Thayer, Margorie. *A Mother for Mother's Day.* Childrens Press, 1980. When Michael's classmates discover that he is an orphan, they decide to try to find Michael a mother for Mother's Day.

HOW AM I DOING?

Many pupils need encouragement to establish better self-discipline for independent reading. Ask yourself the following questions to gauge your teaching effectiveness in this area.

	Yes	No	Some-times
1. Have I taken pupils to the library?	☐	☐	☐
2. Have I provided time for independent silent reading?	☐	☐	☐
3. Have I encouraged an independent reading program for pupils that praises them for their efforts?	☐	☐	☐
4. Have I suggested guidance for reading at home such as finding a special time and place to read?	☐	☐	☐

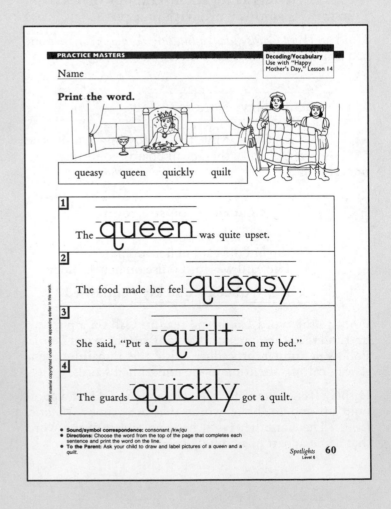

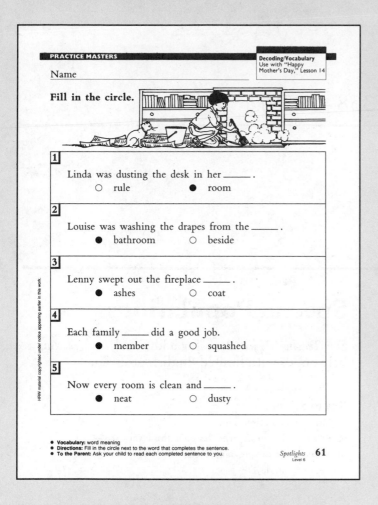

Name _____

Fill in the circle.

1 Linda was dusting the desk in her _____ .
○ rule ● room

2 Louise was washing the drapes from the _____ .
● bathroom ○ beside

3 Lenny swept out the fireplace _____ .
● ashes ○ coat

4 Each family _____ did a good job.
● member ○ squashed

5 Now every room is clean and _____ .
● neat ○ dusty

● **Vocabulary:** word meaning
● **Directions:** Fill in the circle next to the word that completes the sentence.
● **To the Parent:** Ask your child to read each completed sentence to you.

Spotlights **61**
Level 6

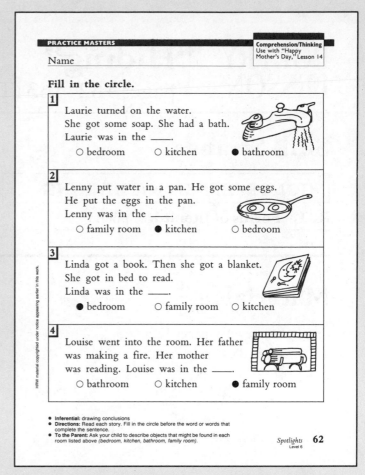

Name _____

Fill in the circle.

1 Laurie turned on the water.
She got some soap. She had a bath.
Laurie was in the _____ .
○ bedroom ○ kitchen ● bathroom

2 Lenny put water in a pan. He got some eggs.
He put the eggs in the pan.
Lenny was in the _____ .
○ family room ● kitchen ○ bedroom

3 Linda got a book. Then she got a blanket.
She got in bed to read.
Linda was in the _____ .
● bedroom ○ family room ○ kitchen

4 Louise went into the room. Her father
was making a fire. Her mother
was reading. Louise was in the _____ .
○ bathroom ○ kitchen ● family room

● **Inferential:** drawing conclusions
● **Directions:** Read each story. Fill in the circle before the word or words that complete the sentence.
● **To the Parent:** Ask your child to describe objects that might be found in each room listed above (*bedroom, kitchen, bathroom, family room*).

Spotlights **62**
Level 6

Name _____

Print the word.

| hot snow grass cold sun frost |

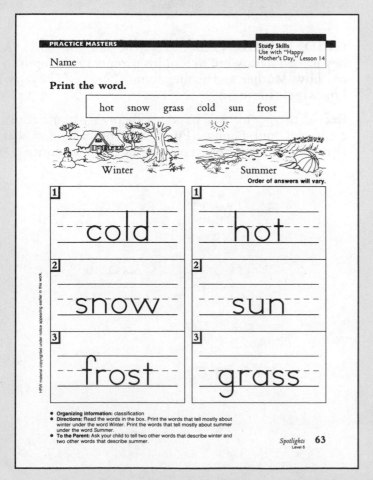

Winter Summer

Order of answers will vary.

1 cold
2 snow
3 frost

1 hot
2 sun
3 grass

● **Organizing information:** classification
● **Directions:** Read the words in the box. Print the words that tell mostly about winter under the word *Winter*. Print the words that tell mostly about summer under the word *Summer*.
● **To the Parent:** Ask your child to tell two other words that describe winter and two other words that describe summer.

Spotlights **63**
Level 6

Name _____

Print the word.

| quickly Laurie Louise room job |

1 Laurie and Louise
cleaned the house.

2 The girls quickly
swept the kitchen.

3 The girls did a very good
job

4 Then every
room was clean.

● **Vocabulary:** word meaning
● **Directions:** Read the words in the box. Choose the word or words that complete each sentence and print the word on the line.
● **To the Parent:** Ask your child to read each completed sentence to you.

Spotlights **23**
Level 6

POETRY LESSON

"Hiding"
pages 162–163 (T358–T359)

Skill Strands

COMPREHENSION/THINKING

R, T **Forms of literature:** poetry

Materials

Spotlights, Level 6: pages 162–163
Teacher's Idea Book

Special Populations

See *Teacher's Idea Book* for additional suggestions to help pupils with limited English proficiency.

Key to Symbols
I Introduced in this lesson
R Reinforced from an earlier lesson in this level
M Maintained from previous levels
T Tested in this level

COMPREHENSION/THINKING

M **Forms of literature:** poetry

DIRECT INSTRUCTION Remind pupils that in the story "Happy Mother's Day," the family members hid from Mother as she found her surprises. Ask why they might have hidden. (to surprise her)

Have pupils find pages 162 and 163 in their books and tell them that the poem on this page is called "Hiding." Have pupils listen as you read aloud the poem to find out who is hiding.

GUIDED PRACTICE Ask who hid and why. (A boy named Benny hid to fool his parents.) Ask pupils to tell how Mother and Father found Benny. (They saw him wiggle his toes.)

Reread the poem. Ask pupils if Benny's parents really could not find Benny. (Pupils will probably say that Benny's parents were just playing a game with him.)

(To be read by the teacher)

Hiding

I'm hiding, I'm hiding,
And no one knows where;
For all they can see is my
Toes and my hair.

And I just heard my father
Say to my mother—
"But, darling, he must be
Somewhere or other;

"Have you looked in the inkwell?"
And Mother said, "Where?"
"In the INK WELL," said Father. But
I was not there.

"We've hunted," sighed Mother,
"As hard as we could
And I AM so afraid that we've
Lost him for good."

Then I laughed out aloud
And I wiggled my toes
And Father said—"Look, dear,
I wonder if those

Toes could be Benny's.
There are ten of them. See?"
And they WERE so surprised to find
Out it was me!

Dorothy Aldis

162   163

LESSON 15

"Gifts to Make"
pages 164–169 (T360–T377)

Skill Strands

DECODING/VOCABULARY

R, T **Sound/symbol correspondence:** consonant /kw/ *qu* (initial, medial)

I, T **Sound/symbol correspondence:** consonant /z/ *z, zz* (initial, medial, final)

M **Vocabulary:** homophones

I **Vocabulary:** word building

I, T **Vocabulary:** word meaning

COMPREHENSION/THINKING

Focus ——————————————
M **Literal:** details

STUDY SKILLS

M **Graphic aids:** illustrations

LANGUAGE

M **Writing:** language-experience stories

Lesson Vocabulary

Decodable words: *caddy, cotton, fuzzy, homemade, kitty, magnet, marker, paste, puzzle, shapes, strip, yarn*

Special words: *paper, scissors*

Materials

Spotlights, Level 6: pages 164–169
Workbook: pages 100–105
Practice Masters: pages 64–67
Instructional Charts: pages 109–114
Resource Box: Letter Cards b, e, f, i, l, p (2), r, s, u, y, z (2)
 Word Cards paper, scissors
Pocket Chart
Teacher's Idea Book
Reteach Masters: page 24

Language Applications

USING LANGUAGE

Oral reading: directions
Independent reading: following written directions

EXTENDING SELECTION CONCEPTS

Independent reading: following written directions (Cooperative Learning)

Special Populations

See *Teacher's Idea Book* for additional suggestions to help pupils with limited English proficiency.

Key to Symbols
I   Introduced in this lesson
R   Reinforced from an earlier lesson in this level
M   Maintained from previous levels
T   Tested in this level

Idea Center

MATERIALS

This selection provides step-by-step directions for making three simple projects. You may wish to provide cotton balls, paper scraps, craft magnets, scissors, paste, colored paper, yarn, felt, paints, and markers, as well as juice cans and boxes. After the selection has been read, pupils will be invited to select a project to complete on their own.

BIBLIOGRAPHY

Add to your reading corner or reading table various books about craft projects and about children making things. A suggested bibliography follows. Suggestions for reading aloud and annotations appear in the lesson plan.

Conaway, Judith. *Springtime Surprises, Things to Make and Do.* Troll Associates, 1986.

Roser, Clare. *Making Presents.* Usborne, Ltd., 1984.

Supraner, Robyn. *Fun with Paper.* Troll Associates, 1981.

Planning Chart

		Instruction	Written Practice	Extending
Step 1 Preparing for the Selection	I, T	**Sound/symbol correspondence:** consonant /z/ z, zz (initial, medial, final)	*Workbook* page 100 *Practice Masters* page 64	
	I	**Vocabulary:** word building		
	I, T	**Vocabulary:** word meaning	*Workbook* page 101 *Practice Masters* page 65 *Reteach Masters* page 24	
	M	**Literal:** details		
Step 2 Reading for Comprehension		**Oral reading:** directions **Independent reading:** following written directions **Literal:** details **Story comprehension**	*Workbook* page 102	
Step 3 Developing Reading and Thinking Skills	M	**Vocabulary:** homophones	*Workbook* page 103 *Practice Masters* page 66 *Workbook* page 104	**Independent reading:** following written directions (Cooperative Learning)
	R, T	**Sound/symbol correspondence:** consonant /kw/ qu (initial, medial)		
	M	**Literal:** details	*Workbook* page 105 *Practice Masters* page 67	
	M	**Graphic aids:** illustrations		
	M	**Writing:** language-experience stories		

1 PREPARING FOR THE SELECTION

DECODING/VOCABULARY

I, T **Sound/symbol correspondence:** consonant /z/z, zz (initial, medial, final)

DIRECT INSTRUCTION Print the following rhyme and words on the chalkboard:

IC 109

> The bumblebee has lots of fuzz.
> It goes zigzag as it sings "Buzz, buzz."
>
> zip buzz puzzle
> fuzzy zap buzzer
> squeeze freeze

Read the rhyme and then ask pupils to read the rhyme with you.

Point to the word *zigzag* and explain that this word tells how the bumblebee flies.

SAY **The word *zigzag* begins with letter *z*. Letter *z* stands for the /z/ sound. Say /z/ with me: /z/. Read this word with me: *zigzag*. *Zigzag* begins with the /z/ sound. Where else do you hear the /z/ sound in *zigzag*?** (in the middle)

Point to the word *fuzz* and ask pupils to read it with you. Ask where the /z/ sound is heard in *fuzz*. (at the end) Point out that there are two letter *z*'s at the end of the word *fuzz*. Remind pupils that when two of the same consonants are together, they often stand for one sound.

Call on a pupil to find another word in the rhyme that ends with the /z/ sound. (*buzz*) Then ask pupils to read the rhyme.

GUIDED PRACTICE Ask pupils to listen to the following words and to raise their hands if the word has the /z/ sound: *razor, list, dizzy, fountain, share, crazy.*

Then direct pupils' attention to the three rows of words on the chalkboard. Call on pupils to read each word as you point to it and to tell where the /z/ sound is heard. Point out that when the letters *ze* come together at the end of a word, the final *e* is silent.

WB 100 **INDEPENDENT PRACTICE** *Workbook* page 100 may be used to practice identifying sound/symbol correspondence /z/z, zz.

PM 64 **ADDITIONAL PRACTICE** *Practice Masters* page 64 may be used as an optional practice for identifying sound/symbol correspondence /z/z, zz. (See page T376 for reduced pages with answers.)

✱ **RETEACH** For those pupils who need additional instruction, see "Reteaching Lesson Skills," page T375, under "Reteaching and Extending."

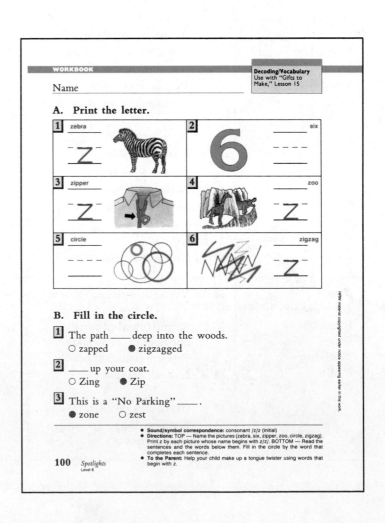

I Vocabulary: word building

DIRECT INSTRUCTION Use *Letter Cards* to make the word *zip* in the *Pocket Chart* and then ask pupils to read the word with you. Add letters *p,e,r* to *zip* and have the new word read. (*zipper*)

GUIDED PRACTICE Display *Letter Cards b, f, l, s, u, y, z.* Ask a pupil to change *zipper* to *zip.* Have the new word read. Continue by giving the following instructions:

1. **Change *z* to *s*. What is the word?** (*sip*)
2. **Take off *p* and add *zzle*. What is the word?** (*sizzle*)
3. **Change *si* to *pu*. What is the word?** (*puzzle*)
4. **Take off *le* and change *p* to *f*. What is the new word?** (*fuzz*)
5. **Add *y* to the end of the word. What is the new word?** (*fuzzy*)
6. **Take off *y* and change *f* to *b*. What is the new word?** (*buzz*)
7. **Add *er* to the end of the word. What is the new word?** (*buzzer*)

I, T Vocabulary: word meaning

DIRECT INSTRUCTION Print the following words and sentences on the chalkboard, omitting the underlining.

> **paper   scissors**
>
> You need <u>scissors</u> to cut <u>paper</u>.
>
> **caddy   fuzzy   puzzle   yarn**
>
> 1. I like to make things with <u>paper</u>.
> 2. Sometimes, Mom lets me use <u>scissors</u> to cut <u>yarn</u> and cotton.
> 3. I made a <u>fuzzy</u> <u>puzzle</u> and a pen <u>caddy</u>.

Read the sentence. Then point to the word *scissors* and read it. Ask why you need scissors. (to cut paper) Point to the word *paper* and read it. Have pupils read the sentence with you. Then ask them to find and read the words *scissors* and *paper*.

The words in the second set are new words that contain known phonic elements. You may wish to ask pupils to read the words, using what they know about letters and sounds.

GUIDED PRACTICE Provide opportunities for pupils to practice reading the new special words and some of the new decodable words in the numbered sentences on the chalkboard by following the suggestions below.

Sentence 1: Have the sentence read. Ask pupils to find and read the word *paper*.

Sentence 2: Ask pupils to find and read the word *scissors*. Then have the sentence read aloud. Ask what materials the person uses scissors to cut. (yarn and cotton)

Sentence 3: Have the sentence read. Ask what the person made. (a fuzzy puzzle and a pen caddy) Ask what a pen caddy is. (a container that holds pens)

Have pupils find and read the words that contain the /z/ sound. (*fuzzy, puzzle*)

Invite pupils to choose a sentence to read aloud.

WB 101 INDEPENDENT PRACTICE *Workbook* page 101 may be used to practice reading selection vocabulary.

Name _____

Print the word.

| paper | scissors | caddy | magnet |

1 Lee can make a ___caddy___ for his pens.

2 He pastes ___paper___ on a can.

3 Lee uses ___scissors___ to cut some paper.

4 Lee puts clips on a ___magnet___.

- **Vocabulary:** word meaning
- **Directions:** Read the words in the box. Print the word that completes each sentence.
- **To the Parent:** Have your child use some of the words in the box to describe how he or she would make a pen-and-pencil holder.

Spotlights **101**
Level 6

PM 65 **ADDITIONAL PRACTICE** *Practice Masters* page 65 may be used as an optional practice for reading selection vocabulary. (See page T377 for reduced pages with answers.)

✳ **RETEACH** For those pupils who need additional instruction, see "Reteaching Lesson Skills," page T376, under "Reteaching and Extending."

COMPREHENSION/THINKING

Focus

M Literal: details

DIRECT INSTRUCTION Print the following sentences and story on the chalkboard:

IC 111

> 1. Mother has a hat.
> 2. Mother has a big blue hat.
> 3. Mother has a big blue hat with a green plume.
>
> The fluffy, black kitten woke from its nap.
> Then it hopped off the big red pillow and went to the tan chair.
> It jumped up on Mom's lap.
> It purred softly.

Have Sentences 1–3 read. Ask which sentence tells the most about Mother's hat. (the last sentence)

SAY **The last sentence tells the size of the hat, the color of the hat, and how the hat is decorated. The hat is big and blue, and has a green plume, or feather. Each bit of information about the hat is called a detail. When you read a story, the author gives details. The details help you to picture what is happening.**

GUIDED PRACTICE Direct pupils' attention to the story on the chalkboard and have it read. Then call on pupils to answer the following questions about the details in the story.

1. **Which details tell how the kitten looked?** (It was fluffy and black.)
2. **Which details tell about the pillow?** (The pillow was big and red.)
3. **Which details tell about the chair?** (It was tan.)
4. **Which detail tells how the kitten sounded?** (It purred softly.)

2 READING FOR COMPREHENSION

Background for the Teacher

SUMMARY This is a nonfiction selection that gives directions for making three simple items—a decorative craft magnet, a pen caddy, and a puzzle.

Using Prior Knowledge

Explain that the next selection in *Spotlights* tells how to make some simple projects. Develop a discussion by asking questions such as those that follow.

1. **When you read directions that tell you how to do something, why should you read all the directions before you begin?** (You should read all the directions so that you know what to do next and so that you can be sure to have all the materials that you need.)
2. **Most written directions give you a list of the things you will need. Why is this important?** (so you know what you will need to complete the project)

Setting a Purpose for Reading

Ask pupils to find page 164 in their books and tell them that this selection is called "Gifts to Make." Point out the headnote at the top of the page. Remind pupils that this note will help them think about the selection as they read. Have the headnote read. Then ask pupils to tell some things that they or others have made as gifts.

Reading Silently

Some pupils may be able to read this story independently. Direct them to read the whole story to find out more about gifts they can make for family and friends.

For those pupils who need more guidance, suggestions for directed reading follow.

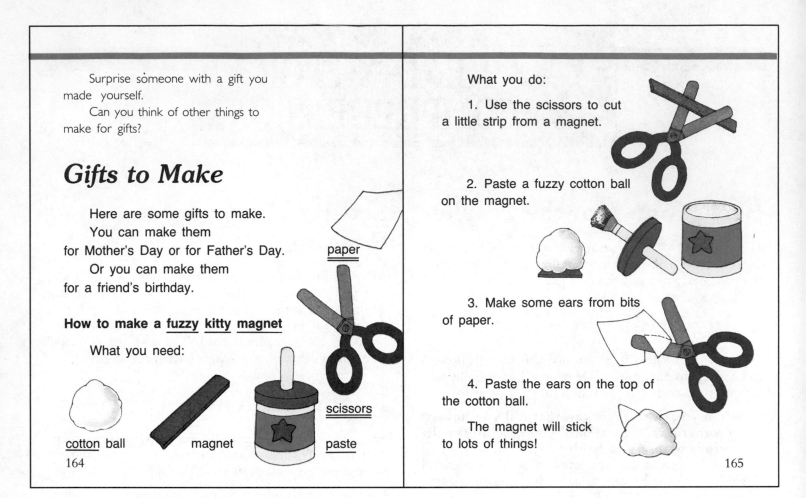

Surprise someone with a gift you made yourself.

Can you think of other things to make for gifts?

Gifts to Make

Here are some gifts to make.
You can make them
for Mother's Day or for Father's Day.
Or you can make them
for a friend's birthday.

How to make a <u>fuzzy</u> <u>kitty</u> <u>magnet</u>

What you need:

<u>cotton</u> ball   magnet   <u>scissors</u>   paste

paper

164

What you do:

1. Use the scissors to cut a little strip from a magnet.

2. Paste a fuzzy cotton ball on the magnet.

3. Make some ears from bits of paper.

4. Paste the ears on the top of the cotton ball.

The magnet will stick to lots of things!

165

Before reading pages 164–165

SAY The first gift that you might make is a magnet to hold messages on a stove or a refrigerator. What do you think you will need? Read pages 164 and 165 to yourself.

After reading pages 164–165

1. **What do you need to make a fuzzy kitty magnet?** (a cotton ball, pieces of paper, a magnet, paste, scissors) Literal

2. **How do you make the magnet?** (Paste a cotton ball on a magnet; paste paper ears on the cotton ball.) Inferential

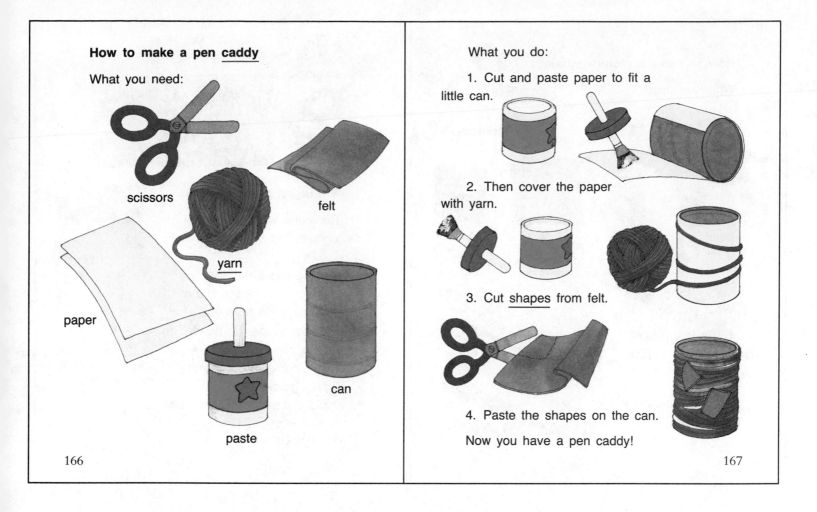

How to make a pen caddy

What you need:

scissors

felt

yarn

paper

can

paste

166

What you do:

1. Cut and paste paper to fit a little can.

2. Then cover the paper with yarn.

3. Cut shapes from felt.

4. Paste the shapes on the can.

Now you have a pen caddy!

167

Before reading pages 166–167

| SAY | A pen caddy is used to hold pens and pencils on a desk. How do you think you might make a pen caddy? Read pages 166 and 167 to yourself.

After reading pages 166–167

1. **What do you need to make the pen caddy?** (a juice can, colored paper, yarn, scissors, paste, felt) Literal
2. **How do you make a pen caddy?** (Put colored paper on a can; paste yarn over the paper; paste felt shapes on the caddy to decorate it.) Inferential

How to make a picture puzzle

What you need:

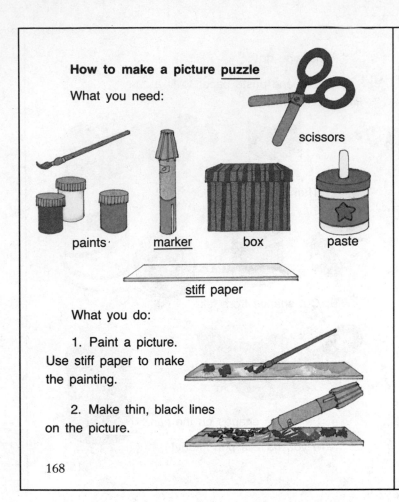

paints·   marker   box   paste

stiff paper

What you do:

1. Paint a picture. Use stiff paper to make the painting.

2. Make thin, black lines on the picture.

168

3. Now cut along the lines with the scissors.

4. Put the puzzle in a box.

Someone will have lots of fun playing with the puzzle!

Discussing the Selection

1. Why would someone like a homemade gift from you?
2. Tell what things are needed to make a pen caddy.
3. What other gifts could you make to surprise someone?
4. Would the mother in the story "Happy Mother's Day" like these gifts? Why?

169

Before reading pages 168–169

SAY **Have you ever made a puzzle? Read pages 168 and 169 to find out how to make a puzzle.**

After reading pages 168–169

1. **What do you need to make a puzzle?** (stiff paper, paints, marker, box, scissors, paste) Literal
2. **How do you make the picture puzzle?** (Paint a picture on stiff paper; make black lines on the paper; cut the paper apart on the lines; put the puzzle in a box.) Inferential

Discussing the Selection

Questions preceded by a number appear in *Spotlights* after the selection. Questions preceded by a bullet are additional questions for extending discussion.

MAIN IDEA

1. **Why would someone like a homemade gift from you?** (Possible answers include: When you make a gift, you show that you care about the person and want to do something special for them.) Critical

SUPPORT

2. **Tell what things are needed to make a pen caddy.** (a juice can, colored paper, yarn, felt, scissors, paste) Literal

• **Tell what things are needed to make a fuzzy kitty magnet.** (cotton ball, magnet, paste, scissors, paper) Literal

THEME-RELATED

3. **What other gifts could you make to surprise someone?** (Answers will vary, but may include: gifts made from paper or household items, gifts of food.) Critical

SELECTION-RELATED

4. **Would the mother in the story "Happy Mother's Day" like these gifts? Why?** (Answers will vary, but may include: yes, because she was so pleased with the things that her family had done for her; making a gift is another way of doing something special for a person.) Critical

Using Language

ORAL READING: DIRECTIONS Ask pupils to turn to page 164 and have the sentences read that tell why you might want to make the gifts in the selection. (Here are some gifts to make. You can make them for Mother's Day or for Father's Day. Or you can make them for a friend's birthday.)

Follow a similar procedure for the remaining pages by following the suggestions below.

Page 165: Ask pupils to read each step that should be followed to make the magnet. Then call on pupils to tell in their own words how to make the magnet.

Page 167: Ask pupils to read the steps that should be followed to make the pen caddy. Then have them tell in their own words how to make the pen caddy.

Page 168: Ask what is needed to make a picture puzzle. (stiff paper, paints, marker, box, scissors, paste)

Page 169: Have pupils read the steps that should be followed to make the picture puzzle. Then ask them to tell in their own words how to make the picture puzzle.

INDEPENDENT READING: FOLLOWING WRITTEN DIRECTIONS Provide materials for pupils to make one or more of the projects in the selection "Gifts to Make." Let pupils choose a project to complete on their own, following the instructions in their books.

Applying the Focus Skill

LITERAL: DETAILS Remind pupils that details are bits of information that describe something. Have pupils look at the magnet at the bottom of page 165 in their books and tell some details about the magnet. (Possible answers include: It is soft and fuzzy; it has ears like a kitten; it does not have eyes.)

Have pupils give details about the finished pen caddy and the finished puzzle. (Possible answers include: The pen caddy is a can with blue yarn wrapped around it for decoration; the puzzle is a picture of two cats in a garden.) Tell them that details may include words that describe the size, shape, and color of something and also how it may be used.

Evaluating Comprehension

WB 102 **INDEPENDENT PRACTICE** *Workbook* page 102 may be used for an informal evaluation of selection comprehension.

WORKBOOK

Comprehension/Thinking
Use with "Gifts to Make," Lesson 15

Name _____

Fill in the circle.

1 ● You can make gifts for people.

2 ○ You need yarn to make a fuzzy kitty magnet.

3 ● A fuzzy kitty magnet will stick to lots of things.

4 ● You paste cotton on a magnet to make a kitty.

5 ○ A caddy is another name for a fuzzy magnet.

6 ● For a caddy, you need to cut paper to fit a can.

7 ● To make a pen caddy, you need a small can.

8 ○ You need a magnet to make a picture puzzle.

9 ● You use stiff paper to make a picture puzzle.

10 ● You cut a picture to make a picture puzzle.

- **Selection comprehension:** "Gifts to Make"
- **Directions:** Fill in the circle by each sentence that tells something you read in "Gifts to Make."
- **To the Parent:** Have your child tell how to make one of the gifts in "Gifts to Make." Then ask him or her to describe what would happen if the steps were followed out of order.

102 *Spotlights*
Level 6

HRW material copyrighted under notice appearing earlier in this work.

T370 *Spotlights,* Level 6

DECODING/VOCABULARY

M Vocabulary: homophones

DIRECT INSTRUCTION Print the following sentences on the chalkboard:

> 1. The car went down the <u>road</u>.
> 2. Mandy <u>rode</u> her bike.
>
> 3. The pig has a curly <u>tail</u>.
> 4. This book has a funny <u>tale</u>.
>
> 5. We got all wet playing in the <u>creek</u>.
> 6. "<u>Creak</u>" went the steps as I went upstairs.
>
> 7. Bill <u>knows</u> what happens in the story.
> 8. I have an itchy <u>nose</u>.

Indicate Sentences 1–2 and have them read. Then call on a pupil to read the underlined word in each sentence. (*road, rode*) Remind pupils that some words sound exactly alike, but they have different meanings and are spelled differently. These kinds of words are called homographs. Ask which word means "a path or highway." (*road*) Ask which word means "to ride on something." (*rode*)

GUIDED PRACTICE Direct pupils' attention to the remaining sentences on the chalkboard.

Have each sentence pair read. Ask pupils which words are homographs in each sentence pair. (*tail, tale; creek, creak; knows, nose*)

Then have pupils read the sentence that answers each of the following questions.

1. **In which sentence does the underlined word mean "a story"?** (*This book has a funny tale.*)
2. **In which sentence does the underlined word mean "a squeaking noise"?** (*"Creak" went the steps as I went upstairs.*)
3. **In which sentence does the underlined word mean "a part of your face"?** (*I have an itchy nose.*)
4. **In which sentence does the underlined word mean "a part of an animal's body"?** (*The pig has a curly tail.*)

INDEPENDENT PRACTICE *Workbook* page 103 may be used to practice recognizing homographs.

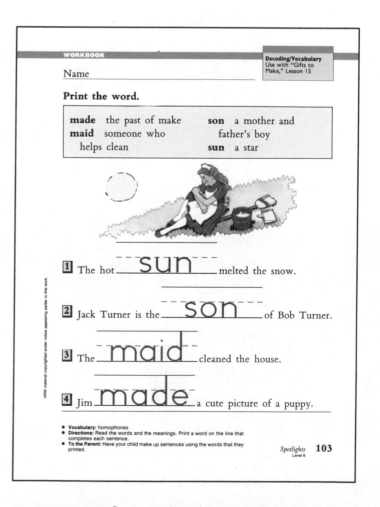

ADDITIONAL PRACTICE *Practice Masters* page 66 may be used as an optional practice for recognizing homographs. (See page T377 for reduced pages with answers.)

R, T **Sound/symbol correspondence:** consonant /kw/*qu* (initial, medial)

DIRECT INSTRUCTION Print the following words on the chalkboard:

IC 113

queen	quick	quit
squash	squirt	quail

Point to the first word and have it read. Ask what two letters are at the beginning of the word *queen*. (*qu*) Remind pupils that letters *qu* stand for the /kw/ sound.

GUIDED PRACTICE Have the remaining words read. Then call on pupils to read the word that answers each of the following questions:

1. **Which word means "fast"?** (*quick*)
2. **Which word means "stop"?** (*quit*)
3. **Which word names a woman who rules a country?** (*queen*)
4. **Which word names a kind of bird?** (*quail*)
5. **Which word means "to squeeze together"?** (*squash*)
6. **Which word tells what a hose can do?** (*squirt*)

WB 104 **INDEPENDENT PRACTICE** *Workbook* page 104 may be used to practice identifying sound/symbol correspondence /kw/*qu*.

✳ **RETEACH** For those pupils who need additional instruction, see "Reteaching Lesson Skills," page T375 under "Reteaching and Extending."

COMPREHENSION/THINKING

Focus
M   Literal: details

DIRECT INSTRUCTION   Have pupils read page 165 in *Spotlights* to themselves.

ASK   **What do you cut from a magnet?** (a little strip) **The words** *little* **and** *strip* **are details that tell what you are to cut. What should you paste on the magnet?** (a fuzzy cotton ball) **What details tell the kind of ball to paste on the magnet?** *(fuzzy, cotton)*

GUIDED PRACTICE   Print the following story on the chalkboard and have it read. Tell pupils that you will ask them to tell about the details in the story.

> Pat made a gift for his sister.
> First, he got a shoe box and painted it red.
> Then he got a soft cloth from his mom.
> He cut the cloth to fit the box.
> When Pat was finished, he had a bed for his sister's doll.

Tell pupils that you will read some sentences and pupils should tell if the sentence is about the gift Pat made.

1. **Pat used a hat box.** (no)
2. **Pat painted a shoe box.** (yes)
3. **Pat made a green doll bed.** (no)
4. **The bed was for a real baby.** (no)
5. **Pat made a blanket for the doll bed.** (yes)

WB 105   INDEPENDENT PRACTICE   *Workbook* page 105 may be used to practice recognizing details.

PM 67   ADDITIONAL PRACTICE   *Practice Masters* page 67 may be used as an optional practice for recognizing details. (See page T377 for reduced pages with answers.)

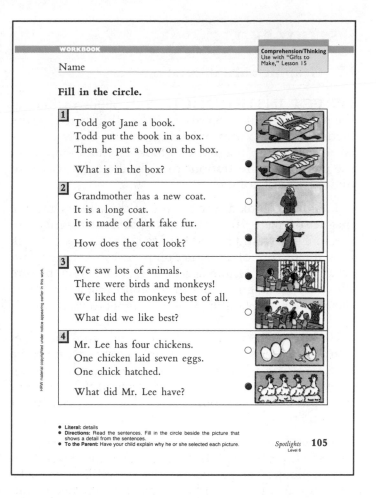

WORKBOOK

Comprehension/Thinking
Use with "Gifts to Make," Lesson 15

Name _____

Fill in the circle.

1. Todd got Jane a book.
    Todd put the book in a box.
    Then he put a bow on the box.

    What is in the box?

2. Grandmother has a new coat.
    It is a long coat.
    It is made of dark fake fur.

    How does the coat look?

3. We saw lots of animals.
    There were birds and monkeys!
    We liked the monkeys best of all.

    What did we like best?

4. Mr. Lee has four chickens.
    One chicken laid seven eggs.
    One chick hatched.

    What did Mr. Lee have?

- **Literal:** details
- **Directions:** Read the sentences. Fill in the circle beside the picture that shows a detail from the sentences.
- **To the Parent:** Have your child explain why he or she selected each picture.

Spotlights **105**
Level 6

M Graphic aids: illustrations

DIRECT INSTRUCTION Ask pupils to look at the picture on page 165 of *Spotlights*. Tell them that the picture at the bottom of this page shows how the finished fuzzy kitty magnet will look. Authors sometimes use pictures or illustrations to make directions easier to understand and follow.

Ask pupils to look at the picture of the scissors and the magnet on page 165. Point out that most magnets are metal. They would be too hard to cut with scissors. Ask how the picture of a magnet on page 165 helps explain what to do. (Possible answers include: The picture shows a craft magnet that can be cut because it is soft; the picture helps explain the kind of magnet to use.)

GUIDED PRACTICE Have pupils look at pages 166 and 167. Ask them to explain how the picture at the bottom of page 167 would help someone who did not know what a pen caddy was. (The picture shows a finished pen caddy, so people can see that it is a place to put pens and pencils.)

Have pupils turn to pages 168 and 169. Tell them that the directions on page 168 say to make thin, black lines on the picture. The directions do not tell how to make the lines. Ask how the illustration may help people understand the directions. (The illustration shows that the lines should be all over the picture to divide it into pieces to make a puzzle.)

M Writing: language–experience stories

DIRECT INSTRUCTION Help pupils to recall that the family in "Happy Mother's Day" did not give Mom store-bought gifts.

Develop a discussion about gift-giving. Then have pupils work together to make up the beginning of a story about giving a gift to someone. Display chart paper on which to print the dictated story for everyone to read.

Begin the story by asking what kind of gift pupils might like to give and to whom they will give the gift. Continue by asking the following questions:

1. **Where will you get the gift?**
2. **How will you keep the gift a secret?**
3. **How will you wrap the gift?**
4. **When will you give the gift?**

GUIDED PRACTICE After the beginning of the story has been written, tell pupils that they each are going to write an ending for the story. Have pupils answer the following questions in their story endings.

1. **What will the person say when you give the gift?**
2. **How will the person act?**

When the story endings have been completed, encourage pupils to read aloud the beginning of the story from the chart paper along with the story endings they have written.

✳ RETEACHING AND EXTENDING

Reteaching Lesson Skills

The activities that follow provide reteaching of skills developed in this lesson. Not every pupil needs to complete these activities. Choose only the activities that are needed to provide for the individual differences in your classroom.

DECODING/VOCABULARY

R, T Sound/symbol correspondence: consonant /kw/ *qu* (initial, medial)

✳ **RETEACH** Print the following words on the chalkboard:

**IC
113**

queen	quick	quit
squash	squirt	quail

Point to the first three words and read them. Explain that the words *queen, quick* and *quit* each begin with the /kw/ sound. The letters *qu* stand for the /kw/ sound.

Call on a pupil to point to and read a word. Continue until all the words have been read.

I, T Sound/symbol correspondence: consonant /z/*z, zz* (initial, medial, final)

✳ **RETEACH** Print the following words on the chalkboard:

**IC
109**

zip	buzz	puzzle
fuzzy	zap	buzzer
squeeze	freeze	

Point to the first word and read it.

SAY	The word *zip* begins with the /z/ sound. Letter *z* stands for the /z/

sound in *zip*. Read this word with me: *zip*.

Call on a pupil to find and read another word that begins with letter *z*. (*zap*)

SAY	This is the word *zap*. Say *zap* with me: *zap*. What letter does *zap* begin

with? (*z*) The letter *z* stands for the /z/ sound.

Have pupils point to and read each of the remaining words. Ask where the /z/ sound is heard in each word. Point out that when the letters *ze* come at the end of a word, the *e* is silent.

I, T Vocabulary: word meaning

 RETEACH Print the following words and sentence on the chalkboard, omitting the underlining.

> paper   scissors
> You need <u>scissors</u> to cut <u>paper</u>.
> **caddy   fuzzy   puzzle   yarn**

Point to the words *scissors* and *paper* and read each word. Then have pupils read the sentence aloud. Have them find and read the words *scissors* and *paper*.

Display *Word Cards* for the underlined words. Have pupils hold up and read the card that answers each of the following questions:

1. **Which word names a tool that cuts paper?** (*scissors*)
2. **Which word names something you write or draw on?** (*paper*)

Have pupils read the second set of words and use them in sentences.

RM 24 Distribute *Reteach Masters* page 24 and explain the directions on the page.

HOW AM I DOING?

Many pupils need help in clarifying their ideas so they can set them down in a well-organized, logical, and interesting fashion. Ask yourself the following questions to gauge your teaching effectiveness in this area.

	Yes	No	Some-times
1. Do I respond positively to pupils' questions?	☐	☐	☐
2. Do I help them understand the importance of writing clear descriptions?	☐	☐	☐
3. Do I encourage pupils to read informational articles outside of the classroom and to share interesting articles with the class?	☐	☐	☐
4. Do I point out particularly good examples of descriptive writing as models for them to emulate?	☐	☐	☐

Extending Selection Concepts

INDEPENDENT READING: FOLLOWING WRITTEN DIRECTIONS (Cooperative Learning) Provide several books that contain simple crafts projects. Have pupils work in small groups to select something to make and work together to complete the project. Some pupils may prefer to make an individual project. Make sure that the group members follow the directions carefully. Invite each group to show its project to the class and to explain how the project was completed.

Conaway, Judith. *Springtime Surprises, Things to Make and Do.* Troll Associates, 1986. This book contains easy directions for things to make from paper and common household items. It even has simple foods.

Roser, Clare. *Making Presents.* Usborne, 1984. Here are simple gifts to make, including how to make wrapping paper and wrap the gift.

Supraner, Robyn. *Fun with Paper.* Troll Associates, 1981. The projects in this book are easy and fun to make from paper and household items.

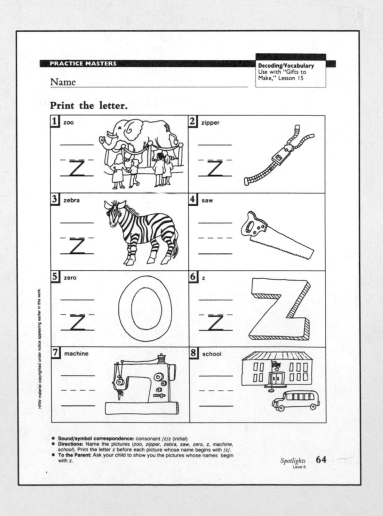

Name

Print the word.

paper	scissors	paste

1 You want to cut shapes from felt.

scissors

2 You want to cover the table.

paper

3 You want to make yarn stick to a can.

paste

4 You want to cut one big sheet of paper.

scissors

- **Vocabulary:** word meaning
- **Directions:** Read the words in the box. Print the word that tells what is needed for each activity. A word may be used more than once.
- **To the Parent:** Ask your child to read the sentences and the answers to you.

Spotlights **65**
Level 6

Name

A. Draw a line.

1 Linda <u>rode</u> on a horse.

2 The horse went up the <u>road</u>.

3 This present is <u>for</u> Lenny.

4 Lenny got <u>four</u> presents.

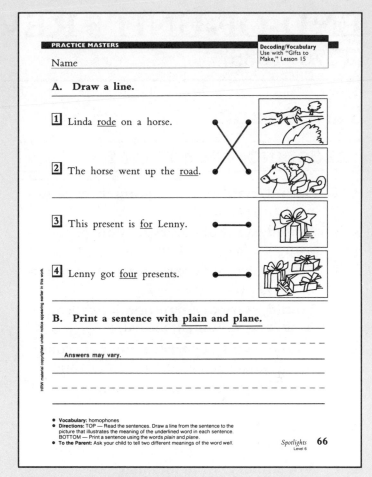

B. Print a sentence with <u>plain</u> and <u>plane</u>.

Answers may vary.

- **Vocabulary:** homophones
- **Directions:** TOP — Read the sentences. Draw a line from the sentence to the picture that illustrates the meaning of the underlined word in each sentence. BOTTOM — Print a sentence using the words *plain* and *plane*.
- **To the Parent:** Ask your child to tell two different meanings of the word *well*.

Spotlights **66**
Level 6

Name

Print the words.

A Kitty
This kitty is little.
It has a long tail.
The kitty drinks milk.
It runs and jumps.

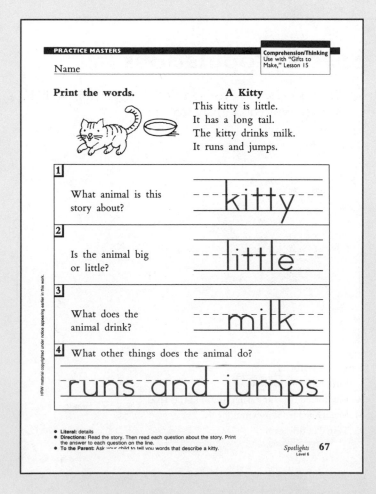

1 What animal is this story about?

kitty

2 Is the animal big or little?

little

3 What does the animal drink?

milk

4 What other things does the animal do?

runs and jumps

- **Literal:** details
- **Directions:** Read the story. Then read each question about the story. Print the answer to each question on the line.
- **To the Parent:** Ask your child to tell you words that describe a kitty.

Spotlights **67**
Level 6

Name

Print the word.

scissors	Paste	markers	puzzle

1 Make a mouse picture with your

markers

2 Use scissors

to cut the paper.

3 Paste

yarn whiskers on your mouse.

4 Cut your mouse into shapes to make a

puzzle

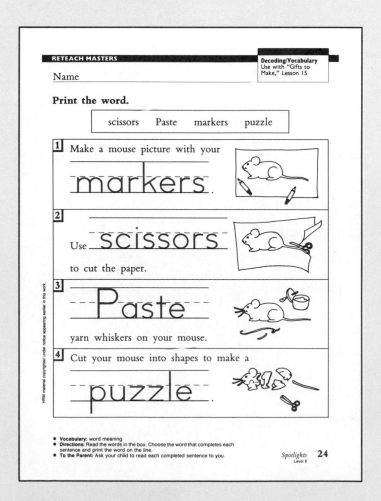

- **Vocabulary:** word meaning
- **Directions:** Read the words in the box. Choose the word that completes each sentence and print the word on the line.
- **To the Parent:** Ask your child to read each completed sentence to you.

Spotlights **24**
Level 6

END-OF-UNIT 3 REVIEW

(T378–T385)

Skill Strands

DECODING/VOCABULARY

R, T   **Sound/symbol correspondence:** consonant /m/*mb* (final)

R, T   **Sound/symbol correspondence:** consonant /kw/*qu* (initial, medial)

R, T   **Sound/symbol correspondence:** consonant /v/*v* (initial)

R, T   **Sound/symbol correspondence:** consonant /z/*z, zz* (initial, medial)

R, T   **Sound/symbol correspondence:** consonant digraph /ch/*ch, tch* (initial, final)

R, T   **Sound/symbol correspondence:** vowel /yoo/, /oo/*u-e*

R, T   **Word structure:** suffix *-ly*

R, T   **Vocabulary:** antonyms and synonyms

R, T   **Vocabulary:** word meaning

COMPREHENSION/THINKING

R, T   **Literal:** pronoun referents (*he, it, she, they, we*)

Materials

Workbook: pages 106–110

Practice Masters: pages 68–72

Instructional Charts: pages 115–118

Resource Box: Word Cards cub, cube, cup, cute, flute, mud, tub, tube, tune

Pocket Chart

Teacher's Idea Book

End-of-Unit 3 Test

End-of-Book Test

Special Populations

See *Teacher's Idea Book* for additional suggestions to help pupils with limited English proficiency.

Key to Symbols

I   Introduced in this lesson

R   Reinforced from an earlier lesson in this level

M   Maintained from previous levels

T   Tested in this level

DECODING/VOCABULARY

R, T **Sound/symbol correspondence:** consonant /v/*v* (initial)

R, T **Sound/symbol correspondence:** consonant /z/*z, zz* (initial, medial)

GUIDED PRACTICE Print the following words and sentences on the chalkboard:

> van   zipped
>
> 1. Val's van zipped up the street.
> 2. Vic painted a zigzag line.
> 3. The bumblebee is very fuzzy.
> 4. The buzzer made a buzzing noise.

Point to the word *van* and read it. Tell pupils that the letter *v* stands for the /v/ sound at the beginning of *van*. Point to *zipped* and read it. Tell pupils that letter *z* stands for the /z/ sound at the beginning of *zipped*. Point to each word and have pupils read it with you.

Call on a pupil to read each sentence. Ask which words in each sentence contain the /v/ sound and which words contain the /z/ sound.

WB 106 **INDEPENDENT PRACTICE** *Workbook* page 106 may be used to practice identifying sound/symbol correspondences /v/*v* and /z/*z, zz*.

PM 68 **ADDITIONAL PRACTICE** *Practice Masters* page 68 may be used as an optional practice for identifying sound/symbol correspondences /v/*v* and /z/*z, zz*. (See page T384 for reduced pages with answers.)

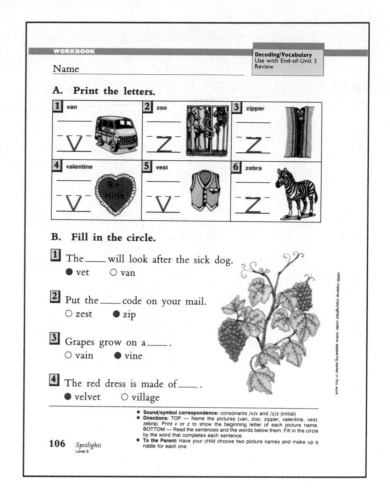

R, T **Sound/symbol correspondence:** consonant /m/*mb* (final)

GUIDED PRACTICE Print the following words on the chalkboard:

> crumb
>
> thumb   lamb   numb

Point to the word *crumb* and read it aloud. Ask what sound is heard at the end of *crumb*. (/m/) Tell pupils that when the letters *mb* are together at the end of a word, the *b* is silent. The sound we hear at the end of *crumb* is /m/.

Have pupils read the remaining words. Then call on pupils to read a word and to use the word in a sentence.

R, T   Sound/symbol correspondence: consonant /kw/*qu* (initial, medial)

GUIDED PRACTICE   Print the following words on the chalkboard:

> queen
>
> quick   quite   squirt
> quit   squeeze   quilt

Point to the word *queen* and have it read. Ask what two letters stand for the sound at the beginning of *queen*. (*qu*)

Call on pupils to read the remaining words and tell which letters stand for the /kw/ sound. Then call on pupils to read the words as you randomly point to them.

WB 107   INDEPENDENT PRACTICE   *Workbook* page 107 may be used to practice identifying sound/symbol correspondence /kw/*qu* and /m/*mb*.

R, T   Sound/symbol correspondence: consonant digraph /ch/*ch, tch* (initial, final)

GUIDED PRACTICE   Print the following words and sentences on the chalkboard:

> chip   patch
> 1. Chuck will catch the chimp.
> 2. Chester is the champ.
> 3. Pitch the ball to Mitch.
> 4. A chipmunk lives in the pumpkin patch.

Point to the word *chip* and read it. Tell pupils that the letters *ch* stand for the /ch/ sound at the beginning of *chip*.

Point to the word *patch* and read it. Tell pupils that some words end with the letters *tch*. The letters *tch* together stand for the /ch/ sound as in *patch*. Point to each word and have pupils read it with you.

Then call on pupils to read the sentences and tell which words in each sentence contain the /ch/ sound. Ask pupils to name the letters that stand for the /ch/ sound in each word. *(ch, tch)*

PM 69   ADDITIONAL PRACTICE   *Practice Masters* page 69 may be used as an optional practice for identifying the consonant digraph /ch/*ch, tch*. (See page T384 for reduced pages with answers.)

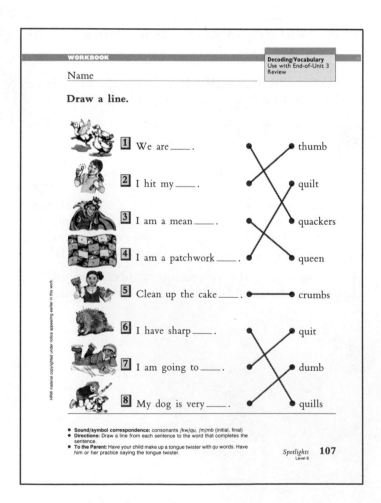

R, T   Sound/symbol correspondence: vowel /yo͞o/, /o͞o/u-e

GUIDED PRACTICE   Place the following pairs of *Word Cards* in the *Pocket Chart*: tub, tube; cub, cube.

Point to and read the first pair of words. Ask how the second word is different from the first word. (It has letter *e* at the end; the letter *u* stands for the /o͞o/ sound.) Tell pupils that when a word has letter *u*, followed by a consonant, and letter *e* is at the end of the word, letter *u* stands for the long *u* sound.

Point to the next pair of words and read them. Ask how the words *cub* and *cube* are different. (In *cub*, *u* stands for the short *u* sound; in *cube*, *u* stands for the long *u* sound.) Ask why *u* in *cube* stands for the long *u* sound. (*Cube* has a *u*, followed by a consonant, and ends with *e*.)

Have pupils read each word and tell what sound letter *u* stands for and why as you hold up the following *Word Cards: tune, mud, cute, flute, cup*. (Letter *u* stands for the long *u* sound in *tune, cute*, and *flute* because each word has *u*, followed by a consonant, and ends with *e*.)

WB 108   **INDEPENDENT PRACTICE**   *Workbook* page 108 may be used to practice identifying sound/symbol correspondence /yo͞o/, /o͞o/u-e.

PM 70   **ADDITIONAL PRACTICE**   *Practice Masters* page 70 may be used as an optional practice for identifying sound/symbol correspondence /yo͞o/, /o͞o/ u-e. (See page T384 for reduced pages with answers.)

R, T   Vocabulary: antonyms and synonyms

GUIDED PRACTICE   Print the following words on the chalkboard, omitting the answers in parentheses.

IC 117

1. slow   quick
2. jump   leap (synonyms)
3. start   stop (antonyms)
4. finish   end (synonyms)
5. hot   cold (antonyms)

Have the first pair of words read. Then ask which word means almost the same thing as the word *fast*. (*quick*) Tell pupils that when two words have almost the same meaning, the words are called synonyms.

Ask which word is the opposite of the word *fast*. (*slow*) Tell pupils that when two words have opposite meanings, they are called antonyms.

Direct pupils' attention to the remaining word pairs on the chalkboard. Have each pair of words read and ask if the words are antonyms or synonyms. Then ask pupils to think of some other pairs of words that are synonyms or antonyms. (Possible answers include: synonyms—*harm/ hurt, mad/angry*, antonyms—*in/out, up/down*.)

WB 109   **INDEPENDENT PRACTICE**   *Workbook* page 109 may be used to practice recognizing antonyms and synonyms.

PM 71   **ADDITIONAL PRACTICE**   *Practice Masters* page 71 may be used as an optional practice for recognizing antonyms and synonyms. (See page T384 for reduced pages with answers.)

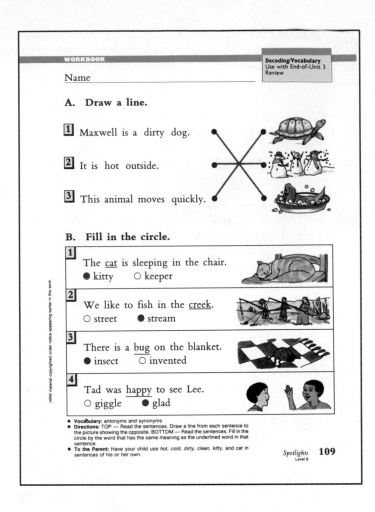

Name _____

A. Draw a line.

1 Maxwell is a dirty dog.

2 It is hot outside.

3 This animal moves quickly.

B. Fill in the circle.

1 The <u>cat</u> is sleeping in the chair.
● kitty   ○ keeper

2 We like to fish in the <u>creek</u>.
○ street   ● stream

3 There is a <u>bug</u> on the blanket.
● insect   ○ invented

4 Tad was <u>happy</u> to see Lee.
○ giggle   ● glad

• **Vocabulary:** antonyms and synonyms
• **Directions:** TOP — Read the sentences. Draw a line from each sentence to the picture showing the opposite. BOTTOM — Read the sentences. Fill in the circle by the word that has the same meaning as the underlined word in that sentence.
• **To the Parent:** Have your child use *hot, cold, dirty, clean, kitty,* and *cat* in sentences of his or her own.

Spotlights Level 6   **109**

R, T   Vocabulary: word meaning

GUIDED PRACTICE   Make a list of some of the vocabulary words from this unit. (See pages 184–186 of the pupil's edition.) Write the list of words, including the word *scary,* on the chalkboard.

Tell pupils that they are going to play a game called "I'm thinking of . . ." Start out the game by saying "I'm thinking of a word that means the same thing as *frightening.*" Call on a pupil to come to the chalkboard to circle and read the word that means "frightening." (*scary*) Then have the pupil choose a word and give a clue beginning with the phrase "I'm thinking of . . ."

Follow a similar procedure until all the words have been circled.

R, T   Word structure: suffix *-ly*

GUIDED PRACTICE Print the following words and sentences on the chalkboard:

IC
117

soft   softly
1. The kitten purred softly.
2. The mouse ate quickly.
3. The train went slowly up the hill.
4. Mike will gladly open the gift.

Point to the two words and have them read. Ask what was added to the word *soft* to make the word *softly.* (*-ly*) Explain that the ending *-ly* can be added to a word to make it tell how something is done. Have the first sentence read and ask how the kitten purrs. (*softly*)

Have the remaining sentences read. After each sentence is read, ask the question from below that goes with the sentence.

Sentence 2: **How did the mouse eat?** (*quickly*)
Sentence 3: **How did the train go up the hill?** (*slowly*)
Sentence 4: **How will Mike open the gift?** (*gladly*)

After the sentences have been read, ask pupils to suggest other words that tell how Mike may have opened the gift. (Possible answers include: *secretly, happily, quickly, slowly.*)

PM 72   **ADDITIONAL PRACTICE**   *Practice Masters* page 72 may be used as an optional practice for reading words with the suffix *-ly.* (See page T385 for reduced pages with answers.)

COMPREHENSION/THINKING

R, T Literal: pronoun referents (*he, it, she, they, we*)

GUIDED PRACTICE Print the following sentences on the chalkboard, omitting the answers in parentheses.

> 1. Dave went to visit his grandparents.
> 2. <u>They</u> live on a farm. (grandparents)
>
> 3. Matt invited Beth to dinner.
> 4. <u>He</u> hoped <u>she</u> would come. (Matt, Beth)
>
> 5. Sam and I like to go swimming.
> 6. <u>We</u> have a lot of fun. (Sam and I)

Have the first two sentences read. Point to the underlined word in the second sentence and have it read. Ask pupils who "they" are. (Dave's grandparents) Tell pupils that the word *they* takes the place of the words *Dave's grandparents.* A word that takes the place of the name of a person or a thing is called a pronoun.

Continue in the same manner with the remaining pairs of sentences by having them read and then asking which word or words are replaced by the underlined words.

INDEPENDENT PRACTICE *Workbook* page 110 may be used to practice recognizing pronoun referents.

* Administer *End-of-Unit 3 Test.*
* Administer *End-of-Book Test.*

Name _____

Print the word.

| zipper | puzzle | lizard | vase | beaver | vine |

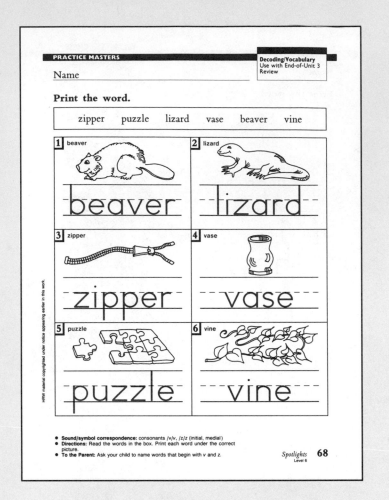

1 beaver — beaver

2 lizard — lizard

3 zipper — zipper

4 vase — vase

5 puzzle — puzzle

6 vine — vine

- **Sound/symbol correspondence:** consonants /v/v, /z/z (initial, medial)
- **Directions:** Read the words in the box. Print each word under the correct picture.
- **To the Parent:** Ask your child to name words that begin with *v* and *z*.

Spotlights
Level 6
68

Name _____

Circle the words.   Print the words.

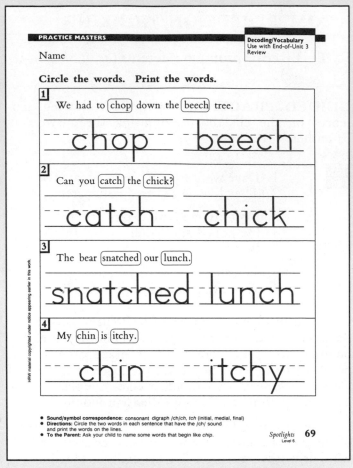

1 We had to ⬚chop⬚ down the ⬚beech⬚ tree.

chop   beech

2 Can you ⬚catch⬚ the ⬚chick?⬚

catch   chick

3 The bear ⬚snatched⬚ our ⬚lunch.⬚

snatched   lunch

4 My ⬚chin⬚ is ⬚itchy.⬚

chin   itchy

- **Sound/symbol correspondence:** consonant digraph /ch/ch, tch (initial, medial, final)
- **Directions:** Circle the two words in each sentence that have the /ch/ sound and print the words on the lines.
- **To the Parent:** Ask your child to name some words that begin like *chip*.

Spotlights
Level 6
69

Name _____

Circle the word.   Print a sentence.

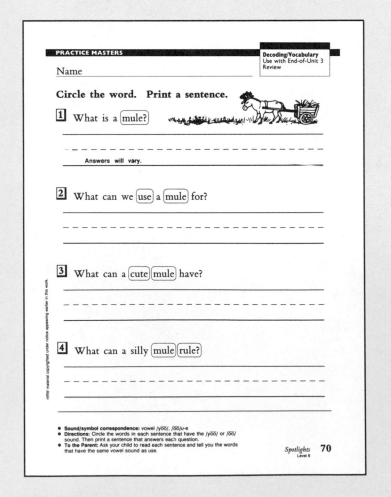

1 What is a ⬚mule?⬚

_____

Answers will vary.

2 What can we ⬚use⬚ a ⬚mule⬚ for?

_____

_____

3 What can a ⬚cute⬚ ⬚mule⬚ have?

_____

_____

4 What can a silly ⬚mule⬚⬚rule?⬚

_____

_____

- **Sound/symbol correspondence:** vowel /yōō/, /ōō/u-e
- **Directions:** Circle the words in each sentence that have the /yōō/ or /ōō/ sound. Then print a sentence that answers each question.
- **To the Parent:** Ask your child to read each sentence and tell you the words that have the same vowel sound as *use*.

Spotlights
Level 6
70

Name _____

A. Draw a line.

1 Laurie ran up the hill.   The shoes are off.

2 Cars go on green.   Cars stop on red.

3 I have on the shoes.   Laurie ran down the hill.

B. Print the word.

| plate | plane | boat | bug |

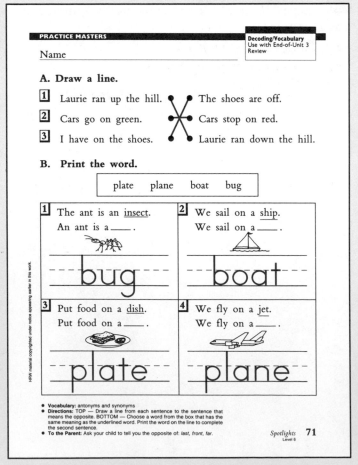

1 The ant is an <u>insect</u>.
  An ant is a ___.

  bug

2 We sail on a <u>ship</u>.
  We sail on a ___.

  boat

3 Put food on a <u>dish</u>.
  Put food on a ___.

  plate

4 We fly on a <u>jet</u>.
  We fly on a ___.

  plane

- **Vocabulary:** antonyms and synonyms
- **Directions:** TOP — Draw a line from each sentence to the sentence that means the opposite. BOTTOM — Choose a word from the box that has the same meaning as the underlined word. Print the word on the line to complete the second sentence.
- **To the Parent:** Ask your child to tell you the opposite of: *last, front, far.*

Spotlights
Level 6
71

Name ·

Fill in the circle.

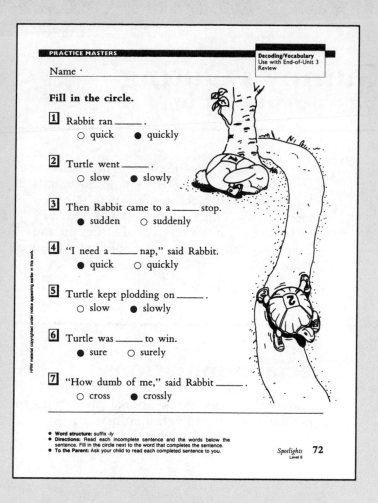

1 Rabbit ran _____ .
   ○ quick   ● quickly

2 Turtle went _____ .
   ○ slow   ● slowly

3 Then Rabbit came to a _____ stop.
   ● sudden   ○ suddenly

4 "I need a _____ nap," said Rabbit.
   ● quick   ○ quickly

5 Turtle kept plodding on _____ .
   ○ slow   ● slowly

6 Turtle was _____ to win.
   ● sure   ○ surely

7 "How dumb of me," said Rabbit _____ .
   ○ cross   ● crossly

● **Word structure:** suffix -ly
● **Directions:** Read each incomplete sentence and the words below the sentence. Fill in the circle next to the word that completes the sentence.
● **To the Parent:** Ask your child to read each completed sentence to you.

Spotlights
Level 6
72

BONUS "Mr. Gumpy's Outing"
pages 170–181 (T386–T394)

Skill Strands

The vocabulary words introduced in the Bonus can be decoded by pupils, using skills that they have learned. No skills are presented in this lesson.

> **Note:** The Bonus Selection is designed to foster independent reading enjoyment. Many pupils will be ready to read the entire Bonus Selection independently. Those pupils should be encouraged to do so. The directed reading lesson and questioning strategies are for pupils who need further direction and teacher assistance to understand and enjoy the selection.

Lesson Vocabulary

Decodable words: *across, chase, chickens, flap, Gumpy, muck, owned, pester, river, squabble, tea, tipped, trample*

Materials

Spotlights, Level 6: pages 170–181
Teacher's Idea Book

Special Populations

See *Teacher's Idea Book* for additional suggestions to help pupils with limited English proficiency.

READING FOR COMPREHENSION

Background for the Teacher

SUMMARY Everyone wants to go for a ride in Mr. Gumpy's boat. Mr. Gumpy tells each passenger how to behave, but they all forget. The boat tips, so they end the outing by having some tea at Mr. Gumpy's house.

INFORMATON "Mr. Gumpy's Outing" is an adaptation of a book of the same title. John Burningham won several awards for his illustrations, some of which have been included in this selection.

Using Prior Knowledge

Tell pupils that the next story tells about a rowboat ride. Ask what might happen to a boat when it is overloaded. (It might sink.) Explain that in this story, the boat is just big enough for all its passengers. Ask pupils to predict if all will go well on this boat ride. (Answers will vary.)

Setting a Purpose for Reading

Have pupils read the title of the story on page 170. Explain that an outing is a short trip away from home. A picnic in a nearby park or a short boat ride might be called an outing.

Point out the headnote at the top of page 170 and have it read aloud. Ask if Mr. Gumpy is going on this outing alone. (No, some friends go with him.) Have pupils predict what might happen on the boat ride. (Possible answers include: The boat might tip over; Mr. Gumpy and friends might go swimming.)

Reading Silently

Some pupils may be able to read this story independently. Direct them to read the whole story to find out more about what happens during Mr. Gumpy's outing.

For those pupils who need more guidance, suggestions for directed reading follow.

What happens when Mr. Gumpy and some friends go for an outing?

Mr. Gumpy's Outing

by John Burningham

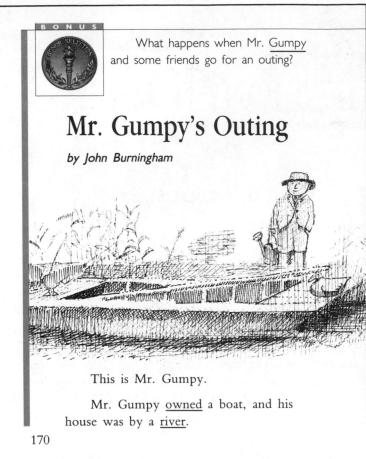

This is Mr. Gumpy.

Mr. Gumpy owned a boat, and his house was by a river.

170

One day, Mr. Gumpy went out in his boat.

"May we come with you?" said the children.

"Yes," said Mr. Gumpy, "if you don't squabble."

171

Before reading pages 170–173

SAY **What friends do you think will join Mr. Gumpy? Read pages 170 to 173 to yourself.**

"Can I come along, Mr. Gumpy?"
said the rabbit.

"Yes, but don't hop about."

"I would like a ride,"
said the cat.

"Very well," said Mr. Gumpy,
"but you're not to <u>chase</u> the rabbit."

172

173

After
reading
pages
170–173

1. **Who joined Mr. Gumpy on his boat?**
   (the children, the rabbit, the cat)
   Inferential
2. **What did Mr. Gumpy tell the children before they got on the boat?** (He
   told them that they must not squabble.)
   What does *squabble* mean? (It means
   "argue or fight.") Inferential
3. **What did Mr. Gumpy make each animal promise?** (The rabbit must not
   hop about; the cat must not chase the
   rabbit.) Inferential

"Will you take me with you?"
said the dog.

"Yes," said Mr. Gumpy, "but don't
pester the cat."

"May I come, please, Mr. Gumpy?"
said the pig.

"Very well, but don't muck about."

174

175

Before
reading
pages
174–176

SAY **The boat was getting pretty
crowded. Do you think any
more friends will want to go along?
Read pages 174 to 176 to yourself.**

"Have you a place for me?"
said the sheep.

"Yes, but don't keep bleating."

"Can we come, too?"
said the chickens.

"Yes, but don't flap,"
said Mr. Gumpy.

176

"Can you make room for me?"
said the calf.

"Yes, if you don't trample about."

"May I go with you, Mr. Gumpy?"
said the goat.

"Very well, but don't kick."

For a time they all went along
just fine, but then . . .

the goat kicked.
The calf trampled.
The chickens flapped.
The sheep bleated.
The pig mucked about.
The dog pestered the cat.
The cat chased the rabbit.
The rabbit hopped.
The children squabbled.
The boat tipped . . .

177

After reading pages 174–176
1. **What other animals joined the group on the boat?** (the dog, the pig, the sheep, the chickens) Literal
2. **What did Mr. Gumpy make each animal promise?** (The pig must not muck about; the sheep must not bleat; the chickens must not flap.) Inferential

Before reading page 177

After reading page 177

SAY **Do you think there could possibly be any more room on the boat? Read page 177 to yourself.**

1. **What other animals did Mr. Gumpy let on the boat?** (the calf and the goat) Literal
2. **What did the calf and the goat have to promise? Why?** (The calf must not trample; the goat must not kick; everyone must sit still so the boat does not tip.) Inferential
3. **What went wrong?** (Everyone on the boat did what they were told not to do; the boat tipped, and they all fell into the water.) Inferential

and into the water they fell.

178   179

Before
reading
pages
178–181

SAY **Do you think Mr. Gumpy was angry with his friends? Read pages 178 to 181 to yourself.**

Then Mr. Gumpy and the goat and the calf and the chickens and the sheep and the pig and the dog and the cat and the rabbit and the children all swam to the bank.

180

"We'll walk home <u>across</u> the fields," said Mr. Gumpy. "It's time for <u>tea</u>."

181

After reading pages 178–181

1. **Was Mr. Gumpy angry? How could you tell?** (No, he was not angry because he asked his friends to come for tea.) Inferential
2. **How did Mr. Gumpy and his friends get home from their outing?** (They walked across the fields.) Literal
3. **Why do you think they did not get back in the boat and ride home?** (Possible answers include: They might tip it over again.) Critical

Discussing the Selection

PURPOSE Remind pupils that at the beginning of the story, they predicted what might happen on the outing. Ask what happened when Mr. Gumpy took his friends for an outing? (The friends forgot what they promised Mr. Gumpy, and they tipped the boat over.) Literal

STORY MAPPING

1. **What did Mr. Gumpy tell each of his friends before he let them on the boat?** (He told the children not to squabble; he told the rabbit not to hop about; he told the cat not to chase the rabbit; he told the dog not to pester the cat; he told the pig not to muck about; he told the sheep not to bleat; he told the chickens not to flap; he told the calf not to trample about; he told the goat not to kick.) Inferential

2. **Why did Mr. Gumpy tell his friends how to behave on the boat?** (Mr. Gumpy knew that if they misbehaved, the friends would cause the boat to tip.) Inferential

3. **Where in the story did you guess that Mr. Gumpy's boat would tip? What part of the story helped you guess what would happen?** (The sentence in the middle of page 177: For a time they all went along just fine, but then . . .) Inferential

CRITICAL THINKING

- **What lesson do you think Mr. Gumpy's friends learned from their outing?** (Possible answers include: They learned that if they had done as Mr. Gumpy told them, the boat wouldn't have tipped over.)

New Words

These are the new words in Level 6, *Spotlights*.
Words printed in regular type are decodable.
Words printed **boldface** are special words.

4 **neighbors**	mud	21 nodded
Dilly	13 slacks	anyone
yet	real	22 Faith
people	name	Kim
5 purr	14 problem	blackest
toast	Jack	23 **next**
fresh	**Minx**	Patty
milk	**Jinx**	furry
hurry	**surprise**	softest
sunny	mother	**live**
6 **cars**	jeep	24 alike
trucks	mail	**both**
7 bus	15 Tabby	runners
hello	16 gray	jumpers
8 Billy	Dusty	25 **Mrs.**
Candy	Jet	pleaded
Tommy	just	26 **Mr.**
9 discussion	**their**	least
selection	twin	27 **telephone**
12 Pesty	17 every	rang
play	19 drink	Jane
inside	dish	Turner
Renny	jump	28 bet
rain	lap	29 yelled
Shaggy	everywhere	30 bell
Milly	20 weeks	Jean

182

31 any	mile	62 fox
32 **Bear**	pride	boats
spells	48 **Maria's**	floats
trouble	**chili**	63 Max
woods	pot	ax
swim	different	bats
place	49 they're	64 mix
33 **Squirrel**	**even**	65 fix
Chipmunk	everyone	win
sunrise	50 these	66 dip
spent	you're	rip
time	51 table	67 life
pine	52 **Tina**	70 **babies**
side	55 please	**baby**
34 fine	we're	**carried**
nap	plenty	arms
smile	56 bowls	71 cannot
35 rid	bite	**carry**
met	land	pocket
36 sneak	57 **been**	72 father
37 dropped	60 whoever	frog
tickle	**invented**	safe
ha	**wheel**	until
38 **began**	**great**	wiggle
43 plan	**idea**	wet
44 Mike's	three	73 throats
slide	**four**	harm
thin	61 **five**	dart
wide	six	74 piggyback
pile	**seven**	ride
45 glide	**more**	

183

76 named	forgetting	hillside
Morty	family	branches
broke	**except**	fire
kept	93 sister	103 fetch
77 woke	Tammy	ripe
snow	94 simple	luck
78 upon	**else**	reaching
liked	tennis	104 treat
smelled	joke	watched
smoke	forgot	105 stole
79 yummy-looking	95 workout	riches
evening	class	106 far
hungry	Hope	107 nuts
snack	96 date	chattered
80 **gone**	yourself	108 chirped
now	97 outside	109 bark
83 **scary**	98 party	scratch
those	present	110 army
84 alone	100 handstands	match
85 broken	cartwheels	swam
87 better	backward	112 row
than	flips	**pictures**
88 mole's	everything	116 Clayton
start	101 **about**	Desmond
rope	102 outsmart	**mice**
scamper	**giant**	pumpkin
pole	Peach	**love**
rose	**woman**	**village**
stones	hut	vine
92 **Fiona**	stream	garden
		sure

184

very	128 **Thumbelina**	141 farm
contest	**Prince**	damp
117 **field**	129 thumb	finished
become	shell	Grandma
jack-o'-lantern	petals	142 rapping
carved	asleep	**door**
118 dark	130 bank	dinner
crept	131 numb	OK
gave	cute	143 hollered
fed	use	cross
119 within	housework	suddenly
120 shrugged	crumbs	Ferris
skill	132 often	fair
fact	134 spoke	rode
van	bride	really
121 frost	wed	145 sweetly
cover	135 sunshine	146 weekend
blanket	136 faraway	fondly
hummed	rule	tickets
123 explained	137 felt	147 suspect
deal	138 **Larry**	150 Jenny
124 tracks	**imagines**	spend
hundred	**toot**	chugged
126 save	front	151 exclaimed
vase	139 visit	seatbelt
vest	140 slowly	152 **room**
vet	speed	beside
127 vote	park	153 quickly
wave	bench	drank
cave	**calf**	Lenny
dive	**horses**	P.S.

185

154 Linda's
bookshelf
Laurie's
neat
155 washing
desk
Louise's
156 queen
drapes
children
157 fireplace
overflowing
ashes
swept
job
158 bathroom

159 squashed
bathtub
160 kitchen
161 member
cost
164 fuzzy
kitty
magnet
cotton
paste
scissors
paper
166 caddy
yarn
167 shapes
168 puzzle

stiff
marker
169 homemade
170 Gumpy
owned
river
171 squabble
173 chase
174 pester
175 muck
176 chickens
flap
177 trample
tipped
181 across
tea

186

Level 6 Word List

The list that follows includes the words that are introduced in Level 6, *Spotlights*. The number following each word indicates the page on which the word first appears in the pupil's edition.

about	101	both	24	cute	131	family	92
across	181	bowls	56	damp	141	far	106
alike	24	branches	102	dark	118	faraway	136
alone	84	bride	134	dart	73	farm	141
any	31	broke	76	date	96	father	72
anyone	21	broken	85	deal	123	fed	118
arms	70	bus	7	desk	155	felt	137
army	110	caddy	166	Desmond	116	Ferris	143
ashes	157	calf	140	different	48	fetch	103
asleep	129	Candy	8	Dilly	4	field	117
ax	63	cannot	71	dinner	142	fine	34
babies	70	carried	70	dip	66	finished	141
baby	70	carry	71	discussing	9	Fiona	92
backward	100	cars	6	dish	19	fire	102
bank	130	cartwheels	100	dive	127	fireplace	157
bark	109	carved	117	door	142	five	61
bathroom	158	cave	127	drank	153	fix	65
bathtub	159	chase	173	drapes	156	flap	176
bats	63	chattered	107	drink	19	flips	100
Bear	32	chickens	176	dropped	37	floats	62
become	117	children	156	Dusty	16	fondly	146
been	57	chili	48	else	93	forgetting	92
began	38	Chipmunk	33	even	49	forgot	93
bell	30	chirped	108	evening	79	four	60
bench	140	chugged	150	every	17	fox	62
beside	152	class	95	everyone	49	fresh	5
bet	28	Clayton	116	everything	100	frog	72
better	87	contest	116	everywhere	19	front	138
Billy	8	cost	161	except	92	frost	121
bite	56	cotton	164	exclaimed	151	furry	23
blackest	22	cover	121	explained	123	fuzzy	164
blanket	121	crept	118	fact	120	garden	116
boats	62	cross	143	fair	143	gave	118
bookshelf	154	crumbs	131	Faith	22	giant	102

Word	Page	Word	Page	Word	Page	Word	Page
glide	45	kitchen	160	nap	34	Prince	128
gone	80	kitty	164	neat	154	problem	14
Grandma	141	land	56	neighbors	4	pumpkin	116
gray	16	lap	19	next	23	purr	5
great	60	Larry	138	nodded	21	puzzle	168
Gumpy	170	Laurie's	154	now	80	queen	156
ha	37	least	26	numb	131	quickly	153
handstands	100	Lenny	153	nuts	107	rain	12
harm	73	life	67	OK	142	rang	27
hello	7	liked	78	often	132	rapping	142
hillside	102	Linda's	154	outside	97	reaching	103
hollered	143	live	23	outsmart	102	real	13
homemade	169	Louise's	155	overflowing	157	really	143
Hope	95	love	116	owned	170	Renny	12
horses	140	luck	103	P.S.	153	riches	105
housework	131	magnet	164	paper	164	rid	35
hummed	121	mail	14	park	140	ride	74
hundred	124	Maria's	48	party	98	rip	66
hungry	79	marker	168	paste	164	ripe	103
hurry	5	match	110	Patty	23	river	170
hut	102	Max	63	Peach	102	rode	143
idea	60	member	161	people	4	room	152
imagines	138	met	35	pester	174	rope	88
inside	12	mice	116	Pesty	12	rose	88
invented	60	Mike's	44	petals	129	row	112
Jack	14	mile	45	pictures	112	rule	136
jack-o'-lantern	117	milk	5	piggyback	74	runners	24
Jane	27	Milly	12	pile	44	safe	72
Jean	30	Minx	14	pine	33	save	126
jeep	14	mix	64	place	32	scamper	88
Jenny	150	mole's	88	plan	43	scary	83
Jet	16	more	61	play	12	scissors	164
Jinx	14	Morty	76	pleaded	25	scratch	109
job	157	mother	14	please	55	seatbelt	151
joke	93	Mr.	26	plenty	55	selection	9
jump	19	Mrs.	25	pocket	71	seven	61
jumpers	24	muck	175	pole	88	Shaggy	12
just	16	mud	12	pot	48	shapes	167
kept	76	name	13	present	98	shell	129
Kim	22	named	76	pride	45	shrugged	120

side	33	stream	102	thumb	129	vine	116
simple	93	suddenly	143	Thumbelina	128	visit	139
sister	93	sunny	5	tickets	146	vote	127
six	61	sunrise	33	tickle	37	washing	155
skill	120	sunshine	135	time	33	watched	104
slacks	13	sure	116	Tina	52	wave	127
slide	44	surprise	14	tipped	177	we're	55
slowly	140	suspect	147	toast	5	wed	134
smelled	78	swam	110	Tommy	8	weekend	146
smile	34	sweetly	145	toot	138	weeks	20
smoke	78	swept	157	tracks	124	wet	72
snack	79	swim	32	trample	177	wheel	60
sneak	36	Tabby	15	treat	104	wide	44
snow	77	table	51	trouble	32	wiggle	72
softest	23	Tammy	93	trucks	6	win	65
speed	140	tea	181	Turner	27	within	119
spells	32	telephone	27	twin	16	woke	77
spend	150	tennis	93	until	72	woman	102
spent	33	than	87	upon	78	woods	32
spoke	134	their	16	use	131	workout	95
squabble	171	these	50	van	120	yarn	166
squashed	159	they're	49	vase	126	yelled	29
Squirrel	33	thin	44	very	116	yet	4
start	88	those	83	vest	126	you're	50
stiff	168	three	60	vet	126	yourself	96
stole	105	throats	73	village	116	yummy-looking	79
stones	88						

Cumulative Vocabulary

The list that follows includes the introduced words that have appeared in *READING TODAY AND TOMORROW* through the end of *Spotlights*. Words introduced in this level are followed by a number that indicates the page on which the word first appears in the pupil's edition.

a		ax	63	beside	152	bugs	
about	101	babies	70	best		bump	
across	181	baby	70	bet	28	bun	
act		back		better	87	bus	7
after		backpack		big		but	
again		backward	100	Billy	8	by	
ago		bad		birdhouse		caddy	166
alike	24	badgers		birds		cake	
all		bags		birth		calf	140
alone	84	bait		birthday		came	
along		bake		bit		camp	
am		ball		bite	56	can	
an		band		black		can't	
and		bang		blackbird		Candy	8
animal		bank	130	blackest	22	cannot	71
another		bark	109	blanket	121	cap	
ant		base		bleat		capes	
ants		bathroom	158	blocks		carried	70
any	31	bathtub	159	boats	62	carry	71
anyone	21	bats	63	bone		cars	6
anyway		be		book		cartwheels	100
apple		beamed		bookshelf	154	carved	117
are		Bear	32	both	24	cast	
arms	70	beast		bowls	56	cat	
army	110	beat		box		cave	127
as		become	117	boy		Charlie	
ashes	157	bed		brakes		chase	173
asked		beehive		branches	102	chattered	107
asleep	129	been	57	bride	134	cherries	
at		began	38	bring		chickens	176
ate		bell	30	broke	76	chicks	
awake		bellowed		broken	85	children	156
away		bench	140	brushes		chili	48

Chipmunk	33	Dean		else	93	fireplace	157
chirped	108	Dee		elves		first	
chugged	150	deep		Elvira		fished	
city		den		end		fishing	
class	95	desk	155	even	49	fit	
Clayton	116	Desmond	116	evening	79	five	61
clean		did		ever		fix	65
clock		Diddle's		every	17	flag	
closer		different	48	everyone	49	flap	176
coat		dig		everything	100	flips	100
cold		Dilly	4	everywhere	19	floats	62
come		dinner	142	except	92	flow	
contest	116	dip	66	exclaimed	151	fly	
cost	161	dirt		explained	123	follow	
cot		discussing	9	fact	120	fondly	146
cotton	164	dish	19	fair	143	food	
could		dive	127	Faith	22	for	
cover	121	do		family	92	forgetting	92
Crab		does		far	106	forgot	93
crashed		dog		faraway	136	four	60
crate		doghouse		farm	141	fox	62
creek		don't		fast		free	
crept	118	door	142	father	72	fresh	5
crisp		Dot		feast		friends	
cross	143	down		fed	118	frog	72
Crow		dragon		feed		from	
crumbs	131	drank	153	feel		front	138
cut		drapes	156	feet		frost	121
cute	131	drink	19	fell		fun	
Dad		dropped	37	fellow		fur	
Daddy-longlegs		dug		felt	137	furry	23
Dale		dust		Ferris	143	fusses	
damp	141	Dusty	16	fetch	103	fuzzy	164
Dane's		each		field	117	Gail	
dark	118	ear		filled		game	
dart	73	eat		find		garden	116
dashed		eating		fine	34	gasped	
date	96	eats		finished	141	gate	
days		eek		Fiona	92	gather	
deal	123	eggs		fire	102	gave	118

get	had	horns	job 157
giant 102	ham	horses 140	joke 93
gift	hand	hose	jump 19
giggle	handstands 100	hot	jumpers 24
girl	happens	house	just 16
girlfriend	happy	housework 131	Kate
glad	harm 73	how	keep
glass	has	however	keeper
glee	hat	huff	kept 76
glide 45	hatches	hugged	kicked
glow	have	hummed 121	Kim 22
go	hay	hundred 124	king
goat	haystack	hungry 79	kingdom
gobble	he	hunt	Kip
going-away	heap	hurry 5	kiss
gone 80	hello 7	hurt	kisses
good	help	hut 102	kitchen 160
got	hen	I	kitten
grabbed	her	I'm	kitty 164
Grandfather	here	idea 60	knows
Grandma 141	here's	if	ladder
Grandmother	herself	imagines 138	lake
Grandson	hid	in	land 56
grasped	hide	insects	lane
grass	hill	inside 12	lap 19
gray 16	hillside 102	into	Larry 138
great 60	hilltop	invented 60	last
green	him	is	late
grew	himself	isn't	Laurie's 154
grinned	hint	it	lays
groan	his	it's	leaf
groaning	hit	its	leap
grow	hole	Jack 14	least 26
grown	hollered 143	jack-o'-lantern 117	leather
grub	home	Jane 27	Lee
grumble	homemade 169	Jean 30	Lee Ann
grunt	honey	jeep 14	left
guards	Hooray	Jenny 150	legs
Gumpy 170	hop	Jet 16	Lenny 153
ha 37	Hope 95	Jinx 14	let's

lick		mean		nap	34	pan	
lid		meat		neat	154	pancake	
life	67	meet		neck		panting	
lifted		member	161	need		paper	164
like		mess		needs		parade	
liked	78	met	35	neighbors	4	park	140
Linda's	154	mice	116	nest		party	98
Lion		middle		never		passed	
little		Mike's	44	new		past	
live	23	mile	45	next	23	paste	164
lived		milk	5	no		pat	
long		Milly	12	nodded	21	path	
look		Minx	14	noise		Patty	23
lost		miss		not		pay	
lot		mitt		note		Peach	102
Louise's	155	Mitzie		now	80	peak	
love	116	mix	64	numb	131	pecking	
low		moan		nuts	107	peeking	
luck	103	moaning		OK	142	pen	
mad		mole's	88	oak		people	4
made		mom		of		perhaps	
magic		money		off		pester	174
magnet	164	Monkey		often	132	pests	
maid		more	61	oh		Pesty	12
mail	14	Morty	76	on		pet	
main		mother	14	one		petals	129
make		mouse		onto		petted	
man		move		or		picked	
map		moved		other		pictures	112
Maria's	48	Mr.	26	out		piggyback	74
marker	168	Mrs.	25	outside	97	pigpen	
mat		much		outsmart	102	pigs	
match	110	muck	175	overflowing	157	pile	44
Matt		mud	12	owned	170	pin	
Max	63	must		P.S.	153	pine	33
Maxwell		my		packed		pink	
Maxwell's		name	13	paid		place	32
may		named	76	paint		plan	43
maybe		Nan		pair		plane	
me		Nan's		Pam		planks	

plants		riches	105	seatbelt	151	six	61
plate		rid	35	see		skates	
play	12	ride	74	seed		skill	120
pleaded	25	rip	66	seeds		skipped	
please	55	ripe	103	seen		slacks	13
plenty	55	river	170	sees		slam	
pocket	71	road		selection	9	slap	
pole	88	robin		sell		sled	
pond		rocks		send		sleeping	
pot	48	rode	143	sent		slide	44
present	98	room	152	sentences		slip	
press		rope	88	set		slowly	140
pride	45	Rosa		seven	61	smack	
Prince	128	rose	88	shade		smash	
problem	14	row	112	Shaggy	12	smelled	78
puff		rug		shame		smile	34
pull		rule	136	Shane		smoke	78
pumpkin	116	runners	24	shapes	167	snack	79
purr	5	running		she		snap	
put		rushes		she's		sneak	36
puzzle	168	sack		sheep		sniff	
queen	156	sad		shell	129	snow	77
quickly	153	safe	72	ship		so	
rabbit		said		shoemaker		sobbed	
raft		sail		shoes		soft	
rain	12	Sam		shop		softest	23
rainbow		same		show		some	
ran		Samson		shown		someone	
rang	27	sand		shrub		something	
rapping	142	sang		shrugged	120	song	
reaching	103	sat		shut		speak	
read		save	126	side	33	speed	140
Reader		saw		simple	93	spells	32
real	13	say		sing		spend	150
really	143	scamper	88	singing		spent	33
red		scary	83	sinking		spin	
remember		scissors	164	sir		spoke	134
Renny	12	scratch	109	sister	93	spot	
rest		sea		sit		spring	
ribbon		seat		sitting		spun	

squabble	171	swim	32	thorn		twig	
squashed	159	swing		those	83	twin	16
Squirrel	33	Tabby	15	three	60	twists	
stacked		table	51	throats	73	two	
Stan		tack		thumb	129	umbrellas	
stand		Tad		Thumbelina	128	under	
standing		tail		thump		until	72
start	88	take		tick		up	
stay		Tam		tickets	146	upon	78
steep		Tammy	93	tickle	37	upset	
stem		tan		tilt		us	
steps		tap		time	33	use	131
stick		taste		Tina	52	van	120
stiff	168	tea	181	tipped	177	vase	126
still		team		to		very	116
sting		teeth		toad		vest	126
stole	105	telephone	27	toast	5	vet	126
stones	88	tell		tock		village	116
stop		ten		today		vine	116
story		tennis	93	Todd		visit	139
stream	102	tent		Tommy	8	vote	127
street		than	87	too		wags	
strips		thank		toot	138	waited	
stuck		that		top		wake	
sudden		that's		toss		walk	
suddenly	143	the		tracks	124	want	
summer		their	16	train		was	
sun		them		trample	177	washing	155
sundown		then		trap		watched	104
sunny	5	Theodore		treasure		water	
sunrise	33	there		treat	104	wave	127
sunset		these	50	trees		way	
sunshine	135	they		trip		we	
sunup		they'll		trouble	32	we'll	
sure	116	they're	49	trucks	6	we're	55
surprise	14	thin	44	trunk		wed	134
suspect	147	thing		turn		weekend	146
swam	110	think		Turner	27	weeks	20
sweetly	145	thirteen		turnip		weeps	
swept	157	this		tweet		well	

Index of Skills

Teacher's Notes

Teacher's Notes

Teacher's Notes

Teacher's Notes

Teacher's Notes

Teacher's Notes

Acknowledgments

For permission to reprint copyrighted material, grateful acknowledgment is made to the following sources:

William Collins Sons & Company, Ltd.: "The Little Elfman" by John Kendrick Bangs from *The Child's Book of Poems*.

Grosset & Dunlap, Inc.: "Choosing a Kitten" written anonymously.

Instructor Publications, Inc.: "A House for One" by Laura Arlon and "A Pumpkin Seed" by Alice Crowell Hoffman from *Poetry Place Anthology*. Copyright © 1983 by Instructor Publications, Inc.